GW00832940

Web Services Development with Delphi

Peter Darakhvelidze
Eugene Markov

A-LIST, LLC

295 East Swedesford Rd.

PMB #285

Wayne, PA 19087

702-977-5377 (FAX)

mail@alistpublishing.com

http://www.alistpublishing.com

This book is printed on acid-free paper.

Web Services Development with Delphi
By Peter Darakhvelidze, Eugene Markov

ISBN: 1-931769-08-7

Printed in the United States of America

02 03 7 6 5 4 3 2 1

A-LIST, LLC titles are distributed by Independent Publishers Group and are available for site license or bulk purchase by institutions, user groups, corporations, etc.

Book Editor: Jessica Mroz

Contents

Introduction

The first time developers came across Delphi 6, they probably noticed that the majority of new capabilities and components were geared towards creating distributed web applications. And this is surely not just because Borland was following some fleeting fashion, but rather because circumstances truly necessitated these additions.

It's interesting to follow the evolution of the developer community's ideas concerning the capabilities of the Internet. Their initial notion of the Global Network as a "technological toy" that had huge possibilities not only for communications, but for the world of business as well, spurred the inevitable Internet boom. Later, a stir caused by the wrong people trying to use the Internet for the wrong purposes couldn't help but produce some disappointment and backsliding. Nonetheless, the sharp decrease in the interest in the Internet as a multi-purpose and global means of business communication, and the subsequent stagnation, somewhat helped in bringing about the realization that the Internet could not only be used as an extremely important technological tool, but as a system-forming factor for planning modern distributed applications.

The entire history of the development of business applications — from mainframes to the modern state of affairs — can be seen as a sequence of steps, each of which made applications more global. Certainly, this opinion might seem a bit one-sided, and not necessarily what you might call unbiased historical research, but within the framework of this book it is completely justified, since it allows us to better focus on the issue at hand. In this context, the widespread use of the Internet as a network environment for distributed business applications is an appropriate and solidly grounded solution.

The popularity of the Internet as a system-forming basis for distributed applications is also based on the very recent appearance of the XML language, which allows for the unification of the data structure presentation process. Presenting XML data is done using a different language — eXtended Stylesheet Language (XSL), as well as a modification of it — XSL Transformations (XLST). This is very important, since developers now have a universal means of presenting these data in the sea of various client applications, web browsers, protocols, and their extensions.

In this book, we try to illustrate in detail all the basic aspects of developing web applications using the abundant means for this that are provided in the Delphi development environment. However, this is not the main advantage (or rather not the only main advantage) of using Delphi as a development environment for creating web applications. Yet another important factor is that Delphi allows you to go through the entire development cycle for complex applications with a distributed infrastructure using various technological solutions.

Indeed, the variety of technologies and components allows you to create applications for any kind of customer and to be able to comply with most of their wishes. So as not to leave our claim unsubstantiated, let's take a little tour of the modern Internet technologies that will be covered in this book.

COM and COM+

We'll begin with a brief survey of the Component Object Model (COM) technology and its child technologies. Right about now, the experienced reader is probably groaning something along the lines of "Oh no, not COM again!". However, we thought that it was absolutely necessary to touch on this issue, even though COM and similar technologies seem to have relatively little to do with web applications. Still, de facto, many "100% Internet" technologies use COM capabilities as the final link in data exchange, something akin to the "last mile" of the network infrastructure.

Of no less importance is the COM+ technology (and its closely related ancestor, the good old Microsoft Transaction Server), which helps solve scale problems for applications on a Windows 2000 platform.

DataSnap

In discussing web applications, we shouldn't forget about the fact that the Internet is without a doubt wonderful and promising, but still only a "means of transport" for the data received by clients of distributed business applications. Therefore, the features of the architecture of such applications and issues of their interaction with database servers are still relevant.

The DataSnap technology, having inherited and developed the capabilities of the MIDAS technology unfamiliar to developers who work in Delphi, is intended for solving just such problems. In particular, this concerns multi-layer distributed applications and means of accessing various data sources.

Here, we must say a few words about the data access object model ActiveX Data Objects (ADO), which has become the de facto standard in this area. It allows you to solve the problem of distributing and installing software of intermediate level data access for the Windows platform.

XML

Everyone has heard the term "XML," and many know the language itself, but far from everyone realizes the practical possibilities this language holds. XML stands for eXtensible Markup Language. It is currently being developed by the World Wide Web Consortium (W3C, **www.w3c.org/XML**). This consortium includes representatives from the largest vendors, research organizations, and educational institutions.

XML is called "extensible" because it gives anyone the opportunity to define and build their own system of tags to describe a particular area of expertise.

Besides the irrefutable value that XML has in and of itself, XML is also the basis upon which many other technologies used in Delphi for creating web applications are built.

SOAP

Since the time web applications came into being up until the present day, web application developers have been running into the problem of web application interoperability, some of which function only on different software and hardware platforms. There have been many proposed solutions to this problem. For example, the Common Object Request Broker Architecture (CORBA) allows you to create full-fledged multi-platform solutions, but requires that special client software be installed. If you want to distribute solutions based on VisiBroker — the object request broker that comes with Delphi — you have to make sure to acquire the proper license for it. (By the way, CORBA is supported in Delphi, and the set of corresponding components, tools, and utilities are included in the DataSnap technology.)

The Simple Object Access Protocol (SOAP) is supported by all the main platforms on the Internet, does not require a complicated client part, and provides for safe data exchange over the Net. SOAP came about in order to solve the common problem of interoperability of applications that work on various platforms. In the two short years of SOAP's existence, it has already been approved by the majority of the IT community.

The set of Delphi components that implement SOAP allows you to construct complete client and server parts of a web application. Besides this, we will examine the Microsoft SOAP Toolkit — a tool for publishing Automation objects as web services — and we will also discuss issues of creating web services.

WebSnap and WebBroker

And finally, Delphi developers were able to unite all the main steps of creating a web application into one whole technological solution. The WebSnap and WebBroker technologies simplify and accelerate going through the "routine" operations for creating an application's user interface, data access, and user authentication. Besides which, developers will undoubtedly appreciate the ease with which VBScript and JScript scripts can be included into source code.

The widespread use of HTML and XML templates is unquestionably an advantage of WebSnap, since it makes the modernization of finished applications in the most fickle and changeable area — the user interface — much simpler.

Cryptography and Data Security

The Internet network is by definition an open, decentralized, and minimally controllable one. In the early stages of Internet programming, the problem of data security was not a concern of very many, and talk of creating industry standards in this area was all theoretical. Today, the paradigm of protecting any important data sent through the Internet is no longer a subject to be only talked about.

We couldn't completely ignore such an important topic in this book. We will examine some applied tasks of cryptography, and then introduce you to the concepts of digital signatures and certificates. Then, in an example of a certificate manager, we'll look at the features of the CryptoAPI interface, and end our discussion with some issues of configuring web tools and components used in distributed applications for cryptographic protection.

PART I

COM and COM+ Applications

Chapter 1

COM Mechanisms
in Delphi

M any of the technologies described in this book are based on the Component Object Model (COM) technology and those technologies created based on it. Therefore, we shall start by reviewing COM's basic capabilities.

One of the most pressing tasks software developers can encounter has always been the interaction, or lack thereof, between certain applications. To solve this problem, a large number of various methods and techniques have been employed.

At the dawn of Windows, shared files, the clipboard, and the Dynamic Data Exchange (DDE) technology were introduced.

To provide data exchange and services, the first version of the Object Linking and Embedding technology — OLE 1 — was developed. It was intended for the creation of compound documents, to which we have been accustomed for a long time already. As a result of its many imperfections, this technology has been replaced by the OLE 2 technology. This solves a more common problem: how to make applications allow other applications to perform their functions (services), and how to use these functions properly.

To solve this problem, a whole range of other technologies has been developed besides OLE. The core of all of them was the basic Component Object Model technology. It described means of interaction for any number of applications. One part of the software renders its own services, while the other gets access to them, and the location of these parts is absolutely unimportant — within one process, in different processes on one computer, or on different computers.

In addition, for applications created using COM technology, it is not important what programming language was used in the course of its development — if the COM standard is observed, interaction should go on without a hitch.

A modification of basic technology — Distributed COM, or DCOM — provides developers of the distributed applications with additional options.

Currently, COM is widely used in various fields of software development. The technologies of Automation, ActiveX, ActiveForm, and Microsoft Transaction Server are COM-based. Distributed applications would not function without COM objects, whether they operate in a local network or on the Internet.

Delphi provides the developer with a set of tools for creating valuable COM applications.

Later, this chapter will deal with the main parts of the COM specification and the methods for creating COM objects and interfaces in Delphi. Much space is allotted to the Type Library Editor — the main tool facilitating work with COM objects in the project.

This chapter deals with the following issues:

❏ Objects and interfaces

❏ The IUnknown interface

❏ Type libraries

❏ Class factories

❏ Server types

Basic Concepts

Using COM technology, an application provides its services via *COM objects*. Every application contains at least one object. Each object has at least one, but perhaps several, *interfaces*. Each interface combines the *methods* of the object that enable access to the *properties* (data) and the execution of operations. The interface usually combines all the methods that perform operations of one type, or those dealing with homogeneous properties.

The client gains access to the object's services through the interface and its methods only. This is a key routine. In order to obtain comprehensive information on the properties and methods of the object, it is enough for the client to know just a few basic interfaces. Therefore, any client may work with any object irrespective of their development environment. According to the COM specification, an existing interface cannot be changed by any means. This guarantees continuous performance of COM-based applications, despite any changes.

The object always operates within the *COM server*. The server may be a dynamic library or an executable file. The object may have its own properties and methods or use data and services from the server.

To gain access to an object's methods, the client must get the pointer to the corresponding interface. Each interface has its own pointer. After that, the client may use the services by simply calling their methods. Access to the objects' properties is possible through their methods only.

Suppose a COM object is integrated into a worksheet and provides access to mathematical operations. It would be logical to divide the mathematical functions into groups according to their types, and create an individual interface for each group. For example, you can separate them into linear, trigonometric, aggregate functions, etc. The object in Fig. 1.1 is within the server — a worksheet. The interfaces are represented by small bubbles linked with the object. Let the linear functions' interface be called `ILinear`, and aggregate ones `IAggregate`.

NOTE

According to the rules of naming accepted in Delphi, the names of interfaces begin with a capital letter I. The names of classes, however, begin with a capital letter T.

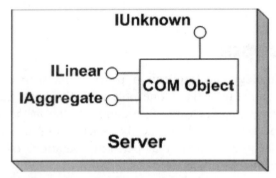

Fig. 1.1. A server and an object with its interface

NOTE

According to the rules for marking COM objects, the basic `IUnknown` interface that each object has is marked as a bubble on the upper side of the object rectangle. The remaining interfaces are marked to the right or to the left.

Fig. 1.2 shows the schema of interaction between the client and the COM object.

Suppose that among the methods of the `IAggregate` interface there is a method for calculating averages. To gain access to the aggregate function that calculates an average, the client must get the pointer to the `IAggregate` interface, and only then can it call this function.

The interaction between the client and the object is provided by the basic COM mechanisms. At the same time, the exact location of the object is concealed from the client: in the address space of the same process, in another process, or on another computer. Therefore, from the point of view of the client software developer, the using worksheet functions looks like a general call to the object's method. The mechanism of the interaction among the remote COM elements is called *marshaling.*

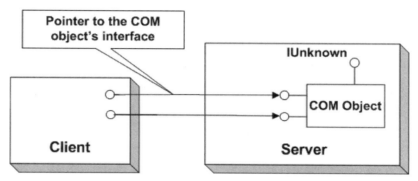

Fig. 1.2. Schema for the interaction of the client and the COM object

Here an appropriate question might emerge: how is a COM object created and initialized upon the client's first call? It is doubtful that the OS independently creates instances of all the classes registered within it, hoping that one of them may be of use at some point. Moreover, the performance of an object relies on the servers. Imagine that every time you start Windows, Word, Excel, Internet Explorer, etc, were all automatically launched.

Any COM object is a normal instance of some class, describing its properties and methods. Information on all COM classes registered and available in this OS is collected in the special *COM Library* used for launching the class instance — the object.

First, the client refers to the COM Library, communicating the name of the required class and the name of the interface needed first. The library finds the required class and initiates a server process that creates an object — a class instance. Then the library returns the object pointer and the interface to the client. From now on, the client may interact directly with the object and its interfaces.

After this, it is time for initialization; the object should load the necessary data, read the settings from the System Registry, etc. All of this falls under the responsibility of special COM objects called *monikers.* Their performance is concealed from the client. Usually, the moniker is created along with the class.

It is quite possible that several clients will simultaneously call the same object. Providing that certain settings have been established, a separate instance of the class is created for each client. A special COM object called a *class factory* performs this operation.

And the last issue to be considered is how the client obtains information about the object. For example, a client software developer is aware that a worksheet is created in accordance with the COM specification, but has no idea about the COM objects that provide its services to clients. To avoid such situations, the COM object developer can distribute the type information together with the object. This includes interface data, their properties and methods, and the methods' parameters.

This information is contained in the *type library* created using the Interface Definition Language (IDL).

Objects

An object is the central element of COM. Applications supporting COM have one or more COM objects within them. Each object is an instance of the corresponding class, and contains one or more interfaces. So what exactly is a COM object?

Without going into a lot of detail on implementing COM objects in Delphi, it is possible to say that a COM object differs somewhat from ordinary objects.

Any object is an instance of a certain class, i.e., a variable of an object type. Therefore, an object has a range of properties and methods that operate with these properties. Three main characteristics are applicable to objects: encapsulation, inheritance, and polymorphism. COM objects meet all these demands (there are some features of inheritance).

With reference to objects as a whole, the notion of the object interface explained above is not used. As a first approximation, it is possible to say that all of an object's methods make up its one and only interface, the object pointer being the interface pointer as well.

A COM object may have any number of interfaces (more than zero), each one having its own pointer. This is the first difference between COM objects and ordinary ones.

NOTE

Some programming languages, e.g., Java, allow an object to have several interfaces.

COM objects have another peculiarity: inheritance. In general, there are two ways of inheritance. Implementation inheritance transfers the entire software code from the ancestor to the descendant. Interface inheritance refers transferring the declaration of methods only, and the descendant has to get the methods' program code independently.

COM objects support only interface inheritance, thus avoiding possible violations of the ancestor's encapsulation. Nevertheless, implementation inheritance cannot be simply disregarded. Instead, COM objects use the mechanism of *containment*, i.e., when needed, the descendant calls for the required method of the ancestor. Also, the mechanism of *aggregation* may be used, when one or several interfaces of one object are temporarily included in another object by transferring the pointers.

Thus, from the point of view of Object-Oriented Programming (OOP), a COM object is definitely an object. Being the key element of COM technology, however, it possesses a few peculiarities when implementing basic routines.

Interfaces

If the COM object is the key element of COM implementation, then the interfaces are the central link of COM ideology. How can two fundamentally different objects interact? The answer is simple: they must agree on the way they will interact beforehand. (We deliberately avoided the word "language," since it might provoke an objectionable association with a programming language, which has nothing to do with the interaction of COM elements.)

An interface is the means of enabling a client to refer correctly to the COM object, and how to get the the object to react so that the client understands.

This can be illustrated by an example. Two people meet on the street: a local (COM object) and a foreigner (client). The foreigner has a dictionary with him (type library or `IUnknown` interface). The foreigner needs, however, the local's knowledge of the city. He takes a pen and paper, looks into the dictionary, makes up a phrase and diligently copies the strange words onto the paper. The local reads the phrase, takes the dictionary, makes up his own phrase, and writes it on the paper.

The story ends happily: the pleased client (the foreigner) receives from the COM object (the local) the result of the service performance (the route), and the local leaves with the dictionary.

As you might guess, the interface in this example is the pen and the paper: the foreigner does not know the native's language, but does know how to ask correctly in order to obtain the right answer.

Each interface has two attributes for identification. The first is its name, which is made up of symbols according to the rules of the programming language used. Each name should begin with the symbol "I." This name is used in the program code. The second is the *Globally Unique IDentifier* (GUID), which is a truly unique combination of symbols that is never reproduced on any computer in the world. For interfaces, such an identifier is called Interface IDentifier (IID).

In general, the client may not know what interfaces the object has. To obtain a list of interfaces, the basic `IUnknown` interface is used, which every COM object has.

The client then needs to find out the methods of the interface he or she has selected. For this purpose, the developer should distribute the method descriptions together with the object. This problem is solved with the help of the Interface Definition Language (IDL) (which is also used in the type libraries). Its syntax is very much like that of C++.

The most important part is yet to come: to call the method itself correctly. For this, the interface implementation definition in COM is used based on standard binary format. This provides independence from the programming language.

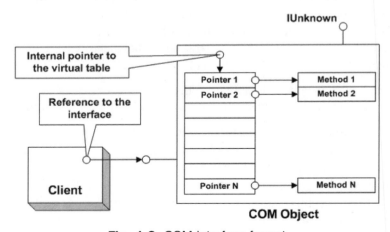

Fig. 1.3. COM interface format

The interface pointer that is available for the client refers to the inner pointer of the object and then to the special virtual table (Fig. 1.3). This table contains the pointers for all methods of the interface. (It looks very much like the table of the object's virtual methods in OOP, doesn't it?)

> **NOTE**
>
> The first three rows of the interface table are always allotted to the methods of the IUnknown interface, since any COM interface is a descendant of this interface.

As a result, the client's call to the method goes through a chain of pointers, gets the pointer for the specified method, and the appropriate program code is executed.

The *IUnknown* Interface

Each COM object contains an interface called IUnknown. This interface has three methods that play a key role in the functioning of the object.

The QueryInterface method returns the pointer to the interface of the object, and its IID identifier is communicated in the parameter of the method. If the object has no such interface, the method returns NULL.

Upon the first call to the object, the client usually obtains the interface pointer. Since every interface is a descendant of IUnknown, every interface has the QueryInterface method. It's not particularly important which interface the client uses. With the help of the QueryInterface method, the client may gain access to any of the object's interfaces.

The IUnknown interface also performs another important routine of the COM object: the reference counting method. The object must exist if it is used by at least one client. And no client may dispose of the object on its own, insofar as other clients may still work with it.

Therefore, the object increases the special unit reference count upon when the next interface pointer is transferred. If one client gives another pointer to the interface of this object, then the client receiving the pointer should increment the reference count once again. For this, the method AddRef of the IUnknown interface is used.

After closing the session with the interface, the client should call the Release method of the IUnknown interface. This method decreases the unit reference count. Once the reference count reaches zero, the object disposes of itself.

Server

The COM server is an executable file: an application or dynamic library that may contain one or several objects of the same or different classes. There are three types of servers.

An *in-process server* is enabled by the dynamic libraries connected to the client application and operates in the same address space.

A *local server* is created by a separate process operating on the same computer with the client.

A *remote server* is created by a process operating on a computer other than the client's.

Let's consider a local server. Here, the interface pointer received by the client refers to the special *COM proxy object* (we shall call it the *substitute*), which operates within the client's process. The substitute provides the client with the same interfaces as the COM object called on the local server. Once the client's call is received, the substitute bundles its parameters and sends the call to the server process through the OS services. The local server has another special object to communicate the call: the *stub*, which unpacks the call and sends it to the required COM object. The result of the call is sent back to the client in reverse order.

Now let's look at a remote server. It operates in the same way as the local one, except for that call transfer between two computers is provided by the DCOM facility with the help of the *Remote Procedure Call* (RPC) routine.

To enable local and remote servers, the mechanism of marshaling and demarshaling is used. *Marshaling* implements the COM integrated packaging format of the call parameters, while *demarshaling* takes care of the unpacking. In the server implementations described above, these operations are enabled by the stub and the proxy. These object types are created jointly with the main COM object, using IDL.

COM Libraries

To provide for the fulfillment of basic functions and interfaces, there is a special COM library within the Operating System (the specific implementation varies). Access to the library is gained in the standard way, via a function call. According to the specification, the names of all the library functions begin with the prefix "Co."

When installating an application that supports COM, the information for all COM objects being implemented is written into the System Registry:

❏ The Class Identifier (CLSID), which uniquely defines the object class.

❏ The type of object server: in-process, local, or remote.

❏ The file path of the DLL or local executable file is retained for local and in-process servers.

❏ The full network address path is written for remote servers.

Suppose the client is trying to use a COM object that heretofore has not been used. The client obviously has no pointer for the required object or the interface. The client must thus refers to the COM library and calls the special CoCreateInstance method (see the "*Class Factory*" section), transferring CLSID of the required class, the IID of the interface, and the required type of server as a parameter.

Using the Service Control Manager (SCM), the library refers to the System Registry, uses the class identifier to locate the server information, and launches the server. The server creates the class instance — an object — and returns the pointer for the called interface to the library.

The COM library communicates the pointer to the client who, later on, may refer directly to the object. A diagram of the creation of the first instance of the object using the COM library and the System Registry is shown in Fig. 1.4.

NOTE

In Fig. 1.4, the client uses the CoCreateInstance method by invoking the COM object with GUID CLSID_2 and calling the IID2_A interface. The appropriate record is found in the System Registry by the global identifier CLSID_2, and the client sends the pointer back to the required interface.

To implicitly initialize the created object (set up the property values), a special object — a moniker — may be used. The client may also initialize the object on his or her own, using special interfaces (IPersistFile, IPersistStorage, IPersistStream).

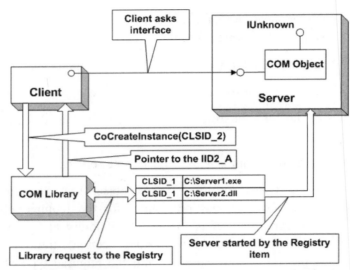

Fig. 1.4. Creation of the first instance of the object using the COM library and the System Registry

Class Factories

Objects are created by a special type of object called a *class factory*. With the help of the class factory, it is possible to create a single object, as well as several copies of it. An individual class factory must exist for each class.

According to the COM specification, a class factory is also a COM object. A COM object is entitled to be called a class factory if it supports the IClassFactory interface. Only two methods are implemented here:

❏ CoCreateInstance creates a new class instance. Besides the IID, this method obtains all the necessary parameters from the class factory. This is what distinguishes the library from the general function of the same name.

❏ LockServer leaves the server operating after the creation of an object.

NOTE

In fact, the general CoCreateInstance method calls the corresponding class factory and CoCreateInstance method of the IClassFactory interface, using the CLSID transferred to it.

CoGetClassObject is a special function used to call the class factory:

```
function CoGetClassObject(const clsid: TCLSID; dwClsContext: Longint;
pvReserved: Pointer; const iid: TIID; var pv): HResult; stdcall;
```

The necessary class of CLSID and the IID interface (IClassFactory) is transferred as a parameter. The function searches for the required factory and returns the pointer to the interface. With its help, the client makes the factory class create the object using the CoCreateInstance method.

Type Library

In order to document the object interfaces for the users, the developer creates information on the object types using the IDL language. All information is integrated into a special type library. It can describe the properties and the methods (as well as their parameters) of the interfaces, and contain the information on the necessary stubs and proxies. Information on the specific interface is designed as a separate object within the library.

To create the type library described by the IDL statements, a special compiler is used. Access to the library is gained via the CLSID of the object class. Besides this, the library has its own GUID that is saved in the System Registry when the object is registered.

Each type library has the ITypeLib interface, which enables it to work with the library, as well as with a single object. To get access to the information on a particular interface, the ITypeInfo interface is used.

To access the library via GUID, the LoadRegTypeLib function is used. If the client knows the file name of the library, it is possible to use the LoadTypeLib function.

COM Objects in Delphi

Now let's look at how to create COM objects in Delphi. As mentioned above, a COM object should provide for the creation of an arbitrary number of interfaces, interfaces being understood as a combination of methods accessed via the interface pointer.

It used to be quite difficult, however, to implement such a requirement directly using standard OOP approaches. Then Delphi developers found the following solution.

The COM object itself is described by the standard class TComObject, which is generated directly from the TObject. All the properties and methods implementing the object assignment are declared and described in its declaration. Therefore, the class of the new COM object is not significantly different from any other.

When a COM object is created, an auxiliary class that describes all the interfaces is linked to it. This class is generally called CoClass, and when a real object is created, its name is prefixed by Co. CoClass combines all the information on the types presented in the library. The declaration and description of the CoClass can be found in the type library.

Thus, the standard class declaration in Object Pascal provides for the creation of the object code; this is exactly what is compiled in binary code. The CoClass is the superstructure, or shell, of this code, providing for the presentation of the object instance according to the COM specification and guaranteeing the correct processing of the client's reference to the object.

The TComObject class, together with the CoClass instance created for each object, possesses all the features of the COM object considered above. It may support any number of the interfaces, including the basic one: IUnknown.

To allow the COM object to work with the type library, the new TTypedComObject class has to be generated from the basic TComObject class. It has another interface in addition: IProvideClassInfo. Should this interface have access to the type library, knowledge of its class identifier will be sufficient to obtain complete information on the object. This class is used to create objects with the use of the type library.

The *TComObject* Class

The TComObject class provides for the implementation of the basic functions of the object, those that actually make it a COM object. Its properties and methods encapsulate the functionality of the IUnknown interface. It also stores the CLSID class identifier.

Like any other object, a COM object is created by the constructor

```
constructor Create;
```

which creates an independent instance of the class.

At the same time, the constructor

```
constructor CreateAggregated(const Controller: IUnknown);
```

creates the new object as part of the aggregate. Here the aggregate is a range of objects that have their own interfaces, with the exception of the one general interface. This general interface is IUnknown, which, as is well known, implements the object call counter and controls all the objects of the aggregate. The object with the general controlling interface is called the controller.

In the CreateAggregated constructor, the Controller parameter defines the controlling interface and, after the reference to the constructor, it is communicated into the property

```
property Controller: IUnknown;
```

To actually create an object and initialize its parameters, the following constructor is used:

```
constructor CreateFromFactory(Factory: TComObjectFactory;
const Controller: IUnknown);
```

The Factory parameter enables the definition of the property

```
property Factory: TComObjectFactory;
```

which defines the class factory for the object. While the object is being created, the method

```
procedure Initialize; virtual;
```

performs the initialization. For the TComObject class this method is empty, but it could well be overflowing with descendants.

Both of the other constructors simply invoke the CreateFromFactory constructor, each in its own way initializing the Controller variable, which defines the affiliation with the aggregate:

```
constructor TComObject.Create;
begin
  FNonCountedObject := True;
  CreateFromFactory(ComClassManager.GetFactoryFromClass(ClassType), nil);
end;
constructor TComObject.CreateAggregated(const Controller: IUnknown);
begin
```

```
    FNonCountedObject := True;

CreateFromFactory(ComClassManager.GetFactoryFromClass(ClassType),
Controller);
    end;
```

After the object is created, the property

```
property RefCount: Integer;
```

is available for reading, which returns the number of opened references to the object. The meaning of this property is defined by the calls of the IUnknown interface

The methods of the IUnknown object interface may be used by calling the analogous methods of the TComObject class.

The method

```
function ObjAddRef: Integer; virtual; stdcall;
```

increases the reference counter by one. Accordingly, the property RefCount is increased.

The method

```
function ObjQueryInterface(const IID: TGUID; out Obj): HResult;
virtual; stdcall;
```

enables definition if the object uses the interface defined by the IID parameter.

And the method

```
function ObjRelease: Integer; virtual; stdcall;
```

reduces the reference counter by one. The RefCount property is also reduced.

The *TtypedComObject* Class

This class is the direct descendant of the TComObject class, and is used to create COM objects using the type library. This class has the additional interface IProvideClassInfo, which allows you to use an additional method:

```
function GetClassInfo(out TypeInfo: ITypeInfo): HResult; stdcall;
```

This function returns the pointer to the `CoClass` of a particular class, thus opening access to all information about the types.

The *IUnknown* Interface in Delphi

The `TComObject` class has methods that correspond to those of the encapsulated `IUnknown` interface.

As the general ancestor of all the interfaces in Delphi, the following interface is used

```
IInterface = interface
  ['{00000000-0000-0000-C000-000000000046}']
  function QueryInterface(const IID: TGUID; out Obj): HResult; stdcall;
  function _AddRef: Integer; stdcall;
  function _Release: Integer; stdcall;
end;
```

which, as you can see from the declaration, contains all three methods that allow the `IUnknown` interface to work. Therefore, the `IUnknown` interface is declared as follows:

```
IUnknown = IInterface;
```

The method

```
function QueryInterface(const IID: TGUID; out Obj): HResult; stdcall;
```

returns the pointer to the `IID` interface, if it is available.

The method

```
function _AddRef: Integer; stdcall;
```

increases the call counter by one.

The method

```
function _Release: Integer; stdcall;
```

reduces the call counter by one.

According to the COM specification, all interfaces in Delphi are descendants of the `IUnknown` interface.

Globally Unique Identifier Type

To represent the Globally Unique Identifier (GUID) in Delphi, a special type is defined in the System module:

```
TGUID = record
    D1: LongWord;
    D2: Word;
    D3: Word;
    D4: array[0..7] of Byte;
  end;
```

In order to generate a new identifier, it is possible to use the CoCreateGUID function from Win API. To convert the identifier into a string, the following function is used:

```
function GUIDToString(const ClassID: TGUID): string;
```

To reverse the operation, the following function is used:

```
function StringToGUID(const S: string): TGUID;
```

The *TInterfacedObject* Class

Especially for work with COM objects that encapsulate interfaces, the hierarchy of basic Delphi classes provides the TInterfacedObject class, which creates a class descendant that inherits not only the properties and methods of the class ancestor, but also the methods of the ancestor interface:

```
TInterfacedObject = class(TObject, IInterface)
```

The declarations of all classes descending from the TInterfacedObject class should indicate not only the class ancestor, but also the interface ancestor. As a result, the new class inherits the methods of the interface ancestor.

The creation of an instance of such class is done not with the class factory, but by using a common constructor:

```
type
  TSomeInterfacedObject = class(TInterfacedObject, IUnknown)
  end;
```

```
. . .
var SomeInterfacedObject: TSomeInterfacedObject;
. . .
SomeInterfacedObject := TSomeInterfacedObject.Create;
```

Since the `TInterfacedObject` class is inherited from the `IInterface` interface (also `IUnknown`), it contains the property of the call counter

```
property RefCount: Integer;
```

and three basic methods:

```
function _AddRef: Integer; stdcall;
function _Release: Integer; stdcall;
function QueryInterface(const IID: TGUID; out Obj): HResult; stdcall;
```

Memory allocation for the new object is carried out by the method of the `NewInstance` class. For the `TInterfacedObject` class, the method

```
class function NewInstance: TObject; override;
```

aside from the main function, also initializes the call counter.

> **NOTE**
>
> The methods of this class may be called without creating an object instance if you indicate the class name where they are described. Before the description of the method, the reserved word "class" should be inserted.

Class Factories in Delphi

When creating of COM objects in Delphi, the developer needn't worry about creating a factory for each class. As you can see below (see Listing 1.1), in addition to the object, not only the `CoClass` is created, but also the class factory as well — a special COM object with the `IClassFactory` interface that is used for the creation of COM objects.

Careful readers will have already noted that when creating the basic class `TComObject` instance, the `CreateFromFactory` constructor, which is charged with calling the corresponding factory class, is invoked in any case. The COM object contacts its class factory via the `Factory` property, which has the `TComObjectFactory` type. The TComObjectFactory class is the basic one when using class factories in COM applications in Delphi.

In cases where there are several class factories functioning within one server, a special COM class manager is used. It is created on the basis of the TComClassManager class, and used mainly for in-process operations where the server needs to perform certain actions with all the class factories, e.g., to delete them correctly.

To create a factory for the declared class with the help of the TTypedComObject class, the TTypedComObjectFactory class is used.

The *TComObjectFactory* Class

This class encapsulates the functions of a multipurpose class factory for COM objects created as instances of the TComObject class. It provides for the functioning of the IUnknown, IClassFactory, and IClassFactory2 interfaces. The IClassFactory interface is the defining interface in the operation of the class factory.

Usually, the class factory is created on the operating server of the object that the factory has created. The factory constructor is described in the section of the module initialization that includes the corresponding server (see Listing 1.1).

To create the factory, the following constructor is used:

```
constructor Create(ComServer: TComServerObject; ComClass:
TComClass; const ClassID: TGUID; const ClassName, Description:
string; Instancing: TClassInstancing; ThreadingModel:
TThreadingModel = tmSingle);
```

The ComServer parameter defines the server where the object will function.

The ComClass parameter defines the type of the class used to identify the class factory while the GetFactoryFromClass procedure of the TComClassManager class is functioning.

The ClassID parameter specifies the class identifier created using this class factory.

The Instancing parameter defines the means for creating the object creation.

The ThreadingModel parameter defines the technique of the interaction between the object and the client.

After the class factory is created, the main parameters of its COM object are available via properties.

The property

```
property ClassID: TGUID;
```

returns the GUID of the object class.

The property

```
property ClassName: string;
```

contains the name of the object class.

The property

```
property ComClass: TClass;
```

defines the type class used for identification of the class factory.

The means for creating the object is defined by the property

```
type TClassInstancing = (ciInternal, ciSingleInstance, ciMultiInstance);
property Instancing: TClassInstancing;
```

And the property

```
property ThreadingModel: TThreadingModel;
```

specifies the means of interaction between the object and the client.

The key method of the class is the function

```
function CreateComObject(const Controller: IUnknown): TComObject;
```

It performs the operations of the CoCreateInstance function of the IClaccFactory interface. This method calls the CreateFromFactory constructor that is linked to this class factory, transferring the necessary parameters.

The method

```
procedure RegisterClassObject;
```

registers the class of the object created. This is done by launching the executable file encapsulating the COM object.

The method

```
procedure UpdateRegistry(Register: Boolean); virtual;
```

registers or unregisters the COM object. For executable applications, this is done upon the first startup or upon startup with the `/regserver` key. This method allows for the saving of the main parameters of the COM object and the location of the executable file in the System Registry.

After the COM object is created, the developer may provide for a special interface responsible for error handling. Its `GUID` is defined by the property

```
property ErrorIID: TGUID;
```

and the property

```
property ShowErrors: Boolean;
```

switches on or off the display of error data from the object's creation.

When distributing the COM object, the developer may include license information and information about the developer in the executable code.

The textual description of the COM object may be defined upon entering the property

```
property Description: string;
```

The property

```
property ProgID: string;
```

contains the name of the developer, class, and version.

The property

```
property LicString: WideString;
```

must contain the license information on the object.

If the developer provides for a user registration procedure and license agreement, the property

```
property SupportsLicensing: Boolean;
```

makes it possible to define the startup mode with the licensing. For this purpose, the property must be defined as `True`.

The *TTypedComObjectFactory* Class

This class is generated from the `TComObjectFactory` class, and is used to create the class factories for classes declared using the `TTypedComObject` class — i.e., this class is used to describe the class factory in the type library. The `TTypedComObjectFactory` class has one additional method:

```
function GetInterfaceTypeInfo(TypeFlags: Integer): ITypeInfo;
```

This function returns the pointer to the `ITypeInfo` interface, which contains information about a certain type.

The *TComClassManager* Class

This class is used to manage the class factories within a particular COM server. This is the class of the `ComClassManager` variable within the ComObj module.

It is possible to obtain a reference to the class instance using a function of the same module:

```
function ComClassManager: TComClassManager;
```

The developer may make use of the class method

```
function GetFactoryFromClassID(const ClassID: TGUID): TComObjectFactory;
```

which performs a search by `ClassID` among the functioning class factories of the server.

The method

```
function GetFactoryFromClass(ComClass: TClass): TComObjectFactory;
```

returns a reference to the class factory for the `ComClass` class. In particular, this method is used in the COM object constructor to obtain a reference to the class factory.

COM Servers in Delphi

When a COM object is created, the ComServ module is automatically added to the module with its description. This module describes the `TComServer` class that encapsulates the properties of the COM server where the corresponding object is operating. The reference to the properties and methods of this class makes it possible to obtain information about the objects operating within the server, their status, and the status of the server itself.

When the ComServ module is included in the object module, an instance of the `TComServer` class is automatically created, the pointer to which is assigned to the variable

```
var ComServer: TComServer;
```

Using this variable, it is possible to obtain information from the server.

The server class is used to create instances of the class factories, i.e., it takes part directly in the interaction of clients and COM objects. Global functions are declared and described in the ComServ module, and these are automatically exported to each in-process server, where they perform basic operations of registration, re-registration, and server rollout. It is not necessary to call them directly.

The *TComServer* Class

This class combines the properties and methods that make it possible to obtain information about the server itself and the object functioning within the COM server. This class is the descendant of the `TComServerObject` abstract class.

This class is used for in-process and local servers.

If the property

```
property IsInprocServer: Boolean;
```

has a value of `True`, then the server is in-purpose. A more accurate definition of the server type is obtained using the property

```
property ServerKey: string;
```

If it contains the value `'InprocServer32'`, then the server is in-purpose and DLL. If you see the value `'LocalServer32'`, then this is the local server in the form of an executable file.

The server file startup technique is defined by the property

```
type TStartMode = (smStandalone, smAutomation, smRegServer, smUnregServer);
property StartMode: TStartMode;
```

which can have the following values:

❏ `smStandalone`: the server is started as a separate application.

❏ `smAutomation`: the server is started as an Automation server (see *Chapter 2, "Automation"*).

❑   smRegServer: the server is started with the /regserver key (or started for the first time) to be registered in the Registry.

❑   smUnregServer: the server is started with the /unregserver key for unregistration.

Upon startup of the server, the following method is called:

```
procedure Initialize;
```

It registers (upon the first startup or upon the use of the /regserver key) all the COM objects related to this server. These may be the principal or subsidiary remote data modules — special COM objects used in the DataSnap technology (see *Chapter 9, "An Application Server"*).

The name is defined by the read-only property

```
property ServerName: string;
```

It can also be defined by the method

```
procedure SetServerName(const Name: string);
```

Note, however, that if the server uses a type library, then it defines the server name. The reference to the type library is available via the property

```
property TypeLib: ITypeLib;
```

which returns the ITypeLib interface — the main interface of the type library.

It is possible to load a type library via the method

```
procedure LoadTypeLib;
```

The full filename is in the property

```
property ServerFileName: string;
```

and if there is a help file, its full name is defined by the property

```
property HelpFileName: string;
```

Another useful read-only property

```
property ObjectCount: Integer;
```

is used in the process of the server's operation. It returns the total number of COM objects operating on this server.

Type Libraries in Delphi

Type libraries store information about objects, interfaces, functions, etc. They are used in Delphi projects that use COM-based technologies.

Traditionally, type libraries are created using the Interface Description Language – IDL. As the basic option, the syntax and operators of the Object Pascal language are used. You may, however, export this code into IDL format, thus providing for the use of your own objects in any Windows application.

Clients may use the type library upon calling an object in order to obtain initial information about the available identifiers, interfaces, and methods. Basically, these data may be obtained by programmatic means using the System Registry and the options of the main COM interfaces. It is not always convenient, however, to supplement the application with such a complicated block of code because you need use a small object for auxiliary purposes.

Usually, a version of the library in Object Pascal is used within the project and, when the objects are distributed, the type library is exported into IDL format. The version of the type library in Object Pascal is saved as a file with the PAS extension and a file name ending in _TLB.

In Delphi, the code of the type library is generated automatically when an object is created. To work with the library, the special Type Library Editor is used (Fig. 1.5). All the operations here modify the source code of the type library and corresponding objects and interfaces, so the developer needs not study the peculiarities of the library code's construction thoroughly.

NOTE

The developer can either use the type library in the project or not. To include the type library when a new COM object is created, it is necessary to set the **Include Type Library** checkbox (Fig. 1.6). Or, you could use the Delphi Object Repository, where the type library is available on the **ActiveX** page.

The Type Library Editor provides the developer with a full toolkit, enabling him or her to automate the process of creating objects and interfaces. The **Editor** window is divided into three main parts (Fig. 1.5).

On top, there is a narrow toolbar. Using the toolbar's buttons, one may create COM elements and perform general operations for the entire library. The toolbar is divided into four parts. On the left we find buttons of new types that may be added to the type library:

 (Interface) creates a new interface.

 (Dispatch) creates a new dispinterface (see details in the next chapter).

(CoClass) creates a new `CoClass` for the COM object.

(Enum) creates a new enumerator. It may contain constants. It is used for object initialization.

(Alias) creates new aliases (do not confuse with database aliases). It is basically the naming of an existing data type. It has its own identifier.

(Record) creates a new record, which is understood as a list of fields — types of data that have been named but do not have their own identifiers.

(Union) creates a new union, presented as an indexed and ordered list of fields.

(Module) creates a new module combining separate functions and constants.

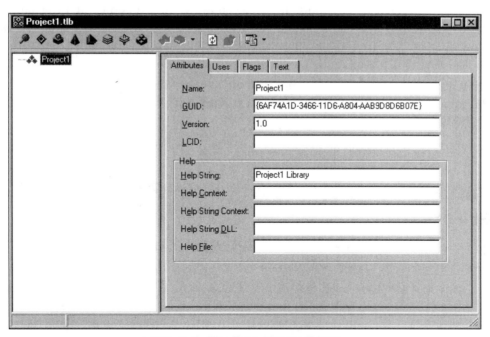

Fig. 1.5. The Type Library Editor

Then come two buttons that alter their assignment depending on the current library type selected from the tree on the left. These buttons are for creating the new elements of the type. For example, new methods and variables may be created for the interface.

Then come two groups of buttons that provide for the functioning of the general operations of the library.

❑ The [icon] (Refresh) button updates the source code of the library, objects, and interfaces in other modules.

❑ The [icon] (Register) button registers the type library in the Registry.

❑ The [icon] (Export) button exports the library code in the format of the Microsoft IDL or CORBA IDL language.

On the left, there is a hierarchical list of the project parts available in the type library. It is used to select the required type and type handling — the pop-up menu contains the main commands of the Editor.

On the right, there is an information bar showing the properties of the element selected from the list and enabling the handling of its parameters. Its multipage notebook changes the settings and contents of the pages, depending on the current type.

There are always two pages for any type on the bar. The **Attributes** page specifies the main parameters of the type. The **Text** page can contain a textual description of the type.

An example using a type library for the interface's methods is considered below.

Simple COM Objects within In-Process Servers

Now let us consider an example that, despite its simplicity, encompasses all the main stages of work with COM objects.

To demonstrate the operation of a COM object, we have to create an in-process server and, within it, a simple COM object to represent its interface. The object will contain a few methods that perform very simple mathematical operations.

Object Creation

To create a COM object within an in-process server (dynamic library), it is necessary to carry out the following actions.

On the **ActiveX** page of the Delphi Object Repository, you must click on the **ActiveX Library** icon. As a result, a new project will be created, called ClientInProcCOM. The source code of the new dynamic library will be created automatically, and is presented in Listing 1.1.

Listing 1.1. Source Code of the InProcCOM Dynamic Library

```
library InProcCOM;

uses
  ComServ,
  ClientInProcCOM_TLB in 'ClientInProcCOM_TLB.pas',
  uSimpleCOM in 'uSimpleCOM.pas' {SImpleCOM: CoClass};

exports
  DllGetClassObject,
  DllCanUnloadNow,
  DllRegisterServer,
  DllUnregisterServer;

{$R *.TLB}

{$R *.RES}

begin
end.
```

The following four functions exported by the library provide for its interaction with COM:

☐ DllGetClassObject provides access to the class library.

☐ DllCanUnloadNow manages the server depending on the state of the objects.

☐ DllRegisterServer registers the server in the System Registry.

☐ DllUnregisterServer deletes the server information from the System Registry.

You should then click on the **COM Object** icon on the **ActiveX** page in the repository. After clicking on the icon, a dialog box will open where the initial parameters for the new object may be specified (Fig. 1.6).

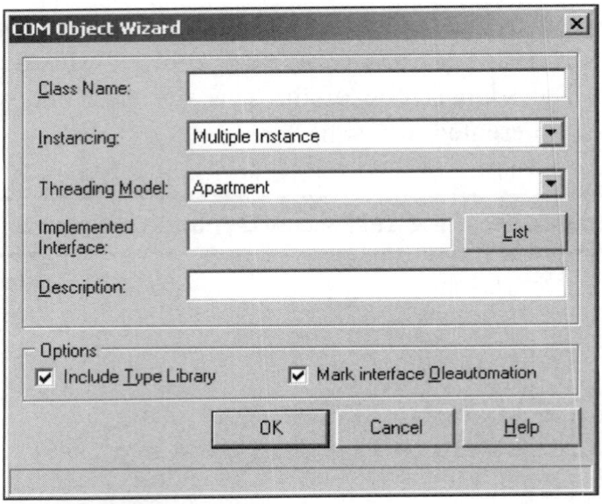

Fig. 1.6. Window for setting the initial parameters of a COM object

The **Class Name** string editor must contain the name of the new class.

The **Instancing** combined list defines the means of creating the object:

❒ **Internal** — the object is used in the process.

❒ **Single Instance** — if several clients call the object, the necessary number of objects are created on a single instance of the server.

❒ **Multiple Instance** — if several clients call the object, a separate instance of the object server is created for each call.

If the object is used within the process, this list's settings are of no importance.

The **Threading Model** combined list defines the method of interaction between the object and clients:

❒ **Single** — the server can service client calls sequentially, one by one.

❒ **Apartment** — a call for the object is performed only in the thread in which the COM object itself was created, and the object can serve only one client at a time; several objects may simultaneously work in this mode in the server.

❏ **Free** — an object can simultaneously serve an arbitrary number of clients.

❏ **Both** — an object can work with clients using both the Apartment and Free models.

❏ **Neutral** — an object may serve several clients in various threads, but does not resolve conflicts that occur; used only for COM+ technology.

The **Implemented Interfaces** string editor contains the name of the interface encapsulated by the object being created. By default, a separate interface is created for an object, whose name consists of the object name and the prefix "I." The developer may, however, attribute to the object an existing COM interface. You may specify the required interface manually or select it from the **Interface Selection Wizard** dialog box, which opens when you press the **List** button.

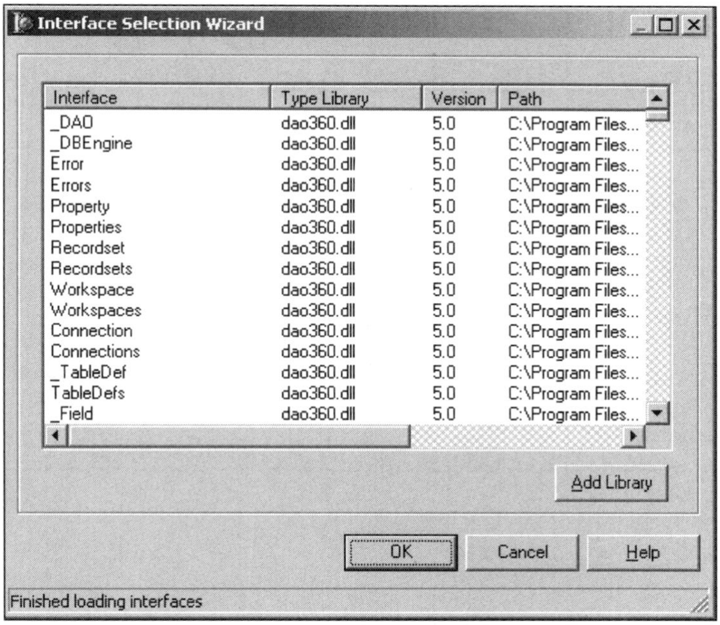

Fig. 1.7. The **Interface Selection Wizard** window

The **Description** string editor contains a description of the object.

The **Include Type Library** checkbox handles the creation of the type library for an object. It is inaccessible, however, unless you select an existing interface for the object.

The **Mark Interface OleAutomation** checkbox makes an object suitable for use within Automation. If the checkbox is checked, a dispinterface is created for the object interface (see *Chapter 2*, *"Automation"*).

The set parameters of the SimpleCOM object are shown in Table 1.1.

Table 1.1. Parameters of the TSimpleCOM Object

Parameter	Value
Class Name	SimpleCOM
Instancing	tmApartment
Threading Model	ciMultiInstance
Implemented Interfaces	ISimpleCOM
Description	Simple COM Object Sample
Include Type Library	Enabled
Mark Interface OleAutomation	Disabled

After the parameters are set and the **OK** button is pressed, the project will be supplemented with a new module that includes the source code of the new class.

The source code of the COM object module immediately after its creation is presented in Listing 1.2.

Listing 1.2. Source Code of the TSimpleCOM COM Object Immediately after Creation

```
unit uSimpleCOM;

{$WARN SYMBOL_PLATFORM OFF}

interface

uses
  Windows, ActiveX, Classes, ComObj, ClientInProcCOM_TLB, StdVcl;

type
  TSImpleCOM = class(TTypedComObject, ISImpleCOM)
  protected
```

```
    end;

  implementation

  uses ComServ;

  initialization
    TTypedComObjectFactory.Create(ComServer, TSImpleCOM, Class_SImpleCOM,
      ciMultiInstance, tmApartment);
  end.
```

As is seen in the declaration, the nearest ancestor of the new object class is the `TTypedComObject` class, since, according to the initial settings of the object, a class factory is created for it.

The object constructor `TSimpleCOM` contains the name of the class factory and the basic interface, which has the same name as the class. There is also a class factory constructor in the initialization section. It should be noted that the class of the class factory was created automatically.

To provide for the server's operation, the `ComServ` module and the `ComServ` variable indicating the COM server class are used. The variable is used in the constructor of the class factory.

You can see that only the `TSimpleCOM` class is described in the module of the COM object, this class being the basis of the COM object's functioning. The interfaces `ISimpleCOM` and `CoClass` are declared in the type library in the ClientInProcCOM_TLB.PAS file.

The source code of the library was created automatically, together with the new COM object, and is saved in the ClientInProcCOM_TLB.PAS file.

Listing 1.3. Type Library Source Code for the TSimpleCOM COM Object

---

```
unit InProcCOM_TLB;

// ********************************************************************* //
// WARNING
```

```
// -------
// The types declared in this file were generated from data read from a
// Type Library. If this type library is explicitly or indirectly (via
// another type library referring to this type library) re-imported, or the
// 'Refresh' command of the Type Library Editor activated while editing the
// Type Library, the contents of this file will be regenerated and all
// manual modifications will be lost.
// ********************************************************************** //

// PASTLWTR : $Revision:   1.130.3.0.1.0  $
// File generated on 11.03.2002 17:46:03 from Type Library described below.

// ********************************************************************** //
// Type Lib: C:\Mark\Bin\Books\d6WEB\DemosE\01_1\Server\InProcCOM.tlb (1)
// LIBID: {246D6A47-D078-498C-8E4C-9D94B76BFE22}
// LCID: 0
// Helpfile:
// DepndLst:
//   (1) v2.0 stdole, (C:\WINNT\System32\stdole2.tlb)
//   (2) v4.0 StdVCL, (C:\Program Files\Common Files\SuperCollect\stdvcl40.dll)
// ********************************************************************** //
{$TYPEDADDRESS OFF} // Unit must be compiled without type-checked pointers.
{$WARN SYMBOL_PLATFORM OFF}
{$WRITEABLECONST ON}

interface

uses Windows, ActiveX, Classes, Graphics, StdVCL, Variants;


// **********************************************************************//
```

```
// GUIDS declared in the TypeLibrary. Following prefixes are used:
//    Type Libraries     : LIBID_xxxx
//    CoClasses          : CLASS_xxxx
//    DISPInterfaces     : DIID_xxxx
//    Non-DISP interfaces: IID_xxxx
// *****************************************************************//
const
  // TypeLibrary Major and minor versions
  InProcCOMMajorVersion = 1;
  InProcCOMMinorVersion = 0;

  LIBID_InProcCOM: TGUID = '{246D6A47-D078-498C-8E4C-9D94B76BFE22}';

  IID_ISimpleCOM: TGUID = '{76247090-8BCD-4AAD-8EE3-EEE4DE68872C}';
  CLASS_SimpleCOM: TGUID = '{E76AE0BE-14DD-431D-B923-324EBA987770}';
type

// *****************************************************************//
// Forward declaration of types defined in TypeLibrary
// *****************************************************************//
  ISimpleCOM = interface;

// *****************************************************************//
// Declaration of CoClasses defined in Type Library
// (NOTE: Here we map each CoClass to its Default Interface)
// *****************************************************************//
  SimpleCOM = ISimpleCOM;

// *****************************************************************//
// Interface: ISimpleCOM
```

```
// Flags:      (0)
// GUID:       {76247090-8BCD-4AAD-8EE3-EEE4DE68872C}
// ********************************************************************//
  ISimpleCOM = interface(IUnknown)
    ['{76247090-8BCD-4AAD-8EE3-EEE4DE68872C}']
  end;


// ********************************************************************//
// The CoSimpleCOM Class provides a Create and CreateRemote method to
// create instances of the default interface ISimpleCOM exposed by
// the SimpleCOM CoClass. The functions are intended to be used by
// clients wishing to automate the CoClass objects exposed by the
// server of this typelibrary.
// ********************************************************************//
  CoSimpleCOM = class
    class function Create: ISimpleCOM;
    class function CreateRemote(const MachineName: string): ISimpleCOM;
  end;

implementation

uses ComObj;

class function CoSimpleCOM.Create: ISimpleCOM;
begin
  Result := CreateComObject(CLASS_SimpleCOM) as ISimpleCOM;
end;

class function CoSimpleCOM.CreateRemote(const MachineName: string): ISimpleCOM;
begin
```

```
    Result := CreateRemoteComObject(MachineName, CLASS_SimpleCOM) as ISimpleCOM;
end;

end.
```

The type library contains the automatically generated GUID of the ISimpleCOM interface, and then comes the declaration of the interface itself. The CoSimpleCOM class provides for the operation of the SimpleCOM object's interfaces. So far, it contains only one interface. There are two functions created in this class: Create is used for work on a server within the process and on a local server; CreateRemote is used for work on a remote server. Both functions return pointers to the ISimpleCOM interface.

Creation of Interface Methods

Having created the new COM object, we are now going to develop the methods used to implement its functions. Let's suppose the object is intended to perform simple mathematical functions.

It is necessary to show how the several interfaces of one object are used. Otherwise, the COM object will not differ in principle from a regular object. Let the first and second interfaces implement a number of simple linear and power functions.

We already have the first interface, ISimpleCOM, which was created together with the COM object in the previous step.

In order to create the second interface and all the required methods, we use the Type Library Editor (Fig. 1.5). For this purpose, we have to perform the following actions.

1. Select the ISimpleCOM interface from the hierarchical list and press the **New Method** button on the toolbar (Fig. 1.7).

2. Rename the resulting method (Method1) in the hierarchical list to LinearX. Note that only methods' names may be specified in the **Attributes** menu.

3. Go to the **Parameters** menu in the right part of the Editor and specify the type long in the **Return Type** list (the type returned by the result method) instead of the standard HResult type.

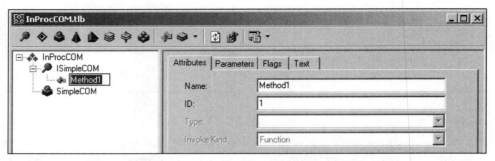

Fig. 1.7. Creating new method in the Type Library Editor

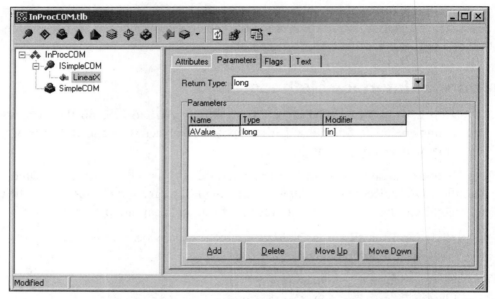

Fig. 1.8. Setting the method's parameter

4. Now press the **Add** button on the bottom of the page to add the first parameter to the method. In the resulting line in the **Name** cell, change the name of the parameter to AValue (Fig. 1.8).

5. The data type of the parameter is specified in the **Type** column. The drop-down list of the column contains all permissible types of data. For our parameter, select the long type.

6. The type of the parameter itself is specified in the **Modifier** column. After pressing the button, the **Parameter Flags** window appears (Fig. 1.9), in which you

can specify the parameter type and, if necessary, the default value. In our case, the parameter must be incoming, so the **In** checkbox should be ticked in the window.

Fig. 1.9. The **Parameter Flags** window

Once the above operations are completed, the method declaration is finished.

Now let's perform the same sequence of operations for another method: squareX.

In order to create the source code for these methods, press the **Refresh** button on the toolbar of the Type Library Editor. As a result, the source code for the created methods will automatically appear in the SimpleCOM object module. Only the corresponding mathematical functions are left to be entered into them (Listing 1.4).

To create the second interface and all the required methods, we use the Type Library Editor. To do this, we have to perform the following actions.

Press the **Interface** button on the toolbar. The new interface appearing in the hierarchical list is to be renamed ISimpleCOM2.

A GUID for the new interface is generated on the **Attributes** page (Fig. 1.10), and IUnknown — the name of the ancestor interface — is to be selected from the **Parent Interface** list. Besides this, the **Dual** and **OleAutomation** checkboxes should be disabled on the **Flags** page. For the newly created interfaces, these checkboxes are switched on by default, since the ActiveX dynamic library was selected as the basis of the in-process server (see *Chapter 3, "ActiveX Components"*).

Then, the Linear2X and CubeX methods are created using the same operations as for the new ISimpleCOM2 interface described above.

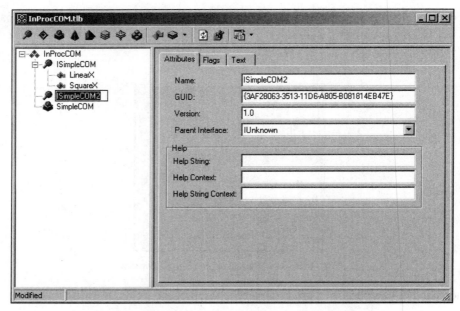

Fig. 1.10. Creating a GUID for the new interface

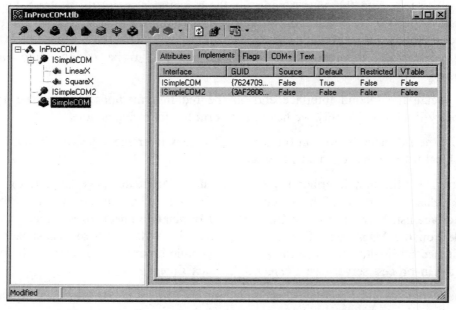

Fig. 1.11. Connecting the interface with the COM object

Now the created interface is to be connected to the TSimpleCOM COM object. For this, the object is selected from the hierarchical list, and on the right side of the window, the **Implements** page should be chosen. Here you can find a list of all the interfaces of the object, though there will be only one basic interface here as of yet. Click the right mouse button on the list and select the **Insert Interface** command from the pop-up menu. Select the ISimpleCOM2 interface from the list that appears, and press **OK**. The new interface will appear within the object.

To conclude, press the **Refresh** button to create the corresponding source code. Then you may shift to the uSimpleCOM.PAS module and create a very simple source code for the new methods (Listing 1.4). Each method performs a simple arithmetical operation.

Listing 1.4. The uSimpleCOM Module of the SimpleCOM Object after the Second Interface Has Been Created

```
unit uSimpleCOM;

{$WARN SYMBOL_PLATFORM OFF}

interface

uses
  Windows, ActiveX, Classes, ComObj, InProcCOM_TLB, StdVcl;

type
  TSimpleCOM = class(TTypedComObject, ISimpleCOM, ISimpleCOM2)
  protected
    function LinearX(AValue: Integer): Integer; stdcall;
    function SquareX(AValue: Integer): Integer; stdcall;
    function CubeX(AValue: Integer): Integer; stdcall;
    function Linear2X(AValue: Integer): Integer; stdcall;
  end;

implementation

uses ComServ;
```

```
function TSimpleCOM.LinearX(AValue: Integer): Integer;
begin
 Result := AValue;
end;


function TSimpleCOM.SquareX(AValue: Integer): Integer;
begin
 Result := AValue*AValue;
end;


function TSimpleCOM.CubeX(AValue: Integer): Integer;
begin
 Result := AValue*AValue*AValue;
end;


function TSimpleCOM.Linear2X(AValue: Integer): Integer;
begin
 Result := AValue*2;
end;


initialization
  TTypedComObjectFactory.Create(ComServer, TSimpleCOM, Class_SimpleCOM,
    ciMultiInstance, tmApartment);
end.
```

It should be noted that the code presented does not suggest any connection whatsoever between the methods and the various interfaces. This division is done in the Type Library (Listing 1.5.). But note that a second interface — ISimpleCOM2 — has appeared in the TSimpleCOM class declaration.

Listing 1.5. Source Code of the Type Library after the Second Interface Has Been Created (Comments Deleted)

```
unit InProcCOM_TLB;

{$TYPEDADDRESS OFF}
{$WARN SYMBOL_PLATFORM OFF}
{$WRITEABLECONST ON}

interface

uses Windows, ActiveX, Classes, Graphics, StdVCL, Variants;

const
  InProcCOMMajorVersion = 1;
  InProcCOMMinorVersion = 0;

  LIBID_InProcCOM: TGUID = '{246D6A47-D078-498C-8E4C-9D94B76BFE22}';

  IID_ISimpleCOM: TGUID = '{76247090-8BCD-4AAD-8EE3-EEE4DE68872C}';
  IID_ISimpleCOM2: TGUID = '{3AF28063-3513-11D6-A805-B081814EB47E}';
  CLASS_SimpleCOM: TGUID = '{E76AE0BE-14DD-431D-B923-324EBA987770}';
type

  ISimpleCOM = interface;
  ISimpleCOM2 = interface;

  SimpleCOM = ISimpleCOM;

  ISimpleCOM = interface(IUnknown)
    ['{76247090-8BCD-4AAD-8EE3-EEE4DE68872C}']
    function LinearX(AValue: Integer): Integer; stdcall;
    function SquareX(AValue: Integer): Integer; stdcall;
  end;

  ISimpleCOM2 = interface(IUnknown)
```

```
    ['{3AF28063-3513-11D6-A805-B081814EB47E}']
    function Linear2X(AValue: Integer): Integer; stdcall;
    function CubeX(AValue: Integer): Integer; stdcall;
  end;


  CoSimpleCOM = class
    class function Create: ISimpleCOM;
    class function CreateRemote(const MachineName: string):
ISimpleCOM;
  end;


implementation


uses ComObj;


class function CoSimpleCOM.Create: ISimpleCOM;
begin
  Result := CreateComObject(CLASS_SimpleCOM) as ISimpleCOM;
end;


class function CoSimpleCOM.CreateRemote(const MachineName: string): ISimpleCOM;
begin
  Result := CreateRemoteComObject(MachineName, CLASS_SimpleCOM) as ISimpleCOM;
end;


end.
```

Let's now look at the changes in the Type Library.

First, the declaration of a second interface, ISimpleCOM2, has appeared in the library. Its GUID has been generated and the necessary variables have been declared.

Second, the methods created in the Type Library Editor are declared in the corresponding interfaces. It should be noted that the long data type specified for the method parameters in the Type Library Editor was converted into the integer type.

In-Process Server Registration

After completing the development of the object and the compiling of the library, the library must be registered as the server. In order to do this, the **Register ActiveX Server** command is selected from the **Run** menu of the Delphi main window. The in-process server information is located in the System Registry.

When the TSimpleCOM COM object is created, the InProcCOM dynamic library is loaded into the address space of the client application and operates as the in-process server. As a result, if the client application has references to the interfaces of the COM object, it may use the methods of these interfaces.

We are now finished creating the SimpleCOM object, and may turn to the client part of the project.

Using In-Process COM Server Interfaces

The simple ClientInProcCOM application, which has only the fmMain form, will play the part of the client application. It is necessary to adjust it so that the performance of the two interfaces of the created object can be tested (Fig. 1.12).

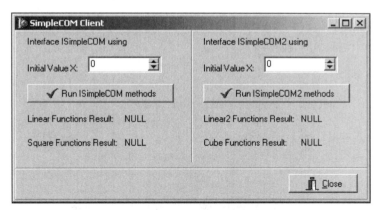

Fig. 1.12. The main form of the ClientInProcCOM project

The TSpinEdit components are intended to specify the x value for the functions performed in the methods of the ISimpleCOM and ISimpleCOM2 interfaces. The values from these visual components will be communicated to the methods as parameters.

The buttons should call the methods of the object interfaces. To display the result, the TLabel components are used.

In order for the client application to make use of the interfaces of the InProcCOM in-process server, it is necessary to add the InProcCOM_TLB.PAS Type Library file to the client's project.

After this, you can declare two variables for the TSimpleCOM COM object interfaces:

```
Interface1: ISimpleCOM;
Interface2: ISimpleCOM2;
```

Listing 1.6 shows the source code of the client that allows you to use the COM object methods.

Listing 1.6. Section Implementation of the uMain Module of the ClientInProcCOM Project

```
implementation

uses InProcCOM_TLB;

var
   Interface1: ISimpleCOM;
   Interface2: ISimpleCOM2;

{$R *.dfm}

procedure TfmMain.FormShow(Sender: TObject);
begin
 Interface1 := CoSimpleCOM.Create;
 Interface1.QueryInterface(ISimpleCOM2, Interface2);
end;

procedure TfmMain.bbRunSimpleCOMClick(Sender: TObject);
begin
 laLinearRes.Caption := IntToStr(Interface1.LinearX(seSimpleCOMValue.Value));
 laSquareRes.Caption := IntToStr(Interface1.SquareX(seSimpleCOMValue.Value));
end;

procedure TfmMain.bbRunSimpleCOM2Click(Sender: TObject);
```

```
begin
  laLinear2Res.Caption := IntToStr(Interface2.Linear2X(seSimpleCOM2Value.Value));
  laCubeRes.Caption := IntToStr(Interface2.CubeX(seSimpleCOM2Value.Value));
end;

end.
```

When the form is opened in the FormShow method handler, the CoClass of the TSimpleCOM class — CoSimpleCOM — is created. Its constructor returns the pointer to the main ISimpleCOM interface to the Interface1 variable of the ISimpleCOM type. All these operations are performed by the InProcCOM dynamic library. Its record in the System Registry can be found by the global identifier from the InProcCOM_TLB.PAS Type Library.

Since any interface is a descendant of IUnknown, you may use the QueryInterface method to get the pointer to the second interface. The identifier of the required interface and the variable to which the pointer will be returned are indicated in the method's parameters. In our example, this is the ISimpleCOM2 interface and the Interface2 variable.

After these operations are completed, the client gets pointers to both interfaces of the SimpleCOM object. To execute the methods of these interfaces, the method handlers of the bbRunSimpleCOM and bbRunSimpleCOM2 buttons are used.

The result is displayed on the form by appropriating the results of the work of the interface methods of the TSimpleCOM COM object of the InProcCOM.DLL in-process server.

Summary

COM technology is a basic concept necessary to understand the topics considered in this book. It helps the objects created by various programming means in various programming languages to interact.

The key COM notions are "object," "interface," and "class factory."

❑ An interface combines several methods and provides access to them via a general pointer.

❑ An object encapsulates one or several interfaces and presents them to the clients.

❑ A class factory creates instances of COM objects.

Chapter 2

Automation

The COM technology considered in *Chapter 1* is the basis of many other technologies. One of them — Automation — was created some time ago and is widely used in the most common client applications of the Windows OS.

This technology enables certain applications to use the functions of other applications. The interaction is performed using specially created interfaces. The basic interface is IDispatch.

Such widely used applications as Word, Excel, and Internet Explorer support Automation. It is not necessary to list the advantages of this technology. For example, any user program that has information on the functions provided by the Microsoft Word Automation interface gains access to the numerous text editing options.

From the programmer's point of view, creating applications that use Automation is very similar to the technique considered in *Chapter 1* for COM objects. This chapter deals with the peculiarities of programming in Delphi using Automation. Among them, the following issues are stressed.

❑ Automation interfaces

❑ Automation objects

❑ Creation of the Automation server

❑ Creation of the Automation controller

❑ Automation examples

Basic Concepts of Automation

As a COM-based technology, Automation provides certain applications with the functions of other applications. Naturally, this is done with interfaces. These interfaces are contained by various Automation objects which, in turn, are located in Automation servers.

The main difference between Automation and its ancestor technology COM is the way methods of interfaces are called.

In COM, the pointers to the interface methods are contained in the special Virtual Tables only (see Fig. 1.3). This access technique is called *early binding*.

In Automation, access to the interface methods is performed both in the traditional COM way, and using a special method that searches for the called method by a special identifier. This access technique is called *late binding*.

In all other respects, Automation technology is similar to COM technology. Let's consider the main entities used in Automation.

Automation Interfaces

All Automation interfaces have a common ancestor, the interface IDispatch, which provides the unique functionality of the technology. Of course, the common ancestor of any Automation interface is the IUnknown interface (see *Chapter 1, "COM Mechanisms in Delphi"*).

The interfaces considered here may be divided into two groups — dispinterfaces and dual interfaces.

The *IDispatch* Interface and Dispinterfaces

The basic interface of Automation is the IDispatch interface. This is a quite common COM interface, although it has some methods that are very important for Automation. Like all similar interfaces, it is implemented by a virtual table of pointers to its methods (see *Chapter 1, "COM Mechanisms in Delphi"*).

The distinguishing feature of the IDispatch interface is the special method Invoke, which provides for the calls of other methods. Besides this method, IDispatch has three important methods. These are GetTypeInfoCount, GetTypeInfo, and GetIDsOfNames. All of them provide the late binding mechanism.

The object operating with the IDispatch interface must define an additional interface where the methods that can be called via the Invoke method are listed. This interface is called a *dispatching interface*, or *dispinterface.*

It does not use a virtual table. Instead, the Invoke method is used to access the methods. A realization of the Invoke method is the case operator: here the required method is selected based on the method passed in the identifier parameter.

With this call, each method must have a unique identifier, called the *dispatch identifier* (DISPID).

The methods of the dispinterfaces are somewhat limited in the data types of the parameters; the values of all parameters are converted to the variant type when the methods are called. The reverse procedure takes place when the results are returned.

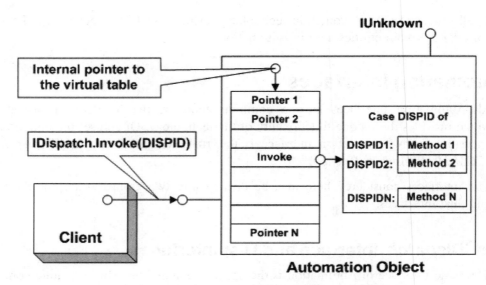

Fig. 2.1. The call mechanism of the dispinterface methods

Let's look at the late binding mechanism (Fig. 2.1).

When the client needs to use a method of the Automation interface, it calls the Invoke method, passing it the dispatcher identifier of the required method as a parameter. Then the Automation object finds the pointer to the Invoke method using the virtual table and calls it. The Invoke method starts a search for the required method by its dispatcher identifier. The pointer found is returned to the main interface and used for processing the client's query.

Like any other interface, each dispinterface has its own unique identifier. It is used in cases when there are several dispinterfaces in the application. As the interface IDispatch is the descendant of the IUnknown interface, you can use the inherited method QueryInterface to call another dispinterface.

As a result, interaction between Automations applications is simplified — only one virtual table is needed for successful performance of the IDispatch interface; all other methods are called by the mechanisms described above.

There is one more advantage of dispinterfaces. You can directly define the methods that return and specify property values. The method returning the value of the property reads only. The method specifying the value writes only.

Dual Interfaces

However, dispinterfaces perform somewhat slower than standard interfaces. Therefore, there is another type of interface used in Automation applications — a *dual interface*. Its methods may be called by both Invoke and the virtual table.

The dual interface must be a descendant of IDispatch. Its virtual table includes references to three methods of IUnknown, four methods of IDispatch, and the methods of the corresponding dispinterface.

Type Library

Since the client should possess information on the dispatcher identifiers of the methods called when the dispinterface methods are called, the Type Library plays an important role when creating interfaces (see *Chapter 1, "COM Mechanisms in Delphi"*). The method identifiers provided in the Type Library, as well as information on the parameters and the interfaces themselves, are used by the client when the Invoke method of the IDispatch interface is called.

Automation Interface Marshaling

Marshaling and demarshaling mechanisms are also used to support the operation of local and remote Automation servers. Marshaling is responsible for packing the call parameters, while demarshaling unpacks them (see *Chapter 1, "COM Mechanisms in Delphi"*).

Like any interface with a virtual table of methods, the IDispatch interface and its descendants make use of two additional objects for marshaling and demarshaling — proxy and stub (see *Chapter 1, "COM Mechanisms in Delphi"*). This pair, however, can only process the method parameters of one interface. But the methods of the dispinterface called by the Invoke method may have parameters that differ greatly from those of the basic interface.

In this case, additional processing is done by the Invoke method itself, which converts the parameters into variables of the variant type. The marshaling of dispinterfaces has a special feature: to pass the different-type parameters via the Invoke method, the parameters are converted to the variant type and back. The methods of the Automation interfaces thus use a limited set of data types suitable for conversion through the variant.

It is only because no proxy and stub are needed in the dispinterface marshaling that dispinterfaces support late binding.

Automation Object

Within the Automation technology (just as in COM) all the methods are contained in the Automation object, which may have one or more interfaces. Like the COM object, the Automation object operates within the Automation server providing the clients with the methods of its interfaces. All Automation object interfaces should be dispatching interfaces.

Automation Server

An application that provides its functions via the IDispatch interface is called an *Automation server*. The server must include an *Automation object* — a common COM object that has an IDispatch interface and dispinterfaces.

The Automation server is an executable file — an application or dynamic library that may contain one or several objects of the same or different classes. Like COM servers, Automation servers can be of three types: In-process server, Local server, and Remote server (see *Chapter 1, "COM Mechanisms in Delphi"*).

Automation Controller

Any standard COM client referring to the Automation server via IDispatch is called an *Automation controller*.

Automation Implementation in Delphi

Let's see how Automation technology is implemented in Delphi. The basis of any software implementation of Automation in Delphi is the TAutoObject class — a descendant of the TComObject class. It provides the methods of the IDispatch interface. Accordingly, the Automation objects have all the capabilities of Delphi COM objects.

When Automation applications are developed, type information is used. The Automation Type Library is created in the same way as for common COM applications (see *Chapter 1, "COM Mechanisms in Delphi"*).

Automation Interfaces

All the Delphi interfaces used in the Automation (both standard and those created by developers) have a common ancestor — the IDispatch interface. Besides the usual methods, it is possible for them to declare properties with read and write methods. This option is implemented in the Type Library Editor.

The *IDispatch* Interface

For Automation technology, IDispatch is the most important interface. It is declared in the System.pas module:

```
IDispatch = interface(IUnknown)
   ['{00020400-0000-0000-C000-000000000046}']
    function GetTypeInfoCount(out Count: Integer): HResult; stdcall;
    function GetTypeInfo(Index, LocaleID: Integer; out TypeInfo):
HResult; stdcall;
    function GetIDsOfNames(const IID: TGUID; Names: Pointer;
      NameCount, LocaleID: Integer; DispIDs: Pointer): HResult;
stdcall;
    function Invoke(DispID: Integer; const IID: TGUID; LocaleID:
Integer;
      Flags: Word; var Params; VarResult, ExcepInfo, ArgErr: Pointer):
HResult; stdcall;
   end;
```

Besides the methods inherited from the IUnknown interface, it contains four additional methods.

The main method of the interface

```
function Invoke(DispID: Integer; const IID: TGUID; LocaleID: Integer;
Flags: Word; var Params; VarResult, ExcepInfo, ArgErr: Pointer):
HResult; stdcall;
```

is used to call all the methods of the dispinterface. For this purpose, you must pass the dispatcher identifier of the called method in the DispID parameter. The GUID of the interface whose method is called is defined by the IID parameter. The LocaleID parameter specifies the localization of the passed values. The Flags parameter specifies whether a usual method is called, or if it is a reading and writing method of the property. The Params parameter contains the pointer to an array of the TDispParams type that contains the parameters of the called method. The VarResult parameter returns the value passed back by the called method.

If an error occurs during the call, the ExcepInfo parameter contains information about it. The ArgErr parameter contains the index of a parameter wrongly specified from the Params array.

The method

```
function GetTypeInfoCount(out Count: Integer): HResult; stdcall;
```

tells us whether this object can return the type information during execution. The Count parameter returns the number of object interfaces supporting the type information.

The method

```
function GetTypeInfo(Index, LocaleID: Integer; out TypeInfo): HResult;
stdcall;
```

returns the pointer to the ITypeInfo Type Library interface (if there is one). If the method is successfully executed, the TypeInfo parameter contains a pointer to the ITypeInfo structure containing the type information.

The method

```
function GetIDsOfNames(const IID: TGUID; Names: Pointer; NameCount,
LocaleID: Integer; DispIDs: Pointer): Hresult; stdcall;
```

returns the dispatcher identifier by the specified name of the dispinterface method. The name array is passed in the Names parameter with the number of NameCount elements. The DispIDs pointer defines the array of identifiers.

Dispatching Interfaces

When full-fledged Automation servers that controllers may refer to without full information on the server functions are created, it is necessary to implement dispatching interfaces. These are descendants of the IDispatch interface, but the keyword dispinterface should be used when they are declared:

```
ISomeDisp = dispinterface
['{AEE41D32-9FFE-94D0-4395-1120AA74DE39}']
function Method1: OleVariant; dispid 1;
function Method2: OleVariant; dispid 2;
procedure Method3; dispid 3;
procedure Method4; dispid 4;
end;
```

Each method of the dispatching interface must have a dispid unique identifier. The properties must have a read-only or write-only attribute. The parameters and the returned results of the methods can only have the following types: Byte, Currency, Real, Double, Real48, Integer, Single, Smallint, AnsiString, ShortString, TDateTime, Variant, OleVariant, WordBool.

The methods GetIDsOfNames and Invoke are used to call the methods and properties of dispatching interfaces. Dispatching interfaces operate using late binding.

Dual Interfaces

The dual interfaces used in Delphi Automation applications are created based on IDispatch. When declared, their methods must use the safecall directive. The parameters and the returned results of the methods can only have the following types: Byte, Currency, Real, Double, Real48, Integer, Single, Smallint, AnsiString, ShortString, TDateTime, Variant, OleVariant, and WordBool.

These interfaces provide for both the binding done by application compilation (virtual table), and binding during execution (or late binding) used in Automation (the Invoke method).

The first three methods of the dual interface are inherited from IUnknown, the next four methods are inherited from IDispatch, and then come the individual methods of the interface.

Automation Object

The capabilities of the Automation object in Delphi are contained by the class TAutoObject. It inherits from the classes TCOMObject and TTypedCOMObject.

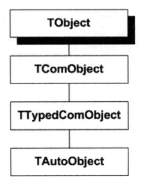

Fig. 2.2. Ancestor hierarchy of the TAutoObject class

Let's consider its main properties and methods. Below in this chapter, you'll find an example of creating an Automation object.

The *TAutoObject* Class

Since the TAutoObject class of the Automation object contains the IDispatch interface, it has four methods similar to those of the interface. These are Invoke, GetTypeInfo, GetTypeInfoCount, and GetIDsOfNames. And, of course, as a descendant of the TComObject class, the class of the Automation object inherits three methods of the IUnknown interface (see *Chapter 1, "COM Mechanisms in Delphi"*).

To create an Automation object instance, as for any COM object, a class factory is needed. The factory used in the created object is indicated by the property

```
property AutoFactory: TAutoObjectFactory;
```

When creating the object, the method is called

```
procedure Initialize; override;
```

It is empty for the class TAutoObject, although developers may cover it in the class-descendants and implement the necessary actions there when the object is initialized.

Use the Delphi Repository to create a new Automation object. After the **Automation Object** icon is clicked, the window for Automation object creation appears on the **ActiveX** page.

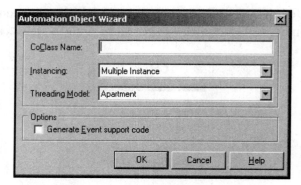

Fig. 2.3. Automation object creation window

The field **CoClass Name** is used for naming the new object.

The **Instancing** list defines the way the server is started. The **Threading Model** list defines the means of interaction between the object and the controllers. The possible values of these parameters are described in detail in *Chapter 1, "COM Mechanisms in Delphi."*

The checkbox **Generate event support code** adds an additional interface to the code of the Automation object being created, which enables management of the object events from the server.

A CoClass with the same name as the Automation object and two interfaces are created at the same time as the Automation object inself. One interface has the same name as the object inherited from the IDispatch interface, and the other is the dispinterface.

Like any other COM object, the CoClass of the Automation object has two class methods — Create and CreateRemote — for creation of an instance of the object's class factory.

For example, when the Automation object SomeAuto is created, the following type will be generated in the new module:

```
type
  TSomeAuto = class(TAutoObject, ISomeAuto)
  protected
    { Protected declarations }
  end;
```

which inherits from the class TAutoObject and implements the methods of the interface of the same name created to support the new object.

Like COM objects, the class factory instance is created in the initialization section of the new object module:

```
initialization
  TAutoObjectFactory.Create(ComServer, TSomeAuto, Class_SomeAuto,
    ciMultiInstance, tmApartment);
```

The new interface is declared in the Type Library (if it already exists in the project, then the new entities are added to the Library; otherwise it is created):

```
ISomeAuto = interface(IDispatch)
  ['{9C2A1E76-391E-11D6-A80B-BA576D9FB37E}']
end;

ISomeAutoDisp = dispinterface
  ['{9C2A1E76-391E-11D6-A80B-BA576D9FB37E}']
end;
```

Note that a dispinterface is also created for the main interface. Later, when methods are added to the main interface, the same methods will be added to the dispinterface, and dispatching identifiers will be assigned to them.

Also, here, in the Type Library, `CoClass` is declared for the new Automation object.

Automation Object Event Handling

If the checkbox **Generate event support code** is activated during the creation of the Automation object, the event handling mechanism will be added to the new object. This mechanism allows the events generated in the Automation object to be passed to the controller.

To allow the server to refer to the controller, the Automation object (and any other COM object) must support at least one *outgoing interface*.

The property

```
property EventSink: IUnknown;
```

represents this interface. It allows for transfer of the events happening within the object to be passed to the controller.

An object with outgoing interfaces is called an *object with connection* and must support the `IConnectionPointContainer` interface, from which the client can find available outgoing interfaces.

Each outgoing interface must have a special corresponding object that implements its methods. This object is called a *sink*.

Let's consider the source code that is generated automatically when the **Generate event support code** checkbox is activated.

Listing 2.1. Automation Object Type Library (Comments Excluded)

```
unit Project1_TLB;

interface

uses Windows, ActiveX, Classes, Graphics, OleCtrls, StdVCL;

const
  LIBID_Project1: TGUID = '{B2211452-E7A8-11D2-80F3-008048A9D587}';
  IID_ISomeObj: TGUID = '{B2211453-E7A8-11D2-80F3-008048A9D587}';
  DIID_ISomeObjEvents: TGUID = '{B2211455-E7A8-11D2-80F3-008048A9D587}';
```

```
    CLASS_SomeObj: TGUID = '{B2211457-E7A8-11D2-80F3-008048A9D587}';
type
  ISomeObj = interface;
  ISomeObjDisp = dispinterface;
  ISomeObjEvents = dispinterface;

SomeObj = ISomeObj;
ISomeObj = interface(IDispatch)
    ['{B2211453-E7A8-11D2-80F3-008048A9D587}']
  end;

ISomeObjDisp = dispinterface
    ['{B2211453-E7A8-11D2-80F3-008048A9D587}']
  end;

ISomeObjEvents = dispinterface
    ['{B2211455-E7A8-11D2-80F3-008048A9D587}']
  end;

  CoSomeObj = class
    class function Create: ISomeObj;
    class function CreateRemote(const MachineName: string): ISomeObj;
  end;

implementation

uses ComObj;

class function CoSomeObj.Create: ISomeObj;
begin
  Result := CreateComObject(CLASS_SomeObj) as ISomeObj;
end;

class function CoSomeObj.CreateRemote(const MachineName: string): ISomeObj;
begin
  Result := CreateRemoteComObject(MachineName, CLASS_SomeObj) as ISomeObj;
end;

end.
```

Listing 2.1 shows that there are three interfaces created for the Automation object. The dual interface `ISomeObj` is designed to work with the `TSomeObj` object. The dispatching interface `ISomeObjDisp` provides for the Automation. The `ISomeObjEvents` interface provides for object event handling in the controller.

Listing 2.2. An Automation Object Module

```
unit Unit2;

interface

uses ComObj, ActiveX, AxCtrls, Project1_TLB;

type
  TSomeObj = class(TAutoObject, IConnectionPointContainer, ISomeObj)
  private
    FConnectionPoints: TConnectionPoints;
    FEvents: ISomeObjEvents;
  public
    procedure Initialize; override;
  protected
      property ConnectionPoints: TConnectionPoints read
FConnectionPoints
      implements IConnectionPointContainer;
    procedure EventSinkChanged(const EventSink: IUnknown); override;
  end;

implementation

uses ComServ;

procedure TSomeObj.EventSinkChanged(const EventSink: IUnknown);
begin
  FEvents := EventSink as ISomeObjEvents;
end;

procedure TSomeObj.Initialize;
begin
  inherited Initialize;
  FConnectionPoints := TConnectionPoints.Create(Self);
```

```
  if AutoFactory.EventTypeInfo <> nil then
    FConnectionPoints.CreateConnectionPoint(AutoFactory.EventIID,
      ckSingle, EventConnect);
end;

initialization
  TAutoObjectFactory.Create(ComServer, TSomeObj, Class_SomeObj,
    ciMultiInstance, tmApartment);
end.
```

Within the object itself, the interface ISomeObjEvents is passed to the FEvents field. To have it initialized, the EventSinkChanged method is automatically covered. The ISomeObjEvents interface is based on the options of the interface IConnectionPointContainer, which is included in the class declaration.

Note that the initialization of additional objects is carried out by the covered method Initialize.

The program code presented in Listings 2.1 and 2.2 is created automatically. If the developer wants to pass the event to the controller, he or she must do the following:

❐ A method of the event handler interface must be created for each event handler.

❐ The CoClass is created for the event handler interface.

❐ When the Automation object is initialized, an event handler class instance must be created.

Let's consider the above steps in more detail with examples from the source code of the Automation object TSomeObject.

Creating Methods (Event Analogs)

The interface of the event handler should have methods that correspond to the events handled:

```
ISomeObjEvents = dispinterface
    ['{B2211455-E7A8-11D2-80F3-008048A9D587}']
    procedure Open; dispid 1;
    procedure Close; dispid 2;
  end;
```

Creating *CoClass*

You should create the CoClass for the event handler interface manually. This class should contain the selected events and allow them to be handled in the Invoke method:

```
TSomeEventSink = class(TInterfacedObject, IUnknown, IDispatch)
  private
  {...}
  FOwner : TObject;
  FOnOpen : TNotifyEvent;
  FOnClose : TNotifyEvent;
  {...}
  protected
  function Invoke(DispID: Integer; const IID: TGUID; LocaleID: Integer;
  public
  {...}
  property OnOpen: TNotifyEvent read FOnOpen write FOnOpen;
  property OnClose: TNotifyEvent read FOnClose write FOnClose;
  end;

  ...

function TSomeEventSink.Invoke(DispID: Integer; const IID: TGUID;
LocaleID: Integer; Flags: Word; var Params; VarResult, ExcepInfo,
ArgErr: Pointer): HRESULT;
begin
  ...
  case dispid of
  5: if Assigned(FOnOpen) then FOnOpen(FOwner);
  6: if Assigned(FOnClose) then FOnClose(FOwner);
  end;
  ...
end;
```

Initializing the Automation Object

During initialization, the Automation object should create the TSomeEventSink class instance and use the analogous events of the event handler class in its own events.

```
TSomeObject = class
  private
```

```pascal
    {...}
    FEventSink: TSomeEventSink;
    function GetOnOpen: TNotifyEvent;
    procedure SetOnOpen(Value: TNotifyEvent);
    function GetOnClose: TNotifyEvent;
    procedure SetOnClose(Value: TNotifyEvent);
  public
    constructor Create;
    {...}
published
    {...}
    property OnOpen: TNotifyEvent read GetOnOpen write SetOnOpen;
    property OnClose: TNotifyEvent read GetOnClose write SetOnClose;
end;

{...}

function TSomeObj.GetOnOpen: TNotifyEvent;
begin
  Result := FEventSink.OnOpen;
end;

procedure TSomeObj.SetOnOpen(Value: TNotifyEvent);
begin
  FEventSink.OnOpen := Value;
end;

function TSomeObj.GetOnClose: TNotifyEvent;
begin
  Result := FEventSink.OnClose;
end;

procedure TSomeObj.SetOnClose(Value: TNotifyEvent);
begin
  FEventSink.OnClose := Value;
end;
```

Class Factory

The class factory for the Automation object is created based on the TAutoObjectFactory class. The Automation class factory inherits from the standard COM class factory.

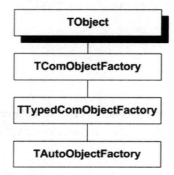

Fig. 2.4. Hierarchy of the ancestor classes of the Automation class factory

The Automation class factory is created by the constructor

```
constructor Create(ComServer: TComServerObject; AutoClass: TAutoClass;
const ClassID: TGUID; Instancing: TClassInstancing;
ThreadingModel: TThreadingModel = tmSingle);
```

As you can see from the declaration, assigning its parameters is done the same as for the parameters of the COM class factory constructor (see *Chapter 1, "COM Mechanisms in Delphi"*).

After creation, the class factory provides access to information on the object dispatching interface. The property

```
PInterfaceEntry = ^TInterfaceEntry;
  TInterfaceEntry = packed record
    IID: TGUID;
    VTable: Pointer;
    IOffset: Integer;
    ImplGetter: Integer;
  end;
property DispIntfEntry: PInterfaceEntry;
```

returns a reference to the corresponding structure.

The method

```
function GetIntfEntry(Guid: TGUID): PInterfaceEntry; virtual;
```

will return information on the dispinterface specified by the GUID parameter.

The type information of the dispinterface created by the Automation object factory is returned by the property

```
property DispTypeInfo: ITypeInfo;
```

To support the event handler interface considered above, the following property is used

```
property EventIID: TGUID;
```

which returns the GUID of the event handler interface. The type information for this interface is contained in the property

```
property EventTypeInfo: ITypeInfo;
```

The *TAutoIntfObject* Class

If an Automation object needs to be used within an application, then the TAuto-IntfObject class may be used, which does not require a class factory for class instance creation. It supports the IDispatch and ISupportErrorInfo interfaces, and performs a number of functions intrinsic to the class factory.

Its constructor

```
constructor Create(const TypeLib: ITypeLib; const DispIntf: TGUID);
```

creates an Automation object with the global identifier DispIntf on the basis of information on the TypeLib type.

After creation, the dispinterface of the Automation object is available through the property

```
property DispIID: TGUID;
```

The type information of the dispinterface is provided by the property

```
property DispTypeInfo: ITypeInfo;
```

And the structure TInterfaceEntry is available through the property

```
property DispIntfEntry: PInterfaceEntry;
```

Automation Server

How is an Automation server created in Delphi? Any application with a normally functioning Automation object and that is properly registered in the OS becomes an Automation server.

According to the COM canons, three types of Automation servers may be created:

❐ In-process

❐ Out-process

❐ Remote

The Automation object is contained in the TAutoObject class, which is a descendant of the base COM class — TCOMObject. To include the Automation object into an application, use the wizard opened by clicking on the **Automation Object** icon on the **ActiveX** page in the Delphi Repository. This is described below.

> **NOTE**
>
> COM objects, and therefore Automation objects, contain the program code for the methods of the interfaces connected with them.

The application is registered in the OS as an in-process Automation server by the command **Register ActiveX Server** from the **Run** menu. To cancel registration, use the command **Unregister ActiveX Server**.

The out-process server is registered by the /regserver key when the application is launched. To cancel registration, use the /unregserver key.

After registration, any application with information on the methods of its interface may call the server.

Automation Controller

The Automation controller manages the server using the methods of the server interfaces. Information on the interfaces is usually distributed in the form of Type Libraries (see *Chapter 1, "COM Mechanisms in Delphi,"* for details on Type Library languages). Any application with access to the corresponding Type Library may become the Automation controller.

To include a Type Library into the project, the command **Import Type Library** in the **Project** menu may be used. Or, if the library was created in Delphi, it is possible to include the name of its file in the uses section of the module.

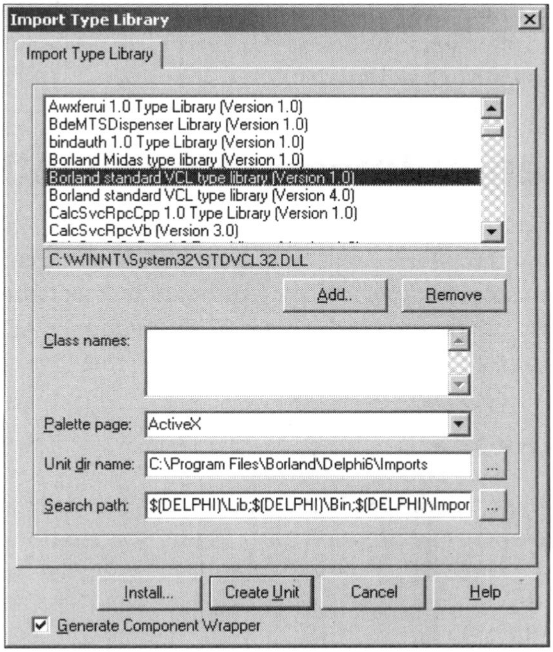

Fig. 2.5. The **Import Type Library** dialog box

The list in the **Import Type Library** dialog box (Fig. 2.5) contains all the Automation servers registered in the system. A Type Library may be imported for any of them. The list may be edited using the **Add** and **Remove** buttons.

Next, it is necessary to create the shellclass instance of the interface (CoClass) in the controller and apply the needed methods of the Automation server where necessary.

If the Type Library is inaccessible, the developer should do the following:

1. The Automation object is created in the controller application based on a variable of the OleValiant type. For this, the following function is used:

   ```
   function CreateOleObject(const ClassName: string): IDispatch;
   ```

   which returns a pointer to the IDispatch interface. The ClassName parameter defines the name of the Automation class. This is a program identifier, which is the Automation server, and corresponds to the identifier of the CLSID class. This function is used both for in-process and out-process servers. Naturally, the server for which the object is created should be registered.

2. After the Automation object is created, the methods of its interfaces may be used in the controller application. If the server does not function on the first call, it is automatically started by the OS.

Example of an Automation Application

Now let's consider the simplest example of creating a server and an automation controller. The out-process server will be the model. Since it is important to demonstrate the performance principle of the Automation mechanism in Delphi, the server will be limited to performing the simplest functions. Afterwards, you may add real operations to this extremely simple working server.

Automation Server

The creation of a server begins with the opening of a regular application project in Delphi. The developer may program any necessary operations for it. The application becomes the Automation server after it is included in the Automation object.

The Object Repository is used for this purpose. Select the **Automation Object** icon on the **ActiveX** page.

While creating the new Automation object, the **Automation Object Wizard** dialog box appears (see Fig. 2.3). The process of object creation is considered in detail above in this chapter. The TSimple object was created strictly according to this description (Table 2.1).

Table 2.1. TSimple Object Parameters

Parameter	Value
CoClass Name	Simple
Instancing	tmApartment
Threading Model	ciMultiInstance
Generate Event support code	Enabled

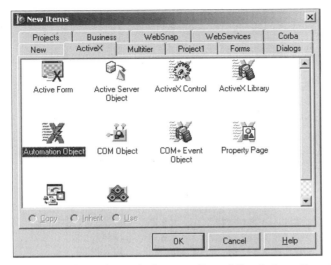

Fig. 2.6. Delphi Repository during creation of the Automation object

Creating and setting the properties and methods of the object interfaces is done in the Type Library Editor. Here the declarations for two methods were created: `Method1` and `Method2`. See *Chapter 1, "COM Mechanisms in Delphi,"* for more details on the creation of interface methods.

Note that the `ISimple` interface of the Automation object fully conforms to the requirements of the dual interface (see Listing 2.3). Along with it, the dispatcher interface `ISimpleDisp` is automatically created. In all other respects, the source code of the Type Library corresponds to a standard COM object.

Listing 2.3. Type Library of the `TSimple` Automation Object (Comments Excluded)

```
unit DemoAutoServer_TLB;

interface

uses Windows, ActiveX, Classes, Graphics, OleCtrls, StdVCL;

const
  LIBID_DemoAutoServer: TGUID = '{F290AEE0-E858-11D2-80F3-008048A9D587}';
  IID_ISimple: TGUID = '{F290AEE1-E858-11D2-80F3-008048A9D587}';
  CLASS_Simple: TGUID = '{F290AEE3-E858-11D2-80F3-008048A9D587}';
```

```
type
ISimple = interface;
  ISimpleDisp = dispinterface;

Simple = ISimple;

ISimple = interface(IDispatch)
    ['{F290AEE1-E858-11D2-80F3-008048A9D587}']
    procedure Method1; safecall;
    procedure Method2; safecall;
  end;

ISimpleDisp = dispinterface
    ['{F290AEE1-E858-11D2-80F3-008048A9D587}']
    procedure Method1; dispid 1;
    procedure Method2; dispid 2;
  end;

  CoSimple = class
    class function Create: ISimple;
    class function CreateRemote(const MachineName: string): ISimple;
  end;

implementation

uses ComObj;

class function CoSimple.Create: ISimple;
begin
  Result := CreateComObject(CLASS_Simple) as ISimple;
end;

class function CoSimple.CreateRemote(const MachineName: string): ISimple;
begin
  Result := CreateRemoteComObject(MachineName, CLASS_Simple) as ISimple;
end;

end.
```

Like the conventional COM interface, the dual automation interface should have a special corresponding shell object in which the properties and methods of the `CoClass` interface are implemented.

Listing 2.4. TSimple Automation Object Module

```
unit SimpleObj;

interface

uses
  ComObj, ActiveX, Dialogs, DemoAutoServer_TLB;

type
  TSimple = class(TAutoObject, ISimple)
  protected
    procedure Method1; safecall;
    procedure Method2; safecall;
  end;

implementation

uses ComServ;

procedure TSimple.Method1;
begin
 ShowMessage('Method2 executed');
end;

procedure TSimple.Method2;
begin
 ShowMessage(' Method2 executed');
end;

initialization
  TAutoObjectFactory.Create(ComServer, TSimple, Class_Simple,
    ciMultiInstance, tmApartment);
end.
```

After the development of the server application is complete, it is necessary to register it in the OS. To do this, just launch the application with the /regserver key. It can be placed in the **Start Parameters** dialog box (the **Parameters** command in the **Run** menu).

Automation Controller

The Automation controller application should have information on the capabilities of the interfaces provided by the Automation server. For this, it should import the Type Library or include the corresponding modules into the uses section. The second method works well if the server and controller are developed simultaneously. It is used in our example, as both the server and controller are located in one group of projects.

The form of the controller includes only two buttons, which will be used to call the methods of the Automation server.

Listing 2.5. Automation Controller Main Form Module

```
unit ContrMain;

interface

uses
  Windows, Messages, SysUtils, Classes, Graphics, Controls, Forms,
  Dialogs, StdCtrls, Buttons, DemoAutoServer_TLB;

type
  TContrForm = class(TForm)
    Label1: TLabel;
    BitBtn1: TBitBtn;
    BitBtn2: TBitBtn;
    procedure FormCreate(Sender: TObject);
    procedure BitBtn1Click(Sender: TObject);
    procedure BitBtn2Click(Sender: TObject);
  public
    Simple: ISimple;
  end;

var ContrForm: TContrForm;

implementation
```

```
{$R *.DFM}

procedure TContrForm.FormCreate(Sender: TObject);
begin
 Simple := CoSimple.Create;
end;

procedure TContrForm.BitBtn1Click(Sender: TObject);
begin
 Simple.Method1;
end;

procedure TContrForm.BitBtn2Click(Sender: TObject);
begin
 Simple.Method2;
end;

end.
```

When the controller form is created, the `CoClass` instance for the Automation object is created in the `FormCreate` method. The constructor returns a pointer to the `ISimple` interface.

By pressing the buttons of the Automation controller form, the appropriate methods of the `ISimple` interface of the `DemoAutoServer` server are called. If the server is not working at the moment, the OS starts it automatically.

Summary

Automation is based on COM technology. The basis of Automation is the `IDispatch` interface.

The Automation server provides clients with its interfaces, and should be registered in the OS. The Automation controller makes use of the server's capabilities.

To organize interaction between the server and the controller, the interface should comply with a number of conditions. This may be either a dispatcher interface or a dual interface.

Chapter 3

ActiveX Components

The previous chapters dealt with the issues of object creation for COM and Automation technologies. These objects provide clients with sets of standard (defined within the corresponding specification) and custom interfaces. The methods and properties of these interfaces may be used by other applications. Therefore, a programmatic COM interface is implemented for such objects.

Now it is time to expand the field of application of the COM objects to the visual user interface of the application. Indeed, if the object provides its methods for use, why not do the same for its visual functionality?

Of course, the visual presentation of the COM objects still needs to be implemented. This task is carried out by another child COM technology — *ActiveX*.

The processes of development and distribution of controls based on COM objects — *ActiveX* controls — are done within the ActiveX technology. These controls can implement various additional functions of the visual interface of the applications, providing users with additional features and options.

The Delphi Component Palette contains the ActiveX page, where there are four components that are ActiveX controls. In Delphi notation, all the controls available for the programmer in the development environment are components. In Delphi, the ActiveX controls do not differ from traditional components, so in the future we will call them *ActiveX components*.

Let's turn to the history of this issue.

Component programming began with Microsoft Visual Basic. It was in this environment that 16-bit Visual Basic eXtension (VBX) modules were used for the first time. The developers were very interested in this feature, and over a short period of time, the options of this programming environment were considerably expanded thanks to the appearance of hundreds and thousands of new VBXs.

The idea behind component development was elaborated, and soon other products (e.g., Delphi) were built on this principle. When 32-bit programming was introduced, the component approach was developed even further, and now has a common standard — ActiveX. Alongside with these processes, Internet and WWW technologies were actively developing. It turned out that the first controls based on COM objects were a poor match for these new fields of application. The core of the problem was that, according to the specification, the first controls (then called "OLE controls") had to support too many standard interfaces. And most of these interfaces had never been used in most of the controls. As a result, the controls were cumbersome, and took too long to load using Internet technologies.

The requirements were also considerably simplified. As a result, the controls became more compact and spurred the development of a range of adjacent technologies, and were named ActiveX controls.

From the programmer's point of view, ActiveX is a black box with its own properties, methods, and events. ActiveX is integrated into Delphi so well that you can know nothing about COM objects but still make exhaustive use of their features. From the point of view of the COM objects model, the ActiveX control is a server that supports automation, is implemented as a dynamic library, is executable in the address space of your application, and allows visual editing.

This chapter deals with the following issues:

❑ How ActiveX controls work

❑ How to include and use in Delphi the preprepared controls created by third-party developers

❑ How to convert standard Delphi components into ActiveX components

❑ How to convert a form into an ActiveX form

How ActiveX Controls Work

The ActiveX control is a COM object that operates most often in the in-process server (see *Chapter 1, "COM Mechanisms in Delphi"*). Of course, there are a number of additional requirements imposed on the controls by the ActiveX technology, but all of them are conditional upon the necessary mechanisms for the loading and functioning of the controls.

As part of the visual interface of the application, the controls must interact with the application by giving it the relevant information about the user's actions, react to these actions independently, and correctly change their own state according to the application's commands.

For example, if the user presses an ActiveX control's button, this control must depict this button being pressed and inform the application about it. If, for example, the application considers it necessary to make its controls inaccessible, then our control must also be able to do this, reacting to the command of the application.

From a formal point of view, the ActiveX control only has to support the IUnknown interface. However, to implement the principal functions intrinsic by definition to the ActiveX controls, it must implement a subset from the set of basic ActiveX interfaces. These are listed in Table 3.1.

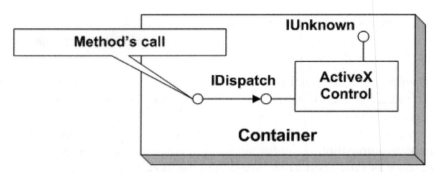

Fig. 3.1. Dispinterfaces are used to access ActiveX controls

Table 3.1. Basic Interfaces of the ActiveX Controls

Interface	Description
IOleObject	Provides the most important methods for the interaction of the control with the container.
IOleControl	Supports the basic functionality of the control: property settings and the reaction to events.
IOleInPlaceObject	This interface manages the activation and deactivation of the control in the container.
IOleInPlaceActiveObject	Provides a direct interaction channel between the control and the frame window of the container with this control.
IObjectSafety	This interface provides two ways to set the safe mode of the control. If this mode is set, then, when loaded via the Internet, the browser will obtain information on whether this control is safe both for the environment into which it is loaded and for the data used.
IPersistPropertyBag	Provides methods for saving and loading the individual properties of the control into storage.
IPersistStreamInit	Provides for the initialization of the storage area used for saving the property values of the control, based on the use of the streams within the storage area.
IPersistStorage	Provides the control with a reference to the storage area instance provided by the container for saving the control's properties.

continues

Table 3.1 Continued

Interface	Description
IPerPropertyBrowsing	Provides methods for passing the property values of the control to the property page.
ISimpleFrameSite	Allows the control to function as a frame site for placing other ActiveX Controls.
ISPecifyPropertyPages	Contains a method that returns data on the availability and support of the property page by this control.
IViewObject	Provides the interaction between the control and the container when it is necessary to inform the container of changes to the appearance of the control.
IViewObject2	An extension of the IViewObject interface. Provides information on the size of the drawing area of the control.

Interface methods are accessed by the Invoke method of the IDispatch interface.

Thus, the main tasks for ActiveX controls may be defined as follows:

❒ Registering the control

❒ Implementing the user interface and visualization

❒ Providing its own methods and properties to the application

❒ Notifying the application of the events occurring

❒ Getting information on the application's properties

It is the ActiveX technology which defines and implements the component's behavior's standards in the user interface of the application.

Let's see how these tasks are accomplished.

Containers and ActiveX Control Registration

The tasks listed above are accomplished thanks to the fact that all ActiveX controls provide standard interfaces. These interfaces are able to support COM objects in the specified state and efficiently interact with an application that uses this control.

An application that has ActiveX components, and that is able to use them, is called a *control container*. Users work with many programs without even suspecting that they are full-fledged ActiveX containers. These programs include Microsoft Internet Explorer, Microsoft Visual Basic, and Microsoft Word. Of course, Delphi is also a container.

Just as ActiveX controls are not obliged to support all the standard interfaces, the containers don't have to allow the application of every ActiveX component. If the application can only implement a small part of the features of the ActiveX component — for example, its visualization and its reaction to the user's actions — it is still a container. The list of basic interfaces for ActiveX containers is shown in Table 3.2.

Table 3.2. Basic Interfaces of ActiveX Controls

Interface	Description
IAdviseSink	Gives the container the option to keep track of changes to controls, bound documents, etc.
IOleClientSite	By means of this interface, attached objects may obtain information on container resources
IOleDocumentSite	Used for activation of OLE Documents
IOleInPlaceSite	Manages the interaction between the container and the site of its control
IOleUIObjInfo	Provides information on the container controls for use in the dialogs for setting the container properties

The containers also implement their functions by providing methods of standard interfaces.

For an ActiveX control to be used by an application, it must be registered on the computer. For this purpose, the ActiveX controls enter data on themselves into the System Registry during installation.

Providing Methods

All standard interfaces of the containers and ActiveX components are dispatch interfaces that originate from IDispatch. Correspondingly, any calls of the methods of controls from the container are carried out by the Invoke method of the IDispatch interface (see *Chapter 2, "Automation"*). This means that in reality, the container uses only the IDispatch interface, and nothing else.

To obtain information on the methods of the dispinterfaces, the container uses the Type Library provided by the control.

Events

When the ActiveX control reacts to the user's actions, it sends the container information about the events, making it possible for the container to react. In this way, the ActiveX controls perform their main assignment.

So how does notification work in ActiveX?

When an event occurs, the control simply calls the necessary method of the container. In this case the container provides its own interfaces, and the control is the client. For this simple schema to work, the control should have a reference to the container interface.

The control should provide each event with a corresponding method of the container interface. The set of these methods is called the *outgoing interface*. Any regular interface is called an *incoming interface*.

In this case, however, a complete, correctly written container should have the methods for all possible events, for any component types. It is obvious that such an extensive implementation procedure would be extremely ineffective.

Therefore, the ActiveX controls must provide the container with a Type Library with interface descriptions — both incoming and outgoing. After the container obtains information about its methods that are being used by the ActiveX control in the outgoing interfaces, it must dynamically implement the `IDispatch.Invoke` method that supports these methods.

Properties

Since the ActiveX control use dispinterfaces, they can use the properties of interfaces (see *Chapter 2, "Automation"*).

There are two methods which may be defined for the property — the reading method and the writing method. Like all other dispinterface methods, they are called via `IDispatch.Invoke`.

Property Pages

To standardize the display of the ActiveX control properties, *property pages* are implemented in them. These property pages are a set of objects that can display the values of the control's properties in the form of a dialog box with a multipage notebook.

If the control supports the ISpecifyPropertyPages interface, then, with the only method of this interface — GetPages — the container can obtain information about the properties provided by this interface. Next, the container creates a frame object to map the property page. Then the frame object creates a *property sheet object*. Each such object will correspond to a page of the property pages notebook.

The frame object and the property sheet object interact via two interfaces: the first is the IPropertyPageSite interface, and the second is the IPropertyPage interface.

If the user has changed the value of the property in the property page dialog, then the corresponding tab object passes the new value to the control.

Licensing

For ActiveX controls, just as for regular applications, illegal use is a major problem. *Licensing* is used to solve this problem.

When a control is created, a license key is generated for it, which is saved in a file with the LIC extension. This is *static* key creation.

If the control is loaded via the Internet, a license key batch file is created for it, having the LPK extension. A reference to this file should be included on the corresponding HTML page. When the page is opened, the browser loads the batch file, obtains the key, and compares it with the existing key. This method of licensing is called *dynamic*.

When a control instance is created, the container checks for the presence of a license to use this control on this computer with the help of the methods of the IClassFactory2 interface.

The GetLicInfo method checks for the presence of a global license. If there is such a license, then the element is created in the usual way. If there is no such license, then the container must call the CreateInstanceLic method, where the number of the license must be passed as the parameter. The class factory of the control checks the license key and, if it is valid, creates an instance of the control.

In order to obtain the license key to use the above method, the container must use another method — RequestLicKey — which returns the required key (if there is one).

Implementing ActiveX Components in Delphi

The ActiveX components in Delphi use the same mechanisms as regular COM objects. The classes of the components inherit from the class ancestor and interface ancestor. The ActiveX components provide clients with their interfaces that descend from IDispatch. To create ActiveX component instances, class factories are used. Information about the component is contained in the Type Library.

The common ancestor of all classes of ActiveX controls in Delphi is the TActiveXControl class. It contains basic functions that enable ActiveX components to interact with the container and provide for the component's reaction to events. It also contains all the basic interfaces of the ActiveX control.

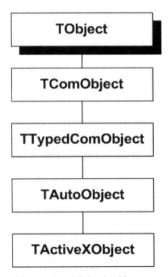

Fig. 3.2. Class hierarchy of ActiveX components in Delphi

As is obvious from Fig. 3.2, the hierarchy of the class ancestors of ActiveX components shows that the ActiveX technology is based on the functionality of its parent technologies — COM and Automation.

The process of creating ActiveX components in Delphi is considerably simplified thanks to the wizard that generates the entire source code necessary for the new component, its class factory, and the Type Library.

Additionally, a special class superstructure, which is created for ActiveX components, allows the ActiveX component to interact with its container, Delphi. Class superstructures are generated from the TOleControl class.

The ActiveX Component Class

Thus, the direct ancestor of any ActiveX component in Delphi is the TActiveXControl class. Originating from the basic classes of the COM objects and Automation, it encapsulates for its descendants the mechanism of using the dispinterfaces necessary for the operation of ActiveX controls.

Additionally, it contains all the ActiveX basic interfaces listed in Table 3.1.

Since the class factory is used to create an ActiveX component instance, there is no need to use the class constructor. But while creating the component, the method

```
procedure Initialize; override;
```

will be called, which you can override and use for setting initial values and for initialization of auxiliary objects in the ActiveX control.

The class provides a ready-to-use mechanism for notification upon actions with the component. If it is necessary to change the value of a property in response to the user's actions, you must make sure that this property can be changed. For this purpose, the overload method is used:

```
function PropRequestEdit(const PropertyName: WideString): Boolean; overload;
function PropRequestEdit(DispID: TDispID): Boolean; overload;
```

You must specify the PropertyName property name or its DispID dispatch identifier as a parameter. If the property can be edited, the function returns True.

When you change the value of a property, you can call the overload method:

```
procedure PropChanged(const PropertyName: WideString); overload;
procedure PropChanged(DispID: TDispID); overload;
```

passing it the name of the PropertyName property or its DispID dispatch identifier as a parameter. The method will generate the OnChanged event.

> **NOTE**
>
> When using the above methods, try to use the dispatch property identifiers, since the names of the properties are handled within methods of the TActiveXControl class and are still converted into identifiers.

After the component instance is created, you can access the VCL class instance that is implementing your ActiveX component. For this, the following property is used:

```
property Control: TWinControl;
```

To obtain pointers to the required interfaces, you can use the method

```
function ObjQueryInterface(const IID: TGUID; out Obj): HResult; override;
```

Note that this is only an implementation of the corresponding IUnknown interface method, which is of course supported by the TActiveXControl class.

The Class Factory of the ActiveX Component

To create ActiveX component instances in Delphi, a class factory is used. Its functionality is inherited from the analogous Automation technology factory. The class factory for ActiveX components is contained in the TActiveXControlFactory class.

The Delphi Environment as an ActiveX Container

The Delphi environment serves as the ActiveX container.

When a new ActiveX component is created in Delphi using the **ActiveX Control Wizard**, a special shell class is automatically created. Its purpose is to allow all the interface methods of the ActiveX component to interact with the development environment. And thus the mechanism for adequate presentation and behavior of ActiveX controls within the Delphi environment is implemented.

The main functions of the class superstructure are implemented in the TOleControl class. Its properties and methods provide the necessary control of the ActiveX component. As a rule, there is no need for the developer to use the methods of this class directly.

Registration of ActiveX Components

To register ActiveX controls created in Delphi, you can use the capabilities of either the OS or the development environment.

In the OS, you can use the regsvr32.exe system utility.

In Delphi, use the tregsvr utility, which is supplied with Delphi in the source texts (..\Demos\ActiveX\TRegSvr folder), or you can use special menu items.

To register a component as an ActiveX control, select the **Register ActiveX Server** command from the **Run** menu.

To unregister the control, select the **Unregister ActiveX Server** command from the **Run** menu.

Using Preprepared ActiveX Components

A number of ActiveX components created by third-party developers (ChartFX, VSSpell, and others) are supplied with Delphi. However, you will probably have to install other controls as well, to expand the capability of the environment. Let's describe this path and the pitfalls that may occur along the way.

Installing Preprepared ActiveX Controls

First of all, you must ensure that the information about the ActiveX controls you require is available in the System Registry. Select the **Component/Import ActiveX Control** menu item. In the list at the top of the dialog box (Fig. 3.3), information on all the ActiveX controls registered in the system is presented. The line under the selection list shows what files they are contained in.

As a rule, all the ActiveX controls distributed on large-scale software are automatically registered during installation. If you have downloaded the file from the Internet or borrowed it from a friend, then there are at least three ways to register:

❑ By pressing the **Add** button in the **Import ActiveX** dialog box

❑ By calling the regsvr32.exe system utility (included in the OS)

❑ By calling the tregsvr utility, which is delivered with Delphi in the source texts (..\Demos\ActiveX\TRegSvr folder)

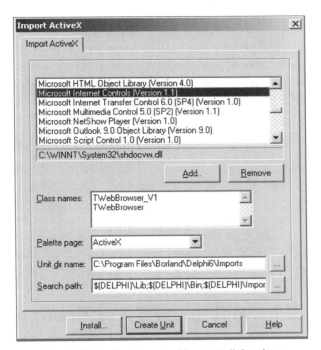

Fig. 3.3. ActiveX control import dialog box

The control is unregistered by pressing the **Remove** button.

When you have stopped at one of the controls, all the classes that this file contains will be listed in the **Class names** field. Then you are offered the option to select the "landing ground" in the **Palette page** list for the future use of the control selected in Delphi — the Component palette page.

If you decide to continue working with this ActiveX control, the next step is to create a *wrapper*. This file is the description of the type library — all the methods, properties, and events contained in the control — written in the Object Pascal language. Its name is formed from the name of the ActiveX and the "_TLB.PAS" line. Pressing the **Create Unit** button creates this file (for purposes of familiarization and testing), and pressing the **Install** button continues the installation process.

The control being installed should be located in one of the *packages*. You may select one of the existing DPK files or create a new one. After the package is compiled, the ActiveX control is at your disposal.

> **NOTE**
>
> If you are going to perform numerous experiments with all possible ActiveXes, determining to what extent they fit your needs, you should create a new package. You will also need a new package if you have already selected the ActiveX and do not want to waste any more memory.

Uninstalling Preprepared ActiveX Controls

The uninstallation of an ActiveX control should begin by removing the references to it. Open the required DPK file, remove the unnecessary controls, and re-compile the package. Then the control (or controls) will disappear from the Component palette page. If you are sure that this control is not being used by anyone, you may remove the information about it from the System Registry (with the **Remove** button in the **Import ActiveX** dialog box). Only then may you remove the OCX file or the dynamic library containing it from the disk.

An Example of Installing the *TWebBrowser* Control

As an example, let's examine the use of the TWebBrowser control from the Microsoft Internet controls (SHDOCVW.DLL file). This is the core of the Microsoft browser, which is most likely already installed on your computer. Additionally, using it is easy and only requires some common sense.

After you have completed all the above operations, you will have the SHDOCVW_TLB.PAS file to work with. This file, among other things, contains the description of the IWebBrowser interface. Apart from the interface, this file contains the description of the TWebBrowser_V1 Delphi object, which is the superstructure over the IWebBrowser interface, and contains methods and properties that correspond exactly to the methods and properties of the interface.

Why is this done? Well, it's done so that all the added-in components have a common foundation and provide them with similar behavior from the point of view of Delphi. Basically, all the class superstructures above ActiveX are generated by the TOleControl class. This class contains the OleObject property, which is a reference to the interface you need. However, it is more reliable to call the methods in the usual way — via the methods of the corresponding Delphi class.

The methods of the IWebBrowser interface execute the main operations for the Internet browser. All the names of the properties and methods of IWebBrowser are simple and clear, aren't they? The IWebBrowser interface is described in the SCHDocVv.pas module, and the methods of the interface are presented in Listing 3.1.

Listing 3.1. IWebBrowser Interface Declaration in the SCHDocVv.pas Module

```
IWebBrowser = interface(IDispatch)
    ['{EAB22AC1-30C1-11CF-A7EB-0000C05BAE0B}']
    procedure GoBack; safecall;
    procedure GoForward; safecall;
    procedure GoHome; safecall;
    procedure GoSearch; safecall;
    procedure Navigate(const URL: WideString; var Flags: OleVariant;
var TargetFrameName: OleVariant; var PostData: OleVariant; var
Headers: OleVariant); safecall;

    procedure Refresh; safecall;
    procedure Refresh2(var Level: OleVariant); safecall;
    procedure Stop; safecall;
    function  Get_Application: IDispatch; safecall;
    function  Get_Parent: IDispatch; safecall;
    function  Get_Container: IDispatch; safecall;
    function  Get_Document: IDispatch; safecall;
    function  Get_TopLevelContainer: WordBool; safecall;
    function  Get_Type_: WideString; safecall;
    function  Get_Left: Integer; safecall;
    procedure Set_Left(pl: Integer); safecall;
    function  Get_Top: Integer; safecall;
    procedure Set_Top(pl: Integer); safecall;
    function  Get_Width: Integer; safecall;
    procedure Set_Width(pl: Integer); safecall;
    function  Get_Height: Integer; safecall;
    procedure Set_Height(pl: Integer); safecall;
    function  Get_LocationName: WideString; safecall;
    function  Get_LocationURL: WideString; safecall;
    function  Get_Busy: WordBool; safecall;
    property Application: IDispatch read Get_Application;
    property Parent: IDispatch read Get_Parent;
    property Container: IDispatch read Get_Container;
    property Document: IDispatch read Get_Document;
    property TopLevelContainer: WordBool read Get_TopLevelContainer;
```

```
    property Type_: WideString read Get_Type_;
    property Left: Integer read Get_Left write Set_Left;
    property Top: Integer read Get_Top write Set_Top;
    property Width: Integer read Get_Width write Set_Width;
    property Height: Integer read Get_Height write Set_Height;
    property LocationName: WideString read Get_LocationName;
    property LocationURL: WideString read Get_LocationURL;
    property Busy: WordBool read Get_Busy;
  end;
```

Now, let's use the data on the capabilities of the TWebBrowser ActiveX component that we have obtained in practice. We will try to create our own simple browser in the space of a few minutes.

We first create a new project — a common application — and use its form. The TWebBrowser ActiveX component is transferred onto the form, and we follow a simple recipe.

Ingredients: a form, a selection list, and several buttons of your choice (see Fig. 3.3). The buttons may correspond to commands that you are accustomed to, like in Microsoft Internet Explorer, for example.

For the buttons in our example, we create click handlers, including in them the appropriate methods from the IWebBrowser interface provided by the TWebBrowser ActiveX component.

Listing 3.2. Method Handlers of Events for a Browser Based on the TWebBrowser Control

```
procedure TForm1.BackToolButtonClick(Sender: TObject);
begin
 WebBrowser_V11.GoBack;
end;

procedure TForm1.GoToolButtonClick(Sender: TObject);
var ov1,ov2,ov3,ov4: OleVariant;
begin
 WebBrowser_V11.Navigate(ComboBox1.Text,ov1,ov2,ov3,ov4);
end;

procedure TForm1.FrwToolButtonClick(Sender: TObject);
begin
```

```
WebBrowser_V11.GoForward;
end;

procedure TForm1.StopToolButtonClick(Sender: TObject);
begin
 WebBrowser_V11.Stop;
end;

procedure TForm1.HomeToolButtonClick(Sender: TObject);
begin
 WebBrowser_V11.GoHome;
end;

procedure TForm1.SrchToolButtonClick(Sender: TObject);
begin
 WebBrowser_V11.GoSearch;
end;
```

Fig. 3.4. A browser compiled based on Microsoft ActiveX controls

Here is the result. After the compilation and startup of the application, we have an efficient Internet browser with a set of the most important functions (see Fig. 3.3). And all we did was link the methods of the ActiveX component with buttons.

If you put a little more effort in, you will have a full-fledged browser. It may be of use to you while debugging applications; examples will be given later on.

Developing Custom ActiveX Components

COM-based technologies are as attractive as they are complicated. Or, to be more precise, as complicated as they are laborious. Building objects on your own takes a lot of time. Therefore, both advanced users and beginners do this in Delphi with a set of wizards. We will say outright that there is no wizard for "direct" creation, or creation of ActiveX components from scratch. You may choose one of two options instead — converting either one of the common Delphi components or a whole form into a control.

Converting Delphi Components into ActiveX Components

The first of the features provided by Delphi is conversion of any window component (descendant of the TWinControl class) into an ActiveX component. This wizard is available by clicking the **ActiveX Control** icon on the **ActiveX** page of the Delphi Repository (Fig. 3.5). You may initially think its name to imply wider capabilities, but it can do only what it can.

Using it is very simple.

1. Select the VCL component from the **VCL Class Name** list.

2. The wizard offers you names for the future ActiveX component and related files. You may either accept this name or specify your own in the **New ActiveX Name**, **Implementation Unit**, and **Project Name** fields.

3. Select the method of interaction between the object and the client from the **Threading Model** list (see details in *Chapter 1, "COM Mechanisms in Delphi"*).

4. There are three additional options available: **Include About Box** — includes in the project a dialog box with information about the developer; **Include**

Version Information — includes information about the version of the control (this is required by some containers); finally, if you do not want to allow your product to be freely distributed, you can include licensing information, and only users with the key will be able to use it in development mode (i.e., in all environments like Delphi or Visual Basic). Use the **Make Control Licensed** checkbox for this.

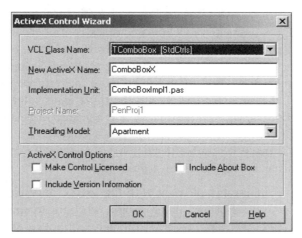

Fig. 3.5. ActiveX component conversion wizard

After you have edited the suggested parameters, the wizard will automatically generate all the necessary files:

❑ The project itself (note that the ActiveX controls are always in the form of DLL libraries — in this case with the OCX extension)

❑ The Type Library with its representation in Object Pascal

❑ One more file with the source text — the implementation file

The implementation file and the classes specified here also play the role of a bridge, but if the TOleControl class provided the connection between the features of the ActiveX and Delphi requirements in the case of TLB, then here, the descendants of the TActiveXControl class establish a correspondence between the former component and its new "hosts" — the containers in which the ActiveX that is created will be located.

We stress this because you will find two classes of the same name in the files (say, when working with the TCheckBox component, this will be the TCheckBoxX class).

But the one that is the descendant of TOleControl will be needed during import of the ActiveX, and the descendant of TActiveXControl will be needed during export.

Thus, after all the files created have been saved, the ActiveX component is ready for export and use in other applications.

Converting Forms into ActiveX Forms

Even more interesting is to create in Delphi a complex control consisting of many simple controls. This is an object of envy with developers who work in other environments. No one will be very impressed if you convert a standard Delphi component into ActiveX. If you develop your own, there will be more interest, but almost all the necessary ideas are still already implemented. On the other hand, after searching through dozens of created controls, you will most likely find a feature or detail in each one that makes that particular control unsuitable for you needs. Only the creation of an ActiveX based on a form will make it possible to combine abundance of features with simple implementation. This technology is called *Active Forms*.

We will now try to combine the pleasant with the useful, and select a practical example to illustrate Active Forms. Many people who create graphic applications need to be able to select the parameters for the pen and brush. At the same time, it is not good to transfer routine code from application to application. The alternative is to combine it within our control.

Thus, the following sequence of operations should be performed to create it.

There is a special wizard designed for creating an ActiveX form in Delphi. To call it, select the **ActiveForm** icon on the **ActiveX** page in the Delphi Repository.

Enter the name of the class of the new form in the **New ActiveX Name** field, or accept the default setting. Accept the defaults or change the names of the form and project module. Finally, select the model of interaction between the object and the client (see details in *Chapter 1*, "*COM Mechanisms in Delphi*") in the **Threading Model** list.

We're going to change the name of the new control — PenX. Note that the rest of the names are changed along with it.

Now save the project. It now consists of PENIMPL1.PAS files (this is actually the implementation code of our ActiveX component), the Type Library file connected with it — PENPROJ1_TLB.PAS, and the project file PENPROJ1.PAS (the DLL header is contained here).

Now the whole surface of the TPenX form (module PENIMPL1.PAS) is available.

Put two TComboBox components and one TtrackBar on it. Place them as you wish (but approximately as shown in Fig. 3.7) and reduce the size of the form so that our ActiveX control doesn't get too big.

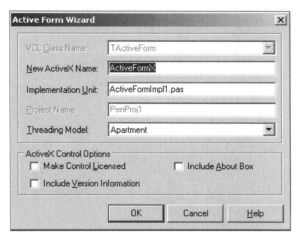

Fig. 3.6. The **Active Form Wizard** dialog box

Fig. 3.7. The appearance of the TPenX object

The drop-down lists are designed for color and pen style selection, and the TTrackBar component is to select the thickness. Set the Min and Max properties of the TUpDown component to 1 and 8, respectively. The lists will visually demonstrate the fixed properties of the pen, so assign the csOwnerDrawFixed values (redrawn by the user) to their Style properties, and specify the event handlers (Listing 3.3).

Listing 3.3. Method Handlers of the Standard Components on the ActiveX Form

---

```
const DefColors : array [0..15] of TColor =( clBlack,
    clMaroon, clGreen, clOlive, clNavy, clPurple, clTeal, clGray, clSilver,
    clRed, clLime, clYellow, clBlue, clFuchsia, clAqua,
```

```
  clWhite);

var GblWidth: Integer;

procedure TPenX.FormCreate(Sender: TObject);
var i: Integer;
begin
 for i := Low(DefColors) to High(DefColors) do
  ClrComboBox.Items.Add(IntToStr(i) );
 ClrComboBox.ItemIndex := 0;

 for i := 0 to 7 do
  StyleComboBox.Items.Add(IntToStr(i) );
 StyleComboBox.ItemIndex := 0;
end;

procedure TPenX.ClrComboBoxDrawItem(Control: TWinControl; Index: Integer;
  Rect: TRect; State: TOwnerDrawState);
begin
 with ClrComboBox.Canvas do
 begin
  Brush.Color := DefColors[Index];
  FillRect(Rect);
 end;
end;

procedure TPenX.StyleComboBoxDrawItem(Control: TWinControl; Index: Integer;
  Rect: TRect; State: TOwnerDrawState);
var FPos: Integer;
begin
 FPos := Rect.Top + (Rect.Bottom - Rect.Top) div 2;
 with StyleComboBox.Canvas do
 begin
  Brush.Color := clWhite;
  FillRect(Rect);
  Pen.Style := TPenStyle(Index);
  Pen.Width := WidthTrackBar.Position;
  MoveTo(Rect.Left, FPos);
  LineTo(Rect.Right, FPos);
 end;
```

```
  end;

  procedure TPenX.ComboBoxChange(Sender: TObject);
  begin
    (Sender as TWinControl).Repaint;
    if FEvents<>nil then FEvents.OnPenChanged;
  end;

procedure TPenX.WidthTrackBarChange(Sender: TObject);

begin

  if WidthTrackBar.Position > 1 then StyleComboBox.ItemIndex:=0;

  ComboBoxChange(StyleComboBox);

end;
```

When the button of the `ClrComboBox` list is pressed, a selection of 16 main colors appears; when the button of the `StyleComboBox` list is pressed, the selection of all possible types of lines appears.

Formally, the ActiveX control is ready. But to get any use out of it, it still needs an interface with the user. We don't need the selection of colors and styles just to be there for no particular reason, but rather to pass them to the user.

Select the **Type Library** command from the **View** menu of the development environment. Open the `IPenX` interface in the window of the Type Library Editor that appears.

NOTE

Pay attention to the methods of the `IPenX` interface that are created automatically. They execute the standard functions of the ActiveX control, and are based on the corresponding methods of the interfaces described in Table 3.1.

Add three properties to the interface — `PenWidth`, `PenStyle`, and `PenColor`. See the details on the Type Library and its Editor in *Chapter 1, "COM Mechanisms in Delphi."*

The new properties will be displayed as three pairs of methods — for reading and for writing (Fig. 3.8).

Press the **Refresh Implementation** button on the upper toolbar. The property description appears in both files of the project, and the code templates for their implementation appear in PENIMPL1.PAS.

NOTE

There is another way of adding properties to ActiveX in Delphi — via the **Edit/Add to Interface** menu.

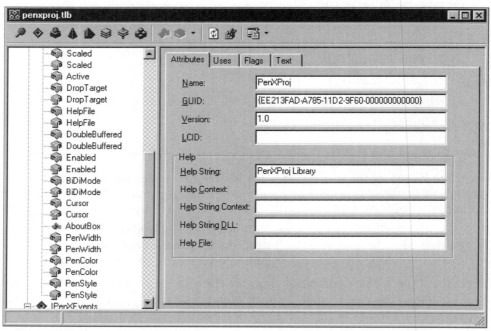

Fig. 3.8. The Type Library Editor with properties added to the IPenX interface

Below is the implementation for reading methods only. Programmatically resetting the value of these properties is not planned.

Listing 3.4. Reading Methods of the New Properties of the IPenX Interface

```
function TPenX.Get_PenColor: Integer;
begin
 Result := DefColors[ClrComboBox.ItemIndex];
end;


function TPenX.Get_PenStyle: Integer;
begin
 Result := StyleComboBox.ItemIndex;
```

```
end;

function TPenX.Get_PenWidth: Integer;
begin
  Result := WidthTrackBar.Position;
end;
```

We are now another step closer to our goal — you could stop further development of the control, compile it, install it, and find in the Object Inspector the three properties we created and work with them further. But when are users supposed to reset the parameters of their pen? So far, they haven't even been informed that anything has happened inside the control.

This will be the final touch.

Once again, refer to the Type Library, this time to the IPenXEvents interface. Not the property, but the method should be added here, and it should be named OnPenChanged. Unlike the properties, in this case only the reference to the method appears, not the template for it. It is up to the programmer to implement the reaction to the event using our ActiveX control, so our task is to initiate this event at the right time. This code must be placed everywhere that at least one of the pen parameters is changed:

```
procedure TPenX.ComboBox1Change(Sender: TObject);
begin
  if FEvents <> nil then FEvents.OnPenChanged;
end;
```

The ActiveForm control is basically ready (Fig. 3.9).

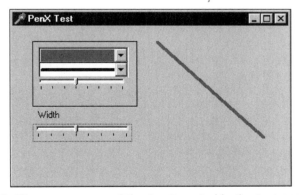

Fig. 3.9. The appearance of the PenX control in the test application

All we have to do now is register the control, include it in one of the packages, and enjoy the capabilities offered by the component approach to programming.

Summary

Developing ActiveX controls is based on the capabilities of the COM and Automation technologies.

ActiveX controls are COM objects, and are subject to the rules for such objects. They may operate within the in-process server (dynamic library) only.

To use the control, the application should possess the capabilities of the ActiveX container. There are many applications that are containers. Among them are Microsoft Internet Explorer, Microsoft Visual Basic, Microsoft Word, and Delphi.

Using the classes and Delphi wizards, you can create your own controls or forms and distribute them.

Chapter 4

COM+ Technology
(Microsoft Transaction
Server)

The issues of reliability, efficiency, and scalability are of great importance for distributed applications. The Microsoft Transaction Server (MTS) software is intended for the support of transaction system handling, allowing you to create an environment for highly efficient and reliable distributed applications for Internet and Intranet.

MTS can be installed on computers with Windows 95/98, Windows NT, and Windows 2000 operating systems. The product was adapted for the Windows 2000 family and given the name "COM+."

MTS technology is based on COM functions, and provides support of distributed applications on a component basis. MTS transactional objects have the basic properties of COM objects. Additionally, the transactional objects implement specific capabilities inherent to MTS objects only:

❑ Transaction handling

❑ Security

❑ Resource pooling

❑ Object pooling

NOTE

The MTS system of transaction security is not implemented for Windows 95/98 operating systems, due to the objective limitations imposed by these systems.

To manage the transactional objects and parameter settings of MTS, a range of applications and utilities is used:

❑ Distributed Transaction Coordinator — DTC — is a service for handling low-level transactions using the two-phase transaction commitment protocol.

❑ The MTS Explorer administrative application allows you to set the parameters of the MTS environment, kept in the System Registry; it also handles MTS packages and roles.

❑ The MTS utilities are for work in the command line or batch file.

❑ The MTX.EXE executive file implements automatic transactions, security, and activation (Just-In-Time — JIT).

Besides the means listed above, you can also use the standard system means for managing MTS. Here, to perform any operation, you need to have administrator rights on the given computer.

However, a discussion of component installation and setting the MTS environment for the server and clients is beyond the scope of this book.

This chapter deals with issues of support implementation and the use of MTS technology in Delphi. Below are the main topics:

❑ How transaction objects function

❑ Managing transaction objects

❑ Managing transactions

❑ Transaction security

❑ Resource management

How MTS Works

Microsoft Transaction Server is a set of program facilities providing for the development, distribution, and functioning of distributed applications for Internet and Intranet. MTS includes:

❑ Middleware that allows transaction objects to function during execution

❑ The MTS Explorer utility that enables handling of transaction objects

❑ Application programming interfaces

❑ Means of resource management

The standard model for applications using MTS is a three-tier architecture of distributed applications that consists of servers, clients, and middleware. The business logic of the application is concentrated in the *MTS transactional objects*, and the middleware handling these objects is constructed with the use of the component model.

Developers who use MTS in their applications create business logic objects that meet the requirements of the MTS objects, and then compile and implement them in the MTS environment using packages.

An *MTS package* is a container that groups the objects for the sake of data security, improvement of resource management, and efficiency. MTS packages are managed using the MTS Explorer utility.

The MTS Object

Since the MTS technology is based on COM, MTS objects must meet the main requirements for COM objects. Additionally, MTS objects have a number of special features:

❐ The object must be implemented within the in-process server (dynamic library).

❐ The object must contain a reference to the MTS type library.

❐ The object must use the standard marshaling COM mechanism.

❐ The object must implement the IObjectControl interface.

Based upon the main principles of how MTS works, the created object may be of two types:

❐ Stateful

❐ Stateless

The choice of the object type depends on the specific task and purpose of the object.

Like any COM object, the MTS objects may retain the internal state when using one instance many times. For each use, the object retains the current values of its properties. At each subsequent call, the object can return the current state to the calling client. This kind of object is of the *stateful* type. Objects of this type allow a wider range of tasks to be solved.

For the object state to be saved, the object must remain active and retain valuable resources, such as the connection with the database. In practice, this is nothing less than work with global variables, for it is here that the intermediate state of the object is saved.

If the object can not retain its intermediate state, it is of the *stateless* type. Objects of this type are more efficient.

When the transaction is successfully completed or terminated, all the transaction objects are deactivated, losing the information on their state acquired during the transaction. This helps to ensure that the transaction is isolated and that the database is in compliance, and frees up server resources for use by other transactions. The completion of the transaction allows MTS to deactivate the object and update the resources.

Transactions

The ability of the MTS object to "live" within its own transaction or to be part of a bigger group of similar objects belonging to one transaction is a great advantage of MTS. This enables the component to be used for various tasks in such a way that the developers may use the code again without modernizing the application logic.

MTS transactions guarantee that:

❏ All changes within one transaction will be either accepted or returned to their previous state.

❏ The transaction converts the state of the system correctly and univocally.

❏ Simultaneous transactions do not accept partial and unsaved changes, which may create conflicts.

❏ Confirmation of the changes to the controlled resources (such as the database records) protects from errors, including network and process errors.

❏ Registration of the transactions allows the initial state to be restored, even after disk errors have occurred.

Clients may gain direct control over the transactions by means of the object context, using the `ITransactionContext` interface. However, for user convenience, MTS can automatically handle the transactions.

Using MTS transactions, you may employ the business logic of the application in server objects. Server objects can implement business logic in such a way that the client does not have to know anything about the rules of the business logic.

There are three ways to set the attributes of transactions:

❏ During the development stage

❏ With the help of the Type Library Editor

❏ In the MTS Explorer environment

The transaction is completed by default, after the time specified in the Transaction timeout parameter (set for each object separately via the MTS Explorer utility) runs out. By default, this time is equal to 60 secs. After this time has expired, an incomplete transaction is automatically terminated.

MTS Object Context

For each MTS transactional object, the transaction server automatically creates a special object, called the *object context*. The functionality of the context is supported by the IObjectContext interface.

Two methods of the interface define the way the object leaves the transaction.

The SetComplete method informs the transaction that it is ready to end its work in the transaction.

The use of the SetAbort method means that executing the code of the object has led to circumstances preventing successful completion of the transaction.

After either of these two methods is used, the object ends its participation in the transaction.

The EnableCommit and DisableCommit methods inform you about the current state of the object. The EnableCommit method informs you that the object is allowing the transaction to be completed, although its own functioning has not been completed.

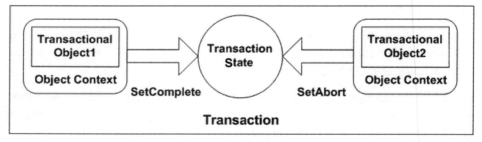

Fig. 4.1. Role of the MTS object context

The call of the DisableCommit method shows that at this moment the current state of the object does not allow the transaction to be completed. If you try to complete the transaction after this method is called, the transaction will be terminated.

Using the methods above, the object context provides the MTS environment with information about the state of the transactional object.

For example, in order to provide services based on the transactions, the resource dispenser may use the context of the MTS object. Let the object be implemented within the transaction that has reserved the connection with the database via the ADO provider. This connection automatically organizes the transaction. All the changes in the database with this connection become part of the transaction, and then are either accepted, or rolled back.

There are several more methods of the `IObjectContext` interface that developers may use.

When the MTS object is used in an open transaction, the `IsInTransaction` function of the context object returns `True`.

If the data security mode is activated for the MTS object or MTS package containing this object, then the `IsSecurityEnabled` method returns the `True` value.

If the application using the MTS object performs some MTS role, then the `IsCallerInRole` method returns the `True` value.

Data Security in MTS

One of the convenient services provided by MTS is the ability to access components (and even separate interfaces), depending on the rights of the client. MTS data security consists of two parts:

❏ Declarative data security

❏ Program data security

In both cases, the MTS environment uses MTS roles to provide security. An *MTS role* is an abstract concept of a certain set of users. These may be separate users or groups of users. Using the MTS Explorer application, the administrator creates the required roles and registers the users and the groups there. Each role is endowed with the necessary rights. The Windows authentification mechanism may be used here.

Declarative Data Security

Declarative data security is created in the MTS environment setting stage using the MTS Explorer utility. It consists of limiting access to a specific object or package to users and groups that are members of certain roles.

By default, there is a System Package built into the MTS environment, for which there are two roles: Administrator and Reader. Before you start work, you need to set the Administrator role to at least one account.

> **NOTE**
>
> The security setting is impossible for Windows 95/98 because of the limited functionality of these operating systems.

Program Data Security

Program data security is provided by the context object and the `IsSecurityEnabled` and `IsCallerInRole` methods of the `IObjectContext` interface of the object. The program data security is planned during the application development stage, and is executed while the application using this MTS object is functioning. When the application tries to use a specific MTS object, it must use the `IsCallerInRole` method. The role executed by the application is communicated as the parameter of the method. If this role is played by the MTS object or package, its use is permitted, and the method returns the `True` value.

If there are several MTS objects used within one process, then the `IsCallerInRole` method always returns `True`. In this case, for more accurate identification, the `IsSecurityEnabled` method is used.

> **NOTE**
>
> For applications requiring stricter security, the object context uses the `ISecurityProperty` interface, the methods of which return the Windows Security Identifier (SID) for the direct call and object creation.

Resources

There are three methods for managing MTS resources:

❒ Just-in-time activation

❒ Resource pooling

❒ Object pooling

We will now consider each of these methods in detail.

Just-In-Time Activation

The ability of the object to be deactivated and activated again while the client has the reference to it is called *just-in-time activation*. During work with the application, it is often necessary to use one instance of the MTS object several times at certain intervals. When the object is called, it is activated, and the application keeps the reference to the unused object for some time after work with the application is completed.

When a COM object is created as part of the MTS environment, the corresponding context of the object is created at the same time. This context of the object exists for the whole "life" of the MTS object, in one or several cycles. The MTS uses the context of the object to save information on it when deactivation takes place.

A COM object is created in the deactivated state, becoming active only after the client's call.

An MTS object becomes inactive if the following events occur:

☐ The call of the SetComplete or SetAbort methods of the IObjectContext interface. If the object calls the SetComplete method once it has successfully completed its operation, then it is not necessary to save the internal state of the object for the next client's call. If the object calls the SetAbort method, then it points out the inability to successfully complete its work, and that the state of the object does not need to be saved. Then the object goes back to the state preceding this transaction. In a normal implementation of a stateless object, deactivation takes place after calling each method.

☐ The transaction is either saved or terminated. After this, the object is also deactivated. Among these objects, the only ones that can continue their existence are objects that have a reference to clients outside this transaction. Subsequently calling these objects will activate them again, and cause them to be executed in the next transaction.

☐ The last client frees the object. This object is deactivated, and the object context is also freed.

Resource Pooling

After the resources are freed during MTS object deactivation, they become available for other server objects. This process is called *resource pooling*.

Consider, for example, the connection to the database via the ADO provider. Of course, allocating resources and opening and closing the connection with the database takes quite a lot of time. Frequent repetition of this operation by various MTS objects to one database will cause an increased waste of resources.

In cases like these, resource pooling is used. If the connection with the database is not used by one server object, it may be used by another object.

For MTS resource pooling, the pooling dispenser is used.

Freeing Up Resources

Freeing up resources is usually done by calling the SetComplete and SetAbort methods after the client's call has been serviced. These methods free up resources reserved by the MTS dispenser.

At the same time, it is necessary to free up references to the other resources, including references to other objects (MTS objects and the object contexts) and memory occupied by component instances. This is not recommended unless you need to save information on the state in between the clients' calls.

Object Pooling

MTS implements not only resource pooling, but *object pooling* as well. This option, however, is only available within the COM+ technology that functions under the Windows 2000 operating system. In the MTS of older versions, object pooling was only declared for future use.

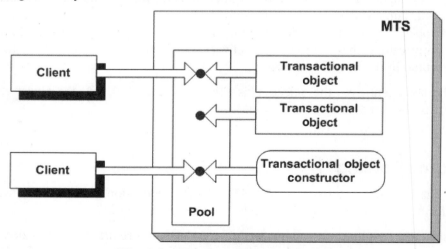

Fig. 4.2. MTS object pooling diagram

The idea behind this mechanism is simple.

When the applications are implemented in the MTS environment, a special pool of objects is created.

The IObjectControl interface is used for handling the pool and positioning objects in it. If the object is intended for pooling use, than the CanBePooled method of the interface should return the True value.

After this object is deactivated, the MTS server places it into the pool. The objects inside the pool are available for immediate use by any other requests of clients. If the object is called and the object pool is empty, MTS automatically creates a new instance of the object.

Creating MTS Applications in Delphi

Delphi provides developers with a wide spectrum of means to create distributed applications using MTS technologies.

Above all, these are the MTS transactional objects, and a special wizard is used for their creation.

To develop the server part of the applications, you can use the MTS data modules that handle the client calls in the MTS environment.

There are also means of resource management in Delphi that may be used while writing programs.

We will look at these tools in more detail.

MTS Transaction Objects

MTS transaction objects are COM objects (see *Chapter 1, "COM Mechanisms in Delphi"*) that possess a range of specific features. These features are implemented by the MTS interfaces. The main interfaces are IObjectControl and IObjectContext.

The MTS transactional objects are normally used for implementing small blocks of the business logic of the application. One object may either work with one transaction exclusively, or share it with the other objects. This depends only on the chosen means of business logic implementation and its algorithms.

The *TMTSAutoObject* Class

The capabilities of the transaction object in Delphi are implemented in the TMTSAutoObject class base (Fig. 4.3).

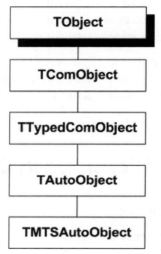

Fig. 4.3. The TMTSAutoObject class hierarchy

Its properties and methods provide for the execution of the main functions of the MTS object:

❐ The transaction's notification on the object's state

❐ Provision of program data security

❐ Object pooling (for COM+ technology only)

All these options were considered above and, since the methods of the TMTSAutoObject class fully coincide with the methods of the interfaces described above, we will just describe them briefly.

The methods

```
procedure SetComplete;

procedure SetAbort;
```

call the methods of the IObjectContext interface of the same name, and provide for transaction saving or rollback.

The methods

```
procedure DisableCommit;
procedure EnableCommit;
function IsInTransaction: Bool;
```

call the methods of the `IObjectContext` interface of the same name, and provide for the transaction's notification on the object's state.

The methods

```
function IsCallerInRole(const Role: WideString): Bool;
function IsSecurityEnabled: Bool;
```

implement the program data security. The `Role` parameter of the `IsCallerInRole` method must contain the name of the MTS role called.

The property

```
property Pooled: Boolean;
```

handles object availability for the pooling. If the property has the `True` value, the object may be placed into the pool for multiple use.

Creating a Transactional Object

In order to create a new MTS transaction object, the **New Transactional Object** wizard is used in Delphi, which is available in the Delphi Repository on the **ActiveX** page.

According to the requirements, MTS transactional objects may be implemented within the in-process server only. Therefore, when a new transactional object is created with the **New Transactional Object** wizard, the type of the project is automatically changed to ActiveX dynamic library (see *Chapter 3, "ActiveX Components"*).

It is necessary to type the name of the transactional object in the **CoClass Name** line, or rather the name of the co-class used for the object's representation in the application.

> **NOTE**
>
> The co-classes are used in Delphi for any COM objects or child technologies. See *Chapter 1, "COM Mechanisms in Delphi,"* for details on the role of coclasses in applications using COM.

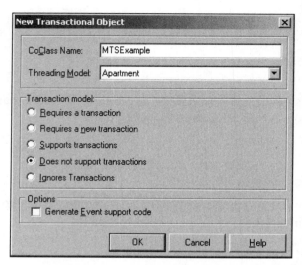

Fig. 4.4. The transactional object creation wizard

The **Threading Model** list allows you to choose the method of interaction between the server and the clients' calls. It is called a thread-oriented model. The possible variants of the model were considered in *Chapter 1, "COM Mechanisms in Delphi."* The features of various models' application for MTS objects are considered below.

The group of **Transaction Model** radio buttons determines the object's behavior in the transaction.

The **Generate Event support code** checkbox enables or disables transactional object event handling. Then, when the source code of the MTS object class is created, the IConnectionPointContainer interface will be created automatically. The notification mechanism is similar to that used for Automation objects. See *Chapter 2, "Automation,"* for more detailed information.

After the parameters of the new object have been specified, and the **OK** button is pressed, Delphi automatically generates the source code for the class of the new object.

Listing 4.1. MTS Transactional Object Class Declaration

```
unit Unit1;
{$WARN SYMBOL_PLATFORM OFF}

interface
```

```
uses
  ActiveX, Mtsobj, Mtx, ComObj, Project1_TLB, StdVcl;

type
  TMTSExample = class(TMtsAutoObject, IMTSExample)
  protected
    { Protected declarations }
  end;

implementation

uses ComServ;

initialization
  TAutoObjectFactory.Create(ComServer, TMTSExample, Class_MTSExample,
    ciMultiInstance, tmApartment);
end.
```

You can see that the code presented in the Listing 4.1 is quite common for COM objects, and, with some variations, was already encountered in previous chapters. Apart from direct class declaration, there is a class factory constructor in the initialization section as well.

At the same time as the class, an interface is created (in our example, this is the IMTSExample interface), which is designed for presenting the methods of the new class. This is the dual interface (it is shown in Fig. 4.3 that the class of an MTS object inherits from the Automation object class).

And at the same time as the class declaration, a corresponding Type Library is created. Here, according to the requirements of the COM and Automation technologies, the main interface and the dispinterface are described, along with the coclass for the new class.

Thread-Oriented Model Types

The MTS object creation wizard requires the type of the thread-oriented model to be specified. Let's take a look at these models.

The **Single** model requires the execution of all the objects created in response to clients' calls in a single thread. This is the default model for all COM objects.

This model is of limited scalability. Objects of the stateful type using this model may cause backups and blocks. You can eliminate this problem by using an object of the stateless type and calling the SetComplete method before exiting it.

The **Apartment** model creates a separate thread for each new instance of the object used during the lifetime of this object.

Within this model, two objects may be executed in parallel as long as they are employed in different activities.

The **Both** model is the same as the **Apartment** model, except that the responses of the objects to calls are handled consecutively, not all at once. This model is recommended as the main model to use with object pooling.

> **NOTE**
>
> The **Free** model used in other COM objects is not applicable to objects run in the MTS environment, since so-called activities are supported. See more detailed information on MTS activities in the "*Optimization of Work with MTS*" section.

The Behavior of MTS Objects in Transactions

The MTS object creation wizard requires that you specify the type of transaction model. There are five available types:

❒ **Requires a transaction**. The MTS objects are to be executed within the transaction. When a new object is created, its object context inherits the transaction from the client context. If the client has no transaction, MTS creates it automatically.

❒ **Requires a new transaction**. The MTS objects must be executed within their transactions. When a new object is created, MTS automatically creates a new transaction for the object, whether the client has it or not. The object is never run within its own transaction. Instead, the system always creates an independent transaction for new objects.

❑ **Supports transactions**. The MTS objects are executed within their client transaction. When a new object is created, its object context inherits the transaction from the client's context. This enables several objects to operate within one transaction. If the client has no transaction, it will be created by the new context.

❑ **Transactions Ignored**. When a new object is created, a linked object of the transaction context is created without a transaction, and independently of whether or not one exists. Applicable for COM+ technology only.

❑ **Does not support transactions**. Depends on the technology used. For MTS, the activity is similar to **Transactions Ignored**. For COM+, the object of the transaction context is created without the transaction. The object still depends on the transaction, but is not activated immediately if a transaction exists.

MTS Data Remote Module

The MTS data remote module allows you to create server parts of distributed applications. It provides the basic functionality of the application server. When correctly registered on the server computer, server created based on the remote module performs the following functions:

❑ It is the MTS transactional object container.

❑ It encapsulates the business logic of the distributed application implemented in the set of MTS transactional objects.

❑ It provides handling of client requests according to the thread-oriented model specified.

❑ It interacts with the MTS environment, providing the operability of the MTS objects with it.

The base functionality of the application server is provided by the IAppServer interface encapsulated by the data module. In the development stage, the MTS data module is the container for all non-visual components.

Detailed information on work with remote data modules and the creation of application servers can be found in *Part III, "Distributed Database Applications."*

The capabilities of the remote data module are encapsulated in the TMTSDataModule class.

To create a new remote MTS data module, the **New Transactional Data Module Object** wizard is used. It is invoked from the Delphi Repository. The icon of the **Transactional Data Module** wizard is on the **Multitier** page of the Repository.

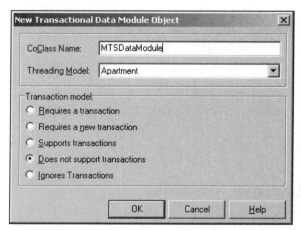

Fig. 4.5. MTS remote data module creation wizard

You must indicate the name of the data module in the **CoClass Name** line.

The **Threading Model** list allows you to choose the method of interaction between the server and the client requests.

The group of **Transaction Model** radio buttons determines the object's behavior in the transaction.

After it is created, the new module is available to the programmer. In the development stage, it is used as common data module. Here it is possible to include any non-visible components and create the source code for them.

In addition to the capabilities of a remote data module inherited from the TRemoteDataModule class, the MTS data module implements the methods of the IObjectContext interface.

Resource Dispensers

There are two resource dispensers in Delphi:

❏ **BDE (Borland Database Engine) resource dispenser**. Handles the pool of connection with the database for MTS components that use BDE's capabilities for work with databases. BDE is middleware that provides the access to several types of databases.

❏ **Shared Property Manager** is used for sharing states among several objects within one server process.

When the Shared Property Manager is used, you do not need to add any code into the application. It also eliminates name conflicts with the help of shared property groups that set unique name spaces for the properties they contain. In using the Shared Property Manager, you mainly use the `CreateSharedPropertyGroup` function to create the shared property group. Then you can save and restore all the properties of this group. Additionally, the state information may be distributed among all the MTS objects installed in the same package.

The next example demonstrates the procedure of adding code to support the Shared Property Manager in the MTS object.

Listing 4.2. Example of Using the Shared Property Manager

```
unit Unit1;
{$WARN SYMBOL_PLATFORM OFF}


interface


uses

  ActiveX, Mtsobj, Mtx, ComObj, Project1_TLB, StdVcl;


type

  TMTSExample = class(TMtsAutoObject, IMTSExample)

  private

    Group: ISharedPropertyGroup;

  protected

    procedure OnActivate; override;

    procedure OnDeactivate; override;

    procedure IncCounter;
```

```
    end;

implementation

uses ComServ;

procedure TMTSExample.OnActivate;
var Exists: WordBool;
    Counter: ISharedProperty;
begin
  Group := CreateSharedPropertyGroup('MyGroup');
  Counter := Group.CreateProperty('Counter', Exists);
end;

procedure TMTSExample.IncCounter;
var Counter: ISharedProperty;
begin
  Counter := Group.PropertyByName['Counter'];
  Counter.Value := Counter.Value + 1;
end;

procedure TMTSExample.OnDeactivate;
begin
  Group := nil;
end;

initialization
  TAutoObjectFactory.Create(ComServer, TMTSExample, Class_MTSExample,
    ciMultiInstance, tmApartment);
end.
```

In this example, the shared property group, called `MyGroup`, and the shared `Counter` property for this group in the `OnActivate` method handler of the `TMTSExample` object are created.

The `CreateSharedPropertyGroup` function is used to create the shared property group and the property group itself. Then, to create the property, use the `CreateProperty` method of `MyGroup`.

In order to get the string value of the property, you need to use the `PropertyByName` method of the group object.

Note that the functionality of the shared property group is contained in the methods of the `ISharedPropertyGroup` interface.

NOTE

All objects with the shared state must be run in the same server process. Objects with shared properties must have the same activation attributes. For example, if one object is configured for running in the client process, and another is configured for the server process, these objects will be launched in different processes even if they are installed in one package.

Testing and Installing MTS Components

When the MTS environment is set up, among the many parameters the administrator may specify is the time for which the transactional object will be active without client calls. This parameter is called the *transaction timeout*. By default, it is equal to 60 seconds.

During the debugging of MTS objects, this parameter must be deactivated (to assign a zero value), otherwise the object may be unloaded by the MTS environment while you work with the source code or the values of the variables during the setup process.

The MTS component cannot be recompiled in the development stage while it is in the memory. The following error message will appear: "Cannot write to DLL while executable is loaded." To avoid this situation, you need to set the "Shut down after being idle for 3 minutes" parameter, changing the time, with the MTS Explorer.

To do this:

1. In MTS Explorer, right click on the package where the MTS transactional object you need is installed, and select the **Properties** command from the pop-up menu.

2. Select the **Advanced** tab in the dialog box that appears.

3. Change the time idle to 0.

4. Press the **OK** button to save the parameters and return to the MTS Explorer environment.

To launch the MTS transactional object for debugging, you need to set the run parameters (Fig. 4.6). To do this:

1. Select **Parameters** from the **Run** menu in Delphi.

2. Specify the full path to the mtx.exe file in the **Host Application** line.

3. Type in the **Parameters** line: the p key and the name of the package where the transactional object is installed —

    /p:"TestPack"

In this example, TestPack is the name of the package where the object is installed.

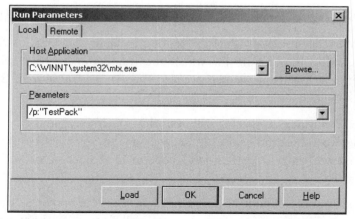

Fig. 4.6. Setting the run parameters of the transactional object

Then, with the breakpoints set in the proper places, you can start the server object and proceed to debugging the application, sending requests from the client.

NOTE

Each package is started in a single instance of the mtx.exe file. This is seen when several packages are started from the **Task Manager** on the **Processes** page.

To install the transactional object into the package from Delphi, you need to do the following. Note that for Windows 2000 the technology is called COM+.

1. Select **Install COM+ Objects** from the **Run** menu.

2. In the **Install COM+ Objects** dialog box (Fig. 4.7), select the MTS object to be installed from the list; for this purpose, check the checkbox to the left of the object's name.

3. When the checkbox is activated, another **Install COM+ Objects** dialog box appears automatically (Fig. 4.8), where you have to select the package into which the MTS transactional object will be installed. Here, to create a new package you must select **Install into new Application**, or **Install into existing Application** for installation into an existing one (selected from the list).

4. Press **OK** to complete the operation.

NOTE

A single object may not be installed into several packages.

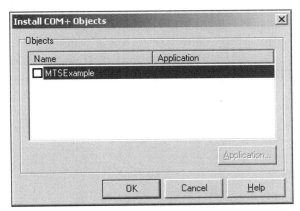

Fig. 4.7. Selecting the MTS transactional object for installation

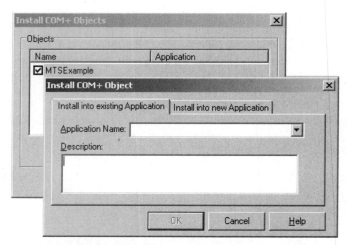

Fig. 4.8. Selecting the application for the MTS transactional object

Optimizing Work with MTS

It is quite easy to develop an application that uses MTS or COM+. More complicated is designing an application in such a way that it is not only functional, but
gives the maximum effect in its work, making full use of all the capabilities of the
technology. For this, it is necessary to clearly understand the performance mechanism of COM objects and the principles of work with transactions.

Transaction Lockout

One of the main principles of competent handling of transactions is their isolation.
To achieve this, various mechanisms of blocking transactions' influence on each
other are used. MTS implements the system of transaction isolation on a high
level. The data will not be visible in one transaction until it has been processed in
another. This reduces system efficiency. To eliminate this problem, it is necessary
to minimize the working period of each transaction and properly use both the
SetComplete and SetAbort methods of the IObjectContext interface.

MTS Activities

Furthermore, one of the most important and fundamental aspects of programming
for MTS is the concept of the *MTS activity*. The correct use of activities is often

neglected, but it is actually the incorrect usage of activities that causes a number of problems and difficulties.

An MTS activity is a set of objects working jointly in the interest of one client. The activity may contain the objects from various packages. Each MTS object exists in one activity only, but the activity may contain several transactions.

Programming for MTS implies that the MTS objects must not be shared among activities. The parallel use of objects within the activity is very dangerous, for a situation may occur in which an object working for one thread may try to accept the transaction, while an object working for another thread is in a process within the same transaction. If the transaction is accepted, this would lead to the commitment of the partially completed transaction.

Example of a Simple Transactional Object

After the main principles and ideas of MTS have been considered, we will create a simple example where the client will request the server for information on current projects. The Microsoft Access database DBDEMOS.MDB will be used as the data source. This is the standard demo database supplied with Delphi. By default, the database file is installed in the **..\Program Files\Common Files\Borland Shared\ Data** folder.

In this simple example, the server will return the total number of orders within the database.

We will create a new group of projects in Delphi, and the first project will be used for server creation.

Server Creation

Using the wizard described above, create an MTS data module called DMTest. Once the data module is created, you must create an **Apartment** thread-oriented model and a **Supports transactions** transactional model in the **New Transactional Data Module Object** wizard.

Here place the group of non-visual components necessary for access to the database via the ADO Microsoft Jet 4.0 OLE DB Provider. In our case, these are the TADOConnection connection component and TADOQuery query component. See *Chapter 7, "ADO Usage in Delphi,"* for details on work with the ADO technology. Now we'll set the connection and request.

ATTENTION

While compiling the example, you need to specify the path to the database on your computer again, using the editor of the ConnectionString property of the TADOConnection component. In our example, this property is blank, as the true location of the database file may vary.

Now, to handle the client's request, create the GetOrderCount method for the IDMTest interface in the type library of the MTS remote data module (Listing 4.3). With the help of the request component, this method will determine the total number of orders.

Listing 4.3. Description of the GetOrderCount Method in the implementation Section

---

```
procedure TDMTest.GetOrderCount(out OrdCount: Integer);
begin
 try
  conDBDemos.Open;
  try
   quOrdCount.Open;
   OrdCount := quOrdCount.Fields[0].AsInteger;
   quOrdCount.Close;
  finally
   conDBDemos.Close;
  end;
  SetComplete;
 except
  OrdCount := DefOrdCount;
  SetAbort;
 end;
end;
```

Pay attention to the use of the SetComplete and SetAbort methods, also implemented for the TMTSDataModule class.

Now, compile the project and install it into the new TestPack package (see Figs. 4.7 and 4.8).

Client Creation

To create the client application, add a new executable application into the group of projects. We'll call it SimpleMTSClient. The main form of the application is shown in Fig. 4.9.

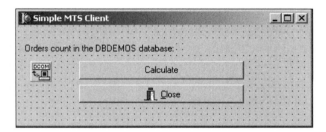

Fig. 4.9. The main form of the MTS client application

The connection between the server and the client may be fixed via various components: TDCOMConnection, TWebConnection, and TSocketConnection. In the example, we will use a component working with Distributed COM, for it is the simplest to set up, and well suited for use on one computer with a server or in a local network. To set it up, you need only indicate the name of the server computer in the ComputerName property, and then select the name of the server from the list of the ServerName property.

ATTENTION

When you work with this example, it is necessary to fill in the values of the ComputerName and ServerName properties of the TDCOMConnection component.

In order to send the call to the server, use the handler method for the buCalculate button click. The source code is very simple:

```
procedure TfmMain.buCalculateClick(Sender: TObject);
var OrdCount: Integer;
begin
  Screen.Cursor := crHourGlass;
  try
    conDCOM.Open;
    conDCOM.AppServer.GetOrderCount(OrdCount);
    laOrdCount.Caption := IntToStr(OrdCount);
    conDCOM.Close;
```

```
finally
 Screen.Cursor := crDefault;
end
end;
```

When the button is pressed, the TDCOMConnection component connects to the database via the server we created.

In the second stage, the AppServer property of the TDCOMConnection component is used. This property is a reference to the IAppServer interface of the remote data module of the MTS server. Apart from its own methods, this interface provides access to all the methods of the IDMTest interface of the remote data module. We are interested, in part, in the GetOrderCount method.

According to Listing 4.3, this method returns the integer in the OrdCount parameter, denoting the number of requests in the database. After type conversion, place this number into the TLabel component.

The connection with the database is closed in the last stage.

After compilation, the application is ready for testing.

Example of Creating a Client and Server in the Case of a Distributed Transaction

In a distributed transaction, several MTS objects must participate in the process.

In our case, these will be two remote MTS data modules. It is not important which database is used with these data modules — the main thing is that the distributed transaction uses different MTS objects. So, for the sake of simplicity, we will use one database in the second connection.

Server Creation

In this example, we will use a connection made with the database by means of BDE. There is a set of files of the dBASE format for the DBDEMOS database in the **..\Program Files\Common Files\Borland Shared\Data** folder. This database is similar to the on used in the previous example.

The previous example will be taken as the basis for the first data module (called DMTest1), and a database request returning the total number of orders will be used.

The structure of this project fully coincides with the above example, except for the data access components.

To provide access to the database via BDE, employ the standard BDE alias DBDEMOS. It is both created and automatically set up when Delphi is installed. Since we are only using one query component, it is sufficient to set the connection parameters in the TQuery component itself, without using the special BDE connection component. For this purpose, select the name of the DBDEMOS alias in the list of the DatabaseName property of the TQuery component. Then enter the text of the request in the SQL property.

Compile the project and register the remote data module in the MTS TestPack package (see Figs. 4.7 and 4.8).

Now, create another MTS remote data module project and name it DMTest2. Its structure fully coincides with the DMTest1 data module, except that the request returns the total number of clients.

Compile the second project and add the new data module to the same TestPack package.

> **NOTE**
>
> For convenience when working with projects, a group of projects will be the best solution in this example.

Developing Distributed Transaction Objects

To implement a distributed transaction, it is necessary to create an additional object to handle distributed transactions.

For this purpose, we will create a new MTS object using the transactional object creation wizard.

Listing 4.4. A Module of a Distributed Transaction Object

```
unit uDistObject;
{$WARN SYMBOL_PLATFORM OFF}

interface

uses
```

```
ActiveX, Mtsobj, Mtx, ComObj, DistrObject_TLB, MTSServer1_TLB,
MTSServer2_TLB, StdVcl;

type
  TDistrObject = class(TMtsAutoObject, IDistrObject)
  private
    DMTest1: IDMTest1;
    DMTest2: IDMTest2;
  protected
    procedure ExecTransaction(out OrdCount, CustCount: Integer); safecall;
  end;

implementation

uses ComServ;

procedure TDistrObject.ExecTransaction(out OrdCount, CustCount: Integer);
var Tr: ITransactionContextEx;
begin
 Tr := CreateTransactionContextEx;
 try
  OleCheck(Tr.CreateInstance(CLASS_DMTest1,IDMTest1, DMTest1));
  OleCheck(Tr.CreateInstance(CLASS_DMTest2,IDMTest2, DMTest2));
  DMTest1.GetOrderCount(OrdCount);
  DMTest2.GetCustCount(CustCount);
  Tr.Commit;
 except
  Tr.Abort;
 end;
end;

initialization
  TAutoObjectFactory.Create(ComServer, TDistrObject, Class_DistrObject,
    ciMultiInstance, tmBoth);
end.
```

We must use two previously created servers in the TDistrObject transactional object. For this purpose, create two variables in the private section pointing to the
interfaces of these servers. Here, the corresponding type libraries must be connected in the uses section.

Create the `ExecTransaction` method, which should return the results of the work of two servers. The method is created in the usual way in the type library of the `TDistrObject` object.

At the beginning of the method, we create an instance of the `ITransactionContextEx` interface, which encapsulates the capabilities of the distributed transaction context. All the work is done by this interface.

The `CreateInstance` method provides for the the creation of instances of server interfaces. The GUIDs of the servers and interface variables are passed as the method's parameters.

Then, using the `GetOrderCount` and `GetCustCount` methods, we receive the information from two servers.

The `Commit` method completes the transaction. In case of error, the `Abort` method rolls the distributed transaction back.

Finally, compile the project and install the object of the distributed transaction in the same `TestPack` package.

Client Creation

The client part of the application is created in the same way as in the previous example, with some slight changes.

You have to use the `TDistrObject` distributed transaction object as the server for the `TDCOMConnection` component. It is specified by the `ServerName` property (see the previous example), or by the `ServerGUID` property, where the GUID of the object must be contained.

So, the handler method of the `buCalculate` button looks as follows:

```
procedure TfmMain.buCalculateClick(Sender: TObject);
var OrdCount, CustCount: Integer;
begin
 Screen.Cursor := crHourGlass;
 try
  conDCOM.Open;
  conDCOM.AppServer.ExecTransaction(OrdCount, CustCount);
  laOrdCount.Caption:=IntToStr(OrdCount);
  laCustCount.Caption:=IntToStr(CustCount);
  conDCOM.Close;
```

```
finally
  Screen.Cursor := crDefault;
 end
end;
```

The returned values are passed to the TLabel components for display.

Summary

Microsoft Transaction Server technology is based on the COM and Automation technologies. The name "MTS" is used for the versions operating in Windows 95/98 and NT. For Windows 2000, a new version has been developed with the name COM+.

Using MTS in distributed applications enhances their efficiency and data security. The main element of the technology, used when the applications are created, is the transactional object. As a rule, it is of moderate size and encapsulates part of the business logic of the application, and the MTS environment "knows" how to work with it. For each transactional object, the MTS environment creates an auxiliary object of the transaction context.

PART II

DATA ACCESS
TECHNOLOGIES

Chapter 5

The Architecture of Database Applications

B y definition, any database application is aimed at interaction with some data source — a database. The interaction involves the following operations:

❏ Retrieving information from a database

❏ Representing data in a specified format for the user

❏ Editing data according to the business algorithms implemented in a program

❏ Returning the changed records back to the database

Along with databases proper, data sources can also be represented by normal files — text files, spreadsheets, etc. However, this chapter deals only with applications that interact with databases.

As you probably know, databases are served by special programs — database management systems — which are divided into local, mostly single-user systems for working with desktop applications, and network systems (often remote), which are multi-user oriented systems that run on specially allocated computers, or servers. The primary criteria for this classification are the database capacity and average database management system load.

However, in spite of the variety of implementations, the basics of database applications remain the same.

The application itself includes a mechanism for receiving and sending data, a mechanism for internal representation of data in some form, a user interface for presenting and editing data, and business logic for processing data.

The *mechanism for receiving and sending data* provides a connection to a data source (often indirectly). This mechanism must "know" the address of the data source, as well as the transfer protocol to use for a two-way data stream.

The *mechanism for internal representation of data* is the core of the database application. It allows received data to be stored in the application and enables these data to be passed to other parts of the application on request.

The *user interface* allows users to browse and edit the data, as well as manage data and the application as a whole.

The *business logic* of the application is a set of data processing algorithms implemented in the program. There is special software between the application and the database that connects the program and the data source and manages the data exchange process. This middleware can be implemented in a wide variety of ways, depending on the database capacity, the system tasks, the number of users, and the techniques used to establish a connection between the application and the database. This middleware can be implemented as an application environment that is essential for the application to work at all, as a set of drivers and DLLs that the application refers to, it can be integrated into the application itself, or it can be a remote server that services thousands of applications.

A data source is the data storage area (the database itself) and a database management system that ensures data integrity and consistency.

This chapter covers in detail the traditional methods of developing database applications with Delphi. Although there are a variety of implementation techniques and an abundance of technical details, the general architecture of Delphi database applications follows the above schema.

Delphi 6 supports quite a large number of various technologies for accessing data (those that are applied with distributed and web applications will be dealt with later in this book). However, the sequence of operations for constructing database applications are still virtually the same. Essentially, the same key components are used, but just slightly adapted in order to suit the requirements of the specific data access technology.

This chapter discusses general approaches to developing Delphi database applications, base classes, and mechanisms which do not change, regardless of whether you choose Borland Database Engine, ADO, or dbExpress for your application.

Thus, this chapter deals with the following issues:

- The structure of Delphi database applications
- The basic components used for developing database applications, as well as their interaction
- The data module
- Programmatic implementation of different parts of a database application
- The concept of a dataset and its role in the basic mechanisms of the database application
- The types of components that contain datasets
- Fields, field types, and field objects
- The use of indexes, and techniques for managing datasets that involve indexing
- The parameters of queries and stored procedures

General Structure of a Database Application

To start with, we will examine how the database application is structured as a whole, and which components and program structures are required by the application. Here we will only concentrate on fundamental issues. All the concepts used here will be considered in more detail later in this chapter.

How a Database Application Works

Delphi Repository doesn't include a separate template for developing database applications. Therefore, like any other Delphi application, the database application starts with a standard form. This approach is undoubtedly justified, as a database application has a *user interface*. This user interface is created by using standard and specialized visual components in conventional forms.

Visual data-aware components are located in the **Data Controls** page of the Component palette. The majority of them are modifications of standard controls, adapted for managing datasets.

An application can contain an arbitrary number of forms and use any interface (MDI or SDI). Usually, one form is responsible for executing a group of similar operations united by the same purpose.

Every database application is based on *datasets*, which are groups of records (they can be conveniently presented in tabular form in the memory) that have been retrieved from the database for browsing and editing. Each dataset is contained in a specific data access component. For data access technology, Delphi VCL implements both a set of base classes that support dataset functionality and sets of child components. These sets are practically identical in their composition, and have a common ancestor in the TDataSet class.

The link between a dataset and data viewing controls is provided by a special component — TDataSource. It manages the data flows between the dataset and the appropriate data controls. This component facilitates data transfer to data controls and returns the results of the editing session to the dataset. It is also responsible for changes in the status of the data controls when the dataset undergoes modifications and passes control signals from the user (of the data controls) to the dataset. The TDataSource component is located in the **Data Access** page of the Component palette.

Thus, the basic data access mechanism is created by three kinds of components:

❑ Components that contain datasets (descendants of the TDataSet class)

❑ TDataSource components

❑ Data controls

Let's examine the interaction between these components in a database application (Fig. 5.1).

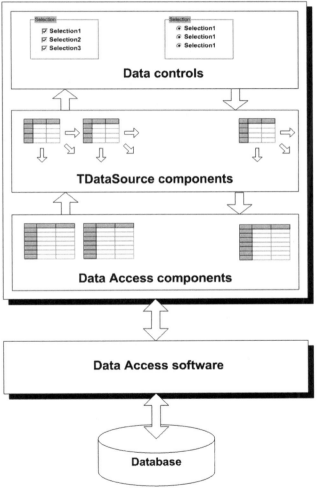

Fig. 5.1. The data access mechanism in a database application

In an application, a data source or middleware interacts with a data access component that contains a dataset and addresses the functions of the corresponding data access technology in order to perform various operations. A dataset component is an "image" of a database table in the application. The permitted number of components in the application is unlimited.

Each data access component can be associated with at least one TDataSource component. The latter provides a link from a dataset to the relevant data controls. The TDataSource component enables the current values of dataset fields to be passed to these components, and returns the changes made.

Another function of the TDataSource component is synchronizing the behavior of data controls with the dataset status. For example, if a dataset is not active, the TDataSource component deletes the data from the data controls and disables these controls. Or, if the dataset is working in read-only mode, the TDataSource component is responsible for informing the data controls that the data cannot be modified.

Each TDataSource component can be connected to several data controls. These components are modified controls designed to display information from datasets.

Once a dataset is open, the component enables the transfer of records from the required database table into the dataset. The dataset cursor is placed at the first record. The TDataSource component passes the values of the specified fields of the current record to the appropriate data controls. While navigating through the records in the dataset, the current values of fields in the data controls are automatically refreshed.

The user can browse and edit data using the data controls. Changed values are immediately passed from the data control to the dataset with the TDataSource component. Subsequently, these changes can either be passed to the database or cancelled.

Now that you have a general idea of how a database application operates, let's move to a step-by-step examination of the process of developing such an application.

Data Modules

It is recommended that a special "form" be used for placing data access components in a database application — the TDataModule class. Note that a data module has nothing in common with the traditional application form, as its direct ancestor is the TComponent class. TDataModule can contain only non-visual components. A data module is available to a programmer in the design stepe, just as any other project module. The user cannot see the data module during runtime.

To create a data module, you can use the Object Repository or the Delphi Main Menu. The **Data Module** icon can be found on the **New** page. As I mentioned before, a data module has little in common with the standard form, if for no other reason than the fact that the TDataModule class is directly derived from the TComponent class. Since non-visual components require practically nothing from the platform, TDataModule has few properties and event handlers of its own — though its descendants that operate in distributed applications perform very important tasks (see *Chapter 8, "The DataSnap Technology. Remote Access Mechanisms"*).

To design a data structure (model, diagram) for your application, you can take advantage of the capabilities provided by the **Diagram** page of the code editor. You can import any element from the hierarchical tree of the data module components that constitute the **Diagram** page and specify its relationship with other components.

With the control buttons you can set a synchronous browsing relationship or a master-slave relationship for the elements in the diagram. As soon as the relationships are specified, the properties of the relevant components are automatically set.

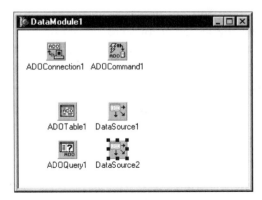

Fig. 5.2. A data module

To call data access components that reside in a data module from any other project module, you need to include the name of this module in the uses clause:

```
...
implementation
```

```
uses uDataModule;
...
DM.Table1.Open;
...
```

The advantage of placing data access components in the data module is that if the value of a property changes, this change is immediately shown in all the regular modules to which this data module is attached. Additionally, all the event handlers of these components — i.e., the entire logic of working with the application — are gathered in the same place, which is also very convenient.

Connecting to Data Sources

The first step for creating a database application is to connect it to a data source. This is what data access components are used for.

The data access component is the foundation of a database application. Using a database table as the base, it creates a dataset and enables you to effectively manage it. This component closely interacts with the functions of the corresponding data access technology. The functionality of the data access technology is usually accessed through a range of interfaces.

All the data access components are non-visual. It is best to place them in the data module. Let's examine the sequence of steps for setting up the database application. As an example, we'll use a tabular component. The following guidelines show you how to customize a table component.

1. *Move the data access component to the data module and attach it to the database.* Depending on the technology, either a special-purpose component establishes a connection, or the data source, driver, interface, or DLL is addressed directly. Techniques for connecting to databases are covered in later chapters.

2. *Attach the component to the database table.* To do this, use the `TableName` property that is available in the **Object Inspector** window. Once you have performed the first step, all the available tables from the database will appear in the list of this property. After the name is selected in the `TableName` property, the component becomes attached to it.

3. *Rename the component.* This is an optional operation. However, in any case, it makes sense to assign pertinent names to your data access components, ones

that correspond to the names of the connected tables. Component names usually duplicate the names of tables (for example, Orders, OrdTable, or tblOrders).

4. *Activate the communication channel between the component and the database table.* To do this, use the Active property. If you set this property to True in the **Object Inspector**, the connection will be activated. This operation can also be performed in the source code of your application. There is also the Open method for opening a dataset, and the Close method for closing it.

Customizing the *TDataSource* Component

At the second stage of development of a database application, you need to place the TDataSource component in a form and customize it for optimal performance. This component allows interaction between the dataset and data controls. For the most part, one component will correspond to one TDataSource component, although there can also be several of them.

To set the properties of the TDataSource component, proceed as follows.

1. *Connect the TDataSource component with the dataset.* Use the DataSet property of the TDataSource component, which is available in the **Object Inspector**. This is a pointer to a DataSet component instance. All the available DataSet components are listed in this property, and can be accessed through the **Object Inspector**.

2. *Rename your component.* This operation is optional, but it is advisable to assign names to your components that correspond to the names of the attached datasets. Usually the name of a component includes the name of the dataset (for example, OrdSource or dsOrders).

> **NOTE**
>
> You can attach the TDataSource component not only to a dataset from the same form, but from any form whose module is declared in the uses clause.

The TDataSource component has a range of useful properties and methods.

The following property enables you to set a connection for your dataset component:

```
property DataSet: TDataSet;
```

And the property below lets you define the current state of a dataset:

```
type TDataSetState = (dsInactive, dsBrowse, dsEdit, dsInsert,
dsSetKey, dsCalcFields, dsFilter, dsNewValue, dsOldValue, dsCurValue,
dsBlockRead, dsInternalCalc);
property State: TDataSetState;
```

By using the property

```
property Enabled: Boolean;
```

you can activate or disable all the connected data controls. If this property is set to False, none of the connected data controls are active. For example, if you need to implement accelerated navigation through records in a large dataset, you may want to disable all connected data controls.

The property

```
property AutoEdit: Boolean;
```

if set to True, will always switch a dataset to edit mode as soon as it receives the focus of one of the connected data controls.

Similarly, the method

```
procedure Edit;
```

activates the edit mode for the connected dataset.

The following method

```
function IsLinkedTo(DataSet: TDataSet): Boolean;
```

returns True if the component indicated in the DataSet parameter is truly connected to the given TDataSource component.

The event handler

```
type TDataChangeEvent = procedure(Sender: TObject; Field: TField) of object;
property OnDataChange: TDataChangeEvent;
```

is called when you edit data in one of the connected data controls.

The event handler

```
property OnUpdateData: TNotifyEvent;
```

is called prior to updating data in the database.

The event handler

```
property OnStateChange: TNotifyEvent;
```

is called when the state of the connected dataset is changed.

Displaying Data

In the third stage of developing a database application, you have to design a user interface on the basis of data controls. These components are specifically designed for viewing and editing data. Outwardly, most of these components do not look any different from traditional controls. Moreover, many data controls descend from standard controls.

Data controls must be connected to the TDataSource component, and through it to the data access component. To do this, use the property

```
property: TDataSource;
```

This property can be found in every data control.

Most data controls are used for displaying data from a single field. These type of components have an additional property —

```
property DataField: String;
```

Here, the dataset field to be displayed in the control is specified.

You thus need to perform the following operations for every data control:

1. *Connect the data control to the TDataSource component.* Use the DataSource property, which must point to the required TDataSource instance. A data control can only be connected to one TDataSource component. The required component can be selected from the list of this property in the **Object Inspector**.

2. *Define the field in the dataset.* Use the DataField property of the TFields type. In this property, you should specify the name of the field of the attached dataset. If the DataSource property is set, you can select the field name from the list. This step is only applicable for components that display a single field.

Datasets

A set of records from one or more database tables that is passed to an application as the result of activating a data access component, from this point on will be referred to as a *dataset.* Obviously, to represent a group of records in an object-oriented environment, an application must use the capabilities of a certain class. This class should contain a dataset and be equipped with methods for managing records and fields.

The TDataSet class is the base class in the hierarchy; it contains an abstract dataset and implements the most general methods for handling it. You can pass either a record from a database table or a string from a traditional text file to it — the dataset will function equally well either way.

Special VCL components for various data access technologies are implemented based on the base class. These allow the developer to create database applications using identical techniques and setting the same properties. Thus, by studying the capabilities of the TDataSet class, we obtain information that is equally applicable to all components that contain a dataset.

An Abstract Dataset

The TDataSet class forms the basis for the hierarchy of classes that implement the functionality of datasets in Delphi database applications. In spite of the fact that this class contains almost no methods that actually support the work of the main dataset mechanisms, its importance is difficult to overestimate.

This class sets the structural foundation needed for any dataset to function. In other words, it serves as the dataset skeleton, which provides methods that need only to have the required calls for the functions of this technology added to them.

You do not need to use the TDataSet class for solving more routine programming tasks while developing database applications. However, developers can use the class as a basis for creating their own custom components.

A dataset is opened and closed by the property

```
property Active: Boolean;
```

which should be set to True or False, respectively. Similar operations are performed by the methods

```
procedure Open;
procedure Close;
```

Navigating through a Dataset

Once a dataset is open, you can navigate through its records. The current record corresponds to the concept of the *cursor* in database servers. As soon as a dataset is open, the cursor is placed at the first record.

The following methods move the cursor next or to the previous record, respectively:

```
procedure Next;
procedure Prior;
```

You can move to the beginning or to the end of a given dataset using the method

```
procedure First;
procedure Last;
```

You have reached the last record in a given dataset if the value of the property

```
property Eof: Boolean;
```

is True.

A similar function for the first record is performed by the property

```
property Bof: Boolean;
```

Moving forward and backward by a specified number of records is performed by the method

```
function MoveBy(Distance: Integer): Integer;
```

The Distance parameter defines the number of records. If its value is negative, the cursor moves to the beginning of the dataset; otherwise it moves to the end.

The following method is used for disabling all the data controls in order to accelerate navigation:

```
procedure DisableControls;
```

The reverse operation is performed by the method

```
procedure EnableControls;
```

The total number of records in the dataset is returned by the property

```
property RecordCount: Integer;
```

However, this property should be used carefully, because every call for it leads to an update of the dataset, which can cause problems with large tables or complex queries. If you need to determine whether dataset is empty (a common operation), you can use the method

```
function IsEmpty: Boolean;
```

which returns True if the dataset is empty. Or, you could use the above-mentioned properties

```
...
if MyTable.Bof AND MyTable.Eof
```

```
then ShowMessage('DataSet is empty');
...
```

The number of the current record is returned by the property

```
property RecNo: Integer;
```

The record size (in bytes) is returned by the property

```
property RecordSize: Word;
```

Dataset Fields

Every dataset record is a set of table field values. Depending on the type of the component and its settings, the number of fields in a dataset can vary. Note that a dataset doesn't necessarily include all the fields of a database table.

The collection of dataset fields is contained in the property

```
property Fields: TFields;
```

while all the required parameters of these fields are contained in the property

```
property FieldDefs: TFieldDefs;
```

The total number of fields in a dataset is returned by the property

```
property FieldCount: Integer;
```

and the total number of BLOB fields is contained in the property

```
property BlobFieldCount: Integer;
```

The property below lets you access the values of the fields in the current record:

```
property FieldValues[const FieldName: string]: Variant; default;
```

where the FieldName parameter sets the name of a field.

The developer very often refers to dataset fields in the process of programming. If the structure of the fields in a dataset is fixed and never changes, this can be done as follows:

```
for i := 0 to MyTable.FieldCount − 1 do
 MyTable.Fields[i].DisplayFormat := '#.###';
```

Otherwise, if the arrangement and composition of dataset fields tend to vary, you can use the method

```
function FieldByName(const FieldName: string): TField;
```

which is done as follows:

```
MyTable.FieldByName('VENDORNO').AsInteger := 1234;
```

The name of a field contained in the `FieldName` parameter is not case-sensitive.

The method

```
procedure GetFieldNames(List: TStrings);
```

returns a full list of the names of dataset fields to the `List` parameter.

Fields and various techniques for handling them will be further discussed later in this chapter.

Editing a Dataset

The `TDataSet` class contains a number of properties and methods that let you edit datasets.

But it is first useful to find out if a dataset can be edited at all. Use the property

```
property CanModify: Boolean;
```

If the value of this property is `True`, then the dataset supports editing. Before you begin editing, make sure that the dataset is set to edit mode, using the method

```
procedure Edit;
```

To save the changes made to the dataset, use the method

```
procedure Post; virtual;
```

The developer can either call the `Post` method manually, or have the dataset call it itself when there is a move to another record.

If necessary, all the changes made after the `Edit` method was last called can be cancelled with the method

```
procedure Cancel; virtual;
```

A new empty record is appended to the end of the dataset with the method

```
procedure Append;
```

A new empty record is inserted in place of the current one with the method

```
procedure Insert;
```

while the current record as well as all the following records are shifted one position down.

> **NOTE**
>
> When the `Append` and `Insert` methods are used, the dataset switches to edit mode automatically.

Additionally, you can add or insert a new record with fields that have already been assigned values. Use the methods

```
procedure AppendRecord(const Values: array of const);
procedure InsertRecord(const Values: array of const);
```

which is done as follows:

```
MyTable.AppendRecord([2345, 'New customer', '+7(812)4569012', 0, '']);
```

Once these methods are called and executed, the dataset automatically returns to the browse state.

You can fill all the fields in the current records in a similar way with the method

```
procedure SetFields(const Values: array of const);
```

The current record is removed by the method

```
procedure Delete;
```

Note that the dataset never prompts you for confirmation, but simply does what it is told.

The contents of all the fields in the current record can be deleted by the method

```
procedure ClearFields;
```

Note that all the fields are cleared (`Null`), not reset to the `nil` value.

The following property informs you whether the current record has been edited:

```
property Modified: Boolean;
```

If the value of the property is `True`, it has.

You can update a dataset without closing and reopening it. Use the method

```
procedure Refresh;
```

However, this method works only with tables and those queries that cannot be edited.

Handling Dataset Events

Event handlers for the `TDataSet` class provide the developer with a huge range of capabilities for tracking events that occur with a dataset.

A pair of event handlers (one for before and one for after the event) is supplied for the following dataset events:

❏ Opening and closing a dataset

❏ Activating edit mode

❏ Activating insert mode

❏ Saving changes made

❏ Canceling changes

❏ Navigating through the records

❏ Refreshing a dataset

Note that in addition to the insert mode event handlers, you can use another method

```
property OnNewRecord: TDataSetNotifyEvent;
```

which is called directly when inserting or adding a record.

Additionally, you can use event handlers for errors that occur. These event handlers are provided for errors in deletion, editing, and saving changes.

The event handler:

```
property OnCalcFields: TDataSetNotifyEvent;
```

is very important when you set values for calculated fields. It is called for every record displayed in the data controls that a dataset uses each time the values of the fields in the data controls are changed.

If the calculations performed by the OnCalcFields event handler are too complicated, you can avoid calling it too frequently with the property:

```
property AutoCalcFields: Boolean;
```

By default, this property is set to True and fields are recalculated every time the values of fields are changed. But if you assign a value of False, the OnCalcFields event handler will be called only when you open a dataset, activate edit mode, or refresh a dataset.

All the above event handlers belong to the same type:

```
type TDataSetNotifyEvent = procedure(DataSet: TDataSet) of object;
```

And the event handler

```
type TFilterRecordEvent = procedure(DataSet: TDataSet; var Accept:
Boolean) of object;
property OnFilterRecord: TFilterRecordEvent;
```

is called for every dataset record if the property `Filtered = True`.

Standard Components

If you examine the data access components in the Component palette, you will notice that the sets for each of the various data access technologies are basically identical. Every set includes a component that contains tabular functions, an SQL query component, and a stored procedure component. And although they have different direct ancestors, the functions of these components in different technologies are still practically identical.

Therefore, it makes sense to examine the properties and methods common to the components by pretending that the table, query, and stored procedure components in each of the above groups descend from the same virtual ancestors.

Table Components

Table components provide access to entire database tables by creating datasets in which the structures of the fields completely duplicate the database table. This feature means that the component is easy to set-up and has a number of extra functions that enable the use of table indexes.

However, in practice programming rarely involves using an entire database table. And when you work with database servers, the middleware used by the data access technologies always translates a request for a table data into a simple SQL query, for example:

```
SELECT * FROM Orders
```

In this situation, using table components becomes less productive than using queries.

Once the connection to the data source has been established, you need to indicate the name of the table in the property

```
property TableName: String;
```

Sometimes, the `TableType` property also specifies the type of table (for example, Paradox tables).

If the connection with the data source has been set correctly, the name of the table can be selected from the drop-down list of the `TableName` property in the **Object Inspector** window.

Table components have the advantage of supporting indexes, which accelerates the whole process of working with a table. All indexes created for a table in the database are automatically loaded to the component. Their parameters can be accessed through the property

```
property IndexDefs: TIndexDefs;
```

The `TIndexDefs` class will be described later in this chapter.

The developer can manipulate indexes while working with the given component.

An existing index can be selected from the **Object Inspector** list with the property

```
property IndexName: String;
```

or the property

```
property IndexFieldNames: String;
```

where you can specify a random combination of names of the indexed fields of a table. Field names are delimited by semicolons. You can thus using the `IndexFieldNames` property specify composite indexes.

The `IndexName` or `IndexFieldNames` properties cannot be used simultaneously.

The number of fields used in the current index of a table component is returned by the property

```
property IndexFieldCount: Integer;
```

The property

```
property IndexFields: [Index: Integer]: TField;
```

is an indexed list of the fields included in the current index:

```
. . .
for i := 0 to MyTable.IndexFieldCount - 1 do
 MyTable.IndexFields[i].Enabled := False;
. . .
```

Table components have a number of methods that allow you to manipulate tables and indexes.

The method

```
procedure CreateTable;
```

creates a new table in the database using the defined name and description of the fields and indexes from the `TFieldDefs` and `TIndexDefs` properties. If any table with this name already exists in the database, it will be deleted and overwritten by the new version with a new structure and data.

The method

```
procedure EmptyTable;
```

deletes all the records from a dataset and a database table.

The method

```
procedure DeleteTable;
```

deletes the database table associated with a component. The dataset must be closed.

The following method:

```
type
   TIndexOption = (ixPrimary, ixUnique, ixDescending,
ixCaseInsensitive, ixExpression, ixNonMaintained);

   TIndexOptions = set of TIndexOption;
procedure AddIndex(const Name, Fields: String; Options: TIndexOptions,
const DescFields: String='');
```

adds a new index to a database table. The `Name` parameter sets the name for the index. The `Fields` parameter lists the names of the fields contained in the index, which are delimited by semicolons. The `DescFields` parameter specifies the description of the index from the constants declared in the `TIndexOption` type.

The method

```
procedure DeleteIndex(const Name: string);
```

deletes an index.

For more information on table components, refer to the *"Mechanisms for Managing Data"* section in this chapter.

Query Components

Query components are designed for creating SQL queries, preparing parameters for these queries, passing them to a database server, and presenting the result of the query in a dataset. Sometimes the dataset can be edited, and sometimes it cannot.

If every single string in the dataset of a query component uniquely corresponds to a string in a database table, you can edit this component. For instance, the query

```
SELECT * FROM Country
```

can be edited. If the above rule does not hold, this dataset can be used only for viewing, and the capabilities of components are irrelevant. Where, for example, should the results of editing a record of the following query be recorded?

```
SELECT CustNo, SUM(AmountPaid)
FROM Orders
GROUP BY CustNo
```

Every record in this query is the sum of other records, the exact number of which is unknown in advance.

However, query components represent a powerful and flexible tool for handling data. You can solve far more difficult tasks with query components than you can with table components.

All in all, a query component works faster, since the structure of the fields returned by a query can change, and `TFieldDef` class instances that store information on field properties can be created on demand at run time.

> **NOTE**
>
> A table component creates all the classes used for describing fields, which accounts for its slower performance as compared to a query in a client-server application.

Let's now take a look at the general properties and methods of query components.

The text of a query is defined by the property

```
property SQL: TStrings;
```

The property

```
property Text: PChar;
```

contains the final version of the query text which will be passed to the server.

A query can be executed using one of three approaches.

If the query is to return a result set, use either the method

```
procedure Open;
```

or the property

```
property Active: Boolean;
```

which you should set to `True`. Once your query has been processed, the dataset of the component is open. The query is closed by the method

```
procedure Close;
```

or the same `Active` property.

If the query doesn't return a result to the dataset (as is the case with the `INSERT`, `DELETE`, and `UPDATE` statements), use the method

```
procedure ExecSQL;
```

and, after your query has been processed, the dataset of the component will not be opened. Any attempt to use the `Open` method or the `Active` property for such a query will produce an error of a pointer to the dataset cursor being created.

Once a query has executed, the property

```
property RowsAffected: Integer;
```

returns the number of records processed by the query.

To enable editing of a query's dataset, set the following property

```
property RequestLive: Boolean;
```

to `True`. This property can be specified, but does not work for a query that returns a result which cannot be modified because of the query itself.

To prepare a query for execution, use the method

```
procedure Prepare;
```

which allows you to allocate the necessary server resources, and provides optimization.

The method

```
procedure UnPrepare;
```

releases the resources used for preparing a query.

The result of these two operations is reflected in the property:

```
property Prepared: Boolean;
```

where a `True` value indicates that the query is ready to run.

The `Prepare` and `UpPrepare` methods are optional, because your component will do this automatically. However, if you plan to run this query several times in a row, you need to prepare it manually prior to the first run. Then the server will not waste time on useless operations in subsequent execution, as the resources have already been allocated.

Quite often, queries have parameters that can be set, the values of which are determined immediately before running the query.

The property

```
property Params: TParams;
```

is a list of TParam objects, each one of which includes settings for a particular parameter. The Params property is automatically refreshed when the text of a query is changed. The TParams class will be discussed in more depth later in this chapter.

> **NOTE**
>
> In the TADOQuery component, the counterpart of the Params property described above is called Parameters and has the TParameters type.

The property

```
property ParamCount: Word;
```

returns the number of query parameters.

The property

```
property ParamCheck: Boolean;
```

determines whether the Params property should be refreshed when the content of the query is changed at run time. If the value is set to True, then the property is updated.

Additionally, query components contain several properties and methods described in the "*Mechanisms for Managing Data*" section of this chapter.

Stored Procedure Components

Stored procedure components are designed for determining stored procedures, setting their parameters, executing these procedures, and returning the results to the component.

Depending on the data access technology selected, each stored procedure component has its own technique for connecting to the server. As soon as the connection to the data source has been established, you can select the name of the stored procedure from the list by the property:

```
property StoredProcName: String;
```

After this, the property

```
property Params: TParams;
```

which is designed for storing parameters of a procedure, is automatically filled.

It is important to divide parameters for stored procedures into two input and output parameters. The former contain basic data, and the latter give the results of procedures.

The TParams class is discussed at greater length later in this chapter.

The total number of parameters is returned by the property

```
property ParamCount: Word;
```

To prepare a stored procedure, use the method

```
procedure Prepare;
```

or the property

```
property Prepared: Boolean;
```

by setting it to True.

The method

```
procedure UnPrepare;
```

or the Prepared := False property reverse the above operation.

Additionally, by checking the value of the Prepared property you can learn whether or not a given procedure has been prepared for execution.

WARNING

After executing a stored procedure, the initial order in which the parameters of a given procedure are arranged in the Params list may change. Therefore, to access any particular parameter, the following method is recommended:

```
function ParamByName(const Value: String): TParam;
```

If a stored procedure returns a dataset, the component can be opened by the method

```
procedure Open;
```

or by the property

```
property Active: Boolean;
```

Otherwise, use the method

```
procedure ExecProc;
```

which will assign the calculated values to the output parameters.

Dataset States

A dataset can perform extremely varied operations from the moment it is opened by the Open method until it is closed by the Close method. You can simply navigate through its records, edit data and delete records, make searches by different parameters, etc. Here, of course, it is desirable that all operations are executed as quickly and as effectively as possible.

A dataset is always in a certain state, i.e., it is ready to perform actions of a strictly defined kind. For every group of operations, a dataset performs a sequence of preliminary actions.

All states of a dataset fall into two groups:

❑ The first group comprises the states which a dataset assumes automatically, including short-term states that accompany various operations on the fields in a dataset (Table 5.1).

❑ The second group includes the states that can be controlled from applications — for example, switching a dataset to edit mode (Table 5.2).

Table 5.1. Automatic States of Datasets

State Constant	Description
dsNewValue	Activated when the NewValue property of a dataset field is addressed
dsOldValue	Activated when the OldValue property of a dataset field is addressed
dsCurValue	Activated when the CurValue property of a dataset field is called
dsInternalCalc	Activated when the values of the fields for which FindKind = fkInternalCalc are calculated
dsCalcFields	Activated when the OnCalcFields method is called
dsBlockRead	The block read mode, which enables accelerated navigation through a dataset
dsOpening	Exists when a dataset is opened by the Open method or the Active property
dsFilter	Activated when the OnFilterRecord method is called

Table 5.2. Controllable States of Datasets

State Constant	Method	Description
dsInactive	Close	The dataset is closed
dsBrowse	Open	The dataset can be accessed only for browsing; the data in it cannot be edited
dsEdit	Edit	The dataset can be edited
dsInsert	Insert	New records can be added to the dataset
dsSetKey	SetKey	The mechanism for searching by key is activated; ranges also can be used

The base TDataSet class that contains the properties of a dataset allows you to check the current state of a given dataset, and also to change this state.

The current state of a dataset is passed to the State property of TDataSetState type:

```
type TDataSetState = (dsInactive, dsBrowse, dsEdit, dsInsert,
dsSetKey, dsCalcFields, dsFilter, dsNewValue, dsOldValue, dsCurValue,
dsBlockRead, dsInternalCalc);
```

Dataset states are managed through the Open, Close, Edit, and Insert methods.

Now let's see how the state of a dataset changes when standard operations are performed.

A closed dataset always has the dsInactive state.

Once a dataset is open, its state changes to dsBrowse. This state permits a user to move around the dataset and view its content, but does not allow the data to be edited. This is the main state for any open dataset; a dataset can move from this state into other states, but any changes in state occur through the browsing of data (Fig. 5.3).

If a dataset needs to be edited, it should be switched to edit mode (dsEdit) using the Edit method. Once the method has executed, you will be able to modify values of the fields in the current record. When you move to the next record, the dataset automatically assumes the dsBrowse state.

If you need to insert a new record in the dataset, use the dsInsert method, which adds a new empty record at the location of the current cursor. After the move to the next record, the primary key (if it exists) is checked for uniqueness, and the dataset resumes the dsBrowse state.

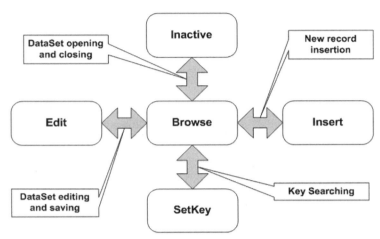

Fig. 5.3. The schema of changes in dataset states

The `dsSetKey` state is used only for table components if you need to use the `FindKey` and `FindNext` method to search, and also if you use ranges (the `SetRange` method). This state is preserved until either the method for searching by key or the method for canceling a range is called. Then the dataset resumes the `dsBrowse` state.

The `dsBlockRead` state can be used for a dataset if you need to navigate quickly through large arrays of records without displaying intermediate data in data controls and without calling the event handler for navigating through records. This can be done with the `DisableControls` and `EnableControls` methods.

Indexes

One of the most pressing problems for any database is to provide the highest possible level of performance and to maintain this level as the amount of data stored increases. This task can be solved by using indexes.

An *index* is a database entity that contains information on the organization of data in database tables.

Unlike keys that just serve as identifiers for individual records, indexes take up extra memory resources (quite a substantial amount) and can be stored either together with tables or as separate files. Indexes are created at the same time as the associated table, and are changed when the data in this table undergoes any modification. Updating indexes for a big database table usually requires significant resources, which makes it worthwhile to limit the number of indexes for such tables if the data in them need updating often. An index includes unique identifiers of records, as well as extra information on the organization of data. Obviously, if a server or local database management system uses indexes to process a query, it takes significantly less time, as indexes "know" how the records are arranged and can speed up processing by clustering records by the values of their parameters.

Naturally, Delphi VCL uses all the capabilities of such a powerful tool as indexes in data access components. It should be mentioned, though, that the properties and methods for handling indexes can be found only in table components, because query components handle indexes with SQL.

You can also manipulate a dataset without using indexes, but to do so the table must not have a primary key — which is rather uncommon. Therefore, datasets use default primary indexes.

Setting Indexes

In order to set secondary indexing for a dataset, you need to indicate the name of the index using the property

```
property IndexName: String;
```

If no value has been specified for this property, it means that the dataset uses a primary index.

Alternatively, you can specify an index by the property

```
property IndexFieldNames: String;
```

where the names of the fields that comprise the required index are listed; the field names are delimited by semicolons. Moreover, lists of fields for all existing indexes are created automatically for this property in the **Object Inspector**, so the developer can make the choice. This property also lets you create composite indexes, but this is possible only if all the fields in the list are indexed.

> **NOTE**
>
> You can change the current index without closing the dataset, which makes sorting by indexes very convenient. This method of adjusting indexes is referred to as "on-the-fly" indexing.

Once indexing is set, the number of fields in the index is passed to the following property:

```
property IndexFieldCount: Integer;
```

Index Definition Lists

All the information on the indexes of a dataset is stored in the property of the TDataSet class:

```
property IndexDefs: TIndexDefs;
```

Here, each index is supplied with a unique definition in the form of a TIndexDef object. The following property enables you to access the information on indexes

```
property Items[Index: Integer]: TIndexDef; default;
```

which is a list of TIndexDef objects.

Objects of the TIndexDef type can be added to the list by calling the method

```
function AddIndexDef: TIndexDef;
```

To search for the index description object, use the method

```
function Find(const Name: String): TIndexDef;
```

which returns the object that matches the index name specified by the Name parameter.

The following pair of methods:

```
function FindIndexForFields(const Fields: string): TIndexDef;
function GetIndexForFields(const Fields: String; CaseInsensitive:
Boolean): TIndexDef;
```

lets you find the required definition object by the list of the fields that constitute a given index. If the index has not been found, the first index that begins with the specified fields will be looked for. If the search has failed, the first method generates the EDatabaseError exception, and the second one returns nil.

The list is automatically updated every time you open a dataset. However, you can update the IndexDefs list of index definitions without opening the dataset by using the method

```
procedure Update; reintroduce;
```

Index Definition

The parameters for every individual dataset index are declared in the `TIndexDef` class, while the full list of these parameters for the entire dataset can be accessed through the `IndexDefs` property of the `TDataSet` class.

The property

```
property Name: String;
```

defines the name of the index.

The list of the fields of the index is contained in the property

```
property Fields: String;
```

The fields are delimited by semicolons.

The property

```
property CaseInsFields: String;
```

lists all the fields which can be treated as case-insensitive when they are being sorted. The fields are delimited by semicolons. All the fields in this list must be included in the `Fields` property. By default, every dataset uses case-sensitive sorting for its records, but some database servers support a combined technique of sorting fields — both case-insensitive and case-sensitive.

The property:

```
property DescFields: String;
```

contains the list of fields that are sorted in descending order. The fields are delimited by semicolons. All the fields in this list must be included in the `Fields` property. The default sorting order for fields is ascending. Several database servers support both ascending and descending sorting order.

The property:

```
property GroupingLevel: Integer;
```

enables you to limit the area of indexing. If this property is set to `nil`, then indexing is applied to all the records in a dataset. Otherwise, only those groups of records that have identical values for the number of fields specified by the property are indexed.

The parameters of an index are specified by the property

```
property Options: TIndexOptions;
```

An index can have the following combinations of parameters:

❏ `ixPrimary` — the primary index.

❏ `ixUnique` — the values of this index are unique.

❏ `ixDescending` — this index sorts in descending order.

❏ `ixCaseInsensitive` — this index uses case-insensitive sorting.

❏ `ixExpression` — this is an expression index (used for dBASE indexes).

❏ `ixNonMaintained` – this index is not automatically updated when the table is opened.

The method

```
procedure Assign(ASource: TPersistent); override;
```

fills the properties of an object with the values set for the analogous properties of the `ASource` object.

For example, you can use properties and methods of index definition objects in this way:

```
with Table1 do
begin
...
 with IndexDefs do
 begin
  Clear;
  AddIndexDef;
  with Items[0] do
  begin
   Name := 'Primary';
   Fields := 'Field1';
   Options := [ixPrimary, ixUnique];
  end;
  AddIndexDef;
  with Items[1] do
  begin
   Name := 'SecondIndex';
   Fields := 'Field1;Field2';
   Options := [ixCaseInsensitive];
  end;
 end;
end;
```

When descriptions for indexes are created, the AddIndexDef method is used, which adds a new TIndexDef object to the Items list of the TIndexDefs object. This technique is used first for setting primary indexes, and afterwards for specifying secondary indexes (SecondIndex). Every description must be supplied with the fields that comprise the index, as well as with the index parameters (the Fields and Options properties).

Parameters of Queries and Stored Procedures

The property

```
property Params: TParams;
```

contains a set of customizable parameters for a query or a stored procedure. This property is a collection of TParam objects that contain individual parameters.

Consider the following SQL query:

```
SELECT SaleDat, OrderNo
FROM Orders
WHERE SaleDat >= '01.08.2002' AND SaleDat <= '31.08.2002'
```

This query selects the numbers of the orders that were placed in August, 2002. Naturally, the user may require a similar report for a different month, or for the first ten days in August, etc.

In this case, you can act as follows:

```
...
with Query1 do
begin
 Close;
 SQL.Clear;
 SQL[0] := 'SELECT PartDat, ItemNo, ItemCount, InputPrice';
 SQL[1] := 'FROM Parts';
 SQL[2] := 'WHERE PartDat>= '+chr(39)+Date1Edit.Text+chr(39)+
  ' AND PartDat<='+chr(39)+Date2Edit.Text+chr(39);
  Open;
end;
```

Here, an SQL property is used to modify the text of a query in accordance with the date values specified by the Date1Edit and Date2Edit single-line editors.

To solve tasks like these, parameters are used. In this case, the text of the query will look as follows:

```
SELECT PartDat, ItemNo, ItemCount, InputPrice
FROM Parts
WHERE PartDat>= :PD1 AND PartDat<= :PD2
```

The colon before the PD1 and PD2 names denotes parameters. The name of a parameter is arbitrary. The first parameter in the list of the Params property is the parameter that comes first in the text of the query.

Once you have entered the text of the query in the SQL property, a TParam object is automatically created for each one of the parameters. These objects can be accessed through the specialized editor called by pressing the button of the Params property in the **Object Inspector** (Fig. 5.4). You have to specify the type of data for every parameter, which should match the type of data of the corresponding field.

Fig. 5.4. The specialized editor for handling query parameters

Now you can use the Params property to set current date boundaries:

```
...
with Query1 do
begin
 Close;
 Params[0].AsDateTime := StrToDate(Date1Edit.Text);
 Params[1].AsDateTime := StrToDate(Date2Edit.Text);
 Open;
end;
...
```

The parameters are used for specifying the current values of the date boundaries.

You can also set the values for the parameters of your query from another dataset. To do this, you need to use the DataSource property of the DataSet component. The TDataSource component that is specified in this property must be linked to the dataset whose field values need to be passed to the parameters. The names of parameters should match the names of the fields in this dataset, and then the DataSource property will begin to work. When you navigate through the dataset records, the current values of the parameters of the same name are automatically passed to the query.

For instance, the SQL property of the first query component looks as follows:

```
SELECT OrderNo, CustNo, SaleDate, AmountPaid FROM Orders
```

It should be linked to a component of the TDataSource type.

The SQL property of the second query looks like this:

```
SELECT CustNo, Company FROM Customer
WHERE CustNo = :CustNo
```

Note that the name of the parameter matches the name of the field in the Orders table, which contains the customer number. This condition is essential. The DataSource property of the second query component must point to the TDataSource component of the first query. As soon as both datasets are open, the current value of the CustNo field of the Orders dataset is automatically passed to the query parameter of the Customers component. In this way, a one-to-many relationship is implemented for these two datasets through the field that contains the customer number.

To conclude our discussion of query parameters, let's examine the properties and methods of the TParams class, part of the Params property, and the TParam class, which contains an individual parameter.

The *TParams* Class

The TParams class is a list of parameters.

The elements in this list can be accessed via the indexed property

```
property Items[Index: Word]: TParam;
```

while the values of these parameters are contained in the property

```
property ParamValues[const ParamName: String]: Variant;
```

A new parameter can be added by the method

```
procedure AddParam(Value: TParam);
```

However, to do this you need to create a parameter object using the method

```
function CreateParam(FldType: TFieldType; const ParamName: string;
ParamType: TParamType): TParam;
```

where `FldType` indicates the type of data used by the parameter, `ParamName` defines the name of the parameter, and `ParamType` indicates the type of parameter (see below).

Both these methods can work in tandem:

```
MyParams.AddParam(MyParams.CreateParam(ftInteger, 'Param1', ptInput));
```

Instead of setting these parameters one at a time, you can use the method

```
function ParseSQL(SQL: String; DoCreate: Boolean): String;
```

which, if `DoCreate = True`, parses the text of an `SQL` query and builds a new list of parameters.

Alternatively, you can set all the parameters at once using the method

```
procedure AssignValues(Value: TParams);
```

A parameter can be deleted from the list by the method

```
procedure RemoveParam(Value: TParam);
```

It is useful to call your parameters by their names when you need to identify them; just as when handling stored procedures, their order can change after they execute. The same is also true for dynamic queries (their **SQL** text can change during the execution process).

Use the following method to call a parameter by its name:

```
function ParamByName(const Value: String): TParam;
```

When the developer deals with complex **SQL** queries, or when multiple corrections have been made to a query, it is possible to create two different parameters with the same name by mistake. In such a case, when the query executes, these parameters are treated as a single parameter, and are both set to the value of the first query. To ensure that all the names assigned to parameters are unique, use the following method:

```
function IsEqual(Value: TParams): Boolean;
```

which returns `True` if a duplicate of the `Value` parameter has been found.

The *TParam* Class

The TParam class contains the properties of an individual parameter.

The following property specifies the name of the parameter:

```
property Name: String;
```

The type of data used by the parameter is defined by the property

```
property DataType: TFieldType;
```

The types of data used in the parameter and in the related field must coincide.

The type of a parameter is defined by the set

```
type
   TParamType = (ptUnknown, ptInput, ptOutput, ptInputOutput, ptResult);
   TParamTypes = set of TParamType;
```

which has the following values:

❑ ptUnknown — the type is unknown.

❑ ptInput — this is an input parameter used for returning values from an application.

❑ ptOutput — this is an output parameter used for passing values to a application.

❑ ptInputOutput — this parameter is used for both passing and returning values.

❑ ptResult — this parameter is used for passing information on the status of an operation.

The property

```
property ParamType: TParamType;
```

sets the type of parameter.

It is often necessary to ascertain whether the value of a parameter is Null. To do this, use the property:

```
property IsNull: Boolean;
```

This property returns True if the value of the parameter has not been set or if the value of the parameter is Null.

The property:

```
property Bound: Boolean;
```

returns True only if the parameter has not been assigned any value.

The method

```
procedure Clear;
```

sets a parameter to Null.

The value of a parameter is specified by the property

```
property Value: Variant;
```

However, when you require maximum speed, using variants is not very effective. In this case, you can use the whole set of As… properties, which not only return the value, but also cast it into the required type. For example, the property

```
property AsInteger: LongInt;
```

returns an integer that denotes the value of a field.

> **NOTE**
>
> You need to be careful when using type cast properties, as an attempt to cast an invalid value will generate an exception.

The following methods allow you to read a parameter value from and write it to the buffer:

```
procedure SetData(Buffer: Pointer);
procedure GetData(Buffer: Pointer);
```

and the method below lets you set the necessary data size when you write data to the buffer:

```
function GetDataSize: Integer;
```

You can copy the type of data, the name, and the value for a parameter directly from the data field using the following method:

```
procedure AssignField(Field: TField);
```

while the method below lets you assign a name and a value to a parameter:

```
procedure AssignFieldValue(Field: TField; const Value: Variant);
```

The total number of characters for numeric values is set by the property

```
property Precision: Integer;
```

The property

```
property NumericScale: Integer;
```

determines the number of decimal places.

The size of a string parameter can be set by the property

```
property Size: Integer;
```

Mechanisms for Managing Data

Related Tables

Database tables can be connected by *one-to-many* or *many-to-many* relationships, and these relationships must be set between indexed fields of two tables.

When a relationship between database tables is created, any component that encapsulates a dataset can be used as a master table, while only table components can be used to set a detail table.

One-to-Many Relationships

To create a one-to-many relationship in a dataset, we use two properties, MasterSource and MasterFields, which are set for a detail table. The dataset of a master table doesn't require any specific settings, and the connection created will work only when you navigate through the records in the master table.

The property

```
property MasterSource: TDataSource;
```

defines the TDataSource component that is linked to the master table.

Then, by using the property:

```
property MasterFields: String;
```

you can specify the relationship between the fields of the master and detail tables. This property contains the name of the indexed field that serves as the link between the tables. If there are several such fields, their names are delimited by semicolons. Note that it is not necessary to use all the fields of the index to establish a relationship.

The MasterFields property can be set by the **Field Link Designer**, called by pressing the button in the edit field of this property in the **Object Inspector**.

Here you can select the required index for the detail table from the list of indexes that can be accessed through the **Available Indexes** drop-down list. However,

it should be noted that some data access technologies do not provide you with the
Available Indexes list.

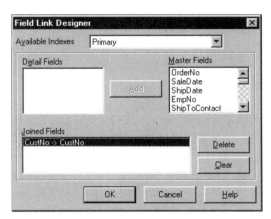

Fig. 5.5. The **Field Link Designer** window

After that, the names of all the fields that constitute this index appear in the **Detail
Fields** list. The **Master Fields** list shows the fields of the master table.

Now you have to create the link between the fields. Select the field of the detail
table from the list on the left and then choose the corresponding field of the master
table from the list on the right. After this, the **Add** button is activated — press it to
create the relationship between the two fields of the master and detail tables. This
link will be displayed in the **Joined Fields** list.

> **NOTE**
>
> Once a link between two indexed fields is created, the given index becomes the current
> index for the dataset. Depending on the type of database management system, either
> the `IndexName` or `IndexFieldNames` property is filled automatically.

You can also delete any existing link. The **Delete** button deletes a selected link,
while the **Clear** button deletes all existing links.

As soon as you've set a link between the fields, a one-to-many relationship is established. You just need to open both datasets to make sure that the relationship
works.

Many-to-Many Relationships

A many-to-many relationship differs in that the detail table is linked to another detail table as a master table using a sequence of operations similar to the one used when creating a one-to-one relationship.

Searching Data

To search through a random selection of fields, you can use the Lookup and Locate methods.

```
function Locate(const KeyFields: string; const KeyValues: Variant;
Options: TLocateOptions): Boolean;
function Lookup(const KeyFields: string; const KeyValues: Variant;
const ResultFields: string): Variant;
```

When you work with the Locate method, you need to pass it a list of the fields that will be searched (the KeyFields parameter — the names of the fields are separated by semicolons), their required values (the KeyValues parameter — the values are delimited by semicolons) and the search settings (the Options parameter). You can specify the loCaseInsensitive option, which disables checking the case of characters, and the loPartialKey option, which activates a search with partial-match retrieval. If the search was successful, the cursor is positioned on the matching record, and the method returns True.

```
Table1.Locate('Last_Name;First_Name', VarArrayOf(['Edit1.Text',
'Edit2.Text']), []);
```

When you deal with the Lookup method, you need to pass it a list of the fields that will be searched (the KeyFields parameter — the names of the fields are separated by semicolons) and their required values (the KeyValues parameter — the values are delimited by commas). If the search was successful, the method returns the array of values of variant type for the fields whose names are contained in the ResultFields parameter.

```
Table1.Lookup('Last_Name;First_Name', VarArrayOf(['Edit1.Text',
'Edit2.Text']), 'Last_Name;First_Name');
```

Both these methods can automatically implement a quick index search if you specify fields of an index in the KeyFields parameter.

Filtering Data

The most effective way to extract information (especially from large database tables) in order to populate a dataset is to create and run a corresponding SQL query. But what if a dataset is based on a table component? Here the filtering mechanism — an integral part of a dataset — comes to the rescue.

Filtering is based on two basic properties, as well as one additional one. The text of the filter should be contained in the `Filter` property, and the `Filtered` property activates and disables the filter. The parameters for a filter are set by the `FilterOptions` property.

> **NOTE**
>
> Query components also support filters. This feature at times allows developers to easily and elegantly solve complex problems that would otherwise require the text of the query to be changed and/or a new query component to be created.

When you use a filter, its text is translated into SQL syntax and passed to the server or through the appropriate driver to the local database management system.

You can create a filter in two ways:

❑ Simple filters that can be implemented by the native syntax of the filtering mechanism are created by using the `Filter` property

❑ More sophisticated filters that require full use of all the capabilities of the given programming language are created using the `OnFilterRecord` dataset event handler

All filters can be divided into two categories: *persistent* and *dynamic*.

Persistent filters are created at design time and can use both the `Filter` property and the `OnFilterRecord` method.

Dynamic filters can be built and edited at run time; they use only the `Filter` property.

The text of a filter for the `Filter` property is compiled from the names of the fields in the relevant database table; the comparison criteria are specified by utilizing all comparison operators (>, >=, <, <=, =, <>) as well as the logical operators AND, OR, NOT:

```
Field1 > 100 AND Field2 = 20
```

You cannot compare two fields. The following filter will generate an error if you attempt to use it:

```
ItemCount = Balance AND InputPrice > OutputPrice
```

Dynamic filters can be created by changing an entire filter expression and its constituent parts. For example, a constraint value for a field can be set by using the controls of a form, which lets the application user manage the dataset filtering.

```
procedure TForm1.Edit1Change(Sender: TObject);
begin
 with Table1 do
 begin
  Filtered := False;
  Filter := 'Field1 >=' + TEdit(Sender).Text;
  Filtered := True;
 end;
end;
```

Filters can select parts of strings for string fields — use an asterisk:

```
ItemName='A*'
```

The filter will work only if the `Filtered` property is set to `True`. If you need to modify the text of a dynamic filter or disable a filter, set the `Filtered` property to `False`.

You can set the parameters for a filter with the `FilterOptions` property:

```
property FilterOptions: TFilterOptions;
TFilterOption = (foCaseInsensitive, foNoPartialCompare);
TFilterOptions = set of TFilterOption;
```

By activating the `foCaseInsensitive` parameter, you specify a case-insensitive pattern of comparing string values. The `foNoPartialCompare` parameter enables selection of string values by comparing parts of strings.

The `OnFilterRecord` event handler is declared as follows:

```
type TFilterRecordEvent = procedure(DataSet: TDataSet; var Accept: Boolean) of object;

property OnFilterRecord: TFilterRecordEvent;
```

If this event handler is created for a dataset, then it is called for every record of this dataset. The program code of the `OnFilterRecord` event handler must assign either the `True` or `False` value to the `Accept` parameter. As a result, the record is either passed to the dataset or rejected:

```
procedure TForm1.TableFilterRecord(DataSet: TDataSet; var Accept: Boolean);
begin
  Accept := Orders.FieldByName['SaleDate'].AsString >= DateEdit1.Text;
end;
```

The most important advantage of `OnFilterRecord` over the `Filter` property is that this event handler enables you to compare fields and calculate their values.

The disadvantage of this method is that event handler lacks flexibility, although this filter can be modified by assigning an event handler a procedure variable that provides a link to a new method.

Using Bookmarks

A bookmark is another tool for handling datasets, which enables you to quickly move to the required record. A dataset can contain an unlimited number of bookmarks, each one of which is a pointer to a particular record. A bookmark can be created only for the current record of a dataset.

A bookmark is simply a pointer to a database record:

```
type TBookmark = Pointer;
```

A dataset has the property

```
type TBookmarkStr: string;
property Bookmark: TBookmarkStr; Bookmark,
```

which contains the name of the current bookmark.

Bookmarks are handled by three basic methods.

The method

```
function GetBookmark: TBookmark; virtual;
```

creates a new bookmark for the current record.

The method

```
procedure GotoBookmark(Bookmark: TBookmark);
```

implements a move to the bookmark specified in the parameter.

The method

```
procedure FreeBookmark(Bookmark: TBookmark); virtual;
```

removes the bookmark specified in the parameter.

Additionally, you can use the method

```
function BookmarkValid(Bookmark: TBookmark): Boolean; override;
```

which checks if the bookmark points to an existing record. The method

```
function CompareBookmarks(Bookmark1, Bookmark2: TBookmark): Integer;
override;
```

lets you compare two bookmarks:

```
var Bookmark1, Bookmark2: TBookmark;
...
if Table1.CompareBookmark(Bookmark1, Bookmark2) = 1
then ShowMessage('The bookmarks are the same').
```

> **NOTE**
>
> The TDBGrid component also supports bookmarks. It has the SelectedRows property of TBookmarkList type, which is a list of bookmarks that point to simultaneously selected records.

Fields

Every database table, and consequently every dataset, has its own structure determined by its collection of fields. Each *field* in a dataset is an object that contains a description of the type of data that must correspond to the value located in a particular place in a record. In other words, a field can be thought of as an accumulation of cells which contain data of a particular type and have a fixed place in every record of the dataset. Or, to put it even more simply, a field is a column in a table.

In a dataset of a Delphi database application, each field is associated with its own object. All field objects are based on the TField class, which contains the fundamental properties of an abstract field that does not depend on the data type. This base class is the common ancestor for all the classes providing the functionality of actual field objects that depend on the type of data.

Field Objects

Field objects contain properties and methods of various types of data. These objects operate in close cooperation with a dataset. For example, to retrieve the values of fields in the current dataset record, the developer has to write code such as the following:

```
Edit1.Text := Table1.Fields[0].AsString;
```

The property of a dataset component

```
property Fields: TFields;
```

represents an indexed list of the field objects of a dataset. If the developer doesn't change the arrangement of the fields in the dataset, the order of field objects in the Fields list corresponds to the structure of the database table.

Every field object stores a number of parameters that describe this field. For example, you can address a field object in a dataset if all you know is the name of this field:

```
Edit1.Text := Table1.FieldByName('SomeField').AsString;
```

To assign a value to a field in the current record, you can either use the techniques described earlier, or if the data type is unknown, use the FieldValues property:

```
Table1.FieldValues['SomeField'] := Edit1.Text;
```

The simplest way to access the current value of a field is by using the name of this field:

```
Table1['SomeField'] := Edit1.Text;
Edit1.Text := Table1['SomeField'];
```

NOTE

When you assign values to dataset fields, always check the state of this dataset.

All the classes that describe the hierarchy of the fields with typified names are based on the TField class. It is the ancestor of classes that enable the functioning of groups of fields organized by data type.

So, what is a field object and what capabilities does it have to offer to developers?

First, the purpose of having the TField class as the base field class is to be able to interact with data controls to correctly present data. For example, a field object stores techniques of alignment, font parameters, heading text, etc.

Second, from the point of view of a dataset, a field object is a storage area for the current value of a field (and not for the entire column of data, as its name seems to suggest).

It is with fields that data controls interact when they work with a dataset. For instance, if no special settings have been made, the columns in the TDBGrid component correspond to the arrangement of the field objects in the connected dataset.

Persistent and Dynamic Fields

Delphi supports two techniques for creating field objects.

Dynamic fields are used by the program if objects for them have not been explicitly created at design time. Every such object is automatically created in conformity with the structure of the database which it is linked to as soon as the dataset is open. Each field object directly descends from the TField class, and its type depends on the type of data used for the fields of the database table. The properties of a dynamic field are determined by the parameters of the fields in the database table.

If no additional settings have been specified, a data access component uses only dynamic fields once it is connected to a database table. You can call properties and methods of dynamic fields programmatically, using the indexed Fields property of a data access component that contains all the dataset fields, or by the FieldByName method.

Dynamic fields are used when the characteristics of the fields in a database table are satisfactory for the developer, and there is no need to consider any field outside the dataset.

Persistent fields are created by the programmer during the design stage; their properties can be accessed through the Object Inspector and their names can be selected from the list of objects of the active form in the top part of the Object Inspector's window. The name of a persistent field object usually combines names of the table and field, for example, OrdersCUSTNO.

Persistent field objects are designed using the special-purpose Field Editor, called by double-clicking the data access component, or with the **Fields Editor** command that can be selected from the pop-up menu of this component.

The Field Editor is essentially a list of existing persistent fields; all manipulations here are performed through the commands of the pop-up menu. The top part of the editor features the navigation buttons for navigating through datasets; these buttons are active only if a dataset is open. If a dataset has aggregate fields (Fig. 5.6), they are grouped in a separate list in the bottom part of the Field Editor's window.

Fig. 5.6. The window that shows a separate list of aggregate fields

You can add a new field to the list of already available persistent database fields using the **Add fields** command, which can be selected from the Field Editor's pop-up menu. To remove a field, just hit the <Delete> key. You can rearrange the positions of the items in a list by dragging them with the mouse. In this way you can create random combinations of persistent fields.

NOTE

As soon as the very first persistent field object is created for a given dataset, the dataset is assumed to contain only those fields, which are available from the list of persistent fields. This feature can be used to artificially limit the data structure of tables. All the fields of a dataset are arranged in the order specified by the Field Editor's list, irrespective of their actual location in the database table.

The **New field** command in the Field Editor's pop-up menu lets you create a virtual persistent field that doesn't actually exist in the data structure of the table (see Fig. 5.7). The type of such fields can be selected via the set of radio buttons — **Field Type**: **Data**, **Calculated**, **Lookup**.

Data fields, which must be based on actually existing table fields, are less common. If the table field, which corresponds to an object, is deleted, or if the type of data used for this field is changed, an exception is generated as soon as the dataset is opened.

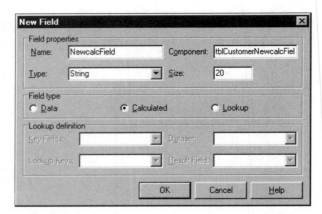

Fig. 5.7. The dialog for creating a new persistent field in the Field Editor's dataset

NOTE

The dialog for creating a new field, which is used for client datasets in multi-tier applications, enables you to select two extra field types — aggregate fields (the **Aggregate** radio button) and internal calculated fields (the **InternalCalc** radio button).

The *TField* Class

As mentioned earlier, the TField class performs the role of a base class in the big hierarchy for fields with various data types, and contains the properties and methods of an abstract data field. It is from the TField class that all the classes of typed fields are derived. Although this class is never used for solving real-world problems, its significance is difficult to overestimate. Practically all fundamental properties of classes of typified fields are inherited from the TField class without any additional modifications, and a set of extra properties and methods facilitate the functioning of each individual type of data.

As far as event handlers are concerned, four basic handlers declared in the TField class are inherited by all descendants without any changes or additions.

Following is the summary of the properties and methods of the TField class.

The name of an object is contained in the property

```
property Name: TComponentName;
```

The name of a field object is created at design time by combining the respective names of the data access component and the field.

The property

```
property FieldName: String;
```

returns the name of a field of a database table.

The property

```
property FullName: string;
```

is used if the current field is a child field in relation to another field. In this case, the property contains the names of all parent fields.

The name of the field in the database table is contained in the property

```
property Origin: String;
```

The property

```
property FieldNo: Integer;
```

returns the initial order number of a field in the dataset. If field objects are persistent, their actual arrangement can be changed in the Field Editor. The property

```
property Index: Integer;
```

contains the index of a field object in the `Fields` list.

The functionality of a field is specified by the property:

```
type TFieldKind = (fkData, fkCalculated, fkLookup, fkInternalCalc,
fkAggregate);
```

```
property FieldKind: TFieldKind;
```

As a rule, the value of this property is set automatically when a field object is created. It is, in fact, unlikely that the real data field will ever need to be made a calculated type. Attempts to modify the value of the `FieldKind` property usually generate an error. Let's look at the possible values which can be assigned to this property:

❑ `fkData` — a data field

❑ `fkCalculated` — a calculated field

❑ `fkLookup` — a lookup field

❑ `fkInternalCalc` — an internal calculated field

❑ `fkAggregate` — an aggregate field

If the field belongs to a calculated type, the property:

```
property Calculated: Boolean;
```

assumes the `True` value.

The connected dataset is indicated by the property

```
property DataSet: TDataSet;
```

which is filled automatically when the object is created with the means of the development environment.

The property

```
property DataType: TFieldType;
```

returns the type of data which is used for the data field, and the property

```
property DataSize: Integer;
```

specifies the amount of memory required for storing the value of the field.

One of the most important tasks of the TField class is providing access to the current value of a field. In this situation, the TField class interacts with the buffer of the current dataset record, and the value itself can be returned by using a number of properties.

The property

```
property Value: Variant;
```

always contains the value saved after the most recent execution of the Post method of the dataset:

```
with Table1 do
begin
 Open;
 while Not EOF do
 begin
  if Fields[0].Value > 10 then
  begin
   Edit;
   Fields[1].Value := Fields[1].Value*2;
   Post;
  end;
  Next;
 end;
 Close;
end;
```

In this example, all the records within the dataset are searched using the `Next` method. If the value of the first field is more than 10, the value of the next field is doubled. The `Value` property of the dataset field objects is used to do this.

However, because of the use of variants the `Value` property is relatively slow. To recast the current field value to the required type, you can use the entire `As...` group of rapid properties, which contain a value in a particular data type. Among these properties, `AsString` is the most widely used — for example, it can be used for displaying numeric values of fields in data controls:

```
Edit1.Text := Table1.Fields[0].AsString;
```

NOTE

It is advisable to use properties from the `As...` group while handling persistent field objects, since implicit setting of the type by the `Value` property may result in invalid conversion of variant type data.

If the property

```
property CanModify: Boolean;
```

is set to `False`, the values of a field cannot be edited. This property, however, is just a means of establishing whether a field supports editing. The property

```
property ReadOnly: Boolean;
```

enables you to forbid editing (`ReadOnly := True`) or allow it (`ReadOnly := False`).

A large group of properties is responsible for representing and formatting field values.

The property

```
property DisplayText: String;
```

contains the values of the field in string format before editing.

The property

```
property Text: String;
```

is used by data controls during editing. Therefore, these two properties can have different values if the string value of the field in string format differs during editing and browsing. With descendant classes of the `TField` class, this effect can be achieved by simply setting the corresponding templates for displaying field data (the `DisplayFormat` property) and editing field data (the `EditFormat` property).

For example, a real number can have separators for thousands during browsing and not have them during editing. The above properties will then look as follows:

```
DisplayText = '1 452.32'

Text = '1452.32'
```

The `Text` and `DisplayText` properties determine the operation of the `OnGetText` event handler. If the `DisplayText` parameter has the `True` value, then the `Text` parameter contains the value of the `DisplayText` property; otherwise, this event handler is passed the value of the field in string format.

If no value has been assigned to a field, then you can specify a certain default value which will be displayed when the field is empty with the `DefaultExpression` property. If a default value contains any characters besides numbers, then the entire expression must be enclosed in single quotation markes.

If an exception arises while you are working with a field, a message that uses the value of the `DisplayName` property as the name of the field is generated. If the `DisplayLabel` property has been set, then `DisplayName` automatically assumes the same value; otherwise you need to use the `FieldName` property to specify the value for the `DisplayName` property. There is no other way to set the `DisplayName` property.

The property

```
property DisplayWidth: Integer;
```

defines the number of characters for displaying a field value in the data controls.

The property

```
property Visible: Boolean;
```

determines if a field is visible in the data controls. Components that display one field no longer show its value, and `TDBGrid` components no longer show the columns related to this field.

> **NOTE**
>
> Several more `TField` class properties and event handlers will be covered later in this chapter.

Types of Fields

We will now examine the classification of dataset fields according to their functionality. The most widely used fields are data fields based on real database table fields. The properties of these field objects are set in conformity with the parameters of database table fields.

Additionally, in practice, programming often involves using lookup fields and calculated fields.

The techniques for creating all types of dataset fields are practically the same (see above). Nevertheless, this diversity allows developers to create extremely complex database application programming tasks.

In this section, we will only examine lookup and calculated fields, as data fields do not present any particular problems for users.

From the point of view of a dataset, there is no crucial difference between these two types of fields. However, values for all lookup fields are calculated before the same operation is performed for calculated fields. Therefore, you can use lookup fields in expressions for calculated fields, but cannot do the reverse.

Lookup Fields

To create a new lookup field for the original dataset, you need to use the following properties.

The property

```
property LookupDataSet: TDataSet;
```

specifies the reference dataset.

The property

```
property LookupResultField: String;
```

indicates the string field from the LookupDataSet reference dataset, the data from which will be shown in the newly created field.

The property

```
property LookupKeyFields: String;
```

specifies the field (or fields) from the LookupDataSet reference dataset, the value of which is used to select the value in the LookupResultField.

The property:

```
property KeyFields: String;
```

sets the field (or fields) in the original dataset for which the lookup field is created.

Lookup fields are very convenient in the TDBGrid component. If you create such a field for a column of this component, the appropriate lookup list will be automatically filled. The elements of this list are stored in the PickList property supplied for every column. Now, in order to obtain the list of all possible values that can replace the current one, you just need to select the required column and click the button that appears in the current cell. The value of the foreign key field (the KeyFields property) of the original dataset is replaced by the value of the current LookupResultField field.

> **NOTE**
>
> You do not necessarily need to open the lookup reference dataset if you use lookup fields in a TDBGrid component. Howerer, the LookupCache property must have the False value.

You can identify a lookup field using the Boolean Lookup property of the base TField class, which assumes the True value for such fields.

The property

```
property LookupCache: Boolean;
```

sets the operating mode for the lookup cache. If its value is True, the lookup cache is activated.

The performance of this lookup cache is founded on the property

```
property LookupList: TLookupList;
```

As soon as the original dataset is open, each lookup field is assigned its value; simultaneously, the lookup cache is filled with the appropriate values that correspond to the values of all key fields of the original dataset. From this point on, while you are moving to the next record, the lookup value is taken from the lookup cache rather than from the reference dataset itself. If the lookup values are of small size, this technique allows you to speed up work with the original dataset, particularly in remote access mode under low-speed network conditions.

During changes in the lookup dataset, use the method

```
procedure RefreshLookupList;
```

which updates the current field value in the cache.

For developers' convenience, the base TField class has the following property:

```
property Offset: Integer;
```

which returns the cache size in bytes.

The easiest way to create lookup fields is to use the Field Editor of the data access component for this purpose. After you have selected the **New field** command from the pop-up menu in the dialog with the same name (see Fig. 5.7) and performed the conventional operations relevant to creating any data field, you also need to set the values of the properties in the **Lookup definition** group. The controls of this group become available once you've selected the type of the field (the **Lookup** radio button in the **Field type** group).

The **Dataset** list shows all the available datasets in the module, from which you need to select the lookup dataset (the LookupDataSet property). The lookup field (the LookupResultField property) is selected from the **Result Field** list. The **Lookup Keys** list indicates the key field of the lookup dataset (the LookupKeyFields property). Finally, the **Key Fields** list defines the key field of the original dataset (the KeyFields property).

Calculated Fields

Calculated fields effectively facilitate the process of developing database applications, as they make it possible to obtain additional data on the basis of already existing data without changing the structure of the database table. The expressions for obtaining values for calculated fields must be included in the OnCalcFields event handler of a dataset. Here you can use any arithmetic and Boolean operations and expressions, any language statement, as well as the properties and methods of any components, including SQL queries:

```
procedure TForm1.Table1CalcFields(DataSet: TDataSet);
begin
 with Table1 do
 Table1CalcField1.Value := Fields[0].Value + Fields[1].Value;
 with Query1 do
 begin
  Params[0].AsInteger := Table1.Fields[0].AsInteger;
  Open;
  Table1CalcField1.AsString := Fields[0].AsString;
  Close;
 end;
end;
```

The OnCalcFields event handler executes when you open a dataset, switch to edit mode, move a focus between data controls or grid columns, or delete a record. Note, however, that for this event handler to execute, the AutoCalcFields property of the dataset must always be set to True.

NOTE

You need to take into account the fact that including complex calculated fields tends to considerably slow down the performance of the dataset (particularly if you use SQL queries with it). Additionally, every editing operation (including modifying field values, saving changes, or moving to another record) results in the recalculation of the calculated fields. By setting AutoCalcFields := False you can reduce the number of calls for the OnCalcFields event handler.

If you choose to create a calculated field, just specify a calculated type as the selected type for your new field in the **New Field** dialog of the Field Editor, and then continue with the usual procedure for creating a data field.

Other calculated fields can be used in expressions for calculated fields, but they must be defined in the OnCalcFields method beforehand.

Calculated fields cannot be used when you filter data with the OnFilterRecord event handler, because this handler is called before the OnCalcFields event handler, and the values of calculated fields are not saved.

Internal Calculated Fields

Internal calculated fields (FieldKind = fkInternalCalc) are a variety of calculated fields used in client datasets (TClientDataSet components). They are distinctive in that the values of such fields are saved in a dataset.

Internal calculated fields can also be used for filtering data by the OnFilterRecord event handler.

Aggregate Fields

Aggregate fields are designed for calculating field values of datasets by employing various SQL aggregate functions. Functions of this kind are:

❑ AVG — calculates the average value

❑ COUNT — returns the number of non-null values

❑ MIN — returns the minimum value

❏ MAX — returns the maximum value

❏ SUM — returns the sum of the values

Aggregate fields are not part of the field structure of a dataset, as aggregate functions imply processing multiple records in a table to obtain a result. Consequently, a value of an aggregate field cannot be bound to any particular field, it is associated with either all records or a number of records.

You can use aggregate fields only with the TClientDataSet component or one of its counterparts, as these components support data caching, which is essential for performing calculations (see *Chapter 10, "A Client of a Multi-Tier Distributed Application"*).

Aggregate fields are not displayed with all other fields in TDBGrid components; they make up a separate list in the Field Editor, and their Index property (mentioned above) is always set to −1. You can represent the value of an aggregate field with a single-field data-aware component (for instance, TDBText or TDBEdit) or by using the properties of this particular field:

```
Label1.Caption := MyDataSetAGGRFIELD1.AsString;
```

Aggregate fields are created by selecting the **New field** command from the pop-up menu of the Field Editor.

Object Fields

Along with traditional types of data (strings, integers, etc.), you can use more complex data types while handling dataset fields. These are usually a combination of a number of simpler types.

Delphi supports four classes of object fields: TADTField, TArrayField, TDataSetField, and TReferenceField. Their common ancestor is the TObjectField class. The TADTField and TArrayField classes provide access to a set of child fields of a particular type from their common parent field. These types of fields can be used if the database server supports object types and the appropriate fields are present in the dataset in use. This means that, like simple fields, object fields can be persistent and dynamic.

These classes access child fields by the properties

```
property Fields: TFields;
```

which contains an indexed list of child field objects, and

```
property FieldValues[Index: Integer]: Variant;
```

which includes values of child fields.

The property

```
property FieldCount: Integer;
```

returns the number of child fields.

The `TReferenceField` and `TDataSetField` classes provide access to data in the connected datasets.

The following property provides a pointer to the dataset in use:

```
property DataSet: TDataSet;
```

Data Types

The Delphi development environment enables developers to create applications used in work with extremely diverse databases. This universality implies the necessity of using means to ensure that the many types of data used in these databases can be handled.

Naturally, there are many data types whose practical implementation does not differ from one platform to another. These types include strings, characters, real numbers, integers, etc.

However, there are certain data types that are not supported by any platform. And, finally, there are also unique types of data.

In order to meet developers' demands, Delphi implements the following technique for handling various types of data.

A data type is uniquely associated with a particular field of a database table. Without this field, the very concept of a data type has no practical meaning. With Delphi, the behavior of an abstract field is contained by the `TField` class, which does not have a specific type of data. From this class, a whole family of classes for typified fields is derived, which are specifically designed for handling individual data types.

NOTE

The `TField` class contains the `DataType` property, which is responsible for the type of data. This property, however, cannot be modified.

The full list of all available types of data is contained in the `TFileldType` type:

```
type TFieldType = (ftUnknown, ftString, ftSmallint, ftInteger, ftWord,
ftBoolean, ftFloat, ftCurrency, ftBCD, ftDate, ftTime, ftDateTime,
ftBytes, ftVarBytes, ftAutoInc, ftBlob, ftMemo, ftGraphic, ftFmtMemo,
ftParadoxOle, ftDBaseOle, ftTypedBinary, ftCursor, ftFixedChar,
ftWideString, ftLargeInt, ftADT, ftArray, ftReference, ftDataSet,
ftOraBlob, ftOraClob, ftVariant, ftInterface, ftIDispatch, ftGuid,
ftTimeStamp, ftFMTBcd);
```

> **NOTE**
>
> Delphi doesn't provide direct support for the BCD data type. This type is implemented through the `ftCurrency` type. This is why BCD's precision is limited to 20 decimal places. However, this restriction can be overcome by using the FMTBcd type, which enables the required accuracy.

Along with traditional types of data, Delphi uses specialized types, thus further enhancing the functionality of applications. Specifically, the `ftInterface`, `ftIDispatch`, and `ftGuid` types allow you to build full-fledged database applications for COM and OLE DB.

Almost all database servers provide users with the ability to create their own custom data types. With Delphi, you can do this by employing an abstract data type and the `TADTField` class. An abstract data type can include any scalar type of data (numbers, dates, references, arrays, datasets).

An autoincremental type of data, `ftAutoInc`, has long been used by various database management systems. A field of the autoincremental type automatically increases its value by one for every new record. This means that every record has a unique identifier that is often used as a primary key.

The Binary Large Object (BLOB) data type `ftBlob` — is a binary array of arbitrary size. A BLOB field itself contains only a pointer to an individual database file that stores the binary array. Therefore, BLOB fields are essentially universal carriers for any data that has a scalar or non-scalar structure and that can be converted to binary representation.

The Memo type `ftMemo` represents a sets strings of random length (a formatted Memo is a variety of this type), based on the **BLOB** format. It is used for saving text from a `TMemo` component or word editor.

The graphic data type is utilized for storing images, and based on the BLOB format. A `TGraphicField` field directly interacts with a data-aware control (for example, `TDBImage`). Images must be saved in BMP format.

The data types `ParadoxOle` and `dBaseOle` were specially developed to facilitate handling OLE data in the Paradox and dBASE database management systems. In Delphi, both these types are also based on the BLOB format.

The CLOB and BLOB data types are specially designed for work with Oracle 8 servers.

The `ftArray` type is used for organizing an array from data of any structure, except for arrays of the same kind. Each element in this array can be supplied with a `TField` object of its own. This mechanism is managed through the `SparseArrays` property of the `TDataSet` class.

Another special data type, `ftDataSet`, as well as the `TDataSetField` class, lets you use any arbitrary dataset as a field in the context of another dataset. This pattern also allows you to manage every single field in the integrated dataset.

The data type `ftReference` also uses external datasets, but it only enables you to attach and use individual fields.

Summary

A database application can access data sources using a wide range of data access technologies, many of which are also used in Delphi applications. However, every Delphi database application has a standard core with a structure that is determined by the database application architecture.

Data access technologies are based on the same set of core components and development methods. This has made it possible to unify the process of developing database applications.

The following three components form the basis of the development process:

❑ Non-visual data access components

❑ Non-visual `TDataSource` components

❑ Visual data-display components

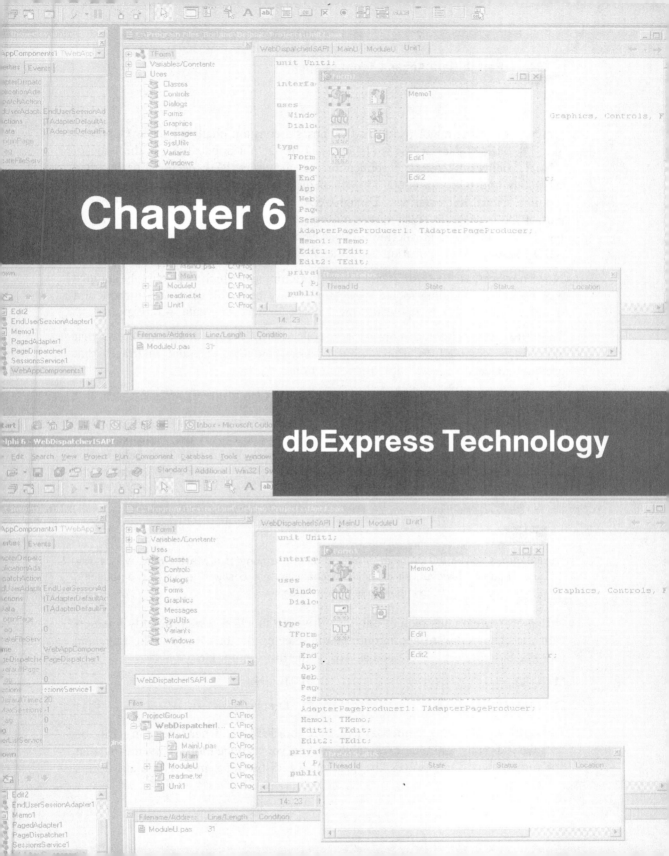

Chapter 6

dbExpress Technology

One of the major problems that poses a constant challenge to developers of various data access strategies used by Delphi applications is the issue of delivering complete applications to end users. BDE needs to be installed separately and takes up about 15 MB of disk space; additionally, this technology requires special alias settings. Though ADO comes with the operating system as part of the package, it still requires customized data providers (see *Chapter 7, "Using ADO in Delphi"*). Furthermore, when you are eventually forced to update your ADO version, your application will "put on" an extra 2 MB at the very least.

Now, however, all these difficulties and shortcomings (which considerably complicate the task of building robust applications) have been solved by the introduction of a new, easy-to-use but powerful mechanism for accessing data — dbExpress.

The dbExpress technology consists of a collection of drivers and components that encapsulate connections, transactions, queries and datasets, and interfaces that provide universal access to dbExpress functions.

dbExpress components are stored in the **dbExpress** tab of the Component palette.

The dbExpress strategy enables interaction between an application and database servers through a set of specialized drivers. dbExpress drivers use exclusively SQL queries for retrieving data. As there is no data caching on the client side in this schema, the technique involves using only forward-only cursors and prohibits direct editing of datasets.

> **NOTE**
>
> dbExpress solves the problem of editing data in a number of ways (which will be discussed later). However, all of these mechanisms are costly in terms of programming efforts, and also tend to impair code performance.

dbExpress components require only one driver to function, which directly interacts with the client software appropriate to the selected database server. The following four database drivers are shipped as part of the distribution kit:

- ❑ DB2
- ❑ MySQL
- ❑ InterBase
- ❑ Oracle

These drivers are implemented as dynamic libraries and, if need be, can easily be compiled directly into an executable file of your application. This means that dbExpress successfully solves the problem of distributing means of data access along with your applications. Of course, this doesn't do away with the necessity of installing the client software appropriate to the SQL server on your system.

In addition, owing to the fact that this technology is used in identical ways both in Delphi and in Kylix, it provides Windows and Linux applications with reliable access to data on all major computing platforms.

Thus it is obvious that the dbExpress data access strategy is the best choice for applications that require a fast and easy mechanism for browsing data on SQL servers. On the other hand, you will find dbExpress inadequate for sophisticated client-server or multilink applications that involve handling data in a more complicated way.

This chapter covers the following issues:

❐ Techniques of configuring connections with diverse database servers, installing drivers and specifying their settings

❐ Mechanisms of using dbExpress components for browsing data and the process of creating a user interface for your applications

❐ Methods of programmatic data editing

❐ Approaches to handling data in update caching mode and using the `TSQLClientDataSet` component

❐ Utilizing interfaces

❐ Principles of distributing applications with the integrated dbExpress technology

Accessing dbExpress Data

Access to data in the dbExpress framework is organized through the use of three constituent parts:

❐ Client software that is relevant to the database server which you mean to access

❐ A dbExpress driver

❐ dbExpress components that are contained in an application which uses the database server

Properly installed and configured client software for the database server is a primary prerequisite for accessing data. Installation processes for each of the four servers that are supported by dbExpress vary slightly, but these technicalities are beyond the scope of this book.

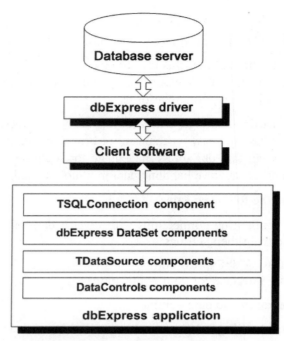

Fig. 6.1. A schematic diagram that illustrates the mechanism for accessing data used within the framework of dbExpress technology

In order to implement interaction with the client software, the dbExpress technology uses special drivers that enable the passing of queries from applications to servers.

An application must contain at least one component that provides a connection to a server, as well as the required number of components to encapsulate the dataset. In all other aspects the application is similar to a traditional database application.

All necessary components can be found in the **dbExpress** tab of the Component palette.

Data Access Drivers

The dbExpress technology enables customers to access a database server by using a driver implemented in the form of a dynamic library. Every server has its own dynamic library.

The files listed in Table 6.1 are stored in the ..\Delphi6\Bin directory.

Table 6.1. dbExpress Drivers

Database Server	Driver	Client Software
DB2	Dbexpdb2.dll.	db2cli.dll
InterBase	Dbexpint.dll	GDS32.DLL
MySQL	Dbexpmy.dll	LIBMYSQL.DLL
Oracle	Dbexpora.dll	OCI.DLL

In order to provide access to data on a server, a driver must first be set up on the client PC. This driver interacts with the server's client software, which also must be installed on the client side.

Standard settings for each driver are stored in the ..\Program Files\ Common Files\Borland Shared\DBExpress\dbxdrivers.ini file.

Connecting to a Database Server

The data dbExpress access strategy enables you to establish a connection with a server by using a `TSQLConnection` component. This component is an absolutely indispensable link: all other components are interconnected with it and utilize it for retrieving data from databases.

As soon as you have included this component in a data unit or form, you need to select the desired server type and specify the connection settings.

The following property

```
property ConnectionName: string;
```

enables you to select any already-set connection from a drop-down list. By default, the developer is permitted one set connection to each database server. Once the desired connection is selected, relevant values are automatically assigned to the following properties (see Table 6.1).

The property

```
property DriverName: string;
```

indicates the driver that is being used.

The property

```
property LibraryName: string;
```

defines the dynamic library of the dbExpress driver.

The property

```
property VendorLib: string;
```

indicates the dynamic library of the client-side software for the server.

And, finally, the property

```
property Params: TStrings;
```

encapsulates parameters for the connection and contains a list of the settings for the selected connection.

If necessary, you can set all the above properties manually.

The developer is free to extend and modify the list of the connections that have been set by using the special **dbExpress Connections** edit window (Fig. 6.2). This edit window is opened as soon as you double-click the TSQLConnection component or select the **Edit Connection Properties** command from the component's pop-up menu.

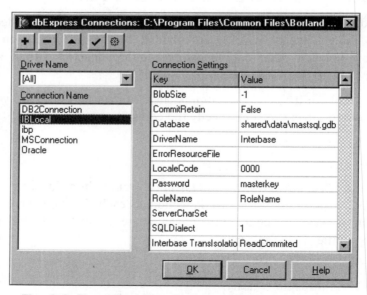

Fig. 6.2. The edit window that shows the connections set for the TSQLConnection component

The list on the left shows all the existing connections, while the list on the right includes the current settings for the selected connection. Using the buttons of the toolbar, you can create, rename, and remove connections. Additionally, you are able to modify existing settings.

The items listed in the left part of the window correspond to the items included in the ConnectionName property list in the Object Inspector. The settings in the right part of the window are contained in the Params property.

The names of the configured connections and the settings that have been specified for them are saved in the ..\Program Files\Common Files\Borland Shared\ DBExpress\dbxconnections.ini file.

The particular settings of any connection depend on the database server used and on the application's requirements (Table 6.2).

Table 6.2. Setting a dbExpress Connection

Parameter	Value
General Settings	
BlobSize	Sets the limit for the size of a BLOB package.
DriverName	The name of the driver.
ErrorResourceFile	The file that stores error messages.
LocaleCode	The locale code that specifies how a particular national character set affects the data sorting schema.
User_Name	The name of the user.
Password	The password.
DB2	
Database	The name of the client kernel.
DB2 TransIsolation	The level of isolation for transactions.
InterBase	
CommitRetain	Specifies the behavior of the cursor after completing the transaction. If this argument is set to True, the cursor is refreshed; otherwise it is deleted.
Database	The name of the GDB file (a database file).
InterBase TransIsolation	The level of the transaction's isolation.

continues

Table 6.2 Continued

Parameter	Value
RoleName	The role of the user.
ServerCharSet	The server character set.
SQLDialect	The SQL dialect used. InterBase 5 supports only one value — 1.
WaitOnLocks	The permission to wait for resources that are currently in use.
MySQL	
Database	The name of the database.
HostName	The name of the computer on which the server runs MySQL.
Oracle	
AutoCommit	The flag that specifies the end of the transaction. It can be installed by the server only.
BlockingMode	Specifies the mode for completing processing queries. If this argument is set to True, the connection waits for the current query to be completed before beginning the execution of the next one (synchronous mode); otherwise, it starts processing the next query immediately (asynchronous mode).
Database	The database record in the TNSNames.ora file.
Oracle TransIsolation	The level of transactions' isolation.

As soon as you have selected the connection (or the type of server and your own settings for the connection parameters), your TSQLConnection component is ready for work.

The property

```
property Connected: Boolean;
```

opens a connection to the server if it is set to the True value. The same effect is achieved by using the following method:

```
procedure Open;
```

Once the connection is opened, all the dbExpress components that encapsulate datasets and are linked to the open TSQLConnection component get access to the database.

A connection is closed either by using the same property, where `Connected = False`, or by using the method

```
procedure Close;
```

During the process of opening and closing an application, the developer can use event handlers, called before and after opening and closing the connection:

```
property BeforeConnect: TNotifyEvent;
property BeforeDisconnect: TNotifyEvent;
property AfterConnect: TNotifyEvent;
property AfterDisconnect: TNotifyEvent;
```

For instance, you can organize an authentication procedure for application users from the client side:

```
procedure TForm1.MyConnectionBeforeConnect(Sender: TObject);
begin
 if MyConnection.Params.Values['User_Name']) <> DefaultUser then
 begin
  MessageDlg('Wrong user name', mtError, [mbOK], 0);
  Abort;
 end;
end;
```

The property

```
property LoginPrompt: Boolean;
```

defines whether the dialog for user authorization should be displayed before opening the connection. In the property is set to `True`, the dialog is displayed.

The value of the following property indicates the current state of your application:

```
TConnectionState = (csStateClosed, csStateOpen, csStateConnecting,
csStateExecuting, csStateFetching, csStateDisconnecting);
property ConnectionState: TConnectionState;
```

You can specify the settings for your connection in the design stage by using the **Object Inspector** or the **Connection Editor** (see Fig. 6.1). Alternatively, you can do this immediately before opening the connection either by using the `Params` property, or with the following method:

```
procedure LoadParamsFromIniFile( AFileName : String = '' );
```

which loads the parameters that have been loaded in advance from the INI file.

The property below enables you to check if the operation was a success:

```
property ParamsLoaded: Boolean;
```

where the `True` value notifies you about a successful loading.

```
procedure TForm1.StartBtnClick(Sender: TObject);
begin
  if MyConnection.Params.Values['DriverName'] = '' then

MyConnection.LoadParamsFromIniFile('c:\Temp\dbxalarmconnections.ini');
  if MyConnection.ParamsLoaded then
  try
   MyConnection.Open;
  except
   MessageDlg('Database connection error', mtError, [mbOK], 0);
  end;
end;
```

Managing Datasets

An additional `TSQLConnection` component enables you to perform a number of operations on connected datasets and control their status. Let's take a closer look at them.

```
property DataSetCount: Integer;
```

returns the number of connected datasets.

But these include only open datasets that have been passed to linked components. The total number of queries being executed at any given time can be obtained by using the following property:

```
property ActiveStatements: LongWord;
```

If the database server has specified a maximum number of concurrent queries that can be processed in the connection, you can learn this upper limit using the property

```
property MaxStmtsPerConn: LongWord;
```

This is why, just to be on the safe side, you can use the following piece of code, which will further ensure that your application is runnung smoothly before opening a connection to a dataset:

```
if MyQuery.SQLConnection.ActiveStatements <=
   MyQuery.SQLConnection.MaxStmtsPerConn
     then MyQuery.Open
     else MessageDlg('Database connection is busy', mtWarning, [mbOK], 0);
```

In case of emergency, all datasets that have been opened through the connection can be quickly closed by using the method

```
procedure CloseDataSets;
```

without closing the connection.

If necessary, the TSQLConnection component can process SQL queries on its own, without resorting to the TSQLQuery or TSQLDataSet component. The function given below is designed for this purpose:

```
function Execute(const SQL: string; Params: TParams;
ResultSet:Pointer=nil): Integer;
```

If you are dealing with a parameterized query, you first need to create a TParams object and enter all the required details in it. As the TParams object exists in its own right and is not yet linked to any query, you should be especially careful and ensure that the parameters are listed in the same order in TParams and in the SQL statement.

If the query returns a result, the method in question automatically creates a TCustomSQLDataSet object and returns a pointer to it in the ResultSet parameter. The function gives you the number of records that have been processed by your query. The code fragment below illustrates this using the Execute function.

```
procedure TForm1.SendBtnClick(Sender: TObject);
var FParams: TParams;
    FDataSet: TSQLDataSet;
begin
 FParams := TParams.Create;
 try
  FParams.Items[0].AsInteger := 1234;
  FParams.Items[1].AsInteger := 6751;
  MyConnection.Execute('SELECT * FROM Orders WHERE OrderNo >=
  :Ord AND EmpNo = :Emp', FParams, FDataSet);
  if Assigned(FDataSet) then
  with FDataSet do
  begin
   Open;
   while Not EOF do
   begin
    {...}
    Next;
   end;
```

```
   Close;
  end;
 finally
  FParams.Free;
  end;
 end;
```

If the query has no parameters that must be specified prior to running it and does not return a dataset, you can use the following function:

```
function ExecuteDirect(const SQL: string ): LongWord;
```

which returns either zero — if the query has been successfully completed, or an error code.

The method:

```
procedure GetTableNames(List: TStrings; SystemTables: Boolean = False);
```

returns a list of database tables. The `SystemTables` parameter enables you to include system tables in the list that is being constructed.

The `GetTableNames` method also handles such properties as

```
TTableScope = (tsSynonym, tsSysTable, tsTable, tsView);
TTableScopes = set of TTableScope;
property TableScope: TTableScopes;
```

which allow you to specify the type of the tables whose names are incorporated into the list.

You can obtain a list of the fields contained in each table by using the following method:

```
procedure GetFieldNames(const TableName: String; List: TStrings);
```

and a list of indexes by using the method

```
procedure GetIndexNames(const TableName: string; List: TStrings);
```

Both the above methods return the resulting list in their `List` parameter.

In a similar fashion, the method

```
procedure GetProcedureNames(List: TStrings);
```

returns a list of the available stored procedures, whereas the method

```
procedure GetProcedureParams(ProcedureName: String; List: TList);
```

determines the parameters for a specific procedure.

Transactions

Like its counterparts in **BDE** and **ADO,** the `TSQLConnection` component supports transactions and implements them in much the same way.

The methods listed below are responsible for beginning, committing, and rolling back a transaction:

```
procedure StartTransaction(TransDesc: TTransactionDesc);
procedure Commit(TransDesc: TTransactionDesc);
procedure Rollback(TransDesc: TTransactionDesc);
```

while the parameters of the transaction are returned by the `TtransactionDesc` record:

```
TTransIsolationLevel = (xilDIRTYREAD, xilREADCOMMITTED,
xilREPEATABLEREAD, xilCUSTOM);
  TTransactionDesc = packed record
     TransactionID    : LongWord;
     GlobalID         : LongWord;
     IsolationLevel   : TTransIsolationLevel;
     CustomIsolation  : LongWord;
     end;
```

This record contains characteristics such as `TransactionID`, which is unique within the framework of the connection, as well as `IsolationLevel`. If the isolation level is set to `xilCUSTOM`, the `CustomIsolation` parameter must be specified. `GlobalID` is used when you work with an Oracle server.

Some database servers don't support transactions, and this feature is defined by using the following property:

```
property TransactionsSupported: LongBool;
```

If the connection is already being used for conducting another transaction, the property

```
property InTransaction: Boolean;
```

is set to the `True` value. Thus, the server does not support multiple transactions on a single connection, it is worth making sure that the connection in question is not currently being used by another transaction:

```
var TransInfo: TTransactionDesc;
{...}
if Not MyConnection.InTransaction then
```

```
try
 MyConnection.StartTransaction(TransInfo);
 {...}
 MyConnection.Commit(TransInfo);
except
 MyConnection.Rollback(TransInfo);
end;
```

Using Dataset Components

The collection of dbExpress components that encapsulate datasets is typical, and comparable to analogous components used in BDE, ADO, and InterBase Express. The dbExpress collection includes such components as TSQLDataSet, TSQLTable, and TSQLQuery, TSQLStoredProc.

> **NOTE**
>
> Although the TSQLClientDataSet component also belongs to this group, it will be discussed separately, as it uses a number of specific functions.

However, the necessity of developing an easy-to-use strategy for accessing data — which is what the dbExpress technology is — has imposed certain restrictions on these components.

Although all the components discussed in this section descend from the same TDataSet ancestor class, which provides a complete toolkit for handling datasets, dbExpress components use forward-only cursors exclusively and do not support data editing. Forward-only (or non-scrollable) cursors only allow you to navigate through a dataset by moving to the record following your current position, or to the beginning of the dataset. These cursors do not support operations that involve buffering data — i.e., searching, filtering, and synchronous browsing.

As a result, another intermediate class — TCustomSQLDataSet — has been introduced with the purpose of disabling a number of the mechanisms of the TDataSet class.

Certain limitations are also imposed on data display when using the components from the **Data Controls** page. You cannot utilize components such as TDBGrid and `TDBCtrlGrid` at all, and you must not forget to disable the buttons that allow you to move to the previous record and the last record in `TDBNavigator`. Attempting to use the components for synchronous browsing is also of no use. The rest of the components on this page can be employed in the regular way.

All the components under consideration implement access to data using the same pattern — through a connection that is encapsulated by the `TSQLConnection` component. The following property is responsible for linking components to the connection:

```
property SQLConnection: TSQLConnection;
```

Let us now discuss the dbExpress components in more depth.

The *TCustomSQLDataSet* Class

Owing to the fact that all dbExpress components ultimately descend from the `TDataSet` class, the designation of the `TCustomSQLDataSet` class is to correctly limit the capabilities which are inherent to `TDataSet`, rather than to add a new functionality to already existing ones. Although this class is not used directly in applications, you may find information about it helpful in order to gain a better understanding of the behavior of other dbExpress components and to create your own custom components from it.

The `TCustomSQLDataSet` class is a common ancestor for those components that encapsulate queries, tables, and stored procedures. The properties given below provide support for all these components.

```
TSQLCommandType = (ctQuery, ctTable, ctStoredProc);
property CommandType: TSQLCommandType;
```

specifies the type of a command which is passed to the server;

```
property CommandText: string;
```

contains the text of the command.

If an SQL query is passed to the server (`CommandType` = `ctQuery`), the `CommandText` property contains the textual content of this query. If a command for retrieving a table is issued to the server, the `CommandText` property contains the name of the required table, which enables this property to automatically create an SQL query to get all the fields of the table using this table name. If a procedure must be performed, the `CommandText` property contains the name of this procedure.

The text of a command that is actually passed to the server for execution is contained in the following protected property:

```
property NativeCommand: string;
```

The property below is utilized specifically for handling tabular datasets:

```
property SortFieldNames: string;
```

and for specifying the sorting order for the records in a tabular dataset. This property must contain a list of fields delimited by semicolons. The property in question is used for building an ORDER BY expression for the command being generated.

In order to handle exceptions that occur in descendant classes, the following protected property can be used:

```
property LastError: string;
```

This property returns the text of the most recent dbExpress error.

You can speed up the process of executing a user's request for data by disabling the function that retrieves the metadata that pertain to a specific queried object (a table, procedure, fields, or indexes), which, as a rule, are passed to a client along with the queried data. If you choose to do this, assign the True value to the following property:

```
property NoMetadata: Boolean;
```

However, avoid overusing this method, as there is a certain category of commands that require metadata (for example, operations with indexes).

The developer can control the process of retrieving metadata. This can be done by using the following method:

```
TSchemaType = (stNoSchema, stTables, stSysTables, stProcedures,
stColumns, stProcedureParams, stIndexes );
  TSchemaInfo = record
    FType      : TSchemaType;
    ObjectName : String;
    Pattern    : String;
  end;
```

which is available from the protected property with the syntax

```
property SchemaInfo: TSQLSchemaInfo;
```

which in turn means that it can be used only when you derive new components from TCustomSQLDataSet.

The FType parameter indicates the type of required data. The ObjectName parameter specifies the name of a table or stored procedure if the FType parameter contains fields, indexes, or parameters of procedures.

NOTE

If you want a component to get the resulting dataset, the FType parameter must always be set to the stNoSchema value. This condition is fulfilled automatically once the value of the CommandText property is changed.

The Pattern parameter indicates the type of restrictions imposed on the metadata. It contains a character mask that is similar to the property of many visual components. A sequence of characters in a mask is defined by the % character, while a single character is specified by the _ character.

If you need to use control characters for masking, utilize the corresponding double characters — %% and __ .

Like the Tag property of the TComponent class, the TCustomSQLDataSet class possesses a string property

```
property DesignerData: string;
```

which can be used by a developer for storing various information. Essentially, it is just an extra string property that doesn't really need to be declared.

The *TSQLDataSet* Component

The TSQLDataSet component is universal, and allows you to execute SQL queries (like TSQLQuery), browse through entire database tables (like TSQLTable), and execute stored procedures (in the same manner as TSQLStoredProc).

The CommandType property of this component sets the mode that it works in.

If this property is set to ctTable, you will be able to select the name of the table from the CommandText property's list — if, of course, the component is attached to a connection. Selecting the ctQuery value from the CommandText property requires that you define the text of an SQL statement. In order to work in stored procedure mode, assign the ctStoredProc value to the CommandType property, and you will then be able to select the desired procedure from the CommandText list.

Traditional techniques are used to open and close a dataset: the `Active` property and the `Open` method. If an SQL query or a stored procedure doesn't return a dataset, the method below can be invoked to execute them:

```
function ExecSQL(ExecDirect: Boolean = False): Integer; override;
```

The `ExecDirect` parameter determines whether or not any parameters must be set prior to executing a command. If a query or procedure does have parameters, the `False` value must be assigned to the `ExecDirect` parameter.

In addition, you can use an extra property — `SortFieldNames` (see earlier in this chapter), which specifies the filtering order for the records in a table.

The `Params` or `ParamCheck` property is used to specify parameters in query or stored procedure mode.

Details on the indexes used in the resulting dataset are stored in the following property:

```
property IndexDefs: TIndexDefs;
```

For more information on `TIndexDefs`, refer to *Chapter 5, "The Architecture of Database Applications."*

The *TSQLTable* Component

The `TSQLTable` component is designed for browsing through entire tables, and its functionality is analogous to components such as `TTable`, `TADOTable`, and `TIBTable`. *Chapter 5* covers the issue of working with table components in more depth.

Use the property below in order to set a name for your table:

```
property TableName: string;
```

If the component is attached to the connection, you can select the name of a table from the list. As soon as the name for the table is chosen and the connection is properly configured, your component is ready for work. Once you have activated it (by using the traditional `Active` property or the `Open` method), the dataset from the selected table will be passed to this component.

In order to obtain a tabular dataset, the `TSQLTable` component queries the server by utilizing the capabilities that it inherited from its ancestor, `TCustomSQLDataSet`.

The method

```
procedure PrepareStatement; override;
```

generates the query text for the selected table, which the component prepares for passing to the server.

The major advantage of all table components is their ability to work with indexes. To activate simple or composite indexes, use the IndexFieldNames, IndexFields, and IndexName properties. And the method

```
procedure GetIndexNames(List: TStrings);
```

returns a list of the indexes being used to the List parameter.

The master-slave link between datasets is implemented using the MasterFields and MasterSource properties.

Additionally, the TSQLTable component provides a developer with a sort of editing tool. The following method is used for clearing all the records from a database table linked to the component:

```
procedure DeleteRecords;
```

The *TSQLQuery* Component

The TSQLQuery component generates client SQL queries to be executed on the server. Its capabilities are standard for all components of this type (see *Chapter 5*, *"The Architecture of Database Applications"*).

The connection to the server is configured using the following property:

```
property SQLConnection: TSQLConnection;
```

in which the TSQLConnection component is selected.

The content of a query is contained in the property below:

```
property SQL: TStrings;
```

And its string representation is stored in the following property:

```
property Text: string;
```

The text of queries can be edited by utilizing a standard editor, which is activated when you click the property button in the **Object Inspector** window.

The parameters of a query must be contained in the indexed property with the following syntax:

```
property Params: TParams;
```

In order to prepare the parameters and the query as a whole, use the property

```
property Prepared: Boolean;
```

If this property is set to `True`, resources for the query are allocated on the server, which significantly accelerates its performance:

```
...
SQLQuery.Prepared := False;
SQLQuery.ParamByName('SomeParam1').AsString := 'SomeValue';
SQLQuery.ParamByName('SomeParam2').Clear;
SQLQuery.Prepared := True;
...
```

The following property

```
property ParamCheck: Boolean;
```

defines whether or not the parameter list of the query will be updated if the query text has been modified. As an example, consider this scenario: a query is used for creating stored procedures, and the source text of the procedures in question is passed to the server in this query. The body of the stored procedure may contain its own parameters which, while the query is being processed, may be interpreted as the parameters of the query itself. In this case, parameters are likely to be created in error. It is situations like these that justify using the `ParamCheck` property:

```
...
SQLQuery.ParamCheck := False;
SQLQuery.SQL.Clear;
SQLQuery.SQL.Add('SomeSQLTextForNewStoredProc');
SQLQuery.ExecSQL();
...
```

If your query returns a dataset, it is executed using either the `Active` property or the `Open` method. Otherwise, use the method

```
function ExecSQL(ExecDirect: Boolean = False): Integer; override;
```

The `ExecDirect = False` parameter means that the query doesn't have parameters that should be specified.

The *TSQLStoredProc* Component

The `TSQLStoredProc` component encapsulates the functionalities of stored procedures in order to execute them in the framework of the dbExpress technology.

All the functions of this component are standard. For more details on the subject of component functions of stored procedures, refer to *Chapter 5.*

Configure the connection to the server by using the following property:

```
property SQLConnection: TSQLConnection;
```

where the TSQLConnection component is selected.

The name of a stored procedure is specified by the following property:

```
property StoredProcName: string;
```

If the connection is already properly configured, the name of a stored procedure can be selected from the corresponding drop-down list in the Object Inspector.

In order to work with input/output parameters, use the property

```
property Params: TParams;
```

NOTE

When you work with parameters, it is advisable to call an individual parameter by name using the ParamByName method. This is because when you work with several servers simultaneously, the order of parameters before and after executing the procedure may be different.

The property

```
property ParamCheck: Boolean;
```

specifies whether the list of parameters will be modified if the stored procedure is changed. To enable this kind of change, this property must be set to True.

A procedure is performed by using the method below

```
function ExecProc: Integer; virtual;
```

if it doesn't return a dataset. Otherwise, either the Active property or the Open method should be utilized.

If a stored procedure returns several linked datasets (as which is a case with hierarchical ADO queries), the next dataset can be accessed by using the method

```
function NextRecordSet: TCustomSQLDataSet;
```

which automatically creates an object of the TCustomSQLDataSet type for encapsulating new data. You can return to the previous dataset if you have specified the object variables for each dataset:

```
var SecondSet: TCustomSQLDataSet;
```

```
...
MyProc.Open;
while Not MyProc.Eof do
   begin
    {...}
    Next;
   end;
SecondSet := MyProc.NextRecordSet;
SecondSet.Open;
{...}
SecondSet.Close;
MyProc.Close;
```

The *TSQLClientDataSet* Component

The TSQLClientDataSet component provides client-side caching of returned data, and updates and subsequently passes them to the server so they can be put in place. Unlike the TClientDataSet component, which is designed primarily for servicing a dataset that has been returned from a remote server using DataSnap server components, the TSQLClientDataSet component is intended simply as an editing tool in the dbExpress framework.

Unlike other dbExpress components, the TSQLClientDataSet component uses a bi-directional cursor (i.e., a cursor that allows backward scrolling) and enables you to edit data, although only when working in caching mode. In other words, a dataset is buffered locally in the component, and all the current updates are saved in it. If you need to save changes on the server, use the special method that passes updates to the server.

Thus, in a way the TSQLClientDataSet component makes up for major deficiencies of dbExpress.

Connecting to a Database Server

In order to connect to a data source, use the following property:

```
property DBConnection: TSQLConnection;
```

which enables you to link the data source to the TSQLConnection connection (see earlier in this chapter). As an alternative, you can utilize the property

```
property ConnectionName: string;
```

which allows you to directly select the type of dbExpress connection.

However, this component lacks a mechanism for creating a remote connection, which is provided by the `TClientDataSet` component in its `RemoteServer` and `ProviderName` properties (for more information on the subject, see *Chapter 10, "A Client of a Multi-Tier Distributed Application"*).

As soon as the connection to a database server is established, you can specify the type of command in use, somewhat like you do for the `TSQLDataSet` component.

The type of command is defined by the following property:

```
TSQLCommandType = (ctQuery, ctTable, ctStoredProc);

property CommandType: TSQLCommandType;
```

The contents of this command are specified by using the property

```
property CommandText: string;
```

After that, a component can be linked to the components that are responsible for displaying data in order to browse and edit the data.

Saving Updates

In order to pass updates that have been cached locally to the server, use the following method:

```
function ApplyUpdates(MaxErrors: Integer); Integer; virtual;
```

where the `MaxErrors` parameter specifies the maximum permissible number of errors that may occur when the updates are being saved. If the actual number of errors exceeds the `MaxErrors` value, the process of saving is terminated. As a rule, this parameter is set to -1, which lifts the restriction on the number of errors.

The method with the following syntax:

```
function Reconcile(const Results: OleVariant): Boolean;
```

deletes updates that have been successfully saved on the server from the local cache of the component. Generally, you don't have to use this method, since it is called by the `ApplyUpdates` method.

Before and after saving the updates that you have made to the server, the following event handlers are called:

```
type
  TRemoteEvent = procedure(Sender: TObject; var OwnerData: OleVariant)
  of object;
```

```
property BeforeApplyUpdates: TRemoteEvent;
property AfterApplyUpdates: TRemoteEvent;
```

You can cancel local updates using the method

```
procedure CancelUpdates;
```

Note that the component uses such traditional dataset methods as `Edit`, `Post`, `Cancel`, `Apply`, `Insert`, and `Delete`. However, these methods are applicable only to records that have been cached locally. You are free to make changes to a dataset using these methods, but all these changes will affect only the content of the cache. Only the `ApplyUpdates` method actually updates the data on the server.

The data exchange between a server and the `TSQLClientDataSet` component is conducted in the form of packets. You can get access to the required packet using the following property:

```
property Data: OleVariant;
```

The changes that you have made are contained in the property with the following syntax:

```
property Delta: OleVariant;
```

The developer can modify the size of a packet as he or she chooses. For example, if the connection's performance is deteriorating you can reduce the size of the packets. The size of a packet can be specified by setting the following property:

```
property PacketRecords: Integer;
```

which determines the number of records to be included in the packet. Packetizing is done automatically if `PacketRecords := -1`.

If `PacketRecords` is set to `0`, the client and client server exchange only metadata.

If the `PacketRecords` property has a positive value, you need to organize data swapping from the server manually. Use the following method:

```
function GetNextPacket: Integer;
```

Before and after executing this method, the event handlers presented below are called:

```
property BeforeGetRecords: TRemoteEvent;
property AfterGetRecords: TRemoteEvent;
```

For instance, you can use the `AfterScroll` event handler in order to implement this swapping:

```
procedure TDM.SQLClientDataSetAfterScroll(DataSet: TDataSet);
begin
 if SQLClientDataSet.Eof
   then SQLClientDataSet.GetNextPacket;
end;
```

Working with Records

The `TSQLClientDataSet` component incorporates means for working with individual records. You can learn the number of records from the following property:

```
property RecordCount: Integer;
```

The number of the current record is contained in the property

```
property RecNo: Integer;
```

The size of any particular record is saved in the property with the following syntax:

```
property RecordSize: Word;
```

All the changes made to the current record can be cancelled using the method

```
procedure RevertRecord;
```

You can refresh the values of the fields of the current record with the method

```
procedure RefreshRecord;
```

Before and after calling the `RefreshRecord` method, the following event handlers are called:

```
property BeforeRowRequest: TRemoteEvent;
property AfterRowRequest: TRemoteEvent;
```

Processing Exceptions

Processing exceptions for the `TSQLClientDataSet` component involves two stages.

First, you need to track down client-side errors — these may include invalid entries, caching errors, etc. Here you can use all standard mechanisms that are commonly applied to datasets. You can also use `try ... except` blocks:

```
...
try
```

```
    DM.SQLClientDataSet.Edit;
    DM.SQLClientDataSet.Fields[1].AsString := SomeString;
    DM.SQLClientDataSet.Post;
except
    on E: EDatabaseError do DM.SQLClientDataSet.Cancel;
  end;
  ...
```

Second, errors can occur when you save updates on the server. And since the event that triggered the exception takes place on another machine or in another process, this type of errors requires a special event handler:

```
    TReconcileErrorEvent = procedure(DataSet: TCustomClientDataSet;
    E: EReconcileError; UpdateKind: TUpdateKind;
    var Action: TReconcileAction) of object;

    property OnReconcileError: TReconcileErrorEvent;
```

This handler starts if an error message is passed from the server. Information on an error is contained in the E: EReconcileError parameter. For example:

```
    procedure TDM.SQLClientDataSetReconcileError(DataSet: TCustomClientDataSet;
    E: EReconcileError; UpdateKind: TUpdateKind;
    var Action: TReconcileAction);
    begin
     if (E.ErrorCode = SomeCode)and(UpdateKind = ukModify) then
        begin
         MessageDlg('Server Error', mtError, [mbOK], 0);
         Action := raCorrect;
        end
     else
        begin
         Action := raCancel;
        end;
end;
```

Client datasets are discussed in more depth in *Chapter 10, "A Client of a Multi-Tier Distributed Application."*

Data Editing Methods

Despite the above-mentioned deficiencies of the dbExpress technology — forward-only cursors and the lack of support for editing — there are ways to get around these problems, or even solve them altogether.

First, you have the `TSQLClientDataSet` component, which enables you to implement a scrolling cursor, and allows you to edit data by caching it on the client side.

Second, editing can be done by specifying the settings and running such SQL queries as `INSERT`, `UPDATE`, and `DELETE`.

Both of these approaches have their advantages and drawbacks.

The `TSQLClientDataSet` component is by all means a very effective tool. It is standardized, relatively easy-to-use, and most importantly, it hides its functionality from the user behind several properties and methods. The problem here, however, is that not all applications support local caching of updates.

For instance, you may experience certain difficulties with maintaining data integrity and adequacy when you edit data by caching it locally in an environment where multiple users are accessing the same data source. Consider a typical example: at Christmas time, a salesperson in a department store reserves a number of items for you that are currently in great demand. While you are racking your brain over the most suitable present to buy for your old aunt, another salesperson (on account of the fact that the goods been reserved for you are still located in the local cache) has already sold some of the items that you requested.

True, you could update the data on the server every time you save a record locally, but this will result in a connection overload and an overall performance loss.

On the one hand, using modifier queries enables you to quickly update data on the server, but on the other hand, you will have to pay the price — extensive programming efforts and more tedious debugging. The code will be much more complex in such a case.

Let's now consider a sample application that implements both these approaches. The Demo DBX application is connected to the ..\Program Files\Common Files\ Borland Shared\Data\MastSQL.gdb database, located on an InterBase server.

Listing 6.1. A Sample dbExpress Application with Edited Datasets

```
implementation

{$R *.dfm}

procedure TfmDemoDBX.FormCreate(Sender: TObject);
begin
```

```
 tblVens.Open;
 cdsCusts.Open;
end;

procedure TfmDemoDBX.FormDestroy(Sender: TObject);
begin
 tblVens.Close;
 cdsCusts.Close;
end;

{Editing feature with updating query}

procedure TfmDemoDBX.tblVensAfterScroll(DataSet: TDataSet);
begin
 edVenNo.Text := tblVens.FieldByName('VENDORNO').AsString;
 edVenName.Text := tblVens.FieldByName('VENDORNAME').AsString;
 edVenAdr.Text := tblVens.FieldByName('ADDRESS1').AsString;
 edVenCity.Text := tblVens.FieldByName('CITY').AsString;
 edVenPhone.Text := tblVens.FieldByName('PHONE').AsString;
end;

procedure TfmDemoDBX.sbCancelClick(Sender: TObject);
begin
 tblVens.First;
end;

procedure TfmDemoDBX.sbNextClick(Sender: TObject);
begin
 tblVens.Next;
end;

procedure TfmDemoDBX.sbPostClick(Sender: TObject);
begin
 with quUpdate do
 try
   ParamByName('Idx').AsInteger := tblVens.FieldByName('VENDORNO').AsInteger;
   ParamByName('No').AsString := edVenNo.Text;
   ParamByName('Name').AsString := edVenName.Text;
   ParamByName('Adr').AsString := edVenAdr.Text;
   ParamByName('City').AsString := edVenCity.Text;
```

```
   ParamByName('Phone').AsString :=  edVenPhone.Text;
   ExecSQL;
 except
   MessageDlg('Vendor''s info post error', mtError, [mbOK], 0);
   tblVens.First;
 end;
end;


{Editing feature with cached updates}

procedure TfmDemoDBX.cdsCustsAfterPost(DataSet: TDataSet);
begin
 cdsCusts.ApplyUpdates(-1);
end;

procedure TfmDemoDBX.cdsCustsReconcileError
(DataSet: TCustomClientDataSet;
   E: EReconcileError; UpdateKind: TUpdateKind;
   var Action: TReconcileAction);
begin
 MessageDlg('Customer''s info post error', mtError, [mbOK], 0);
 cdsCusts.CancelUpdates;
end;

end.
```

In the above example, two tables — **VENDORS** and **CUSTOMERS** — have been selected for browsing and editing. The first table is connected to the `tblVens` component of the `TSQLTable` type through the established connection (the `cnMast` component). The values of five fields are displayed in traditional `TEdit` components, because the data display components — which are linked to a dbExpress component through the `TDataSource` component — can operate only in browse mode, and do not support data editing.

The `AfterScroll` event handler provides an effective and easy solution to the problem of filling `TEdit` components when you navigate through the dataset. The `quUpdate` component of the `TSQLQuery` type is used for saving updates (by pressing the `sbPost` button). The current values of the fields from the `TEdit` components are passed as query parameters. As a forward-only cursor is used in this case, the problem of refreshing the data after a modifier query is executed does not arise, and the dataset in question is updated only when you call the `First` method of the `tblVens` component.

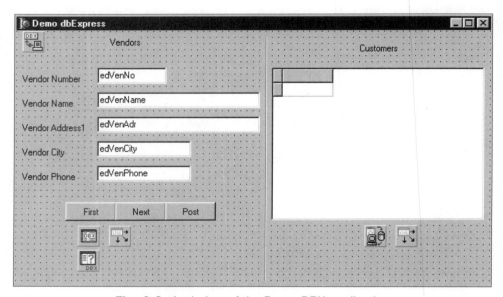

Fig. 6.3. A window of the Demo DBX application

The second table is connected to the `cdsCusts` component of the `TSQLClientDataSet` type through the same `cnMast` component, which operates in tabular mode. Data is displayed in a regular `TDBGrid` component.

Here, all updates are saved by calling the `ApplyUpdates` method located in the `AfterPost` handler, when the updates in question have already been cached locally. `AfterPost` is called every time a move to the next line is performed in the `TDBGrid` component.

A simplistic technique of handling exceptions that occur on the server is also provided for the `cdsCusts` component.

Notice also the settings of the `cnMast` component of the `TSQLConnection` type. By assigning the `False` value to the `KeepConnection` and `LoginPrompt` properties, you ensure opening of the required datasets when creating a new form, and the automatic closing of the connection as soon as you have closed your application with minimum source code.

dbExpress Interfaces

The dbExpress technology is based on the use of four major interfaces, whose methods are used by all dbExpress components. If you intend to use the technology seriously or to develop your own custom components, you will certainly find information on these interfaces helpful in your work.

The *ISQLDriver* Interface

The ISQLDriver interface encapsulates just three methods for handling a dbExpress driver. An interface instance is created in order to establish a connection and provide its link to the driver.

The following methods:

```
function SetOption(eDOption: TSQLDriverOption; PropValue: LongInt):
SQLResult; stdcall;
function GetOption(eDOption: TSQLDriverOption; PropValue: Pointer;
MaxLength: SmallInt; out Length: SmallInt): SQLResult; stdcall;
```

let you work with the parameters of the driver. And the following method:

```
function getSQLConnection(out pConn: ISQLConnection): SQLResult;
stdcall;
```

returns a pointer to the interface that is linked to the driver of the ISQLConnection connection.

You can access the ISQLDriver interface by using the

```
property Driver: ISQLDriver read FSQLDriver;
```

property of the TSQLConnection component.

The *ISQLConnection* Interface

The ISQLConnection interface is responsible for the connection's performance. It is used for passing queries to the server and for returning results while building ISQLCommand interface instances; in addition, it manages transaction processing and supports metadata passing via the ISQLMetaData interface.

The method below is invoked in order to open a connection to the server:

```
function connect(ServerName: PChar; UserName: PChar; Password: PChar):
SQLResult; stdcall;
```

where `pszServerName` is the name of the database, while `pszUserName` and `pszPassword` is the name and password of the user.

The following method is used for closing a connection:

```
function disconnect: SQLResult; stdcall;
```

You can modify the parameters of your connection by calling such methods as

```
function SetOption(eConnectOption: TSQLConnectionOption; lValue:
LongInt): SQLResult; stdcall;
function GetOption(eDOption: TSQLConnectionOption; PropValue: Pointer;
MaxLength: SmallInt; out Length: SmallInt): SQLResult; stdcall;
```

In order to process a query that passes through a connection, an `ISQLCommand` interface instance is created.

```
function getSQLCommand(out pComm: ISQLCommand): SQLResult; stdcall;
```

Transaction processing is done using three methods:

```
function beginTransaction(TranID: LongWord): SQLResult; stdcall;
function commit(TranID: LongWord): SQLResult; stdcall;
function rollback(TranID: LongWord): SQLResult; stdcall;
```

Exceptions that occur in the `TSQLConnection` component are handled by the method

```
function getErrorMessage(Error: PChar): SQLResult; overload; stdcall;
```

It implements the protected `SQLError` procedure that can be utilized in your custom components and in order to enhance the functionality of your code.

For instance, you can write your own custom procedure for checking errors. It will probably look something like this:

```
procedure CheckError(IConn: ISQLConnection);
var FStatus: SQLResult;
    FSize:SmallInt;
    FMessage: pChar;
begin
 FStatus := IConn.getErrorMessageLen(FSize);
 if (FStatus = SQL_SUCCESS)and(FSize > 0) then
 begin
  FMessage := AllocMem(FSize + 1);
  FStatus := IConn.getErrorMessage(FMessage);
  if FStatus = SQL_SUCCESS
   then MessageDlg(FMessage, mtError, [mbOK], 0)
```

```
    else MessageDlg('Checking error', mtWarning, [mbOK], 0);
   if Assigned(FMessage)
   then FreeMem(FMessage);
  end;
 end;
```

The ISQLConnection interface can be accessed through the

```
property SQLConnection: ISQLConnection;
```

property of the TSQLConnection component.

The *ISQLCommand* Interface

The ISQLCommand interface provides for the functioning of a dbExpress query. Components of dbExpress that work with datasets utilize it to implement their methods.

The parameters of a query can be set using the method

```
function setParameter(ulParameter: Word ; ulChildPos: Word ;
eParamType: TSTMTParamType ; uLogType: Word; uSubType: Word;
iPrecision: Integer; iScale: Integer; Length: LongWord ; pBuffer:
Pointer; lInd: Integer): SQLResult; stdcall;
```

where ulParameter is the ordinal number of the parameter. If the parameter is a child parameter for complex data types, then its number is specified by ulChildPos. eParamType defines the type of the parameter (input, output, mixed), uLogType sets the data type of the parameter, and uSubType indicates the subparameter of the data type. iScale determines the maximum value in bytes, iPrecision sets the maximum precision of the data type, Length sets the size of the buffer, pBuffer indicates the buffer that contains the value of the parameter, and finally, lInd sets the flag that determines if the parameter can be set to zero.

This method is called for each parameter.

You can obtain information on a parameter by calling the method

```
function getParameter(ParameterNumber: Word; ulChildPos: Word; Value:
Pointer; Length: Integer; var IsBlank: Integer): SQLResult; stdcall;
```

where ParameterNumber is the ordinal number of the parameter. If the parameter in question is a child parameter for complex data types, its number is set by ulChildPos. Value is a pointer to the parameter value's buffer, Length specifies the size of the buffer, and IsBlank indicates that the parameter is currently blank.

The method

```
function Prepare(SQL: PChar; ParamCount: Word): SQLResult; stdcall;
```

prepares a query for processing on the basis of the specified parameters.

A query is executed by calling the method

```
function Execute(var Cursor: ISQLCursor): SQLResult; stdcall;
```

which returns the interface of the cursor in the Cursor parameter if the query has been executed.

Or, the following method can be used instead:

```
function ExecuteImmediate(SQL: PChar; var Cursor: ISQLCursor):
SQLResult; stdcall;
```

This method executes a query that doesn't require preparation (i.e., doesn't have any parameters). It also returns a prepared cursor interface in the Cursor parameter if the query has been processed successfully. The text of the query is defined by the SQL parameter.

And finally, the method

```
function getNextCursor(var Cursor: ISQLCursor): SQLResult; stdcall;
```

defines the cursor of the next dataset in the Cursor parameter if a stored procedure has been executed that returns several datasets.

The ISQLCommand interface is used by the TCustomSQLDataSet component, and is not available to descendants.

The *ISQLCursor* Interface

The ISQLCursor interface contains a number of methods that provide information on cursor fields and their values. All these methods look exactly the same. To get the required information, indicate the ordinal number of a field in the cursor structure.

The method

```
function Next: SQLResult; stdcall;
```

updates the cursor by inserting the information contained in the next string of the dataset into it.

This interface is used by the `TCustomSQLDataSet` component, and is not available to descendants.

Debugging Applications with dbExpress Technology

Along with the traditional methods for debugging your code, dbExpress enables you to control queries which are passed to the server through the connection. This is achieved by using the `TSQLMonitor` component.

By using the property

```
property SQLConnection: TSQLConnection;
```

the component is linked to the connection being debugged.

The component is then activated by setting `Active = True`.

While the application is running, and as soon as the connection is opened, information on all the commands that are passed will be given by the property

```
property TraceList: TStrings;
```

The contents of a list can be saved to a file using the method

```
procedure SaveToFile(AFileName: string);
```

You can also add this information to a text file, which can be specified by the following property:

```
property FileName: string;
```

but this is only if the

```
property AutoSave: Boolean;
```

property is set to `True`.

The property

```
property MaxTraceCount: Integer;
```

defines the maximum number of controllable commands and manages the process control. If the value is `-1`, all restrictions are lifted, and if the value is 0, control is disabled.

The current number of commands that have been traced is contained in the following property:

```
property TraceCount: Integer;
```

Before adding a command, the following handler is invoked to the list:

```
TTraceEvent = procedure(Sender: TObject; CBInfo: pSQLTRACEDesc;
var LogTrace: Boolean) of object;

property OnTrace: TTraceEvent;
```

Immediately after it is added to the list, the following procedure is called:

```
TTraceLogEvent = procedure (Sender: TObject; CBInfo: pSQLTRACEDesc) of object;
property OnLogTrace: TTraceLogEvent;
```

As a result, the developer obtains a compact code which allows him or her to effortlessly access the information on whether the commands have succesfully passed through the connection, etc.

If the TSQLMonitor component cannot be used for some reason, utilize the method

```
procedure SetTraceCallbackEvent(Event: TSQLCallbackEvent; IClientInfo:
Integer);
```

of the TSQLConnection component. The Event parameter of the procedure type specifies the function that will be called during the execution of each command. The IClientInfo parameter must contain a number.

It enables the developer to manually declare a function of the TSQLCallbackEvent type:

```
TRACECat = TypedEnum;
TSQLCallbackEvent = function(CallType: TRACECat; CBInfo: Pointer):
CBRType; stdcall;
```

This function will be called every time a command is passed, and the text of this command will be given to the CBInfo buffer. The developer simply needs to perform the necessary operations with the buffer inside the function.

By way of example, let's consider the following source code:

```
function GetTraceInfo(CallType: TRACECat; CBInfo: Pointer): CBRType; stdcall;
begin
  if Assigned(Form1.TraceList) then Form1.TraceList.Add(pChar(CBinfo));
end;


procedure TForm1.MyConnectionBeforeConnect(Sender: TObject);
begin
  TraceList := TStringList.Create;
```

```
end;

procedure TForm1.MyConnectionAfterDisconnect(Sender: TObject);
begin
 if Assigned(TraceList) then
 begin
  TraceList.SaveToFile('c:\Temp\TraceInfo.txt');
  TraceList.Free;
 end;
end;

procedure TForm1.StartBtnClick(Sender: TObject);
begin
   MyConnection.SetTraceCallbackEvent(GetTraceInfo, 8);
   MyConnection.Open;
   {...}
   MyConnection.Close;
end;
```

An object of the `TStringList` type is created in the `BeforeConnection` method before opening a connection. Once the connection is closed, this object is saved to a file and deleted.

Before opening a connection (the event handler for the pressing of the **Start** button), the `GetTraceInfo` function is joined to the connection using the `SetTraceCallbackEvent` method.

Thus, information on the commands will be accumulated in the list as each is passed. Once the connection is closed, the list is saved as a text file.

NOTE

The `TSQLMonitor` component also uses calls for the `SetTraceCallbackEvent` method. This means that you cannot use this component and your own functions simultaneously.

Distributing dbExpress Applications

A dbExpress application that is ready for work can be delivered to its users in two ways.

The DLL for the selected server comes with the dbExpress application (see the **Driver** column in Table 6.1). This DLL is contained in the ..\Delphi6\Bin directory.

Additionally, if the application uses the `TSQLClientDataSet` component, you need to include the midas.dll dynamic library.

An application is compiled with the following DCU files: dbExpInt.dcu, dbExpOra.dcu, dbExpDb2.dcu, and dbExpMy.dcu (depending on the selected database server). If the application uses the `TSQLClientDataSet` component, you need to add the Crtl.dcu and MidasLib.dcu files. As a result, only the executable file of your application need be delivered.

The dbxconnections.ini file doesn't need to be included if your application doesn't require additional settings for connections.

Summary

The dbExpress technology is intended for developing applications that require fast and easy access to databases stored on SQL servers. This access is achieved by using compact drivers implemented as DLLs. Currently, drivers for four database servers have been created:

❑ DB2   ❑ InterBase

❑ MySQL   ❑ Oracle

The dbExpress technology is based on using standard types of data access components, and it also allows for lightweight distribution (as a single executable application file or as a couple of DLLs). It supports cross-platform development for Linux, and can easily be integrated into CLX applications.

However, the technology does have a number of deficiencies, among them the use of non-scrollable cursors only, and certain limitations that are imposed on editing data. (You can edit data only by locally caching it on the client side, or by executing special modifying queries.)

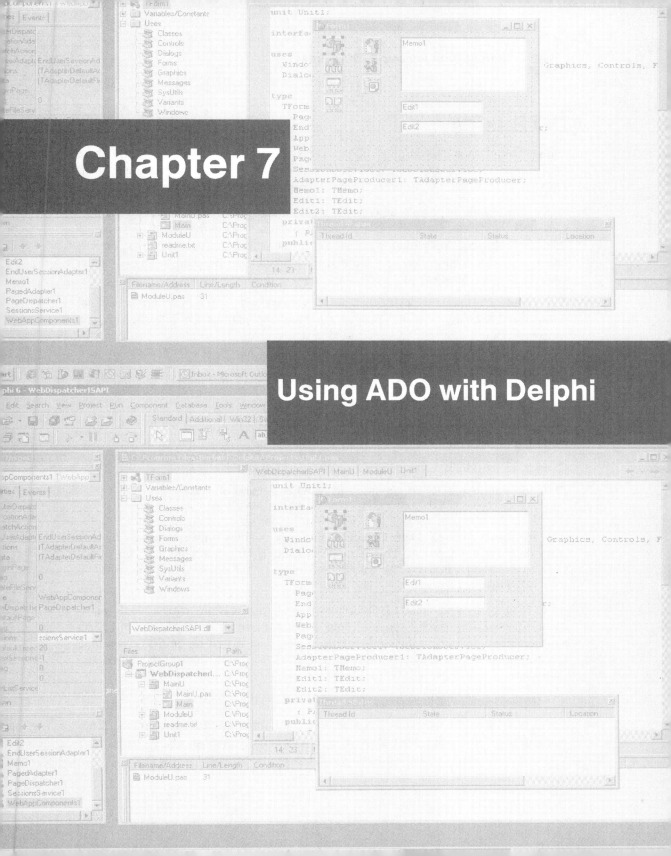

Chapter 7

Using ADO with Delphi

ADO Basics

Along with such traditional data access methods as Borland Database Engine and ODBC, Delphi applications support Microsoft ActiveX Data Objects (ADO) based on COM resources, or more specifically, OLE DB interfaces.

ADO gained wide popularity among developers thanks to its versatility: a basic set of OLE DB interfaces comes with every modern Microsoft operating system. This means that to enable your application to access a data source, all you need to do is correctly specify the ADO connection provider and then transfer the program to any computer with the required database (of course, the compoter must also have ADO installed).

The Delphi Component palette has an ADO page with a set of components that allow for the creation of full-fledged database applications for referring to data through ADO.

This chapter covers the following issues:

❒ A brief overview of ADO, available ADO providers, and objects and interfaces that work with ADO

❒ Establishing a connection to a database using ADO in Delphi applications

❒ Using an ADO dataset object in an application

❒ How to use tables, SQL queries, and stored procedures

❒ Understanding ADO commands and ADO command objects

❒ ADO Basics

The Microsoft ActiveX Data Objects technology enables universal access to data from database applications. This is made possible by the functions of a set of interfaces designed based on the general model of COM objects, and described in the OLE DB specification.

ADO technology and the OLE interfaces provide applications with a single technique for accessing diverse kinds of data. For example, an application using ADO can perform equally complicated operations with data stored on an SQL corporate server, and with spreadsheets and a local DBMS. An SQL query directed to any data source using ADO will be successful.

This raises a question: how can data sources process this query?

There is no need to worry about database servers: processing SQL queries is their main responsibility. But what about the series of files, spreadsheets, e-mails, etc.? It is here that ADO mechanisms and OLE DB interfaces come to the rescue.

OLE DB is a set of specialized COM objects that contain standard functions for processing data and specialized functions of specific data sources, and interfaces that provide for data exchange between objects.

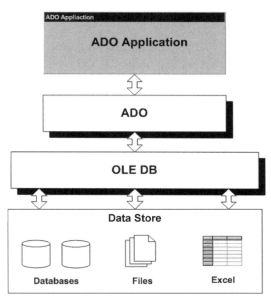

Fig. 7.1. The process of ADO data access

According to ADO terminology, any data source (a database, spreadsheet, or file) is called a data store if an application interacts with it through a data provider. The minimum set of application components can include a connection object, a dataset object and a request processing object.

As a result, the application doesn't refer to a data source directly, but rather to the OLE DB object, which can represent data (for instance, from an e-mail file) in the form of a database table or an SQL query result.

The ADO technology as a whole incorporates not just OLE DB objects, but also mechanisms that allow for interaction between data objects and applications. On this level, the most important role is played by ADO providers, which coordinate the operations of applications with data stores of various kinds.

This architecture enables the set of objects and interfaces to be open and extensive. The set of objects and a corresponding provider can be created for any data store without changing the primary ADO structure. Here, the very concept of data is significantly widened, as a set of objects and interfaces for handling non-traditional tabular data can be developed. These can include graphic data of geoinformation systems, tree structures of system registries, data of CASE tools, etc.

As ADO is based on the standard COM interfaces that are part of the Windows system mechanism, the overall amount of system code is reduced, allowing for the distribution of database applications without accessory programs and libraries.

NOTE

The OLE DB specification described below is presented in compliance with the official Microsoft terminology for this subject area.

The OLE DB specification distinguishes the following types of objects that will be examined below:

❏ An *enumerator* searches for data sources or other enumerators. It is used to support the functioning of ADO providers.

❏ A *data source object* is a data store.

❏ A *session* combines a collection of objects that refer to one data store.

❏ A *transaction* contains the mechanism for executing transactions.

❏ A *command* contains the text of a command and enables its execution. A command can be an SQL query, a call to a database table, etc.

❏ A *rowset* is a collection of data lines that are the result of the execution of an ADO command.

❏ An *error* contains information on an exceptional situation.

Let's examine the functional capabilities of the basic OLE DB objects and interfaces.

Enumerators

Enumerator objects search for any ADO objects that provide access to data sources. Other enumerators are also visible in the enumerator.

The primary search for data sources is conducted in the ADO provider. The enumerators can only select data sources of specific types, and so the provider can provide access only to a specific type of data source.

ADO has a system root enumerator that does a basic search for other enumerators and data source objects. It can be used if you know its class identifier, CLSID_OLEDB_ENUMERATOR.

> **NOTE**
>
> In Delphi, the GUID of the global enumerator object is stored in the ..\Delphi6\Source\Vcl\OleDB.pas file:
>
> CLSID_OLEDB_ENUMERATOR: TGUID = '{C8B522D0-5CF3-11CE-ADE5-00AA0044773D}';

The functions of the enumerator are contained in the ISourcesRowset interface. The method:

```
function GetSourcesRowset(const punkOuter: IUnknown; const riid:
TGUID; cPropertySets: UINT; rgProperties: PDBPropSetArray; out
ppSourcesRowset: IUnknown): HResult; stdcall;
```

returns a pointer to the rowset object that contains information on found data sources or enumerators.

Connection Objects with Data Sources

The internal ADO mechanism that provides a connection with data stores uses two types of objects — data source objects and session objects.

The data source object presents detailed information on the required real data source and provides a connection to it.

The IDBProperties interface is used to input information about a data store. The required information must be supplied to make a successful connection. It is likely that for any data source, the name, user name, and password will be needed.

However, each type of data store has its own unique settings. To obtain a list of all the required parameters for connecting to a data store, you can use the method:

```
function   GetPropertyInfo(cPropertyIDSets:   UINT;   rgPropertyIDSets:
PDBPropIDSetArray;   var pcPropertyInfoSets:   UINT;   out   prgPropertyInfoSets:
PDBPropInfoSet; ppDescBuffer: PPOleStr): HResult; stdcall;
```

that returns the completed DBPROPINFO structure.

```
PDBPropInfo = ^TDBPropInfo;
  DBPROPINFO = packed record
    pwszDescription: PWideChar;
    dwPropertyID: DBPROPID;
    dwFlags: DBPROPFLAGS;
    vtType: Word;
    vValues: OleVariant;
  end;
  TDBPropInfo = DBPROPINFO;
```

The DBPROPFLAGS_REQUIRED value is set for each required parameter in the element dwFlags.

To initialize a connection, you must use the method:

```
function Initialize: HResult; stdcall;
```

of the IDBInitialize interface of the data source object.

Sessions

A session object can be created from a data source object. In order to do this, use the method

```
function CreateSession(const punkOuter: IUnknown; const riid: TGUID;
out ppDBSession: IUnknown): HResult; stdcall;
```

of the IDBCreateSession interface. The session is designed for managing transactions and rowsets.

Transactions

Transaction management in OLE DB is implemented at two levels.

First, the session object has all the necessary methods. It has the ITransaction, ITransactionJoin, ITransactionLocal, and ITransactionObject interfaces.

Within the session, a transaction is controlled by the `ITransactionLocal`, `ItransactionSC`, and `ITransaction` interfaces, and their methods — the `StartTransaction`, `Commit`, and `Rollback`.

Second, you can create a transaction object for the session object with the method

```
function GetTransactionObject(ulTransactionLevel: UINT;
out ppTransactionObject: ITransaction): HResult; stdcall;
```

of the `ITransactionObject` interface, which returns a pointer to the interface of the transaction object.

Rowsets

The rowset object is the main ADO object that handles data. It contains a collection of rows from the data source, as well as mechanisms for navigating the rows and keeping them in an active state.

The session object must have the `IOpenRowset` interface with the method

```
function  OpenRowset(const  punkOuter:  IUnknown;  pTableID:  PDBID;
pIndexID: PDBID; const riid: TGUID; cPropertySets: UINT; rgPropertySets:
PDBPropSetArray; ppRowset: PIUnknown): HResult; stdcall;
```

which opens the required rowset.

Depending on the capabilities of the data source, the rowset can support diverse interfaces. But five of them are essential:

- `IRowset` navigates through the rows.
- `IAccessor` presents information on the format of the rows stored in the rowset buffer.
- `IRowsetInfo` receives information on rowsets (for example, the number of rows or the number of updated rows).
- `IColumnsInfo` receives information on the columns of rows (their names, the data type, update capability, etc.).
- `IConvertType` contains the single method `CanConvert`, which determines the conversion capability of data types in a rowset.

NOTE

In contrast with the usual practice of developing interfaces within the COM model, OLE DB interfaces often have only one or two methods. As a result, a large group of interfaces implement several fully standard functions.

The following interfaces provide additional features for managing rowsets:

❏ IRowsetChange carries out changes in rowsets (makes changes, adds new rows, deletes rows, etc.).

❏ IRowsetIdentity compares rows from different sets.

❏ IRowsetIndex allows the use of indexes.

❏ IRowsetLocate searches in a rowset.

❏ IRowsetUpdate implements the mechanism for caching changes.

Commands

The ADO development kit would be incomplete if it didn't use SQL in working with data. DML and DDL statements, and a range of special ADO statements, known as text commands.

A command object contains the textual command itself and the mechanism for processing and transferring this command. The command object performs the following operations:

❏ Analyzing the text of a command

❏ Binding a command to the data source

❏ Optimizing a command

❏ Transferring a command to the required data source

The main ICommand interface of the command object uses three methods:

```
function Cancel: HResult; stdcall;
```

which cancels the command,

```
function  Execute(const  punkOuter:  IUnknown;  const  riid:  TGUID;
var pParams: DBPARAMS;
       pcRowsAffected: PInteger; ppRowset: PIUnknown): HResult; stdcall;
```

which executes the command, and

```
function GetDBSession(const  riid:  TGUID;  out  ppSession:  IUnknown):
HResult; stdcall;
```

which returns a pointer to the session interface that issued the command.

In addition to the main interface, the command object enables access to additional interfaces:

❏ ICommandPrepare contains two methods (Prepare and Unprepare) for preparing a command.

❏ `ICommandProperties` sets the properties for a command that should be supported by the dataset returned by this command.

❏ `ICommandText` manages the text of a command (this interface is required for the command object).

❏ `ICommandWithParameters` handles the parameters of a command.

ADO Providers

ADO providers establish a connection between an ADO-compliant application and a data source (an SQL server, a local DBMS, a file system, etc.). Each type of data store must have an ADO provider.

The provider "knows" the location and contents of data stores, and can refer queries to data and interpret returned service information and the results of queries for the purpose of transferring them to the application.

A list of the providers installed on the system can be made available for selection by setting the connection through the `TADOConnection` component.

The following standard providers are installed on the operating system when Microsoft ActiveX Data Objects is installed.

Microsoft Jet OLE DB Provider provides a connection with the Access database using DAO technology.

Microsoft OLE DB Provider for Microsoft Indexing Service provides read-only access to file systems and Microsoft Indexing Service Internet resources.

Microsoft OLE DB Provider for Microsoft Active Directory Service provides access to the Active Directory Service.

Microsoft OLE DB Provider for Internet Publishing allows you to use the resources provided by Microsoft FrontPage, Microsoft Internet Information Server, and HTTP files.

Microsoft Data Shaping Service for OLE DB allows you to utilize hierarchical datasets.

Microsoft OLE DB Simple Provider is designed to organize access to the data sources that support only basic OLE DB capabilities.

Microsoft OLE DB Provider for ODBC drivers provides access to any data that have already been registered by ODBS drivers. In practice, however, making a connection in such an unusual way can be problematic. ODBC drivers are already notorious for their slow performance, so an additional layer of services here is undesirable. *Microsoft OLE DB Provider for Oracle* allows you to establish a connection to an Oracle server.

Microsoft OLE DB Provider for SQL Server is used to connect to a Microsoft SQL server.

Realizing ADO in Delphi

The mechanism for accessing data using ADO and a wide range of objects and interfaces is realized in Delphi VCL in the form of a set of components that reside on the **ADO** page. All the interfaces necessary for working with these components are described in the OleDB.pas and ADODB.pas files stored in the ..\Delphi6\Source\Vcl directory.

ADO Components

The TADOConnection component combines the capabilities of enumerator, data source, and session with transaction service capabilities.

ADO text commands are realized in the TADOCommand component.

Rowsets (a Microsoft notation) can be gotten using the components TADOTable, TADOQuery, and TADOStoredProc. Each of them lets you access a particular type of data presentation in a data store. From here on, when referring to Delphi applications, the set of rows returned from a store of data lines will be called a recordset. This is in keeping with the Borland documentation (see **www.Borland.com**) and the style of the previous chapters.

The set of ADO properties and methods allows for realization of all the functions required by database applications. Ways of using ADO components are somewhat different from standard VCL data access components (see *Chapter 5, "The Architecture of Database Applications"*).

However, if necessary, the developer can use all the capabilities of ADO interfaces by addressing them through the appropriate ADO objects. Pointers to these objects can be found in components.

The Mechanism for Connecting to an ADO Data Store

ADO data access components can use two methods for connecting to a data store. These are the standard ADO method and the standard Delphi method.

In the first scenario, components use the ConnectionString property to refer to a data store directly. In the second case, the special TADOConnection component is used, which allows for extended management of a connection, and enables several components to refer to the same data store simultaneously.

The ConnectionString property is designed for storing information on a connection with an ADO component. It lists all the required parameters, delimited by semicolons. At the very least, the list should contain the names of the provider for the connection or remote server:

```
ConnectionString:='Remote Server=ServerName;Provider=ProviderName';
```

If necessary, the path to the remote provider can be specified:

```
ConnectionString:='Remote Provider=ProviderName';
```

and the parameters required by the provider as well:

```
'User Name=User_Name;Password=Password'
```

Every component that refers to an ADO data store independently by specifying the parameters for the connection in the ConnectionString property opens its own connection. The more ADO components an application contains, the more connections can be open at once.

Therefore, it is advisable to implement the ADO connection mechanism using a special component — TADOConnection. This component opens the connection that is also set by the ConnectionString property, and provides the developer with extra tools for managing the connection.

The components that operate on an ADO data store through the connection connect to the TADOConnection component using the property

```
property Connection: TADOConnection;
```

which can be found in every component that contains an ADO dataset.

The *TADOConnection* Component

The TADOConnection component is designed for managing a connection with ADO data store objects. It enables ADO components that contain datasets to access a data store.

Using this component gives the developer a number of advantages:

❐ All ADO data access components address the data store through one connection

❐ Direct specification of the connection provider object

❐ Access to the ADO connection object

❐ Execution of ADO commands

❐ Execution of transactions

❐ Extended connection management using event handlers

Connection Setup

Before opening a connection, you have to set its options. To do this, use the property

```
property ConnectionString: WideString;
```

which was examined in detail in the previous section. It only remains to add here that the set of parameters can vary depending on the type of provider, and can be set both manually and by using an editor to specify the connection parameters. Call the editor by double-clicking the TADOConnection component tranferred to the form, or by clicking the button in the ConnectionString edit field in the **Object Inspector** window.

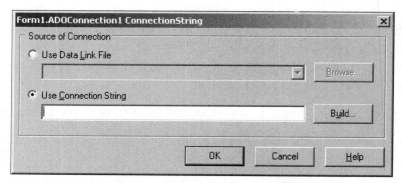

Fig. 7.2. The ADO connection setup editor

Here you can set the connection using the ConnectionString property (the **Use Connection String** radio button) or by loading the connection parameters from a UDL extension (the **Use Data Link File** radio button).

A UDL file (Listing 7.1) is a regular text file that contains the name of a parameter and its value after the equals sign. The parameters are delimited by semicolons.

Listing 7.1. A Demo DBDEMOS.UDL File

```
[oledb]
; Everything after this line is an OLE DB initstring
Provider=Microsoft.Jet.OLEDB.4.0;Data Source=C:\Program Files\
Common Files\Borland Shared\Data\DBDEMOS.mdb
```

If the file with connection parameters is not available, you will have to make the settings manually. Press the **Build** button, and the **Data Link Properties** dialog will be displayed in which you can set the connection parameters manually. The dialog is a four-tab window that allows you to specify all the necessary parameters step-by-step.

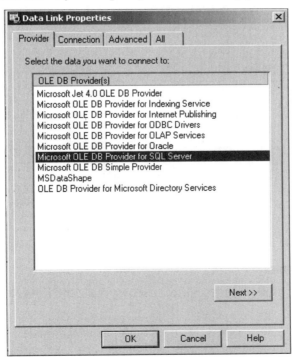

Fig. 7.3. The dialog for setting connection parameters on the **Provider** selection tab

The first tab, **Provider**, lets you select the OLE DB provider for a particular type of data source from the providers installed on your system. Here you can see the providers not only for database servers, but also for services installed on the operating system. The controls for managing the following tabs depend on the type of a data source, but the difference is not that great. Further on, at almost every stage, you will need to assign the data source (server name, database, file, etc.) and the user authentication mode, and define the user name and password.

Let's examine the setup process using the OLE DB provider for the Microsoft SQL Server as an example.

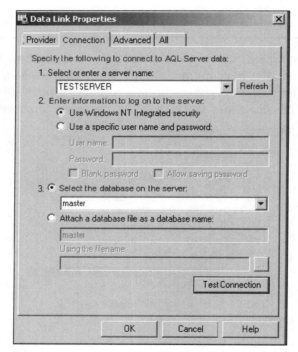

Fig. 7.4. The dialog for setting connection parameters on the **Connection** tab

The next tab, **Connection** (Fig. 7.4), allows you to set the data source.

The first step is to select the name of a server from the servers available on your computer.

The second step is to specify the user authentication mode. This is either the Windows integrated security system or the server's own authentication system. You also need to define the user name and password.

The third step is to select the database of the server.

After you have made the settings for the data source, you can test the connection by pressing the **Test Connection** button.

Now you can move to the next tab.

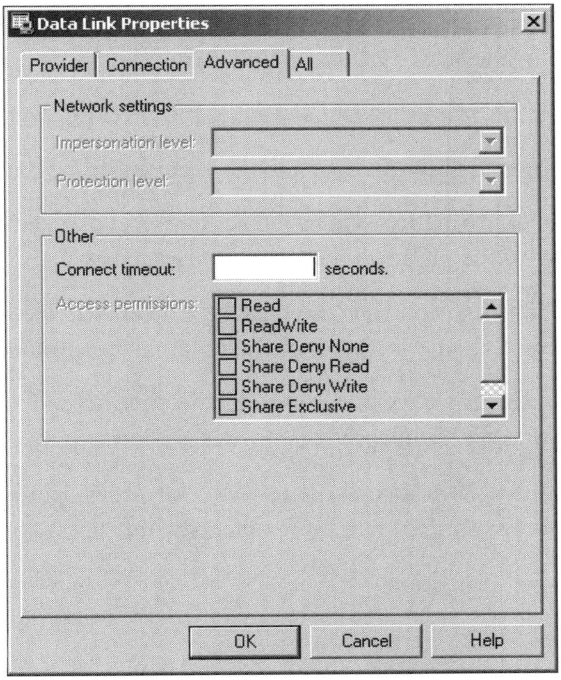

Fig. 7.5. The dialog for setting connection parameters on the **Advanced** tab

The **Advanced** tab (Fig. 7.5) allows you to set additional connection parameters. Depending on the data store, some elements in this tab may be unavailable.

The **Impersonation Level** list specifies the level of impersonation for clients according to the authority of their roles. The following values can be selected for this list:

❑ **Anonymous** — the client role is inaccessible to the server.

❑ **Identify** — the client role is recognized by the server but the client is not granted permission to access system objects.

❑ **Impersonate** — the server process can be represented by the protected context of the client.

❑ **Delegate** — the server process can be represented by the protected context of the client, but the server can also carry out other connections.

The **Protection Level** list allows you to set the security level for the data. The following values can be selected for this list:

❑ **None** — no confirmation is required.

❑ **Connect** — confirmation is required only when connecting.

❑ **Call** — confirmation from the data source is required for every query.

❑ **Pkt** — confirmation that all data have been received from the client.

❑ **Pkt Integrity** — confirmation that all data have been received from the client and the integrity of the data has been maintained.

❑ **Pkt Privacy** — confirmation that the data have been received from the client in encoded form and that the integrity of the data has been maintainted.

In the **Connect Timeout** field you can specify the time to wait for the connection in seconds. After the time has elapsed, the process is interrupted.

If necessary, the **Access Permissions** list lets you set access permissions for specific operations. The following values can be selected for this list:

❑ **Read** — read-only permission

❑ **ReadWrite** — read/write permission

❑ **Share Deny None** — read/write permission for all users

❑ **Share Deny Read** — read permission denied to all users

❑ **Share Deny Write** — write permission denied to all users

❑ **Share Exclusive** — read/write permission denied to all users

❑ **Write** — write-only permission

The last tab, **All** (Fig. 7.6), enables you to view and, if necessary, change all the settings for the selected provider (the **Edit Value** button is designed for this).

As soon as you have confirmed the settings made in the dialog, a new ConnectionString property value is given to them.

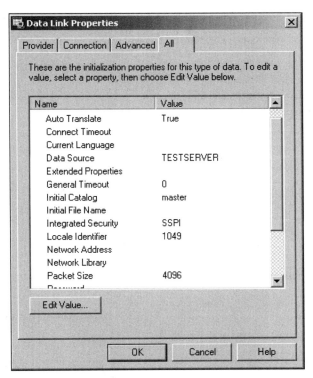

Fig. 7.6. The dialog for setting connection parameters on the **All** tab
for viewing the settings

Managing Connections

A connection to an ADO data store is opened and closed using the property:

```
property Connected: Boolean;
```

or the methods:

```
procedure Open; overload;

procedure Open(const UserID: WideString; const Password: WideString);
overload;
```

and

```
procedure Close;
```

The Open method can be overloaded if you need to use a remote or local connection. For a remote connection, you have to use the option with the UserID and

`Password` parameters. Before and after opening and closing a connection, the developer can use the corresponding standard event handlers:

```
property BeforeConnect: TNotifyEvent;
property BeforeDisconnect: TNotifyEvent;
property AfterConnect: TNotifyEvent;
property AfterDisconnect: TNotifyEvent;
```

Additionally, the `TADOConnection` component has a number of extra event handlers. After the provider has confirmed that the connection will be opened, and before its actual opening, the following method is invoked:

```
TWillConnectEvent = procedure(Connection: TADOConnection;
var ConnectionString, UserID, Password: WideString; var
ConnectOptions: TConnectOption; var EventStatus: TEventStatus)
of object;

property OnWillConnect: TWillConnectEvent;
```

The `Connection` parameter contains a pointer to the component that has called this event handler.

The `ConnectionString`, `UserID`, and `Password` parameters define the parameter string and the user name and password.

The connection may be synchronous or asynchronous, which can be determined using the `ConnectOptions` parameter of the type `TConnectOption`:

```
type TConnectOption = (coConnectUnspecified, coAsyncConnect);
```

❑ `coConnectUnspecified` — a synchronous connection that always waits for the result of the last request

❑ `coAsyncConnect` — an asynchronous connection that can execute a new request without waiting for an answer from the previous request

Finally, the `EventStatus` parameter determines the success of the connection request:

```
type
  TEventStatus = (esOK, esErrorsOccured, esCantDeny, esCancel,
  esUnwantedEvent);
```

❑ `esOK` — the connection request connection was successfully executed.

❑ `esErrorsOccured` — an error occurred in the process of executing the request.

❑ `esCantDeny` — the connection cannot be interrupted.

❐ esCancel — the connection was cancelled before opening.

❐ esUnwantedEvent — an internal ADO flag.

For example, if the connection is successful, you can select a synchronous operating mode for the component:

```
procedure TForm1.ADOConnectionWillConnect(Connection: TADOConnection;
var ConnectionString, UserID, Password: WideString;
var ConnectOptions: TConnectOption; var EventStatus: TEventStatus);

begin
  if EventStatus = esOK
    then ConnectOptions := coConnectUnspecified;
end;
```

Incidentally, the parameter for synchronous/asynchronous mode can also be set using the property

```
ConnectOptions property ConnectOptions: TConnectOption;
```

Once the connection is opened, you can use the following event handler for executing your custom code:

```
TConnectErrorEvent = procedure(Connection: TADOConnection; Error:
Error; var EventStatus: TEventStatus) of object;

property OnConnectComplete: TConnectErrorEvent;
```

Here, if an error has occurred in the process of opening the connection, the EventStatus parameter will assume the esErrorsOccured value, and the Error parameter will contain the ADO Error object.

Let's now move to additional properties and methods of the TADOConnection component that safeguard the connection.

To limit the connection opening time for slow communication channels, use the property:

```
property ConnectionTimeout: Integer;
```

which specifies how many seconds to wait for the connection to open. The default value is 15 seconds.

You can also determine a component's reaction to an unused connection. If no active component uses this connection, the property

```
property KeepConnection: Boolean;
```

keeps the connection open when the value is set to `True`. Otherwise, as soon as the last active `TCustomADODataSet` component is closed, the connection is also closed.

If necessary, you can directly indicate the ADO connection provider using the property

```
property Provider: WideString;
```

The default name of the data source is set by the property

```
property DefaultDatabase: WideString;
```

However, if the same parameter is specified in the `ConnectionString` property, it overrides the value of the property.

If necessary, an **OLE DB** connection object can be accessed directly using the property

```
property ConnectionObject: _Connection;
```

When a connection is opened, the user name and password must be entered. The standard dialog for this operation is managed with the property

```
property LoginPrompt: Boolean;
```

You can specify the same parameters without this dialog using the `ConnectionString` property, the `Open` method, or the following event handler

```
type TLoginEvent = procedure(Sender:TObject; Username, Password:
string) of object;
property OnLogin: TLoginEvent;
```

The property

```
type TConnectMode = (cmUnknown, cmRead, cmWrite, cmReadWrite,
cmShareDenyRead, cmShareDenyWrite, cmShareExclusive, cmShareDenyNone);
property Mode: TConnectMode;
```

sets the operations that are accessible to the connection:

❑ `cmUnknown` — permission is unknown or cannot be determined.

❑ `cmRead` — read-only permission.

❑ `cmWrite` — write-only permission.

❑ `cmReadWrite` — read/write permission.

❑ `cmShareDenyRead` — read permission denied to other connections.

❑ cmShareDenyWrite — write permission denied for other connections.

❑ cmShareExclusive — opening permission denied for other users.

❑ cmShareDenyNone — opening other connections with permission is denied.

Accessing Connected Datasets and ADO Commands

The TADOConnection component provides access to all the components that use it for access to an ADO data store. All datasets opened in this way can be accessed with the indexed property

```
property DataSets[Index: Integer]: TCustomADODataSet;
```

Each item in this list contains the index of an ADO data access component (of the TCustomADODataSet type). The total number of components connected to datasets is returned by the following property:

```
property DataSetCount: Integer;
```

The following property enables you to centralize the type of cursor used for these components:

```
type TCursorLocation = (clUseServer, clUseClient);
property CursorLocation: TCursorLocation;
```

The clUseClient value sets the client-side local cursor, which allows you to perform any operations with data, including operations not supported by the server.

The clUseServer value specifies the server-side cursor that only realizes the capabilities of the server, but allows for fast processing of large amounts of data.

For instance:

```
...
for i := 0 to ADOConnection.DataSetCount − 1 do
  begin
    if ADOConnection.DataSets[i].Active = True
      then ADOConnection.DataSets[i].Close;
    ADOConnection.DataSets[i].CursorLocation := clUseClient;
  end;
...
```

In addition to handling datasets, the TADOConnection component enables the processing of ADO commands. Each ADO command is contained in a special TADOCommand component, which will be explained in detail later in this chapter. All ADO commands that work with the data store through the connection can be managed with the following indexed property:

```
property Commands[Index: Integer]: TADOCommand
```

Each item in this list is represented by an TADOCommand class instance.

The total number of available commands is returned by the following property:

```
property CommandCount: Integer
```

For example, you can execute all the linked ADO commands immediately after the connection has been opened by using the following script:

```
procedure TForm1.ADOConnectionConnectComplete(Connection:
TADOConnection; const Error: Error; var EventStatus: TEventStatus);
var i, ErrorCnt: Integer;
begin
  if EventStatus = esOK then
  for i := 0 to ADOConnection.CommandCount - 1 do
   try
   if ADOConnection.Commands[i].CommandText <> ''
    then ADOConnection.Commands[i].Execute;
   except
    on E: Exception do Inc(ErrorCnt);
   end;
  end;
```

Besides datasets, the TADOConnection allows you to execute ADO commands. The ADO command contains a special component, TADOCommand, which is examined below. All ADO commands that work with a data source through a connection can be accessed through the indexed property

```
property Commands[Index: Integer]: TADOCommand
```

Each element of this list is an example of the TADOCommand class.

The total amount of accessible commands are returned by the property

```
property CommandCount: Integer
```

For example, immediately after closing a connection you can execute all connected ADO commands with the following script:

```
procedure TForm1.ADOConnectionConnectComplete(Connection:
TADOConnection; const Error: Error; var EventStatus: TEventStatus);
```

```
var i, ErrorCnt: Integer;
begin
 if EventStatus = esOK then
 for i := 0 to ADOConnection.CommandCount - 1 do
  try
  if ADOConnection.Commands[i].CommandText <> ''
   then ADOConnection.Commands[i].Execute;
  except
   on E: Exception do Inc(ErrorCnt);
  end;
end;
```

However, the `TADOConnection` component can execute ADO commands independently, without help from other components. To do this, we use the overload method

```
function Execute(const CommandText: WideString; ExecuteOptions:
TExecuteOptions = []): _RecordSet; overload;
procedure Execute(const CommandText: WideString; var RecordsAffected:
Integer; ExecuteOptions: TExecuteOptions = [eoExecuteNoRecords]);
overload;
```

Commands are executed by the `Execute` procedure (if the command doesn't return a recordset) or the `Execute` function (if the command does return a recordset).

The `CommandText` parameter should contain the text of the command. The `RecordsAffected` parameter returns the number of the records processed by the command (if there are any). The parameter

```
type
 TExecuteOption = (eoAsyncExecute, eoAsyncFetch,
eoAsyncFetchNonBlocking, eoExecuteNoRecords);
 TExecuteOptions = set of TExecuteOption;
```

specifies the conditions for the execution of the command:

❑ `eoAsyncExecute` — the command is executed asynchronously (the connection will not wait for the command to be executed, but continue operating and process the command completion signal command when it arrives).

❑ `eoAsyncFetch` — the command receives the required records asynchronously.

❑ `eoAsyncFetchNonBlocking` — the command receives the required records asynchronously, but the created thread is not blocked.

❑ `eoExecuteNoRecords` — the command does not return any records.

As soon as a data source has received a command and informed the connection, the following event handler is called:

```
TWillExecuteEvent = procedure(Connection: TADOConnection; var
CommandText: WideString; var CursorType: TCursorType; var LockType:
TADOLockType; var ExecuteOptions: TExecuteOptions; var EventStatus:
TEventStatus; const Command: _Command; const Recordset: _Recordset)
of object;

property OnWillExecute: TWillExecuteEvent;
```

Immediately after execution of the command, the following event handler is called:

```
TExecuteCompleteEvent = procedure(Connection: TADOConnection;
RecordsAffected: Integer; const Error: Error; var EventStatus:
TEventStatus; const Command: _Command; const Recordset: _Recordset)
of object;

property OnExecuteComplete: TExecuteCompleteEvent;
```

Errors

All run-time errors that occur while the connection is open are saved in the special ADO object that contains the collection of error messages. This object can be accessed using the property

```
property Errors: Errors;
```

See "*ADO Error Object*" section for more information on the ADO errors.

Transactions

The TADOConnection component allows you to carry out transactions. The methods

```
function BeginTrans: Integer;
```

```
procedure CommitTrans;
```

```
procedure RollbackTrans;
```

enable the start, commission, and completion of a transaction. The event handlers:

```
TBeginTransCompleteEvent = procedure(Connection: TADOConnection;
TransactionLevel: Integer; const Error: Error; var EventStatus:
TEventStatus) of object;

property OnBeginTransComplete: TBeginTransCompleteEvent;
```

```
TConnectErrorEvent  =  procedure(Connection:  TADOConnection;  Error:
Error; var EventStatus: TEventStatus) of object;
```

```
property OnCommitTransComplete: TConnectErrorEvent;
```

are called after the start and commission of the transaction. The property

```
type TIsolationLevel =  (ilUnspecified,  ilChaos,  ilReadUncommitted,
ilBrowse,    ilCursorStability,    ilReadCommitted,    ilRepeatableRead,
ilSerializable, ilIsolated);
```

```
property IsolationLevel: TIsolationLevel;
```

enables you to specify the level of isolation for the transaction:

❑ `ilUnspecified` — the level of isolation is not specified.

❑ `ilChaos` — changes to more secure transactions cannot be overwritten.

❑ `ilReadUncommitted` — uncommitted changes to other transactions are visible.

❑ `ilBrowse` — uncommitted changes to other transactions are visible.

❑ `ilCursorStability` — changes to other transactions are visible only after they have been committed.

❑ `ilReadCommitted` — changes to other transactions are visible only after they have been committed.

❑ `ilRepeatableRead` — changes made to other transactions are not visible, but can be accessed during data updating.

❑ `ilSerializable` — the transaction is executed in isolation from other transactions.

❑ `ilIsolated` — the transaction is executed in isolation from other transactions.

The property

```
TXactAttribute = (xaCommitRetaining, xaAbortRetaining);
```

```
property Attributes: TXactAttributes;
```

sets the technique for managing transactions during commission and rollback:

❑ `xaCommitRetaining` — as soon as the current transaction is committed, the next one is automatically started.

❑ `xaAbortRetaining` — once the current transaction is rolled back, the next one is automatically started.

ADO Datasets

In addition to connection components, the **ADO** tab of the Delphi Component palette contains standard components that encapsulate a dataset and are adapted for work with ADO data stores. These components are:

- ❏ TADODataSet — the universal dataset
- ❏ TADOTable — a database table
- ❏ TADOQuery — an SQL request
- ❏ TADOStoredProc — a stored procedure

As can be expected of all components that contain datasets, their common ancestor is the TDataSet class, which provides basic functions for managing datasets (see *Chapter 5, "The Architecture of Database Applications"*).

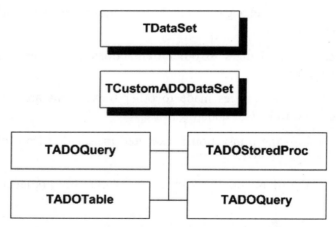

Fig. 7.7. The hierarchy of ADO DataSet classes

ADO components have a standard set of properties and methods, and inherit the mechanism for data access through ADO from their common ancestor, the TCustomADODataSet class. Additionally, the TCustomADODataSet class contains a range of properties and methods common to all its descendants that it would be useful to examine here. Therefore, we will first study the TCustomADODataSet class, and then proceed to ADO components.

The *TCustomADODataSet* Class

The `TCustomADODataSet` class contains the mechanism for accessing stored data with ADO. This class combines the abstract methods of its common ancestor, `TdataSet`, with the functions of a specific mechanism for accessing data.

Therefore, here we will examine only the unique properties and methods of the `TCustomADODataSet` class that support ADO.

A dataset is connected to an ADO data store using the `TADOConnection` component (the `Connection` property), or by setting the connection parameters with the `ConnectionString` property (see above).

Datasets

Prior to opening a dataset, you need to specify the type of lock that will be used during editing. Use the following property:

```
type TADOLockType = (ltUnspecified, ltReadOnly, ltPessimistic,
ltOptimistic, ltBatchOptimistic);

property LockType: TADOLockType;
```

where:

☐ `ltUnspecified` — the lock is specified by the data source and not by the component.

☐ `ltReadOnly` — the dataset is opened in read-only mode.

☐ `ltPessimistic` — the record remains locked throughout the editing session until it has been saved in the data store.

☐ `ltOptimistic` — the record is locked only while changes are being saved in the data store.

☐ `ltBatchOptimistic` — the record is locked while its is being saved in the data store using the `UpdateBatch` method.

> **NOTE**
>
> To guarantee that the lock is correctly implemented, the `LockType` property must be modified before opening a dataset.

A dataset is opened and closed with the `Open` and `Close` methods. You can also use the property

```
property Active: Boolean;
```

The current state of any dataset can be determined by the property

```
type
    TObjectState = (stClosed, stOpen, stConnecting, stExecuting, stFetching);
    TObjectStates = set of TObjectState;
property RecordsetState: TObjectStates;
```

A dataset in ADO components is based on the use of an ADO recordset object, which can be accessed directly using the property

```
property Recordset: _Recordset;
```

But as all key methods of the ADO recordset object interfaces are overlapped by methods of the class, you don't normally need to access this object directly.

The following event handler is called every time a dataset is refreshed:

```
TRecordsetEvent = procedure(DataSet: TCustomADODataSet; const Error:
Error; var EventStatus: TEventStatus) of object;
property OnFetchComplete: TRecordsetEvent;
```

where `Error` is a link to the ADO error object, if any error has occurred.

If a dataset operates in asynchronous mode, the following event handler is invoked every time it is refreshed:

```
TFetchProgressEvent = procedure(DataSet: TCustomADODataSet; Progress,
MaxProgress: Integer; var EventStatus: TEventStatus) of object;
property OnFetchProgress: TFetchProgressEvent;
```

where the `Progress` parameter indicates how the operation is progressing.

Dataset Cursors

The type and location of the cursor you use for ADO datasets will depend on their function.

The location of the cursor is set by the property

```
type TCursorLocation = (clUseServer, clUseClient);
property CursorLocation: TCursorLocation;
```

The cursor can be located either on the server (`clUseServer`) or on the client side (`clUseClient`).

❑ A *server cursor* is used for handling large datasets that are inexpedient to send to the client as a whole. Here, the performance of the client dataset is somewhat slowed down.

❑ A *client cursor* enables the dataset to be transferred to the client. This considerably accelerates the performance, but this type of cursor is only worth using with small datasets that do not increase network load.

When you use a client cursor, you need to specify an additional property —

```
TMarshalOption = (moMarshalAll, moMarshalModifiedOnly);
property MarshalOptions: TmarshalOption
```

which controls data exchange between the client and the server. If the connection that you are using is fast enough, you can use the `moMarshalAll` value, which permits you to return all the records in the dataset to the server. Otherwise, you can speed up the performance of the component by using the `moMarshalModifiedOnly` property, which ensures that only records modified by the client will be returned to the server.

The type of cursor is specified by the property:

```
TCursorType = (ctUnspecified, ctOpenForwardOnly, ctKeyset, ctDynamic,
ctStatic);

property CursorType: TCursorType;
```

❑ `ctUnspecified` — the cursor is unspecified, the type of cursor is determined by the capabilities of the data source.

❑ `ctOpenForwardOnly` — a forward-only cursor that enables only forward navigation; it is used when you require fast single movement through all the records in a dataset.

❑ `ctKeyset` — a keyset (bidirectional) local cursor that does not allow you to look at records added or deleted by other users.

❑ `ctDynamic` — a dynamic (bidirectional) cursor that displays all changes, but also takes up many resources.

❑ `ctStatic` — a static (bidirectional) cursor that ignores all changes made by other users.

NOTE

Client-side cursors (`CursorType` = `clUseClient`) support only one type — `ctStatic`.

Before and after every move of the cursor within a dataset, the following event handlers are called:

```
TRecordsetReasonEvent = procedure(DataSet: TCustomADODataSet;
const Reason: TEventReason; var EventStatus: TEventStatus) of object;
```

```
property OnWillMove: TRecordsetReasonEvent;
```
and
```
TRecordsetErrorEvent = procedure(DataSet: TCustomADODataSet;
const Reason: TEventReason; const Error: Error; var EventStatus:
TEventStatus) of object;
```
```
property OnMoveComplete: TRecordsetErrorEvent;
```
where the `Reason` parameter informs you which method caused this move.

Local Buffer

As soon as the dataset records are transferred to the client, they are cached in the local buffer, the capacity of which is defined by the property:

```
property CacheSize: Integer;
```

The value of this property indicates the number of records in the local buffer, and cannot be less than 1. Obviously, if the buffer is large enough, a component need not refer to the data source very often, but on the other hand, a large cache will significantly slow down the opening of a dataset.

Furthermore, in selecting the size of the local buffer, it is necessary to take into account the amount of memory available to a component. This can be done with simple calculations:

```
CacheSizeInMem := ADODataSet.CacheSize * ADODataSet.RecordSize;
```

where `RecordSize` is the property

```
property RecordSize: Word;
```

that returns the size of a single record in bytes. As you can see, ADO components face a problem common to all client data — with a poor connection, the application slows down. However, there is still something you can do. If you don't need to display data in the visual components of a user interface while navigating through records, the property

```
property BlockReadSize: Integer;
```

enables the block transfer of data. This property specifies the number of records that can constitute a single block. The status of the dataset changes to `dsBlockRead`. By default, block transfer is not used, and the value of this property is 0.

You can also limit the maximum size of a dataset. The property

```
property MaxRecords: Integer;
```

sets the maximum number of records that can be contained in a dataset. The default value of this property is 0, which means that the number of records is unlimited. The total number of records at any given moment is returned by the read-only property

```
property RecordCount: Integer;
```

Once the last record of a dataset is detected, the following event handler is called:

```
TEndOfRecordsetEvent = procedure (DataSet: TCustomADODataSet; var
MoreData: WordBool; var EventStatus: TEventStatus) of object;

property OnEndOfRecordset: TEndOfRecordsetEvent;
```

The MoreData parameter indicates whether the record is really the last one. If MoreData = True, this means that there are still more records in the data store that have not yet been sent to the client.

Handling Record Status

The TCustomADODataSet class has additional capabilties that allow it to monitor the status of every single record.

You can define the status of every current record by using the property:

```
TRecordStatus = (rsOK, rsNew, rsModified, rsDeleted, rsUnmodified,
rsInvalid, rsMultipleChanges, rsPendingChanges, rsCanceled,
rsCantRelease, rsConcurrencyViolation, rsIntegrityViolation,
rsMaxChangesExceeded, rsObjectOpen, rsOutOfMemory, rsPermissionDenied,
rsSchemaViolation, rsDBDeleted);

property RecordStatus: TRecordStatusSet;
```

where:

❒ rsOK — the record has been saved.

❒ rsNew — the record has been added.

❒ rsModified — the record has been modified.

❒ rsDeleted — the record has been deleted.

❒ rsUnmodified — the record has not been modified.

❒ rsInvalid — the record cannot be saved because it is invalid.

❒ rsMultipleChanges — the record cannot be saved because of multiple changes made to it.

❏ rsPendingChanges — the record cannot be saved because it references unsaved changes.

❏ rsCanceled — the operation with the record has been cancelled.

❏ rsCantRelease — the record is locked.

❏ rsConcurrencyViolation — the record cannot be saved because of the type of current lock.

❏ rsIntegrityViolation — referential integrity has been violated.

❏ rsMaxChangesExceeded — too many changes have been made.

❏ rsObjectOpen — a conflict with a database object has occurred.

❏ rsOutOfMemory — lack of memory.

❏ rsPermissionDenied — access denied.

❏ rsSchemaViolation — the data structure has been violated.

❏ rsDBDeleted — the record has been deleted in the database.

As you can see, thanks to this property, the status of an individual record can be determined with great accuracy.

Additionally, the following method:

```
type
  TUpdateStatus = (usUnmodified, usModified, usInserted, usDeleted);
function UpdateStatus: TUpdateStatus; override;
```

returns details on the status of the current record.

Accordingly, before and after a record is updated, the relevant event handlers are called:

```
TWillChangeRecordEvent = procedure(DataSet: TCustomADODataSet; const
Reason: TEventReason; const RecordCount: Integer; var EventStatus:
TEventStatus) of object;

property OnWillChangeRecord: TWillChangeRecordEvent;
```

and

```
TRecordChangeCompleteEvent = procedure(DataSet: TCustomADODataSet;
const Reason: TEventReason; const RecordCount: Integer; const Error:
Error; var EventStatus: TEventStatus) of object;

property OnRecordChangeComplete: TrecordChangeCompleteEvent;
```

where the Reason parameter indicates the method used for updating the record, and the RecordCount parameter returns the number of modified records.

Managing Filtering

In addition to traditional filtering based on the `Filter` and `Filtered` properties and the `OnFilterRecord` event handler, the `TCustomADODataSet` class provides the developer with a number of additional functions.

The property

```
TFilterGroup = (fgUnassigned, fgNone, fgPendingRecords,
fgAffectedRecords, fgFetchedRecords, fgPredicate,
fgConflictingRecords);

property FilterGroup: TFilterGroup;
```

sets a group filter for records based on information on the update status of every record in the dataset, much like the `RecordStatus` property that we examined earlier.

Filtering is possible with the following parameters:

❏ `fgUnassigned` — the filter is not specified.

❏ `fgNone` — all restrictions specified by the filter are removed, and all records of the dataset are displayed.

❏ `fgPendingRecords` — modified records that have not been saved in the data source using the `UpdateBatch` or `CancelBatch` method are displayed.

❏ `fgAffectedRecords` — the records that were processed during the most recent save in the data source are displayed.

❏ `fgFetchedRecords` — records received during the most recent update in the data source are displayed.

❏ `fgPredicate` — only deleted records are displayed.

❏ `fgConflictingRecords` — modified records that caused an error to occur when they were saved in the data source are displayed.

For batch filtering to work, two additional conditions are required. First, filtering must be activated — the `Filtered` property should be set to `True`. And secondly, the `LockType` property must be set to `ltBatchOptimistic`.

```
with ADODataSet do
  begin
    Close;
    LockType := ltbatchOptimistic;
```

```
Filtered := True;
FilterGroup := fgFetchedRecords;
Open;
end;
```

The method:

```
procedure FilterOnBookmarks(Bookmarks: array of const);
```

activates filtering based on the existing bookmarks. To do this, you must set bookmarks beforehand at all the records that you are interested in, using the `GetBookmark` method. The `FilterOnBookmarks` method automatically clears the `Filter` property and assigns the `gUnassigned` value to the `FilterGroup` property.

Running Searches

The following method provides a fast and versatile search through the fields of the current dataset index:

```
SeekOption = (soFirstEQ, soLastEQ, soAfterEQ, soAfter, soBeforeEQ,
soBefore);

function Seek(const KeyValues: Variant; SeekOption: TSeekOption =
soFirstEQ): Boolean;
```

The `KeyValues` parameter must list all the required values of the indexed fields. The `SeekOption` controls the search process:

❑ `soFirstEQ` — the cursor is positioned at the first record found.

❑ `soLastEQ` — the cursor is positioned at the last record found.

❑ `soAfterEQ` — the cursor is positioned at the matching record or, if such a record is not found, immediately after the place where the record would have been located.

❑ `soAfter` — the cursor is positioned immediately after the record found.

❑ `soBeforeEQ` — the cursor is positioned at the matching record or, if such a record is not found, immediately before the place where the record would have been located.

❑ `soBefore` — the cursor is positioned immediately before the record found.

Sorting

The property

```
property Sort: WideString;
```

provides a simple method of sorting through a random collection of fields. This property must contain the names of the required fields delimited by semicolons, and also must specify the sorting order (ascending or descending):

```
ADODataSet.Sort := 'FirstField DESC';
```

The default sorting order is ascending.

ADO Command Object

To run a request to any data source, every ADO component should contain the special ADO Command object.

If you use components descended from the `TCustomADODataSet` class, there is usually no need to employ the Command object directly. Although all the actual interaction between an ADO Dataset object and a data source is accomplished through the Command object, the settings and command execution are hidden in the properties and methods of ADO components. Nevertheless, you can access the Command object in the `TCustomADODataSet` class using the property:

```
property Command: TADOCommand;
```

> **NOTE**
>
> If the developer needs to execute a ADO command that is not directly linked to any particular dataset, he or she can utilize the special `TADOCommand` component, which is also located in the **ADO** tab of the Component palette.

The type of command is set by the property

```
type
    TCommandType = (cmdUnknown, cmdText, cmdTable, cmdStoredProc,
cmdFile, cmdTableDirect);
property CommandType: TCommandType;
```

where:

❑ `cmdUnknown` — the type of command is unknown and will be specified by the data source.

❑ `cmdText` — a text command (for example, an SQL request) interpreted by the data source; the textual content must be compiled in compliance with the rules for the specific data source.

❑ `cmdTable` — a command for receiving a table dataset from the data store.

❑ cmdStoredProc — a command to execute a stored procedure.

❑ cmdFile — a command for receving a dataset saved in a a file with the format used by a specific data source.

❑ cmdTableDirect — a command for receiving a table dataset directly, for example from a file of this table.

The text of the command is set by the property

```
property CommandText: WideString;
```

and must match the command type.

To restrict the time of waiting for the execution of a command, use the property:

```
property CommandTimeout: Integer;
```

ADO Dataset components execute commands using the following operations:

❑ Opening and closing datasets

❑ Processing requests and stored procedures

❑ Updating datasets

❑ Saving datasets

❑ Performing batch operations

The developer can modify the way a command is processed by changing the following property:

```
type

   TExecuteOption = (eoAsyncExecute, eoAsyncFetch,
eoAsyncFetchNonBlocking, eoExecuteNoRecords);

   TExecuteOptions = set of TExecuteOption;

property ExecuteOptions: TExecuteOptions;
```

where:

❑ eoAsyncExecute — the command executes asynchronously.

❑ eoAsyncFetch — the command for updating datasets executes asynchronously.

❑ eoAsyncFetchNonBlocking — the command for updating datasets executes asynchronously, and subsequent operations are not blocked.

❑ eoExecuteNoRecords — the command does not demand the return of a dataset.

Batch Operations

As mentioned above, ADO Dataset components use a client-side local cache for storing data and changes. Thanks to this, it is possible to implement batch operations. In this mode, all the changes made are accumulated in the local cache instead of being immediately passed to the data source. This speeds up performance and allows you to save an entire batch of modified records at once.

The downside to this method is that while the changes are located on the client, they are unavailable to other users. Data could be lost in this way.

In order to switch a dataset to group operations mode you need to proceed as follows.

The dataset must use the client cursor:

```
ADODataSet.CursorLocation := clUseClient;
```

The cursor must have the ctStatic type:

```
ADODataSet.CursorType := ctStatic;
```

The lock must be set to the ltBatchOptimistic value:

```
ADODataSet.LockType := ltBatchOptimistic;
```

To pass changes made in the data store, ADO components use the method

```
procedure UpdateBatch(AffectRecords: TAffectRecords = arAll);
```

To cancel all changes made but not saved using the UpdateBatch method, use the method

```
procedure CancelBatch(AffectRecords: TAffectRecords = arAll);
```

The TAffectRecords type used by these methods enables you to define the type of records processed by the operation:

```
TAffectRecords = (arCurrent, arFiltered, arAll, arAllChapters);
```

where:

❏ arCurrent — the operation processes only the current record.

❏ arFiltered — the operation processes only records that match the current filter.

❏ rAll — the operation processes all records.

❏ arAllChapters — the operation processes all the records in the current dataset (including records which are not visible because of the active filter), as well as all the embedded datasets.

Parameters

Many ADO Dataset components that contain recordsets must supply parameters to requests. To do this, the special `TParameters` class is used.

An individual `TParameter` class is created for each parameter in the `TParameters` collection.

This class is a descendant of the `TCollection` class and contains an indexed list of individual parameters. Remember that in working with regular request parameters in request and stored procedure components, you need to use the `TParams` class (for example, in dbExpress components), which also descends from the `TCollection` class.

The methods used by these two classes coincide, while their properties have some differences. To display command parameters, ADO uses a special parameter object that is actively used by all ADO components that encapsulate datasets.

This is why ADO components in VCL had their own class of parameters created for them.

The *TParameters* Class

The main purpose of the `TParameters` class is to contain a list of parameters. An indexed list of parameters is represented by the property

```
property Items[Index: Integer]: TParameter;
```

The current values of parameters can be obtained from the indexed property

```
property ParamValues[const ParamName: String]: Variant;
```

You can access a particular value by the name of the parameter

```
Edit1.Text := ADODataSet.Parameters.ParamValues['ParamOne'];
```

A list of parameters can be updated using the methods

```
function AddParameter: TParameter;
```

and

```
function CreateParameter(const Name: WideString; DataType: TDataType;
Direction: TParameterDirection; Size: Integer; Value: OleVariant):
TParameter;
```

The first method simply creates a new `Parameter` object and adds it to the list.

The next step is to specify all the properties of the new parameter:

```
var NewParam: TParameter;
  ...
  NewParam := ADODataSet.Parameters.AddParameter;
  NewParam.Name := 'ParamTwo';
  NewParam.DataType := ftInteger;
  NewParam.Direction := pdInput;
  NewParam.Value := 0;
```

The `CreateParameter` method creates a new parameter and sets its properties:

❏ `Name` — the name of the parameter

❏ `DataType` — the data type of the parameter corresponding to the the field type of the database table (`TFieldType`)

❏ `Direction` — a parameter type that is an addition to the standard types `dUnknown`, `pdInput`, `pdOutput`, `pdInputOutput`; `TParameterDirection` also has the additional type `pdReturnValue` value, which determines any returned value

❏ `Size` — the maximum size of the parameter value

❏ `Value` — the value of the parameter

When you work with parameters, it is more convenient to call them using names, and not the absolute indexes from the list. You can do this using the method

```
function ParamByName(const Value: WideString): TParameter;
```

The list of parameters must always match a request or procedure. To refresh the list, use the property

```
procedure Refresh;
```

You can also create a list of parameters for a request that is not linked to a `Parameter` object. Use the method:

```
function ParseSQL(SQL: String; DoCreate: Boolean): String;
```

where `DoCreate` defines whether existing parameters should be deleted prior to parsing the request.

The *TParameter* Class

The `TParameter` class contains an individual parameter.

The name of the parameter is set by the property

```
property Name: WideString;
```

The type of data which must express the value of the parameter is specified by the property

```
TDataType = TFieldType;
property DataType: TDataType;
```

Finally, since parameters interact with fields of database tables, the parameter data type must coincide with the field data type. The size of the parameter depends on the data type:

```
property Size: Integer;
```

which can be modified for a string and character data type and the like.

The value of the parameter is contained in the property

```
property Value: OleVariant;
```

And the property

```
type
  TParameterAttribute = (paSigned, paNullable, paLong);
  TParameterAttributes = set of TParameterAttribute;
property Attributes: TParameterAttributes;
```

controls the values assigned to parameters:

❑ paSigned — the value can be a character value.

❑ paNullable — the value can be empty.

❑ paLong — the value can contain **BLOB** type data.

The following property sets the direction of a parameter:

```
type TParameterDirection = (pdUnknown, pdInput, pdOutput,
pdInputOutput, pdReturnValue);

property Direction: TParameterDirection;
```

where:

❑ pdUnknown — an unknown parameter — the data store must try to determine the type independently.

❑ pdInput — an input parameter used in requests and stored procedures.

❑ pdOutput — an output parameter used in stored procedures.

❏ pdInputOutput — an input/output parameter used in stored procedures.

❏ pdReturnValue — a parameter for returning any value.

If a parameter must pass large binary arrays (images or files, for example), the value for this parameter can be loaded using the methods

```
procedure LoadFromFile(const FileName: String; DataType: TDataType);
```
and

```
procedure LoadFromStream(Stream: TStream; DataType: TDataType);
```

The *TADODataSet* Component

The TADODataSet component is used for representing datasets from ADO data stores. This component is easy-to-use, with just a few properties and methods of its own. It mostly uses the functions of its direct ancestor, the TCustomADODataSet class.

This is the only ADO component that contains a dataset with published properties that enable it to manage ADO commands. The properties in question (see above) are

```
property CommandText: WideString;
```
and

```
property CommandType: TCommandType;
```

As a result, the component is a flexible tool that enables you (depending on the type and text of the command) to receive data from tables, SQL requests, stored procedures, files, and so on. For example, you can select the necessary value of the property CommandType = cmdText and enter the text of an SQL request in the CommandText property from the editor:

```
ADODataSet.CommandType = cmdText;
ADODataSet. CommandText := Memo1.Lines.Text;
```

and the SQL request is ready to execute.

NOTE

Only the Data Manipulation Language can be used for SQL queries (use only SELECT).

The ConnectionString and Connection properties are used for establishing connection with databases.

A dataset can be opened and closed by the Active property or the Open and Close methods.

This component can be used in applications just as all other usual data access components — by linking the dataset that it contains to visual data-aware components through the `TDataSource` component.

The *TADOTable* Component

The `TADOTable` component allows Delphi applications to use database tables through OLE DB providers. The functional capabilities and use of this component are similar to the standard Table component (see *Chapter 5, "The Architecture of Database Applications"*).

As you already know, the component is based on the ADO command, however, the properties of the command are set in advance and cannot be modified.

The name of the required database table is set by the property

```
property TableName: WideString;
```

Other properties and methods of the component are provided by indexing (which any other query component lacks).

Since not all ADO providers support direct handling of database tables, an SQL request is required to get access to them. If the property:

```
property TableDirect: Boolean;
```

has the `True` value, you can directly access a database table. Otherwise, the component will generate the appropriate query.

The property

```
property ReadOnly: Boolean;
```

allows you to activate or disable the read-only mode for the table.

The *TADOQuery* Component

The `TADOQuery` component allows applications that use ADO to run SQL queries. Its functionality is similar to the standard query component (see *Chapter 5, "The Architecture of Database Applications"*).

The text of the query is specified by the property

```
property SQL: TStrings;
```

The parameters of the query are defined by the following property:

```
property Parameters: TParameters;
```

If the query is to return a dataset, use the following property to open it:

```
property Active: Boolean;
```

or the method

```
procedure Open;
```

Otherwise, you can use the method

```
function ExecSQL: Integer; ExecSQL
```

The number of records processed by the query is returned by the property:

```
property RowsAffected: Integer;
```

The *TADOStoredProc* Component

The TADOStoredProc component enables Delphi applications that connect to databases through ADO to use stored procedures. This component is similar to the standard stored procedure component (see *Chapter 5, "The Architecture of Database Applications"*).

The name of the stored procedure is specified by the property

```
property ProcedureName: WideString;
```

The following property defines the input/output parameters for the stored procedure

```
property Parameters: TParameters;
```

If the procedure is to be used many times without changes, it makes sense to prepare its execution on the server in advance. This can be done by setting the following property to True:

```
property Prepared: Boolean;
```

ADO Commands

The ADO command, which we have already devoted so much attention to in this chapter, corresponds to the TADOCommand component in Delphi VCL. The methods of this component in many ways coincide with the TCustomADODataSet class, although this class is not an ancestor of the component. It is used to execute commands that do not return datasets.

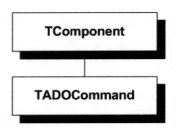

Fig. 7.8. The TADOCommand component hierarchy

As the TADOCommand component doesn't require dataset handling, its direct ancestor is the TComponent class. It has simply gained the mechanism for connecting to databases through ADO and means of implementing commands.

A command passes to an ADO data store through either its own connection or the TADOConnection component, just like to other ADO components.

The text of the command must be contained in the property

```
property CommandText: WideString;
```

However, you can also specify a command using another technique. A direct pointer to the required ADO command can be defined by the property

```
property CommandObject: _Command;
```

The type of command is set by the property

```
type TCommandType = (cmdUnknown, cmdText, cmdTable, cmdStoredProc,
cmdFile, cmdTableDirect);
```
```
property CommandType: TCommandType;
```

Since the TCommandType type is also used in the TCustomADODataSet class, where it is necessary to display all possible types of command in relation to the TADOCommand component, this type is redundant. Here, you cannot set the values cmdTable, cmdFile, cmdTableDirect, and the cmdStoredProc type can be assigned only to stored procedures which do not return datasets.

If the command must contain the text of an SQL query, the CommandType property must have the value cmdText.

To call a stored procedure, the cmdStoredProc type must be specified, and the name of the procedure must be entered in the CommandText property.

If parameters must be specified for the command to execute, use the property

```
property Parameters: TParameters;
```

Commands are executed with the `Execute` method:

```
function Execute: _RecordSet; overload;

function Execute(const Parameters: OleVariant): _Recordset; overload;

function Execute(var RecordsAffected: Integer; var Parameters: OleVariant;
ExecuteOptions: TExecuteOptions = []): _RecordSet; overload;
```

The developer can use any of the above overload method notations.

The `RecordsAffected` parameter returns the number of records processed.

The `Parameters` parameter indicates the parameters of the command.

The `ExecuteOptions` parameter specifies the conditions for executing the command:

```
TExecuteOption = (eoAsyncExecute, eoAsyncFetch,
eoAsyncFetchNonBlocking, eoExecuteNoRecords);
   TExecuteOptions = set of TExecuteOption;
```

where:

❏ `eoAsyncExecute` — the command is executed asynchronously.

❏ `eoAsyncFetch` — data are fetched asynchronously.

❏ `eoAsyncFetchNonBlocking` — data are fetched asynchronously without blocking the stream.

❏ `eoExecuteNoRecords` — if the command returns a dataset, the records are not passed to the component.

The `eoExecuteNoRecords` option is recommended for handling the `TADOConnection` component.

The following method is used to abort a command:

```
procedure Cancel;
```

The current state of a command can be defined by the following property:

```
type
   TObjectState  =  (stClosed,  stOpen,  stConnecting,  stExecuting,
stFetching);
   TObjectStates = set of TObjectState;

property States: TObjectStates;
```

ADO Error Object

We have encountered the ADO error object in this chapter quite often while discussing various ADO components. ADO error objects contain information on errors that occur during the execution of any ADO object.

Delphi doesn't provide any specific type for the error object, but developers can use the methods of the `Error` interface, which provides many methods for other ADO objects. For example, the type

```
TRecordsetEvent = procedure(DataSet: TCustomADODataSet; const Error:
Error; var EventStatus: TEventStatus) of object;
```

which is used for the event handler called after a dataset has been refreshed, contains the `Error` parameter that supplies us with the sought-after link.

Let's examine some useful properties of the ADO error object.

The property

```
property Description: WideString read Get_Description;
```

returns the error description passed from the object in which the error occurred.

The property

```
property SQLState: WideString read Get_SQLState;
```

contains the text of the command that caused this error.

The property

```
property NativeError: Integer read Get_NativeError;
```

returns the code of the error, passed from the object in which the error occurred.

Developing a Sample ADO Application

Now let's try to put this information on using ADO in Delphi into practice. As an example, we'll create a simple application, ADO Demo, that can access a couple of database tables, save changes with the help of batch operations, sort records, and place filters on selected records.

Let's use the dBase files stored in the ..\Program Files\Common Files\ Borland Shared\Data demo Delphi database as the data source. We will select the INDUSTRY and MASTER tables to use in the new application. These tables are linked by a foreign key in the columns IND_CODE and INDUSTRY.

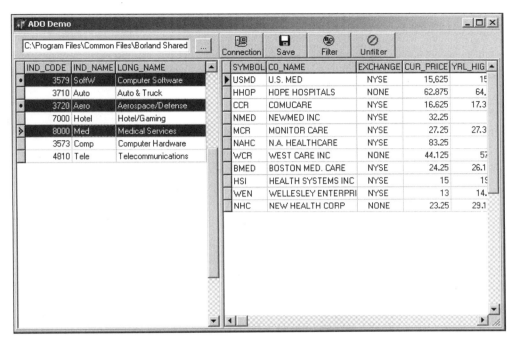

Fig.7.9. The main window of the ADO Demo application

The INDUSTRY table can be edited; it is contained in the `tblIndustry` component of the `TADOTable` type and is displayed in the left `TDBGrid` component. As for
the MASTER table, it is contained in the `tblMaster` component designed for
viewing only. These two components are related to each other by a one-to-many
dependence through the `MasterSource` and `MasterFields` properties.

Listing 7.1. The implementation Section of the uMain Unit of the ADO Demo Application

```
implementation

uses IniFiles, FileCtrl;

const sIniFileName: String = 'ADODemo.ini';
      sEmptyDefDB:  String = 'Database path is empty';
```

```
      sEmptyFilter: String = 'Records for filter are not selected';

{$R *.dfm}

procedure TfmMain.FormShow(Sender: TObject);
begin
 with TIniFile.Create(sIniFileName) do
 try
  DefDBStr := ReadString('DefDB', 'DefDBStr', '');
  edDefDB.Text := DefDBStr;
 finally
  Free;
 end;
 SetLength(Bookmarks, 0);
end;

procedure TfmMain.FormClose(Sender: TObject; var Action:
TCloseAction);
begin
 with TIniFile.Create(sIniFileName) do
 try
  WriteString('DefDB', 'DefDBStr', edDefDB.Text);
 finally
  Free;
 end;
end;

procedure TfmMain.sbDefDBClick(Sender: TObject);
begin
 if SelectDirectory(DefDBStr, [], 0)
  then edDefDB.Text := DefDBStr;
end;

procedure TfmMain.tbConnectClick(Sender: TObject);
begin
 ADOConn.Close;
 ADOConn.DefaultDatabase := '';
 if DefDBStr = '' then
 begin
  MessageDlg(sEmptyDefDB, mtError, [mbOK], 0);
  Abort;
```

```
   end
  else
  begin
   ADOConn.DefaultDatabase := DefDBStr;
   ADOConn.Open;
  end;
end;

procedure TfmMain.tbSaveClick(Sender: TObject);
begin
 tblIndustry.UpdateBatch();
end;

procedure TfmMain.tbFilterClick(Sender: TObject);
var i: Integer;
begin
 if dbgIndustry.SelectedRows.Count > 0 then
 begin
  SetLength(Bookmarks, dbgIndustry.SelectedRows.Count);
  for i := 0 to dbgIndustry.SelectedRows.Count - 1 do
  begin
   Bookmarks[i].VType := vtPointer;
   Bookmarks[i].VPointer := pointer(dbgIndustry.SelectedRows[i]);
   end;
   tblIndustry.FilterOnBookmarks(Bookmarks);
  end
  else
   MessageDlg(sEmptyFilter, mtWarning, [mbOK], 0);
end;

procedure TfmMain.tbUnFilterClick(Sender: TObject);
begin
 tblIndustry.Filtered := False;
 dbgIndustry.SelectedRows.Clear;
end;

procedure TfmMain.dbgIndustryTitleClick(Column: TColumn);
begin
 if tblIndustry.Active then
  if (Pos(Column.FieldName, tblIndustry.Sort) > 0)
  and(Pos('ASC', tblIndustry.Sort) > 0)
```

```
         then tblIndustry.Sort := Column.FieldName + ' DESC'
         else tblIndustry.Sort := Column.FieldName + ' ASC';
    end;

    procedure TfmMain.ADOConnAfterConnect(Sender: TObject);
    var i: Integer;
    begin
      for i := 0 to adoConn.DataSetCount - 1 do
       ADOConn.DataSets[i].Open;
    end;

    procedure TfmMain.ADOConnBeforeDisconnect(Sender: TObject);
    var i: Integer;
    begin
      for i := 0 to adoConn.DataSetCount - 1 do
       ADOConn.DataSets[i].Close;
    end;

    end.
```

Connecting to the Data Source

Use the TADOConnection component to connect the application to the data source, and then set the connection options by pressing the ConnectionString property button in the **Object Inspector** window.

The next step is to move to the **Data Link Properties** editor and select Microsoft OLE DB Provider for OLE DB Drivers (see Fig. 7.3). As a rule, this editor is part of the operating system, unless you have gone to the trouble of removing it. Then, on the **Connection** page (see Fig. 7.4), select the **Use data source name** radio button, and choose the dBase files from the list. Now the application is fully prepared to connect to the ODBC provider.

Let's look at other properties of the TADOConnection component.

The LoginPrompt property must be set to False in order to disable the display of a user authorization dialog, which is unnecessary for dBase files.

Leave the DefaultDatabase property empty for the time being. We will use it later to indicate the path to the database files, using elements of the application user interface.

The `CursorLocation` property is set to the `clUseClient` value to ensure the use of dataset cursors on the client side.

The default value of the `ConnectOptions` property is `coConnectUnspecified`, which means that all commands will execute synchronously. This means that the connection will wait for a response to every command.

Set the `Mode` property to the `cmShareDenyNone` value to prevent other connections from setting any restrictions, as we do not plan on giving multiple-users access to the data source in this case.

Once you have started your application, you need to indicate the location of the data store to open the connection. Use the corresponding button and the single-line editor in the **Control** bar. After the path is selected, its value is saved to the `DefDBStr` variable and to the `edDefDB` editor. This variable is used for establishing the connection. Press the `tbConnect` button to open the connection. The appropriate event handler checks the state of the `DefDBStr` variable and assigns the proper value to the `DefaultDatabase` property of the `TADOConnection` component.

> **NOTE**
>
> The `DefaultDatabase` property will work because the path to the data store was not specified in the process of setting the options for the connection. Otherwise, the value of this property would be overwritten by the settings of the `ConnectionString` property.

The application accesses the ADO dataset through the `ADOConnAfterConnect` event handler, which is called as soon as the connection has been established. Similarly, the datasets are closed before disconnecting with the `ADOConnBeforeDisconnect` event handler.

The current value of the path to the data store is saved to the DemoADO.ini file and uploaded when the application is opened.

Batch Operations

The `tblIndustry` component is designed for performing batch operations. This is why the `LoclType` property has the value `ltBatchOptimistic`. The `CursorLocation` property is set to `clUseClient` to enable you to use the client dataset. The type of cursor (the `CursorType` property) must be set to `ctStatic`.

All changes can be saved to the data store using the `UpdateBatch` method in the event handler for the `tbSave` button.

Filtering

The records in the `tblIndustry` dataset are filtered by the `FilterOnBookmark` method. The user should select the required records in the `dbgIndustry` component (which operates in the `dgMultiSelect` mode). Then, when the `tbFilter` button is pressed, the bookmarks specified in the `SelectedRows` property of the `dbgIndustry` component are passed to the `Bookmarks` array of the `TVarRec` type, which in turn is passed as a parameter of the `FilterOnBookmark` method for filtering.

The `Bookmarks` array serves here as an intermediate link for converting the `dbgIndustry` component's boolmark type into a parameter of the `FilterOnBookmark` method.

Sorting

Sorting is also applied to the `tblIndustry` dataset. When you click the heading of a column in the `dbgIndustry` component, the `dbgIndustryTitleClick` event handler is called. Depending on the current state of the `tblIndustry.Sort` sorting property (which indicates the fields to be sorted, as well as the sorting order), this event handler gives a new value to the `Sort` property.

Summary

The ADO technology provides you with a universal strategy for accessing heterogeneous data sources. As the ADO functions are based on OLE DB and COM interfaces, applications don't require any additional libraries. All they need is for ADO to be installed on the system.

The `TADOConnection` component provides connections to data sources through OLE DB providers. The `TADODataSet`, `TADOTable`, `TADOQuery`, and `TADOStoredProc` components enable you to use recordsets in applications. The properties and methods of these components allow you to develop full-fledged applications.

The `TADOCommand` component contains ADO text commands.

Besides the standard capabilities for handling data, required ADO interfaces and objects can be directly accessed from components as well.

PART III

DISTRIBUTED DATABASE APPLICATIONS

Chapter 8

DataSnap Technology. Remote Access Mechanisms

I n the chapters of the previous part, we covered issues of developing traditional database applications that access databases on local machines or on a local network. However, we have not examined situations where we need an application that is equally well prepared for dealing both with computers in a local network and with multiple remote machines.

Obviously, in this case the access model for data should be widened, since with a large number of remote machines, traditional schemas for creating database applications are ineffective.

This chapter discusses the model of a distributed database application, called multi-tiered, and specifically, its simplest version — a three-tier distributed application. The parts of this application are:

❑ Database server

❑ Application server (middleware)

❑ Client-side application

All three parts are united by the transaction mechanism (the transport level) and the mechanism of processing data (the business logic level).

In generalizing a three-tier model, it should be noted that increasing the number of tiers doesn't affect the database server or the client-side part of the application. All additional tiers actually only complicate the middleware, which can include, for example, a transaction server, a secure server, etc.

All Delphi components and objects that enable the development of multi-tier applications are collectively referred to as DataSnap.

NOTE

> In earlier versions of Delphi (Delphi 4 and 5), these components were called MIDAS (Multi-tier Distributed Applications Services).

Most of the components discussed in the following chapters are available from the special **DataSnap** page of the Delphi Component palette. However, we will need a number of extra components for designing multi-tier applications, and these additional components are also given due attention here.

This chapter covers the following issues:

❑ The structure of multi-tier applications

❑ The DataSnap strategy for accessing remote databases

❑ Remote data modules

❏ Provider components

❏ Transaction components of DataSnap remote connections

❏ Extra components — connection brokers

Structure of a Delphi Multi-Tier Application

The multi-tier architecture of database applications came into being because of the necessity of processing requests from multiple remote clients on the server. On the face of it, this task can be adequately solved by using traditional client-server applications, the key elements of which were covered in the previous section. However, with a large number of clients, the entire processing burden is placed on the database server, which has rather meager resources for implementing sophisticated business logic (stored procedures, triggers, views, etc.). Developers are forced to significantly complicate the program code of client-side software, which is extremely undesirable when multiple remote client machines are accessing the same server. With more complex client-side software, the probability of errors is increased, and service becomes more difficult.

The multi-tier architecture of database applications was introduced in order to correct the above defects. A multi-tier database application (Fig. 8.1) consists of:

❏ "Thin" client applications that provide only transmission, presentation, and editing of services, as well as very basic data processing

❏ One or more middle software tiers (an application server), which can function either on a single machine or be distributed in a local network

❏ A database server (Oracle, Sybase, MS SQL, InterBase, etc.) that supports the functioning of data in a database and processes requests

Thus, within this architecture, *"thin" clients* are very simple applications that provide only data transmission services, local caching, presentation services by means of a user interface, editing, and very basic data processing.

Client applications never access a database server directly; they do it through the middleware. The middleware can be a single intermediary layer (in the simplest three-tier model) or a more complex structure.

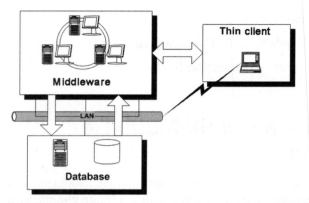

Fig. 8.1. The multi-tier architecture of database applications

Middleware receives requests from clients, processes them according to programmed rules of business logic, converts them to a format convenient for the database server if necessary, and sends them to the server.

Database servers execute requests received and send the results to the application server, which addresses the data to the clients.

A simpler three-tier model contains the following elements:

❏ "Thin" clients   ❏ An application server

❏ A database server

Our discussion here will focus on the three-tier model. In the Delphi development environment, there is a set of tools and components for building client and middleware software. The server section is covered in *Chapter 9, "An Application Server,"* while *Chapter 10, "A Client of a Multi-Tier Distributed Application,"* covers issues of designing client software. An application server interacts with a database server using one of the technologies for accessing data implemented by Delphi (see *Part II, "Data Access Technologies"*). These are ADO, BDE, InterBase Express, and dbExpress. The developer can select the most suitable technology based on the nature of the task at hand and the parameters of the database server.

For an application server to interact with clients, it must be developed on the basis of one of the following standards that support distributed access:

❏ Automation   ❏ MTS

❏ WEB   ❏ SOAP

❏ CORBA

Remote client applications are created using a special set of components collectively called DataSnap. These components contain standard transports (DCOM, HTTP, CORBA, and sockets) and establish a connection between a client application and the application server. Additionally, DataSnap components allow a client to access the functions of the application server through the interface `IAppServer` (see *Chapter 9, "An Application Server"*).

An important role in developing client applications is played by the component that contains client datasets. This also depends on the data access technology, and is examined in *Chapter 10, "A Client of a Multi-Tier Distributed Application."*

Along with the benefits listed above, an intermediary level — an application server — also provides several additional bonuses that can be very useful as far as increased reliability and enhanced performance are concerned.

As client computers are often rather weak machines, the use of sophisticated business logic on the server side helps to considerably speed up the overall system performance. This is not just the work of more powerful hardware, but also thanks to the optimization of executing similar user requests. For example, if the load on the database server is excessive, the application server can execute requests from users on its own (queue these requests or cancel them), without putting an additional load on the database server.

Using an application server enhances your security system, as you can organize user authorization as well as any other security measures without direct access to data.

Additionally, you can easily use protected data communication channels — HTTPS, for instance.

Three-Tier Delphi Applications

Let's take a closer look at the parts of a three-tier distributed Delphi application. As mentioned above, in Delphi, it makes sense to develop both the client part of a three-tier application and application server middleware.

The parts of three-tier applications are developed using DataSnap components, along with a number of other special components that are mainly responsible for client operation. Data is accessed using one of the data access technologies implemented in Delphi (see *Part II, "Data Access Technologies"*).

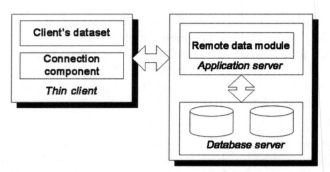

Fig. 8.2. Diagram of a multi-tier distributed application

It makes sense to develop a three-tier application using a set of projects in the development environment rather than just a single project. This is what the Project Manager utility is used for (**View\Project Manager**).

Data is transmitted between the application server and clients by the IAppServer interface provided by the application server. This interface is used by both server-side provider components — TDataSetProvider — and client-side TClientDataSet components.

Let's now examine the parts of a three-tier application in more depth.

Application Servers

An application server contains the bulk of business logic of a distributed application and enables clients to access a database.

From the point of view of the developer, by far the most important part of any application server is its *remote data module*. Let's try to find out why.

First, depending on the implementation, a remote data module contains a ready remote server, which only needs to be registered and have some parameters set. Delphi comes with five types of remote data modules. To create them, use the **Multi-tier**, **WebSnap**, and **WebServices** pages of the Delphi Repository (Fig. 8.3).

❑ *Remote Data Module* — a remote data module that contains the Automation server. It is used for establishing connections via DCOM, HTTP and sockets. For more detail, see *Chapter 9, "An Application Server."*

❑ *Transactional Data Module* — a remote data module that contains a Microsoft Transaction Server (MTS).

❑ *CORBA Data Module* — a remote data module that contains a CORBA server.

❑ *Soap Server Data Module* — a remote data module that contains a SOAP server (Simple Object Access Protocol).

❑ *WebSnap Data Module* — a remote data module that uses web services and a web browser as a server.

Second, a remote data module enables interaction with clients. The module supplies a client application with the methods of the special IAppServer interface or its descendant. The methods used by this interface help to organize the process of transmitting and receiving data packets for a client application.

Third, like a traditional data module (see *Chapter 5*, "*The Architecture of Database Applications*"), a remote data module is a platform for the placement of non-visual data access components and provider components. All connection and transaction components, as well as components that contain datasets placed in a remote data module, provide a connection between the three-tier application and the database server. These can be sets of components for various data access technologies.

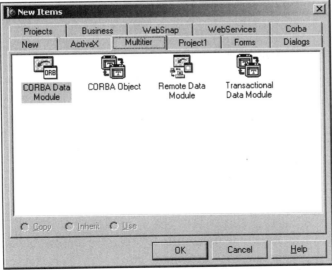

Fig. 8.3. Selecting a remote data module in the Delphi Repository

Besides the remote data module, another integral part of any application server is the TDataSetProvider provider components. Each component that contains a dataset designed to be passed to the client must be associated with a provider component in the remote data module.

To do this, the remote data module must contain the required number of TDataSetProvider components. These components pass data packets to the client application, or more precisely, to the TClientDataSet components. They also provide access to the methods of their own IProviderSupport interface. Using the methods of this interface, you can manage packets of sent data at a low-level.

Usually, the developer does not have to do this. You simply need to know that all components that handle data — both on the client side and on the server side — use this interface. However, if you intend to create your own version of DataSnap, you will find the description of the interface very useful (see *Chapter 9, "An Application Server"*).

Client Applications

A client application in a three-tier model should have only the minimum required set of functions, and delegate the majority of data processing operations to the application server.

Above all, a remote client application must provide a connection to the application server. DataSnap connection components are used:

❏ TDCOMConnection — uses DCOM

❏ TSocketConnection — uses Windows sockets

❏ TWebConnection — uses HTTP

❏ TCORBAConnection — uses a connection within the CORBA architecture

NOTE

The TSOAPConnection component is discussed separately.

DataSnap connection components use the IAppServer interface, which utilizes the server-side provider components and client-side TClientDataSet components for passing data packets.

Data are handled using `TClientDataSet` components that operate in data caching mode.

Data are presented and a user interface is created in a client application by using the standard controls from the **Data Controls** page of the Component palette.

For more information on how to design client applications for multi-tier database applications, refer to *Chapter 10, "A Client of a Multi-Tier Distributed Application."*

DataSnap Remote Access Mechanism

For data packets to be passed between a provider component and a client dataset (Fig. 8.2), a transport link, which provides physical transmission of data, must be established from the client to the server. This can be accomplished by using a variety of transport protocols supported by the operating system. Different types of connections that allow you to configure the communication channel and begin passing and receiving information are contained in several DataSnap components. To create a connection by using a specific transport protocol on the client side, the developer simply needs to place the appropriate component in a form and set a number of properties correctly. This component can interact with the remote data module of the same, which is part of an application server.

Below we'll look at transport protocols for connection components that use DCOM technology, TCP/IP sockets, HTTP, and CORBA.

The *TDCOMConnection* Component

The `TDCOMConnection` component implements data transmission on the basis of the Distributed COM technology, and is used primarily for establishing connections within the local network.

To configure a DCOM connection, you first need to specify the name of the machine where the application server is installed. For `TDCOMConnection` components, it must be a registered Automation server. The name of the computer is specified by the property

```
property ComputerName: string
```

If it is correct, in the list of the property

```
property ServerName: string;
```

you can select one of the servers available in the **Object Inspector**.

When a server is selected, the property

```
property ServerGUID: string;
```

is filled automatically with the global identifier of the registered Automation server.

For a client to connect with the application server successfully, both properties must be given in the required order. Only giving the server name or the server GUID will not guarantee access to the remote COM object.

A connection is opened and closed by the property

```
property Connected: Boolean;
```

or the methods

```
procedure Open;
procedure Close;
```

Data transmission between a client and a server is organized by the IAppServer interface of the TDCOMConnection component:

```
property AppServer: Variant;
```

which can also be accessed using the method

```
function GetServer: IAppServer; override;
```

The property

```
property ObjectBroker: TCustomObjectBroker;
```

lets you use a TSimpleObjectBroker component instance to obtain the list of available servers at run time.

The event handlers for the TDCOMConnection component are listed in Table 8.1.

Table 8.1. The Event Handlers for the TDCOMConnection Component

Declaration	Description
property AfterConnect: TNotifyEvent;	Called after a connection is established.
property AfterDisconnect: TNotifyEvent;	Called after a connection is closed.
property BeforeConnect: TNotifyEvent;	Called before establishing a connection.

continues

Table 8.1 Continued

Declaration	Description
`property BeforeDisconnect: TNotifyEvent;`	Called before closing a connection.

`type TgetUsernameEvent = procedure(Sender: TObject; var Username: string) of object;`
 	
`property OnGetUsername: TGetUsernameEvent;`
	Called immediately prior to displaying the logon dialog for authorization of a remote user. This is achieved if the `LoginPrompt` property is set to `True`. The `Username` parameter can contain the default name of a user, which will then appear in this dialog.

`type TLoginEvent = procedure(Sender:TObject; Username, Password: string) of object;`
 	
`property OnLogin: TLoginEvent;`
	Called after a connection is established if the `LoginPrompt` property is set to `True`. The `Username` and `Password` parameters contain the user name and password entered at authorization.

The *TSocketConnection* Component

The `TSocketConnection` component provides a connection between a client and an application server using TCP/IP sockets. For a connection to open successfully, the server part must be equipped with a socket server (a ScktSrvr.exe application).

For successful connection, the property

```
property Host: String;
```

must contain the name of the server computer. Additionally, the property

```
property Address: String;
```

must contain the IP address of the server.

To open a connection, both these properties must be specified.

The property

```
property Port: Integer;
```

sets the name of the port in use. The default port is 211, but the developer is free to change the port, for example, to allow it to be used by different categories of users, or to create a protected communication channel.

If the name of the computer has been correctly specified in the property list

```
property ServerName: string;
```

the **Object Inspector** will show a list of the available Automation servers. Once you have selected the server, the property

```
property ServerGUID: string;
```

which contains the GUID of the registered server, is set automatically, though it can also be set manually.

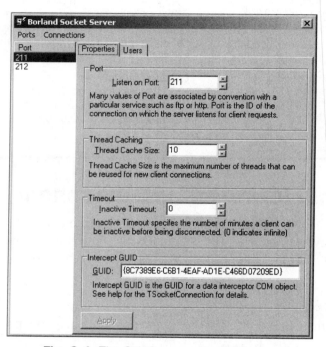

Fig. 8.4. The ScktSrvr.exe Socket Server

The method

```
function GetServerList: OleVariant; virtual;
```

returns a list of registered Automation servers.

Open and close a connection using the property

```
property Connected: Boolean;
```

or one of the corresponding methods:

```
procedure Open;
procedure Close;
```

The channel of a TCP/IP socket can be encrypted using the property

```
property InterceptName: string;
```

which contains the program identifier of the COM object that provides encryption/decryption data services for a channel, and the property

```
property InterceptGUID: string;
```

contains the GUID of this object.

This COM object intercepts data in the channel and processes it according to its own program code. This can be encryption, compression, noise manipulation, etc.

> **NOTE**
>
> The COM object that provides additional processing of data in the channel must be created by the developer. The intercepting object should support the standard IDataIntercept interface.

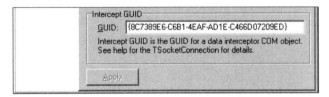

Fig. 8.5. Registering an Interceptor COM Object in a Socket Server

Of course, on the server side there must be a registered COM object that performs the reverse operation. The socket server is used for this (Fig. 8.5). The **Interceptor GUID** string in this page must contain the GUID of the intercepting COM object.

The method

```
function GetInterceptorList: OleVariant; virtual;
```

returns a list of the intercepting objects registered on the server.

The TSocketConnection component provides the IAppServer interface that organizes the process of data transmission between a client and a server:

```
property AppServer: Variant;
```

which can also be gotten by the method

```
function GetServer: IAppServer; override;
```

The property

```
property ObjectBroker: TCustomObjectBroker;
```

lets you use a `TSimpleObjectBroker` instance to obtain the list of the available servers at run time.

The event handlers of the `TSocketConnection` component are identical to the event handlers of the component `TDCOMConnection` (see Table 8.1).

The *TWebConnection* Component

The `TWebConnection` component connects a client to the server based on the HTTP transport. To manage this component, the wininet.dll library must be registered on the client computer. This does not usually require any extra effort, as this file is contained in the Windows system folder if Internet Explorer is installed on the computer.

A server computer needs to have Internet Information Server 4.0 or higher installed, or Netscape Enterprise 3.6 or higher. This software enables the `TWebConnection` component to access the HTTPsrvr.dll dynamic library, which should also be located on the server. For instance, if the HTTPsrvr.dll file is located in the Scripts IIS 4.0 folder on the www.someserver.com web server, then the property

```
property URL: string;
```
should contain the following value:

```
http://someserver.com/scripts/httpsrvr.dll
```

If the URL is correct and the server is properly configured, then the following property list:

```
property ServerName: string;
```
will show the names of all registered application servers in the **Object Inspector**. One of the names must be contained in the `ServerName` property.

Once the server name is set, its GUID automatically appears in the property

```
property ServerGUID: string;
```
The properties

```
property UserName: string;
```
and

```
property Password: string;
```
can, if necessary, contain the user name and password that will be used during authorization.

The property

```
property Proxy: string;
```

contains the name of the proxy server used.

You can include the name of an application in an HTTP message header using the property

```
property Agent: string;
```

A connection is opened and closed using the property

```
property Connected: Boolean;
```

Similar operations are performed by the methods

```
procedure Open;
procedure Close;
```

The IAppServer interface is accessed either through the property

```
property AppServer: Variant;
```

or the method

```
function GetServer: IAppServer; override;
```

The list of available application servers is returned by the method

```
function GetServerList: OleVariant; virtual;
```

The property

```
property ObjectBroker: TCustomObjectBroker;
```

lets you use a TSimpleObjectBroker component instance to obtain the list of available servers at run time.

The event handlers for the TWebConnection component are identical to the event handlers of the TDCOMConnection component (see Table 8.1).

The *TCORBAConnection* Component

The TCORBAConnection component enables a client application to access a CORBA server. Here, you need just set a single property to configure the connection to a server.

```
type TRepositoryId = type string;
property RepositoryId: TRepositoryId;
```

where the names of a server and a remote data module are specified, separated by a slash. For example, the property for the CORBAServer server and the CORBAModule module will have the following value:

```
CORBAServer/CORBAModule
```

Alternately, the address of a server can be presented in IDL (Inteface Definition Language) notation:

```
IDL: CORBAServer/CORBAModule:1.0
```

The property

```
property HostName: string;
```

should contain the name of a server computer or its IP address. If no value has been specified for this property, the TCORBAConnection component connects to the first server found, which has the parameters specified by the RepositoryId property. The name of the CORBA server is contained in the property

```
property ObjectName: string;
```

A connection is opened and closed using the property

```
property Connected: Boolean;
```

Similar operations are executed by the methods

```
procedure Open;
procedure Close;
```

If, for some reason, a connection fails to open, using the following property can prevent the application from hanging up:

```
property Cancelable: Boolean;
```

When this property is set to True, the connection is canceled after waiting for more than one second for a connection to establish. You can also set this event handler:

```
type TCancelEvent = procedure(Sender: TObject; var Cancel: Boolean;
var DialogMessage: string) ofobject;
```

```
property OnCancel: TCancelEvent;
```

which is called prior to canceling a connection.

Once a connection is open either using the property

```
property AppServer: Variant;
```

or the method

```
function GetServer: IAppServer; override;
```

the client has access to the IAppServer interface.

Event handlers for the TCORBAConnection component are inherited (except for the OnCancel method described above) from the ancestor TCustomConnection class. These event handlers are described in Table 8.1.

Additional Components — Connection Brokers

The DataSnap collection includes a set of additional components that are designed to facilitate managing connections between remote clients and application servers. Let's take a look at them.

The *TSimpleObjectBroker* Component

The `TSimpleObjectBroker` component contains a list of servers available to the clients of the multi-tier distributed application. The list is created in the design stage. If necessary (if the server shuts down or overloads, etc.), a connection component of the client application can use one of the extra servers from the `TSimpleObjectBroker` component list directly during runtime.

To enable this function, fill in the list of `TSimpleObjectBroker` component servers and specify a pointer to it in the `ObjectBroker` property of your connection component (see above). Thus, if the connection is reestablished, the server name can be acquired from the `TSimpleObjectBroker` component list.

The list of servers is defined by the property

```
property Servers: TServerCollection;
```

At design time, a list of servers is compiled by a special editor (Fig. 8.6), which is called by pressing the property button in the **Object Inspector** window.

The `Servers` property is a collection of `TServerItem` class objects. This class has several properties which allow you to describe the key parameters of the server.

The property

```
property ComputerName: string;
```

defines the name of the machine on which the application server is working. Additionally, you can set the name of the server to be displayed in the server list:

```
property DisplayName: String;
```

By using the following property, you can make the server record accessible or inaccessible for selection:

```
property Enabled: Boolean;
```

Once an attempt to use a record of this list for connecting has failed, the property

```
property HasFailed: Boolean;
```

is assigned the `True` value, and from this point on, the record is ignored.

The property

```
property Port: Integer;
```

contains the number of the port used for connecting to the server.

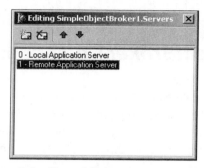

Fig. 8.6. The server list editor of the `TSimpleObjectBroker` component

When the connection is being established, the values of these properties are substituted for relevant properties of the connection component:

```
DCOMConnection.ComputerName :=
TSimpleObjectBroker(DCOMConnection.ObjectBroker).Servers[0].ComputerName;
```

Besides the list of servers, a `TSimpleObjectBroker` component has only a few additional properties and methods.

The method

```
function GetComputerForGUID(GUID: TGUID): string; override;
```

returns the name of the machine where the GUID server that is specified by the parameter is registered.

The method

```
function GetComputerForProgID(const ProgID): string; override;
```

returns the name of the computer where the server with the name specified by the `ProgID` parameter is registered.

The property

```
property LoadBalanced: Boolean;
```

selects a server from the list. If its value is `True`, a server is selected at random; otherwise, the first available server name is suggested.

The *TLocalConnection* Component

The TLocalConnection component is used locally for accessing existing provider components.

The property

```
property Providers[const ProviderName: string]: TCustomProvider;
```

contains pointers to all the provider components that reside in the same data module as a given TLocalConnection component. Items in this list are indexed by the names of provider components.

The total number of provider components in the list is returned by the property

```
property ProviderCount: Integer;
```

In addition, by employing TLocalConnection, you can get access to the IAppServer interface locally. Use the property

```
property AppServer: IAppServer;
```

or the method

```
function GetServer: IAppServer; override;
```

The *TSharedConnection* Component

If the IAppServer interface of a remote data module uses a method that returns a pointer to an analogous interface of another remote data module, then the first module is called the parent module, and the second is called the child module (see *Chapter 9, "An Application Server"*). The TSharedConnection component is used to connect a client application to a child data module of the application server.

The property

```
property ParentConnection: TDispatchConnection;
```

should contain a pointer to the connection component with the parent remote data module of the application server. The name of a child remote data module is specified by the property

```
property ChildName: string;
```

which should contain its name. If the interface of the parent remote data module has been configured correctly, the property list in the **Object Inspector** shows the names of all the child remote data modules.

The `IAppServer` interface of a child remote data module is returned by the property

```
property AppServer: Variant;
```

or the method

```
function GetServer: IAppServer; override;
```

The event handlers for the `TSharedConnection` component are inherited from the `TCustomConnection` ancestor class (see Table 8.1).

The *TConnectionBroker* Component

The `TConnectionBroker` component provides centralized control of the connection between client datasets and the application server. The corresponding `ConnectionBroker` properties of all client datasets must point to a `TConnectionBroker` component instance. Then, to change a connection (for example, to switch from HTTP to TCP/IP sockets), you needn't change the value of the `RemoteServer` property of all the `TClientDataSet` components — simply change the following property:

```
property Connection: TCustomRemoteServer;
```

The `IAppServer` interface is accessed by the property

```
property AppServer: Variant;
```

or the method

```
function GetServer: IAppServer; override;
```

The `TConnectionBroker` event handlers fully correspond to Table 8.1.

Summary

Multi-tier distributed applications provide effective interaction between a large number of remote "thin" clients and database servers with the help of middleware. Among multi-tier applications, the most widely-used model is the three-tier model, where the middleware consists of just one application server.

To create three-tier distributed applications in Delphi, DataSnap components and remote data modules are used. All these tools are implemented for various transport protocols.

Also, three-tier distributed applications use `TDataSetProvider` and `TClientDataSet` components, which contain datasets on the client side.

Chapter 9

An Application Server

Multi-tier distributed applications provide remote clients with high-performance access to databases, since they use intermediary-level, special-purpose software. In the most commonly used schema — the three-tier application — this is the application server, which performs the following functions:

❑ Authorizes users

❑ Receives and transfers requests from users and data packets

❑ Coordinates access of client requests to the database server by balancing the processing load on the server

❑ Can contain a part of the business logic of a distributed application, thereby enabling you to use "thin" clients

Delphi supports developing application servers on the basis of a range of different technologies:

❑ Web   ❑ CORBA

❑ Automation   ❑ SOAP

❑ MTS

This chapter covers the following issues:

❑ Program building blocks of Delphi application servers

❑ The structure of an application server

❑ Types of remote data modules

❑ Creating and configuring remote data modules

❑ The role of provider components in the process of passing data to clients

❑ `IAppServer` interface methods

❑ Registering application servers

Application Server Architecture

Thus, as stated above, an application server is the software of the intermediary tier in a three-tier distributed application (Fig. 9.1). The key feature of such a server is the remote data module. Delphi supports five types of remote data modules (which will be discussed later).

The issues surrounding the use of remote data modules that encapsulate the functionality of automation servers will be discussed in more detail later in this chapter. Other types of remote data modules will be discussed later in the book.

Each remote data module encapsulates the IAppServer interface, whose methods are used to enable clients to access a database server (see *Chapter 8, "DataSnap Technology. Remote Access Mechanisms"*).

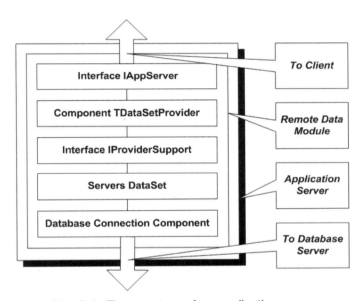

Fig. 9.1. The structure of an application server

In order to exchange data with a database server, a data module is equipped with several data-access components (connection components and components that encapsulate datasets).

To support interaction with clients, the remote data module must have the necessary number of TDataSetProvider components, each of which must be associated with a corresponding dataset.

WARNING

Data exchange between an application server and its clients is provided by the MIDAS.DLL library, which must be registered on the computer where the application server resides.

You can create a new application server by performing the following sequence of rather simple operations:

1. Create a new project (specify its type as a traditional application through **File\New\Application**) and save it.

2. Depending on the technology in use, select the appropriate type of remote data module from the Delphi Repository. Remote data modules are listed on the **Multitier**, **WebSnap**, and **WebServices** pages.

3. Customize the options of the remote data module under creation.

4. Place data access components in the remote data module and customize their settings. The developer can choose one of several available sets of components (see *Part II, "Data Access Technologies"*), depending on the database server used and on the requirements of the application.

5. Place the necessary number of TDataSetProvider components into the remote data module and link them to the components that encapsulate datasets.

6. If necessary, create additional methods for the IAppServer interface descendant that is used by the remote data module. This operation is done by building a new type library.

7. Compile the project and create the executable file for the application server.

8. Register the application server and, if need be, configure the extra software.

The entire remote access mechanism encapsulated in remote data modules and provider components runs automatically, and does not require any additional program code from developers.

The discussion that follows provides you with a simple example of how to implement in practice all the above steps for building application servers.

The *IAppServer* Interface

The IAppServer interface is a core feature of the remote access mechanism that the client application uses to get to application servers. It is through this interface that client datasets communicate with the provider component on the application server. Client datasets get an IAppServer instance from the connection component in the client application (see Fig. 9.1).

When remote data modules are being created, each module will correspond to a newly created interface. This interface will be a descendant of the `IAppServer` interface.

A developer can add a few custom methods to the interface, which, thanks to the capabilities of the remote access mechanism employed by multi-tier applications, will be available to the client application.

In client applications, the property

```
property AppServer: Variant;
```

is available both in remote-connection components and in client datasets.

By default, this interface is stateless. This means that all calls for it are independent and not related to previous calls. This is why the `IAppServer` interface does not have properties that store information on the state between calls.

As a rule, a developer has no need to directly use the methods of this interface, but its significance for multi-tier applications is difficult to overestimate. If you'll be doing detailed work with remote access mechanisms you'll need to use the interface at some point, in any case.

The `IAppServer` interface methods are listed in Table 9.1.

Table 9.1. The Methods of the IAppServer Interface

Declaration	Description
`function AS_ApplyUpdates(const ProviderName: WideString; Delta: OleVariant; MaxErrors: Integer; out ErrorCount: Integer; var OwnerData: OleVariant): OleVariant; safecall;`	Passes updates received from a client dataset to the provider component specified by the `ProviderName` parameter. Changes are stored in the `Delta` parameter. The `MaxErrors` parameter determines the maximum permissible number of errors that can be ignored while saving data before aborting the operation. The actual number of errors is returned by the `ErrorCount` parameter. The `OwnerData` parameter contains additional information exchanged between the client and the server (for example, values that were assigned to event handlers). This function returns the data packet that contains all the records which, for some reason, have not been saved to the database.

continues

Table 9.1 Continued

Declaration	Description
function AS_DataRequest(const ProviderName: WideString; Data: OleVariant): OleVariant; safecall;	Generates the OnDataRequest event for the provider specified in ProviderName.
procedure AS_Execute(const ProviderName: WideString; const CommandText: WideString; var Params: OleVariant; var OwnerData: OleVariant); safecall;	Executes the query or stored procedure defined by the CommandText parameter for the ProviderName provider. Query or stored procedure settings are stored in the Params parameter.
function AS_GetParams(const ProviderName: WideString; var OwnerData: OleVariant): OleVariant; safecall;	Passes the current values of the client dataset's parameters to the ProviderName provider.
function AS_GetProviderNames: OleVariant; safecall;	Returns a list of all remote data module providers that are currently available.
function AS_GetRecords(const ProviderName: WideString, Count: Integer; out RecsOut: Integer; Options: Integer; const CommandText: WideString; var Params: OleVariant; var OwnerData:OleVariant): OleVariant; safecall;	Returns the data packet with records of the server dataset that is linked to the provider component. The CommandText parameter contains the name of the table, the content of the request, or the name of the stored procedure from which records should be fetched. But this works only if the poAllowCommandText option in the Options parameter was activated for the provider. Query or stored procedure parameters are found in the Params parameter. The parameter sets the required number of records, beginning with the current one, if its value is positive. If the value is zero, only metadata are returned; if the value is −1, all records are returned. The RecsOut argument returns the actual number of passed records.
function AS_RowRequest(const ProviderName: WideString; Row: OleVariant; RequestType: Integer; var OwnerData: OleVariant): OleVariant; safecall;	Returns the record of the dataset provided to the ProviderName component and specified in the Row parameter. The RequestType parameter stores the value of the TfetchOptions type.

Most of the interface methods use the `ProviderName` and `OwnerData` parameters. The former specifies the name of the provider component, and the latter contains a set of parameters passed for use in event handlers.

The observant reader has probably noticed that using the `AS_GetRecords` method implies saving information during the course of working with the interface, since this method returns records starting with the current one, even though the `IAppServer` interface has the stateless type. This is why it is recommended that you refresh the client dataset prior to using this method.

The type

```
TFetchOption = (foRecord, foBlobs, foDetails);

TFetchOptions = set of TFetchOption;
```

is used by the `RequestType` parameter of the `AS_RowRequest` method:

❐ `foRecord` returns the field values of the current record.

❐ `foBlobs` returns the values of BLOB fields of the current record.

❐ `foDetails` returns all detail records of the nested datasets for the current record.

Remote Data Modules

Remote data modules are one of the core elements of application servers (see Fig. 9.1) for three-tier distributed applications.

First, remote data modules, depending on their implementation, encapsulate the remote server.

Second, remote data modules encapsulate the `IAppServer` interface, thereby providing the functions of a server and enabling data exchange with remote clients.

Third, they perform the role of a traditional data module, which means that you can use them as containers for various data-access components.

Depending on the technology used, Delphi lets you select any of five available remote data modules.

❐ *Remote Data Module.* The `TRemoteDataModule` class encapsulates the automation server.

❏ *Transactional Data Module.* The TMTSDataModule class is a descendant of the TRemoteDataModule class, and adds MTS functionality to the automation server.

❏ *WebSnap Data Module.* The TWebDataModule class creates an application server that uses Internet technologies.

❏ *Soap Server Data Module.* The TSOAPDataModule class encapsulates a SOAP server.

❏ *CORBA Data Module.* The TCORBADataModule class is a descendant of the TRemoteDataModule class and performs the functions of a CORBA server.

The following sections of this chapter will concentrate on the process of creating an application server on the basis of the TremoteDataModule class. The other data modules (except for CORBA data modules) will be the subjects of in-depth discussions later in the book.

Remote Data Modules for Automation Servers

TremoteDataModule remote data modules are created with the Delphi Repository (through **File\New\Other**). The icon of the TRemoteDataModule class can be found on the **Multi-tier** page. The process of building a new remote data module begins with a dialog box (Fig. 9.2), in which you need to set three options.

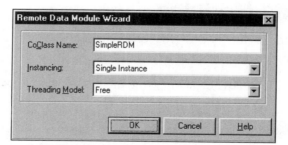

Fig. 9.2. The wizard for creating TRemoteDataModule instances

The **CoClass Name** string must contain the name of the new data module, which will also be used to name the new class built to support the newly created data module.

The **Instancing** list lets you define the method of creating a data module:

❏ **Internal** — the data module only provides for the functioning of an internal automation server.

❑ **Single Instance** — an instance of the remote automation server is created for each client connection in the framework of its own process.

❑ **Multiple Instance** — an instance of the remote automation server is created for each client connection in the framework of one common process.

The **Threading Model** list sets the mechanism for processing client requests:

❑ **Single** — requests from clients are processed in strict order.

❑ **Apartment** — the data module processes one request at a time. Nevertheless, if the DLL creates multiple COM objects to execute queries, then separate threads can be created for these queries, and their processing is carried out in parallel.

❑ **Free** — the data module supports the creation of multiple threads for parallel processing of requests.

❑ **Both** — this pattern is almost identical to the previous one (**Free**), except that all processed requests are returned to the corresponding clients strictly one by one.

❑ **Neutral** — client requests can be passed to data modules using multiple concurrent threads. This pattern is utilized only for the COM+ technology.

When building a new remote data module, a special class — a descendant of the `TRemoteDataModule` class — is created, along with a class factory based on the `TComponentFactory` class.

NOTE

The `TComponentFactory` class is a class factory for Delphi components that encapsulate interfaces. It supports the `IClassFactory` interface.

Let's consider an example of creating the `SimpleRDM` remote data module. Using the Remote Data Module Wizard, specify **Single Instance** as the technique to create your new module, and **Free** as the request processing pattern. Once all the settings are made, press **OK**, and Delphi will automatically generate the source code for your new data module (Listing 9.1).

Listing 9.1. The Source Code for a New Remote Data Module and Its Class Factory

---

```
type
  TSimpleRDM = class(TRemoteDataModule, ISimpleRDM)
  private
```

```
    { Private declarations }
  protected
    class procedure UpdateRegistry(Register: Boolean; const ClassID,
ProgID: string); override;
  public
    { Public declarations }
  end;

implementation

{$R *.DFM}

class procedure TSimpleRDM.UpdateRegistry(Register: Boolean; const
ClassID, ProgID: string);
begin
  if Register then
  begin
    inherited UpdateRegistry(Register, ClassID, ProgID);
    EnableSocketTransport(ClassID);
    EnableWebTransport(ClassID);
  end else
  begin
    DisableSocketTransport(ClassID);
    DisableWebTransport(ClassID);
    inherited UpdateRegistry(Register, ClassID, ProgID);
  end;
end;

initialization
  TComponentFactory.Create(ComServer, TSimpleRDM,
    Class_SimpleRDM, ciMultiInstance, tmApartment);
end.
```

Note that the settings that were initially specified for the new data module are also used in the `initialization` section of the `TComponentFactory` class factory.

NOTE

The `TComponentFactory` class factory is responsible for producing Delphi component instances that support interfaces.

The `UpdateRegistry` class method is created automatically, and used for the registration and invalidation of an automation server. If the `Register` argument is set to `True`, registration is implemented; otherwise, it is canceled.

Since this method is used automatically, the developer should not invoke it manually.

Developing a new data module is always accompanied by creating its interface, a descendant of the `IAppServer` interface. The source code of this interface is stored in the type library of the application server project. The code of the `ISimpleRDM` interface of the `SimpleRDM` remote data module is presented in Listing 9.2. For the sake of convenience, all automatically included comments are removed from the listing.

Listing 9.2. The New Type Library for the Application Server, with the Source Code for the Remote Data Module Interface

```
    LIBID_SimpleAppSrvr: TGUID = '{93577575-0F4F-43B5-9FBE-A5745128D9A4}';

    IID_ISimpleRDM: TGUID = '{E2CBEBCB-1950-4054-B823-62906306E840}';
    CLASS_SimpleRDM: TGUID = '{DB6A6463-5F61-485F-8F23-EC6622091908}';
type

    ISimpleRDM = interface;
    ISimpleRDMDisp = dispinterface;

    SimpleRDM = ISimpleRDM;

    ISimpleRDM = interface(IAppServer)
      ['{E2CBEBCB-1950-4054-B823-62906306E840}']
    end;

    ISimpleRDMDisp = dispinterface
      ['{E2CBEBCB-1950-4054-B823-62906306E840}']
      function  AS_ApplyUpdates(const ProviderName: WideString; Delta:
    OleVariant; MaxErrors: Integer; out ErrorCount: Integer; var
    OwnerData: OleVariant): OleVariant; dispid 20000000;

      function  AS_GetRecords(const ProviderName: WideString; Count:
    Integer; out RecsOut: Integer; Options: Integer; const CommandText:
    WideString; var Params: OleVariant; var OwnerData: OleVariant):
    OleVariant; dispid 20000001;

      function  AS_DataRequest(const ProviderName: WideString; Data:
    OleVariant): OleVariant; dispid 20000002;
```

```
    function  AS_GetProviderNames: OleVariant; dispid 20000003;
    function  AS_GetParams(const ProviderName: WideString; var
OwnerData: OleVariant): OleVariant; dispid 20000004;

    function  AS_RowRequest(const ProviderName: WideString; Row:
OleVariant; RequestType: Integer; var OwnerData: OleVariant):
OleVariant; dispid 20000005;

    procedure AS_Execute(const ProviderName: WideString; const
CommandText: WideString; var Params: OleVariant; var OwnerData:
OleVariant); dispid 20000006;
  end;

  CoSimpleRDM = class
    class function Create: ISimpleRDM;
    class function CreateRemote(const MachineName: string):
ISimpleRDM;
  end;

implementation

uses ComObj;

class function CoSimpleRDM.Create: ISimpleRDM;
begin
  Result := CreateComObject(CLASS_SimpleRDM) as ISimpleRDM;
end;


class function CoSimpleRDM.CreateRemote(const MachineName: string):
ISimpleRDM;
begin
  Result := CreateRemoteComObject(MachineName, CLASS_SimpleRDM) as
ISimpleRDM;
end;

end.
```

Note that the ISimpleRDM interface descends from the IAppServer interface, which we covered earlier.

Since the remote data module implements the automation server, a dispatch interface — ISimpleRDMDisp — is automatically generated to supplement the main dual ISimpleRDM interface. The methods created for this dispatch interface are analogous to the methods of the IAppServer interface.

The `CoSimpleRDM` class provides for the creation of COM objects that support the interface used. Two class methods are automatically created for it.

The first method,

```
class function Create: ISimpleRDM;
```

is used for handling local and in-process servers.

The second method,

```
class function CreateRemote(const MachineName: string): ISimpleRDM;
```

is used in a remote server.

Both methods return a pointer to the `ISimpleRDM` interface.

At this point, if you save the project with the newly created data module and then register it, it will become available in remote client applications as the application server.

However, as long as this application server is empty, it cannot pass any datasets to a client application.

Once created, the remote data module becomes a platform for storing data-access components and provider components (discussed below), which, along with the remote data module, perform the key functions of the application server.

Child Remote Data Modules

A single application server can accommodate several remote data modules, which can perform different operations, deal with different database servers, etc. This does not at all change the process of developing the server part. It simply means that, once you have selected the name of the server in the client-side remote connection component (described in *Chapter 10, "A Client of a Multi-Tier Distributed Application"*), you will have access to the names of all remote data modules that this application server contains.

However, such a scenario means that every module must be supplied with its own individual connection component. If you need to avoid this, you can use the `TSharedConnection` component (see *Chapter 8, "DataSnap Technology. Remote Access Mechanisms"*), but you will have to introduce certain changes to the remote data module interfaces.

To provide access to several data modules in the context of a single remote connection, you have to define one of them as the main data module, while the rest must be specified as child modules.

Let's now consider the implications of this approach on the process of creating remote data modules. Essentially, the idea is very simple. The interface of the main remote data module (which module is to be the main one is up to the developer) must contain properties that point to the interfaces of all other data modules that are to be utilized on the client in the framework of a single connection. Such modules are referred to as child data modules.

If the properties in question (which must have the "read-only" attribute) do exist, then you are able to access all the child modules through the ChildName property of the TSharedConnection component (see *Chapter 8, "DataSnap Technology. Remote Access Mechanisms"*).

For example, if a child data module is named Secondary, the main data module must contain the Secondary property:

```
ISimpleRDM = interface(IAppServer)
    ['{E2CBEBCB-1950-4054-B823-62906306E840}']
    function  Get_Secondary: Secondary; safecall;
    property Secondary: Secondary read Get_Secondary;
  end;
```

The implementation of the Get_Secondary method looks as follows:

```
function TSimpleRDM.Get_Secondary: Secondary;
begin
  Result := FSecondaryFactory.CreateCOMObject(nil) as ISecondary;
end;
```

As you can see, the simplest possible solution is just to return a pointer to the newly created child interface.

A detailed description of the step-by-step development of a child remote data module is provided later in this chapter.

Data Providers

The TDataSetProvider provider component works as a bridge between a dataset of a given application server and a client dataset. This component forms data packets, sending these packets to a client dataset, and receiving datasets that have been changed by the client (Fig. 9.3).

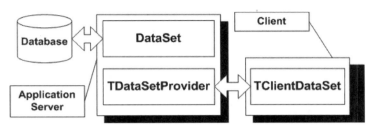

Fig. 9.3. The interaction of a provider component with a client

All necessary operations are performed by this component automatically. The developer just needs to place a TDataSetProvider component inside the remote data module on the server side and establish a link between this component and a dataset of the application server using the following property:

```
property DataSet: TDataSet;
```

Then, provided that the connection options are correctly configured (in the way described earlier), the list of the ProviderName property of the TClientDataSet component, which can be accessed through the **Object Inspector**, will show the names of all provider components of the application server in question. If you connect a client dataset to the provider component, and then open it, the records of the application server dataset specified in the DataSet property of the TDataSetProvider provider component will be passed to the client dataset.

The TDataSetProvider component also contains properties that facilitate data exchange.

The property

```
property ResolveToDataSet: Boolean;
```

coordinates the process of data transmission from a client to the database server. If this property is set to True, the dataset of the application server that is specified in the DataSet property is affected by all the updates received from the client (which means that all these updates are applied to it — its status changes, the appropriate event handlers are invoked, etc.). Otherwise, the updates are passed directly to the database server. If you do not want the application server to process the changes made by the client, set the ResolveToDataSet property to False, which will noticeably accelerate the performance of your application.

The property

```
property Constraints: Boolean;
```

manages the process of passing the constraints imposed on the server dataset to the client dataset. If its value is `True`, the constraints are applied to the client dataset.

The property

```
property Exported: Boolean;
```

enables the client dataset to use the `IAppServer` interface's data. This is done by setting this property to `True`.

The parameters of a provider component are set via the following property:

```
type
   TProviderOption = (poFetchBlobsOnDemand, poFetchDetailsOnDemand,
poIncFieldProps, poCascadeDeletes, poCascadeUpdates, poReadOnly,
poAllowMultiRecordUpdates, poDisableInserts, poDisableEdits,
poDisableDeletes, poNoReset, poAutoRefresh, poPropogateChanges,
poAllowCommandText, poRetainServerOrder);
   TProviderOptions = set of TProviderOption;
```

The `Options` parameter set is assigned by giving it a `True` value.

```
property Options: TProviderOptions;
```

`poFetchBlobsOnDemand` enables the passing of **BLOB** field values to a client dataset. By default, this feature is disabled in order to accelerate performance.

`poFetchDetailsOnDemand` enables the passing of records from a detail dataset that relate to the master dataset in a one-to-many relationship to a client dataset. By default, this option is disabled in order to speed up performance.

`poIncFieldProps` enables the passing of several field properties to the client dataset, specifically: `Alignment`, `DisplayLabel`, `DisplayWidth`, `Visible`, `DisplayFormat`, `EditFormat`, `MaxValue`, `MinValue`, `Currency`, `EditMask`, and `DisplayValues`.

`poCascadeDeletes` enables the automatic removal of detail records in a one-to-many relationship on the server side if the master records of the client dataset have been deleted.

`poCascadeUpdates` enables the automatic updating of detail records in a one-to-many relationship on the server side if the master records of the client dataset have been modified.

`poReadOnly` activates a read-only mode for the server dataset.

`poAllowMultiRecordUpdates` enables concurrent updates for multiple individual records. Otherwise, updates are made consecutively, one by one.

poDisableInserts prevents the client from inserting new records into the server dataset.

poDisableEdits forbids the client from introducing changes to the server dataset.

poDisableDeletes forbids the client from deleting records from the server dataset.

poNoReset disables the updating of records in the server dataset before these records are passed to the client (prior to calling the AS_GetRecords method of the IAppServer interface).

poAutoRefresh enables automatic updating of records in the client dataset. By default, this option is disabled in order to speed up work.

poPropogateChanges — once changes made to the BeforeUpdateRecord and AfterUpdateRecord event handlers are fixed in the server dataset, they are passed to a client. When this feature is activated, it allows you to fully control the process of updating records on the server.

poAllowCommandText lets you modify the text of an SQL query or the names of stored procedures or tables in the appropriate dataset component of the application server.

poRetainServerOrder forbids a client from changing the record sorting order. Disabling this option may result in errors in datasets, or more specifically, in the appearance of duplicate records.

The event handlers for the TDataSetProvider component are listed in Table 9.2.

Table 9.2. The Event Handlers for the TDataSetProvider Component

Declaration	Description
Property AfterApplyUpdates: TRemoteEvent;	Called after updates passed from a client are saved to the server dataset
Property AfterExecute: TRemoteEvent;	Called after an SQL query or stored procedure is executed on the server
Property AfterGetParams: TRemoteEvent;	Called after a provider component forms a set of server dataset parameters to be passed to a client
property AfterGetRecords: TRemoteEvent;	Called after the provider component builds a data packet for passing a server dataset to a client
property AfterRowRequest: TRemoteEvent;	Called after the current record in the client dataset is refreshed by the provider component

continues

Table 9.2 Continued

Declaration	Description
`property AfterUpdateRecord: TAfterUpdateRecordEvent;`	Called immediately after an individual record in the server dataset is updated
`property BeforeApplyUpdates: TRemoteEvent;`	Called before saving updates passed by a client to the server dataset
`property BeforeExecute: TRemoteEvent;`	Called prior to executing an SQL query or a stored procedure on the server
`property BeforeGetParams: TRemoteEvent;`	Called before the provider component compiles a set of parameters for the server dataset to pass them to a client
`property BeforeGetRecords: TRemoteEvent;`	Called before the provider component builds a data packet for passing a server dataset to a client
`property BeforeRowRequest: TRemoteEvent;`	Called before the current record in the client dataset is refreshed by the provider component
`property BeforeUpdateRecord: TBeforeUpdateRecordEvent;`	Called immediately before an individual record in the server dataset is updated
`property OnDataRequest: TDataRequestEvent;`	Called when a client request for data is being processed
`property OnGetData: TProviderDataEvent;`	Called in the interim between receiving queried data from a server and passing them to a client
`property OnGetDataSetProperties: TGetDSProps;`	Called when a set of properties is being created for a server dataset in order to subsequently pass them to a client
`property OnGetTableName: TGetTableNameEvent;`	Called when the provider component receives the name of a table that needs updating
`property OnUpdateData: TProviderDataEvent;`	Called when changes are saved to a server dataset
`property OnUpdateError: TResolverErrorEvent;`	Called when an error occurs while updates are being applied to a server dataset

The *IProviderSupport* Interface

In order to enable data exchange with a dataset located on a server, the provider component uses the `IProviderSupport` interface, which is a necessary feature of every component that descends from the `TDataSet` class. The data access technology used determines the technique that is employed by each component that encapsulates a dataset in order to implement the `IProviderSupport` interface's methods.

The developer may need the methods of this interface when he or she faces the task of designing custom components that encapsulate datasets and descend from the `TDataSet` class.

Registering Application Servers

For a client to "see" an application server, this server must be registered on the computer where it resides. The process of registration itself can vary, depending on the technology used. Later in the book, you will learn how to register MTS, Web, and SOAP servers.

Here we will dwell on the subject of registering only one type of server — automation servers that use `TRemoteDataModule` remote data modules — which is a surprisingly easy operation.

For executable files, you need just launch the server with the `/regserver` key, or simply launch the executable file itself.

In the development environment, the `/regserver` key can be stored in the dialog box of the **Run\Parameters** command.

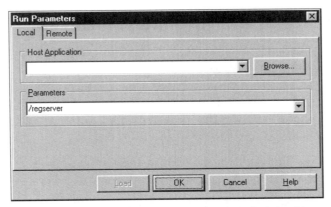

Fig. 9.4. The dialog box for setting an application's launching options

If you choose to cancel a registration, use the `/unregserver` key, but note that you can do this only via the command line.

Dynamic libraries are registered with the `/regsvr32` key.

Creating a Sample Application Server

By way of example, let's discuss developing a simple application server based on TRemoteDataModule. To start, create a new project and save it under the SimpleAppSrvr name. This project is a part of the SimpleRemote project group, to which a client application will subsequently be added.

Table 9.3. Files of the SimpleAppSrvr Project

File	Description
uSimpleAppSrvr.pas	The standard project file
SimpleAppSrvr_TLB.pas	The type library. This contains the declarations of all inter-faces used in a given project
uSimpleRDM.pas	The file of the SimpleRDM remote data module
uSecondary.pas	The file of the Secondary child remote data module

> **NOTE**
>
> Designing a client for the SimpleAppSrvr application server is covered in *Chapter 10,
> "A Client of a Multi-Tier Distributed Application."*

The Main Form of the Application Server

When you run your application server for the first time, you need to customize the ADO connection, which is used to access a data source in the data modules. Specify the real path to the data source in the fmMain main form of the application server (the uSimpleAppSrvr.pas file) by pressing the button of the standard dialog box used to choose files. The selected file will be displayed in the edDataPath single-line editor.

From this point on, this path will be used in the BeforeConnect event handlers of the remote data modules' TADOConnection components to customize connections.

The path to the database is stored in the SimpleApp.ini file.

The Main Remote Data Module

Now, using the Delphi Repository, add a new remote data module to your project (see Fig. 8.3). When the appropriate dialog box is displayed (see Fig. 9.2), specify the name for the module — say, `SimpleRDM` — together with its options, which include:

❑ **Single Instance**, which is the technique for creating individual data modules for each client

❑ **Free**, which is the approach to processing requests (described earlier)

The `UpdateRegistry` class method is created automatically for the data module in order to provide for registration/invalidation of an automation server (see Listing 9.1).

Created at the same time as the remote data module is the new type library, which contains the dual `ISimpleRDM` interface and the `ISimpleRDMDisp` dispatch interface (see Listing 9.2).

NOTE

Every newly created interface is automatically assigned a unique GUID.

Place the components for accessing the **...\Program Files\Common Files\ Borland Shared\Data\dbdemos.mdb** Microsoft Access database demo into the `SimpleRDM` module. We will access data using an OLE DB provider. This is the `TADOConnection` component, which implements the connection, and three `TADOTable` table components, which encapsulate the datasets of the Orders, Customer, and Employee tables.

Prior to opening the connection, the following event handler is called:

```
procedure TSimpleRDM.conMastAppBeforeConnect(Sender: TObject);
begin
  if fmMain.edDataPath.Text <> ''
    then conMastApp.ConnectionString := 'Provider =
Microsoft.Jet.OLEDB.4.0;Persist Security Info=False;Data Source=' +
fmMain.edDataPath.Text
    else Abort;
end;
```

which is used for customizing the `ConnectionString` property.

The `LoginPrompt = False` property disables the display of the logon dialog box when the connection is being opened.

Each table component is linked to the `TDataSetProvider` component. The `ResolveToDataSet = False` property of the provider component prevents the application of updates from a client to the dataset of the connected component. Instead, the updates are saved directly to the database. This feature speeds up the overall performance of the application.

The Child Remote Data Module

In addition to the main data module, let's build a child data module named Secondary. This child module can be linked to the main one by supplying the ISimpleRDM interface with an extra method that returns a pointer to the interface of the child data module. In this example, this is the Get_Secondary method.

This method is created using the type library of the server (Fig. 9.5).

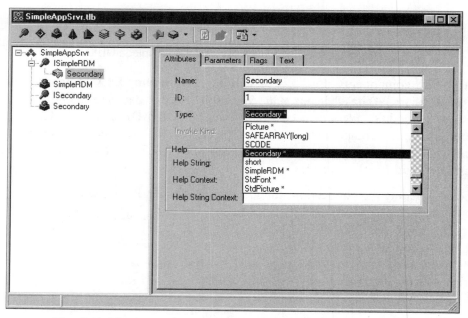

Fig. 9.5. The type library of the SimpleAppSrvr application server

Select the ISimpleRDM interface from the tree in the left part of the window, and create a new read-only property for this interface with the name Secondary. This operation is accompanied by the creation of a method that allows you to read the value of this property. Name this method Get_Secondary. This method must return the Secondary type, set using the **Type** list on the **Attributes** page in the right panel of the type library window.

As soon as the source code of the type library is updated (via the **Refresh Implementation** button), a description of the new property and method of the ISimpleRDM interface appear in the SimpleAppSrvr_TLB.PAS file. Now the declaration of the ISimpleRDM interface looks as follows:

```
ISimpleRDM = interface(IAppServer)
   ['{E2CBEBCB-1950-4054-B823-62906306E840}']
   function Get_Secondary: Secondary; safecall;
   property Secondary: Secondary read Get_Secondary;
end;
```

At the same time, the Get_Secondary method is added to the declaration of the SimpleRDM remote data module included in the uSimpleRDM.pas file. The source code of this method should look like this:

```
function TSimpleRDM.Get_Secondary: Secondary;
begin
  Result := FSecondaryFactory.CreateCOMObject(nil) as ISecondary;
end;
```

As a result, the Secondary data module is now a child module of the SimpleRDM module.

The Secondary module also contains components for accessing a Microsoft Access database. The dbdemos.mdb database, which is used in this example, comes with Delphi. The connection is provided by the TADOConnection component, which is customized using the TSecondary.conMastAppBeforeConnect event handler.

Two TADOTable table components encapsulate the Vendors and Parts tables of the dbdemos.mdb database, respectively. In addition, a one-to-many relationship is established for these table components. The MasterSource property of the tblParts component points to the dsVendors component (the TDataSource class), which is linked to the tblVendors component. The MasterFields and IndexFieldNames properties of the tblParts component contain the name of the VendorNo field that is shared by these two tables.

The one-to-many relationship specified for these two tables will help demonstrate how to use nested datasets in the sample client application (see *Chapter 10, "A Client of a Multi-Tier Distributed Application"*).

Registering the Sample Application Server

Now that your application server is ready to work, you just need to perform the final step — registering. Just run the executable file of the project on the machine on which you mean to place this application server.

Once your application server is registered, it can be accessed from all client applications that have their DataSnap connection component tuned to the computer on which the application server resides.

Summary

An application server is the software of the intermediary tier for three-tier distributed applications. This server enables remote clients to connect to a database server, and implements the bulk of the business logic of a distributed application.

In Delphi, application servers are developed on the basis of remote data modules, which in turn can be created by utilizing various data-access technologies. Remote data modules implement the `IAppServer` interface. Direct access to data is obtained through `TDataSetProvider` components via their `IProviderSupport` interface.

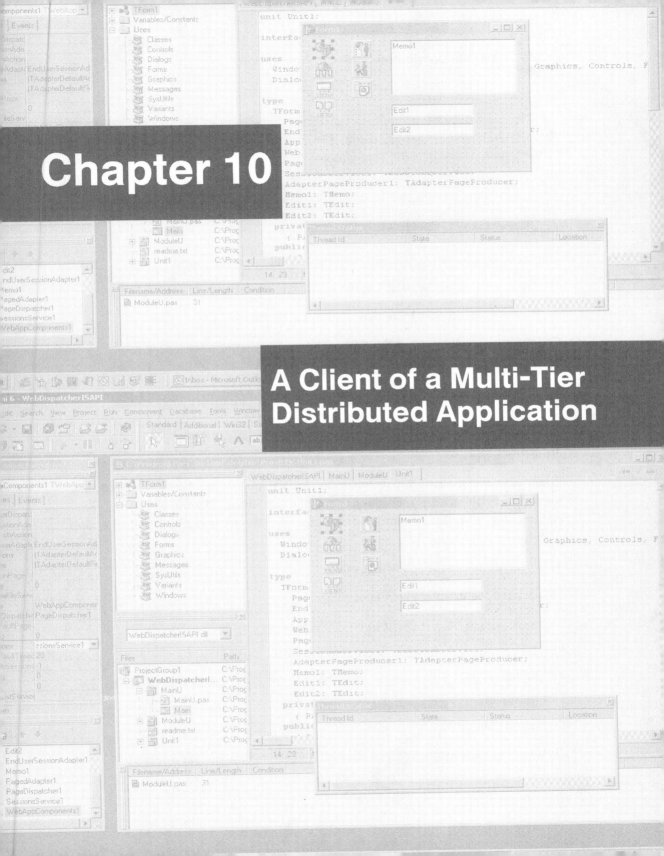

Chapter 10

A Client of a Multi-Tier Distributed Application

C lient software in multi-tier distributed applications has special features of architecture that are dictated by its role, given that the principal part of business logic and data processing logic are centralized on application servers (see *Chapter 9, "An Application Server"*). This schema allows for more efficient processing of requests from multiple remote clients and also simplifies the servicing of client software. Clients that perform only the minimum set of operations are referred to as "thin" clients.

Clients of multi-tier applications perform the following functions:

❏ Connecting to application servers, passing and receiving data

❏ Presentation services by means of user interfaces

❏ Performing elementary editing operations

❏ Caching data locally

Delphi enables developers to create clients for multi-tier applications using DataSnap components (see *Chapter 8, "The DataSnap Technology. Remote Access Mechanisms"*) and the TClientDataSet component, whose role is difficult to overestimate.

When developing client applications, besides the new components, standard data display components are used, along with the traditional pattern of linking visual components with datasets through TDataSource (see *Chapter 5, "The Architecture of Database Applications"*).

This chapter covers the following issues:

❏ The architecture of a client application

❏ Connecting a remote client to an application server

❏ The TClientDataSet component and local data caching

❏ The fundamental operations performed by client datasets that relate to data processing

❏ Nested datasets

❏ Handling local errors in client datasets and errors in application servers

Client Application Architecture

A client application is structurally similar to the conventional database application discussed in *Chapter 5, "The Architecture of Database Applications."*

The connection between a client and an application server is implemented by specially designed `DataSnap` components. Depending on the required transport technology, a developer can utilize the following components:

- `TDCOMConnection` — DCOM

- `TSocketConnection` — TCP/IP sockets

- `TWEBConnection` — Web

- `TCORBAConnection` — CORBA

These components interact with a remote data module contained in a server by calling the methods of the `IAppServer` interface.

Additionally, in a client application, a developer can use additional methods for the interface of a remote data module derived from the `IAppServer` interface. For more detail on these components, and the techniques for setting them up to access a server, refer to *Chapter 9, "An Application Server."*

> **NOTE**
>
> The connection to an application server is enabled using the MIDAS.DLL dynamic library, which must be registered on the client machine.

Like a conventional database application, a client of a multi-tier distributed application must include the components that contain datasets and are linked to the corresponding data controls through `TDataSource` components.

Obviously, a server dataset should be cached locally by the client application. Also, the mechanism used for this purpose should provide high-performance caching of comparatively small portions of information, which considerably reduces the network traffic between a client and the application server.

Caching and editing data in client datasets is done by the special `TClientDataSet` component, which has the `TDataSet` class as its distant ancestor. In addition to the methods inherited from its ancestors, the `TClientDataSet` class contains a number of extra functions that simplify data management.

NOTE

Similar to ordinary database applications, "thin" clients use data modules as containers for non-visual data access components.

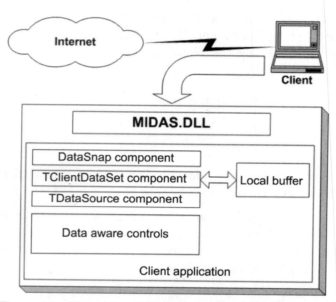

Fig. 10.1. The architecture of the client part of a multi-tier distributed application

To obtain a server dataset, the `TClientDataSet` component interacts with the `TDataSetProvider` component using the methods of the `IProviderSupport` interface (see *Chapter 9*, "*An Application Server*").

Essentially, all the unique functions of a client application are concentrated in the `TClientDataSet` component, which will be the subject of further discussion in this chapter. Otherwise, a client application is not much different from a conventional database application, and can be developed using the standard methods.

Client Datasets

The Delphi Component palette includes a collection of components that contain a client dataset. At the same time, the process of designing a real-world remote client application involves using the `TClientDataSet` component. This point needs to be further clarified. Apart from the `TClientDataSet` component that resides in the **Data Access** page, the Component Palette provides three more components:

❏ The TSQLClientDataSet component is designed for the dbExpress data access technology and is essentially the only full-fledged tool for handling datasets in this technology

❏ The TBDEClientDataSet component is used for developing BDE applications

❏ The TIBClientDataSet component is used by the InterBase Express data access technology

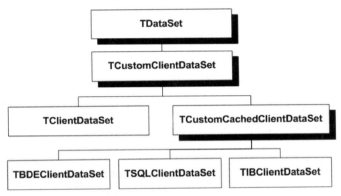

Fig. 10.2. Hierarchy of client dataset classes

All the listed components descend from a common ancestor, the TCustomClientDataSet class (Fig. 10.2), and provide local data caching and interaction with a server dataset by means of the IProviderSupport interface.

The fundamental difference between the TClientDataSet component and other client components lies in the fact that the former is intended for dealing with an *external* provider component. This means that it can interact with a remote data provider.

The other components listed above contain a *native* data provider, thus implementing a high-performance mechanism for local data caching within the particular data-access technology. Using native providers is made possible by the general ancestor class TCustomCachedDataSet.

It has the protected property

```
property Provider: TDataSetProvider;
```

The connection to a data source is implemented not by the RemoteServer property (which will be discussed later as applied to the TClientDataSet component), but by the standard tools of the corresponding data-access technology.

Thus, only the TClientDataSet component can be used for handling remote data (i.e., data which is external in relation to the client), as it can communicate with remote data providers.

The *TClientDataSet* Component

The TClientDataSet component is used by a client of a multi-tier distributed application. This component contains a dataset passed from a remote data source by a provider component. TClientDataSet provides for the following key functions:

❑ Receiving data from a remote server and passing the updates made by a client to this server using a provider component

❑ Presenting datasets using local caching, and supporting the fundamental operations inherited from the TDataSet class

❑ Joining records of a dataset using the aggregate functions for summing data

❑ Saving datasets locally as files, and subsequently restoring them from these files

❑ Converting a dataset to XML format

The TClientDataSet component is a descendant of the TDataSet class, and so the TClientDataSet has the same set of functions as traditional dataset components. The main difference is that it accesses a data source only through a remote data provider. This means that saving and updating datasets is performed locally, without connecting to a data source.

For example, executing the Post method will result only in the local caching of the current record. All updates are easily manageable and are passed to the server only when it is necessary.

Like regular components, TClientDataSet can work in tandem with data controls. The TDataSource component is required for this.

Let's examine the key functions provided by the TClientDataSet component.

Getting Data from a Provider Component

The TClientDataSet component accesses remote data using a DataSnap connection component (see *Chapter 8, "The DataSnap Technology. Remote Access Mechanisms"*). Depending on the data-access technology used, the component could be TDCOMConnection, TSocketConnection, TWebConnection, or TcorbaConnection.

The `TClientDataSet` component connects to a connection component using the property

```
property RemoteServer: TCustomRemoteServer;
```

When a connection is properly configured, the pointer to the `IAppServer` interface, which is indicated in the property

```
property AppServer: IAppServer;
```

coincides with the value of the property

```
property ClientDataSet.RemoteServer.AppServer;
```

Once the connection is set, in the property

```
property ProviderName: string;
```

you can select one of the provider components available on the application server specified in the connection component.

If the provider is correct and properly connected, the read-only property

```
property HasAppServer: Boolean;
```

is automatically set to `True`.

Now the component is ready to receive data. As soon as you call the method

```
procedure Open;
```

or the property

```
property Active: Boolean;
```

the first data packet is passed to the component by the provider.

The size of the packet is determined by the property

```
property PacketRecords: Integer;
```

which specifies the number of records to be passed in one packet. If the property is set to -1 (the default value), then all the records of a dataset are passed. If the value is 0, the client receives just the relevant metadata.

If the connection between the client and server is slow, the number of records per packet can be reduced, but it's best if you do it in such a way that when you use a `TDBGrid` component, the records received as a single packet take up the whole work area of this component.

A developer can manage the process of passing the next packet using the method

```
function GetNextPacket: Integer;
```

For example, this can be done as follows:

```
procedure TDataModule1.ClientDataSetAfterScroll(DataSet: TDataSet);
begin
  if ClientDataSet.EOF then ClientDataSet.GetNextPacket;
end;
```

The property

```
property FetchOnDemand: Boolean;
```

should have the `False` value. If its value is `True`, the component is able to receive new packets on demand, for example if you need to scroll records within a `TDBGrid` component.

Before and after getting a new packet, the corresponding event handlers execute

```
type
  TRemoteEvent = procedure(Sender: TObject; var OwnerData: OleVariant)
of object; property BeforeGetRecords: TRemoteEvent;

property AfterGetRecords: TRemoteEvent;
```

The content of the current packet can be accessed through the property

```
property Data: OleVariant;
```

All the data in it are stored in transport format, ready to be sent. Note that this property can be used not only for reading, but for writing as well, forming a packet to pass to a provider:

```
var  OwnerData: OleVariant;
     MaxErrors, ErrorCount: Integer;
...
MaxErrors := 0;
  ResultDataSet.Data := SourceDataSet.AppServer.AS_ApplyUpdates('',
  SourceDataSet.Delta, MaxErrors, ErrorCount, OwnerData);

...
```

The `AS_ApplyUpdates` method passes the data contained in the `Delta` cache to the provider, and returns the records that failed to be saved. See Table 9.1 for more details on the `AS_ApplyUpdates` method.

The size of the `Data` cache in bytes is returned by the property

```
property DataSize: Integer;
```

Caching and Editing Data

Every new packet received from a provider is locally cached in the memory. Similarly, with the Post method, you save all changes locally without passing them to the server. The cache where the updates are stored can be accessed through the property

```
property Delta: OleVariant;
```

To send updates to the server, use the method

```
function ApplyUpdates(MaxErrors: Integer); Integer; virtual;
```

where the MaxErrors argument sets the number of errors that are ignored when data are saved on the server. If the value of the argument is –1, saving on the server is canceled with the first error. The method returns the number of saved records.

As soon as the ApplyUpdates method executes, all the records that have not been saved are passed back to the client local Delta cache.

If the datasets in your client application are not subject to frequent changes, you can link the operation of saving updates on the server with the AfterPost event handler:

```
procedure TForm1.ClientDataSetAfterPost(DataSet: TDataSet);
begin
 ClientDataSet.ApplyUpdates(-1);
end;
```

The read-only property

```
property ChangeCount: Integer;
```

returns the total number of changes saved to the Delta cache.

You can clear the cache from all updates via the method

```
procedure CancelUpdates;
```

Once the method is called, the ChangeCount property assumes a value of 0.

Before and after updates on the server dataset, the corresponding event handlers are called

```
property BeforeApplyUpdates: TRemoteEvent;
```

and

```
property AfterApplyUpdates: TRemoteEvent;
```

In spite of multiple changes made locally, you can restore the record to its original form. The method

```
procedure RefreshRecord;
```

obtains the initial version of the current record stored on the server. Here (like in all other cases when the component asks for the current record to be refreshed) the following event handlers are called:

```
property BeforeRowRequest: TRemoteEvent;
```

and

```
property AfterRowRequest: TRemoteEvent;
```

But what if you need to restore the deleted record? You cannot do this with a traditional dataset after it has been saved. However, the TClientDataSet component has the method

```
function UndoLastChange(FollowChange: Boolean): Boolean;
```

which restores a dataset to the form it had prior to the last edit, insert, or delete operation. If the FollowChange argument is set to True, the dataset cursor is positioned on the restored record.

The state of the current record can be learned via the method

```
function UpdateStatus: TUpdateStatus; override;
```

which returns a value of the type

```
TUpdateStatus = (usUnmodified, usModified, usInserted, usDeleted);
```

which indicates the state of the current record:

❑ usUnmodified — the record remains unmodified.

❑ usModified — the record was modified.

❑ usInserted — the record was inserted.

❑ usDeleted — the record was deleted.

For example, while a dataset is being closed, you can run the check

```
if ClientDataSet.UpdateStatus = usModified
  then ShowMessage('Record was changed');
```

Also, you can control the visibility of the records in a dataset, depending on their type. The property

```
property StatusFilter: TUpdateStatusSet;
```

defines the type of records to be displayed. For instance:

```
ClientDataSet.StatusFilter := usDeleted;
```

will show only the deleted records of the dataset (here, updates are not saved on the server).

Managing Queries

The `TClientDataSet` component not only allows for effective dataset management, it can influence the performance of the server component to which it is linked via a provider.

The property

```
property CommandText: string;
```

contains the text of an SQL query — the name of a stored procedure or table, depending on the type of the server component.

By modifying the value of this property in the client, you can, for example, change the SQL query on the server. But this is possible only if the `Options` property of the appropriate `TDataSetProvider` component is set to the value

```
PoAllowCommandText := True;
```

A new value of the `CommandText` property is passed to the server only after the client dataset is open, or after running the method

```
procedure Execute; virtual;
```

You can set parameters of queries and stored procedures and save these parameters in the property

```
property Params: TParams;
```

Input parameters are set before running a query, while output parameters are used for presenting the results returned from a server.

Note that when you run a query or a stored procedure, the order in which the parameters are arranged may change. Therefore, it is best to call parameters by their names. For example:

```
Edit1.Text := ClientDataSet.Params.ParamByName('OutputParam').AsString;
```

The current values of the parameters of a server dataset component are returned by the method

```
procedure FetchParams;
```

Before and after getting parameters from a provider, a client dataset calls the event handlers:

```
property BeforeGetParams: TRemoteEvent;
```

and

```
property AfterGetParams: TRemoteEvent;
```

Using Indexes

Generally, using indexes is the prerogative of database servers. Of all Delphi components, only table components support indexing to any extent. Clearly, a remote connection does not allow for the efficient management of dataset indexes on a server. That's why the `TClientDataSet` component allows developers to create and utilize local indexes.

Correctly created and utilized local indexes can significantly speed up operations with a dataset. At the same time, they cannot be saved along with the dataset locally, and must be rebuilt every time the dataset is open or refreshed from the server.

To create a local index, use the method

```
procedure AddIndex(const Name, Fields: string; Options: TIndexOptions;
const DescFields: string = ''; const CaseInsFields: string = '';
const GroupingLevel: Integer = 0 );
```

The `Name` parameter defines the name of a new index. The `Fields` parameter must contain the names of the fields which you mean to include in the index. The names of fields must be delimited by semicolons. The `Options` parameter lets you set the type of your new index:

```
TIndexOption = (ixPrimary, ixUnique, ixDescending, ixCaseInsensitive,
ixExpression, ixNonMaintained);

   TIndexOptions = set of TIndexOption;
```

where:

- [ ] `ixPrimary` — the primary index.

- [ ] `ixUnique` — the index keys are unique.

- [ ] `ixDescending` — the index sorts records in descending order.

- [ ] `ixCaseInsensitive` — the index uses case-insensitive sorting.

- [ ] `ixExpression` — the index uses an expression (for dBASE indexes).

- [ ] `ixNonMaintained` — the index is not updated when the table is opened.

You are also able to specify that the fields be sorted in descending order. These fields, delimited by semicolons, should be listed in the `DescFields` parameter. In a similar way, the `CaseInsFields` parameter allows you to indicate the fields to which case-insensitive sorting should be applied.

The `DescFields` and `CaseInsFields` parameters are used instead of the `Options` parameter.

Finally, the `GroupingLevel` parameter sets the grouping level for the fields of the index. For more information on this parameter, refer to the *"Aggregates"* section in this chapter.

The fundamental properties of the component that allow for managing indexes coincide with the analogous table component properties (*Chapter 5, "The Architecture of Database Applications,"* covers this issue in more depth). So we will only briefly list them here:

This component lets a developer manage indexes. A newly created index is applied to the dataset either by the property

```
property IndexName: String;
```

which must indicate the name of the index, or through the property

```
property IndexFieldNames: String;
```

where you can specify a random combination of the names of the indexed fields in a table. The field names are separated by semicolons. The `IndexName` and `IndexFieldNames` properties must not be used simultaneously.

The number of fields used in the current index of a table component is returned by the property

```
property IndexFieldCount: Integer;
```

And the property

```
property IndexFields: [Index: Integer]: TField;
```

is an indexed list of the fields that are included in the current index.

The parameters of the existing indexes can be accessed through the property

```
property IndexDefs: TIndexDefs;
```

The `TIndexDefs` class is also examined in *Chapter 5, "The Architecture of Database Applications."*

Once a new index is created and activated, the records in the dataset are rearranged according to the values of the indexed fields.

A local index is deleted by the method

```
procedure DeleteIndex(const Name: string);
```

As soon as the current index is deleted or canceled (by setting the `IndexName` property to `0`), the records in the dataset are automatically put back in their original order, which corresponds to the order of datasets on the server.

The names of all available indexes of a dataset can be listed via the method

```
procedure GetIndexNames(List: TStrings);
```

For instance:

```
Memo1.Lines.Clear;
ClientDataSet.GetIndexNames(Memo1.Lines);
```

Saving Datasets to Files

A client application can take advantage of another very convenient feature of the `TClientDataSet` component. Imagine that the connection between the client and the server has a low capacity and also tends to break off frequently. What should a user do if he or she has made a lot of changes and cannot save them to the server?

In such a case, it is possible to save the dataset to a file on the local disk and, as soon as possible, load the changes from this file and pass them to the server.

Saving data (actually the `Data` cache) to a file is implemented by the method

```
procedure SaveToFile(const FileName: string = ''; Format:
TDataPacketFormat=dfBinary);
```

Notice that if the `FileName` parameter is empty, the name of the file is returned by the property

```
property FileName: string;
```

Additionally, you can save data to a stream:

```
procedure SaveToStream(Stream: TStream; Format: TDataPacketFormat=dfBinary);
```

The format in which the data will be stored is defined by the `Format` parameter:

```
type TDataPacketFormat = (dfBinary, dfXML, dfXMLUTF8);
```

where:

❑ `dfBinary` — a binary format

❑ `dfXML` — an XML format

❑ `dfXMLUTF8` — an XML format coded in UTF8

Loading data from files, correspondingly, is performed by the methods:

```
procedure LoadFromFile(const FileName: string = '');
```

and

```
procedure LoadFromStream(Stream: TStream);
```

Once it is loaded, the dataset is ready to work:

```
if LoadFileDialog.Execute then
begin
 ClientDataSet.LoadFromFile(LoadFileDialog.FileName);
 ClientDataSet.Open;
end;
```

Working with BLOB Data

If a server dataset contains large fields (e.g., images), then passing the data through low-speed communication channels can take a lot of time, which undoubtedly impairs the performance of the application. The simplest solution to this problem is to send BLOB data to clients only when they really need it, i.e., only on demand.

The `TClientDataSet` component allows you to control the process of fetching BLOB fields using the property

```
property FetchOnDemand: Boolean;
```

By default, this is `True`, which means that the client dataset "pulls" BLOB data automatically when requires it. This means that the application will stop and receive data again every time data are viewed, scrolled, etc. If the property is set to `False`, the client needs to call the following method explicitly:

```
procedure FetchBlobs;
```

Note, however, that this operation is possible only if the `Options` property of the `TDataSetProvider` component is set to the `True` value:

```
PoFetchBlobsOnDemand := True;
```

Converting Data to XML Format

A client dataset can be easily converted to XML format. You just need to use the property

```
property XMLData: OleVariant;
```

which returns the data stored in the `Data` cache in binary form, in XML format.

For example, a client dataset can be saved as an XML file:

```
if SaveDialog.Execute then
 with TFileStream.Create(SaveDialog.FileName, fmCreate) do
 try
  Write(Pointer(ClientDataSet.XMLData)^,
  Length(ClientDataSet.XMLData));
 finally
  Free;
 end;
```

Aggregates

The availability of a local cache lets the TClientDataSet component implement a variety of extra operations, based on the use of aggregate functions as applied to the fields of the entire cached dataset. The most common aggregate functions include:

❏ AVG — returns an average

❏ COUNT — returns the number of values

❏ MIN — returns the minimum value

❏ MAX — returns the maximum value

❏ SUM — returns the sum of the values

The following features of the TClientDataSet component help implement the above functions:

❏ The indexed list of the objects that encapsulate aggregate expressions — aggregates

❏ Aggregate fields that allow for calculating new values, similar to calculate fields, except with record grouping using aggregate functions

Aggregate Objects

The aggregate expressions for all records within a dataset can be calculated using TAggregate objects. The indexed list of these objects is available from the property

```
property Aggregates: TAggregates;
```

of the TClientDataSet component. The TAggregates class has TCollection as its direct ancestor, which means that it supports all the fundamental techniques for handling collections.

To create a new aggregate, open the **Properties** tab in the Object Inspector and select the **Add** item from the pop-up menu in the Aggregate Editor, or press the **Add New** button (Fig. 10.3).

Fig. 10.3. The `TClientDataSet` component's Aggregate Editor

You can also add a new aggregate dynamically:

```
var NewAgg: TAggregate;
...
NewAgg := ClientDataSet.Aggregates.Add;
...
```

Let's examine the properties of the `TAggregate` class.

The name of an aggregate is contained the property

```
property AggregateName: string;
```

which can be used for displaying the aggregate in data controls.

The expression to be calculated using aggregate functions must be contained in the property

```
property Expression: String;
```

For instance, it is possible to calculate the total area of the countries of North and South America from the Country.db table stored in the Delphi demo database (the areas of the countries are contained in the `Area` field):

```
ClientDataSet.Aggregates[SomeIndex].Expression:= 'SUM(Area)';
```

Calculation of the aggregate is managed through the property

```
property Active: Boolean;
```

and the calculated result is returned by the function

```
function Value: Variant;
```

If the user edits a dataset, then the returned values for all activated aggregates (`Active = True`) are automatically recalculated.

For example, you can visualize the new value of an aggregate after the changes made to the dataset have been saved:

```
SomeLabel.Caption := ClientDataSet.Aggregates[0].AggregateName;
SomeEdit.Text := ClientDataSet.Aggregates[0].Value;
```

Besides inspecting the value of the `Active` property, you can also check whether or not the aggregate is active by the property

```
property InUse: Boolean;
```

If it returns a value of `True`, the aggregate expression is being calculated.

The visibility of a given aggregate in data controls is determined by the value of the property

```
property Visible: Boolean;
```

The calculation load on a dataset can be reduced by simultaneously disabling all the aggregates. Set the property

```
property AggregatesActive: Boolean;
```

to `False`. If `AggregatesActive = True`, only active aggregates are calculated, the `Active` properties of which are set to `True`.

If you need to use all active aggregates, then, rather than handling them one by one and checking their `Active` properties, you can use the property

```
property ActiveAggs[Index: Integer]: TList;
```

of the `TClientDataSet` component, which lists the active aggregates of a given dataset.

Aggregate Fields

Aggregate fields are not included in the structure of dataset fields, as aggregate functions imply processing multiple records of a table. Hence, the value of an aggregate field cannot be restricted to any individual record, but relates to either all dataset records or a group of records.

A new aggregate field is created by the **New Field** command from the pop-up menu in the Field Editor of the `TClientDataSet` component.

As soon as you've selected the **Aggregate** radio button from the **Field Type** group, the `TAggregate` field type will automatically appear in the **Type** box. The name for new field is specified in the **Name** single-line editor.

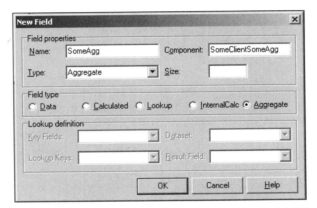

Fig. 10.4. The `TClientDataSet` component's Field Editor

Aggregate fields are not displayed together with all other fields in `TDBGrid` components, but are listed separately at the bottom of the Field Editor's window.

Fig. 10.5. The Field Editor that shows a separate list of aggregate fields

The value of an aggregate field can be presented through one of the available single-field data-aware controls (for example, `TDBText` or `TDBEdit`), or through the native properties of the field:

```
Label1.Caption := MyDataSetAGGRFIELD1.AsString;
```

The `TAggregateField` class is designed to encapsulate the properties and methods of aggregate fields.

Its property

```
property Expression: string;
```

specifies the expression to be calculated.

Calculations are performed only for those fields whose property

```
property Active: Boolean;
```

is set to `True`.

The aggregate fields activated via the `Active` property are calculated only if the `AggregatesActive` Boolean property of the client dataset component has a value of `True`.

By default, every `TAggregateField` class instance is created with the property `Visible = False`.

Grouping and Indexing

Every aggregate (object or field) has the property

```
property GroupingLevel: Integer;
```

which defines the grouping level for the fields of a dataset during calculation. If the value is `0`, all the records in a dataset are calculated. If the property is set to `1`, the records are grouped by the first field of the dataset, and each group is calculated separately. If the value is `2`, the records are grouped by the first and the second fields, etc.

However, grouping at a level higher than 0 is possible only if the dataset uses a grouping fields index. For example, if the property `GroupingLevel = 2` and the dataset begins with the **CustNo** and **OrderNo** fields, then the `IndexName` property of the `TClientDataSet` component and the property

```
property IndexName: String;
```

of the aggregate (object or field) must indicate the name of the index that includes both these fields.

Nested Datasets

Chapter 5, "The Architecture of Database Applications," discussed the issue of organizing a one-to-many relationship between database tables when a record of the master table is linked to several records of a detail table by matching the foreign key in the former to the primary key in the latter. This mechanism, which is extremely popular in database application programming, is implemented in the `TClientDataSet` component using the `TDataSetField` class.

To organize a one-to-many relationship on the client side, you need to use at least two TClientDataSet components — the parent component for the master dataset and the child component for the nested dataset.

Thus there are two table components on the server side, which are related in a one-to-many relationship using the MasterSource and MasterFields properties. There can also be two SQL queries linked to each other by the parameters of the detail query, with master query fields of the same name and the DataSource property.

Now the task is to implement a one-to many relationship for the TClientDataSet component and the master server component using a provider component as an intermediary, and supply TClientDataSet with persistent objects for all fields. Simply double-click the component and select **Add Field** from the pop-up menu in the Field Editor. As a consequence, the Field Editor will show the names of all the server dataset's field objects, as well as an extra object field, TDataSetField. The name of this field will duplicate the name of the server component of the one-to-many relationship.

This field references the detail server component, which can be easily verified by checking its read-only property:

```
property NestedDataSet: TdataSet;
```

while the indexed list of all fields passed from the detail server component can be accessed through the read-only property:

```
property Fields: Tfields;
```

From this point on, it is this field which is used to set the connection between the components on the client side. For the TClientDataSet detail component, you need to select the following property in the Object Inspector:

```
property DataSetField: TdataSetField;
```

The list of this property will contain the name of the newly created object field, TDataSetField. Selecting this name sets a one-to-many relationship for the client datasets. Note that the RemoteServer and ProviderName properties of the nested dataset are automatically cleared, as their values lose their meaning and the component is connected only to the master component of the one-to-many relationship.

Now when you navigate records in the master dataset, connected records will automatically appear in the nested dataset. You can also use all the functions provided by the TClientDataSet for both the master and nested datasets.

Additional Properties of Client Dataset Fields

As you know, all field classes have one common ancestor, the TField class. This section will concentrate on just a few extra field properties which work only in caching mode for traditional components that contain datasets and for the TClientDataSet component. In the TClientDataSet component, these properties are implemented by a local cache.

Thus developers may need properties that return not just the current value, but also the previous values of the fields.

The property

```
property CurValue: Variant;
```

returns the current value of the field.

The property

```
property OldValue: Variant;
```

contains the value of the field before editing began.

The property

```
property NewValue: Variant;
```

contains a new value that can be assigned when a server error is being treated by the OnReconcileError event handler (this will be discussed later).

Handling Errors

Specific methods used for handling the TClientDataSet component extend also to processing errors. Indeed, client datasets must react not only to local errors, but also to errors that occur while saving updates on the server.

The first problem can be solved by traditional means, which include using try ... except blocks or event handlers inherited from the TDataSet class:

```
property OnDeleteError: TDataSetErrorEvent;
```

is called for handling errors in deleting records,

```
property OnEditError: TDataSetErrorEvent;
```

is called for handling errors in editing records,

```
property OnPostError: TDataSetErrorEvent;
```

is called for handling errors in caching records locally.

All these handlers use the procedural type

```
type
   TDataSetErrorEvent = procedure(DataSet: TDataSet; E: EDatabaseError;
var Action: TDataAction) of object;
```

Here, in addition to the `DataSet` and `E` parameters that specify the dataset and the error type, you can set the dataset's reaction to the error via the `Action` parameter:

```
type TDataAction = (daFail, daAbort, daRetry);
```

where:

❏ `daFail` — aborts the current operation and displays an error message

❏ `daAbort` — aborts the current operation without displaying an error messages

❏ `daRetry` — repeats the operation

For instance, you may have to write the following event handler to deal with errors that occur while you are editing data:

```
procedure TForm1.ClientDataSetEditError(DataSet: TDataSet;
E: EDatabaseError; var Action: TDataAction);
begin
  if Not (DataSet.State in [dsEdit, dsInsert]) then
  begin
   DataSet.Edit;
   Action := daRetry;
  end
  else Action := daAbort;
end;
```

Here, if the dataset is not in the edit state, this oversight is corrected and the operation repeats.

Thus local errors are fairly easy to handle. But how can a client dataset learn that an error has occurred on a remote server? Obviously, it does this with the use of its provider component. The `TDataSetProvider` component not only returns all unsaved changes to the client in the `Delta` packet (as mentioned earlier), but also generates an event that is responded to by the event handler:

```
type
   TReconcileErrorEvent = procedure(DataSet: TCustomClientDataSet;
E: EReconcileError; UpdateKind: TUpdateKind; var Action:
TReconcileAction) of object;

property OnReconcileError: TReconcileErrorEvent;
```

Note that all parameters here are similar to their counterparts used for local event handlers, except that they have their own types. Let's take a closer look at them.

The `UpdateKind` argument indicates the type of the operation that produced the error on the server:

```
type
    TUpdateKind = (ukModify, ukInsert, ukDelete);
```

where:

❑ `ukModify` — modifies data

❑ `ukInsert` — inserts data

❑ `ukDelete` — deletes data

The `Action` argument enables a developer to define the reaction of the client dataset to the error:

```
type
    TReconcileAction = (raSkip, raAbort, raMerge, raCorrect, raCancel, raRefresh);
```

where:

❑ `raSkip` — aborts the operation for the records that caused the error and caches these records

❑ `raAbort` — aborts all changes for the operation that has caused the error

❑ `raMerge` — merges the modified records to the matching records on the server

❑ `raCorrect` — saves the changes made to the event handler

❑ `raCancel` — cancels all changes that have caused the error and replaces them with the original local values of the client dataset

❑ `raRefresh` — cancels all changes that have caused the error and replaces them with the original values of the server dataset

As you can see, there is a wide choice of possible reactions to a server error.

The type of error is returned by the `E` argument, for which the special `EReconcileError` class is designed. This class has a number of useful properties.

The property

```
property ErrorCode: DBResult;
```

returns the error code. The available error codes can be found in the ..\Source\Vcl\DSIntf.pas file. The code of the previous error is returned by the property

```
property PreviousError: DBResult;
```

Using the above information, you can handle server errors on the client side manually. However, there is an easier way — using the standard dialog for handling remote errors. The dialog in question can be attached to your project (it is stored in the ..\ObjRepos\RecError.pas module) and called by the procedure

```
function HandleReconcileError(DataSet: TDataSet; UpdateKind:
TUpdateKind; ReconcileError: EReconcileError): TReconcileAction;
```

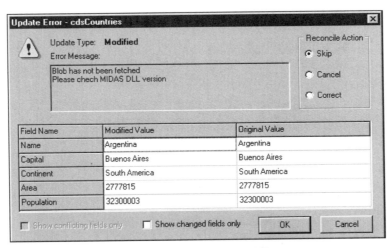

Fig. 10.6. The standard dialog for handling server errors

The parameters of the `OnReconcileError` event handler are substituted for the parameters of this function and return the action selected by the user in the dialog. Thus, using this function is very simple:

```
procedure TForm1.ClientDataSetReconcileError
(DataSet: TCustomClientDataSet;
E: EReconcileError; UpdateKind: TUpdateKind; var Action:
TReconcileAction);
begin
  Action := HandleReconcileError(DataSet, UpdateKind, E);
end;
```

Creating a Sample Thin Client

The sample thin client is a part of the SimpleRemote.bpg group of projects, and is intended for interaction with the `SimpleAppSrvr` application server, which we built in the previous chapter.

The SimpleClient project consists of two files:

❏ Components that provide for a connection with the remote application server and for dataset handling are concentrated in the `DataModule` (the uDataModule.pas file). Note that this is the "standard" data module used in database applications (see *Chapter 5, "The Architecture of Database Applications"*).

❏ The main form of the client application — `fmMain` (the uMain.pas file) — which contains the data controls of the user interface.

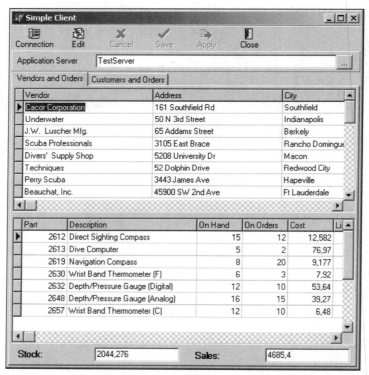

Fig. 10.7. The SimpleClient client application window

Listing 10.1. The DataModule Implementation Section

```
implementation

uses uMain, Variants, Dialogs;
```

```
{$R *.dfm}

procedure TDM.SrvrConAfterConnect(Sender: TObject);
var i: Integer;
begin
 for i := 0 to SrvrCon.DataSetCount — 1 do
  SrvrCon.DataSets[i].Open;
 cdsVendors.Open;
end;

procedure TDM.SrvrConBeforeDisconnect(Sender: TObject);
var i: Integer;
begin
 for i := 0 to SrvrCon.DataSetCount — 1 do
  SrvrCon.DataSets[i].Close;
 cdsVendors.Close;
end;

procedure TDM.cdsVendorsAfterScroll(DataSet: TDataSet);
begin
 fmMain.edCostSum.Text := VarToStr(cdsParts.Aggregates[0].Value);
 fmMain.edPriceSum.Text := VarToStr(cdsParts.Aggregates[1].Value);
end;

procedure TDM.cdsPartsReconcileError(DataSet: TCustomClientDataSet;
E: EReconcileError; UpdateKind: TUpdateKind;
var Action: TReconcileAction);
begin
 cdsParts.CancelUpdates;
 MessageDlg(E.Message, mtError, [mbOK], 0);
end;

end.
```

Connecting the Client to the Application Server

On a local network, the connection between the client application and the server is implemented via the SrvrCon component of the TDCOMConnection class. This type of connection was selected because it is the simplest, and requires only the availability of a local network, or possibly nothing at all. In the demo application, you can use the application server installed on the same machine.

To set the connection to the SrvrCon component, the name of the server computer is specified through the ComputerName property. Next, you can select one of the available registered servers from the list contained in the ServerName property. In this example, the SimpleAppSrvr.SimpleRDM server is used; the name of this server consists of the names of the application server and the main remote data module.

Note that this list also contains the Secondary child module. However, you can save yourself the trouble of creating another connection and simply use the TSharedConnection component, which is specifically designed for such cases. To set it up, just specify the connection component in the ParentConnection property, which will be SrvrCon in this example.

The SrvrCon component is managed by two event handlers (see Listing 10.1) called before activating the connection and after disconnection. All datasets of the client application are opened and closed through these handlers.

Now the datasets of both remote data modules that reside on the application server are available in the client application.

The connection to the server is established through the **Connect** button. When it is pressed, the following simple code executes:

```
procedure TfmMain.tbConnectClick(Sender: TObject);
begin
 try
  DM.SrvrCon.Close;
  DM.SrvrCon.ComputerName := edServerName.Text;
  DM.SrvrCon.Open;
 except
  on E: Exception do MessageDlg(E.Message, mtError, [mbOK], 0);
 end;
 SetCtrlState;
end;
```

The connection is closed, the new name of the server computer is specified, and then the connection is reopened. The specially created SetCtrlState form method is used for controlling the availability of the buttons in the form by analyzing the current state of the datasets.

Client Application Datasets

Every `TClientDataSet` component of `DataModule` is linked to the corresponding provider component located on the server.

The `cdsOrders` component is intended for viewing the information on orders. The additional components — `cdsEmployees` and `cdsCustomers` — store the lists of employees and customers used in the master dataset. The `cdsOrders` component contains the declaration of the `PaidSum` aggregate field calculating the total sum paid for all orders. The `cdsParts` component is used for viewing and editing the data on new supplies. The `cdsVendors` component represents the list of vendors. Since the dataset associated with `cdsVendors` on the application server is treated as the main dataset in the one-to-many relationship, in addition to standard fields, the `cdsVendors` component is automatically provided with the `tblParts` field of the `TDataSetField` type. This field lets you set the nested dataset. This can be done by simply defining the `tblParts` field in the `DataSetField` property of the `cdsParts` component. Now when you navigate the records in the master dataset, `cdsVendors`, the nested dataset — `cdsParts` — will reflect the records associated with the current vendor.

> **NOTE**
>
> To maintain the simplicity and intelligibility of the source code, editing is provided only for the `cdsParts` component. But similar methods for all datasets can be used in developing real-world database solutions.

The `cdsParts` component is provided with two aggregates that sum up the data on supplies and sales. When you move around the records in this dataset, the values of the aggregates are updated in the `AfterScroll` event handler (see Listing 10.1).

As the `cdsParts` component is designed for editing data, it should be allowed to handle the exceptions that occur both on the client and server side. This task is performed by the `cdsPartsReconcileError` event handler (see Listing 10.1). The operation itself is very simple, and serves more to illustrate the ability of creating a custom technique for handling server exceptions than to use the standard `HandleReconcileError` function (see Fig. 10.6). All the records likely to produce errors are canceled here via the `CancelUpdates` method, and an error message is displayed.

Locally editing, saving, and canceling changes for the `cdsParts` component are implemented by the standard dataset methods. Additionally, the `UndoLastChange` method is used for canceling changes, which enables you to restore the last modified record even after changes are saved locally.

The `ApllyUpdates` method is used for passing changes to the server. The `-1` parameter means that the client will be immediately informed about the first error that occurs.

Summary

As a rule, multi-tier distributed applications use thin clients, delegating the bulk of processing logic to the middleware of the intermediary tier. In three-tier applications, application servers are used as middleware.

The core of any client application is the `TClientDataSet` component, which contains a dataset and enables it to function using a local data cache. Client applications connect to the remote application server via DataSnap components.

PART IV

THE BASICS OF DEVELOPING AN INTERNET APPLICATION

Chapter 11

Sockets

This chapter opens a discussion on the various problems pertaining to distributed application development. The common denominator in these applications is that their constituent parts interact with each other through a certain network medium.

Of course, you may choose to look at this medium as a sort of "black box," the details of operation of which are of no concern to you as a user. Besides which, the component approach used by Delphi encourages such a position and hides all the details of network connections.

In spite of the tremendous breakthroughs in the field of networking in recent years, networks still cannot be considered one hundred percent reliable (and in all probability never will be). But what about you, dear reader? Apparently, you intend to design reliable applications, correct? Then you'll have to understand the principles of networking, whether you like it or not. This doesn't mean that you must become a qualified professional in the field of network engineering, of course. We simply hope that this and the following chapters will give you adequate insight into the subject of why and how data are transmitted between applications.

What language do network elements use to talk to each other? The commonly accepted international seven-layered *Open Systems Interconnection* (OSI) model standardizes several aspects of the communication process. Each of these layers — from the first, physical layer up to the highest presentation and application layers — is meant to solve a specific range of tasks and uses its individual toolkit for this purpose. This chapter begins with a brief overview of the OSI model. This overview is essential for the logical presentation of the material covered in this chapter.

We will then proceed to exploring the most popular and universal API used for building network applications — the Winsock specification (Windows Sockets). Delphi of course provides its users with a series of objects and components to facilitate the task of managing sockets — and this aspect will be further emphasized from a practical viewpoint.

So, the following is the full list of issues that we will cover in this chapter.

❑ Introduction to the theoretical principles of network architecture

❑ Utilizing different layers of the OSI model in Internet applications

❑ Sockets: their purposes and methods of using them

❑ The hierarchy of the Delphi classes that encapsulate sockets

❑ Software implementation of a link between client and server sockets

Introduction to Network Architecture

It isn't necessary for you to be a qualified network engineer in order to design distributed applications, but understanding some fundamental network concepts will no doubt do you a world of good. Delphi provides implementations of a huge variety of network protocols, which means that in order to choose the most suitable one you must know the purposes of each of them, understand the way in which they interact, and, should an error occur, be able to quickly and correctly localize it.

Prior to discussing protocols and their characteristics, let's look at the general principles that were employed to systematize them into a unified and consistent architecture. Such a hierarchy exists, and it is usually referred to as the Open Systems Interconnection model. But if you expect us to dive into details on the functions and objects right away — well, then you'll need a little patience, because first of all you have to absorb a number of theoretical postulates.

However, the goal of this chapter is not to give a comprehensive analysis of this extremely complex issue. Those who wish to learn how the OSI model is implemented in Windows can refer to the Resource Kit documentation.

OSI Model

At the dawn of networking, each manufacturer marketed its own closed solutions. However, it soon became obvious to everyone that such a shortsighted policy undermined the very nature of networking, since networks were conceptually meant to unite user, not divide them. In 1978, the International Standards Organization (ISO) ushered in the Open Systems Interconnection standard (OSI), which united all communication protocols into a single, seven-layered structure. Each level provides a solution for a particular aspect of the general communication problem and has rules for implementing these solutions. The layers are numbered from 1 to 7 (the highest layer).

The OSI model is only distributed to the multitude of various communication protocols, not to the physical communication media. Sometimes OSI models are referred to as *protocol stacks*, since each higher layer is preceded by a functionally self-sufficient communication protocol toolkit. Each layer uses its own unique set of protocols, which are intended for solving a clearly defined range of communication tasks.

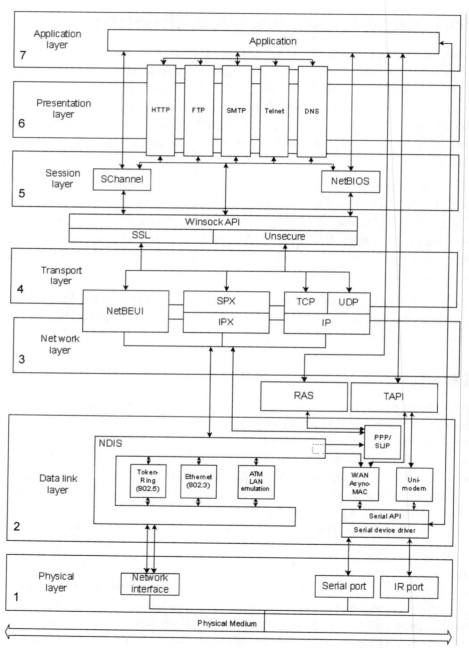

Fig. 11.1. The interaction between OSI layers

The OSI conceptual framework is built on the idea that the role of each layer is to provide a specific interface for the protocols of the next layer. The layers are not actually connected to one another, however: for instance, a protocol of the fourth (transport) layer believes that it is "talking" to the same layer on another computer. In fact, it is addressing the layer immediately below it, while this lower layer in turn "talks" to the layer below it, etc. (Fig. 11.1).

For computers to be able to connect to each other, they must have functionally identical protocol stacks. These stacks ensure the possibility of communication, in spite of the fact that such computers may differ considerably in their architecture. For instance, the byte ordering in Macintosh computers that use Motorola micro-processors begins with the high byte, while Wintel (Windows + Intel) computers utilize a type of byte ordering where the low byte is stored first. As a result, Mac-intoshes and PCs simply cannot communicate in the "ordinary" fashion due to this simple but essential difference in processing data. This is where the communication protocol stacks come in. These stacks perform the task of compiling specific data formats used by different computers into a common language that can be under-stood by all machines connected by means of a given protocol stack.

A Macintosh that uses the TCP/IP stack can directly connect to a PC that also uses the TCP/IP stack. But replacing the TCP/IP stack with the IPX/SPX stack on one of these computers will break the connection. In such a case, you'll have to utilize an appropriate router.

The following is a brief overview of all the layers that constitute the OSI model. This overview will hardly make a professional of you — but we hope it will help you better understand certain basic things that you will need to grasp before setting out to develop distributed applications.

Physical Layer

In the framework of OSI, the physical layer directly deals with the network com-munication medium — be that an electric or optical cable, a telephone network, certain radio communication devices, etc.

The physical layer is not meant to handle structured data — blocks, packets, rec-ords, and so on. It is responsible only for converting a sequence of bits into an electrical signal when sending data, and vice versa when receiving them.

On the physical layer, information can be transmitted in the form of both digital and analog signals. Computers often convert signals from one form into the other.

The process of converting digital information into its analog form is called *modulation*. The reverse conversion is referred to as *demodulation*. A combination of both terms was used to coin the term *modem* (*mo*dulator/*dem*odulator), a common device used for transmitting information over analog (telephone) communication paths.

Analog signals change continuously, and therefore can assume an arbitrary set of values. Digital signals change discretely; a (binary) signal can assume a value of either 0 or 1. For example, ISDN adapters are digital link devices that enable computers to connect to each other without using the modulation/demodulation processes.

Since in a real network a physical medium can be shared by two or more machines simultaneously, decisions about the topology design and shared access to the medium must also be made at this layer. Most of you have probably in one way or another dealt with networks based on the Ethernet standard (which will be discussed in detail later). This standard can implement both a bus network (multiple machines connected by a common coaxial cable) and a star network (each machine is connected to a hub or a switch through its individual network cable).

As a rule, all the user needs to know about the physical layer is how to correctly connect the network cable to the adapter. This layer only utilizes a hardware approach to handle the communication process, and doesn't use any program interfaces or protocols.

Link Layer Protocols

This layer solves the following network connection tasks:

❏ Identifying computers in the network

❏ Implementing network access control by determining the appropriate moment for starting the data transmission

❏ Establishing a connection between two physical devices

❏ Managing data flow — alternating transmission and exchanging data frames

❏ Confirming the receipt of a frame, initializing a repeat transmission of unconfirmed fragments, and resolving conflicts

❏ Tracking down and handling physical layer errors

Both the physical and the link layer were further detailed once the OSI standard had been set. They were elaborated within the framework of so-called Project 802, implemented by the Institute of Electrical and Electronics Engineers (IEEE). Since then, these standards have been referred to as IEEE 802 standards, despite the fact that they were subsequently approved by US and international standardization organizations. The numbers 802 denote the year and month when work on the standard began (February 1980). The date of its formal approval can be thought of as the birthday of modern local networks. Originally, the specification consisted of 10 sections (802.1—802.10); section 802.3 was used as a basis for developing such networks as Ethernet, 802.4 was used for ArcNet, and 802.5 was the basis for Token Ring.

According to IEEE 802, the link layer is comprised of two sublayers:

❏ The *Media Access Control (MAC)* sublayer defines the way in which multiple devices can share the same communication path.

❏ The *Logical Link Control (LLC)* sublayer sets and maintains the link between connecting devices.

Implementing Media Access Control

The MAC sublayer specifies the technique for transmitting signals over the medium. For example, it can be implemented in the form of computers taking turns to transmit their information (Ethernet), passing a special token from one machine to another around a ring (Token Ring), by a bus (ArcNet), or by way of voting (mainframes).

It may be worth mentioning that every device in the context of a given network (for example, the Ethernet adapter card on your computer) has a unique address. This is the device's physical address (also called the MAC address); it is used to unambiguously identify each hardware device in a given network.

If you want to learn the MAC address of the network card installed on your own machine, run the ipconfig utility (for the Windows NT/2000/XP operating system) or winipcfg (for Windows 9x).

You can also run the arp utility from the command line with the -a parameter; this particular utility comes with all currently used Windows versions (if the TCP/IP protocol is installed on the computer). It will show you the state of the Address Resolution Protocol (ARP) protocol cache that is responsible for mapping the IP addresses to the MAC addresses of the computers in your local network.

While physical layer protocols implement bitwise data transmission, the data link layer operates with groups of bits — so-called frames.

Another important issue that needs understanding as far as the MAC sublayer is concerned is the principle of synchronizing the process of data transmission. There are three types of transmission synchronization used to manage these bit groups:

❏ Asynchronous data transmission

❏ Synchronous data transmission

❏ Isochronous data transmission

Asynchronous Data Transmission

A classical example of asynchronous data transmission is illustrated by the process of establishing a connection between modems. Both modems use a start bit that lets the receiving device tune to the signal. A typical asynchronous frame consists of four components:

❏ A start bit

❏ A data bits

❏ A parity bit

❏ A stop bit

The start bit and stop bit signal the beginning and the end of each frame, respectively. Data bits carry the information being passed to the receiving device. The parity bit provides the most elementary means used for detecting errors. A device can detect an error that distorted one bit in a given frame, but it cannot spot an error that affects two or more bits simultaneously.

Synchronous Data Transmission

Synchronous data transmission is much faster than asynchronous communication, since the transmission and reception of data by both parties are synchronized. This can be achieved in two ways:

❏ Passing a synchronizing signal within the data flow

❏ Utilizing a separate communication path for passing timing signals

Using timing at both ends of a communication link allows you to transmit very large data frames. In this context, a simple parity check is obviously inadequate. Thus a Cyclic Redundancy Check (CRC) is used for synchronizing communication links.

Synchronous data transmission is normally used, for instance, in most local area networks.

Isochronous Data Transmission

Isochronous data transmission implies using a timer that sends a timing signal to all the devices connected to it. But due to the fact that PCs are independent and self-sufficient entities supplied with timers of their own, the probability of running across such a technique of data transmission is very low.

You may wonder when you, as a programmer, may have to deal with all these concepts. Well, all network adapter drivers operate on the MAC layer. But presumably you're not reading this book to find information on how to develop drivers (for this you'd be better off referring to the Driver Development Kit), so let's proceed to the discussion of the next sublayer.

Logical Link Control

As stated earlier, this layer is responsible for establishing and maintaining connections between machines; it is defined in the IEEE 802.2 standard. This layer provides data flow management, and implements error check and transmission sequence control.

What Windows component operates on the link layer? The API of the LLC layer is called the Network Driver Interface Specification (NDIS). All drivers for network adapters and other end devices are developed on the basis of this specification. Moreover, NDIS is a common platform that incorporates both connection-oriented network devices (the ATM and ISDN networks, for example) and connectionless devices (this category includes such networks as Ethernet, Token Ring, etc.).

In addition to data transmission, NDIS performs a range of various service functions — for instance, Plug-and-Play and power control; and should you choose to configure your computer so that it wakes up when a network event approaches, such notification will be provided by NDIS.

Besides NDIS, the link layer in Windows supports another protocol: Point-to-Point Protocol (PPP). PPP is used to implement remote access, as a rule using a serial port. In such a case, the modem plays the role of the physical device.

NOTE

Windows remote clients also support an older protocol — Serial Line Internet Protocol (SLIP), which is an ancestor of PPP.

Functions of Network Layer

While the link layer is responsible for establishing a connection between physical devices within the context of a single network, the network layer implements the logic enabling connections between end devices located in physically detached networks. This layer provides the foundation for inter-network communication.

Since inter-network communication is very widespread, and involves using the most diverse kinds of network equipment, the network layer contains routing algorithms for delivering packets from the sender to the recipient.

A network layer uses the concept of a *datagram*. A datagram is an individual, independent data packet. Datagrams are adequately equipped to travel all the way from the sender to the recipient.

> **NOTE**
>
> In the following discussion, we will also use the term *packet*, alongside datagram. Though these concepts denote information units that are actually quite dissimilar, the differences between them are too complex to be examined in this chapter. Besides this, the physical and link layers also use the term *frame*.

All devices participating in network communication must be identified by their unique network address in order to coordinate routing. In the global network, all potential addressees are referred to as *hosts*. To put it simply, a host can be thought of as a computer; for a simple workstation with a single network adapter, this is a fair description. However, there are servers that can have several network interfaces, and various special devices (routers) that, if they even can be thought of as computers, then only very specialized ones.

Different protocols implement individual approaches to the task of assigning network addresses; for obvious reasons, we are not able to discuss all of them, so we will focus on exploring in detail just the Internet Protocol (IP) network protocol as the basic standard used for data transmission over the Net.

Every host in the IP is identified by a unique parameter — its *address*. Datagrams are sent using this address to the specified network and to the defined host participating in inter-network communication. It goes without saying that every such address must be unique, even in the context of the Internet. This issue is monitored by a special organization.

Most of our readers are sure to have dealt with IP addressing in one way or another — so we won't dwell on the obvious here. We'll just remind you that an IP address, which consists of four blocks represented by numbers ranging from 0 to 255, contains not just the unique address of a given host, but also the unique address of the network in which this host is located. Depending on the network class, it can take up one, two, or three out of four bytes.

Were you to look up the IP specification in the official standards, you would find the following definition: *IP is a connectionless, unreliable datagram protocol primarily responsible for addressing and routing packets between hosts.* What do these seemingly vague and confusing terms — *connectionless* and *unreliable* — mean?

There are three types of protocols:

❐ Connection oriented protocols

❐ Unacknowledged connectionless protocols

❐ Acknowledged connectionless protocols

Using connection oriented protocols is very similar to communicating through ordinary telephone lines. Such a protocol functions along a well worked out route, which exists only as long as the connection exists.

This kind of a protocol allows you to manage data flow and error check and transmission sequence control by acknowledging the receipt of every portion of data (this is done by passing a special acknowledgement packet back to the sender). Such a two-way exchange reduces the communication channel's capacity, but contributes to a higher reliability.

Unacknowledged connectionless protocols assume the network connection to be reliable in advance; this pertains, for example, to various local networks. Due to this assumption, issues of data flow management and error check are none of their concern, leaving these tasks to protocols at other layers. The lack of an acknowledgement of the receipt of datagrams is offset by a gain in performance speed.

How about an example from the "analog" world? OK, just think of an ordinary postal service. Postal services in developed countries can now be considered 99.99% reliable, and having sent a letter, you can rest assured that it will be safely delivered to the addressee. Yet another feature shared by a postal service and an IP is that mailed letters are passed through a number of consecutive nodes until they arrive at the actual recipients.

However, a hundred years ago or so, postal services were far from reliable; the reliability of the Internet, accordingly, is nowhere near ideal. You can use the ping or pathping utility (which comes with Windows 2000) to check the reliability of passing your data packets to the selected host. If the channel used by the addressee server to connect to the Net is not reliable enough or has inadequate capacity, you may lose up to 100% of your packets.

Acknowledged connectionless protocols contirm the fact of receiving data in order to manage data flow, but these protocols do not require the establishing of a connection as an essential prior condition. The difference between these protocols and those discussed above can be illustrated by the difference between traditional and registered mail — in case of the latter, the sender receives the appropriate notification.

So, you needn't worry yourself too much about the IP's alleged "unreliability." This shortcoming is made up for by other protocols.

As follows from the above definition, the ultimate purpose of IP is to implement routing. Every host supports its own routing table, which contains such information as:

❐ A list of all known hosts and networks, together with the masks that define the IP address as belonging to the given network.

❐ A gateway used as a link to the given network.

❐ The network interface from which to send data to this network.

❐ The metric, which is the number of hops that a data packet must make on this route in order to hit the specified target network. The metric is also often referred to as the cost of the route; if several routes can be used for traveling to this network, then the lowest-cost route is selected.

If you have ever configured TCP/IP on your machine, you certainly remember using the Default gateway parameter. In local networks, the routing tables of the computers are customized in such a way that packets addressed to neighboring computers are sent to them directly. All packets that cannot be passed directly are forwarded to the default gateway.

But, in order to allow data to be sent in local networks, somebody must give the IP protocol information as to how the IP addresses of the hosts are mapped to their MAC addresses. This job is performed by a special auxiliary protocol — the Address Resolution Protocol (ARP) — which is a part of the IP standard.

Before proceeding to the next layer, it should be emphasized that IP is absolutely adequate for sending data from any point connected to the Internet to any other point. Connection problems, which are typically tackled by system administrators, are ultimately due, as a rule, to the incorrect setting up of the routing on this important layer.

Transport Layer

The fact that TCP/IP is by far the most widely used standard often results in the common misconception that all connections over the Internet are established using just two protocols — Internet Protocol and Transmission Control Protocol. But this is not exactly the case. Besides TCP, the transport layer also uses, User Datagram Protocol (UDP). At this point, we are shifting from our purely theoretical discussion to applied issues; both these protocols are used by particular Delphi components. These protocols serve different purposes: while TCP is a connection-oriented protocol that logically enhances IP with means for providing high reliability, UDP is a very elementary wrapper over the IP, which doesn't establish connections. UDP is used in specific situations, when the highest possible performance speed is the most important criterion and the loss of some portions of data is tolerable — for example, when video/audio data are transmitted. Another example is provided by the Quake network game that uses UDP to coordinate communication between the players.

You can think of TCP's task as fitting together various pieces of a puzzle. On the sender side, the original "picture" is broken into fragments. By the way, when reading the previous section, did you even think about the importance of such a factor as the size of the data fragment being passed? Obviously, the techniques used must be different when sending 10 KB and 10 MB. TCP can handle messages of any length by receiving them from higher-level protocols, breaking them into fragments, and passing them to the recipients as IP packets.

> **NOTE**
>
> Fragment size can vary from one to tens of kilobytes, and can be customized depending on the characteristics of the transmission medium.

As we already know, in the course of their travel over the net, your packets can be lost, delayed, stolen, damaged, duplicated, and lastly — which is quite typical — they can be delivered to the receiver in an order different from the original one.

So, on the recipient's side, TCP carefully and thoroughly verifies the packets and arranges them in the initial order. Packets are verified by checking their control sums. If the packet is received correctly, the receiver sends the corresponding acknowledgement (ACK) to the sender; otherwise, the transmission is repeated.

This layer is also responsible for procedures providing reliable message delivery. Lower-layer protocols report errors, and the transport layer analyzes these errors and decides whether to demand that the transmission be repeated, or inform higher-layer protocols about the need to take appropriate measures.

While IP delivers messages by passing them from one host to another, a transport layer is used for passing data between processes that run on network devices. That's why yet another parameter is added to an IP address at the transport layer — the *port number.*

Datagrams are sent to a particular process running on the addressee server by the port number. If we draw a parallel between a host and a radio station, the part performed by the port is akin to the frequency at which this radio station communicates with another radio station. An operating system running in multitask mode can service multiple network applications at once. When a datagram arrives at the target computer, the port tells the operating system which of the tasks is the recipient of the data just received. A port is represented by a number ranging from 0 to 65,535.

The port number is often called a *well-known port.* Internet standards specify a number of well-known ports for such services as HTTP (port 80), FTP (20, 21), telnet (23), and others; numbers up to 1023 are reserved for standard ports. Well-known ports are defined in the Winsock.PAS modules as constants beginning with the prefix IPPORT_ (for instance, IPPORT_FINGER).

It is quite possible to use a port different from a well-known one for a standard protocol. However, in such a case, both sides must be aware of this change. In fact, a well-known port is called "well-known" because it allows the client to find the recipient without any prior notification.

The Concepts of Session, Presentation, and Application Layer

Well-known Internet applications, protocols, and services are all included into the three upper layers of the OSI reference model. The division of responsibilities between these layers is relatively random. For example, the specification refers to all functionalities and services located on top of the transport layer as the "application layer." Indeed, the recipient is specified, the connection is established, data integrity is insured, errors are handled — what is then left for the upper layers? They need only be able to talk to each other using a common language.

The following is a brief overview of the functions provided by these layers.

Session Layer

The session layer manages the dialog between two interacting devices. Every act of two interacting parties connecting to each other, exchanging data, and, once the exchange is acknowledged, closing the connection, will be referred to as a session. During a session, the sides identify themselves and set the parameters for the session (this particular procedure is often called handshaking) as well as the type of data exchange (one-way, two-way, synchronous, or asynchronous).

Presentation Layer

The presentation layer does the job of reducing data formats to a common denominator.

Lower-layer protocols implement connections using bitwise data transmission. The presentation layer sets a unified pattern of data conversion for all interacting parties. This might mean:

❏ Converting character coding schemas

❏ Converting data formats (integers, floating-point numbers, strings, etc.)

❏ Compressing data so that they take up less space

❏ Encrypting data (to prevent unauthorized reading or alteration; this issue is covered in more detail in *Chapter 12*)

Application Layer

Finally, at this point, our long-suffering participants in the network connection have settled all real and potential problems. Now they can proceed to what was the original goal of all their networking activity: solving a specific task.

You have most certainly heard of such "languages" as File Transfer Protocol (FTP), Simple Mail Transfer Protocol (SMTP), and Terminal Emulation (telnet): all of them are included in these upper layers.

Once again, it needs to be stressed that this division into session/presentation/ application layers is quite arbitrary. This division is theoretical — in practice, however, real protocols often combine the functions of all three layers. Let's take the commonly used HTTP as an example. It incorporates a handshake procedure, session identification, and user authorization, defines the format used by the client for sending requests to the HTTP server, and sets the language for these requests (GET/POST, etc.). HTTP is the foundation of the browser, its application layer. On the other hand, from the point of view of SOAP (on which all web services are based), HTTP is no more than a session protocol, an instrument for transmitting the data of its own, higher level.

The Client/Server Model and Sockets

The thoroughly described OSI model sets unified guidelines for every device that wishes to take part in networking. But OSI fails to explain the role performed by each interacting entity. The client/server model is meant to fill this gap by dividing a network application into two parts and designating one of them as the client and the other as the server.

The *client side* generates requests for information and services. The *server side* analyzes the network in order to find out whether any new requests have been submitted and, if so, responds to them appropriately. All of the following chapters will teach you to develop applications that can perform both of these functions.

The client/server relationship works on the assumption that there is a "point-to-point" link between the client and the server. The client can be positioned at a distance of several meters from the server, or even be located on the other side of the world. The client/server model is founded on OSI network concepts, which provide a virtual channel for the connection.

Both ends of this virtual channel have a virtual end-point device called a *socket*. If we once again make a comparison with analog communication and draw a parallel between TCP/IP and a telephone service, sockets can be thought of as a pair of phones or faxes. One of these you use for dialing the number and waiting for a reply, and the other one is used by your friend: who, when he or she hears it ringing, picks it up — and thus establishes the connection channel.

To the programmer, sockets are just another familiar and highly convenient paradigm that let you put data into and collect them from a "black box," without bothering to know the details of how it works. On the one hand, using sockets allows for an abstraction from the technicalities of work on lower layers, and on the other hand, it lets developers solve a broad range of tasks that cannot be handled by special-purpose protocols.

The term "socket" — as well as this API's specification, for that matter — was introduced into the UNIX operating system, version Berkeley Software Distribution (BSD). In the eighties, when the Internet was beginning to take its current shape, all computers with this OS installed on them formed the backbone for the emerging Internet (this also explains the term Berkeley Sockets). The very concept of a communication channel as a sort of a "pipe" for downloading data is notably close to UNIX; but sockets are also used for Windows, since they fit into this OS pretty well too. Having created a socket, you obtain its handle, which later can be used in such familiar functions as `ReadFile/WriteFile`, along with files, named pipes, and serial ports. Look at the icons denoting socket components in Delphi: each of them is represented by a plug and socket. You insert the plug into the socket and the "current" of data begins to circulate around your application.

Sockets provide network software developers with a truly cross-platform API interface. They also ensure binary-level compatibility, which means that applications that use API sockets can use any other appropriate implementation from other vendors. Essentially, sockets are middleware that is responsible for translating the calls generated by the application into the instruction language used by network protocols.

So, in a nutshell, every active connection uses two sockets. The socket that requests the connection performs the role of the client. The socket that satisfies the connection requirement does the job of the server. Nevertheless, once two systems are connected, the roles of the client and the server often tend to become more indistinguishable, since either side is able to solve tasks initially thought to be the responsibility of the other party.

The client performs the active role: it initiates the link by generating a request to the server. The server is more passive: it waits for requests — and typically does nothing else, except for some insignificant background procedures, until the first request arrives. As soon as a request is received, the server "comes to life" and responds to the request. Having satisfied the request, the server resumes its role of a passive network listener.

Microsoft Windows and Sockets

Those programmers who "grew up" on Intel + Microsoft platforms have probably heard very little about Berkeley sockets; but every one of them knows the term Winsock. This is what socket implementations for Microsoft Windows are known as.

The first versions of Winsock were 16-bit. The current version of Windows Sockets (2.0) is notable for its ability to operate not only on top of TCP/IP, but also on top of many other transport protocols (IPX/SPX, NetBEUI). However, since the topic of our discussion is programming for the Internet, here we are interested in this capability only to a certain degree.

The Winsock API is programmatically compatible and contains the same calls that were originally included in the Berkeley Sockets specification. However, Microsoft wouldn't have lived up to its reputation if it hadn't provided a number of extensions of its own. Were you to analyze the API structure, you will find these extensions easily recognizable. All basic native functions and structures do not have prefixes and begin with a lower-case letter, for example: `accept`, `connect`, `htonl`, `listen`, etc. All extensions begin with the WSA prefix: `WSAAccept`, `WSAConnect`. Actually, the basic set of functionalities would suffice to provide effective performance — except for two functions, `WSAStartup` and `WSACleanup`, which you need to use in order to start and stop working with Winsock.

Winsock implies support for multithreading in Windows, where every process contains one or more concurrent threads. We will explain operating modes of sockets and the socket threads connected with them later in this chapter.

And, in conclusion, just a few words need to be added about alternatives to Winsock — or rather, about the lack of them. As we will touch on later, most Microsoft implementations of higher-layer protocols have counterparts in third-party solutions. However, practically none of these independent developers has managed to provide a custom implementation of sockets. For one thing, this is because sockets are extremely closely integrated with the operating system and network drivers; third-party sockets would necessitate a colossal endeavor, one requiring much time and effort. That's why all the components and protocol stacks that you will deal with in Delphi are based on Winsock. Borland Kylix relies on the implementation of sockets provided with all Linux releases.

Handling Sockets with Delphi

Delphi developers have a vast choice of various tools for working on the socket level. Why is this and where do they come from?

To begin with, you can certainly work with this API "tête-à-tête," without intermediary components and objects. Prototypes of functions are provided as a part of the Delphi suite in the WINSOCK.PAS file. There are not that many of these functions: the size of WINSOCK.PAS is only about 40 KB. But such issues as manipulating modes of socket operation, organizing a waiting state, handling errors, etc., are not so simple, and require intimate knowledge of networking. On the whole, if your particular problem is not too specific, using the components and objects that encapsulate the socket API appears to be the most reasonable solution.

Delphi Components Encapsulating Sockets

The very first components of this kind were `TClientSocket` and `TServerSocket` (the `ScktComp` module). Understandably enough, they all were WinSock 2 library-oriented. The object model is relatively simple and logical: a number of properties corresponding to the initial settings of a socket, methods determining its functionalities (establishing/breaking a connection, reading/writing), and events that occur when socket states are changed. These objects will be described in detail later in this chapter.

However, with Delphi 6, new components that would be compatible with the CLX library for Kylix had to be inroduced. The `ScktComp` module was tied in too closely with Windows. For this (or maybe some other) reason, Borland offered a new implementation of a socket wrapper — the `TTCPClient`, `TTCPServer`, and `TUDPSocket` components (the `Sockets` module).

Also, we cannot help but mention here two solutions that were contributed by programmers outside of Borland. For some years, the pressing necessity of providing their product with an alternate protocol suite — which would allow the developing of applications independent of Microsoft Internet solutions — has been a matter of considerable concern to Delphi management. The FastNet protocol suite (Net-Masters LLC, **www.netmastersllc.com**) was the first attempt to solve this problem. Delphi 6 still does support this product — but only due to compatibility considerations; in any event, the old version of the FastNet library (5.3.0, build 1055) has not been modified since Delphi 5. Among the most glaring faults of this library, we can name the enormous amount of errors and the lack of source code.

These were soon replaced by a new implementation of a protocol suite provided by Nevrona (**www.nevrona.com**) — Internet Direct (Indy). This product was originally developed under the name Internet Component Suite, and was available in the form of source code, which helped correct and prevent a lot of errors.

Here we are going to explore the capabilities of the `TServerSocket` and `TClientSocket` components, which can be found on the **Internet** page of the

Delphi 6 Component Palette. Unless stated otherwise — and we will make a point of specifically mentioning those cases — the differences between these components and their analogs are minimal, and amount mostly to variations in the names for the same properties and methods.

Establishing a Connection

The mechanism for connecting via sockets is as follows. The client socket is created on one side. To initiate the link, the client socket needs to be given the path to the server socket that is to set up the connection.

As we already know, a path in TCP/IP networks is specified by two parameters: the address or hostname (usually referred to simply as the host) and the port. In this case, by the host we mean the system where the application containing the socket is running. A hostname, as a rule, is represented by a character string in UNC format, which can be translated into a given address — for example, **http://www.microsoft.com**. The particular technique used for implementing mutual correspondence between names and addresses can vary, depending on the size of the network and the operating system in use. On the Internet, there is the Domain Naming System (DNS), which consists of special servers that store and maintain the correspondence tables that indicate how addresses are interpreted into DNS names. A self-explanatory name is more easily remembered, but using addresses to establish a connection is still considered to be the simplest and most reliable approach, since no additional information is required.

> **NOTE**
>
> Most likely, you will begin debugging both the client and the server side on the same machine. If so, you can indicate that the server resides on the same computer and bind the sockets in one of four ways:
>
> ❏ By specifying the network name of your computer (which can be learnt through the "Network" applet on the Control Panel).
>
> ❏ By indicating the IP address of your computer (which is available from the TCP/IP properties. Your machine must have this protocol installed and have its permanent IP address on hand).
>
> ❏ By specifying the predefined localhost name (which always corresponds to the given host, and thus means that the recipient and the sender in this case are represented by the same entity).
>
> ❏ By specifying the IP address 127.0.0.1 (which also always indicates the host).

A port number is a simple instrument that allows you to maintain multiple concurrent connections between two hosts. Prior to setting and using his or her host value, the programmer should inspect the list of already reserved ports.

And so, the address on the client side is set through the Address and Port properties of the TClientSocket component.

The server socket is started on one of the two connected sides. Initially, it waits in *listening* state, ready to accept the connection specified by the assigned port. Once it receives the first request from the other side (the client) the connection is established. At the same time, a new listening socket is created for detecting new requests.

Synchronizing Sockets

When using sockets, the stage where you specify their type — either blocking (synchronous) or non-blocking (asynchronous) — is of critical importance. Essentially, working with sockets is the same as input/output operations, which, as you know, can also be either synchronous or asynchronous (delayed). In the first case, calling an input/output function blocks the application until the input/output operation is completed. For asynchronous sockets, the input/output operation is initiated and the application continues to run. The completion of the input/output action will be marked in the system by the occurrence of a certain event. The WinSock 2.0 library supports both approaches to handling sockets; accordingly, Delphi components also can be set to the required type via their ServerType and ClientType properties, which will be studied later in this chapter.

One specific feature of the TServerSocket and TClientSocket components is that they are "two-layered" wrappers of API sockets. Both components have the property:

```
property Socket: TClientWinSocket;
```

for the TClientSocket component, and

```
property Socket: TServerWinSocket;
```

for the TServerSocket component.

This property is an object, essentially a socket wrapper, with all the functions necessary to support the establishment of a connection, reading, and writing. They share responsibility like this: on the TServerSocket (TClientSocket) level, all main published properties and events whose processing can be implemented programmatically are stored, while the `TServerWinSocket` (`TClientWinSocket`) level contains various functions, including those of reading from and writing to the socket.

Let's discuss the components and objects beginning with the server side, and then proceeding to the client side.

The *TServerWinSocket* Object

A list of connections with the client sockets is made on the level of this object. This list is stored in the property

```
property Connections[Index: Integer]: TCustomWinSocket;
```

The total number of connections (and the number of elements in the `Connections` property) is returned by the property

```
property ActiveConnections: Integer;
```

The above list and counter are very handy if you need to broadcast some general information across all your clients simultaneously, for example:

```
for i := 0 to ServerSocket.Socket.ActiveConnections - 1 do
    ServerSocket.Socket.Connections[i].SendText('Hi!');
```

The type of the server (blocking or non-blocking) is set through the property

```
type TServerType = (stNonBlocking, stThreadBlocking);
property ServerType: TServerType;
```

Since it is difficult to imagine a server that would be blocked by every read/write operation, Borland developers applied the following approach. The blocking mode was replaced by the `stThreadBlocking` mode. As a result, as soon as a new connection is set, a separate thread (a `TServerClientThread` object) starts. This thread is responsible for the connection with this particular client, and its blocking doesn't affect the performance of other connections.

If you don't want to generate `TServerClientThread`, and instead choose to declare a custom thread class and use it to work with the socket, you need to generate the event handler

```
property OnGetThread: TGetThreadEvent;
type TGetThreadEvent = procedure (Sender: TObject; ClientSocket:
TServerClientWinSocket; var SocketThread: TServerClientThread) of
object;
```

Unlike `stThreadBlocking`, the behavior of `stNonBlocking` is similar to that described earlier: all operations are performed asynchronously, and the programmer only has to specify the response to the events that occur upon their completion.

You probably know that building and destroying a new thread always has its price in terms of the system overhead. To avoid such waste, the object under discussion supports a thread cache. Upon completion of a connection, the threads are not destroyed, but rather switch to a waiting state until the next connection is activated.

The property

```
property ThreadCacheSize: Integer;
```

indicates the number of free threads that might be waiting, ready for a connection with the client. This number is determined by the duration and intensity of the contact with the clients. Redundant threads waste system resources — above all memory and CPU time. To optimize the performance of the free thread cache, it is useful to examine the values of two properties:

```
property ActiveThreads: Integer;
property IdleThreads: Integer;
```

which return the number of active (serving the clients) and idle (waiting) threads, respectively.

The start and completion of a thread that works with sockets are marked by the events

```
property OnThreadStart: TThreadNotifyEvent;
property OnThreadEnd: TThreadNotifyEvent;
type TThreadNotifyEvent = procedure (Sender: TObject; Thread:
TServerClientThread) of object;
```

Threads competing for some system resource are likely to cause problems when they operate in a multiuser environment. (See *Chapter 13*, which is devoted to multithread applications.) The following methods let you avoid such clashes when dealing with sockets:

```
procedure Lock;
procedure Unlock;
```

If your application contains a code fragment that may negatively affect the manageability of a multitasking environment, insert it between the calls for the `Lock` and `Unlock` methods — by doing so you block all other threads working with sockets for this period.

The reading and writing methods used for working in blocking mode are essentially different from the same methods utilized in non-blocking (asynchronous) mode. Let's first look at the methods called when you work in non-blocking (asynchronous) mode.

The mechanisms for reading are represented by a group of three methods:

❑ `function ReceiveLength: Integer;` — returns the number of bytes that can be received in response to the client's notification of sent data.

❑ `function ReceiveText: string;` — returns the text string read from the socket.

❑ `function ReceiveBuf(var Buf; Count: Integer): Integer;` — returns `Count` bytes of data that were read from the socket to the `Buf` buffer.

Similarly, the methods

```
function SendBuf(var Buf; Count: Integer): Integer;
procedure SendText(const S: string);
function SendStream(AStream: TStream): Boolean;
```

send the buffer, text string, and data stream to the client. Additionally, the method

```
function SendStreamThenDrop(AStream: TStream): Boolean;
```

sends the data stream to the client and then closes the connection.

> **NOTE**
>
> The `AStream` data stream, which is given as a parameter for the last two functions, is passed "under the supervision" of the `TServerWinSocket` object, and is removed by this object as the process of data transmission progresses. The developer should be careful not to attempt removing `AStream` after calling either the `SendSrteam` or `SendSrteamThenDrop` method.

Using the method

```
function GetClientThread(ClientSocket: TServerClientWinSocket):
TServerClientThread;
```

you can get the pointer to the thread that is currently serving a particular socket.

The events

```
property OnClientConnect;
property OnClientDisconnect;
property OnClientRead;
property OnClientWrite;
```

share the same type:

```
TSocketNotifyEvent = procedure (Sender: TObject; Socket:
TCustomWinSocket) of object;
```

They take place upon connecting to and disconnecting from the client, and also during reading or writing. Should an error occur, the following event is generated:

```
property OnClientError: TSocketErrorEvent;
TErrorEvent = (eeGeneral, eeSend, eeReceive, eeConnect, eeDisconnect,
eeAccept);
   TSocketErrorEvent = procedure (Sender: TObject; Socket:
TCustomWinSocket; ErrorEvent: TErrorEvent; var ErrorCode: Integer) of
object;
```

Its parameters are as follows: `ErrorEvent` indicates the type of the operation in the course of which the error occurred, and `ErrorCode` contains the Windows error code. If you have handled the error manually and do not wish the system to take measures for further treatment, just set the `ErrorCode` parameter to 0.

The *TServerSocket* Component

The key property of this component is the pointer to the object (mentioned above):

```
property Socket: TServerWinSocket;
```

It is this object that lets you take advantage of all the socket's functionalities. The component itself was created only for publishing all necessary properties and events. It has events of its own — `OnClientConnect`, `OnClientDisconnect`, `OnClientRead`, `OnClientWrite`, `OnClientError` — but they are not self-sufficient; instead, they contain pointers to the corresponding properties of the `TServerWinSocket` object. The same applies to the `ServerType` and `ThreadCacheSize` properties.

The component also provides the following events:

❒ `property OnListen: TSocketNotifyEvent;` — occurs after the address and port of the socket are set and before the socket is switched to listening mode (the state of readiness to accept a connection).

❒ `property OnAccept: TSocketNotifyEvent;` — occurs immediately after the connection is established.

The `Active: Boolean;` property is responsible for the socket state. Changing its value for the client socket means connecting to or disconnecting from the server. With the server socket, it means activating or disabling the listening state. Using this property produces an effect identical to using the following methods:

```
procedure Open;
procedure Close;
```

The property

```
property Service: string;
```

will help you identify the purpose of the socket. This property stores the character name of the service that uses this socket (ftp, http, telnet, etc.).

The *TClientWinSocket* Object

Many events and methods of this object were described earlier when we discussed the `TServerWinSocket` object, since both of these objects are derived from the same ancestor. However, some differences do exist and need to be commented on. Like the server socket, the client socket can be one of two types:

```
type TClientType = (ctNonBlocking, ctBlocking);
property ClientType: TClientType;
```

But, unlike the situation with the server socket, blocking the client socket cannot do much harm. If the `ctBlocking` mode is running, the client application is blocked until the operation is completed. Of course, if this scares you, you can always create a thread for working with the socket in `ctBlocking` mode manually. In `ctNonBlocking` mode, all operations are performed asynchronously.

The *TClientSocket* Component

In the discussion of this component, the primary focus will be the logical sequence of events that occur while establishing a connection between the server and the client socket. The sequence in question is as follows:

1. The `Open` method is called (or the `Active` property is set to `True`).

2. The `property OnLookup: TSocketNotifyEvent;` event is generated before initializing the socket.

3. At this stage, it is still possible to change the properties of the `TClientWinSocket` object — the address, the port number, etc.

4. The socket is completely initialized and begins the search for the server socket. Once it is found, the following event takes place:

```
property OnConnecting:TSocketNotifyEvent;
```

5. As soon as the client's request is satisfied by the server and the connection is established, the `property OnConnect: TSocketNotifyEvent;` event occurs.

Let's illustrate this chain of events with a sample code, in which we send information about the time and date. The process of connecting to the server looks like this:

```
procedure TClientForm.FileConnectItemClick(Sender: TObject);
var sHost: string;
begin
if ClientSocket.Active then ClientSocket.Active := False;
   if InputQuery('Choose Host', 'Name or Address', sHost) then
     if Length(sHost) > 0 then
       with ClientSocket do
       begin
         Host := sHost;
         Active := True;
       end;
end;
```

Once the connection is established, the client responds to the `OnClientRead` event:

```
procedure TClientForm.ClientSocketRead(Sender: TObject; Socket:
TCustomWinSocket);
   var s: string;
begin
   s:= Socket.ReceiveText;
   if ((s[1]='T') and (TimeSpeedButton.Down)) then
     TimeSpeedButton.Caption := Copy(s,2,Length(s))
   else if ((s[1]='M') and (MemSpeedButton.Down)) then
     MemSpeedButton.Caption := Copy(s,2,Length(s));
end;
```

In the server application, the socket is set to active (listening) state as soon as the program starts. All connected clients are automatically registered as elements of the list (the `Connections` property). The information about the date and time is sent by the server through the timer as formatted text strings:

```
procedure TServerForm.Timer1Timer(Sender: TObject);
var i: Integer; s : string;
 ms : TMemoryStatus;
begin
 with ServerSocket.Socket do for i := 0 to ActiveConnections - 1 do
  Connections[i].SendText('T'+TimeToStr(Now));

 GlobalMemoryStatus(ms);
 s := Format('%10dK',[(ms.dwAvailPageFile + ms.dwAvailPhys) div
1024]);
 with ServerSocket.Socket do for i := 0 to ActiveConnections - 1 do
  Connections[i].SendText('M'+s);
end;
```

You can make the server respond to a message received from the client. The answer must be sent via the `Socket` parameter of the `OnClientRead` event that occurred.

```
procedure TServerForm.ServerSocketClientRead(Sender: TObject;
  Socket: TCustomWinSocket);
begin
  Memo1.Lines.Add(Socket.ReceiveText);
  Socket.SendText('All right');
end;
```

A full listing of this example is provided on the companion CD.

Summary

Having studied the basics — sockets — you are now well-equipped to explore the various protocols and interfaces used for building present-day distributed applications and web services. Now that you are familiar with the concept of a network protocol suite and the socket API, you should be ready to detect and handle errors that occur on any layer of interaction.

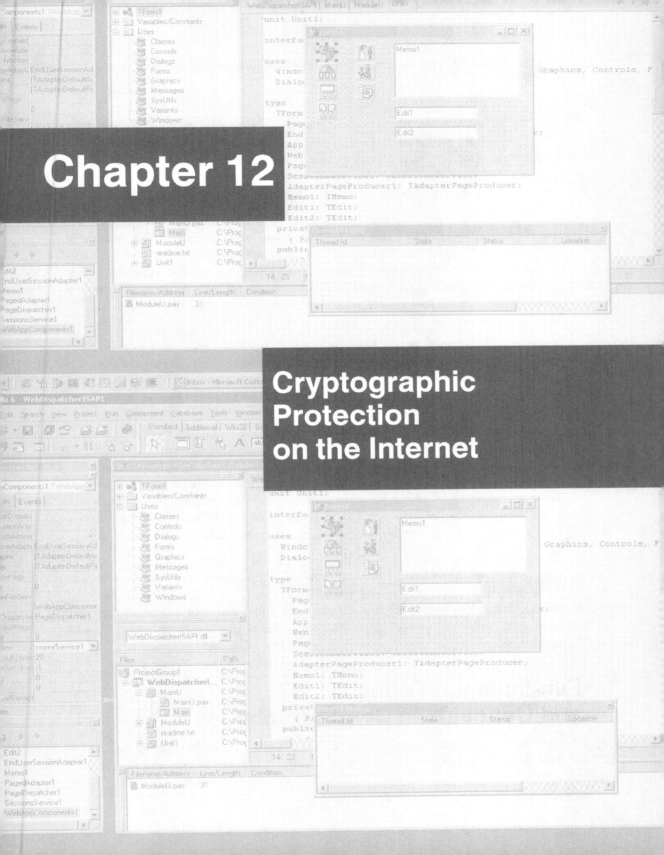

Chapter 12

Cryptographic Protection on the Internet

T he last decade has witnessed the rapid evolution of the Internet from a simple means of communication used mainly by enthusiasts, to its present state, in which it is increasingly becoming an arena for important business transactions. And no serious business can be conducted without observing a set of precise formal procedures devised in order to minimize possible risks and losses.

By definition, the Internet is a decentralized and uncontrollable (well, minimally controllable) environment, and besides your business partners, here you are likely to run across practically anybody, including all kinds of malicious individuals. This is why adequate precautions must be taken to protect all important information sent through the Internet against unauthorized access, damage, and alteration.

The name of the discipline that deals with such problems is *cryptography*. Originally, it was a weapon in the hands of various opposing secret services, but cryptography has gradually become a tool used by virtually every computer user. Of course, the technical details of protected systems are kept secret from laymen as much as possible. But it is really a necessity for a developer to acquire a fairly good knowledge of the major principles and methods of cryptography. Hundreds of programmers do their best to invent and implement their own custom-made "codes," "encoders," and "access-restriction systems," not thinking that in just a few hours — if not minutes — they will inevitably become the victim of a hacking. Moreover, not only individual developers find themselves in such a precarious situation: all passwords used in Windows 95, older Microsoft Office versions, and popular archive programs can be figured out quickly and easily. This is why only developers who are well-versed in modern cryptography will be able to cope with these tasks.

This chapter begins with a look at the range of applied tasks solved by cryptography. Then, we will discuss the concepts of digital signatures and certificates. After that, using a certificate manager as an example, we will explore the features of the CryptoAPI interface. And finally, you will learn how to customize web tools and components used in distributed applications to enforce cryptographic security.

Fundamental Terms and Concepts in Cryptography

Novices often confuse cryptography with the basic encryption and decryption of data. This is certainly the first and most important task of cryptography, which has been around for about a thousand years. Cryptography has, however, a much broader range of uses:

- ❐ Privacy (that is to say, protection of information against unauthorized access)
- ❐ Authentication of information and identification of legitimate system users
- ❐ Controlling the integrity of information

Privacy

Privacy is ensured by using encryption algorithms. The concept of privacy is very simple: data being transferred must not be read by anyone for the duration of a reasonable period of time, even if the data were to get stolen. Actually, as far as sending data through the Internet goes, a case like this is more often the rule than the exception. In the course of its travel between two remote computers, IP packets can pass dozens of hosts, and you cannot identify them and determine the route the data will take in advance.

Every encryption algorithm is in essence a rule used for scrambling the content of a source message (which is also often referred to as plain text) into an encrypted sequence of data (cipher text). The use of the word "text" in the definition is simply tradition. You can encrypt any kind of data: the contents of a database, an audio or video file, or an executable code.

Information is encrypted with a key — a specific sequence of data that, after being "mixed" with the source data according to a specific algorithm, ensures that the source information is modified until it cannot be decrypted without a second key. In any case, any type of encryption must be a reversible operation. And if you have the key, you can decrypt the content of the message into its original form and all the information in it will be unambiguously restored (Fig. 12.1).

The observant reader will have certainly noticed that we mentioned "a second key" rather than "the same key." Indeed, once you have locked the door to your house, you can rest assured that nobody who does not have the same set of keys as you can unlock it (of course, this is only if your door is solid enough and cannot be easily opened by a burglar armed with a sledgehammer and a lock-pick).

Fortunately, the situation is different in digital cryptography. There are cryptographic algorithms that use the same key both for encryption and for decryption. This kind of cryptosystem is referred to as symmetrical. The key used for both operations is called a private key. This private key is possessed only by the sender and the recipient of the message, which means that any outsider who has learned this private key is able to read the information encrypted with the key. In addition — and this possibility is by far more dangerous — a malicious intruder can encrypt and send misinformation by pretending to be a bona fide sender.

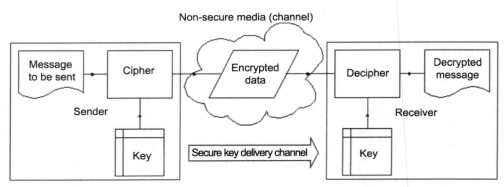

Fig. 12.1. Schematic diagram illustrating the method for sending confidential information

This is how matters stood when a work by W. Diffie and M. Hellman published in 1976 heralded in the era of asymmetrical encryption: or, in other words, encryption that uses a public key. There are various techniques for creating pairs of keys, in which one of them, which is called an open or public key, is utilized for encrypting information. This key can be made available to the general public. The other key — private — is used for decryption. Only the owner of this second key can read confidential messages. And because this key is known to just one person (while in the first case the same key is used by two parties), it need not be passed or transported anywhere, which significantly enhances the reliability of the whole system.

Mathematically speaking, the whole schema can easily be inverted. In other words, a private key can be used for encryption and a public key for decryption. You may well ask here: what sort of privacy is that if anyone is able to decrypt and read certain messages? This is a good point, of course: actually, this operation is not exactly encryption but it probably rings a bell to those readers who are familiar with the idea of electronic signatures. It's OK if you are unfamiliar with this concept, since we are going to discuss it later in more detail. As you can see, the entire edifice of modern cryptography is founded on the simple idea of using two different keys.

However paradoxical it may seem to an inexperienced novice, users throughout the world prefer to use public and well-known encryption algorithms. This tendency can be explained primarily by the fact that the collaborative efforts made by a community of cryptographers help detect and mend potential "holes" and deficiencies in such algorithms. A private algorithm, though it certainly makes life harder for malicious analysts, can become vulnerable and virtually useless as soon as any bugs are found in it. In addition, the cat will inevitably be let out of the bag somehow — sooner or later — and therefore it seems rather naive to rely heavily on the policy of keeping your algorithm secret in order to guard your privacy. As far back as in the nineteenth century, the Dutch scientist Kirchhoff advanced a criterion according to which the security of tamper-proof encryption should be preserved even in case all the encryption mechanisms and source data — except for the private key — fell into the hands of the opponent. The key in question is no more than just a system parameter and can be comparatively easily changed if it is lost without introducing any modifications to the entire system.

You do not have to be a mathematician to understand that your opponent, who has literally unlimited computational resources and all the time in the world at his or her disposal, will sooner or later inevitably decrypt any message with a finite length, if only by resorting to the banal method of checking all the possibilities. The core idea here is to use an algorithm that is secure enough to make the idea of "trying all the possibilities" senseless. In truth, any secret — be it commercial, state, or romantic — is destined to become outdated sooner or later. And if the goal cannot be achieved while this secret is still important, nobody will consider the decryption of it a worthy investment.

Mathematical formulas for precisely calculating stability do not exist: it can only be roughly estimated using various methods. Of course, stability depends on the length of the key — the longer the key the higher the stability. It should also be remembered that the computational power of modern computers is growing rapidly. For example, the Digital Encryption Standard (DES) designed in 1977 for U.S. governmental organizations, which uses 56-bit keys, had, by the end of the twentieth century, become an easy victim to an attack by a team of amateur cryptographers, who joined together to crack hundreds of computers around the world. To achieve this goal, they worked in tandem and used the Internet. The time it took them to wreak havoc on global systems amounted to just tens of hours.

But the development of cryptography never stops either. The newest highly sophisticated algorithms provide you with a number of possibilities that exceeds the number of atoms in the universe. The probability of guessing the correct answer is negligibly small. And for this reason, such algorithms are referred to as computationally secure.

Authentication

Another vital issue for any kind of information circulating within a secure channel is the problem of *authentication*. Authentication is used to prove that the object (a person, a computer system) is who or what he, she, or it claims to be. The source of a confidential message must be established and verified. Otherwise, one will not be able to protect oneself from a flood of misleading messages.

Authentication uses a number of methods:

❏ Password verification

❏ Checking essential attributes that are inherent to and inseparable from the object being verified

❏ Verifying the fact that the object possesses some kind of confidential information (a key, for instance)

❏ Establishing the fact that the object really was in the specified place at the specified moment of time

❏ A recommendation issued by a third, trusted party

At the present time, new authentication trends born in our digital era are beginning to replace older ones that had prevailed for centuries, including traditional paper passports and various credentials. Many of these new innovations, such as smart cards (portable cards containing detailed information about their owners), fingerprint readers, iris-identification devices, and other biometric devices have already received broad acceptance.

You undergo the procedure of authentication all the time when logging on to a network or a local computer. The deceptive outward simplicity of the password verification procedure in Windows hides a sufficiently complex algorithm that ensures that your password security is not being passed around the Internet.

Authentication is closely intertwined with the issue of *non-repudiation*. In the era of symmetrical cryptosystems, both the sender and the recipient within the framework of a single secure channel use the same key and are assumed to trust one other. Asymmetrical methods allow developers to extend the applications by including scenarios where the parties do not or cannot trust one other. These methods not only help establish who the sender is but also furnish unambiguous proof of the fact that the message was signed by this and only this sender.

Integrity

It is quite possible that any message sent through the Internet may, in whole or in part, fall into the wrong hands and undergo alterations. *Information integrity* implies that the message is received by the recipient in exactly the same form as it was forwarded by the sender, without any intentional or accidental modifications.

Sealed envelopes are meant to guarantee information integrity in conventional letter exchange. Digital information is treated in a similar fashion. A specific control code (hash or digest) is added to the message that is to be transferred. A hash is a sequence of data with a small (in comparison to the message), fixed length, which performs the role of a seal.

> **NOTE**
>
> Modern cryptography uses 128-, 160-, and 192-bit hashes.

A hash function generating such a code must possess two essential properties:

❑ It must be computationally irreversible, which means that you can unambiguously calculate the value of the hash for any given message, but you cannot reconstruct the source message itself using its hash (unless, of course, you are ready to check all the possibilities).

❑ The probability that the same hash will be used for different messages must be negligibly small.

In addition, your opponent part should not be able to calculate the correct value of the hash in order to prove the validity of his or her own false message. Since we have pretty much dismissed the usefulness of secret algorithms, the only way to cope with this problem is to introduce hash-calculating algorithms that use a variable parameter: a key. Only the legitimate sender and recipient of the message — who are the owners of the key — should be able to calculate the hash for a given message and thereby confirm its integrity.

Digital Signatures, Certificates, and How to Use Them

The advent of asymmetrical cryptographic methods was a landmark in the sphere of authentication and integrity control, which brought about dramatic developments in this field. Though mathematicians have long been able to calculate and exploit hashes, the subtlety here is to use a *signed hash*.

As stated above, a cryptosystem that uses two keys can provide encryption with both a public and a private key. In the first case, anyone can encrypt a message, but only one user is able to read it. In the second scenario, on the contrary, only the user who has the secret key can encrypt a message, while anyone who has the public key can effortlessly decrypt this message. The term "encryption" is hardly appropriate in this case. Rather, here we can speak of the process of signing a message. Thus you can see that the very same algorithms can be used both to provide privacy and to generate a *digital signature*.

A message using a private key that also carries a digital signature unambiguously identifies the person who has created (signed) it, just as a traditional signature on any document does.

> **NOTE**
>
> It has been argued that there is a crucial difference between a traditional and a digital signature. A traditional signature always and under all circumstances belongs to the same person. As for a digital signature, it is just data stored in a computer, and can be in the possession of any person who currently owns this computer. This is why some people have suggested that a digital signature should be called an "electronic seal," which can be borrowed, stolen, etc.
>
> In order to overcome this argument, the laws of some countries stipulate that only natural persons can use digital signatures, while legal entities are not allowed. However, regulations of certain other countries allow for both natural and legal "persons" to use digital signatures.

The basic stages involved in generating an electronically signed document are shown in Fig. 12.2.

1. The sender selects the hashing algorithm and constructs the hash for the document.

2. The pair of keys and the encryption algorithm to be used for the digital signature are specified.

3. The newly generated hash is processed (that is to say, signed) with the sender's secret key.

4. The message to be sent is compiled from the document body, the signed hash, the hash function identifiers, the encryption function, and the sender's public key.

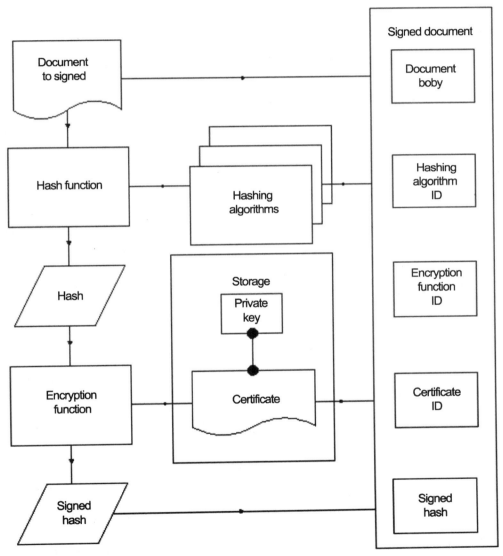

Fig. 12.2. The procedure for creating a digital signature

The recipient begins by calculating the hash using the same algorithm as the sender. Then, the recipient decrypts the hash value that was passed to him or her before the message transmission took place, with the sender's public key. If these two values are identical, the message has not been tampered with and has been delivered in its original form.

The suggested schema contains only one small bug concerning the authentication of the author of the signature. The signature is verified using a public key. Just how can we be sure that the public key that you have belongs in fact to the author of this signature?

In the early stages of using electronic signatures, various methods of publishing open keys were used — those that appeared most effective in terms of the ability to inform the widest possible sector of the public — including publishing these keys on book covers, attaching them to thousands of e-mail messages, etc. This, of course, helped deter potential substitution of these keys.

But a complete and adequate solution to this problem was provided only by digital certificates (which from here on out will be referred to simply as certificates). Such certificates contain information about a person or organization, along with this person's or organization's public key signed by a trusted authority, the Certification Authority (CA). The CA issues the certificate after proper authentication of the requester, that is, after the information that this requester has provided about himself or herself, as well as about his or her ownership of a given pair of keys, is duly verified and confirmed.

But here the obvious question needs to be settled as to why CAs can be trusted and who is responsible for CA authentication. This is a good question that can be answered only partially. CAs are well-ordered and have their own hierarchy. Each CA has its own certificate that must be issued and signed by a CA with a higher rank. And who is at the top of this hierarchical structure? The uppermost rank is formed by a comparatively small group of companies that make it their business to verify requesters and to provide them with such certificates. Number one among them is VeriSign (**www.verisign.com**).

Since a recommendation from a highly reputed certificate authority costs money, certificates, as a rule, are not issued for free. However, a personal certificate given to a natural person can be rather cheap, if not free. Moreover, some countries, Sweden, for instance, have launched their own programs aimed at certifying their citizens.

The situation is completely different when certificates are issued to companies for business purposes, the most expensive being those provided to various subsidiary CAs.

The size and profitability of the certification business can be inferred from the fact that in April 2002, Mark Shuttleworth, the founder of a well-known CA (Thawte, Inc. in South Africa), became the second space tourist and paid tens of millions of dollars for the pleasure of a week's visit to the International Space Station.

At this point, we will switch from our theoretical discussion to technical issues and take a little learning tour that will provide you with first-hand experience in the subject under discussion. Open your Internet Explorer and go to the **Contents** tab of the **Internet Options** window (the **Tools/Internet Options** item of the menu). Here, press the **Certificates** button, which activates the Certificate Manager.

> **NOTE**
>
> The same manager is provided as a part of Microsoft Platform SDK in the form of a separate program (CertMgr.exe).

The main part of the Certificate Manager window is taken up by four tabs: **Personal, Other People, Intermediate Certification Authorities**, and **Trusted Root Certification Authorities**. These tabs correspond to the four certificate storage areas that were preinstalled on your system. Each of these tabs lists the certificates contained in a given storage area (Fig. 12.3).

The last tab, **Root**, is used for storing certificates issued by the root CA (of the highest rank), which were originally provided as a part of the system distribution kit and are registered automatically. Only those Windows users who have administrator rights can add more certificates to and remove certificates from this list. The Microsoft certificate is also included in this list.

> **NOTE**
>
> Microsoft does not provide commercial certification services in the ordinary sense, that is to say, authentication services for individuals and organizations. However, all developers and companies who provide various solutions for Windows, including hardware drivers, cryptosystems, etc., must be certified by Microsoft. The Windows 2000 operating system does support a digital signature driver, though the signature itself is optional here. In Windows XP, however, all drivers must be signed.

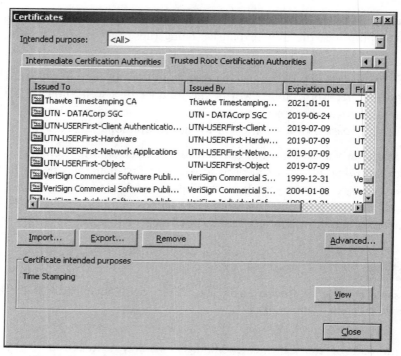

Fig. 12.3. The certificate list contained in the root storage

On top of the set of tabs is the **Intended purpose** option list, which lets you filter the certificate collection. By the intended purpose of a given certificate, we mean the list of potentially feasible tasks that can be accomplished using this certificate, such as:

- Server authentication
- Client authentication
- Signing an executable code
- Protecting e-mail messages
- Timestamping
- The Windows 2000 cryptographic utilities: IPSec and EFS
- Signing drivers and other Windows component parts

A full list of capabilities can be accessed by pressing the **Advanced** button.

Ensuring safety always involves getting rid of redundant features, and, as a consequence, the application range of every certificate is usually limited to a couple of related tasks.

Double-clicking a table row results in activating a specific window for viewing certificate properties in order to better explore the inherent potentialities of this particular certificate (Fig. 12.4).

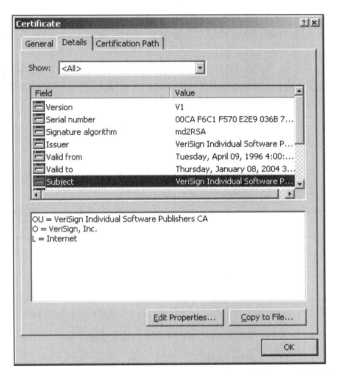

Fig. 12.4. The tab showing the properties of the certificate

Of the three tabs of the displayed dialog, the first one provides general information in a form legible even for a novice, while the third tab includes the entire chain of certificates up to the root one. Let's now concentrate on the second tab. The list of fields displayed here is actually the entire content of the certificate.

At this point, a few words need to be said as to what standards are used to manage the certificate system. A standard format for electronic certificates was approved by the recommendation of the International Telecommunications Union (ITU-T) X.509;

the same requirements are specified in ISO/IEC 9594-8. This standard has become commonly accepted.

Besides this, an invaluable contribution to the field of generating standards was made by the RSA company (named for Rivest, Shamir, and Adelman, who developed one of the first public-key encryption algorithms, and also owned the patent on it). By now, the patent has expired and the RSA method has been openly published in a public repository (at the site **www.rsa.com**). Of all the Public Key Cryptography Standard (PKCS) industry standards designed by them, you will most likely come across PKCS #10 (a standard format for a certificate request message sent by a client to a certification authority) and PKCS standard #7 (the standard response to this request, which contains the resulting certificate). It should be noted that these industry standards are supported by Microsoft Certificate Services.

According to X.509, every certificate must have a set of mandatory fields (listed in Table 12.1). In addition, it may include a number of optional extensions (an identifier of the CA and the certificate owner, the flags of the certificate's uses, etc.).

Table 12.1. The Fields of an X.509 Certificate

Name	Content
Version	The certificate version number: V1...V3. The Microsoft certification server that will be discussed elsewhere in this chapter issues V3 certificates.
Serial Number	The certificate's serial number, the uniqueness of which is guaranteed by the CA that issued it. Its length can vary.
Signature algorithm	The algorithm used for the digital signature.
Issuer	The name of the CA that issued the certificate.
Valid from	The date and time from which the certificate is valid.
Valid to	The date and time until which the certificate is valid.
Subject	The name of the individual/organization to whom/which the certificate is issued. This field often contains additional information about the country, region, or other subdivision.
Public key	The public key: 512- or 1024-bit binary data.

Information contained in a certificate is encoded using a specific coding schema, depending on the certificate version and on the type of fields. The steps involved in the processes of extracting and using this information will be covered in the next section, which discusses a demo application.

Introduction to CryptoAPI

The CryptoAPI program interface was first marketed as part of Microsoft Internet Explorer 3.02. The formal pretext for integrating cryptography into the popular web browser was the necessity of securing connections between HTTP clients and the server. Unofficially, the actual reason for this originates during a time of prolonged litigation between Microsoft and Netscape, when the former was forced to prove in court that Internet Explorer is an integral part of the system. Binding such an essential feature as cryptography to the browser was undeniably a strong trump.

Up until a certain moment, CryptoAPI had not been used almost anywhere in the Microsoft operating system environment except for the browser. Starting with Windows 2000, however, dramatic developments occurred. Currently, cryptography is used for designing the Encrypting File System (EFS) in the Internet Protocol Security (IPSec) secure-transport protocol, for remote authorization based on the Kerberos protocol, for encrypting e-mail, etc.

This chapter seeks to encompass two core aspects of managing CryptoAPI. The first aspect relates to the functional features of the interface and its capabilities that can be successfully utilized in your Delphi solutions. The second issue to be discussed is customizing and employing various ready-to-use cryptographic utilities that come as parts of the operating system and can be very handy for developing distributed information systems.

CryptoAPI Structure

CryptoAPI is a two-level structure. The upper level contains two system DLLs — advapi32.dll and crypt32.dll — which provide for the overwhelming majority of CryptoAPI functions. It is these DLLs that are called from a customer's programs. Bear in mind, though, that these dynamic libraries do not perform encryption as such, nor do they provide the service of signing documents — they just redirect all calls to a lower level.

The lower level houses a specific cryptographic service provider (CSP), which is a sort of a "black box" and is called by all cryptographic functions in order to implement actual encryption, the signing of a document, etc. The implementation mechanism used for the cryptographic algorithms is hidden from the user.

It can be based in certain hardware components or designed programmatically. Alternatively, it can combine both approaches. Each vendor is represented by either a dynamic library or a set of libraries, which support the lower-level API, CryptoSPI.

This model can be compared to modern 3D graphics accelerators (this is a comparison that Microsoft likes to make). Indeed, while programming using API OpenGL or Direct3D, you do not care about what 3D graphics methods are being utilized in every particular case. Most often, these methods are implemented through certain hardware features of the graphics processor on your video card, such as Riva GeForce or ATI Radeon. But if your video card does not provide full hardware support for all the capabilities, it does not mean that these capabilities are lost for you. It just means that they will simply be emulated programmatically.

Normally, the standard Windows 2000 toolkit includes several CSPs. It should be noted that not all of them are necessarily full-fledged providers. Besides different sets of supported functionalities, these providers vary significantly depending on the algorithms they use for encryption/signing, as well as on the length of the key, etc. Thus, the very first provider that gained broad recognition — the MS Base Cryptographic Provider — uses 40-bit symmetric key encryption and 512-bit public key encryption. This provider was used as the basis for developing such providers as Strong and Enhanced Cryptographic Provider, which use 128-bit and 1024-bit keys, respectively.

Theoretically speaking, almost anyone can develop their own customized cryptographic service provider. In order to install and operate this provider in the Windows environment, however, you need to submit exhaustive information on it to Microsoft, undergo the certification process, and obtain from them a digital signature. Apparently, all these procedures are extremely complicated, and therefore not feasible for the ordinary user. Thus, you in fact have to choose between two options: either use CryptoAPI with multiple built-in providers, or borrow a solution developed by independent programmers.

For those programmes who work in C and C++, the WinCrypt.h header file is supplied as a part of Platform SDK and other products. Programmers writing in Visual Basic and other script languages are provided with the CAPICOM utility, an Automation object that is essentially a COM wrapper for CryptoAPI.

One of the most sophisticated and important functions of CryptoAPI is the storage of private keys. In fact, it is this aspect that happens to be the weak point in most cryptosystems. If any malicious intruder can effortlessly get access to private keys and get hold of them, then all the brilliantly conceived and skillfully implemented algorithms turn out to be useless. The key storage methods are becoming increasingly more complex with every new Microsoft operating system. In Windows 95, private keys were stored in the Registry; in Windows 2000, they are stored as files inside the user profile, but here they are encrypted with a specific session key that is generated and supported by the Protected Storage service on the basis of the data about the user and the computer.

> **NOTE**
>
> For a detailed explanation of how the methods for storing private keys are implemented in Windows 2000, refer to *Chapter 13*, "*Security*" in the Windows 2000 Resource Kit. It should also be noted that there are certain CSPs that support hardware-only techniques for storing keys (for instance, inside a smart card).

Of course, you do not necessarily need to put all the above information to practical use in your program. Its purpose is just to help you better understand the underlying principles of the work of CryptoAPI. Each user is supplied with a unique key storage within the system, which is represented by a named part of the whole key storage. This is a logical entity that lets the programmer not be tied to the specific physical location of the key.

> **NOTE**
>
> At times, — when the consideration of extra security and reliability calls for it — it may be reasonable not to rely too heavily on Crypto API. It is recommended that you make several copies of all rarely used private keys (such as the emergency recovery key in the Encrypting File System (EFS)) on removable information carriers, keep them in a safe place, and remove those keys from the computer. This is particularly important for laptop computers, which often fall victim to theft.

So, what exactly can a programmer find for him- or herself among CryptoAPI's capabilities?

❑ Working with the providers (obtaining a list, selecting them, creating the context for accessing the key container)

❏ Basic cryptographic operations (encrypting, decrypting, generating and verifying electronic signatures)

❏ Managing keys (generating symmetrical keys and asymmetrical key pairs, exporting/importing/removing keys)

❏ Managing certificates (working with storage areas, viewing and searching in storage areas, exporting/importing certificates)

❏ Validating certificates, working with lists of trusted and revoked certificates

All in all, CryptoAPI provides about 300 functions, and with every new version and improvement that number is growing (the current CryptoAPI version is Crypto API 2.0). More detailed information on them is stored in MSDN, where you can easily find the required functions by their prefixes, crypt- and cert-. All basic operations are illustrated there by examples in C.

Using CryptoAPI: the Certificate Manager

To be able to use CryptoAPI with Delphi, you will need the file where all its functions are described. Unfortunately, Borland does not include a translation of the WinCrypt.h. header file into Pascal in the Delphi toolkit. This means that in order to utilize CryptoAPI, you will have to rely on the products of independent developers who have managed to do the translation in question themselves. You can find two such examples at **http://codecentral.borland.com**: ID 15979, by Massimo Maria Ghisalberti, and ID 17597, by Oleg Starodub. The files — wcrypt2.pas and wincrypt.pas, respectively — will enable you to call the required functions. Both these files work with CryptoAPI Version 2, though the wcrypt2.pas file is somewhat incomplete.

Our sample manager is very similar to the Certificates Manager that comes as a part of Windows and was described earlier. Nevertheless, in our opinion, it is just this example that is particularly worthy of discussion: whatever problems you will need to tackle, the task of arranging and managing certificates will inevitably be one of them.

The manager user interface is surprisingly simple: the `TTabControl` component that contains the list proper (the `TListView` component) and several buttons for performing the basic functions (Fig. 12.5).

Our manager works with standard system storage areas such as MY (corresponding to the **Personal** page of the Certificates Manager), TRUST (**Other People**), ROOT (**Trusted Root Certification Authorities**), and CA (**Intermediate Certification Authorities**). Besides this, a new function — `CertEnumSystemStore` — was added starting with Windows NT4 SP4, which gives you a list of all the storage areas on a given computer. In this example, the version of the operating system is being checked, and if this function is supported, then the number of `TTabControl` tabs — every one of which denotes a storage area — is increased to the actual number of these storage areas.

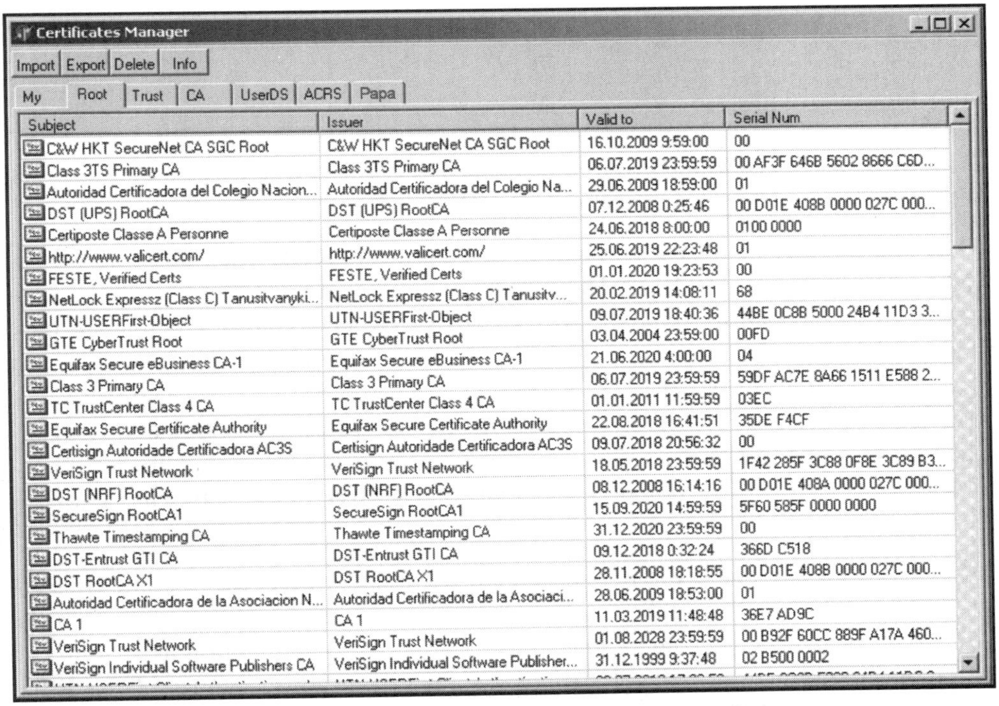

Fig. 12.5. The main **Certificates Manager** window

The **Issuer** and **Subject** fields are encoded using the so-called Distinguished Names (DN) standard. This is a record containing the attributes of a given object, delimited by commas, for example: 'CN = MyServer, OU = UsersUnit'. For certificates, the following DN fields are defined:

Table 12.2. DN Fields for the X.509 Standard Certificates

Abbreviated Name	Full Name	Content
CN	CommonName	The name of a physical person or a legal entity; for certificates issued to computers, this is its DNS
O	Organization	The legal name of an organization
OU	Organizational Unit	The name of an organizational unit, for instance, the Certification Services Division
L	Locality	The locality of an organization
S	State or Province	The full name of the state or province
C	Country	The two-letter abbreviation that denotes the country (US, CA, RU, etc.)
E	E-mail	An e-mail address

The two date fields, **Valid From** and **Valid To**, are encrypted using the common Windows standard for representing time, FILETIME.

Finally, a number of fields, the algorithm identifiers, are represented using the so-called Object Identifier (OID). This coding schema is provided by the ASN.1 (Abstract Syntax Notation) standard (ASN) used in X.509. In this schema, all constants are represented as strings of integers delimited by periods. For instance, the '1.2.840.113549.1.1.5' string is used for generating the SHA1 hash algorithm. But how can we get a conveniently readable name from this bulky and indistinct sequence of numbers? To do this, you need to use a special CryptoAPI function, CryptFindOIDInfo, which, given a specified OID, returns the name of the encrypted entity.

The certificate name and the public key are represented by corresponding byte arrays. You will need the number in order to locate the desired certificate within the storage area. The advantage of the CertFindCertificate function is that it can carry out a search using several attributes simultaneously: the names of the issuer and the subject, the algorithm applied, the key, etc. However, taking into account the fact that each certificate from a given issuer is supplied with a unique number, an unambiguous search result is ensured by using a combination such as the issuer identifier plus the certificate number. This structure is referred to as CERT_ID. While compiling a certificate list, you generate an instance of this structure and establish its relationships with the **Data** fields of every TListItem element of the TListView component.

Our example has a function for returning detailed information on the certificate, which decrypts the essential fields and represents them in a conveniently readable form. Viewing it helps to better understand and handle the variety of these (rather unusual for an ordinary Windows user) coding schemas.

The fundamental structure used by all the functions involved in managing certificates is CERT_CONTEXT:

```
CERT_CONTEXT = record
    dwCertEncodingType: DWORD;
    pbCertEncoded:      PBYTE;
    cbCertEncoded:      DWORD;
    pCertInfo:          PCERT_INFO;
    hCertStore:         HCERTSTORE;
  end;
```

As you can see, CERT_CONTEXT consists of two parts: the encrypted certificate body (the pbCertEncoded array of length cbCertEncoded) and the pCertInfo notation, which contains all the principal fields and extension fields.

Listing 12.1 includes the declaration of just one Certificates Manager function, the import function. Otherwise, the full listing would have been too long. (The full source code is provided on the companion CD.) The procedure has the following parameters: Store, which is the name of the system storage area where we are trying to put the certificate, and FileName, which is the certificate file name. The file must comply with the PKCS #7 format. Such files, for example, are generated by the Microsoft Certificate Services.

NOTE

You can take advantage of another format, PFX, if you choose to export/import a certificate together with the corresponding private key. Private keys are provided for only those certificates that were generated by a CA either for you personally or for your machine.

Listing 12.1. The Certificates Manager: the Import Procedure

```
function InstallCert( const Store, FileName: string ): Integer;
var CertFile: file;
    hStore : HCERTSTORE;
```

```
    PKCS7Length: Integer;
    Buf: pointer;
    pccExisting, pccNewContext: PCCERT_CONTEXT;
    le: Integer;
    Res: boolean;
begin
 Result := -1;
 try
  try
   AssignFile( CertFile, FileName );
   ReSet( CertFile, 1 );
   PKCS7Length := FileSize( CertFile );
   buf := AllocMem( PKCS7Length );
   if not Assigned( buf ) then RaiseLastOSError;
   {$I-}
   Blockread( CertFile, buf^, PKCS7Length, le );
   if PKCS7Length<>le then RaiseLastOSError;
   hStore := CertOpenSystemStore( 0, pChar(Store) );
   if not Assigned( hStore ) then RaiseLastOSError;
   pccNewContext := CertCreateCertificateContext( X509_ASN_ENCODING
   or PKCS_7_ASN_ENCODING,

                                     buf, PKCS7Length );
   if not Assigned( pccNewContext ) then RaiseLastOSError;
   pccExisting := CertFindCertificateInStore( hStore,
   X509_ASN_ENCODING or PKCS_7_ASN_ENCODING, 0,

   CERT_FIND_EXISTING, pccNewContext, nil );
   if Assigned( pccExisting ) then
    begin
     CertFreeCertificateContext( pccExisting );
     Result := 0; //already exists
     Exit;
    end;
   Res := CertAddCertificateContextToStore(hStore,
                                     pccNewContext,
                                     CERT_STORE_ADD_NEW,
                                     nil );
   le := GetLastError;
```

```
     if (Res = False) and (DWORD(le)=$80092005)(*CRYPT_E_EXISTS*) then
      Result := 0
     else
      raise EOSError.CreateResFmt( @SOSError, [le, SysErrorMessage(le) ]
)
   finally
    if Assigned( Buf ) then FreeMem( Buf );
    CloseFile( CertFile );
    CertFreeCertificateContext( pccNewContext );
    CertCloseStore( hStore, 0 );
   end;
   except
    on E:EOSError do
     Result := E.ErrorCode;
    on E:EInOutError do
     Result := E.ErrorCode;
   end;
  end;
```

In the above listing, the user interface and the function for managing certificates are contained in separate modules, Main and CertUtils, respectively. We hope that these utilities may come in handy in your future projects.

Microsoft Certificate Service

To build a system implementing the public key encryption infrastructure, you do not need to accumulate a wide assortment of certificates issued by various third-party organizations. The Windows 2000 operating system server includes a service that supports a full cycle of certificate management: issuing and maintaining them, publishing lists of issued certificates and certificate-revocation lists, etc.

It's important that this service be transport protocol independent. Developers are provided with COM interfaces for all major certificate service modules that can be accessed from various client applications. If you have such a service installed on your computer, go to **http://SERVERNAME/CertSrv** (a web folder with this name is generated by default, but it is possible that your administrator will name it differently). Here, you will find the sample client application of the certificate service that uses the browser as the interface.

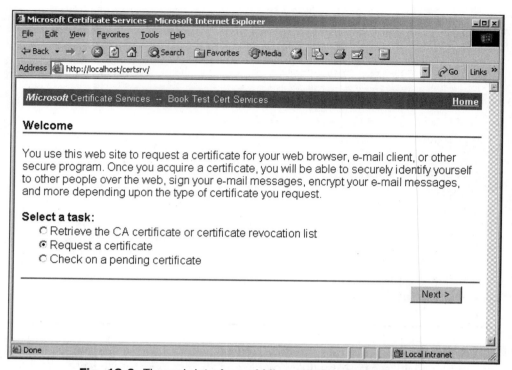

Fig. 12.6. The web interface of Microsoft Certificate Services

The range of tasks performed by this application is typical of those involved in interaction with a certificate authority:

☐ Obtaining and installing root CA certificate

☐ Obtaining a certificate revocation list (CRL)

☐ Submitting a new certificate request

☐ Checking the current status of a request sent earlier

Microsoft CA can use two approaches for distributing certificates: automatic (immediate) and non-automatic (out-of-band or delayed) modes. In the first case, a certificate request is processed immediately and, if the information provided by the requester meets the specified CA criteria, the desired certificate is issued in the form of an output parameter of the corresponding method.

The second scenario implies submitting all requests for subsequent processing by the administrator by means of a specific Certification services tool. The administrator personally grants certificates, rejecting all illegal requests.

> **WARNING**
>
> Remember that if your CA is configured in such a way that it issues certificates automatically, and if the web folder mentioned above is insufficiently protected (with additional security measures, such as, for example, a password-validation mechanism), then anyone can obtain a certificate from your CA. Such a situation is obviously undesirable at the very least, and as often as not may become critical.

The CertCli COM object is responsible for processing certificate requests on the server side, while on the client side this task is performed by xenroll.dll.

At a later stage, when discussing the SOAP protocol, we will discuss a specific demo Web service that distributes certificates by calling Microsoft Certificate Services.

Implementing a Secure Network Connection with Internet Protocols

The Secure Sockets Layer (SSL) protocol was one of the first protocols to be developed (in 1994) with the explicitly stated purpose of server authentication. In 1996, its new version (3.0) was submitted to the IETF for formal approval. So don't be surprised if you happen to come across this out-of-date version while browsing the official SSL site (**http://www.netscape.com/eng/ssl3**). And what about the protocol itself? Has it undergone any changes in the course of the last eight years? In 1999, it was formally adopted as the recommended standard (RFC 2246), but still under the name of Transport Layer Security (TLS 1.0), and with only minor improvements and extensions. Microsoft tends to use the term TLS in its documentation, but the abbreviation SSL is far more widely accepted. Besides this, you might run across the term SChannel, which pertains to the Windows toolkit designed for implementing both twin protocols.

Now we have to position SSL correctly within the framework of the seven-layer protocol stack, OSI/ISO. This is the wrapper covering the transport layer that is responsible for encrypting data packets and signing them electronically, as well as for generating and exchanging keys. Certainly, normal operation requires that these packets be transferred using a network protocol (most often TCP/IP). SSL, which is a higher-level protocol, is utilized for handling encrypted information. SSL is often confused with the HTTPS protocol, which is definitely incorrect, since HTTPS is just a variation of HTTP that uses SSL encryption to implement secure connections. Typically, HTTP uses Port 80, while the default HTTPS port is 443.

The SSL protocol supports two authentication modes: server authentication and mutual authentication. In the first scenario, only the server has to prove its identity (with the help of its certificate), while in the second case, each client connecting to the server is required to do the same.

So, how exactly does the communication channel implemented with the SSL protocol work? Once a connection is established, handshaking takes place, which consists of four steps. Two steps are fulfilled by the client, and two by the server.

1. The client sends a `ClientHello` message to the server, which contains:

    - A list of the cryptographic algorithms for encryption and digital signature generation that are supported by the client

    - The session identifier, if the client wants to resume the interrupted session

    - A random number used to initialize the first state

    - A list of compression algorithms, if it is possible to use them

2. The server selects one of the algorithms from the list provided by the client (the list is arranged in such a way that the preferred algorithms are put on top of it). If the server does not support any of the listed algorithms, it signals a denial-of-connection failure. In addition, the server sends its certificate (the basis for all subsequent actions) and another random number.

    If mutual authentication is required in order to successfully establish the connection, then at this stage, the server must also request the client certificate.

3. The client generates the session key based on these random numbers. This is the secret key used for symmetrical encryption. Such a session key can be 40 or 128 bits long, depending on the server settings. This newly generated key is digitally signed by the client with the server public key (which was

, received in the certificate body) and encrypted with the algorithm that was passed in the first stage and confirmed in the second stage. All this together with the specific security mode indicator is sent to the server.

Also, the client has to send its certificate if necessary.

4. The server decrypts the session key with its own private key. If a client certificate has been passed, the server verifies it as well.

Now everything is ready for implementing secure two-way data transmission. The server signals its readiness to start the transaction, and secure information exchange follows, with the data encrypted using the session key.

At this time, provided the **Warn if changing between secure and not secure mode** option of Internet Explorer is set, the user sees the following message (Fig. 12.7).

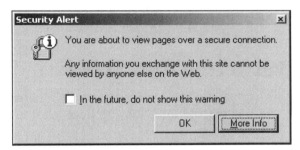

Fig. 12.7. The Internet Explorer message that appears once you have switched to SSL mode

If the IE user wishes to view the information on the certificate of the server that is participating in SSL communication, he or she can double-click the icon appearing in the IE status bar when in secure mode (Fig. 12.8).

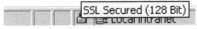

Fig. 12.8. The icon in the Internet Explorer status bar that is activated in SSL mode and enables you to view the server certificate

Among the IE security options related to SSL, there is another less conspicuous but extremely important one. Here we mean the **Check for server certificate revocation (requires restart)** checkbox. This option lets the SSL client request the most recent version of the certificate revocation list (CRL) from the appropriate CA prior to establishing a connection. Just like any other highly sensitive information —

passwords, for example — a certificate's private key can be compromised. If this happens, the entire certificate becomes invalid, since any malicious imposter is able to break into your system. The only thing to do in this case is to inform the CA about the loss of the key. All certificates that have become invalid before the scheduled expiration date are revoked and included in a CRL which in turn is sent by the CA to all users on demand.

By default, this IE option is deactivated: indeed, such lists are databases and can be very large. However, if you are developing an application that you mean to exploit within a corporate network for passing highly confidential information, such extra checking can be very important.

> **NOTE**
>
> Incidentally, a reasonably short validity term for a certificate is also a very efficient preventive measure against possible damages should the certificate be lost.

Configuring SSL on the IIS 5 Server

In this section, we will discuss how to customize the settings for secure web connections using the Internet Information Services v.5.0, which comes with Windows 2000.

As follows from the above description of the underlying principles of SSL functioning, the server certificate is absolutely indispensable for the proper operation of the system. This means that the very first step you need to take in order to enable your server to support communications using the HTTPS protocol is to provide it with a certificate issued by the appropriate certification authority. Of course, you can obtain this certificate from your local CA. But this scenario has a very important flaw: such a certificate must be included in the lists of trusted certificates on the machines of all your clients. Otherwise — depending on the Internet Explorer security settings — at worst, the connection to the server will be denied, and at best the user will be asked whether he or she chooses to proceed with the connection (Fig. 12.9). Most users will answer "No" — and will be absolutely right in doing so.

If your distributed application is meant to be run within a company's intranet, then it is quite easy to provide all users with the appropriate certificates. However, if you do not know all your prospective clients, then the best solution will be to spend the required sum and obtain the server certificate from one of the root CAs included by default in the IE certificate list.

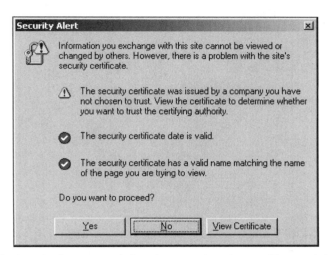

Fig 12.9. A typical message informing you that the certificate of the server
you have tried to connect to using HTTPS is untrustworthy

The lack of a server certificate is immediately evident from two facts:

❑ The **SSL Port** edit field is grayed (Fig. 12.10).

❑ In the **Directory Security** page, only one button in the Secure Communications
set of controls — the **Server Certificate** button, which lets you launch the Certificate Wizard — is active (Fig. 12.10, b).

Since this chapter does not attempt to duplicate the IIS documentation, let us just
briefly outline the steps involved in the process of setting the SSL options on the
server.

You can use one of the certificates that are already installed on your computer
(in other words, those whose lists of intended purposes include the Server
Authentication flag).

You may also choose to generate a new certificate, in which case you need
to launch the wizard for creating new certificates. In fact, the wizard in question
is simply a tool for generating certificate requests in PKCS #10 format, where
the certificate's intended purpose — server authentication — is predefined.
This request is then directed to the specified CA, and, as soon as you get a response, you can run the wizard again to install the certificate and associate it with
the web server.

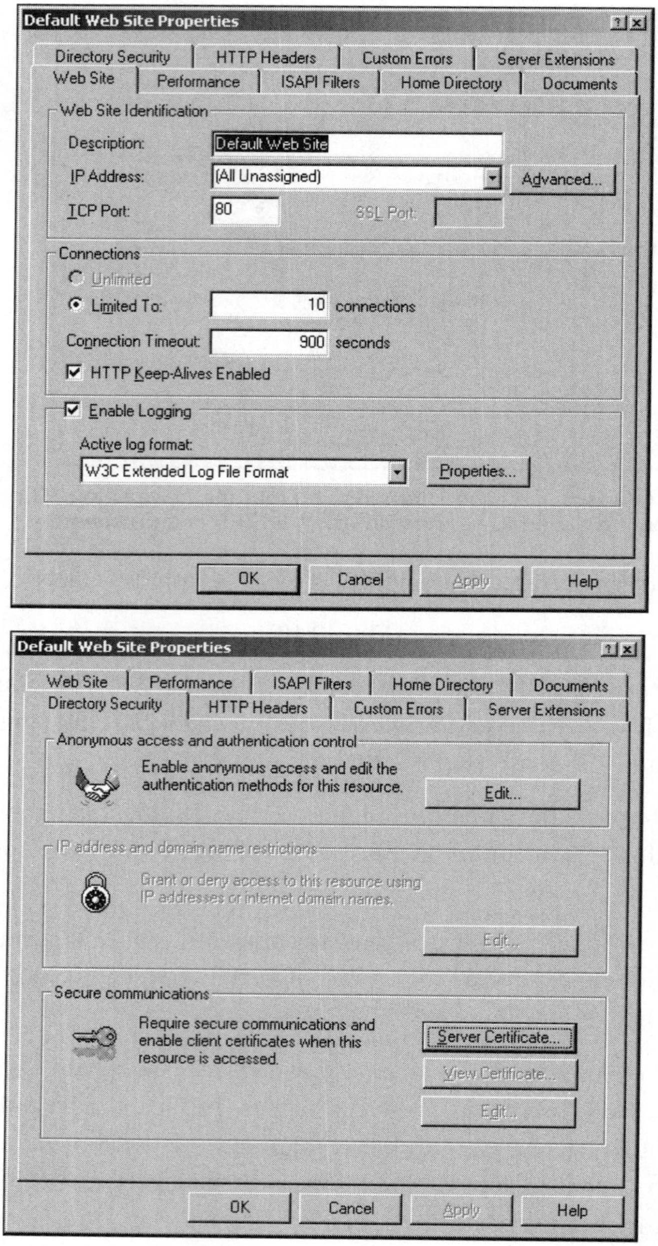

Fig. 12.10. The **Web Site Properties** page, which allows you to customize the settings for a secure communication channel

When working with the wizard, it is important to remember that the **Your Site's Common Name** field must always contain the same URL that will be used by the HTTP clients to access the protected connection. If you mean to make the server accessible through the Internet, you must indicate the server domain name (**www.myserver.com**). In the context of intranets, the name of the server computer can be used. Alternatively, the IP address is also permissible in both cases.

Finally, you can take advantage of the third technique for obtaining the certificate by importing it from a *.key file. This format was widely used in IIS Version 4 (and earlier versions) for exporting certificates and the corresponding private keys.

Each folder of the IIS web site is provided with its individual **Directory Security** page and the corresponding SSL options, but on these pages, the **Server Certificate** button is deactivated. This means that only one common certificate is valid within the entire site, but you are still able to set the SSL options for each folder individually. If, in addition, you want to safeguard a certain portion of information with another certificate, you will have to create a separate site in IIS and specify the relationship between them.

The SSL options can be set after pressing the **Edit** button (Fig. 12.11).

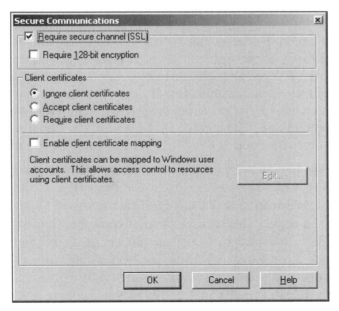

Fig. 12.11. The SSL settings for the web folder
in Internet Information Services 5

Well, that's about it as far as configuring SSL on the server goes, except that the only Windows-specific option — **Enable client certificate mapping** — allows the mapping of certificates electronically signed by clients to Windows user accounts in order to facilitate resource management.

Customizing the SSL Protocol on the Client Side

The client side in this example will also be represented by the Microsoft browser. Even if your client application is not browser-based, it most likely uses some browser features in its work. For instance, the SOAP protocol implementation for Delphi 6 is founded in the WinInet library, which is in fact nothing but the implementation of the HTTP and FTP protocols for Internet Explorer, and therefore shares with it all the options and settings.

> **NOTE**
>
> Competing browsers also have their own HTTPS implementation. Moreover, the SSL protocol was originally developed and implemented by Netscape. Netscape Navigator uses its own functionalities and repositories for handling and storing certificates, which are in no way associated with CryptoAPI.

Under ordinary circumstances — that is to say, when only authentication of the server is required — a connection can be established if the server certificate has not expired or been revoked and was issued by a CA listed among those trusted by the client. If all these requirements are met, the client just needs to change the name of the protocol in the corresponding URL from **http://something/...** to **https://something/**. Those clients who try to access the resource using the old URL will be returned an error: HTTP 403.4 (Forbidden: SSL required).

Besides the server certificate, a secure data transaction can also use certificates issued to the other party: that is to say, client certificates that identify the clients of your application. Information about the certificate is passed with the request and can be read by the server. This scenario is most convenient for managing systems that should only be accessed by a limited number of users. Suppose you have decided to launch a local CA that issues certificates only to those users who are authorized to work with your application. In such a case, you have to select the **Require client certificates** option in Fig. 12.11. Now, only certificate owners will be able to access your resource, while all unauthorized clients will be rejected with the HTTP error code 403.7 (Forbidden: Client certificate required).

If you have more than one certificate that can be used for client authorization on your computer, the browser will display a window with the list of appropriate certificates.

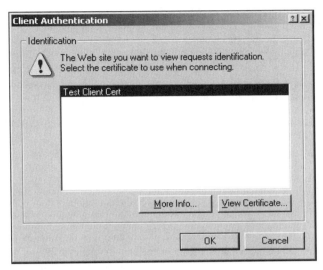

Fig. 12.12. The window through which you can enforce access control by authorizing only appropriately certified clients to access a communication channel secured using SSL

WARNING

It is often necessary to close all the IE windows on your computer after you have obtained a certificate online or introduced changes to the settings.

At this stage, it might be appropriate to provide some useful hints for those readers who intend to utilize SSL without the Microsoft producrs.

An alternative implementation of the HTTP protocol is offered in the Indy component package (**www.nevrona.com/Indy**) that comes with Delphi 6. While establishing secure connections, it, in turn, relies on the OpenSSL package (**www.openssl.org**). Both solutions are distributed in the form of source codes — a security measure that is difficult to overestimate. Moreover, Indy is a cross-platform product and is used as a basis for developing all Internet solutions for Kylix. It is quite possible to recompile all VCL modules for Delphi 6 as well, and do this in such a way as to replace WinInet with Indy.

The OpenSSL package — with corresponding Microsoft products — supports the SSL versions 2 and 3 and TLS 1.0 protocols. This package is continuously being improved and, at the moment of the writing of this book, the latest version available is Version 0.9.6.

NOTE

SSL solutions are subject to US Export Restrictions, which is why new SSL versions for Indy can be found, for example, at a Slovenian server (**www.intellicom.si**). We recommend that you familiarize yourself with the legal aspects of this problem before using and distributing cryptographic solutions.

If you are implementing an HTTPS connection not interactively from the browser, but rather using the SOAP protocol, then you need to specify the client certificate programmatically. The technique for this will be discussed in the following chapters.

Summary

This chapter has discussed the most general underlying principles used for creating secure information systems, which utilize modern cryptography as one form of protection. This is a comparatively new field: on the one hand, a number of comprehensive books have been written on the subject of cryptographic scientific theories, while on the other hand, a plethora of safety manuals for system administrators have been published, where the prevailing methodologies used are essentially something uninformative as "first you do this, then you do that." We hope that this book will help to fill the gap between these two approaches and not only inform you about how to utilize cryptography in your applications, but also provide you with a better understanding of the larger picture.

In no way can security requirements be reduced to just using various cryptographic protection measures. This problem has many dimensions to it — which implies that you will have to solve a lot of tasks that go far beyond the scope of this book — from considering the right time for introducing patches and new packages, to enforcing extra access restrictions.

This chapter has not dealt with the IPSec protocol (Internet Protocol Security). This is a fairly new protocol that was originally implemented by Microsoft in Windows 2000. Besides Windows, it also is used with operating systems provided by other vendors, although so far it has not found the widespread recognition that SSL has. Still, if all the clients of your application support IPSec, you may have to consider employing this protocol, and to do this you should refer to the Windows 2000 Resource Kit, which includes documentation on the subject.

Chapter 13

Threads and Processes

W orking with Delphi, one should bear in mind that this exceptional product not only simplifies the development of complex applications, but also makes use of all the features of the operating system. *Threads* are one of the features supported by Delphi.

Threads allow you to accomplish several tasks simultaneously within one program. PCs operating systems have just recently made this possible.

The *operating system* (OS) provides the application with the use of the CPU for a time, and as soon as the application switches to message wait or frees up the processor, the operating system gives control to another task. Now that computers with more than one processor have dropped drastically in price, and the Windows NT operating system can use several processors, users really can launch more than one task at a time. When planning the time of the CPU, Windows 95 and Windows NT distribute it among threads, not among applications. To use all the advantages provided by several processors in the newest operating systems, the programmer should know how to create threads.

This chapter deals with the following issues:

❏ What are threads?

❏ The difference between a thread and a process.

❏ Advantages of threads.

❏ The `TThread` class in Delphi.

❏ Implementation of a multithread application.

❏ Thread synchronization.

Threads Overview

The definition of a thread is quite simple: *threads* are objects that receive the time of the processor. The time of the processor is allotted by quanta, or time slices. A quantum is the interval at the thread's disposal until the time is transferred to the disposal of another thread.

Note that quanta are allotted not to programs or processes, but to the threads they generate. Each process has at least one (main) thread, but the latest operating systems, beginning from Windows 95 (for followers of Borland Kylix: Linux also), make it possible to launch several threads within a process.

If you are a novice at using threads, then the simplest example of their use is found in Microsoft Office applications. The Excel and Word packages employ several threads. In MS Word, you can correct grammar and type at the same time, entering data both from the keyboard and the mouse; Excel can perform background calculations while typing.

NOTE

In Windows NT/2000, and XP you can find out the number of the threads launched by the application using the utility Task Manager. Select the **Thread Count** option from among the indexes shown in the **Processes** window. As of the writing of these lines, MS Word has used 5 threads, and Delphi has used 3.

It is quite possible that you are reading this chapter out of mere curiosity. But it's more likely that you are looking for solutions to specific problems. What kind of problems can be solved using threads?

If the tasks of the application can be divided into different subsets — event handling, input/output, communication, and others, then the threads may be organically embedded in the software solution. If the developer can divide one complex task into several small ones, this will only enhance the code portability and the options for its multiple use.

In making an application multithreaded, the programmer also gets additional options for managing it by controlling thread priorities, for example. If any of them slows the application down by taking too much processor time, then its priority can be lowered.

Another important advantage of threads is that if the load on the application grows, their number can be increased, thus solving the problem.

Threads make life easier for programmers who are developing applications in the client/server architecture. When a new client needs to be served, the server may specially launch a separate thread. These threads are called *symmetric threads* — they have the same purpose, execute the same code, and can share the same resources. Furthermore, applications designed for a big load may support a pool of threads of the same type. Since the creation of a thread requires some time, to speed-up work it is advisable to have the required number of ready threads to be activated as each new client is connected.

NOTE

This approach is especially characteristic of Web-server Microsoft Internet Information Services and applications handling the calls in its environment. If you create ISAPI applications in Delphi, you can use thread pooling by connecting the `ISAPIThreadPool.pas` module to your project. If you need ideas for other purposes, study the contents of this module.

Asymmetric threads solve various tasks and, as a rule, never divide shared resources. Asymmetric threads are needed:

❏ When lengthy calculations need to be carried out in the application, and a normal input response is needed

❏ When the asynchronous input/output must be handled using various devices (COM port, sound map, printer, etc.)

❏ When you want to create several windows and handle the input there

Threads and Processes

When we say "application," we usually mean the concept that OS terminology labels a "process." A process consists of virtual memory, executable code, threads, and data. A process may contain many threads but it always contains at least one. The thread itself, as a rule, possesses a minimum of resources; it is depend and upon the process that handles the virtual memory, code, files, and other OS resources.

Why do we use threads instead of processes, when, if necessary, the application may consist of several processes? The fact is that switching among processes is a much more laborious operation than switching among threads. Another argument in favor of using threads is that they were specially designed for resource sharing; it is not so easy to share resources among processes with separate address space.

Background Procedures, or How to Do without Threads

Here we consider the option you have of organizing a background job within a single-threaded application, while keeping this thread's ability to react to events from the keyboard and the mouse.

Not so long ago, programmers tried to emulate threads by launching procedures within the Windows message handling cycle. The message handling cycle, or waiting loop, is a special fragment of code in the application controlled by the events. It is executed when the application finds events in the queue which need to be handled; if there are no such events, the application may perform a "background procedure" during this time. This method of thread imitation is quite complicated, since the programmer must keep the state of the background procedure constant between calls to it, and also must decide at which moment it should return the control to the event handler. If this procedure takes a long time, the user may think the application has stopped reacting to external events. The use of the threads eliminates the problem of context toggling; now the context (stack and registers) are saved by the OS.

In Delphi, creating a background procedure is done via the `OnIdle` event of the `Application` object:

```
type TIdleEvent = procedure (Sender: TObject; var Done: Boolean) of object;
property OnIdle: TIdleEvent;
```

The handler of this event may be written by placing the `TApplicationEvents` component from the **Additional** page of the Component palette in the form.

To do any job in background mode, it must be divided into quanta, and one quantum must be performed with each `OnIdle` call — otherwise the application will react slowly to external actions.

Thread Priorities

The Win 32 API interface enables the programmer to manage time distribution among threads; this is also applicable to applications written in Delphi. The OS plans the processor's time according to the thread priorities.

The priority of the thread is a value formed from two component parts: the priority of the process which generated the thread and the thread priority itself. When the thread is created, it is assigned a priority corresponding to that of the process which generated this thread. In turn, processes may have the following priority classes:

❒ Real time   ❒ Normal

❒ High   ❒ Below normal

❒ Above normal   ❒ Idle

NOTE

The Above normal and Below normal classes first appeared in Windows 2000.

The Real time class specifies an even greater priority than many system processes of the OS. This priority is needed for processes that handle high-speed data streams. If this process is not completed in a short period of time, the user may feel that the system is failing to respond, since even the mouse event handling will not get processor time.

High class is limited to processes that need to be completed in a short period of time in order not to cause an error. An example is a process that sends signals to an external device, and unless the signal is received on time, the device is disconnected. If the application has efficiency problems, it would be incorrect to try to solve them merely by raising the priority to High — this process influences the whole performance of the OS. In this case, the computer may simply need to be upgraded.

The majority of processes are launched with Normal priority. Normal priority means that the process does not require any special attention from the OS.

Finally, processes with background priority are launched only if there are no other processes in the Task Manager queue. Common applications that use this kind of priority are screensavers and *system agents*. Programmers can use background processes to complete operations and for data reorganization. Examples are document saving or database backup. The priorities have values from 0 to 31. The process that generated the thread may change its priority later on; in such a situation, the programmer can control the response speed of each thread.

The base priority of the thread is formed of two constituents, although this does not mean it is equal to their sum. Base priority values can be found using Table 13.1. For the thread whose priority is THREAD_PRIORITY_IDLE, the base priority will be equal to 1, regardless of the priority of the generating process.

For the Normal class, two more priorities are added, indicated with the letters B (Background) and F (Foreground).

Table 13.1. Classes of the Processes and Priorities of Their Threads (for Windows 2000 and XP)

	IDLE_PRIORITY_CLASS	BELOW_NORMAL_PRIORITY_CLASS	NORMAL_PRIORITY_CLASS	ABOVE_NORMAL_PRIORITY_CLASS	HIGH_PRIORITY_CLASS	REALTIME_PRIORITY_CLASS
THREAD_PRIORITY_IDLE	1	1	1	1	1	16
THREAD_PRIORITY_LOWEST	2	4	5 (B) 7 (F)	8	11	22

continues

Table 13.1 Continued

	IDLE_ PRIORITY_ CLASS	BELOW_ NORMAL_ PRIORITY_ CLASS	NORMAL_ PRIORITY_ CLASS	ABOVE_ NORMAL_ PRIORITY_ CLASS	HIGH_ PRIORITY_ CLASS	REALTIME_ PRIORITY_ CLASS
THREAD_ PRIORITY_ BELOW_ NORMAL	3	5	6 (B) 8 (F)	9	12	23
THREAD_ PRIORITY_ NORMAL	4	6	7 (B) 9 (F)	10	13	24
THREAD_ PRIORITY_ ABOVE_ NORMAL	5	7	8 (B) 10 (F)	11	14	25
THREAD_ PRIORITY_ HIGHEST	6	8	9 (B) 11(F)	12	15	26
THREAD_ PRIORITY_ TIME_ CRITICAL	15	15	15	15	15	31

Apart from the base priority specified in this table, the scheduler may assign so-called dynamic priorities. For NORMAL_PRIORITY_CLASS processes, when switched from background mode to foreground mode, and in some other cases, the priority of the thread with which the foreground window is created rises. This is the way all Microsoft desktop operating systems work. Server operating systems are optimized for background applications. However, Windows NT and later operating systems with this core allow the optimization mode to be switched using the **Application response** radio buttons of the System applet in the Windows toolbar (Fig. 13.1).

Additionally, Windows 2000 Professional and Windows 2000 Server have different quantum allocation algorithms. The first (desktop) operating system allocates the time using short quanta of variable length in order to accelerate the response of foreground applications. However, reliable performance of system services is of more importance for the server and, therefore in the second OS, long quanta of constant length are distributed.

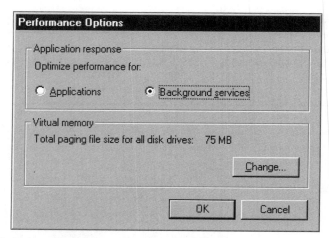

Fig. 13.1. Using the **Performance Options** dialog, it is possible to manage the priority assignment algorithm

Now that thread priorities have been explained, it is necessary to say a few words about the way the job scheduler uses them for processor time distribution. The operating system has various queues ready for thread execution — separate for each priority level. When distributing a new quantum, the system scans the queues — from the highest priority down to the lowest one. The first thread in the queue that is ready for execution obtains this quantum and moves to the end of the queue. The thread will be executed during this quantum, unless one of two events happens:

❏ The thread being executed has stopped to wait.

❏ A new thread with a higher priority is ready for execution.

Now you probably understand more clearly the danger of raising priorities without good reason. If there are active threads with a high priority, not one thread with a lower priority will get processor time! This problem may even catch up to you on the level of your application. Suppose that you have set THREAD_PRIORITY_ABOVE_NORMAL to the computational thread, and THREAD_PRIORITY_BELOW_NORMAL to the thread where the user's input is handled. Then, instead of the planned result — combination of the calculations with a normal response from the application — you will get the exact opposite. The application will cease to respond to the input, and only the OS will be able to cancel it.

Thus, the normal practice for asymmetric threads is to assign a higher priority to the thread handling the input, and assign a lower or even *idle* priority to the rest if this thread can only be executed during system timeout.

The *TThread* Class

Delphi provides the programmer with full access to the programming features of the Win32 interface. Why, then, has Borland provided a special class for thread organization? Generally, the programmer is not obliged to know all the particulars of the mechanisms offered by the operating system. The class should encapsulate and simplify the program interface; the TThread class is a very good example of providing the developer with easy access to programming threads. The API of the threads is not very complicated in itself, and the features offered by TThread are even simpler. In short, all you need do is to span the Execute virtual method.

Another special feature of the TThread class is the guarantee of safe work with the Visual Components Library (VCL). If the TThread class is not used during VCL calls, situations requiring special synchronization may occur (see the "*Thread Synchronization Problems*" section).

From the point of view of the operating system, the thread is its object. When it is created, it gets a descriptor and is traced by the OS. The object of the TThread class is the Delphi construction corresponding to the thread of the OS. This VCL object is created prior to the actual appearance of the thread in the system, and deleted after the thread has disappeared.

Let us begin the study of the TThread class with the Execute method:

```
Procedure Execute; virtual; abstract;
```

This is the code executed in the TThread thread being created.

> **NOTE**
>
> Although the formal description of Execute is abstract, the creation wizard of the new TThread object creates a blank template of this method.

By redefining the Execute method, we can contribute to the new thread class what is to be executed when the class is launched. If the thread was created with the CreateSuspended parameter equal to False, then the Execute method is immediately executed; otherwise the `Execute` method is executed after the call of the `Resume` method.

If the thread is intended for one-time execution of certain actions, then no completion code is needed within `Execute`.

However, if a loop will be executed within the thread, and the thread must end together with the application, then the conditions for the cycle's end should be approximately the following:

```
procedure TMyThread.Execute;
begin
repeat
 DoSomething;
Until CancelCondition or Terminated;
end;
```

Here `CancelCondition` is your personal condition for the thread to end (data has been exhausted, completion of calculations, input of a special character, etc.), and the `Terminated` property indicates the end of the thread (this property may be set on the inside and on the outside of the thread; in all likelihood, the process that generated this thread is being terminated).

The object constructor

```
constructor Create( CreateSuspended: Boolean);
```

gets the `CreateSuspended` parameter. If this value is equal to `True`, the newly created thread does not begin execution until the `Resume` method is called. If `CreateSuspended` has the `False` value, the constructor is finished, and thread stars only after resuming.

```
destructor Destroy; override;
```

The `Destroy` destructor is called when there is no need for the created thread any more. The destructor terminates it and frees up all the resources related to the `TThread` object.

```
function Terminate: Integer;
```

For complete termination of the thread (without a subsequent startup) there is the `Terminate` method. But you would be wrong in thinking that this method forces the thread to stop. All that happens is that the property

```
Property Terminated: Boolean;
```

is set to `True`. Thus, `Terminate` is a "gentle" way of telling the thread to terminate, which allows you to correctly free up the resources. If you need

to terminate the thread immediately, use the Windows API function
`TerminateThread`.

> **NOTE**
>
> The `Terminate` method is also automatically called from the object destructor. The VCL object thread will wait until the OS object thread is terminated. Thus, if the thread can not terminate correctly, calling the destructor may lead to the whole application freezing.

Another useful property is

```
property FreeOnTerminate: Boolean;
```

If this property is equal to `True`, then the thread destructor will be automatically called upon its termination. This is very convenient in cases when you are not sure of the exact moment of the thread's termination, and want to use it on a "fire and forget" basis.

```
Function WaitFor: Integer;
```

The `WaitFor` method is intended for synchronization, and enables one thread to wait for the termination of another one. If you write the code:

```
Code := SecondThread.WaitFor;
```

within the `FirstThread` thread, it means that the `FirstThread` thread stops until the `SecondThread` thread terminates. The `WaitFor` method returns the completion code of the expected thread (see the `ReturnValue` property).

```
Property Handle: THandle read FHandle;
Property ThreadID: THandle read FThreadID;
```

The `Handle` and `ThreadID` properties provide the programmer with direct access to the thread through API Win 32. If the developer wants to refer to the thread and manage it, omitting the features of the `TThread` class, then the `Handle` and `ThreadID` values may be used as arguments of the Win 32 API functions. If, for example, the programmer wants to wait for termination of several threads before resuming the execution of the application, he or she should call the `WaitForMultipleObjects` API function; to call it, a thread handle array is needed.

```
property Priority: TThreadPriority;
```

The `Priority` property allows you to request and set thread priorities. The thread priorities are described in detail above. The allowable priority values for the `TThread` objects are `tpIdle`, `tpLowest`, `tpLower`, `tpNormal`, `tpHigher`, `tpHighest`, and `tpTimeCritical`.

```
procedure Synchronize(Method: TThreadMethod);
```

This method is for the `protected` section, i.e. it may be called from the descendants of the `TThread` only. Delphi provides the programmer with the `Synchronize` method for safe call of VCL methods within threads. To avoid conflicts, the `Synchronize` method guarantees that only one thread at a time has access to each VCL object. The parameter passed to the `Synchronize` method is the name of the method that calls the VCL; calling `Synchronize` with this parameter is the same as calling the method itself. This method (of the `TThreadMethod` class) should not have any parameters and should not return any values. For example, the following function should be provided in the main form of the application

```
procedure TMainForm.SyncShowMessage;
begin
  ShowMessage(IntToStr(ThreadList1.Count));
    //other calls of VCL
end;
```

and in the message display thread don't write

```
ShowMessage(IntToStr(ThreadList1.Count));
```

or even

```
MainForm.SyncShowMessage;
```

but only:

```
Synchronize( MainForm.SyncShowMessage);
```

> **NOTE**
>
> For any call of the VCL object from a thread, ensure that the `Synchronize` method is used; otherwise, the results may be unpredictable. This is true even in cases when you use the means of synchronization described below!

```
procedure Resume;
```

The `Resume` method of the `TThread` class is called when the thread resumes execution after a stop, or for explicitly starting a thread created with the `CreateSuspended` parameter equal to `True`.

```
procedure Suspend;
```

Calling the `Suspend` method suspends the thread with the option of subsequently restarting. The `Suspend` method suspends the thread independently of the code being executed by the thread at that moment; execution resumes from the point at which it was stopped.

```
property Suspended: Boolean;
```

The `Suspended` property enables the programmer to determine if the thread is suspended. Using this property, you can also start and stop the thread. By setting `Suspended` to `True`, you will get the same result as when calling the `Suspend` method — its suspension. Conversely, setting `Suspended` to `False` resumes execution of the thread, just like the call of the `Resume` method.

```
Property ReturnValue: Integer;
```

The `ReturnValue` property makes it possible to find out and set the value returned by the thread after it is terminated. This value is completely determined by the user. By default, the thread returns zero, but if the programmer wants to return another value, then simply resetting the `ReturnValue` property within the thread will help the other threads to obtain this information. For example, this may be useful if there are problems within the thread, or if it is necessary to return the number of words that did not pass the spell check with the help of the `ReturnValue`.

Here we end our comprehensive overview of the `TThread` class. Let's now create a multi-threaded application for closer consideration of threads and the Delphi `TThread` class. All you need to do for this is to write some lines of code and click the mouse a few times.

Example of a Multi-Threaded Application in Delphi

This section contains a description of the steps required to create a simple but demonstrative example of a multi-threaded application. We will try to calculate the value of Pi with the maximum number of digits after the decimal point. Of course, the Pi constant built into Delphi is quite precise, or rather has the maximum precision permitted by the most accurate Extended 10-byte format for floating-point numbers. Thus, we probably won't be able to surpass it. But this example of thread use may serve as a prologue for the solving of real tasks.

The first example contains two threads: the main thread (handling the user's input) and the computation thread. We will be able to change their properties and observe the reaction.

Carry out the following sequence of operations:

1. Open the **File** menu in the Delphi environment and select **New Application**.

2. Arrange the five items and the one toggle on the form as shown in Fig. 13.2.

Fig. 13.2. Threads1 application form

Rename the main form to fmMain.

3. Open the **File** menu and select **Save Project As**. Save the module as uMain, and the project as Threads1.

4. Open the **File** menu and select **New**. Double-click on the thread-type object (the **Thread Object** icon). The **New Items** dialog box shown in Fig. 13.3 is then opened.

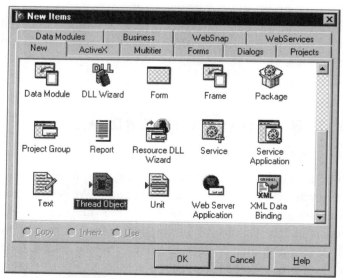

Fig. 13.3. The **New Items** dialog box with the selected thread-type object

5. When the dialog box appears, type `TPiThread` and press <Enter> (Fig. 13.4).

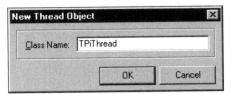

Fig. 13.4. The **New Thread Object** dialog box

Delphi will create a new module and place the template for the new thread in it.

6. The code imported into the `Execute` method calculates Pi using Leibnitz' convergence of an infinite series:

$$\pi = 4 - 4/3 + 4/5 - 4/7 + 4/9 - ...$$

Displaying the new value after each iteration is like shooting sparrows with a cannon. The system will spend 10 times as much time displaying the information as on the actual calculation. We have, therefore, introduced the `Update-Period` constant, which regulates the periodicity of the current value's display.

Below is the code of the `Execute` method:

```
const
  //better to choose odd value, to avoid monotonic increase/decrease effect
  UpdatePeriod = 1000001;

procedure TPiThread.Execute;
var sign : Integer;
  PiValue, PrevValue : Extended;
  i : Int64;
begin
  { Place thread code here }
  PiValue := 4;
  sign := -1;
  i := 0;
  repeat
  Inc(i);
  PrevValue := PiValue;
  PiValue := PiValue + sign * 4 / (2*i+1);
```

```
      sign := -sign;
      if i mod UpdatePeriod = 0 then
       begin
        GlobalPi := PiValue;
        GlobalCounter := i;
        Synchronize( fmMain.UpdatePi );
       end;
     until Terminated or
     (Abs(PiValue - PrevValue)<1E-19) ;
   end;
```

7. Open the **File** menu and select **Save As**. Save the module with the thread as uPiThread.pas.

8. Edit the main file of the uMain.pas module and add the uPiThread module to the list of the modules used in the interface section. It should look as follows:

```
uses
   Windows, Messages, SysUtils, Variants, Classes, Graphics, Controls, Forms,
   StdCtrls,
   uPiThread;
```

9. Add the reference to the thread created in the public section of the TfmMain form:

```
   PiThread : TPiThread;
```

10. Add two local variables to the uMain module

```
   GlobalPi : Extended;
   GlobalCounter : Int64;
```

as well as the UpdatePi method:

```
   procedure TfmMain.UpdatePi;
   begin
     if IsIconic( Application.Handle ) then Exit;
     LaValue.Caption := FloatToStrF( GlobalPi, ffFixed, 18, 18 );
     laIterNum.Caption := IntToStr( GlobalCounter ) + ' iterations';
   end;
```

This method, if you have noticed, is called from the thread via the Syncronize procedure. It reflects the current approximation of Pi, as well as the number of iterations.

To make the calculation more effective, there is no display of the process if the main window is minimized. So after the window is maximized, you may have to wait for refreshing.

11. Double-click anywhere in the working area of the form, and the template of the FormCreate method will be created. Here we represent the value of the system constant Pi:

```
procedure TfmMain.FormCreate(Sender: TObject);
begin
  laBuiltIn.Caption := FloatToStrF( Pi, ffFixed, 18, 18 );
end;
```

12. Select the toggle on the form (called cbCalculate) and assign to the OnClick event a code that creates or deletes the calculation thread, depending on the state of the checkbox:

```
procedure TfmMain.cbCalculateClick(Sender: TObject);
begin
  if cbCalculate.Checked then
   begin
     PiThread := TPiThread.Create( True );
     PiThread.FreeOnTerminate := True;
     PiThread.Priority := tpLower;
     PiThread.Resume;
   end
  else
   begin
     if Assigned( PiThread ) then PiThread.Terminate;
   end;
end;
```

The multi-threaded application is now ready to start. If everything is OK, you will see a picture similar to Fig. 13.5.

Fig. 13.5. The Threads1 application being executed

While one of the authors was writing this text, the launched Threads1 application performed five billion iterations, and came close to the built-in value of Pi, to the tenth decimal place. Exactly how patient are *you*?

This simple example is the first step in understanding how native classes can be generated from the TThread base class. Due to its simplicity, it is not without imperfections; moreover, if there were more than one thread, some of the techniques here would even be erroneous. This, however, is considered below.

Thread Synchronization Problems

Unfortunately, the simplicity of thread creation is sometimes "compensated for" by the complexity of their use. There are two typical problems the programmer may encounter when working with threads — *deadlocks* and *race conditions*.

Deadlocks

Once we witnessed the following amusing scene at the convergence of some trolley tracks:

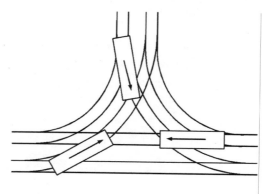

Fig. 13.6. Deadlock situations happen not only in programming

The picture gives a comprehensive explanation of the deadlock situation. *Deadlocks* take place when a thread is waiting for a resource that belongs at that moment to another thread. Here is an example: Thread 1 captures resource A, and to continue operating, waits for a chance to capture resource B. At the same time, Thread 2 captures resource B, and to continue operating, waits for a chance to capture resource A. This scenario will block both threads; neither will be executed. Any shared system objects may serve as resources — files, shared memory arrays, I/O devices, etc.

Fig. 13.6 shows that three trolleys had captured one resource each (an intersection) and tried to capture another one, which is obviously impossible unless the intersections that have already been captured are released. In life, the situation was very easily resolved — the youngest of the drivers had to move back. It is not so easy in information technology. Open any document accompanying the Service Pack of any version of Windows. Often, you may find information there on a couple of deadlocks solved.

Races

A *race condition* occurs when two or more threads try to get access to a public resource and change its state. Let us consider the following example. Suppose Thread 1 has gained access to a resource and modified this resource as it wanted; then Thread 2 was activated and modified the same resource before Thread 1 terminated. Thread 1 supposes that the resource is in the same state as it was before switching. Depending on when the resource was modified, results may vary — sometimes the code will be executed without problems, and sometimes it won't. Programmers should not form any hypotheses about the order of thread execution, as the OS scheduler may start and stop them at any time.

```
Inc( i );
if i = iSomething then
  DoSomething;
```

Here, `i` is the global variable available from both threads. Let's say that two or more threads execute this code simultaneously. Thread 1 has incremented the value of the variable `i` and wants to check its value to execute some condition. Here another thread is activated, which increases the value of `i` even more. As a result, the first thread "skips" the condition, which, it seems, should have been executed.

Both deadlock and race situations may be avoided if the techniques set forth in the *"Means of Thread Synchronization"* section are used.

Means of Thread Synchronization

It is very easy to speak about synchronization if the thread being created does not interact with the resources of other threads and does not call the VCL. Suppose there are several processors on your computer, and you want to perform the calculations in parallel. Then the following code is quite appropriate:

```
MyCompThread := TComputationThread.Create( False );
//do something while second thread computes
```

```
DoSomeWork;
// now can wait
MyCompThread.WaitFor;
```

This schema is absolutely illegal if the `MyCompThread` thread calls the VCL via the `Synchronize` method during the operation. In such a case, the thread is waiting for the main thread to call the VCL, and the main thread, in turn, is waiting for this thread — a typical deadlock!

Here you should refer to the Win 32 program interface for help. It provides a wide range of tools that may be of use in organizing the joint operation of the threads.

The main concepts for understanding the mechanisms of synchronization are *wait functions* and *synchronization objects*. There are a number of functions provided in Windows API that make it possible to terminate the execution of the thread that called this function until the state of some object — called a synchronization object — is modified. (Here this term refers not to the Delphi object, but to an object of the operating system.) The simplest of these functions — `WaitForSingleObject` — is designed for waiting for one object.

Among possible options are four objects specially developed for synchronization: event, mutex, semaphore, and timer.

But you can wait for other objects as well, those whose descriptors are mainly used for other purposes, but can be enabled for waiting. These are: process, thread, change notification, and console input.

Indirectly, the critical section may be added to this group.

> **NOTE**
>
> The means of synchronization listed above are mainly encapsulated in the classes of Delphi. The programmer has two options. One, the SYNCOBJS.PAS module containing the classes for the event (`TEvent`) and critical section (`TCriticalSection`) is included in the VCL. Also, an excellent version of IPCDEMOS is provided with Delphi, which illustrates the problems of interaction of processes and contains the IPCTHRD.PAS module with analogous classes — for event, mutex (`TMutex`), and shared memory (`TSharedMem`).

We now turn to a detailed description of the objects used for synchronization.

Events

An object of the event type is the easiest choice for synchronization tasks. It is similar to a doorbell — it rings while its button is pressed, informing those around it of this fact. Similarly, the object may be in two states, but can be "heard" by many threads at the same time.

The `TEvent` class (SYNCOBJS.PAS module) has two methods: `SetEvent` and `ResetEvent`, which convert the object into the active and passive state, respectively. The constructor looks as follows:

```
constructor Create(EventAttributes: PSecurityAttributes;
ManualReset, InitialState: Boolean; const Name: string);
```

Here the `InitialState` parameter is the initial state of the object, and `ManualReset` is the means of reset (conversion into the passive state). If this parameter is equal to `True`, then the event must be reset manually. Otherwise, the event is reset as soon as at least one thread is started that is waiting for this object.

The third method —

```
TWaitResult = (wrSignaled, wrTimeout, wrAbandoned, wrError);

function WaitFor(Timeout: DWORD): TWaitResult;
```

deserves a more detailed description. It makes it possible to wait for event activation within `Timeout` milliseconds. As you may have guessed, the call of the `WaitForSingleObject` function takes place within this method. There are two typical results upon the output of `WaitFor` — `wrSignaled` if object activation took place, and `wrTimeout` if nothing happened during the timeout.

NOTE

If it is necessary (and permitted!) to wait for an infinitely long time, then the `TimeOut` parameter should be set to the `INFINITE` value.

Here is a small example. Let's include in the new project an object of the `TThread` type, having filled its `Execute` method with the following contents:

```
Var res: TWaitResult;

procedure TSimpleThread.Execute;
begin
    e := TEvent.Create(nil,True,false, 'test');
    repeat
    e.ReSetEvent;
    res := e.WaitFor(10000);
    Synchronize(ShowInfo);
    until Terminated;
```

```
    e.Free;
  end;

procedure TSimpleThread.ShowInfo;
begin
  ShowMessage(IntToStr(Integer(res)));
end;
```

Place two buttons on the main form — pressing one starts the thread, and pressing the other activates the event:

```
procedure TForm1.Button1Click(Sender: TObject);
begin
 TSimpleThread.Create(False);
end;


procedure TForm1.Button2Click(Sender: TObject);
begin
  e.SetEvent;
end;
```

Press the first button. Then the displayed result (ShowInfo method) will depend on whether the second button has been pressed, or if the allotted 10 seconds are up.

Events are used not only for work with threads — some procedures of the operating system automatically toggle them. These procedures include *overlapped* input/output and events related to the communication ports.

Mutexes

An object of the mutex (mutual exclusion) type enables only one thread to possess it at a time. If we continue with the analogies, this object may be compared to a baton.

The class encapsulating the mutex — TMutex — is in the IPCTHRD.PAS module (the IPCDEMOS version). The constructor:

```
constructor Create(const Name: string);
```

specifies the name of the object being created. Initially it does not belong to anything. (But the CreateMutex API function called within it enables the created object to be passed to the thread in which it occurred.) Then, the method

```
function Get(TimeOut: Integer): Boolean;
```

tries to capture the object in `TimeOut` milliseconds (in this case, the result is equal to `True`). If the object is not needed anymore, the following method must be called:

```
function Release: Boolean;
```

The programmer may use mutex in order to avoid the reading and writing the common memory by several threads simultaneously.

Semaphore

The semaphore is similar to mutex. The difference is that a semaphore can manage the number of threads that have access to it. A semaphore is set to the maximum number of threads with enabled access. When this number is reached, subsequent threads will be terminated until one or more threads disconnect from the semaphore and free access.

As an example of using semaphores, consider a case when each one of a group of threads works with a fragment of the shared memory pool. Since the shared memory only permits addressing a determined number of threads, all the rest must be blocked until one or more users of the pool stop its shared use.

Critical Sections

When working in Delphi, the programmer may also use an object of the critical section type. These are generally similar to mutexes, but there are two main distinctions:

❏ Unlike critical sections, mutexes may be shared by the threads in various processes.

❏ If the critical section belongs to another thread, then the waiting thread is blocked until the critical section is emptied. This is unlike mutex, which allows the process to continue after the timeout is up.

At first glance, the benefits of using critical sections instead of mutexes is not obvious. Critical sections, however, are more effective than mutexes, since they use fewer system resources. Mutex may be set for a certain period of time, and execution continues even after this period has expired; the critical section always waits as long as is required.

Let's look at the `TCriticalSection` class (SYNCOBJS.PAS module). The logic of its use is simple — "hold on and don't let go." A critical section common for all threads is created and initialized in the multi-threaded application. When one of the threads reaches the critically important code area, it tries to capture the section by calling the `Enter` method:

```
MySection.Enter;
try
 DoSomethingCritical;
finally
 MySection.Leave;
end;
```

When the other threads reach the capture operator of the `Enter` section and find out that it is already captured, they pause until the first thread frees up the section by calling the `Leave` method. Note that the call of the `Leave` method is located in the `try ... finally` construction — here 100% reliability is needed. Critical sections are system objects, and their deallocation is obligatory, as with the other objects considered here.

Process. How to Spawn a Child Process

An object of the `Process` type may be used to pause a thread's execution if it requires a process to be terminated in order to continue. From the practical point of view, this problem occurs when you need to execute an application created by someone else, or, for example, an MS DOS session within your own application.

Let's consider how one process can generate another. Instead of the obsolete `Win-Exec` function taken from previous versions of Windows and supported for compatibility purposes only, it would be best to use the more powerful function:

```
function CreateProcess(lpApplicationName: PChar; lpCommandLine: PChar;
   lpProcessAttributes, lpThreadAttributes: PSecurityAttributes;
   bInheritHandles: BOOL; dwCreationFlags: DWORD; lpEnvironment: Pointer;
   lpCurrentDirectory: PChar; const lpStartupInfo: TStartupInfo;
   var lpProcessInformation: TProcessInformation): BOOL;
```

The first two parameters are clear — this is the name of the application being started, and the parameters communicated to it in the command line. The `dwCreationFlags` parameter contains flags that define the technique of creating the new process and its future priority. The flags used in the example below mean the following: `CREATE_NEW_CONSOLE` — a new console application with a separate window will be started; `NORMAL_PRIORITY_CLASS` — normal priority.

The TStartupInfo structure contains data about the size, color and location of the application window being created. The wShowWindow field is used in the example below: the SW_SHOWNORMAL flag which indicated that the window will be displayed normal size.

At the function's output, the lpProcessInformation structure is filled in. Here, the programmer is returned the descriptors and identifiers of the process created, as well as its primary thread. We will need a process descriptor: in our example a console application is created, and its completion is then waited for. It is the lpProcessInformation.hProcess object which will inform us of the completion.

Listing 13.1. Spawning a Child Process

```
var
      lpStartupInfo: TStartupInfo;
      lpProcessInformation: TProcessInformation;
begin
 FillChar(lpStartupInfo,Sizeof(lpStartupInfo),#0);
 lpStartupInfo.cb := Sizeof(lpStartupInfo);
 lpStartupInfo.dwFlags := STARTF_USESHOWWINDOW;
 lpStartupInfo.wShowWindow := SW_SHOWNORMAL;
  if not CreateProcess(nil,
                PChar('ping localhost'),
                nil,
                nil,
                false,
                CREATE_NEW_CONSOLE or NORMAL_PRIORITY_CLASS,
                nil,
                nil,
                lpStartupInfo,
                lpProcessInformation)
    then
     ShowMessage( SysErrorMessage(GetLastError) )
    else
     begin
      WaitForSingleObject( lpProcessInformation.hProcess, 10000 );
      CloseHandle( lpProcessInformation.hProcess );
     end;
  end;
```

Thread

One thread can wait for another thread, as well as for another process. The waiting can be organized with API functions (as in the example above), but it is more convenient to do this using the `TThread.WaitFor` method.

Console Input

A *console input* is suitable for threads that are supposed to wait for a response to the user pressing a key on the keyboard. This type of waiting can be used in a duplex communication (chat) program. One thread will wait for the characters, the other will keep track of the user's input and then send the typed text to the waiting application.

File System Changes Notification

This type of waiting object is very interesting and not as well known as it deserves to be. We have considered almost all the variants of how one thread can notify another. But how about getting notification from the operating system on things such as the fact that changes have been made to the file system? This kind of notification is borrowed from the Unix OS, and is available to programmers working with Win 32.

Three functions are used to monitor the file system — `FindFirstChangeNotification`, `FindNextChangeNotification`, and `FindCloseChangeNotification`. The first returns the descriptor of the file notification, which can be passed to the waiting function. The object is activated once changes have taken place in the specified folder (creation or deletion of the file or folder, change of access rights, etc.). The second prepares the object for the reaction to the next change. Finally, the third closes an object that is no longer necessary.

The code of the `Execute` method of the thread created to monitor the file system can look as follows:

```
var DirName : string;
...
procedure TSimpleThread.Execute;
var r: Cardinal;
  fn : THandle;
begin
 fn := FindFirstChangeNotification( pChar(DirName), True,
FILE_NOTIFY_CHANGE_FILE_NAME );
 repeat
```

```
  r := WaitForSingleObject(fn,2000);
  if r = WAIT_OBJECT_0 then
    Synchronize( Form1.UpdateList );
  if not FindNextChangeNotification( fn ) then break;
  until Terminated;
  FindCloseChangeNotification( fn );
end;
```

The main form should contain the components needed to select the examined folder and the TListBox component, where the names of the files will be recorded:

```
procedure TForm1.Button1Click(Sender: TObject);
var dir : string;
begin
 if SelectDirectory(dir,[],0) then
  begin
   Edit1.Text := dir;
   DirName := dir;
  end;
end;
procedure TForm1.UpdateList;
var SearchRec: TSearchRec;
begin
  ListBox1.Clear;
  FindFirst(Edit1.Text+'\*.*', faAnyFile, SearchRec);
  repeat
   ListBox1.Items.Add(SearchRec.Name);
  until FindNext(SearchRec) <> 0;
  FindClose(SearchRec);
end;
```

The application is ready. To make it fully functional, provide it with a reset mechanism when the examined folder is changed.

Local Data of a Thread

If there are several identical threads in the application, an interesting problem occurs. How can we avoid the same variables from being used at once by several threads? The first thing that might occur to us is to add and use fields of an object — a descendant of TThread — which can be added while the object is being created. Each thread corresponds to a separate instance of the object, and their data will not overlap. (By the way, this is one of the greatest advantages of using TThread class). But there are API functions that are completely unaware of Delphi objects and their fields and properties. To support data sharing between threads at a low level, a special directive — threadvar — is included in the Object Pascal language. This directive differs from the directive that describes var variables in that it is applied to the local data of the thread only. The following description:

```
Var
  data1: Integer;
threadvar
  data2: Integer;
```

means that the data1 variable will be used by all threads of this application, and each thread will have its own data2 variable.

How to Avoid the Concurrent Starting of Two Instances of One Application

This problem occurs quite often. Many users, especially novices, do not fully understand that several seconds, or even several dozens of seconds, may pass between clicking on the icon of an application and its actual start. Users begin clicking the icon repeatedly, launching many new instances. And when working with databases and in many other cases, having more than one instance is not only unnecessary, but harmful too.

The idea behing the solution is that the first created copy of the application captures some resource, and all the rest of the copies started try to do the same but terminate if they fail.

An example of such a resource is the common block in the file, which is mapped in the memory. Since this resource has a name, you can make it unique for your application:

```
var UniqueMapping : THandle;
    FirstWindow : THandle;
begin
  UniqueMapping := CreateFileMapping($ffffffff,
  nil, PAGE_READONLY, 0, 32,'MyMap');
  if UniqueMapping = 0 then
    begin
      ShowMessage( SysErrorMessage( GetLastError ) );
      Halt;
    end
```

```
  else if GetLastError = ERROR_ALREADY_EXISTS  then
    begin
      FirstWindow := FindWindowEx( 0, 0, TfmMain.ClassName, nil );
      if FirstWindow<>0 then
         SetForegroundWindow( FirstWindow );
      Halt;
    end;
//no other copies - continue
Application.Initialize;

  . . .
```

Something similar to these lines must be included in the beginning of the text of the project, prior to form creation. The block of shared memory is allotted in the system swap file (the first parameter equal to −1 indicates this, see the description of the `CreateFileMapping` function). Its name is `MyMap`. If the error code `ERROR_ALREADY_EXISTS` is received during block creation, this is evidence that another copy of the application has been started. In such a case, the application refocuses on the main form of another instance and finishes; otherwise the process of initialization is continued.

Summary

Like other powerful tools, threads should be used carefully and must not be misused, as errors may occur that could be very hard to find. There are many arguments for the use of threads, but there are also arguments against them. Working with threads will be easier if the following statements are kept in mind:

❒ If the threads work only with variables declared within their own class, then race and deadlock situations are unlikely. In other words, avoid using global variables and variables of other objects in threads.

❒ If you call fields or methods of VCL objects, do it via the `Synchronize` method.

❒ Do not "oversyncronize" your application, or it will work as a single thread. An excessively synchronized application loses all the advantages that the presence of several threads brings, since they will be constantly paused and waiting for synchronization.

Threads are an elegant solution to several present-day programming problems, but they also make already complicated debugging process even more complicated. Still, the advantages of threads definitely outweigh their shortcomings.

PART V

XML DATA IN DISTRIBUTED APPLICATIONS

Chapter 14

Using XML

The Delphi 6 Component palette includes just under 30 different tabs, each of which contains at least a dozen components. Typically, authors who write on the subject rarely provide more than a brief overview of all the components, instead trying to group them by function because of space restrictions.

This chapter, however, is entirely devoted to a single component — TXMLDocument — and for good reason. First, in spite of the fact that almost everybody is familiar with the term "XML," and many know the language itself, few are fully aware of the entire range of possible applications of this standard. Second, XML serves as the foundation for many other Delphi 6 technologies; without understanding the essentials, these technologies simply cannot be approached.

Let us start by introducing you to the basics of the language — the concepts used in an XML schema and a Document Object Model (DOM). Then we will examine the principles of using XML in the Delphi environment.

Understanding XML

XML stands for eXtensible Markup Language, which is being developed by the World Wide Web Consortium (**W3C, www.w3.org/XML**). W3C is composed of the leading vendors, as well as academic and scientific organizations. Though all the decisions made by the consortium are published in the form of advice, very few developers venture to deviate much from the recommended strategy.

At first glance, an XML document is very similar to an HTML document. Both languages are subsets of the Standardized Generalized Markup Language (SGML). Both HTML and XML use the same elements, and their corresponding definitions, which are enclosed in angle brackets, are called *tags* in both languages. Actually, as far as syntax goes, these languages are closely related to one other, except that XML has stricter rules.

In fact, however, their resemblance is limited to these external similarities. A sharp dividing line becomes evident when you look at the languages from the perspective of their practical use: HTML is designed for *presenting* information, while XML is meant for its universal *definition*.

HTML was introduced, and has been developed, as a language for web browsers, for the presentation of information sent using HTTP. The <FONT> tag made its appearance first; it enabled developers to modify the type face and font size used on a given page. Then, major browser vendors like Netscape and Microsoft started flooding the market with new tags in competition with one another for the creation of new and dramatic effects, though they weren't very concerned with consistency. Those readers who have experience in the field of web design (and I believe almost everyone has tried his or her hand at creating a web page) know how difficult it is to make an HTML document run equally smoothly on different types and versions of browsers. Even those who have never created their own web page have certainly come across recommendations such as "best viewed with Internet Explorer 4.0 and higher" and the like while surfing the Web.

Many new constructs have been introduced, but the essential principles that underlie HTML (which is currently in its fourth version) remain the same:

❐ The language has always used a predefined and fixed set of tags that cannot be extended by the developer.

❐ HTML tags have no bearing on the content of a given HTML document: they simply determine the way this information is presented.

Conversely, XML is called "extensible" because it allows the developer to define and build his or her own custom system of tags that most efficiently describe a given subject area. If you have ever taken part in a project involving the interaction of many diverse information systems, you are certainly aware of the huge amount of time and effort needed to achieve consistency among data-exchange formats used for different applications. Moreover, as often as not, once the project is finished, these formats and protocols are no longer needed: who wants to be troubled by digging into this mountain of binary structures?

But this is not the case with XML. This language is text-based, and it supports the UNICODE standard. These features contribute to the enhanced readability of documents and facilitate their development. One could argue that textual data are bulky compared to binary data, and transferring them is a much more time-consuming task. This is true, of course, but one should take into account that XML can use the entire HTML-implementing infrastructure (including HTTP, servers, and browsers). Many browsers already support XML.

Presenting an XML document is done using another standard: eXtended Stylesheet Language (XSL) and its variation, XSL Transformations (XSLT). It should be noted that XSLT is defined using XML. All these languages, as well as the ways in which Delphi 6 supports them, will be discussed later.

In conclusion, let's examine a diagram illustrating the general steps involved in handling an XML document (Fig. 14.1). In this system, every document should be accompanied by the relevant definition (description). In light of the previous discussion, it is quite understandable why — unlike HTML tags — XML tags are not standardized, which implies that additional information on their types, uses, and the relationships among them is required every time they are used. This definition can be either a so-called Document Type Definition (DTD) or a more recent version, an XML schema. Both definition variations may be contained either in the document body itself or in a separate file specified in the document.

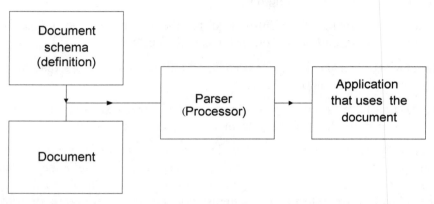

Fig. 14.1. General schema illustrating the handling of XML documents

Before being processed, every document must undergo syntax analysis and be validated for consistency with its DTD. This job is performed by an *XML validating parser.*

From the very beginning, XML developers were concerned with the issue of unified access to various XML documents. The task was even more challenging since they had a poor example before them: the differing implementations of the Dynamic HTML (DHTML) object model by Microsoft and Netscape. These considerations led the W3C to develop and standardize the Document Object Model (DOM) for XML. Essentially, DOM is a collection of interfaces corresponding to the nodes of the tree structure of an XML document. As soon as a DOM-compatible parser has been loaded and analyzes the syntax of a given document, the programmer gains access to the same set of methods and properties — irrespective of the operating system, programming language, and parser implementation.

Currently, several parser implementations are in wide use. For Windows and Internet Explorer, Microsoft has specifically developed a fast, high-performance parser: MSXML. Being aware of the fact that this parser is too closely tied up with other operating system components and, as a result, completely lacks portability, Borland did not run the risk of putting all its eggs in one basket. Delphi 6 comes with a number of alternative parsers and also supports the use of custom parsers. Similar utilities for various operating systems and the Java environment are provided by Sun, Oracle, IBM, and other software vendors.

Finally, the fourth block in the diagram represents the application meant to work with XML. The basic guidelines for its creation are covered in this chapter. First, however, let us discuss the first three blocks in more detail.

Fundamentals of XML Syntax

The basic concept of XML is the *element*. Elements are used as building blocks for constructing a document tree. Each element has its own name, which can contain characters, numbers, hyphens, and underscores.

The beginning and the end of an element are marked with opening and closing tags, respectively. These tags can enclose the textual value of the element or other elements:

```
<first>Hello, World!</first>
```

Here the element named "first" has the "Hello, World!" value.

> **WARNING**
>
> As opposed to HTML, XML is a case-sensitive language. Note that element names like `first`, `First`, and `FIRST` are entirely different elements.

In addition to the name of the element, the opening tag may contain element attributes. These attributes provide extra information about the element:

```
<salary year="2001" currency="USD">100000</salary>
```

The element has a value of 100,000, and the attributes indicate that this number is expressed in U.S. dollars and is dated 2001.

On the other hand, an element might not contain either values or attributes. In the first case, a short notation without a closing tag is permissible:

```
<dummy/>
```

This is the same as

```
<dummy></dummy>
```

Elements can be nested. This structure is used in order to emphasize that, semantically, some elements are child elements in relation to others (Listing 14.1).

Listing 14.1. A Sample XML Document

```
<?xml version="1.0"?>
<!-- First XML sample document -->
<ProjectTeam project="Super">
    <ProjectManager age="35" certification="MCSD">Mark Bose</ProjectManager>
    <Developers>
        <Developer age="25">John Doe</Developer>
        <Developer age="28" certification="MCP">Patrick
Keegan</Developer>
    </Developers>
    <Testers/>
</ProjectTeam>
```

The `ProjectTeam` element has three child elements: `ProjectManager`, `Developers`, and `Testers`. In turn, the `Developers` element contains two other `Developer` elements. The age and certification attributes provide additional information about these elements.

Moreover, it is absolutely imperative that the elements be either totally independent (meaning that they must not overlap) or be completely *nested*. They cannot be partially nested. Constructions like

```
<first_element> <second_element></first_element> </second_element>
```

are invalid, unlike in HTML.

There is another basic difference between XML and HTML that should be noted. It is a hard-and-fast rule in XML that each opening tag *always* be matched with the appropriate closing tag. Otherwise, a document is considered invalid and, consequently, cannot be processed. HTML, on the other hand, is not so particular about this requirement, since a new tag can cancel the action of a previous unclosed tag. Nevertheless, if you create HTML documents and intend to utilize XML parsers, try to avoid taking such liberties, just to be on the safe side.

Let's now move to the general structure of an XML document using the content of Listing 14.1 as an example. An XML document consists of three parts:

❑ The prolog

❑ The definition (optional)

❑ The document body, which begins with the root element

Prolog

A prolog can include certain processing instructions that pertain to the entire document, as well as comments. Processing instructions are represented by special tags enclosed by the `<?` and `?>` character pairs. These instructions are referred to as "processing" because they inform the parser as to what operating modes or options must be activated. As a rule, an XML document begins with an *XML declaration*:

```
<?xml version="1.0"?>
```

Strictly speaking, this processing instruction is optional, but it is recommended by the W3C since it indicates the number of the XML version. Besides the version number, which is mandatory, an XML declaration can include the encoding type definition and the `standalone` attribute:

```
<?xml version="1.0" encoding="UTF-8" standalone="yes"?>
```

The `standalone` attribute indicates whether the document includes its own definition. If the document contains pointers to external DTDs/schemas, it is not a standalone document.

No characters, space characters included, may precede an XML declaration. If they do, the parser will generate an error message.

Another processing instruction commonly used in prologs is a reference to an XML stylesheet, for example:

```
<?xml-stylesheet type="text/xsl" href=
"http://schemas.biztalk.org/BizTalk/g9boxjl2.xsl"?>
```

This instruction specifies the XSL stylesheet used for presenting the document — on a browser, for example.

In addition to these two instructions, the body of the document may contain other instructions specific to a given parser. An unknown instruction will not raise an exception; the parser will simply ignore it.

Any comments in the text of an XML document are marked by the `<!--` and `-->` characters. They can be inserted anywhere in a document, and not just in the prolog, but they definitely cannot be enclosed within other tags. The information within these characters is treated as a comment, and the parser ignores its content. The following sample comment is acceptable:

```
<!-- this is a sample of <element> and <? processing instruction ?> -->
```

Besides this, when dealing with an XML document, you may often encounter what are called CDATA sections. At times, the developer needs to insert content that is not meant to be processed by the parser; this could be, for instance, a certain data thread. It makes no sense to search this thread for reserved characters, such as <, >, etc. Thus the parser simply skips all the content inserted between `<![CDATA[` and `]]>`, without validating its conformity with XML syntax. But this by no means implies that you are absolutely free to write anything you choose here. XML uses text format, and symbols with $0\times0-0\times1F$ hexadecimal values are invalid (except for the tabulation character — 0×9, the line-feed character — $0\times D$, and the carriage-return character — $0\times A$). This means that if you insert binary data into an XML document (compressed or encrypted data, for example), you must use the Base64 encoding schema or a similar method (this will be further detailed in the following chapters).

Definition

By definition, we mean a DTD or XML schema. Both variations solve the same task: they describe the design of a future document, including all the document elements together with their attributes, data types, links, and nesting levels.

Why then is a definition generally treated as an optional part of a document?

For a document to be parsed and made available to your application, the document must meet specific requirements. According to the XML specifications, documents fall into two categories: *well-formed* and *valid*.

A well-formed document contains no syntax errors (that is to say, the rules of using such characters as <, >, &, etc., are observed). Besides this, a well-formed document satisfies three criteria:

1. It contains at least one element.

2. It has a root element that is unique for a given document.

3. All other elements must be nested in the root element and/or in one other without overlapping.

If all these validation criteria are met, the document can be analyzed with a parser and accessed through Document Object Model (DOM) interfaces.

A valid document must first be well-formed. Second, the document design should be in complete agreement with its definition, that is to say, with its DTD or schema.

A Microsoft parser allows you to activate and disable a validation check mode: the ValidateOnParse property specifies whether this check should be run once the document is opened. An eponymous option is available in the TXMLDocument component — the key XML component in the context of the Borland strategy. If you mean to use XML for automated document management systems that enforce rigorous limitations on data format, it makes sense to discard all invalid documents at the very beginning.

In the beginning, the structure of an XML document was described using the corresponding document type definition — DTD — which was borrowed from SGML. The DTD is a set of tags enclosed within the <! and > symbols. The DTD for the sample document from Listing 14.1 might look like this:

```
<!ELEMENT Developer (#PCDATA)>
<!ATTLIST Developer
   age CDATA #REQUIRED
   certification CDATA #IMPLIED
>
<!ELEMENT Developers (Developer+)>
<!ELEMENT ProjectManager (#PCDATA)>
<!ATTLIST ProjectManager
   age CDATA #REQUIRED
   certification CDATA #REQUIRED
>
<!ELEMENT ProjectTeam (ProjectManager, Developers, Testers)>
<!ATTLIST ProjectTeam
   project CDATA #REQUIRED
>
<!ELEMENT Testers EMPTY>
```

A detailed description of a DTD is beyond the scope of this book. This is even more the case since this version has recently given way to others. For in-depth information, refer to the relevant W3C documentation.

The idea of introducing XML schemas was as simple as it was brilliant. Indeed, it seemed quite logical to ask: why not use XML for defining XML documents? As an answer to this question, a new subset of XML was developed specifically to create definitions. This still-evolving subset has a number of varieties, such as XML Schema Definition (XSD) and XML-Data Reduced (XDR). These issues are addressed below.

Document Body. Root Element

Now let us take a look at the so-called *root element*, which sometimes is also referred to as the document element. As mentioned above, a well-formed document must have one element that contains all other elements. Figuratively speaking, this is the main document header that makes the document a document. Its name often determines the subject of the document.

After seeing the name of the root element in Listing 14.1 — ProjectTeam — the reader will understand what this document is about. Now, if you try to add any other element before or after `ProjectTeam` — `<test/>`, for example — this document will be rejected after being parsed.

Suppose in addition to the document itself, an XML file also contains its schema. Typically, a schema has its own root element: `<Schema>`. Then, one more element is added to the existing ones (that is to say, to the document root and the schema root), which is often referred to simply as `<xml>`. This is not to be confused with the prolog — `<?xml?>`.

Now let us sum up our discussion of the XML document structure. If a given document meets the criteria used for determining whether it is well-formed and (possibly) valid, this document is parsed, which involves breaking it down into several parts. As soon as the document is analyzed, the programmer can access any part of it via the tree paradigm.

At this point, another technique for processing XML should be mentioned. Parallel to DOM, another standard — Simple API for XML (SAX) — is also being developed, which is based on an entirely different paradigm. Rather than provide the developer with a ready-to-use document that is already parsed into parts, a SAX parser generates a set of events for the customer: the beginning and end of the elements, the processing command, etc. By creating and specifying the appropriate event handlers, the developer implements the required functionality.

This approach makes sense if:

☐ The document being parsed is rather big (1 megabyte or more) and you need to suspend the whole process until parsing is completed

☐ You do not need to parse the entire document; the necessary decisions can be made after reading just the beginning of the document

Microsoft parsers include objects that support SAX, but these objects have not been integrated into Delphi 6. If you so choose, you can incorporate them manually, thus taking advantage of Delphi capabilities for handling automation objects.

Document Object Model

Suppose you have an XML document that has been properly parsed and loaded. Now you can reference it and access a set of interfaces for handling this document as a tree-like structure, which is usually referred to as the Document Object Model (or DOM). DOM representation is the task of every parser. Fortunately, ongoing efforts aimed at standardization have had a beneficial effect on XML.

The W3C is committed to the issue of enhancing and perfecting DOM. The foundation for all parsers is provided by the DOM Level 1 standard adopted in 1998. Currently, the DOM Level 2 standard is commonly used (**http://www.w3.org/TR/DOM-Level-2-Core**). Note that the latter is not the second version of the same model; it is actually the second level, representing an extended and advanced paradigm.

The reader is sure to ask here: What interfaces does DOM implement? What language and platform do we mean exactly?

We do not mean anything specific at all. In order to achieve portability, DOM was implemented in the Interface Definition Language (IDL), which was developed by the Object Management Group (OMG) for the CORBA specification. IDL lets you define only the interfaces themselves as abstract collections of methods (that is to say, those which cannot be implemented). The W3C published DOM support (language bindings) for Java and ECMAScript (the standardized version of Netscape JavaScript/ Microsoft JScript).

Here we work on the assumption that the definition of interfaces is taken care of by the parser. Once the developer obtains a pointer to any interface from the parser, he or she gets access to the required properties and methods of this interface, while all the work that comes with it is performed by the parser.

Of course, when DOM is used on the Windows platform, it is mapped to COM interfaces, which means that in this book, we will have to work with the already familiar terms associated with COM objects. This mapping was implemented both by Microsoft and by Borland.

Consequently, a Delphi 6 programmer is able to opt for any of the following operating modes when he or she manipulates DOM:

❐ Using just "pure" DOM (the IDOMNode/IDOMDocument interfaces and their derivatives)

❐ Using the TXMLDocument component and the IXMLNode/IXMLDocument interfaces supported by this component

❐ Calling the parser interfaces and functions directly: for instance, for the MSXML parser they are called IXMLDOMNode/IXMLDOMDocument

This wealth of capabilities should not intimidate you. They are all based on the standard DOM and vary a bit in syntax and also due to the availability of certain extra functions.

IDOMNode Interfaces

The prime object of DOM is to present the result of parsing in the form of nodes of a tree-like structure, where each individual object is represented by a node. All types of nodes are derived from a common ancestor: IDOMNode. All interfaces for specific node types, such as IDOMElement, IDOMAttr, etc., descend from IDOMNode.

The node defining the whole document, as one would expect, is located at the uppermost level. Its type, which is IDOMDocument, will be discussed later. A direct descendant of IDOMDocument is the node of IDOMElement type, which corresponds to the root element of the document. In turn, the nodes denoting child elements originate from the root element, and so on. The attributes of each element are also presented as a set of its child elements. But as for these nodes, they form a specific node type that cannot have child nodes.

Here is the DOM representation of the sample XML document given in Listing 14.1 (Fig. 14.2).

This diagram illustrates one specific DOM feature. Each element that contains text points to its child node that represents this text. As often as not, this peculiarity leads to confusion when the developer tries to get the text from the properties of the element itself, while it should be sought in a child element.

The IXMLNode interface provided by Borland has a different structure, which will be covered later.

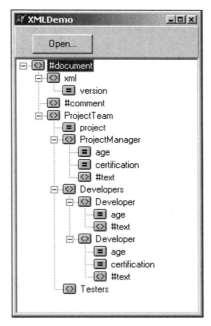

Fig. 14.2. This is the object model representing the sample XML document. The diagram is created using the program to be discussed below

The node generaly corresponds to the IDOMNode interface. This node is defined in the xmldom module, along with its special-purpose descendants. Let us examine them in logical order, moving from general to specific.

The *nodeType, nodeName,* and *nodeValue* Properties

The key to understanding DOM is to grasp the meaning of three important properties — nodeType, nodeName, and nodeValue — that are part and parcel of every node. The nodeType property, which is the most elementary among them, indicates the type of the node. Depending on the nodeType value, the nodeName and nodeValue properties can be interpreted differently. All possible variations are listed in Table 14.1.

Table 14.1. Possible Values of the `nodeType`, `nodeName`, **and** `nodeValue` **Properties for the IDOMNode Interface**

nodeType value		nodeType	nodeName value	Interpretation of the value of the nodeValue property	Name of the corresponding Interface
Numeric value	**Character constant**				
1	`ELEMENT_NODE`	Element	Element name	Nil	IDOMElement
2	`ATTRIBUTE_NODE`	Attribute	Attribute name	Attribute value	IDOMAttr
3	`TEXT_NODE`	Text node	#text	String text	IDOMText
4	`CDATA_SECTION_NODE`	CDATA section	#cdata section	Section content	IDOMCDATASection
5	`ENTITY_REFERENCE_NODE`	Reference to the entity	Entity name	nil	IDOMEntityReference
6	`ENTITY_NODE`	Entity (a DTD element)	Name	nil	IDOMEntity
7	`PROCESSING_INSTRUCTION_NODE`	Processing instruction	Instruction name	Instruction text	IDOMProcessingInstruction
8	`COMMENT_NODE`	Comment	#comment	Comment content	IDOMComment
9	`DOCUMENT_NODE`	Document node	#document	nil	IDOMDocument
10	`DOCUMENT_TYPE_NODE`	DTD header	DTD name	nil	IDOMDocumentType
11	`DOCUMENT_FRAGMENT_NODE`	Fragment	#document fragment	nil	IDOMDocumentFragment
12	`NOTATION_NODE`	DTD part	#notation	nil	IDOMNotation

The node hierarchy is clear enough. The TEXT_NODE, CDATA_SECTION_NODE, ENTITY_NODE, PROCESSING_INSTRUCTION_NODE, COMMENT_NODE, and NOTATION_NODE nodes cannot have child nodes. The DOCUMENT_TYPE_NODE node, which is associated with the DTD header, can have one or several subordinate nodes of the NOTATION_NODE or ENTITY_NODE type.

An element can contain other elements, attributes, comments, processing instructions, CDATA sections, references, and one text node. A document node can contain all the above-mentioned types, but in this case, only one child element is permissible (a root element).

We will not go into detail about all 12 types of nodes used in DOM. Some of them relate to DTD. This standard has been almost completely supplanted by XML schemas. Others are rarely used. As for those types that will be dealt with in the following chapters, they will be examined more thoroughly.

Properties and Methods Used for Managing Other Nodes

To facilitate orientation in the tree structure, IDOMNode provides:

❏ References to the owner document and parent node (the ownerDocument and ParentNode properties)

❏ References to the nearest nodes on the same level of the hierarchy (previousSibling, nextSibling)

❏ Nine methods and properties for handling child nodes

❏ In addition, there is a separate structure containing attributes (the attributes property)

Table 14.2 provides a brief overview of all these methods and properties.

Table 14.2. Methods and Properties of the IDOMNode Interface

Name	Description
property ownerDocument: IDOMDocument;	Reference to the document containing this node.
property parentNode: IDOMNode	Parent node.
property previousSibling: IDOMNode;	Previous node on the same level.
property nextSibling: IDOMNode;	Next node on the same level.

continues

Table 14.2 Continued

Name	Description
`function hasChildNodes: WordBool;`	Indicates whether the node has child nodes.
`property childNodes: IDOMNodeList;`	List of child nodes.
`property firstChild: IDOMNode;`	First child node in the list.
`property lastChild: IDOMNode;`	Last child node in the list.
`function replaceChild(const newChild, oldChild: IDOMNode): IDOMNode;`	Replaces the `oldChild` node with the `newChild` node and returns the pointer to the old node.
`function removeChild(const childNode: IDOMNode): IDOMNode;`	Removes the `childNode` node from the list and returns the pointer to it.
`function appendChild(const newChild: IDOMNode): IDOMNode;`	Appends the `newChild` node to the end of the list of child nodes.
`function insertBefore(const newChild, refChild: IDOMNode): IDOMNode;`	Inserts the `newChild` node before the `refChild` node.
`function cloneNode(deep: WordBool): IDOMNode;`	Copies the current node; the parent node is not defined. The `deep` parameter determines the cloning mode for child nodes: if it is set to `True`, they are also copied.
`property attributes: IDOMNamedNodeMap;`	Interface providing a list of node attributes.
`procedure normalize;`	Normalizes the structure of child nodes by removing empty text nodes.
`function supports(const feature, version: DOMString): WordBool;`	Indicates whether this node supports the specified *feature* property of the specified *version* in the context of the indicated DOM implementation.

You can gain access to the items of the interfaces that store the lists of child nodes (IDOMNodeList) and attributes (IDOMNamedNodeMap) using the same properties:

```
property item[index: Integer]: IDOMNode;
property length: Integer;
```

Due to the fact that those functions listed in Table 14.2 that enable you to add or remove child nodes do not work for attributes, IDOMNamedNodeMap supports an identical functionality for attributes.

After examining the available functions, you will have certainly noticed that they do not include any search functionality. Is it possible that the idea of the necessity of such a function had not occurred to anybody before? Well of course it had, and quite often for that matter. But the search specification is not included in the standard DOM, and therefore is provided by extra documents. We will discuss this important point later.

Namespaces

Names of XML elements and attributes are presented in text notation, which is clearly a great advantage since it makes documents intelligible and readable. But nothing is perfect. Imagine that you need to merge two documents, one of which contains information on vendors and the other describes the goods supplied. If the author of the first document has named one of his or her elements *name* or *class*, and the second author has done the same, how are you supposed to recognize the difference between the name of the vendor and the name of the product?

Elements and attributes can be assigned names that are combinations of two parts: a prefix and the local name itself. For instance, in the name of the element

```
<z:row FullName='GUADELOUPE' Code2='GP' Code3='GLP' NumCode='312'/>
```

z is a prefix and row is the local name. Then, in the above example about vendors and products, you can use such names as vendor:name and product:name.

A prefix denotes the namespace to which a given name belongs. The namespace is set by the construct:

```
xmlns:[prefix]=" URI namespace"
```

Typically, all namespaces used in a document are listed as attributes of the root element. Here, for example, is what the root element of an ADO recordset saved as an XML document looks like:

```
<xml xmlns:s='uuid:BDC6E3F0-6DA3-11d1-A2A3-00AA00C14882'
    xmlns:dt='uuid:C2F41010-65B3-11d1-A29F-00AA00C14882'
    xmlns:rs='urn:schemas-microsoft-com:rowset'
    xmlns:z='#RowsetSchema'>
```

The concept of a name space, along with the methods and properties that are associated with it, was introduced to the standard starting with DOM Level 2.

Name	Description
property namespaceURI: DOMString;	The namespace URI
property prefix: DOMString;	The prefix in the node name
property localName: DOMString	The local name of the node

The *IDOMDocument* Interface

This interface corresponds to an entire document that has been opened and processed with a parser. Not surprisingly, this interface has methods used in its high-level processing.

The property

```
property documentElement: IDOMElement;
```

indicates the root element of the document. In our example, this is ProjectTeam. Another property

```
property doctype: IDOMDocumentType;
```

provides access to the document DTD, if such a DTD is contained in it.

A whole collection of methods:

```
function createElement(const tagName: DOMString): IDOMElement;

function createDocumentFragment: IDOMDocumentFragment;

function createTextNode(const data: DOMString): IDOMText;

function createComment(const data: DOMString): IDOMComment;

function createCDATASection(const data: DOMString): IDOMCDATASection;

function createProcessingInstruction(const target, data: DOMString):
IDOMProcessingInstruction;

function createAttribute(const name: DOMString): IDOMAttr;

function createEntityReference(const name: DOMString):
IDOMEntityReference;
```

lets you create nodes of various types. Note that these will be standalone nodes, which will not be included in any of the child lists associated with already-existing nodes.

Creating a Sample Application That Uses DOM

Now it is time to move on from our rather lengthy theoretical discussion to technical details and experience XML first-hand. With its hierarchy of nodes, XML resembles a tree. So, we should try to load the document in a TTreeView component to visualize this structure.

Place the TXMLDocument components (from the Internet page of the Component Palette), along with TTreeView, the OnClick button and dialog for opening files, and the Filter property (customizing its extension to XML) in the form (Fig. 14.3). Add TImageList with two images inside. We will need them in order to differentiate between elements and attributes.

Fig. 14.3. The appearance of the main form of a simple XML loader

The next step is to write the following code for the OnClick button event (Listing 14.2):

Listing 14.2. The XMLDemo1 Application Code

```
procedure TForm1.Button1Click(Sender: TObject);

function DOMNode2TreeViewNode( ADOMNode : IDOMNode; ParentNode :
TTreeNode ):boolean;

var i: Integer;
    ThisNode : TTreeNode;
```

```
       TVNodes : TTreeNodes;
begin
  if not Assigned( ADOMNode ) then Exit;
  TVNodes := tvXML.items;
  ThisNode := TVNodes.AddChild( ParentNode, ADOMNode.NodeName );
  if not Assigned( ThisNode ) then Abort;
  ThisNode.ImageIndex := 0;
  if Assigned( ADOMNode.attributes ) then
    for i := 0 to ADOMNode.attributes.length - 1  do
     with TVNodes.AddChild( ThisNode,
ADOMNode.Attributes.item[i].NodeName ) do
      ImageIndex := 1;
  ThisNode.SelectedIndex := ThisNode.ImageIndex;
  if Assigned( ADOMNode.ChildNodes ) then
    for i := 0 to ADOMNode.ChildNodes.length - 1  do
     DOMNode2TreeViewNode( ADOMNode.ChildNodes[i], ThisNode );
end;

begin
  if not OpenDialog1.Execute then Exit;
  XMLDocument1.LoadFromFile( OpenDialog1.FileName );
  try
   XMLDocument1.Active := True;
   tvXML.Items.Clear;
   try
    Screen.Cursor := crHourGlass;
    DOMNode2TreeViewNode( XMLDocument1.DOMDocument, nil );
   finally
    Screen.Cursor := crDefault;
   end;
  except
   on E:EDOMParseError do
```

```
  begin
    ShowMessage( 'Parser error. Message:'#13#10 + E.Reason );
  end;
 end;
end;
```

In this listing, the lion's share of the work is performed by the `DOMNode2TreeViewNode` recursive procedure, which

❑ Adds a node to the tree that corresponds to the current node (element) of the XML document

❑ Adds nodes corresponding to the element attributes (if the element has any such attributes)

❑ Recursively calls itself for all child nodes

The sample code above works well enough as far as the simple task of displaying XML files goes. But try to run it on your computer. Surely, you must have noticed that the content of the file quite often differs from the content of the tree.

The discrepancies appear where elements with textual values are used. Can you see a number of nodes named `#text` in the picture? All these nodes have been artificially created by the parser. We mentioned this peculiarity earlier, while discussing DOM.

Implementing DOM in Delphi 6

Before the release of Delphi 6, those developers who used XML had to work mostly with the MSXML parser produced by Microsoft. It does have a number of advantages: high speed (according to various estimates, the speed of its performance is 20—100 percent above that of its competitors) and support for the most recent updates to XML standards. Still, like many other Microsoft solutions, this one is too closely integrated with other parts of the operating system, specifically with Internet Explorer.

NOTE

The MSXML parser comes with Internet Explorer beginning with version 4.01, with every new operating system, starting with Windows 2000 and ME, and with many other products. This means that you cannot install it on a "bare" Windows 95 system. To do this, you need to install the appropriate version of IE in advance.

A history of the gradual evolution of MSXML is complicated. Starting with the second version, MSXML has supported preliminary versions of XSL Patterns. While major improvements have been made to the parser, the language has also changed. By the time the third MSXML version was released, the language was basically different, since it had split into a conversion language (XSLT) and XPath, which is a language designed for implementing searches. Microsoft management decided to support both the old and new language dialects by providing MSXML 3 with the capability to run in two operating modes: the replace mode and the so-called side-by-side mode. One side effect of such a decision is the situation in which new COM objects that support DOM get the same ProgID as was used in the old version. This caused chaos, a classic case of the Tower of Babel, which ruined a great number of projects.

Quite recently, MSXML 4 was released, which was supposed to remedy the situation. All the remains of the functionality that provided support for XSL were removed from this new version with an unwavering hand. It is not even called a parser any more. Now it is referred to as a whole parsing suite. As a result, the product "puts on" an extra 5 megabytes. Besides this, it can only be installed using Windows Installer 2.0, the runtime of which is not even included in the Windows 2000 operating system! This means another 2 megabytes for your client-application installation and many other problems. The general picture appears to be clear: as far as portability is concerned, the usefulness of MSXML is quite doubtful.

In light of this, it seems that Delphi 6 developers were absolutely justified in their determination to enable multiple DOM implementations. The Delphi suite comes with modules for using the MSXML, OpenXML, and IBM XML parsers, with the default parser being MSXML.

But if you are resolved to achieve the greatest possible compatibility (with the least help from Microsoft products), then the best choice would certainly be the OpenXML parser. It is distributed free as a set of source codes written by Dieter Koehler and can be loaded from his website, **www.philo.de/xml**. Borland developers used the 2.3.14 version (the Sources\Internet\xdom.pas file) as a foundation, made minimal changes, and designed the adapter module for attaching to the general infrastructure (oxmldom.pas).

Unfortunately, at the time of the release update pack 6.02, Borland developers had not been able to provide reliable and consistent support for the third parser (IBM), and it cannot currently be used. This task remains, however, high on their agenda.

The XML architecture in Delphi is such that the specific parser functionality is hidden from the customer behind an additional layer of program interfaces. All derivatives of the XML technology in Delphi 6 — SOAP, the XMLMapper utility (the DataSnap technology), and other components — were designed to be completely independent from the type of parser in use.

This dramatic gain in DOM flexibility was achieved at the cost of its growing sophistication, since new intermediary links were to be added to the hierarchical system of objects and interfaces.

Now create a new application and place a single `TXMLDocument` component in the main form. You will see that the pointers to four more modules — `xmldom`, `XMLIntf`, `msxmldom`, `XMLDoc` — have been added to the uses list of your module. It is time to make it clear what is what in the system and to define the role performed by each module.

The *xmldom* Module

This module contains a "pure" declaration of COM interfaces, which is not confined to any specific implementation, and corresponds to XML DOM 2.0: the `IDOMNode` interface and its derivatives, as well as support for a few DOM extensions, which, if not adopted officially, are actually commonly used by developers (see the `IDOMNodeEx` interface).

It also contains mechanisms implementing various DOM parsers and startup procedures for the parsers that are being activated.

The *msxml* Module

This module compiles the type library of the msxml2.dll library to Object Pascal. It also contains declarations of such interfaces as `IXMLDOMNode`, `IXMLDOMDocument`, etc.

If you wish to use the advanced functionality of the most recent Microsoft parsers, create a similar module by importing the type library available from msxml3.dll and msxml4.dll.

The *msxmldom* Module

This module contains no new interfaces (good news), but instead, it defines the objects (such as `TMSDOMNode` and its derivatives) that support the `IDOMNode` interface family. Of course, they are not "bona fide" objects, but only adapters invoking Microsoft parser interfaces. Besides this, the module performs the entire tedious preliminary job of finding the appropriate version of the MSXML parser. The same function of an adapter between Delphi and the parser is fulfilled by the oxmldom (OpenXML) and ibmxmldom (IBM) modules.

The *XMLIntf* Module

This module contains definitions of the IXMLNode and IXMLDocument interfaces — Borland add-on modules for XML DOM — which, on one hand, enhance its functionality, and on the other hand, help take the edge off some pressing problems. These interfaces are directly linked to the TXMLDocument component.

The *XMLDoc* Module

Finally — for dessert — let us take a look at the XMLDoc module and the implementations that it contains: the TXMLNode class and the TXMLDocument component. These classes are simply and elegantly linked to their predecessors. The IXMLNode and IXMLDocument interfaces have the DOMNode/DOMDocument properties, respectively, to which all DOM calls are directed. Thus, on the TXMLDocument component level — the very first level that potential users of this language in Delphi 6 will deal with — formal independence from the parser vendor is achieved.

We should say that this structure, which consists of at least three layers wrapped around each other, might seem a bit too complicated. But here, we nevertheless must give credit to the efforts of Borland developers in combining maximum convenience with maximum compatibility. If you consider certain functional features redundant, just use the parser directly, or even create your own custom parser.

IXMLNode Interfaces

While introducing their own system of interfaces at the same time as DOM, Borland developers no doubt questioned — just like users — the expediency of such a measure. Clearly, the issue of customer convenience was their principal motivation. As compared to DOM, the IXMLNode interface adds a number of major improvements:

☐ Newly added properties: text (the node text) and xml (the content of this node together with the contents of all its child nodes presented in XML).

☐ Unified access to the list of child nodes (the ChildNodes property) and attributes (AttributeNodes). Now both lists have the same IXMLNodeList type.

☐ In addition, both lists were extended by adding access methods (accessors) familiar to Delphi programmers through the TStrings object. The property

```
property ChildValues[const IndexOrName: OleVariant]: OleVariant;
```

is the default property of a node. It is represented by a pseudo-array, the values of which can be accessed both via the index (number) of the child node and by the name of the child node. For our sample XML document, all three constructions are permissible:

```
XMLDocument1.DocumentElement.ChildValues['ProjectManager'];
XMLDocument1.DocumentElement['ProjectManager'];
XMLDocument1.DocumentElement[0];
```

The property

```
property Attributes[const AttrName: DOMString]: OleVariant;
```

provides access to the element attributes by their names.

The Text property needs to be further explained to prevent potential misunderstanding.

This property is not defined for all nodes — there are exceptions, among which are various types of elements. You can check whether a given element can be assigned a value for the Text property using another property:

```
property IsTextElement: Boolean;
```

which is a read-only property.

Here's a rule: the Text property is specified for an element if the element has only one child node of the ntText type (TEXT_NODE for DOM nodes). If the element doesn't yet have any child nodes, then its Text property is available and can be set. The required text node is created as a result.

For instance, for an element such as

```
<element>This is the text</element>
```

the value of the `Text` property will be equal to "This is the text." And if we further modify this example in the following way:

```
<element>This is the text<child>and some additions</child></element>
```

then any attempt to call `Text` will generate the `EXMLDocError` exception.

But is there any way to achieve the desired result? Following is a fragment of a sample code that will be discussed in detail later in this section. We set text for the `AXmlNode` node of the `IXMLNode` type, despite all the obstacles. To do this, we have to process three special cases:

☐ The node is a text node (`IsTextElement=True`); in this elementary scenario we simply update the `Text` property (in this particular case, the text value to be assigned is stored in `EdValue.Text`.

☐ The element has child nodes, and the first of them is a text node. Here we need to update the value of its `nodeValue` property.

☐ The element has child nodes, but the first of them is not a text one. In this case you need to insert such a node via the `Insert` method and assign it the required text value.

Theoretically, a fourth scenario is also possible: a text node does exist, but it is not the first node in the child node list. However, parsers always put the text first, which means that this is possible only after certain programming manipulations. That's why we neglect it.

```
if AXMLNode.IsTextElement then
   AXMLNode.Text := EdValue.Text
 else with AXMLNode do
  begin
   //text added at first
 if (not HasChildNodes) and (EdValue.Text<>'') then
     ChildNodes.Add( OwnerDocument.CreateNode( EdValue.Text, ntText )
 )
   else
    begin
     //already has text
     if ChildNodes[0].NodeType = ntText then
       ChildNodes[0].NodeValue := EdValue.Text
```

```
    //has children but not text
    else if EdValue.Text<>'' then
        ChildNodes.Insert(0, OwnerDocument.CreateNode( EdValue.Text, ntText ) );
    end;
end;
```

The `Text` property poses no problems of this kind as far as all other types of nodes are concerned. There, its value is simply identical to that of the `NodeValue` property.

Understanding the Relationship among All Interfaces

Having exposed you to a choice of several levels of interfaces, we now need to clarify the relationship among them. Why this move from the general idea to particulars? The unified access provided by Borland is efficient enough, but you may still need to use the specific features of a parser that has not been unified.

This is particularly true for a Microsoft parser. Even taking into account all its deficiencies concerning size and lack of portability, it nevertheless remains the most complete tool in terms of functionality. Developers from Redmond stay ahead of W3C standards by augmenting their DOM interfaces with new, and at times non-standard, functionalities. While ignoring whether this is positive or negative, we cannot deny the importance of access to these functional features.

Exactly how is the relationship between interfaces implemented?

1. Moving from `IXMLNode` to `IDOMNode`.

   This move is simple enough: every node of the first type is supplied with the `DOMNode` property, which is an explicit pointer to the DOM node. Similarly, the `IXMLDocument` interface is provided with a pointer to `IDOMDocument`.

2. Moving from `IDOMNode` to the interface implemented by the parser.

   This operation is far less clear. `IDOMNode` hides the Delphi object that implements this interface, along with a number of other objects: `IDOMNodeEx`, `IDOMNodeSelect`, and `IXMLDOMNodeRef` (for a Microsoft parser) or `IOXDOMNodeRef` (for OpenXML). "Ref" at the end of these names must be understood virtually: the only purpose of the last two interfaces is to provide a reference to a lower-level node that is directly implemented by the parser.

This Delphi object belongs either to the `TMSDOMNode` or the `TOXDOMNode` class, respectively. Calling `IDOMNode`, you actually call an instance of this object, and consequently can apply the corresponding typecast rules:

```
MSDOMNode := (DOMNode as IXMLDOMNodeRef).GetXMLDOMNode;
илиOXDOMNode := (DOMNode as IOXDOMNodeRef).GetDOMNode;
```

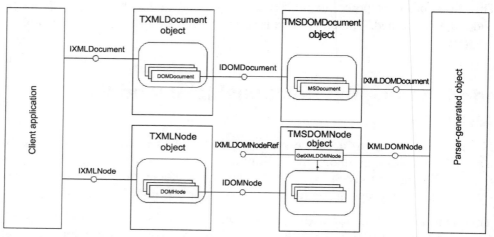

Fig. 14.4. Relationships among interfaces and objects supporting XML in Delphi 6

The interconnection of interfaces of different levels for a Microsoft parser is given in Fig. 14.4.

You need to take into account that a reverse, "bottom-up" move is impossible: you cannot find the `IXMLNode` node that corresponds to a given `IDOMNode` node by using explicit methods. This means that you have to design your project in such a way that uses interfaces of the same level.

Loading XML

The developers addressed the challenge of making the `TXMLDocument` component as universal as possible. The same holds true for the techniques for loading XML, which can be implemented:

❑ From a file. There are two ways to load from a file:

 • By specifying the value of the `FileName` property and then setting the Active property to `True`. If the `FileName` property was set in the development stage, the `Active` property is automatically set to `True` at run time.

- By invoking the `LoadFromFile` method (which also results in changing the `FileName` and `Active` values).

❑ From a stream: calling `LoadFromStream`.

❑ From a string containing XML: calling `LoadFromXML`.

❑ By setting the `XML` property. In this case, you need to set `Active = True` to activate the document.

As you have probably noticed, the `Active` property performs a key function in `TXMLDocument`. It is literally an "off-switch": as soon as the document is activated, the parser is called. Once the parser has processed the document and confirmed that it is well-formed (and, if necessary, valid), the DOM hierarchy is created. The tools for dealing with this hierarchy — that is to say, the `DOMDocument`, `documentElement`, and `ChildNodes` properties, among others — are assigned the required values.

Conversely, by setting `Active` to `False`, you will destroy all internal objects implementing DOM and set the above properties to `nil`.

Sometimes, `Active` is set automatically, and sometimes you have to set it manually.

How is the component linked to a given XML document in the design stage and at run time? The component has two published properties: `FileName` and `XML`. Their relationship is rather complicated:

1. At design time, these properties are mutually exclusive: by setting one of them, you clear the value of the other, and vice versa.

2. If the `FileName` property is set, the value of the `XML` property will reflect the file content once the application has started. But as soon as any changes have been made to the `XML` property, the current value of the `FileName` property is cleared out, which stands to reason, since the content of these properties is not synchronous anymore.

3. To modify the `XML` property, you always set `Active` to `False`. This measure insures the component against the addition of syntactically invalid constructs: once it is repeatedly activated, the parser is called to help find errors.

4. Changing the `FileName` property deactivates the component if two conditions are met: if the component was loaded from this file, and if it is currently active. Otherwise, the document remains active, but the value of the `XML` property is cleared out.

5. If the content of the file specified by `FileName` has been changed at run time, the changes are not shown automatically. In order to track them down, call the `Refresh` method.

> **NOTE**
>
> In version 6.02, the `Refresh` method tends to fail all at times. To prevent this, rather than call `Refresh`, simply set `Active` to `False` and then to `True` again.

6. When you load via `LoadFromXML` and `LoadFromStream`, the value of the `XML` property is identical to that which has been loaded, and the value of `FileName` is not changed.

7. If you wish to enable automatic saving of updates, set the `doAutoSave` option of the `Options` property to `True`. Here we mean the changes introduced by calling appropriate DOM methods and properties. As stated before, DOM structures are destroyed as soon as the document is deactivated. If `doAutoSave` is set, the current state of the whole DOM tree is saved either to the file (if the tree has been loaded from this file) or to the `XML` property (if the content has been loaded from this property). But if the XML text has been loaded from either a string or a stream (see Item 6), then the component quite logically assumes that there is nowhere to save the changes, and consequently, all the updates that you have made will be lost. But be sure to remember that all this holds for the changes made in DOM (adding/deleting elements and/or their attributes, moving them, etc.). If you are just modifying the value of the `XML` property, see Item 3.

8. Finally, if neither the `FileName` property nor the `XML` property has been assigned a value, you will create an empty XML document by setting the `Active` property to `True`.

Loading Asynchronously

At this point, we should say a few words about asynchronous loading. You may find this capability extremely handy when dealing with big and very bulky XML documents. The Microsoft parser supports an asynchronous operating mode, and this support is included in `TXMLDocument`.

Set `poAsyncLoad` for the `ParseOptions` property. As a result, the `OnAsyncLoad` event will be initialized four times — with the `AsyncLoadState` parameter equal to loading (a numeric value) (1), loaded (2), interactive (3), or completed (4). The same value is assigned to the AsyncLoadState property. This event is not generated when you operate synchronously, and the value of AsyncLoadState is always 0 (Uninitialized).

Of course, the information provided by you during asynchronous loading is insufficient. It is enough only for informing the customer as to how the task is progressing, and for displaying the progress bar. If you need to implement more sophisticated processing during the upload, you might consider using SAX parsers.

Functions Implementing a Document

If you need to create an instance of the IXMLDocument component at run time, then, besides the techniques mentioned, you have several more functions at your service (the XMLDoc module):

```
function LoadXMLDocument(const FileName: DOMString): IXMLDocument;
function LoadXMLData(const XMLData: DOMString): IXMLDocument;
overload;
function LoadXMLData(const XMLData: string): IXMLDocument; overload;
function NewXMLDocument(Version: DOMString = '1.0'): IXMLDocument;
```

You get the IXMLDocument interface, but it is, in fact, an TXMLDocument object instance that is being created. When you no longer require it, you can destroy it simply by assigning nil to the interface returned by the function. It should be noted that you do not need to set nil for the interface for those TXMLDocument instances that were placed in a form or module, since, like any other component, this one will have an owner (the Owner property) and will be destroyed by the Delphi Runtime Library (RTL) together with its container form.

Handling Parser Errors

The developers have also addressed the issue of handling errors made by the parser. The collection of DOM interfaces includes the IDOMParseError interface, which provides sufficiently detailed information on any error that occurs in the course of parsing.

The two properties

```
property errorCode: Integer;
property reason: DOMString;
```

answer the question "what?". Each parser certainly has its own numeric values of error codes (the `errorCode` property), as well as its own error messages. The error codes for a Microsoft parser can be found in MSDN, though the MSDN coverage of this particular issue is far from complete.

The properties:

```
property url: DOMString;
property srcText: DOMString;
property line: Integer;
property linePos: Integer;
property filePos: Integer;
```

answer the question "where?". Taken collectively, they let you find where exactly in the XML text an error has occurred. The names of these properties are self-explanatory. It just might be worth mentioning that `url` is the document address and `srcText` is the content of the document string where the error has been found. The `line`, `linePos`, and `filePos` properties provide more exact error coordinates in the string/file.

It should be added that the occurrence of errors depends on the state of the `poValidateOnParse` checkbox of the `ParseOptions` property. This checkbox determines whether the document should be checked just for its correctness or for both correctness and validity. In addition, the validation check is determined by the location of the DTD/schema. The DTD/schema that resides inside the document unambiguously predefines the necessity of such a check. Otherwise, if the DTD/schema is set in the form of a reference to some external document, this document will be checked for its validity only if the `poResolveExternals` option is specified.

Another question arises: how can you obtain access to this interface if a parsing error has taken place? Delphi has an exception class — `EDOMParseError` — that is designed specifically for the purpose of providing you with the necessary information. This class is supplied with the same properties as those that have been listed for `IDOMParseError`. Similar to any other exception, `EDOMParseError` provides the customer with the relevant error message that is contained in the `Message` property. For this purpose, Borland developers placed the concatenation of the corresponding values of the `Reason` and `Line` properties, as well as of the first 40 characters of the `srcText` property, in `Message`. If you need more-detailed information, analyze the values of other properties. An example of how to use them is given in Listing 14.2 as the sample code for a simple XML loader.

As you already know, the parser is invoked as soon as the document is activated. This means that the `try...except` sections, which are responsible for trapping `EDOMParseError`, must enclose:

❑ Explicitly setting the `Active` property to `True`

❑ All possible techniques for loading XML

You may be wondering, however, if there is any way you can access the `IDOMParseError` interface itself directly. Unfortunately, if you deal with `TXMLDocument` and its properties, the answer is no. Should an error occur during parsing, the `IDOMDocument` interface — and all other DOM interfaces for that matter — will assume the `nil` value. We will return to the `IDOMParseError` interface later while discussing the technique for working with a parser directly, without Borland "intermediary service."

In addition, the `TXMLDocument` component is associated with two more types of exceptions: `EXMLDocError` and `DOMException`.

`DOMException` occurs if a certain functionality is not supported by the current parser (the `DOMVendor` property). For instance, this kind of exception is raised for the OpenXML parser if you try to invoke the `SelectNode` or `SelectNodes` methods of the `IDOMNodeSelect` interface or the `TransformNode` method of the `IDOMNodeEx` interface. Neither the search language, Xpath, nor the conversion language, XSL/XSLT, is supported by the parser in question.

The second type of exception is raised for those errors that are in no way related to the parser functionality: for example, if you attempt to load from a non-existent file, modify a read-only document, or create a node of an invalid type. This exception class has no numeric error code or additional properties, which is quite understandable, since, while `EDOMParseError` defines the problems of authors of XML documents, and `DOMException` deals with the problems of authors of parsers, `EXMLDocError` informs you about your own errors that you have made as a programmer.

Using the *IXMLNode* and *IXMLDocument* Interfaces

To better illustrate the capabilities provided by Borland, let's explore one more example. Let's see how to create a simple XML editor using the above interfaces. By the way, such a code may be of more than just informative value for you. There aren't really that many XML editors that are distributed freely, the Microsoft XML Notepad project having been closed.

To make matters worse, the procedures used to manage the nodes of the XML tree (adding, removing, moving, renaming, etc.) are somewhat intricate, even for a seasoned programmer. In light of this, developing a simple editor appears to be the obvious choice for familiarizing yourself with all these operations.

For our would-be editor, let's opt for the already standard schema of arranging controls. In the left part of the window, let's place the tree (the `TTreeView` component), which displays the document structure. In the right pane, let's put `TPage-Control` with two tabs. The first tab will be used for editing the property and a list of the attributes of the current node, and the other tab will show XML itself (the contents of the `IXMLNode` property of the same name).

> ### NOTE
>
> Though the `XML` property is defined for `IXMLNode` and is formally parser-independent, as of yet it is only supported if the `DOMVendor` property points to the Microsoft parser.

The resulting appearance of the window is shown in Fig. 14.5.

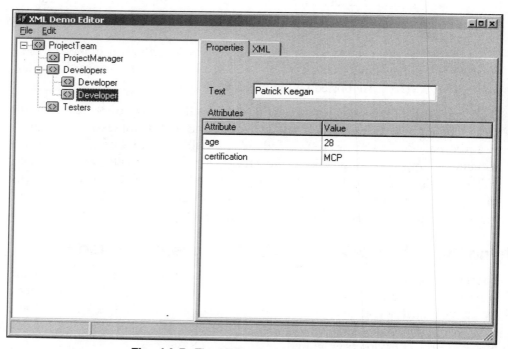

Fig. 14.5. The **XML Demo Editor** window

The full listing "The XML Editor Code" (contained on the companion CD) of the sample code doesn't exceed 500 lines — the size of a program, which, in our opinion, is more like a real application than an example. This explains why it features only the most essential functions: those of reading/writing, editing, and handling the clipboard. However, you are free to add any custom functions that you personally need.

Note some interesting features of the sample code (see CD-ROM): among all the node methods, not a single one allows you to rename nodes. This is quite understandable, considering that the fundamental `NodeName` property is read-only. To rename a node:

❏ Create a new node with the desired name

❏ Copy all attributes and child nodes to the newly generated node

❏ Replace the older node with the new one by calling the `ReplaceNode` function

Microsoft XML Core Services

At the time of the writing of this book, the fourth version of the parser was in wide use. Its key differences from the previous versions are as follows:

❏ Newly added support for XML Schema Definition (XSD, **www.w3.org/TR/ xmlschema-1**).

❏ Support for Schema Object Model (SOM), which is represented by a new set of interfaces similar to DOM but, contrary to the latter, intended for dealing with schema nodes.

❏ Support for XSL was removed (which was provided for in versions 2 and 3); in the fourth version this support has been completely replaced by the improved XSLT version.

❏ The parser-version-independent CLSID and ProgID identifiers were removed. Now, to create a COM object instance of the parser, you must explicitly indicate the version of the would-be object.

At this point, let us digress a little for a brief look at the history of the versions of MSXML. In spite of the fact that the first version of this parser was released (along with Internet Explorer 4.0) as a part of Windows 95 OSR2.5, Microsoft specialists and technical writers prefer to begin their count from version 2, which came with Office 2000 and Internet Explorer 5 (4.01 Service Pack 1, to be precise). All present-day Microsoft documentation on the subject of compatibility refers to MSXML version 2 as the first release — presumably, if you mean to develop commercial applications that use MSXML, you are to make sure that this version is included in the software package. The dynamic library of the second version of the parser, as well as the dynamic library of the next version, 2.5 (Windows 2000, IE 5.01 and 5.5), was called msxml.dll.

Intermediate version 2.6 came only with Microsoft SQL Server 2000 and ADO (MDAC) version 2.6. At this stage, the interface IXMLDOMDocument2 was added to the library — the innovation that was regarded by Microsoft as the most opportune moment for changing the name of the dynamic library to msxml2.dll. However, this version of the library has never been available for download and in- clusion into distribution kits, and happened to be the most short-lived among all the versions.

> **NOTE**
>
> Though we mention here the name of just one DLL, it should by no means be inferred that the parser includes only this library and nothing else. In actuality, it also contains one or two resource libraries, which can be internationalized. In any event, simply copy- ing and including the required DLL into your distribution kit cannot guarantee the appli- cation's proper performance. Microsoft provides redistributable versions of parsers.

Shortly afterwards, version 3 of the parser (msxml3.dll) was released. It added a new feature: support for the XSLT standard. But to simply add a new standard was not enough — the challenge was to ensure the compatibility of this standard with the Microsoft XML flagship, Internet Explorer, which as you probably remember was provided with MSXML version 2. As a result, this new parser supported two operating modes. In side-by-side mode, it could be registered independently, with- out affecting the performance of previous versions; this means that XSLT couldn't be used in IE, because, while trying to generate a COM object, the browser called the old version of the parser.

In replace mode, version 3 of the parser "short-circuited" all the Registry settings on itself, entirely supplanted the older MSXML, and became the main parser for IE. Switching between modes was done with the XmlInst.exe utility; it was provided along with the parser and is currently available for download from the Microsoft site.

But such careless treatment of a product of which millions of copies were released could not but lead to an avalanche of problems. Many web applications simply refused to perform; users and developers were constantly confusing the modes. As a consequence, Microsoft beat a retreat by removing support for the parser-version-independent identifiers from its newly released version 4 (the msxml4.dll dynamic library).

NOTE

Interestingly enough, the beta version of MSXML 4 still supported them. If you have installed this version on your computer, be sure to remove it!

Let's assume you have MSXML versions 2, 3, and 4 on your computer (which is to be expected considering that you are a developer). We can now look more closely at the ID situation from the point of view of a Delphi programmer.

As you may remember, the class ID (CLSID) is a unique ID that indicates the class of a given COM object, while the program ID (ProgID) — a text synonym of the CLSID — was originally introduced to address the needs of Visual Basic users.

With Delphi, you can create an object by calling the CreateCOMObject function:

```
Var Doc : IXMLDOMDocument2;
...
  Doc := CreateCOMObject( CLASS_DOMDocument ) as IXMLDOMDocument2;
```

Here you'll obtain a pointer to the required interface, supported by the newly created instance of the object with the specified CLSID (in this example, CLASS_DOMDocument).

Also, you can utilize the CreateOLEObject function that uses ProgID:

```
Var Doc : OleVariant;
...
  Doc := CreateOLEObject( 'MSXML2.DOMDocument' );
```

This returns the IDispatch interface supported by the object.

And so, version 2 of the Microsoft parser supported the DOMDocument object with the CLASS_DOMDocument class ID and the program IDs "MSXML.DOMDocument," "Microsoft.XMLDOM," and "Microsoft.XMLDOM.1.0" (the first one being by far the most popular).

When the IXMLDOMDocument2 interface was added to versions 2.6 and 3, CLASS_DOMDocument26, CLASS_DOMDocument30, and such program IDs as

"MSXML2.DOMDocument" (version-independent), "MSXML2.DOMDocument.2.6," and "MSXML2.DOMDocument.3.0" appeared along with them.

> **NOTE**
>
> The number 2 in the name "MSXML2.DOMDocument" denotes the interface version rather than the parser version. Program IDs beginning with `'MSXML2'` can be found in versions 3 and 4, but not in version 2.0.

In replace mode, the version 3 parser superceded the Registry setting so that all the version-independent IDs — `CLASS_DOMDocument`, "MSXML.DOMDocument," and "MSXML2.DOMDocument" — pointed to msxml3.dll as a COM server that was generating the required objects. In side-by-side mode, the version-independent IDs (except for "MSXML2.DOMDocument") called the older DLL, while those that contained the number of the version in their names called the most recent version of DLL.

Finally, the parser of version 4 adds `CLASS_DOMDocument40` and "Msxml2.DOMDocument.4.0" to the Registry. And it doesn't affect the settings of other versions either: for instance, if you try to generate "MSXML2.DOMDocument," msxml3.dll will be called.

All this means that if you know exactly what is installed on the client's machine, it's best to develop an instance of the parser with the number of the required version. Otherwise, you can use the function specifically provided by Borland (the `msxmldom` module):

```
function CreateDOMDocument: IXMLDOMDocument;
```

This successively goes through all the class IDs, from 4 through 2, in order to create the most up-to-date object.

Currently, the fourth version of the parser does not come with any operating system or any other product. This means that if you have chosen to rely on its capabilities, you will need to include the parser (about 5 megabytes) and most likely Windows Installer (Version 2) — since the latter is also not yet included as a part of the Microsoft operating system — in your distribution kit together with your product.

Now let us show you how to create an object that would be supported by the parser, and then tell you about this object.

In order to obtain the definition of the necessary interfaces, you can attach the ready-to-use msxml.pas file from the Source\RTL\Win\ directory in Delphi 6, which corresponds to version 2.0. Alternatively, you can choose to take advantage of another possibility and import the type library relevant to the parser that is installed on your machine (the **Project/Import Type library** item of the Delphi menu). Only by using the above approaches can you gain access to the interfaces that were added to the fourth version of the product. In the **Import Type Library** dialog, limit yourself to pressing the **Create Unit** button, and not the **Install** button. Otherwise, you will end up with about 40 COM objects converted by Delphi to components and installed in the ActiveX page of the Component Palette — and you will likely never need about 90 percent of them.

By way of illustration, let's examine the way in which two Microsoft technologies interact: XML and ADO (ActiveX Data Objects, which was discussed earlier in *Chapter 7*). Let's compile the ADO record set to the form of an XML document, edit it, and perform the reverse conversion.

Starting with version 2.5, ADO includes the capability of loading and saving the content of the cursor (the `Recordset` object) in the form of an XML document accompanied by its XDR schema. As you probably know, for the sake of compatibility, Delphi components and objects are based on the ADO libraries corresponding to version 2.1. However, you most likely have a newer version installed on your computer. Version 2.5 comes with Delphi 6 Enterprise (the MDAC_TYP.EXE file). A huge number of Microsoft applications install and use ADO: Office, Internet Explorer, Visual Studio, etc. You can always load the latest ADO version from the Microsoft site, **www.microsoft.com/data**.

If you are not quite sure about which ADO version is installed on your computer, simply open the Registry Editor — regedit.exe — and, among the hive child keys (`HKEY_CLASSES_ROOT`), find all the items beginning with `ADODB.Recordset`. If these items include `ADODB.Recordset.2.5` or higher (currently the latest version is 2.7), then most likely you already have the required version installed on your machine.

Now that you are sure that you have no problems with ADO, you can compile and test the sample code below.

After placing the `TADOConnection` and `TADODataset` components in the form, link them to the **DBDEMOS.MDB** file that is supplied with Delphi as an example of using Microsoft Access databases (it is installed by default to the C:\Program Files\Common Files\Borland Shared\Data\ directory). Besides this, you will need two more components — TDataSource and TDBGrid — for displaying the content of this database in traditional form.

The drop-down list is meant to contain a list of all the tables in the attached database, including such well-known examples as country, employees, parts, etc.

Finally, the TMemo component will be used for storing the XML text, and two buttons will be employed for implementing the compilation proper (Fig. 14.5). Listing 14.3 below includes just the compilation code, while the full source code for this example is contained on the companion CD.

Listing 14.3. Compiling ADO Recordset to and from XML

```
const
 SParserError =
   'Parser error. Message: %s'#13#10'URL: %s; src : %s;'#13#10'Line:
%d, LinePos: %d';


procedure TForm1.btnToXMLClick(Sender: TObject);
var
 rs : OleVariant;
 Doc : IXMLDOMDocument;
begin
 try
 Doc := CreateCOMObject( CLASS_DOMDocument40 ) as IXMLDOMDocument;
 try
  rs := ADODataSet1.Recordset;
  rs.Save( Doc, adPersistXML );
  if Doc.parseError.errorCode <> 0 then
   with Doc.parseError do
    begin
     Memo1.Lines.Clear;
     ShowMessage( Format( SParserError,
     [Reason, URL, srcText, Line, LinePos ]
     ) );
    end
  else
   Memo1.Text := Doc.xml ;
```

```
finally
  rs := UnAssigned;
  Doc := nil;
end;
except
  on E:Exception do
    ShowMessage( E.ClassName + #13#10 + E.Message );
end;
end;

procedure TForm1.btnFromXMLClick(Sender: TObject);
var
  rs : _Recordset;
  Doc : IXMLDOMDocument;
begin
  try
    try
    Doc := CreateCOMObject( CLASS_DOMDocument40 ) as IXMLDOMDocument;
    if not Doc.loadXML( Memo1.Text ) then
      with Doc.parseError do
        begin
          Memo1.Lines.Clear;
          ShowMessage( Format( SParserError,
          [Reason, URL, srcText, Line, LinePos ]
          ) );
          Exit;
        end;
      rs := CreateCOMObject( CLASS_Recordset ) as _Recordset;
      rs.Open( Doc, EmptyParam,  adOpenUnspecified, adLockUnspecified,
      adCmdFile );
      ADODataSet1.Recordset := rs;
    except
      on E:Exception do
        ShowMessage( E.ClassName + #13#10 + E.Message );
    end;
    finally
      rs := nil;
      Doc := nil;
    end;
  end;
```

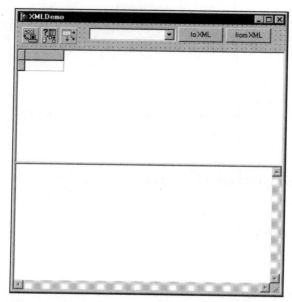

Fig. 14.5. The appearance of the main form of the sample XMLDemo3 document

By pressing the **to XML** button, you will convert the record set to a document that can then be accessed for editing. Add one more element with the name z:row into this document — each element of this type corresponds to a record in the selected table. Edit the attributes of this element; they are associated with the table fields. Setting other values to the attributes is necessary in order to prevent potential collisions that may occur in the table during the reverse compilation.

Finally, by pressing the **from XML** button, you initiate the reverse compilation. All the updates that you have made will be shown in the TDBGrid component but will not be written to the disk.

One of the features of this example, among those fundamentally important for understanding, is the approach used here for handling the IStream interface. The Microsoft implementation of XML documents implies very frequent use of this interface for two reasons: First, it supports the interface in question, and second, it can read/write XML from/to any objects implementing this interface.

An ADO record set can also work with IStream. The Open and Save methods imply the passing of a reference to the object supporting this interface as their parameters. The only Delphi deficiency is that this polymorphism of the Save method is not yet known in the Recordset interface definition (which comes with

Version 2.1, as you may remember). However, this problem is easily settled: assign the pointer to `Recordset` to a `OleVariant` variable and then call the `Save` method via the dispatch interface, as it is illustrated in the code of the `btnToXMLClick` method.

> **NOTE**
>
> An even more radical solution to this problem is to get rid of `TADODataSet` and other Delphi components altogether and handle ADO objects directly by importing the appropriate TLB. However, remember that extremes are dangerous: in this case, you risk losing all advantages afforded by the outstanding achievement of Borland developers — unified data access — which took them quite a while to implement (and certainly must not be overlooked!). You can also choose a compromise approach: to continue using the ADODB module together with all the components contained in it, but at the same time replacing the `ADOInt` module (the imported ADO 2.1 type library) with the appropriate module available from the imported TLB of ADO 2.5 and higher. Bear in mind, however, that if you do, you will be forced to rewrite about a dozen methods and events — a task that requires a certain level of skill.

It should be noted that no Delphi module meant to work with XML (`xmldom`, `msxml`, `msxmldom`, `xmlintf`, and `xmldoc`) is used in this sample code.

Summary

In this chapter we have just begun discussing XML, a language that is increasingly becoming the focus of the strategies pursued by leading IT experts. This discussion is crucial for mastering Delphi 6, and it will be further elaborated in all the chapters that follow.

Chapter 15

Using Data in XML Format

D elphi gives developers the option of using XML data in their applications. This capability can be used in all kinds of applications, including database applications, distributed applications, and web applications.

A collection of tools and components provides for the conversion of XML data into Delphi data packets and back to the original format.

Consequently, Delphi applications can use not only such traditional data sources as databases, spreadsheets, and text files, but XML files as well.

The procedure used to convert the format is surprisingly simple. In the design stage, you can use a special utility for this, *XML Mapper*. At runtime, all necessary tasks are performed by the components responsible for converting data, which are available on the **Data Access** page of the Component palette.

The topics covered in this chapter include:

❑ Prerequisites for using XML data

❑ Requirements for XML schemas

❑ The interaction of XML formats and Delphi data packets

❑ The XML Mapper utility

❑ The TXMLTransform component for converting XML data

❑ Components for providing access to XML data

Converting XML Data

Delphi has a mechanism for converting XML data into Delphi data packets. As you probably remember, data packets are used widely in distributed applications for passing data between clients and servers. (For more information on this issue, see *Part III, "Distributed Database Applications."*)

Why was this particular way of using XML data chosen?

The answer is simple. Because data packets are used, the set of components for transforming XML data is easily integrated into almost any Delphi application. Thanks to the capability of converting XML data for subsequent use in client dataset components, the developer automatically has a powerful tool that can be used for viewing, editing, and saving XML data. Most importantly, learning to use new technologies isn't necessary; the developer can use those with which he or she is already familiar.

At the end of this chapter, we will give you an example of how, by using just a few components (most of which are familiar to you from the other chapters of this book) and performing just a few operations. You can build an application that will not only allow you to view and edit XML data, but also to publish them on a web page.

Now we are going to proceed to a detailed study of the mechanism of converting and using XML data.

A Generalized Schema for Converting XML Data

Let's consider the following task. We have an XML file containing some data as our source file. (For a detailed explanation of the XML format, refer to the previous chapter.) We need to convert these data into Delphi data packet format.

To begin with, the XML document must obviously have an ordered structure that allows you to present the data in tabular format.

Second, we need to build a data packet with a structure that adequately represents the converted data.

Lastly, we need to make sure that every single XML element corresponds to the correct field of the data packet.

And so we can see a generalized schema for transforming XML data into a data packet format taking shape (Fig. 15.1).

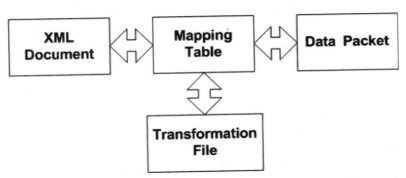

Fig. 15.1. The process of converting XML data into a Delphi data packet presented schematically

Using certain Delphi facilities, a special *transformation file* is built from the source XML file. It describes how the XML nodes are mapped to the fields of the data packet. (Guess what language is used for creating this file? XML, of course.) Besides which, the transformation file will also determine the structure of the resulting document.

If the conversion is to a new data packet, you can specify a one-to-one relationship: that is, each XML node will be associated with a separate field of the data packet. If an existing data packet is being used, the XML nodes should be mapped only to existing fields of the packet.

Once it is converted, the data packet can be used in an application or saved as a file. This is implemented via the method

```
procedure SaveToFile(const FileName: string = '';
  Format TDataPacketFormat=dfBinary);
```

of the client dataset component. The format of the file depends on the value of the Format parameter. If it is dfXML, the data will be saved in XML format.

It should be noted that the above schema, which is implemented in Delphi, pertains equally to XML-to-data packet conversions and vice versa (data packet-to-XML). But each case requires creating an individual transformation file.

Delphi Data Packet Format

Delphi data packets are used for exchanging data between client datasets and their provider components. *Chapter 9, "An Application Server,"* discusses this issue in more depth. A data packet is accessed through a property of the OleVariant type. A data packet can be saved as an XML file using the method

```
procedure SaveToFile(const FileName: string = '';
  Format TDataPacketFormat=dfBinary);
```

of the client dataset, but this is possible only if the Format parameter is set to dfXML. If its value is dfBinary, the packet is saved in binary format as a file with the cdr extension.

For example, the data packet for the Country table of the Delphi demo database looks as follows:

Listing 15.1. The XML File of the Data Packet for the Country Table

```
<?xml version="1.0" standalone="yes"?>
<DATAPACKET Version="2.0">
  <METADATA>
```

```
<FIELDS>
 <FIELD attrname="Name" fieldtype="string" WIDTH="24"/>
 <FIELD attrname="Capital" fieldtype="string" WIDTH="12"/>
 <FIELD attrname="Continent" fieldtype="string" WIDTH="13"/>
 <FIELD attrname="Area" fieldtype="string" WIDTH="7"/>
 <FIELD attrname="Population" fieldtype="string" WIDTH="9"/>
</FIELDS>
<PARAMS/>
</METADATA>
<ROWDATA/>
</DATAPACKET>
```

The XML structure that describes the data packet must contain the mandatory element

```
<DATAPACKET Version="2.0">
```

and should provide descriptions for all the fields included in the dataset. This is done using the <FIELDS> element. If the packet contains actual data, they are described in the <ROWDATA> element in the form of records. An individual <ROW> element is created for each record.

Tools for Converting XML Data

Creating transformation files and passing data in the design stage is done by a special-purpose Delphi utility — XML Mapper.

A set of components stored in the **Data Access** page of the Component palette allows you to use functions for transforming XML files.

Transforming data is the responsibility of the TXMLTransform component. It can be used both for converting XML data into a data packet and for the reverse conversion.

The TXMLTransformProvider component implements access to the XML file. It acts as a bridge between the XML file and the client dataset. TXMLTransformProvider builds and passes data packets to the client application and receives the changes made by the client.

The TXMLTransformClient component is a container for the TXMLTransform component, and converts the data received from TXMLTransformProvider.

Besides which, the **Internet Express** page of the Component palette contains the
TXMLBroker component, which is meant to receive data packets from the provider
component (as well as from the remote application server), and translate them into
XML format for producer components.

Let's examine all these tools more thoroughly and see how they are used in designing applications.

The XML Mapper Utility

The XML Mapper utility is called from the **Tools\XML Mapper** menu. It is responsible for creating transformation files, XML schemas, and data files (both
XML and data packet). All these files will later be available for use in various applications. Transformation files, for instance, are utilized by components that implement data conversion.

In accordance with the schema of converting XML data (see Fig. 15.1), the XML
Mapper window is divided into three panes (Fig. 15.2).

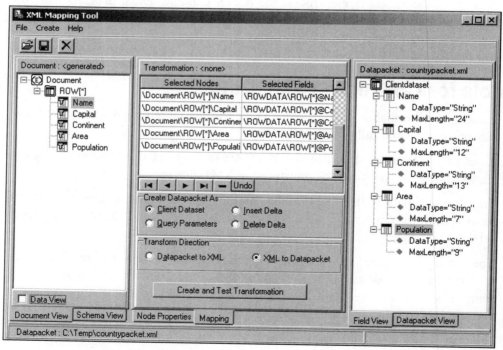

Fig. 15.2. The XML Mapper utility allows you to create transformation files

The left pane is intended for work with the XML document, which is the very first link in the transformation chain. Selecting and loading the file is done with the standard controls. In the **Document View** tab, you can work with the tree of the nodes and elements of the XML document. It is here that you select which elements are to be converted. You can view the document schema in the **Schema View** tab.

The right pane lets you perform various operations on the data packet file. The **Field View** tab shows the packet structure in the form of a field tree. The **Datapacket View** tab contains an XML representation of the packet structure. (As stated earlier, a data packet saved as an external file of the client dataset has the XML format.) Selecting the fields to be mapped to the XML elements is done using both tabs.

The middle pane displays the links set between the XML document and the data packet, and allows you to edit these links. Editing is done in the **Mapping** tab, at the top of which you see the translation table. And finally, the **Node Properties** tab can be used to view the properties of the XML node selected in the left pane.

Selecting the Source File

The XML Mapper utility works with the following data types. The main data types for which conversion is performed are:

❐ XML format

❐ Delphi data packet format

Information on all customized transformation links and additional useful data are represented by the following data types (these types store information in XML format):

❐ A transformation file (XTR) stores mapping information and descriptions of both datasets — XML and data packet.

❐ A repository file (XRP).

❐ An XML schema file (DTD, XDR, XSD) lets you view the structure of the XML file.

XML Mapper supports two-way data transformation: XML-to-data packet and data packet-to-XML. This means that you can open the source file both in the left and in the right pane. This operation can be done using standard Windows tools: the Main Menu, the toolbar button, and the pop-up menu of the given pane.

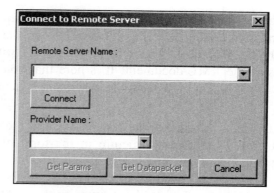

Fig. 15.3. The panel for loading a data packet from a remote server

A data packet can also be obtained directly from the remote server. To do this, use the **Connect To Remote Server** command from the left pane's pop-up menu. Selecting this command results in the display of a panel, in which you need to choose the required server (which must be registered on the computer) and specify the dataset to be loaded from the server (Fig. 15.3).

While loading the transformation file, you will be able to work with the XML Mapper environment, which handles the XML and data packet data as well as the links specified between them (if, of course, they have been saved).

Constructing the Data Packet and XML Document and Saving Converted Data

For the XML Mapper utility to perform its job, it needs at least a data source file, whether it be an XML file or a data packet. Once the source file with the data to be converted is selected, a receiver file has to be opened or created.

If the receiver file already exists, just open it in XML Mapper. If you choose to create a new file, then, after the mapping between the elements and fields is completed (which we will cover shortly), call the appropriate command from the **Create** menu:

❑ **Datapacket from XML** — to create a data packet

❑ **XML from Datapacket** — to create an XML file

If an XML file is made from a data packet, you can also customize the elements being created. This can be done in the special-purpose **Create Xml from ClientDataSet** window, which is automatically displayed as soon as you select the **XML from Datapacket** command. Here you can modify the names of these elements, including the root element (Fig. 15.4).

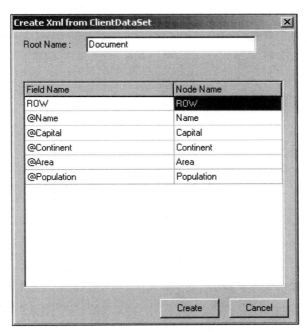

Fig. 15.4. The window for customizing elements
of the XML document being created

If you are building a data packet from an XML document, you can choose the type for this packet. Use the **Create Datapacket As** radio button group in the **Mapping** tab of the middle pane for this (see Fig. 15.2).

Now you can save the newly created structure as a file using the traditional method.

NOTE

Notice that all the above commands only build the data structure, and have nothing to do with the transformation of the actual data. The transformation proper will be covered later.

Mapping XML Elements to the Data Packet Fields

How is the mechanism of mapping implemented? It's a fairly simple process. Just select the necessary XML element or packet field of the source data file in the left or right pane and double-click it. This will result in a new record that will contain the selected element or field appearing in the table in the **Mapping** tab of the middle pane.

Your next move depends on whether a receiver file exists or not. If not, you needn't do anything more; simply perform the same operation on the next element or field.

If the target file does exist, you have to select the necessary field or element in its structure in a similar fashion and double-click it. As a result, a row in the mapping table in the **Mapping** tab will be filled completely and will contain the related XML element and data packet field. This link means that the data included in this element (field) of the source file will be transformed into the corresponding field (element) of the target file.

> **NOTE**
>
> Notice that the rows of the table are filled from top to bottom, irrespective of the location of the current record.

Once the relationships between all the required fields and XML elements have been set, the mapping table will contain the schema for data conversion.

Creating the Transformation File and Converting the Data

As soon as the mapping table is filled, you can begin creating the transformation file. To do this, select the **Transformation** command from the **Create** menu. The **Transformation** command will then become available in the **File\Save** menu. Having selected it, save the newly created transformation file in order to use it later when working with transformation components.

Apart from building the transformation file, you can also move data between the XML and data packet. To do this — and it can only be done once the source file and target file are selected and the fields and XML elements are properly mapped to each other — press the **Create and Test Transformation** button available in the

Mapping tab of the middle pane. The direction of the transformation is set in the **Transform Direction** radio button group.

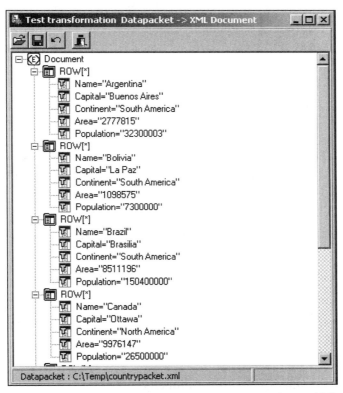

Fig. 15.5. A window showing the result of converting data for an XML document

After that, the data conversion itself takes place and the result appears in a new window. If the direction of transformation indicated the XML document as the data receiver, the result will be presented in an XML tree (Fig. 15.5). For the opposite conversion, the result is displayed in tabular form.

Converting XML Data in Distributed Applications

Now let's turn to the programming aspects of using XML data in distributed applications. First of all, we need to consider the problem of converting XML data.

This task is performed by the TXMLTransform component, which can convert data from XML format into a Delphi data packet and vice versa. This is a base component, since it is used by other components that we have yet to discuss.

In conformity with the transformation schema (see Fig. 15.1), the very first step is to specify the data source and the data receiver, as well as the transformation file.

The role of the data source can be taken on both by XML data and by a data packet.

The property

```
property SourceXml: string;
```

allows you to specify source data as a string; however, don't be so quick to open the file in the stream and export the data from it. Simply define the path to the source file in the property

```
property SourceXmlFile: string;
```

Once it is set, this property takes priority over other properties used to specify the source file.

Besides this, you can open an XML source file using the property

```
property SourceXmlDocument: IDOMDocument;
```

It should contain a reference to the TXMLDocument component in which the source file is set. But this property works only if the SourceXml and SourceXmlFile properties are empty.

The transformation file is set with the property

```
property TransformationFile: string;
```

or, if the transformation schema is defined in the XML document in the TXMLDocument component, you could also use the property

```
property TransformationDocument: IDOMDocument;
```

As soon as the transformation is completed, its result is available from the property

```
property ResultString: string;
```

in XML format.

Once the data source and transformation schema are defined, you are able to convert data just by calling the property

```
property Data: string;
```

Every time this property is called, transformation is performed automatically. Calling this property is accompanied by the invocation of the handler method

```
type
    TTranslateEvent = procedure(Sender: TObject; Id: string; SrcNode:
    IDOMNode; var Value: string; DestNode: IDOMNode) of object;
  property OnTranslate: TTranslateEvent;
```

For example, the dialog for selecting the source XML file and the client dataset can be associated with the following code fragment:

```
procedure TForm1.TransformClick(Sender: TObject);
const DefaultTranslationFile: String = 'CountryTrans.xtr';
begin
 OpenDlg.Filter := 'XML Files|*.xml';
 if OpenDlg.Execute then
 begin
  XMLTransform.SourceXmlFile := OpenDlg.FileName;
  XMLTransform.TransformationFile := DefaultTranslationFile;
  memo1.Lines.Add(XMLTransform.Data);
  ClientDataSet.Close;
  ClientDataSet.XMLData := XMLTransform.Data;
  ClientDataSet.Open;
 end;
end;
```

In the above fragment, the source XML file is selected, and the XMLTransform component, with the help of the transformation file, then converts the data into a data packet. This occurs when the Data property is called, and the result is then passed to the ClientDataSet client dataset (or, to be more specific, to its XMLData property).

Also, you can use the method

```
function TransformXML(const SourceXml: string;
  const AtransformationFile: string = ''): string;
```

but to do this you have to first assign the source file and the transformation file once again using the SourceXml and AtransformationFile parameters.

The above example for this method looks as follows:

```
procedure Tform1.TransformClick(Sender: Tobject);
const DefaultTranslationFile: String = 'CountryTrans.xtr';
```

```
  var S: String;
  begin
   OpenDlg.Filter := 'XML Files|*.xml';
   if OpenDlg.Execute then
   begin
    with TfileStream.Create(OpenDlg.FileName, fmOpenRead) do
    try
     SetString(S, nil, Size);
     Read(Pointer(S)^, Size);
    finally
     Free;
    end;
    XMLTransform.SourceXml := S;
    XMLTransform.TransformationFile := DefaultTranslationFile;
    ClientDataSet.Close;
    ClientDataSet.XMLData :=
    XMLTransform.TransformXML(XMLTransform.SourceXml,
  DefaultTranslationFile);
    ClientDataSet.Open;
   end;
  end;
```

The transformation result can also be saved as an XML document if the property

```
    property ResultDocument: IDOMDocument;
```

is set.

Additionally, the developer can change the schema of the resulting document, which, as you know, is stored in the transformation file. A new schema just needs to be set through the property

```
    property EmptyDestinationDocument: IDOMDocument;
```

The XML schema should be loaded into the TXMLDocument component.

The component has two pairs of handler methods, not counting OnTranslate.

The first pair

```
    type
      TRowEvent = procedure(Sender: TObject; Id: string;
      SrcNode: IDOMNode; DestNode: IDOMNode) of object;
    property BeforeEachRow: TRowEvent;
    property AfterEachRow: TRowEvent;
```

is called before and after a row is processed.

The second pair

```
property BeforeEachRowSet: TRowEvent;
property AfterEachRowSet: TRowEvent;
```

is called prior to and after a record set is processed.

The `Id` parameter contains the ID (name) of the element being converted. The `SrcNode` and `DestNode` parameters are references to the DOM interfaces for the source and target nodes, respectively.

Using XML Data in Distributed Applications

To pass XML data to the client of a distributed application, you need to utilize a provider component, just as with distributed database applications (see *Chapter 9, "An Application Server"*). Needless to say, in order to handle XML data, we require a special provider. The role of this provider will be taken on by the `TXMLTransformProvider` component.

This component descends from the `TCustomProvider` class and provides the client with the `IAppServer` interface. Thanks to this, `TXMLTransformProvider` is able to perform the main function of a provider component: passing data from the data source to the client, accepting the changes made by the client, and then passing them back to the data source. The component uses files in XML format as data sources. The XML file is specified by the property

```
property XMLDataFile: string;
```

For the client dataset (for instance, the `TClientDataSet` component) to be able to use XML data, these data need to be transformed into a Delphi data packet. The reverse operation is performed when the changes made by the client are passed back to the data source.

As you already know, such transformations necessitate using special transformation files. For the `TXMLTransformProvider` component, Borland developers found a simple solution: they integrated two `TXMLTransform` components into one provider component; these two components are thus able to accomplish all the necessary transformations.

The operation of reading data from XML files is performed by the component available via the property

```
property TransformRead: TXMLTransform;
```

The operation of applying changes to the XML file is performed by the component available via the property

```
property TransformWrite: TXMLTransform;
```

To be able to successfully perform its duty, each of the above components needs a transformation file. Both of them are provided with such a file using their respective `TransformationFile` properties.

For example:

```
XMLTransProvider1.TransformRead.TransformationFile :=
OpenDlg.FileName;
```

Besides which, handler methods can be specified for each transformation component.

The `TXMLTransformProvider` component itself has the set of handler methods that is standard for every provider component (see *Chapter 9, "An Application Server"*).

Using the `TXMLTransformProvider` component as a basis, you can develop various distributed applications (Fig. 15.6).

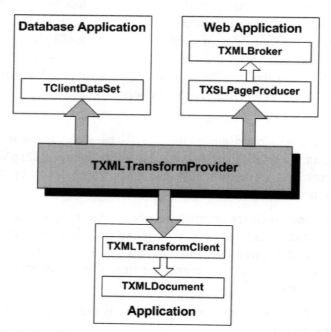

Fig. 15.6. Possible uses of the `TXMLTransformProvider` component in distributed applications

First of all, the component can be used in tandem with client datasets in distributed database applications. It isolates the client application from the data source, and the dataset uses the TXMLTransformProvider provider component to access the XML files in exactly the same way as it accesses any table of a traditional database on the server.

Second, this component allows you to pass XML data to the client application and work with them as you would with XML documents. To do this, you have to use the provider component in combination with the TXMLTransformClient component.

Finally, you will find this component extremely handy when designing distributed web applications. To publish XML data, the appropriate provider component is linked to the necessary HTML page using the TXMLBroker component as a bridge.

Let's take a closer look at these capabilities.

XML Data in the Client Dataset

The TXMLTransformProvider component has all the necessary properties and methods of a standard provider component. As a result, it can work with the TClientDataSet component both locally and via a remote server.

Client datasets connect to data sources in the traditional manner — using the ProviderName property. If the XML data source resides on a remote server, you need to specify the server as well using the RemoteServer property (see *Chapter 10, "A Client of a Multi-Tier Distributed Application"*).

All subsequent operations involved in passing XML data to the client and saving changes are done in the standard manner.

To change data locally, methods for editing datasets are called (Edit, Append, Post, Cancel, etc.), while the changes made by the client are passed to the source XML file using the ApplyUpdates method of the client dataset.

XML Data in an XML Document

In addition to the traditional technique of integrating XML data into a dataset, a client application can also use them directly, in XML document format. The TXMLTransformClient component is used for this.

This component also can work with either a local or remote data provider. The required `TXMLTransformProvider` provider is defined through the property

```
property ProviderName: string;
```

If you have to use XML data on a remote server, you also need to set the property

```
property RemoteServer: TCustomRemoteServer;
```

To provide for the interaction with the XML data source, the `TXMLTransformClient` component encapsulates three `TXMLTransform` components. They are available through the following properties.

The property

```
property TransformGetData: TXMLTransform;
```

returns a reference to the transformation component that services the incoming data stream. Depending on the format of these data, its `TransformationFile` property must point to the transformation file that will correctly implement the data conversion.

To get the data from the provider and convert them into XML format, use the method

```
function GetDataAsXml(const PublishTransformFile: string): string;
```

where the `PublishTransformFile` parameter is the name of the transformation file. If this parameter is empty, the file name will be taken from the `TransformGetData.TransformationFile` property.

For example, a client application can handle an XML document received from a remote server in the following way:

```
...
SomeXMLDocument.XML.Clear;
SomeXMLDocument.XML.Add(XMLTransformClient.GetDataAsXml('SomwFilePath'));
...
```

The property

```
property TransformApplyUpdates: TXMLTransform;
```

provides access to the transformation component that transforms the source flow of modified data. Depending on the format of these data, its `TransformationFile` property should indicate the transformation file that will correctly convert the data.

If the provider associated with the `TXMLTransformClient` component passes data from an SQL query with parameters or a stored procedure, the property

```
property TransformSetParams: TXMLTransform;
```

returns the `TXMLTransform` component that converts the dataset parameters.

If the dataset has parameters, then prior to getting the data from the provider and transforming them, the following method should be invoked for the `TXMLTransformClient` component:

```
procedure SetParams(const ParamsXml, ParamsTransformFile: string);
```

which takes care of the conversion of the dataset parameters.

The `ParamsTransformFile` parameter points to the transformation file, while the `ParamsXml` parameter must reference the XML document for the incoming converted parameters.

XML Data on an HTML Page

The `TXMLTransformProvider` component can also be used for passing and transforming data for web pages. Here, the `TXMLBroker` component from the **Internet Express** page of the Component palette acts as the bridge between the provider component and producer component. Its responsibility is to provide for "mutual understanding" between a web page using predominately HTML and `TXMLTransformProvider`, which works with XML data.

The `TXMLBroker` component uses the standard properties — `ProviderName` and `RemoteServer` — to connect to the provider. To get data from a server, the developer can use the method

```
function GetXMLRecords(var RecsOut: Integer; var OwnerData:
OleVariant; XMLOptions: TXMLOptions): string;
```

although passing data to the web page and saving changes are usually done automatically.

The `TXMLBroker` component itself must interact with the `TXSLPageProducer` component responsible for generating the web page. That's why the `TXMLBroker` reference must be specified in the `XMLData` property of the producer component. For a more detailed discussion of this method of publishing data — as approached from the angle of distributed web application design — refer to *Chapter 19, "WebSnap Technology."*

The `TXMLBroker` component works with the web page using the property

```
property WebDispatch: TWebDispatch;
```

which gives you the encapsulated dispatcher component. It provides the developer with exhaustive information on the HTTP requests that need to be processed.

Additionally, the method

```
function GetDelta(Request: TWebRequest): string;
```

returns a delta packet with the changes found in the HTTP `Request` request. And after that, you can call the method

```
function ApplyXMLUpdates(const Delta: string; out ErrorCount:
Integer): string;
```

which will forward the delta packet to the producer component. For instance, should an error occur in the `SomeXMLBroker` component in the process of passing changes, the modified web page request can be redirected to a reserve `TXMLBroker` component:

```
var DeltaStr: String;
    ErrCnt: Integer;
...
DeltaStr := SomeXMLBroker.GetDelta(SomeWrongRequest);
ReserveXMLBroker.ApplyXMLUpdates(DeltaStr, ErrCnt);
...
```

When passing data from the provider to the web page, and when returning the changes made, two handler methods are called, one for each process:

```
type TRequestRecordsEvent = procedure (Sender: TObject; Request:
TWebRequest; out RecCount: Integer; var OwnerData: OleVariant; var
Records: string) of object;
property OnRequestRecords: TRequestRecordsEvent;
```

and

```
type TRequestUpdateEvent = procedure (Sender: TObject; Request:
TWebRequest; Response: TWebResponse; var Handled: Boolean) of object;
property OnRequestUpdate: TRequestUpdateEvent;
```

The `TXMLBroker` component is able to adjust the size of the data packet passed by the provider to the server. This is implemented via the property

```
property MaxRecords: Integer;
```

which sets the number of records per packet. The default value of this property is -1, which means that the size of the packet is not regulated. If this property is set to 0, the packet will contain no data at all and will be used for passing data structure information only.

The `TXMLBroker` component possesses a representative set of properties and methods for handling potential exceptions.

First, it can use a producer component that is specifically intended for handling errors that may occur in the provider component's process of sending data. If the property

```
property ReconcileProducer: TCustomContentProducer;
```

is filled in, the appropriate producer component will return to the web page responses to requests that generate exceptions.

The property

```
property MaxErrors: Integer;
```

allows you to set the maximum number of errors that will be allowed to occur in the course of the provider's passing of data. This property can be very useful if you have a bad communication channel and need to make repeated attempts to send a packet.

Once an error has occurred, you can get the content of a delta packet via the method

```
function GetErrors: string;
```

and the total number of errors in the packet will be returned by the method

```
function GetErrorCount: Integer;
```

However, the simplest way to do this is by invoking the handler method

```
type TGetErrorResponseEvent = procedure (Sender: TObject; ErrorCount:
Integer; XMLErrors: string; Request: TWebRequest; Response:
TWebResponse; var Handled: Boolean) of object;
property OnGetErrorResponse: TGetErrorResponseEvent;
```

which is called when a data sending error has occurred.

Sample Application Using XML Data

As an example, let's design an application that will allow us to view and edit XML data as a dataset and as an XML document. Here we will use the Country.xml file from the Delphi demo database as the data source, but the user interface of the application allows you to select and load any XML file.

The `TXMLTransformProvider` component provides access to the data source. In order to do this, `TXMLTransformProvider` needs to be passed the full path to the XML file in its `XMLDataFile` property. Besides which, the provider component must use transformation files for reading the data and saving the changes made. That's why, once the source file is opened, the

```
XMLProvider.TransformRead.TransformationFile := edReadFileName.Text;
```

and

```
XMLProvider.TransformWrite.TransformationFile := edWriteFileName.Text;
```

properties of the component are passed the names of the corresponding files.

At this point a few words need to be said about creating these transformation files. For the Country.xml file, the transformation files were built using the XML Mapper utility.

First, the source XML file was loaded into the utility, and then a data packet for this file was created and saved. After that, by pressing the **Create and Test Transformation** button, the CountryRead.xml transformation file for reading the XML data was created and saved. Then, with the **Transform Direction** group of radio buttons, the direction of the transformation was modified in such a way that the data packet file became the data source. The next step is to once again create and save a transformation file, but this time it will be the CountryWrite.xml file for converting the XML data into a data packet (Fig. 15.7).

To present the XML data in the dataset, we use the `TClientDataSet` component, which is connected to the provider using the `ProviderName` property. The client dataset can be viewed and edited in the `TDBGrid` component. And all the updates are applied and saved using the provider component. This is done with the method

```
ClDataSet.ApplyUpdates(-1);
```

To present data in the XML document, the `TXMLTransformClient` and `TXMLDocument` components are used. The former is associated with the provider through the `ProviderName` property. The latter is filled with the data once the `bbOpen` button is pressed. This is implemented using the `GetDataAsXml` method of the `TXMLTransformClient` component:

```
XMLDoc.XML.Clear;
XMLDoc.XML.Add(XMLClient.GetDataAsXml(edReadFileName.Text));
```

To transform the data, you can also use the same transformation file used for reading the XML data of the provider component.

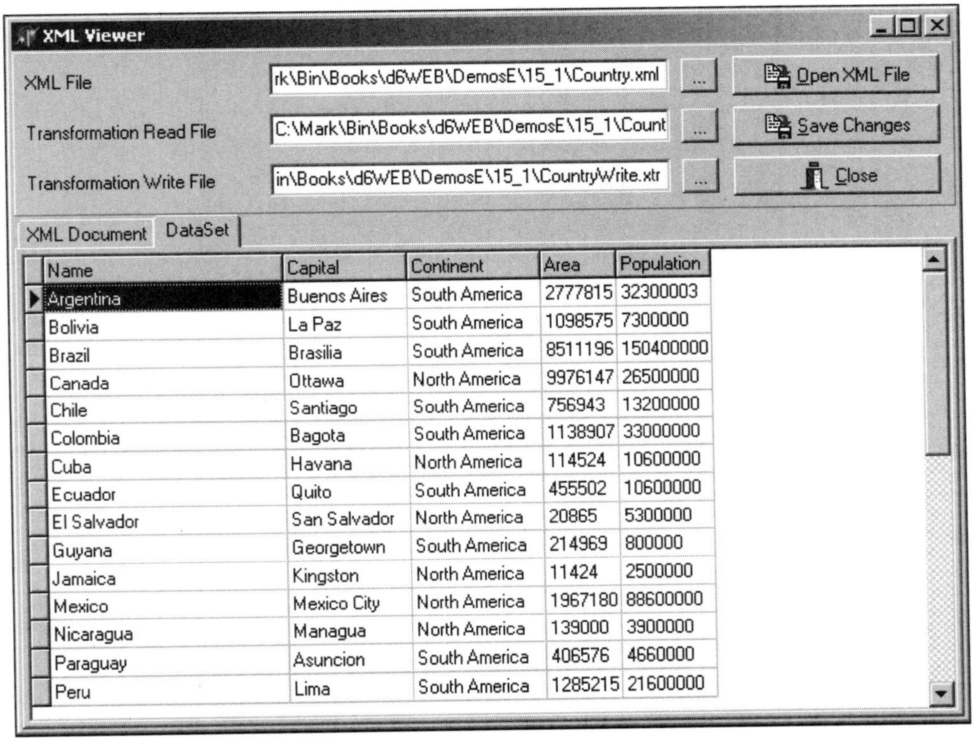

Fig. 15.7. The main window of the XML Viewer application

Then, using the SetXMLNode method, the tree of XML nodes and elements in the TTreeView component is filled in (Listing 15.2).

Listing 15.2. The SetXMLNode Method Builds a Hierarchical Tree of the Nodes and Elements of the XML Document When Opening the XML File

```
procedure TfmMain.SetXMLNode(TreeNode: TTreeNode; XMLNode: IXMLNode);
var i: Integer;
    NewNode: TTreeNode;
begin
 NewNode := tvXMLDoc.Items.AddChild(TreeNode, XMLNode.NodeName);
 if not Assigned(NewNode)
  then Abort;
 if Assigned(XMLNode.AttributeNodes) then
  for i := 0 to XMLNode.AttributeNodes.Count - 1  do
```

```
    tvXMLDoc.Items.AddChild(NewNode, XMLNode.AttributeNodes[i].NodeName +
            '='   +

XMLNode.Attributes[XMLNode.AttributeNodes[i].NodeName]);
  if Assigned(XMLNode.ChildNodes) then
    for i := 0 to XMLNode.ChildNodes.Count - 1   do
      SetXMLNode(NewNode, XMLNode.ChildNodes[i]);
end;

procedure TfmMain.bbOpenClick(Sender: TObject);
var i: Integer;
begin
 if edXMLFileName.Text <> '' then
 begin
  ClDataSet.Close;
  XMLDoc.Active := False;
  tvXMLDoc.Items.Clear;
  XMLProvider.XMLDataFile := edXMLFileName.Text;
  XMLProvider.TransformRead.TransformationFile := edReadFileName.Text;
  XMLProvider.TransformWrite.TransformationFile := edWriteFileName.Text;
  try
   ClDataSet.Open;
   XMLDoc.XML.Clear;
   XMLDoc.XML.Add(XMLClient.GetDataAsXml(edReadFileName.Text));
   XMLDoc.Active := True;
   SetXMLNode(nil, XMLDoc.DocumentElement);
  except
   on E: Exception do
   begin
    tvXMLDoc.Items.Clear;
    ClDataSet.Close;
    XMLDoc.Active := False;
    Application.MessageBox(pChar(E.Message), pChar(AppTitle),
    MB_ICONERROR or MB_OK);
   end;
  end;
 end;
end;
```

As a result, as soon as the XML file is selected, the application displays the data in the form of an XML tree and a dataset table.

NOTE

The XML Viewer application can work with a remote server as well. You just need to use the RemoteServer property of the TClientDataSet and TXMLTransformClient components in addition to the ProviderName property.

Summary

Distributed applications can use data in XML format just the same as it can other data sources. Furthermore, in many cases this capability is implemented using standard or minimally modified components. The key role here is played by the TXMLTransformProvider component.

The components for transforming XML data allow you to pass XML data to the following types of client applications:

❑ Distributed database applications, which can work with XML data that has been converted into a dataset encapsulated by the TClientDataSet component.

❑ Any client applications, which can use XML data passed in the form of an XML document and furnished by the TXMLDocument and TXMLTransformClient components.

❑ Distributed Internet applications, which can publish XML data on web pages.

In order to convert XML data into the Delphi data packet format (which allows you to easily use such data), developers can employ the XML Mapper utility.

PART VI

DISTRIBUTED APPLICATIONS AND WEB SERVICES

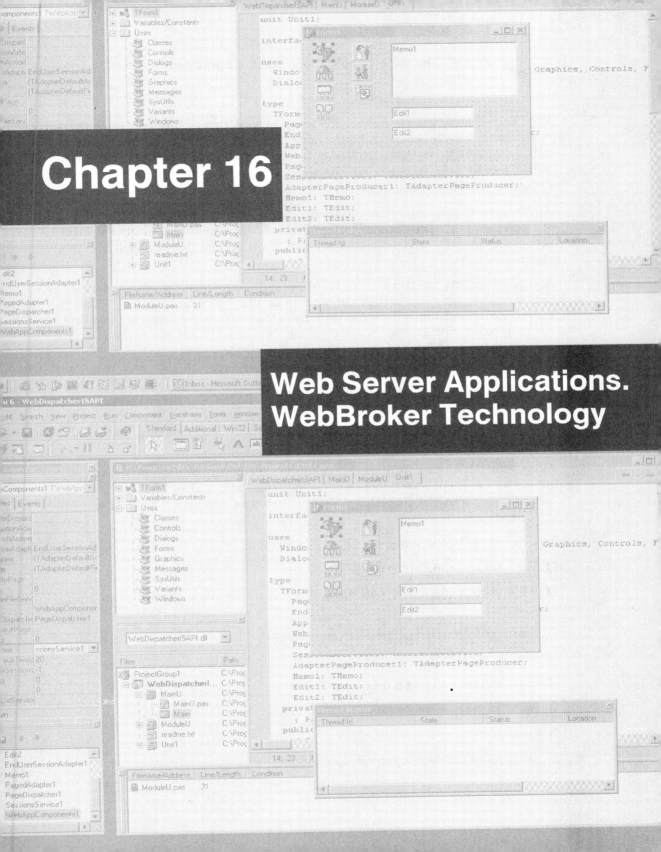

Chapter 16

Web Server Applications. WebBroker Technology

This chapter will discuss creating an application that is capable of interacting with a web server and publishing data on the Internet. By the word *publishing*, we mean the ability to create and place on a web server dynamic data that, for example, are contained in a database and stored in the form of electronic tables or text files.

A web server application's role is to receive and process client requests, and to create responses to these requests. This is done while the application is actively interacting with the web server, which takes care of connecting the web application to clients.

An application can contain a set of HTML pages for the client interface, and must implement its own business logic. In order to do this, you must have a mechanism for processing and dispatching requests. Each request must be identified and sent to the page or module that encapsulates the business logic of the application in order to create a response.

To implement the functions listed above, Delphi includes a set of components, modules, and wizards, all united into the *WebBroker* technology.

Knowledge of HTML will be useful in reading this chapter, but you'll only need just enough to be able to use it directly with questions of programming. The artistic formation of your product is best left to a web designer.

Along with HTML tags, you may choose to use the XML language as well to create the web pages of server applications. We looked at examples of using XML in Delphi in previous chapters. Using XML in web applications will be discussed in the *Chapter 19*.

This chapter will concentrate on the following issues:

❐ The CGI and ISAPI interfaces

❐ What parts make up a web application, and how they interact with each other

❐ Broker components and producer components

❐ How to use HTML in Delphi applications

❐ Creating and designing a data input form

❐ Database access components

❐ Cookie files

❐ Examples of creating server web applications

Publishing Data on the Internet.
Web Servers

Having a mechanism for publishing data on the Internet implies having the following component parts (Fig. 16.1). With the help of specialized applications (the web browser), clients interact with web servers that are accessible over the Internet. The web servers take care of the receipt and dispatch of requests and passing the responses to the client. For this to happen, the request must contain enough information to get itself passed to the requested web server application.

The application, in turn, receives the request and processes it, forming a response and including the requested information into it. In most cases, the data for the response is formed dynamically.

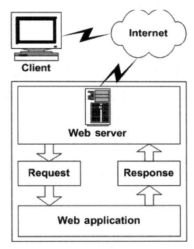

Fig. 16.1. The interaction between a web server and a web server application

The majority of web servers work in UNIX with the Apache server popular on that platform. Microsoft also offers its Microsoft Internet Information Server on the Windows NT Server and Windows 2000 Server platforms (other Microsoft OSs have a simplified version).

Now we'll talk a bit about role of programming in the publication of data.

 The server implements support of the HTTP protocol, taking requests from client browsers and returning them some web page or pages in response. Directly processing requests and forming responses is the job of server applications. But you can't anticipate everything — some pages have to be generated dynamically.

A simple database can be laid out on tens or hundreds of existing pages; but what about for e-shops or an airline ticket reservation system?

In such a case, the application must be able to dynamically form pages using *scripts*. The script's task is to process the request, extract the necessary information from the database or other external source, and put it in the form of an HTML document. Then the application must give it back to the server, which will in turn send it to the client (Fig. 16.1).

Many specialized languages have been created for and are used in developing scripts. In the WebBroker technology (as well as in certain other technologies that we will discuss later in the book), you can use scripts that have been created with the VBScript and JScript script languages.

WebBroker technology allows you to solve this task using specialized producer components that form the HTML page based on the associated script.

Types of Web Server Applications

We will look at the structure of web server applications in detail later in this chapter. Now let's turn our attention to exactly which types of applications are available when working in Delphi.

To create a web server application, go to the **New** page in the Delphi repository and choose **WebServer Application**. You'll then see a dialog in which you need to choose the type of application (Fig. 16.2).

Fig. 16.2. Dialog for choosing the type of web server application

The following types of applications are available:

ISAPI/NSAPI Dynamic Link Library — an application based on a dynamic library. To exchange data, it uses the Internet Services API interface (ISAPI), which we will look at more closely below. Such dynamic libraries work in the address space of the Internet Information Server in multi-user mode, where a thread is created for each request.

CGI standalone executable — an application based on an executable file. For data exchange, it uses a Common Gateway Interface (CGI), receiving control commands through application environment variables. A separate instance of the application is created for each request.

Win-CGI standalone executable — a kind of CGI application adapted for use with Windows.

Apache Shared Module (DLL) — an application based on a dynamic library that works in the address space of an Apache server in a UNIX OS in multi-user mode. A thread is created for each request.

Web App Debugger executable — an application based on an executable file. This type of application interacts with the Web App Debugger utility, which you can launch from the pop-up menu of **Tools\Web App Debugger** in the Delphi main window. This utility is a model of a web server and takes the place of a real web server. This will allow you to speed up the process of debugging web server applications with tools from Delphi without using actual web servers. The ready-to-use application can then be easily moved for use with real servers. All you need to do is include the test application module in the necessary type of application.

Later in the chapter, we will concentrate more on ISAPI server applications as modern and speedy tools for creating applications for Microsoft Internet Information Server.

Introduction to the CGI and ISAPI Interfaces

The first (and conventional) interface for creating extension modules was Common Gateway Interface (CGI), which came into Windows from UNIX. The application in this instance is a typical executable file (EXE) that receives the necessary information from environment variables. In Windows, both of these situations are somewhat inexpedient. First of all, placing the information in a DOS environment and reading it there is not particularly convenient. Second, a separate instance of the application is launched for each request. And launching the executable module every time means a large drop in speed.

The first problem can be solved by changing over to WinCGI, a version of CGI adapted for Windows. In WinCGI, the parameters from the web server are transferred to the application through an INI file.

Both interfaces are among the simpler ones, but neither is particularly convenient for work in Windows. The favorite means of writing CGI scripts is the special Perl language. You can also use C, Basic, and of course Delphi to write such applications.

But there is a certain way in which you can speed up the work of web applications. Microsoft has equipped its Internet Server with the ISAPI interface. It supports applications that are dynamic libraries loaded by the server and working with it in a single address space. One library can process as many requests as arrive to it.

One of these interfaces, Netscape Services API (NSAPI), maintains the efficiency of the application when working with a Netscape web server.

For instance, this request from the client browser

```
http://www.mysite.com/scripts/test.dll/find=someuser
```

means that the user wants to address the web server application test.dll on the www.mysite.com server with the request find=someuser.

The ISAPI/NSAPI library must export certain functions that will be called by the server. There are three of them, and their declaration in the ISAPI DLL project file looks like this:

```
exports
  GetExtensionVersion,
  HttpExtensionProc,
  TerminateExtension;
```

In Delphi, these functions are declared like this:

the function

```
function GetExtensionVersion(var Ver: THSE_VERSION_INFO): BOOL;
```

returns the number of the ISAPI or NSAPI application version as the Ver parameter.

The function

```
function HttpExtensionProc(var ECB: TEXTENSION_CONTROL_BLOCK): DWORD;
```

handles the transfer of the request from the web server to the application.

And the function

```
function TerminateExtension(dwFlags: DWORD): BOOL;
```

returns `True` if the application is ready to be closed.

Structure of a Web Server Application in Delphi

And so, the web application interacts with the web server, receiving the request from it and returning the response to it. Let's find out what exactly is happening during this time inside the application, and which WebBroker components are used here.

First, from the functionality point of view, the web server application consists of three interconnected parts that perform the following operations:

Request dispatch. The application should be able to process the request and get from it information as to which web page to send the request to for a response. The dispatch function is encapsulated by a web module and the specialized `TWebDispatcher` component.

Business logic implementation. The application should be able to do that for which it was created. As a response to a correctly processed request received, the application must call an already existing and debugged procedure that will perform the operation that the client needs done. This can be anything from simply pressing a button that moves the user to another page, to saving a financial transaction, to confirming a ticket reservation, etc.

Special objects — called *actions* — are used to implement business logic. Their handler methods can be called while processing a request. It is by these that the operations necessary to the application must be realized. Actions are encapsulated in web modules.

The second method of implementing business logic is using scripts written in VBScript or JScript. These scripts are placed on the web pages and called when necessary.

Web page formation. In most cases, the server application supplies the client with a user interface based on web pages. And usually, dynamic formation of pages is preferred. To accomplish this, *producer components* are used. Producer components are able to form pages based on HTML or XML *templates*, that is, they create a set of HTML tags and script operators that assure the correct presentation and functioning of the page in the client browser.

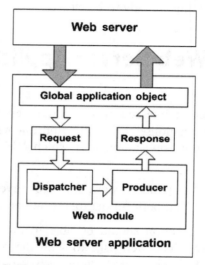

Fig. 16.3. The structure of a web server application

From the viewpoint of the developer, a web server application created with the WebBroker technology consists of the following parts:

The *global application object* encapsulates the functions for the application's interaction with the web server, and takes care of the receipt of requests and sending out prepared responses. After the request is received, it creates a new thread and sends the request to the dispatcher of the web module for processing.

The basis of the application is in its *web modules* — objects similar to data modules, but with additional functions. It is the web modules that take care of request dispatch. Besides this, they also encapsulate actions. But then they also function very well in their traditional role, too — they act as a storage area for non-visual components and their program code.

Finally, *producer components* deal with the dynamic generation of web pages. For this, they have the option of using HTML or XML templates or database tables.

On the **Internet** page of the Component Palette, there are components available that guarantee access to various data sources.

Let's now look at each of the component parts of a web server application in more depth.

The Global Application Object

From the structure and schema of interaction of the application with the web server (see Figs. 16.1 and 16.3), it's obvious that there must be a program code to guarantee the receipt of requests and the sending of responses, along with generally controlling the parts of the application. To fulfill these tasks, each application created with WebBroker technology contains a global application object.

This object is included into the application automatically during the application's creation, and is itself created when the application is launched. Access to it can be had with the help of the `Application` global variable, just as with regular Delphi applications.

Each type of web server application has its own class, whose common ancestor is the `TWebApplication` class (Fig.16.4).

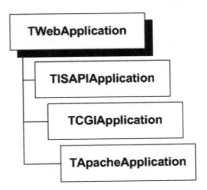

Fig. 16.4. The hierarchy of web server application classes

The global application object performs the following functions:

☐ Interacting with the web server, receiving requests, sending responses

☐ Creating and destroying request and response objects and specifying their properties

❑ Managing the memory and the web module pool (for CGI applications, this boils down to creating and destroying application instances)

❑ Sending requests to dispatchers

Creating and initializing a global object depends on the type of application, and is described above. After creation, the object methods are called by the web server when they are required. Most often this is when sending a request to the application.

Let's look at the way a global object based on an **ISAPI** application works.

> **NOTE**
>
> Apache works in a manner similar to ISAPI, while CGI could be looked at as a simplified version of ISAPI with a single request. The properties of a global object examined below correspond to those for an ISAPI application.

After the request is received, the application object creates a new thread, and in it, either creates an instance of the web module or uses an existing instance. Request and response objects are then created, and their parameters filled in.

After this, the request object is sent to the dispatcher (this may be a web module or the `TWebDispatcher` component). And, at the end of this "technological chain," the prepared response is sent to the web server (if this hasn't already been done by the action object), and the instance of the web module is either destroyed or cached for later use.

Additionally, a global object allows you to get information on the current session of the application.

The read-only property

```
property ActiveCount: Integer;
```

returns the number of requests that are currently being processed.

If you plan on using the web module in a pool, without deleting it, then the property

```
property CacheConnections: Boolean;
```

must be assigned a value of `True`. And if pooling is enabled for the web module, then the property

```
property InactiveCount: Integer;
```

will return the number of currently inactive modules.

The property

```
property MaxConnections: Integer;
```

assigns the maximum possible number of requests that can be processed at once (the size of the web module pool). The number for ActiveCount can't be higher than MaxConnections. If you try to create a web module whose number is higher than MaxConnections, an exception is generated.

The Web Module

The basis of an ISAPI project is the web module, which is represented by the TWebModule class. On it, just as on a foundation, stand all of the applications described in this chapter. This is that same bridge that receives requests, interprets them, and sends them to be executed.

For this, the web module class inherits the functionality of the base request dispatcher — the TCustomWebDispatcher class. The TWebDispatcher component has similar capabilities. Thanks to this, developers can create their own request dispatchers.

NOTE

Attempting to place the TWebDispatcher component on an already open web module will lead to the error message "Only one dispatcher for module."

Besides request dispatch functions, the web module allows you to program the business logic of the application.

The property

```
property Actions: TWebActionItems;
```

contains an indexed list of action objects that take on the role of request processors. Each one is identified by a line of text. The TWebActionItem.PathInfo property

```
http://www.mysite.com/scripts/test.dll/add
```

will call the action whose PathInfo property is equal to add.

To process requests for which no corresponding action names were found, the web module can set an action to be the default. This action's TWebActionItem.Default property is set to True.

The TWebModule class has two events that occur before and after the processing of a request:

```
type
  THTTPMethodEvent = procedure (Sender: TObject; Request:
    TWebRequest; Response: TWebResponse; var Handled: Boolean) of object;
property BeforeDispatch: THTTPMethodEvent;
property AfterDispatch: THTTPMethodEvent;
```

Here you have, respectively, the first and last possibility to change something in the response to the request, or to refuse to process it completely. If you set the Handled parameter to True in BeforeDispatch, the processing of the request will end there:

```
procedure TWebModule1.WebModuleBeforeDispatch(Sender: TObject;
Request: TWebRequest; Response: TWebResponse; var Handled: Boolean);
var i: Integer;
    IsActionExist: Boolean;
begin
 IsActionExist := False;
 for i := 0 to WebModule1.Actions.Count - 1 do
  if Request.PathInfo = WebModule1.Actions[i].PathInfo
  then IsActionExist := True;
 Handled := IsActionExist;
end;
```

The Request and Response parameters of these handler methods represent the access to the request and response objects, respectively. But since the web module receives the link to the request and response objects created by the global application object during its creation or extraction from the pool, access to it can also be obtained using the following properties:

```
property Request: TWebRequest;
property Response: TWebResponse;
```

The following method exists specially to simplify dispatch and to assure access to an action by name:

```
function ActionByName(const AName: string): TWebActionItem;
```

It returns a link to an Action element by its name.

The developer can edit the list of web module actions both in the development stage and using software during the execution. To do this, you must use the methods from the Actions list:

```
function Add: TWebActionItem;
```

and

```
procedure Delete(Index: Integer);
```

For example:

```
var NewAction: TWebActionItem;
    FAddActionExecute: THTTPMethodEvent;
...
 NewAction := WebModule1.Actions.Add;
 NewAction.Name := 'actAdd';
 NewAction.DisplayName := 'Add Action';
 NewAction.MethodType := mtAny;
 NewAction.PathInfo := 'add';
 NewAction.OnAction := FAddActionExecute;
...
```

The events

```
property OnCreate: TNotifyEvent;
property OnDestroy: TNotifyEvent;
```

occur when creating and destroying an instance of TwebModule. You should pay particular attention to the first event — the OnCreate handler method is called before the first HTTP request is processed. It is here that you can do the following:

❏ Read the current server settings from INI files or from the system registry

❏ Initialize global variables

❏ Connect to a database

Actions

The functionality of a particular action is implemented in the properties and methods of the TWebActionItem class.

First of all, the action must be identified and connected to the request. For this, you'll need to compare the URI path of the request with the action property

```
property PathInfo: string;
```

If they are the same, the request is intended for this particular action.

NOTE

The TWebRequest request class has an analogous property that is automatically filled in from the URI string during creation.

The following handler method is used to implement the operation that the action indicates:

```
type
   THTTPMethodEvent = procedure (Sender: TObject; Request: TWebRequest;
   Response: TWebResponse; var Handled: Boolean) of object;

   property OnAction: THTTPMethodEvent;
```

Here is where the application's response to the given request is prepared. If the request can't or shouldn't be processed, Handled is set to False. In such a case, the request is sent to an action whose property

```
   property Default: Boolean;
```

has a value of True.

The process of searching for an action and executing its OnAction handler method is done automatically by the web module.

The HTTP protocol sets a number of request types that come from the client to the server — GET, POST, HEAD, and PUT. They have a corresponding action property:

```
   type TMethodType = (mtAny, mtGet, mtPut, mtPost, mtHead);
   property MethodType: TMethodType;
```

If the given action can respond to any kind of request, the property is set to mtAny.

The action can be enabled or disabled when necessary. The following property is used for this:

```
   property Enabled: Boolean;
```

If this property has a value of False, the request dispatcher skips it when looking for a candidate to process a request.

Requests and Responses

When a request arrives from a web server, the global application object creates the request and response objects.

The TWebRequest class encapsulates the request. The TWebResponse class encapsulates the response. These are the basic classes. But descendants of these classes are used for particular types depending on the type of web server application.

The request class contains a large set of properties that determine the parameters of the heading and contents of the request. Let's look at the most important of them.

First of all, the Universal Resource Identifier (URI) of a request is contained in the property

```
property URL: string;
```

But besides this, there is also a set of properties that contain the main parts of the URI.

The property

```
property Host: string;
```

returns the name of the web server's host.

The property

```
property ScriptName: string;
```

defines the name of a web server application, a script, or an extension module.

The property

```
property PathInfo: string;
```

contains the URI path that in the application will identify the name of the action that is to be used to execute the request.

The property

```
property Query: string;
```

contains the text of the request, along with a list of its parameters and their values.

But it is actually more convenient to use the property

```
property QueryFields: TStrings;
```

which is a list of lines, each of which contains one parameter of the request in the `Name=Value` format.

The request object likewise returns a number of attributes of the client that sent the request. For example, the property

```
property RemoteAddr: string;
```

contains the IP address of the client host.

The type of request is defined by the property

```
type TMethodType = (mtAny, mtGet, mtPut, mtPost, mtHead);
property MethodType: TMethodType;
```

just the same as with the action. Moreover, when sending a request to this or that action, the dispatcher compares the value of this property for them.

The property

```
property Content: string;
```

is the body, or content, of the request. And the property

```
property ContentFields: TStrings;
```

contains a list of parameters for the body of the request and their values.

Since requests and responses are created in pairs, and there is always a request object corresponding to each response object, the TWebResponse class has the property

```
property HTTPRequest: TWebRequest;
```

which contains a link to the object of the corresponding request.

The result of the request's execution is put into the

```
property Content: string;
```

property of the response object.

Producer Components

Included in the WebBroker technology are producer components. They take care of dynamic generation of web pages based on HTML templates, or use databases as a data source.

More general functions of a producer are implemented in the TPageProducer component.

The template for creating pages is given by the property

```
property HTMLDoc: TStrings;
```

If the template is saved in a file, it can be specified with the property

```
property HTMLFile: TFileName;
```

To get a page from the template, you have to call the method

```
function Content: string;
```

but this works only if the template is assigned the properties listed above. If not, you can use the method

```
function ContentFromString(const S: string): string;
```

which forms the HTML text of a page directly from the s string.

And yet another similar method,

```
function ContentFromStream(Stream: TStream): string;
```

forms the result from data from the `Stream` stream.

If the template contains scripts, their language should be indicated in the property

```
property ScriptEngine: string;
```

Delphi's available script languages are VBScript and JScript.

Another property

```
property Dispatcher: IWebDispatcherAccess;
```

contains a link to the web module or the `TWebDispatcher` component that is servicing the current request.

The only handler method of the component,

```
type
  TTag = (tgCustom, tgLink, tgImage, tgTable, tgImageMap, tgObject, tgEmbed);
  THTMLTagEvent = procedure (Sender: TObject; Tag: TTag; const
  TagString: string; TagParams: TStrings; var ReplaceText: string)
  of object;
OnHTMLTag: THTMLTagEvent;
```

is called when it is necessary to interpret an HTML template tag that can't be processed by the HTML interpreter. The complete text of the tag is contained in the `TagString` parameter. The parameters of the tag are found in the `TagParams` parameter in the `Name=Value` format. The transformed text should be saved in the `ReplaceText` parameter.

The `Tag` parameter determines the type of tag encountered. Of the seven types, six are predetermined (Table 16.1).

Table 16.1. Types of Tags for Producer Components

Value of the `Tag` parameter	Tag text	Function
tgLink	LINK	Describes a hypertext link
tgImage	IMAGE	Describes an image
tgTable	TABLE	Describes a table
tgImageMap	IMAGEMAP	Describes an image with context-sensitive areas

continues

Table 16.1 Continued

Value of the Tag parameter	Tag text	Function
tgObject	OBJECT	Describes an ActiveX object built into the page
tgEmbed	EMBED	Describes an embedded Netscape library

When reacting to one of the predefined tags, the producer component must generate the appropriate, correctly described HTML element and place it in the document. If there is a tag found in a document that cannot be considered one of the above, the Tag property will equal tgCustom; you can process such tags any way you see fit.

For example, the handler method

```
procedure TForm1.ppHTMLTag(Sender: TObject; Tag: TTag; const
TagString: String; TagParams: TStrings; var ReplaceText: String);

begin
  if Tag = tgImage then
   if (TagParams.Values['ImgType'] = 'GIF') and
      (TagParams.Values['ImgName'] <> '')
   then ReplaceText := '<IMG SRC="../Images/' +
                          TagParams.Values['ImageName'] + '">';
end;
```

replaces the tag with a link to a specific image.

HTML Pages in Web Server Applications

Now we'll move on to some particulars of programming a user interface for web server application HTML pages. We won't focus so much on the abounding capabilities of the HTML language — there is a wide range of specialized literature for that. And talking about pages with little welcome messages like "Hello, world!" probably won't do us any good either. That's why we're only going to concentrate on certain fine points concerning the use of WebBroker components, those which will help us when actually developing HTML pages.

Displaying Data

If your application generates only one page in response to a request, the response can also be formed directly in the handler method of the OnAction event of the corresponding action:

```
procedure TWebModule1.WebModule1WebActionItem1Action(Sender: TObject;
Request: TWebRequest; Response: TWebResponse; var Handled: Boolean);
begin
  PageProducer1.HTMLFile := FPageFileName;
  Response.Content := PageProducer1.Content;
end;
```

If you get an output of not one, but a set of pages, you must automate this action. You could proceed as follows. When creating the web module, give the typical set of tags for all page headings, and then add on to the beginning and the end of the set for each page you create. Thus they will look similar. Also, you can use this method to regulate the settings for the page display, having read some of the parameters from the initialization (INI) file or the registry (Listing 16.1).

Listing 16.1. Setting the Appearance of the Web Pages

```
var CommonLookStart, CommonLookEnd: String;

procedure TWebModule1.WebModule1Create(Sender: TObject);
var Ini: TINIFIle;
    s: string;
begin
  Ini := TINIFile.Create('SomeApp.ini');
  try
    bgpath := Ini.ReadString('Design','Background','img\star.jpg');
    txtcol := Ini.ReadString('Design','text','white');
    lcol := Ini.ReadString('Design','link','lime');
    acol := Ini.ReadString('Design','alink','olive');
    vcol := Ini.ReadString('Design','vlink','green');
  finally
    ini.Free;
  end;
    CommonLookStart := Format('<HTML><BODY BACKGROUND="%s"
    TEXT=%s LINK=%s ALINK=%s VLINK=%s>',

    [bgpath,txtcol,lcol,acol,vcol]);
```

```
    CommonLookEnd := '</BODY></HTML>';
end;

procedure TWebModule1.WebModule1WebActionItem1Action(Sender: TObject;
   Request: TWebRequest; Response: TWebResponse; var Handled: Boolean);
begin
  SomePageProducer.HTMLFile := FPageFileName;
  Response.Content := CommonLookStart +
                      SomePageProducer.Content +
                      CommonLookEnd;
end;
```

The next problem, which you will likely run into at some point, is having to change the content of pages for some reason or another. Of course, you could do all this directly in the OnAction event code and write a bunch of if...then...else operators, but there is a more graceful solution — use WebBroker producer components.

NOTE

The given components can be used not only in an ISAPI or CGI application, but any time it is necessary to generate a document in HTML format.

Let's say, for example, that you must include some information from the request in the response.

To begin, we need to create an HTML template. We will save the following set of lines in the HTMLDoc property of the producer component:

```
<HTML><HEAD>
<TITLE>Demo 2</TITLE>
<BODY>
Clients request host: <#NAME>!
Request time: <#TIME>
</BODY>
</HTML>
```

Our investigation in this case will focus on the <#NAME> and <#TIME> tags we defined.

The TPageProducer component has the property

```
property Dispatcher: TCustomWebDispatcher;
```

It contains a reference to the web module or the `TWebDispatcher` component that services the current request. The `OnHTMLTag` handler method

```
procedure TWebModule1.PageProducer1HTMLTag(Sender: TObject; Tag: TTag;
  const TagString: String; TagParams: TStrings; var ReplaceText:
String);
begin
 if TagString =' NAME' then
    ReplaceText := TCustomContentProducer(Sender).Dispatcher.Request.RemoteHost
  else if TagString =' TIME' then ReplaceText := TimeToStr(Now);
end;
```

will take care of the interpretation of the NAME and TIME tags, replacing their text with the IP address of the request host and the time when it was sent, respectively. Then the handler method of the action will send the HTML text to the response.

```
procedure TWebModule1.WebModule1WebActionItem1Action(Sender: TObject;
  Request: TWebRequest; Response: TWebResponse; var Handled: Boolean);
begin
  Response.Content := PageProducer1.Content;
end;
```

As a result, the information about the client host and the time sent will be dynamically displayed on the test page.

Data Input and Editing

We've already encountered how to input information to web pages. But that is only half the battle — we also must be able to enter user data. Using the same page mechanism, we can create an input form. There is a special tag for this — <FORM> (as well as its corresponding closing tag — </FORM>). In the tag, specify the URL of your server application that will process the received data, for instance:

```
<FORM method="GET" action="http://localhost/script/some.dll/validate>
```

<INPUT> tags are used to input information. They are specially designed for organizing dialogs with the user in the browser environment, and imitate the basic Windows controls that are used to input information. Each tag must contain a type field (which gives the type of control) and a name field. The basic types of controls are shown in Table 16.2.

Table 16.2. Types of Web Page Controls (the <INPUT> Tag)

Tag	Function
`<input type=TEXT>`	A single-line text editor; intended for entering regular text
`<input type=PASSWORD>`	A single-line text editor for entering encrypted information (passwords)
`<input type=FILE>`	A single-line editor for choosing a file
`<input type=CHECKBOX>`	A button with independent fixation (a checkbox)
`<input type=RADIO>`	A button with dependent fixation (a radio button)
`<input type=HIDDEN>`	An uneditable field that contains official information for the server; hidden from the user
`<input type=SELECT>`	A button that initiates the transfer of information from the browser to the server when pressed
`<input type=RESET>`	A button that, when pressed, clears all input fields and gives them their initial value

Now create a page template that contains a set of controls for inputting user names and passwords (Listing 16.2).

Listing 16.2. An HTML Template for Creating User Authentification Pages

```
<form method="GET" action="/stest/some.dll/validate">
<CENTER>
<h2>Login Page</h2>
</center>
<BR>
<h3>Enter user name:</h3>
<table>
<td><input name="username" type="TEXT"></td>
</table>

<h3>Enter password:</h3>
<table>
<td><input name="password" type="PASSWORD"></td>
</table>

<table>
<td><input type="SUBMIT" value="Login"><</td>
```

```
</table>

<table>
<td><input type="RESET" value="Cancel"></td>
</table>

</form>
```

The template contains four <INPUT> tags — two for entering the name and password, and two mandatory tags — SUBMIT and RESET — which are analogous to **OK** and **Cancel** in Windows. By the way, the text on these buttons can be changed by specifying the value field.

In the end, the page should look something like Fig. 16.5.

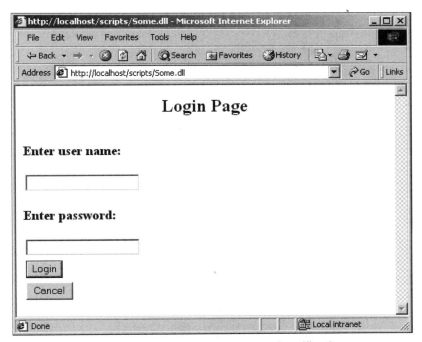

Fig. 16.5. The appearance of a user authentification page

After the user enters the name aaa, the password bbb, and presses the **Login** button, the request line to the server will look like:

```
http://localhost/stest/some.dll/validate?username=aaa&password=bbb
```

> **NOTE**
>
> Note that the password is not passed in encrypted form. This system of passwords will protect you from the guy with nothing to do looking over your shoulder, but not from hackers. For transfer of truly secret information, you'd need to use other protocols, one of them being built on HTTP, called Secure HTTP (HTTPS).

Now let's see which Object Pascal code should be responsible for checking the data entered by the user. The handler method of the `actValidate` action might look somewhat like what is presented in Listing 16.3.

Listing 16.3. Handler Method of the actValidate Action, Responsible for Checking the Name and Password of the User

```
const Admin: Integer = 0;
      User:  Integer = 1;
      Guest: Integer = 2;

procedure TWebModule1.WebModule1actValidateAction(Sender: TObject;
Request: TWebRequest; Response: TWebResponse; var Handled: Boolean);

var UserStatus: Integer;
begin
 with ValidateQuery do
 begin
  SQL.Clear;
  SQL.Add('SELECT * FROM Userbase WHERE UserName = :UserName
  and UserPassword = :Password');
  Params[0].AsString := Request.QueryFields.Values['UserName'];
  Params[1].AsString := Request.QueryFields.Values['Password'];
  Open;
  if RecordCount > 0 then
  begin
   UserStatus := FieldByName('UserCategory').AsInteger;
   Response.Content := '<BR><B>Success</B><BR>';
   if UserStatus = Admin
   then
    Response.Content := Response.Content +
```

```
                         '<BR>You have Full Access permission<BR>' +
                         '<A HREF="http://' +
                         Request.Host +
                         '/WebPages/AdmMenu.htm"><B>Admin Page</B></A>'
    else
      if UserStatus = User
      then
         Response.Content := Response.Content +
                         '<BR>You have Modify permission<BR>' +
                         '<A HREF="http://' +
                         Request.Host +
                         '/WebPages/UserMenu.htm"><B>User Page</B></A>'
      else
        if UserStatus = Guest
        then
           Response.Content := Response.Content +
                         '<BR>You have Read permission<BR>' +
                         '<A HREF="http://' +
                         Request.Host +
                         '/WebPages/GuestMenu.htm"><B>Guest Page</B></A>';

    end
    else
      Response.Content := '<BR><B>Wrong UserName or Password</B><BR>';
    Close;
  end;
end;
```

In our example, the entered data are first checked to see if they exist in the database by the ValidateQuery SQL request component. If the user account exists in the database and the password is correct, the user's authority level is checked. Depending on the category of the user, he or she gains access to the appropriate web page. In order for this to happen, a link to a special page is added to the application response. If the name and password are not found in the database, the user's access is denied.

Cookies

Web server applications can respond to requests of anonymous clients, but it would be much more convenient if they could "remember" just the slightest thing about previous contact with them — what the client requested and when. In such a case, past requests can become a part of the present one.

You can, without burdening the client at all, maintain the appropriate database for this on the server. However, this would require a lot of time and would take up much of your free space. The first alternative to this method was conceived by developers at Netscape, who invented so-called cookie files.

Cookies work like this. Once the application has identified the client, it adds a special, additional field alongside its HTTP response that contains a user identifier and any necessary information to the server, such as the time and text of the last request. If the user's browser supports the cookies mechanism (and all versions of MS Internet Explorer and Netscape Navigator starting with the third version do), this information will be written to a file on the user's drive, and in the future will be attached to every request the user makes to that particular server.

A method of the TWebResponse component is used for sending cookies —

```
procedure SetCookieField(Values: TStrings; const ADomain,
APath: string; AExpires: TDateTime; ASecure: Boolean);
```

Here, Values are a set of lines in Name=Value form; ADomain, APath are the addresses at which cookies should be added; AExpires is the expiration date on the cookie, after which the cookie will no longer be sent.

Let's say that the user has chosen some image from the list of possible images. We will need to process it, now and in the future, and so we need to remember the name of the image and the time it was selected in the cookie:

```
procedure TWebModule1.WebModule1ShowImageAction(Sender: TObject;
   Request: TWebRequest; Response: TWebResponse; var Handled: Boolean);
var CurrentImageName: string;
   MCookies: TStringList;
begin
 CurrentImageName := Request.QueryFields.Values['ImgName'];
 if CurrentImageName<>'' then
  begin
   MCookies := TStringList.Create;
```

```
MCookies.Add('Picture=' + CurrentImageName);
MCookies.Add('Time=' + TimeToStr(Now));
Response.SetCookieField(MCookies, '', '', Date + 1, False);
MCookies.Free;
Response.Content:='<BR><IMG SRC=http://' +
                   Request.Host +
                   GlobalHTMLPath +
                   '/Images/' +
                   CurrentImageName + '>';
  end
 else
  Response.Content := 'Image not found';
end;
```

The request object also has a `Cookies` property. When processing the next request from this user, we already know the name of the image he or she has chosen:

```
CurrentImageName := Request.CookieFields.Values['Picture'];
if CurrentImageName='' then
   begin
   Response.Content := 'Image not selected';
   Exit;
   end;
else
   Response.Content := 'Image: ' + CurrentImageName;
```

Using Databases

Web server applications often must interact with databases, both for taking care of their own functionality and when executing a user request. There are four components within the WebBroker technology used to implement these functions.

❒ The `TDataSetPageProducer` component creates the HTML text of a page using a dataset and an HTML template as a basis.

❒ The `TDataSetTableProducer` component generates the HTML text of a page, presenting data from any dataset in tabular form.

❒ The `TQueryTableProducer` component generates the HTML text of a page, displaying the data from a dataset that was created with BDE by a parameterized component of the SQL request in tabular form.

❐ The `TSQLQueryTableProducer` component generates the HTML text of a page, displaying the data from a dataset created with dbExpress by a parameterized component of the SQL request in tabular form.

Let's now examine all of these in more detail.

Publishing Database Table Records

To include on your page not only information, but information from databases, you have to use the `TDatasetPageProducer` component. Its properties and methods are generally the same as those of a regular producer component.

In addition, it has the following property to connect it to the data set:

```
property DataSet: TDataSet;
```

through which you can get a link to any data access component (see *Part II*, *"Data Access Technology"*). But in order to create a web page with data from the appropriate database table, specifying this property alone is not enough.

Besides which, as with a standard producer component, `TDatasetPageProducer` must have an HTML template. The template is just a regular document or HTML text for web pages, but it must include in the correct places tags with the same names as the fields of that dataset in the `<#FieldName>` format. The component will thus automatically replace the tag with the value of the field of the current dataset record.

For example, for a table called Country in a sample Delphi database, a very simple template could look like this:

```
<HTML>
<HEAD>
   <TITLE>Biolife Data</TITLE>
</HEAD>
<BODY>
 <TABLE BORDER=0 >
 <TR>
  <TD><B>Name:</B></TD>
  <TD><#Name></TD>
 </TR>
```

```
<TR>
 <TD><B>Capital:</B></TD>
 <TD><#Capital></TD>
</TR>
<TR>
 <TD<B>Continent:</B></TD>
 <TD><#Continent></TD>
</TR>
<TR>
 <TD<B>Area:</B></TD>
 <TD><#Area></TD>
</TR>
<TR>
 <TD<B>Population:</B></TD>
 <TD><#Population></TD>
 </TR>
</TABLE>
</BODY>
</HTML>
```

However, as you have probably already noticed, displaying all records of a dataset on a page using the `TDatasetPageProducer` component demands a few tricks on your part: you must create a complex template, be able to move around to all dataset records, etc. To make this easier to do, you can use WebBroker components, which we will talk about shortly.

Generating Reports

When publishing data on the Internet, one of the toughest moments is generating reports and forms. If you did all the tables and their borders manually, you might find yourself turning from a programmer into a web designer. And here is where two components in particular come in very handy — `TDatasetTableProducer` and `TQueryTableProducer`. They act as a kind of tabular report generator on web pages.

> **NOTE**
>
> There are actually three components, but the `TQueryTableProducer` component and the `TSQLQueryTableProducer` component are identical for all practical purposes. Their only difference is that `TSQLQueryTableProducer` can work with dbExpress requests, and `TQueryTableProducer` can work with components of BDE requests. If requests from other data access technologies must be used, developers can use the `TDatasetTableProducer` component, but the parameters must be set by hand.

The first essential property of any report generator on the WWW is the dispatcher component from which the requests come. The second is the component that connects the generator to the data source.

How do these two components that we are examining here differ from one another? They differ in the data source and the way in which it is used.

`TDatasetTableProducer` has the property

```
property DataSet: TDataSet;
```

which provides for a connection with any Delphi dataset.

`TQueryTableProducer` has the property

```
property Query: TQuery;
```

which allows you to gain access to a BDE dataset request component. This narrow specialization is compensated for by having the ability to set the parameters of the `TQuery` request right along with the text of the received HTTP request. Let's say that the text of the `SQL` property in `TQuery` looks like this:

```
SELECT Name, Capital, Area
FROM Country
WHERE Name = :Name
```

This request has the `Name` parameter. If you receive this request:

```
http://localhost/test.dll?Name=Canada
```

then the `Name=Canada` parameter will be automatically passed directly to the request component, and a report will be generated for the value `Canada`.

Remember that parameters of a `GET` type HTTP request are contained in the `Request.QueryFields` property, and parameters of a `POST` request are found in the `Request.ContentFields` property. Both are given to `TQuery`.

If you don't need parameters, and the generated report doesn't depend on the contents of the request, use the `TDatasetTableProducer` component; in most cases, it works faster.

A document generated with the help of `TDatasetTableProducer` and `TQueryTableProducer` consists of four parts:

❐ The caption of the document. It is given by the property:

```
property Caption: string;
```

The value of this property is assigned using the `<CAPTION>` tag of an HTML document. The alignment of the caption is defined with:

```
type THTMLCaptionAlignment = (caDefault, caTop, caBottom);
property CaptionAlignment: THTMLCaptionAlignment;
```

The caption may be dynamically formed. Before beginning its formation, the following event is called:

```
property OnGetTableCaption: THTMLGetTableCaptionEvent;
THTMLGetTableCaptionEvent = procedure (Sender: TObject; var
Caption: string; var Alignment: THTMLCaptionAlignment) of object;
```

❐ The lines that come before the table, or the header. In order to be able to generate complex reports, the developers of the component have allowed you to precede tables with any HTML document:

```
property Header: TStrings;
```

❐ The table itself. Its properties will be described below.

❐ The concluding lines, or footer. These can also be any document, and are contained in the property

```
property Footer: TStrings;
```

To work with tables, it makes sense to assign the `DataSet` (`Query`) property while still in the development stage. After the connection to the database has been set, you need to focus on editing the properties.

```
property Columns: THTMLTableColumns;
```

This property determines which database fields will be included in the table being formed, as well as how they will look. After launching the `Columns` property editor (Fig. 16.6) and adding new columns, we can, first of all, connect them to the fields of the data source indicated in the `DataSet` (or `Query`) property.

Secondly, we have the opportunity to assign them a color (the `BgColor` property), their horizontal and vertical alignment (`Align` and `vAlign`), and to use additional HTML tags (the `Custom` property). We can also have separate colors, alignments, and custom tags for the header of a column.

Fig. 16.6. Editor of the `Columns` property of the `TDatasetTableProducer`
and `TqueryTableProducer` components

NOTE

To make the presentation of the values of these properties more appealing, we must refer to the principles of forming tables in HTML, and in particular to the `<TD>` and `<TR>` tags and the ways in which they can be modified. The values of these properties — `bgColor`, `Align`, and `vAlign` — directly correspond to what will be contained in these tags.

In the left part of the `Columns` property editor, we can change the values of the attributes of all the tables included in the property

```
property TableAttributes: THTMLTableAttributes;
```

These properties have the following meaning (Table. 16.3).

Table 16.3. Properties of the THTMLTableAttributes object

Property	Meaning
`property CellSpacing: Integer;`	The default space between table cells.
`property CellPadding: Integer;`	The default space from the text in the cell to its border.

continues

Table 16.3 Continued

Property	Meaning
`property Border: Integer;`	The thickness of the lines framing the table cells (in pixels). A value of 1 means that these lines are absent.
`type THTMLAlign = (haDefault, haLeft, haRight, haCenter);` `property Align: THTMLAlign;`	The method of aligning the table relative to the browser window.
`property Width: Integer;`	The width of the table as a percentage of the width of the browser window.

For those of you that know HTML, you could say that the value from `TableAttributes` corresponds to the modifier of the `<TABLE>` tag.

You can also assign the formation of the rows individually with a separate property:

```
property RowAttributes: THTMLTableRowAttributes;
```

To keep the report from becoming too long (and the web page from becoming too big and inconvenient to load), you can limit the number of rows (i.e., database records) to be placed in the table:

```
property MaxRows: Integer;
```

The generated report can be called with the `Content` method (or with its variants — `ContentFromString` and `ContentFromStream`), just as in any producer component.

Using the two components described here is actually very simple:

```
procedure TWebModule1.WebModule1Actions1Action(Sender: TObject;
Request: TWebRequest; Response: TWebResponse; var Handled: Boolean);
begin
  Response.Content := MyQueryTableProducer.Content;
end;
```

Let's look at the two remaining events that appear in the `TDatasetTableProducer` and `TQueryTableProducer` components.

Before beginning the report generation, the following event crops up:

```
property OnCreateContent: TCreateContentEvent;
type TCreateContentEvent = procedure (Sender: TObject; var Continue:
Boolean) of object;
```

Here you can check the status of the database, the authorization level of the client, etc. If the report is not to be generated, setting the `Continue` parameter to `False` will prohibit this.

The important event

```
type
THTMLAlign = (haDefault, haLeft, haRight, haCenter);
THTMLVAlign = (haVDefault, haTop, haMiddle, haBottom, haBaseline);
THTMLFormatCellEvent = procedure (Sender: TObject; CellRow,
CellColumn: Integer; var BgColor: THTMLBgColor; var Align: THTMLAlign;
var VAlign: THTMLVAlign; var CustomAttrs, CellData: string) of object;
property OnFormatCell: THTMLFormatCellEvent;
```

will arise when formatting each individual cell of the table. The last parameter —
CellData — contains what was already placed in the cell by the report generator
itself. You can modify its contents; here is an example:

```
procedure TWebModule1.MyQTPFormatCell(Sender: TObject; CellRow,
CellColumn: Integer; var BgColor: THTMLBgColor; var Align: THTMLAlign;
var VAlign: THTMLVAlign; var CustomAttrs, CellData: String);
  var s: string;
begin
 if CellRow <> 0 then
  if (CellRow mod 2 = 0)
   then BgColor:='Silver'
   else BgColor:='Gray';
 if (CellColumn = 0) and (CellRow <> 0) then
 begin
  s := CellData;
  CellData := '<A HREF=' +
     Request.ScriptName +
     '/Parts?Ph_Name=' +
     s +
     ' target="main"> <IMG ALT="[GO!]" SRC="/img/arrow.gif"
  BORDER=0>' +
     s;
 end;
end;
```

Here, first of all, each even row is colored in one color, and each odd row in
another. The table is thus easier to read. Secondly, the information generated
by TQueryTableProducer is transformed from simple text into a hyperlink
to another function of this library. Later, it will become our key for searching
in another table.

Editing Data

To end our discussion on using databases, let's turn to Delphi's data editing abilities. To do this, we'll examine a more complex method of organizing data input that we must use in order to solve a simple task: organizing the cursor in an HTML representation of data. The records are already on the screen in tabular form, and now the user must choose one or more of them on which to perform some action (deletion, modification, etc.).

Here we will again use forms. We recommend that you follow these steps:

1. Add the <FORM> HTML tag with fields pointing to your web server application to the Header property of the TQueryTableProducer component.

2. While generating the table, process the OnFormatCell event to add a single-line editor to one of the table columns. Each control must have a unique number that corresponds to the row number in the table.

```
procedure TWebModule1.StoreQTPFormatCell(Sender: TObject; CellRow,
CellColumn: Integer; var BgColor: THTMLBgColor; var Align: THTMLAlign;
var VAlign: THTMLVAlign; var CustomAttrs, CellData: String);

var s: string;
begin
 if CellRow <> 0 then
  if (CellRow mod 2 = 0)
   then BgColor:='Silver'
   else BgColor:='Gray';
 if (CellColumn = 0) and (CellRow > 0)
  then CellData := '<INPUT TYPE=HIDDEN NAME=H' +
                    IntToStr(CellRow) +
                    ' VALUE="' +
                    CellData +
                    '">' +
                    CellData;
 if (CellColumn = StoreQTP.Columns.Count - 1) and (CellRow > 0) then
 begin
  CellData := '<INPUT TYPE=CHECKBOX NAME=R' +
             IntToStr(CellRow) +
             ' VALUE=1>Order';
  s := '<BR><INPUT TYPE=TEXT NAME=T' +
      IntToStr(CellRow) +
      ' SIZE=5 MAXLENGTH=8 VALUE="';
```

```
    CellData := CellData + s + '">';
  end;
end;
```

In this example, the table is formed so as to give the user the ability to order something from the table shown. For this, there is one checkbox (with the names R1...RN) and one text field (with the names T1...TN) added in the last column for each item. If the user chooses something, he or she must check the box and enter a number in the neighboring field. In the first column, a hidden field is added (Hidden, with names H1...HN), whose value will be equal to the value of the database field that corresponds to the first column in the current record. Why this is so will be explained a bit later.

3. All the rest of the necessary <INPUT> tags are added to the Footer property of the TQueryTableProducer component.

After the page is generated and displayed, and after the user has made a choice, your library will receive a request from it. The idea behind this method is that, from among all the created checkboxes, R1...RN, only those that were chosen by the user will end up in the text of the request. And if checkbox R1 is selected, we extract the values of H1 and T1 from the body of the request.

But why do we need the H1 field, since it doesn't give us any additional information? Well, all we currently know about the chosen record is its number, and as you well know, selecting from a database is not done by the number of the record. But we have the value of the database field in the H1 element, and it is this field taken from the first column that will most likely be the key one. We can always get the necessary record from it.

Example of a Simple Web Server Application

In closing, let's go through a small example. The goal of creating this application is not to demonstrate how to use WebBroker components (enough was said on that topic above), but rather to discuss the process of developing an application as a whole, as well as the methods used to debug it. This is why the example is so very simple.

With the help of the Delphi Repository, we will create a new web server application. Choose the **Web App Debugger executable** type from the dialog box (see Fig. 16.2); this is an application that works under the control of the Web App Debugger utility included with Delphi. We'll call the application Simple Web Server Application.

NOTE

After you have finished developing and debugging, we will move the prepared application to an ISAPI platform.

The Main Window of the Application

After creating the project, two modules are available in the development environment. Unit1.pas is a regular form, and will automatically be used for work with the Web App Debugger utility. But we are more concerned with Unit2.pas, which contains the web module. We will rename it wmMain.

Let's now move the `TpageProducer` component to the web module from the **Internet** page of the Component palette and name it `MainPage`. Its `HTMLDoc` property contains the template for the main page. There are two hyperlinks on it — to the two pages on which the data from the Country table of the sample Delphi database are displayed — one in the form of a list and one as a table.

Listing 16.4. HTML Template of the Main Page of the SimpleWebApp.exe Application

---

```
<BODY>
<H1 ALIGN=center><B>Simple Web Server Application</B></H1>
<P>
<P>
View the dataset as a list
<A HREF="<#APPNAME>/countrylist">Countries list</A>.
<P>
View the dataset as a table
<A HREF="<#APPNAME>/countrytable">Countries table</A>.
<P>
</BODY>
</HTML>
```

We can see from Listing 16.4 that the template includes `<#APPNAME>` tags. In the `OnHTMLTag` handler method of the `MainPage` component, these tags are replaced with the name of the application, thus forming a correct hyperlink (see Listing 16.5).

For the `MainPage` page to open upon launching the application, in the web module we have to create an action (its `Actions` property), connect it with the `TPageProducer` component (the action's `Producer` property), and make it the default (the action's `Default` property). Note that when choosing the producer component in the action, the `PathInfo` property, which allows us to identify the action in requests, is automatically specified. And now, if the web server receives a request like this:

```
http://localhost/SimpleWebApp.exe
```

or like this:

```
http://localhost/SimpleWebApp.exe/MainPage
```

our application will connect it to the `MainPage` producer component using the `actMain` action, and will open the `MainPage` page, whose template is described in the component.

For our hyperlinks to those two different pages to work (see Listing 16.4), we must add two more actions to the web module — `actCountryList` and `actCountryTable`. They must be connected to the appropriate producer components, and their `PathInfo` properties must coincide with the hyperlink requests in the template of the main page.

Viewing the Country Table

Now let's begin working with the Country table. We'll move the `TADOTable` component from the **ADO** page to the web module, and set it to the Country table of the sample Delphi database. To do this, let's use the ..\Program Files\ Common Files\Borland Shared\Data\dbdemos.mdb file from the Microsoft Access database. You can find more on the ADO technology in *Chapter 7, "Using ADO with Delphi."*

Then we move the `TDataSetPageProducer` and `TDataSetTableProducer` components from the **Internet** page to the web module.

Listing 16.5. The *Implementation* Section of the SimpleWebApp Application's Web Module

---

```
implementation

uses WebReq, dialogs;


{$R *.DFM}


procedure TwmMain.WebModuleCreate(Sender: TObject);
begin
  SetString(WebAppName, FilePath, GetModuleFileName(hInstance, FilePath,
  SizeOf(FilePath)));
  WebAppName := ExtractFileName(WebAppName);
end;


procedure TwmMain.MainPageHTMLTag(Sender: TObject; Tag: TTag;
  const TagString: String; TagParams: TStrings; var ReplaceText: String);
begin
  if TagString = 'APPNAME' then
    ReplaceText := WebAppName;
end;


procedure TwmMain.CountryListHTMLTag(Sender: TObject; Tag: TTag;
const TagString: String; TagParams: TStrings; var ReplaceText: String);
var ResponseStr: String;
begin
  if TagString = 'COUNTRYLIST' then
  try
   Country.Open;
   try
    while not Country.EOF do
```

```
    begin
      ResponseStr := ResponseStr + Format('<TABLE><TD WIDTH=280>%s</TD>' +
                                           '<TD WIDTH=280>%s</TD>' +
                                           '<TD WIDTH=280>%s</TD></TABLE>',
        [Country.FieldByName('Name').AsString,
         Country.FieldByName('Capital').AsString,
         Country.FieldByName('Area').AsString]);
      Country.Next;
      end;
    finally
    Country.Close;
    end;
  except
    on E: Exception do ResponseStr := E.Message;
  end;
  ReplaceText := ResponseStr;
end;


procedure TwmMain.CountryTableFormatCell(Sender: TObject; CellRow,
  CellColumn: Integer; var BgColor: THTMLBgColor; var Align: THTMLAlign;
  var VAlign: THTMLVAlign; var CustomAttrs, CellData: String);
begin
 if CellRow = 0
  then BgColor := 'Gray'
   else
    if CellRow mod 2 = 0
     then BgColor := 'Silver';
end;


initialization
```

```
if WebRequestHandler <> nil then

    WebRequestHandler.WebModuleClass := TwmMain;

end.
```

The first component displays the data from the table in the form of a list. For this, we have to connect it with the dataset, i.e., to assign a link to the ADO table component to the DataSet property. Besides this, we will create a simple template in the HTMLDoc property that will provide for a somewhat sorted display of country data.

The template also contains the <#COUNTRYLIST> tag, which, in the component's OnHTMLTag handler method, is replaced by data received from the Country dataset (see Listing 16.5).

The second component provides for the display of the Country dataset in table form. The dataset is also connected to the component through the DataSet property. And now our setup is almost over. We do, however, have a little left to do on the main page. For example, we can specify the TableAttributes.Border and TableAttributes.CellPadding properties. The OnFormatCell handler method takes care of filling in the background of the necessary rows. Thus, during execution, the TDataSetTableProducer component provides for the data display, as shown in Fig. 16.7.

NOTE

Note that the same component of the dataset is used for filling in both pages.

Testing the Application

Now we are finished with the creation of our application. After saving and compilation, we can launch it using the Web App Debugger utility (Fig. 16.8).

The **Start/Stop** button in the upper part of the window allows us to update the list of registered applications of the Web App Debugger. A list of them can be accessed in the web browser window by clicking the hyperlink to the right of the button. Here it's necessary to select our application and launch it. We will then see the MainPage main window.

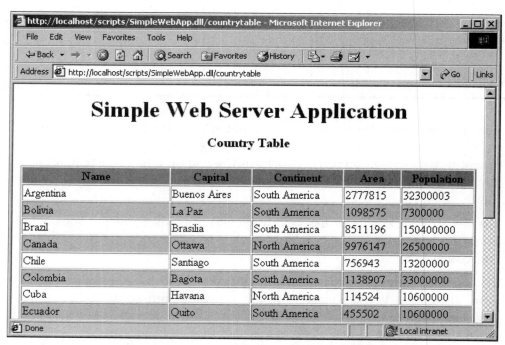

Fig. 16.7. A page of the SimpleWebApp.exe application

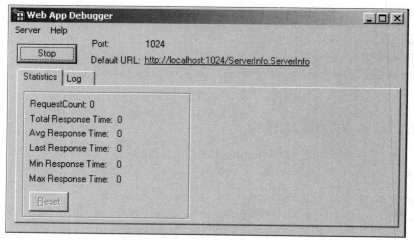

Fig. 16.8. The **Web App Debugger** utility allows us to debug a web server application without actual web servers

Moving the Application to the ISAPI Platform

Using the Web App Debugger executable type of application lets us significantly accelerate the debugging process. But of course this type is not suitable when distribution is necessary. We will thus describe a simple process for moving the application to an USAPI platform.

1. Create a new web server application project and save it in a separate folder, using the same file names that were used for the test application. Don't forget to change the names of the web module classes as well.

2. Move all the modules created from the test project folder (in our case, there is but one — uMain.pas).

3. If necessary, include additional functions in the project (e.g., destroying an instance of the application after it is idle for a certain length of time).

4. Compile the project.

That's it. The ISAPI application is now ready for work.

Summary

WebBroker technology allows you to create web server applications of a few basic types for the Microsoft Internet Information Server and UNIX Apache servers. The set of specialized components and modules give the application the ability to execute the following functions:

❐ Interaction with the web server; exchange of requests and responses

❐ Control over memory allocation and request dispatch

❐ Dynamic creation of web pages based on HTML templates

❐ Access to databases from the application, and being able to use them when creating pages

One peculiarity of the WebBroker technology is the high level of automation of operations. To maintain the efficiency of most components, you simply need to set one or two properties and use a few methods and event handler methods.

In addition, we advise you to study one fundamental document — RFC 2068 — which is a description of the HTTP protocol, version 1.1.

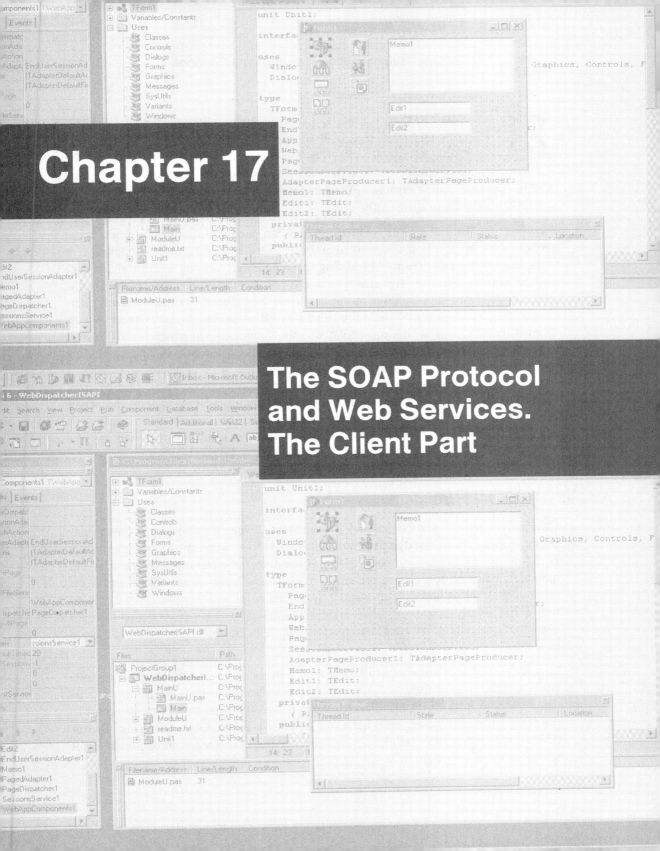

Chapter 17

The SOAP Protocol and Web Services. The Client Part

Having seen in Delphi 6 entire pages complete with new Internet components, folders with dozens of source code files, and hundreds of documentation pages, each user has the right to ask why on earth he or she needs to use all of these, and whether existing, well-tested technologies wouldn't suffice. The question is fair enough: an excessive number of tools is the surest way to end up using them incorrectly.

However, far from being simply attempts to keep pace with the latest trends, these technologies were indeed designed to address a very real problem. The challenge at issue is all too well known — providing interoperability among applications working on various platforms. It seems that in the past two years, a means of calling the methods of remote applications has at last been found, and, most importantly, embraced by the majority of the IT community. It is called Simple Object Access Protocol (SOAP); it is this protocol that this chapter is concerned with. We will begin by substantiating the claims concerning the need for SOAP, and by finding the place it occupies among other solutions. After that, we will discuss the basics of SOAP and the web services that are SOAP-based applications. Then, step-by-step, we will walk you through the entire process of building a SOAP client and server application in Delphi. As for issues associated with the interaction between web services created with Delphi and various third-party solutions, they will be the dominant theme of the next chapter.

Why SOAP?

Obviously, software companies and independent developers did not just yesterday begin working on a language that Windows and UNIX, Macintosh and mainframes could use when speaking to each other on the Internet. Having read the previous chapters dedicated to network protocols, you already know about HTTP and some other high-level protocols. But what if you need to go even higher? What if your task is not simply to request a hypertext and show it to the user, but also to organize the interaction between two concurrent applications running on different platforms?

Certainly, there are solutions to this problem available — CORBA, for example. But CORBA, which truly is a cross-platform technology, has one essential deficiency — you have to install a CORBA client on every end user. If you intend to distribute solutions based on VisiBroker — which is the Object Request Broker (ORB) that comes with Delphi — then you need to take special measures in order to obtain the appropriate license.

At the other end of the spectrum, we find another recent solution from Microsoft — COM Internet Services (CIS). This technology is actually just a trick that allows you to "lengthen the arms" of DCOM remote object calling. As you likely know, when DCOM objects connect to each other over TCP/IP, they use a randomly selected port from the permissible range — 1024 to 65535. CIS lets you establish such a connection and exchange data over HTTP using port 80.

Here we have reached the key point in our discussion. Security requirements on the Internet are becoming increasingly rigid; firewalls, which operate on the principle that "everything that is not explicitly permitted must be forbidden," are becoming more commonly used for filtering network traffic. Many firewalls do not relay anything at all except for TCP packets that use such ports as 80 (which is, as you probably remember, the port specifically designated for HTTP), 443 (HTTPS) and UDP packets that use port 53 (DNS). The rationale behind such limitations is that there are numerous holes in various operating systems that allow hackers to use specific ports to launch a network attack, which will at best just block the server, and at worst launch a "Trojan horse" on it.

Even if you manage to convince your system administrator and some of your clients into lowering their security requirements and opening some of their ports, it would be sheer madness to expect all of your potential clients to do the same if you intend on serving dozens of them, let alone hundreds. In light of this, we have to admit that HTTP still is the only current protocol that is truly commonly used for connecting over the Internet.

In this aspect, CIS lets you circumvent firewalls. But this is an exclusively DCOM oriented solution; it works for no other platform.

Delphi, DataSnap, and *TSomeConnection*: Potential Issues

Let's look at a Delphi component intended for work with remote databases (the DataSnap technology, earlier known as MIDAS, see *Chapter 8*) from the perspective of these global problems. The DataSnap architecture is as follows: the server side has an object implementing the IAppServer interface, while the client side has the TClientDataSet object that contains a reference to IAppServer. The role of the latter is performed by a connection component — TDCOMConnection, TSocketConnection, TWebConnection, etc. Such a component also contains an implementation of IAppServer, but this is only an instrument for marshaling requests from the client to the remote application, rather than a bona fide server. In other words, the client simply addresses `IAppServer`, never giving a thought to how exactly the data are packed, transmitted, verified, and delivered.

The server side can use different approaches for marshaling. The `TDCOMConnection` object does not need the server part at all: called remote interfaces are made by the DCOM system itself. But here, Borland has not provided support for CIS, so we have to rule out `TDCOMConnection` as a candidate for working in global networks.

For `TSocketConnection`, there is a special Borland Socket Server. Its executable module (`scktsrvr.exe`) can be found in Delphi's Bin folder, while the project source codes are stored in Source\Vcl. Data exchange is implemented on top of TCP/IP using port 211 (by default). This is exactly the case referred to above: access via this port is, as a rule, denied.

The next component has a very promising name — `TWebConnection`. And indeed, it implements a connection on top of HTTP: the client part needs the WinInet library, and the server side works with the ISAPI library that translates HTTP requests into calls for server methods — httpsrvr.dll. But the problem here is not with data transmission, but rather with interoperability, since this technology works exclusively with connections between `TClientDataSet` and the application server — and with nothing else. The reader familiar with DataSnap may object: surely we can add our own custom methods to the server application (or, to be more precise, to the interface being generated, a descendant of `IAppServer`) and then expose them to the client side. Well, of course you can, by all means, but this solution is only for special cases: it allows you to fine-tune Windows based clients, but doesn't do a thing for clients on other operating systems.

SOAP: The Principles of Its Operation

So, let's summarize the above discussion. What we need is a protocol that is supported on all major platforms represented on the Internet, and at the same time does not require too complex of a client part and has no problem where delivering messages over the Internet and security are concerned.

Such a protocol "knocked on the door" almost immediately after XML — indeed, if we have such universal language at our disposal, then let's use it for writing letters!

The word "letter" is not used here just by way of metaphor. SOAP transmits data in XML format over HTTP; every message sent both by the client and by the server is enclosed in an envelope — hence the analogy with a letter.

NOTE

Do you remember the chapter about the OSI protocol suite? In this model, higher-level protocols were guided by lower-level calls, without being dependent on the details of implementation. Similarly, there are no unbreakable ties between SOAP and HTTP. SOAP packets can be transported over other protocols as well, such as the SMTP mail protocol. You just need to create and standardize the appropriate binding. However, it is difficult to imagine such an expression as y := sin(x) calculated in response to a mail call. Originally, the SOAP specification documented only one binding, to HTTP. As a consequence, many people still view these two protocols as closely linked.

Let's look at a sample SOAP message:

```
<?xml version="1.0" ?>
<SOAP-ENV:Envelope xmlns:SOAP-
ENV="http://schemas.xmlsoap.org/soap/envelope/"
xmlns:xsd="http://www.w3.org/2001/XMLSchema"
xmlns:xsi="http://www.w3.org/2001/XMLSchema-instance"
xmlns:SOAP-ENC="http://schemas.xmlsoap.org/soap/encoding/">
 <SOAP-ENV:Body SOAP-ENV:encodingStyle=
 "http://schemas.xmlsoap.org/soap/encoding/">
  <NS1:Login xmlns:NS1="http://tempuri.org/message/">
   <Code xsi:type="xsd:string">User</DCode>
   <Passw xsi:type="xsd:string">secret</DPassw>
  </NS1:Login>
 </SOAP-ENV:Body>
</SOAP-ENV:Envelope>
```

The root XML element is called `Envelope` — it is in this "envelope" that the client's request is enclosed. In the request, a certain client calls the `Login` method, passing two string parameters: `Code` and `Passw`. As a response, it receives the value of the `Result` output parameter, 0, which obviously denotes the absence of errors.

```
<?xml version="1.0" encoding="UTF-8" standalone="no" ?>
<SOAP-ENV:Envelope SOAP-ENV:encodingStyle=
"http://schemas.xmlsoap.org/soap/encoding/" xmlns:SOAP-
ENV="http://schemas.xmlsoap.org/soap/envelope/">
 <SOAP-ENV:Body>
 <NS1:LoginResponse xmlns:NS1="http://tempuri.org/message/">
  <Result>0</Result>
 </NS1:LoginResponse>
 </SOAP-ENV:Body>
</SOAP-ENV:Envelope>
```

This envelope — that is to say, the rules for writing letters — is the first part of the standard.

Web Services

Now we can define the concept of a web service. A web service is a server application available on the Internet, whose interface is developed and published in compliance with the SOAP standard. The language used for such a description is called Web Services Description Language (WSDL).

Let's briefly outline the capabilities of web services, without going into the technical details. Imagine this scenario: you want to provide your clients with access to certain services, for example, some specific data from your information system, a language translation utility, a geographical map, a weather forecast for some specific locality, a chess partner — whatever. To this end, you publish a description of your future web service in the standard language. This description informs your prospective customers that there is a "black box" at such and such an address on the Internet. If one puts such and such data in such and such a format into this "box," one will be able to obtain such and such data in such and such a format. The client does not care one bit about how the server is implemented or how the data are processed. As far as he or she is concerned, if the question is correctly formulated he or she should simply get an appropriate answer, and nothing more.

SOAP is often mistaken for just another version of CIS — say, something like the DCOM technology developed on a global scale. This is quite incorrect, since these technologies are fundamentally different.

Having created a COM object, you set its properties and call its methods. As long as you have a reference to the object instance, you can rest assured that the properties that you have specified will preserve their values. Such objects are referred to as stateful (objects that preserve their state).

The client does not know how web services objects are created and destroyed. For instance, having invoked the `SetRate` method with a value of 0.93, you can by no means be sure that the `Rate` property will have the same value by the next call. As a matter of fact, it is not even guaranteed that you will address the same object instance as you did in the first call. SOAP objects are a typical example of a class of stateless objects.

And this all leads us to another basic SOAP limitation — the impossibility of callbacks. It is characteristic of both Win32 API and COM that they pass the address of a certain procedure of theirs to a called function. This procedure is executed when a specified event occurs on the server. Since with SOAP the context is unknown in principle, you can forget about implementing callbacks as well.

For developers' convenience, those who create tools for SOAP are currently trying to imitate the context and supply it with a unique session ID (like Cookie session files). This approach does offer some promise, but don't let this delude you — SOAP is still a fundamentally stateless protocol. If your particular problem requires a stateful protocol, you'd better consider using some other solution.

Description of the WSDL Standard

The WSDL standard (the abbreviation stands for, as you may remember, Web Services Description Language) is the language used by clients and servers of web services for talking to each other. Its current specification — 1.1 — is right now only at the stage of being accepted by the W3C; nonetheless, all service vendors strictly follow it.

Every web service is fully described using the following key concepts:

❏ *List of types.* One of the bases of data exchange is the types standardized for XML. But if your service uses non-standard (custom) types — for example, data structures — they should be declared by indicating or providing the appropriate XML schema (in XSD format).

❏ *Messages.* Every message is an "atom" that is exchanged by the connected sides. A message consists of one or more parts (parameters). Consider an example: let's say that on the server side, you call a function whose declaration in ObjectPascal would look like this: `function GetSomeData(Param1: Integer; Param2, Param3: string): double;` The input message for such a function would consist of three parts — an integer and two string parameters — while the output message would have only one parameter of the `double` type.

❏ *Port type.* The port type is a description of a certain set of operations. An operation is an action performed on an input message that generates an output message — very much like the RPC (Remote Procedure Call) mechanism. For completeness' sake, it should be noted that the WSDL standard also determines the reverse order of the call: the server sends a message and the client responds

❏ *Binding.* The binding specifies the link between the port type and the transport protocol that will be used for delivering messages.

❑ *Port*. The port links all the above concepts with reality. The relationship between the port and the port type can be compared to the one between the class definition and the object that implements it in object-oriented programming. The port indicates that the given port type using the given binding is available for connection at the specified Internet address.

❑ *Service*. It is a named set of ports.

The interconnection between these basic concepts is shown in Fig. 17.1.

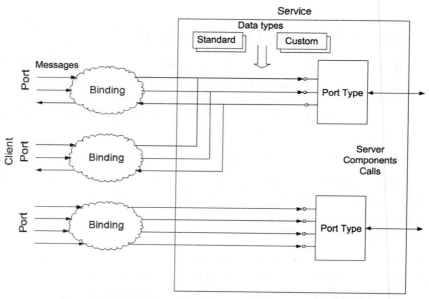

Fig. 17.1. Basic web service elements in WSDL terms

WSDL documents, naturally, are described in XML. Everything that we just described — `<types>`, `<message>`, `<portType>`, `<binding>`, `<port>`, `<service>` — are reserved XML element names. Each component part of a WSDL document is surrounded by the `<definitions>` root element, whose `name` attribute defines the name of the service in use.

NOTE

The WSDL specification also allows the `<document>` element, which is used for including various "human" documentation on the service's content and any of its constituent parts. Here, developers can include their instructions and comments. If you don't know or don't understand the structure or working principles of a service, try to find such elements in its WSDL document.

Let's take a look at a sample WSDL file for a service that can perform two elementary operations: return the string and array of strings that were passed to it for processing in their original, unchanged form (Listing 17.1). Later, we will use the following specification as a foundation for building a web service.

Listing 17.1. A Sample WSDL File of the SimpleEcho Service

```
<?xml version="1.0"?>
<definitions xmlns="http://schemas.xmlsoap.org/wsdl/"
xmlns:xs="http://www.w3.org/2001/XMLSchema" name="ISimpleEchoservice"
targetNamespace="http://tempuri.org/" xmlns:tns="http://tempuri.org/"
xmlns:soap="http://schemas.xmlsoap.org/wsdl/soap/"
xmlns:soapenc="http://schemas.xmlsoap.org/soap/encoding/"
xmlns:ns1="http://www.borland.com/namespaces/Types">
  <types>
    <xs:schema
targetNamespace="http://www.borland.com/namespaces/Types"
xmlns="http://www.borland.com/namespaces/Types">
      <xs:complexType name="TStringDynArray">
        <xs:complexContent>
          <xs:restriction base="soapenc:Array">
            <xs:sequence/>
            <xs:attribute ref="soapenc:arrayType"
n1:arrayType="xs:string[]"
xmlns:n1="http://schemas.xmlsoap.org/wsdl/"/>
          </xs:restriction>
        </xs:complexContent>
      </xs:complexType>
    </xs:schema>
  </types>
  <message name="echoStringRequest">
    <part name="Value" type="xs:string"/>
  </message>
  <message name="echoStringResponse">
    <part name="return" type="xs:string"/>
  </message>
  <message name="echoStringArrayRequest">
```

```xml
    <part name="Value" type="ns1:TStringDynArray"/>
  </message>
  <message name="echoStringArrayResponse">
    <part name="return" type="ns1:TStringDynArray"/>
  </message>
  <portType name="ISimpleEcho">
    <operation name="echoString">
      <input message="tns:echoStringRequest"/>
      <output message="tns:echoStringResponse"/>
    </operation>
    <operation name="echoStringArray">
      <input message="tns:echoStringArrayRequest"/>
      <output message="tns:echoStringArrayResponse"/>
    </operation>
  </portType>
  <binding name="ISimpleEchobinding" type="tns:ISimpleEcho">
    <soap:binding style="rpc"
transport="http://schemas.xmlsoap.org/soap/http"/>
    <operation name="echoString">
      <soap:operation soapAction="urn:SimpleEchoIntf-
ISimpleEcho#echoString" style="rpc"/>
      <input>
        <soap:body use="encoded"
encodingStyle="http://schemas.xmlsoap.org/soap/encoding/"
namespace="urn:SimpleEchoIntf-ISimpleEcho"/>
      </input>
      <output>
        <soap:body use="encoded"
encodingStyle="http://schemas.xmlsoap.org/soap/encoding/"
namespace="urn:SimpleEchoIntf-ISimpleEcho"/>
      </output>
    </operation>
    <operation name="echoStringArray">
      <soap:operation soapAction="urn:SimpleEchoIntf-
ISimpleEcho#echoStringArray" style="rpc"/>
      <input>
        <soap:body use="encoded"
encodingStyle="http://schemas.xmlsoap.org/soap/encoding/"
namespace="urn:SimpleEchoIntf-ISimpleEcho"/>
      </input>
      <output>
```

```
        <soap:body use="encoded"
encodingStyle="http://schemas.xmlsoap.org/soap/encoding/"
namespace="urn:SimpleEchoIntf-ISimpleEcho"/>
        </output>
      </operation>
    </binding>
    <service name="ISimpleEchoservice">
      <port name="ISimpleEchoPort" binding="tns:ISimpleEchobinding">
        <soap:address
location="http://localhost/scripts/simpleecho.dll/soap/ISimpleEcho"/>
      </port>
    </service>
</definitions>
```

What does this file consist of?

☐ Since the `string` type is commonly known and fundamental, the types clause contains just one type; it is described by the element schema `<xs:complexType name="TStringDynArray">`. By the way, such dynamic array types as `TStringDynArray`, `TintegerDynArray`, etc. are declared in Delphi in the `Types` module and registered in the `InvokeRegistry` module.

☐ The message section contains four elements: one element for the input and output parameters of both functions. Their respective names are: `echoStringRequest`, `echoStringResponse`, `echoStringArrayRequest`, and `echoStringArrayResponse`. Theoretically, the same message can be used to describe several port types, but in real-world programming it is considered good practice to avoid this.

☐ The only port type is called `ISimpleEcho` (note this point — it will be used later to explain how the parameters of a Delphi project are related to the parameters of the service). It includes descriptions of two operations: `echoString` and `echoStringArray`.

☐ The binding indicates that the SOAP protocol will be used to deliver messages.

☐ Finally, the last element of the WSDL document shows us that the `ISimpleEchoService` service has only one port — `IsimpleEchoPort` — which can be addressed at the address `http://localhost/scripts/simpleecho.dll/soap/ISimpleEcho`.

Having examined the WSDL standard itself, let's figure out where all the files that describe services come from and how they can be accessed.

Normally, if the author intends his or her service for public use, he or she publishes it. Visit the site at **www.xmethods.com**, which is one of the most popular service repositories. You will see that every service listed there is accompanied by a reference to the relevant WSDL file.

Services built in Delphi automatically publish their descriptions. They all interact with the web server using the ISAPI/CGI standard. The Delphi runtime library is designed in such a way that the default action (without parameters) and the ./wsdl action provide the user with "readable" information in tabular form (Fig. 17.2).

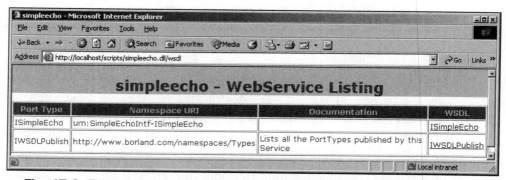

Fig. 17.2. This is how a web service built with Borland tools provides information on its ports in a browser window

If you just need a plain WSDL file in XML format without any fancy design, specify a path such as to **http://myserver/myservice.dll/wsdl/myPortTypeName**. Besides the ports assigned by the developers, the Delphi environment also as a matter of course adds the IWSDLPublish port, which helps the client automatically get information on the service. This port type is defined as follows:

```
IWSDLPublish = interface(IInvokable)
['{45B6B1C5-A872-C07C-DCC0-798B59768E0E}']
  procedure GetPortTypeList(var PortTypes: TWideStringDynArray); stdcall;
  function  GetWSDLForPortType(const PortType: String): String; stdcall;
  procedure GetTypeSystemsList(const TypeSystems:
  TWideStringDynArray); stdcall;
  function  GetXSDForTypeSystem(const TypeSystem: String): String; stdcall;
end;
```

If you know that the server side of the service was written using Delphi tools, you can address its IWSDLPublish and obtain a list of the port types, their WSDL files, and information on the data types programmatically.

If you need a full analysis of the WSDL file, including each message and its data, you could of course rely on the XML parser and do all this work manually. However, it is much simpler to take advantage of ready-to-use facilities. A client built with Delphi 6, once it is successfully connected, automatically gets access to the IWSDLDocument and IWSDLItems interfaces, which let you explore the description of the service to the extent you think necessary.

Suppose you now have the WSDL file of the desired service. What should you do with it next? How can you create a client that would be able to exchange messages of the specified types? The answer depends on the development environment you use. Fortunately, with Delphi, this answer is fairly simple. You will learn it from the following section, which deals precisely with the architecture of the client part.

Architecture of Web Services in Delphi

Like many other technologies, SOAP can be implemented in different guises, depending on the Delphi 6 developer's needs. If your intention is to build a client for remote databases, you can simply take the TSOAPConnection component and use SOAP as one of the possible connection level protocols, along with HTTP, CORBA, DCOM, or sockets. Such a case hardly requires you to have any special knowledge, since all the functionality of SOAP is encapsulated within TSOAPConnection.

If you are writing a service that is not related to DBMS data transmission, or if you choose to add your own custom improvements, then you have at your service such facilities as the SOAP Server Application Wizard on the server side, and the THTTPRIO component on the client side.

If you are not satisfied with even all of this, you can always utilize a whole range of "lower-level" components that directly form and receive SOAP messages.

And finally, both the client and the server can be written using other tools. The next chapter will be devoted to the interaction between Delphi and Microsoft tools for creating web services.

The components that Borland has provided you with for handling web services all reside in the page of the same name. Additionally, while developing a new web service project, begin by opening the Object Repository dialog (**File\New\Others**). The Web-Services page of the dialog contains three templates for building the server part of an application (SOAP Server Application, SOAP Server Data Module, and SOAP Server Interface), as well as the WSDL file import wizard for the web service client.

While installing Delphi, you were warned that SOAP and web services are rapidly evolving technologies and, therefore, the standards in this area are subject to change. This euphemism conceals a highly important practical message: the original version of Delphi 6 — and update 1 too, as a matter of fact — included too "raw" an implementation of SOAP, which, apart from other faults, had various interoperability problems with services built with the Microsoft SOAP Toolkit. Only with Update Pack 2, did this new technology find more or less reliable support in Delphi.

> **NOTE**
>
> Nevertheless, mistakes and inconsistencies are common occurrences, as far as these developing technologies are concerned. Already, after the release of Update Pack 2, some changes have been introduced into the SOAP implementation. Some of them were aimed, for example, at eliminating the incompatibility between Borland SOAP and the installed MSXML4 parser. Unfortunately, if you or your clients use this parser, making manual corrections is absolutely unavoidable — see the article at: **http://community.borland.com/article/0,1410,28514,00.html**. However, it is highly probable that by the time you read this book, Update Pack 3 will already be available. In any event, we recommend that you visit the Borland site often to keep abreast of the most recent improvements.

Web Service Client

We will begin discussing the principles of web service performance with the client part. First, it is quite possible that your task will come down to simply obtaining information from existing services — and not necessarily those built with Delphi 6. Second, a client part is significantly simpler in design and understandability, and so the practice we gain from doing this will make writing the server part much easier.

So, we will start by looking at the client before we create our own server. However, it is assumed that the reader has no problems with access to the Internet: indeed, how could he or she consider using and creating web applications otherwise?

As an example, let's take the BASE test web service creted by Borland as a part of the SOAPBuilders Interoperability Lab project for examining the compatibility of various SOAP implementations. Information about the project itself can be found at **http://www.whitemesa.com/interop.htm** and **http://www.xmethods.net/ilab**. The WSDL file of the Borland implementation of the BASE service is at **http:// soap-server.borland.com/WebServices/Interop/cgi-bin/InteropService.exe/wsdl/ InteropTestPortType/**.

The purpose of BASE is as simple as it is handy: it is an echo that brings back a sent value. The value in question can be of one of the 14 predefined types, from a string to an array of structures. It should be noted that representing various data types in XML can be quite difficult, and most — if not all — tools for building web services are a bit "rough" in this area. At the sites above, you can also find matrices that show the results of testing the interaction of various server and client implementations of the BASE service: all too many cells there show a sad FAILED.

Generating the Web Service Interface

The very first thing you need to do in order to create a client service is to call the WSDL importer wizard from the Object Repository (**File\New\Other**, the **WebServices** page). It is assumed that you already have a ready-to-use project — this can be either a traditional application, DLL, or an ActiveX library.

The role of the wizard can be summed up in just a few words. You specify the full path to the WSDL file that describes the web service, and the wizard generates an interface that lets you call methods of this service.

What's good is that you don't need to think about the technical specifics of the SOAP implementation in Delphi to do this; you might as well know nothing whatsoever about the protocol. You still get an object with methods identical to the service's. And this whole process looks just as if you were manipulating an ordinary Automation object.

So, let's call the wizard and enter the above address for the BASE service into the **Location of WSDL File or URL** field (Fig. 17.3).

The description file can reside both on the Internet and locally, on your computer.

By the second step, the wizard is already prepared to show the results of its work. Take a close look at them: do you see the similarities between them and the result of importing a COM type library (the **Project|Import type Library** item)? The left pane shows the tree of all the service's interfaces together with the methods, as well as specific data types. On the right, you will see the module of the code in Object Pascal that describes the service. Press the **Finish** button and the file generated by the wizard will be added to your current project (Fig. 17.4).

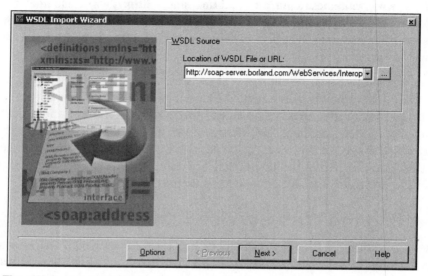

Fig. 17.3. The WSDL importer wizard: the page for specifying the address of a desired service

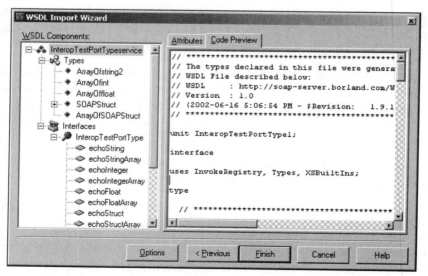

Fig 17.4. The WSDL import wizard: the service interface page

The name of the newly generated PAS file will correspond to the name of the service; it is taken from the `name` attribute of the `<definitions>` element of the WSDL document. If there is no such attribute, the file name will be the name of the document itself. In our scenario, the wizard will create Interop-TestPortType1.pas.

NOTE

Besides the wizard that is launched immediately in the Delphi environment, you can also use the wsdlimp.exe command-line utility stored in the \BIN folder. This utility shares its wsdlimp.ini settings file with the wizard. The file stores a list of the service descriptions that have already been imported. Sometimes this list causes problems when you are trying to enter new addresses in the wizard — and now you know where it can be edited.

Let's save the file and analyze its content. The descriptions of the data structures are followed by the interface we are interested in:

```
InteropTestPortType = interface(IInvokable)
['{426150D1-7C2C-A74F-954B-DB3ADC067CD8}']
  function  echoString(const inputString: String): String; stdcall;
  function  echoStringArray(const inputStringArray: ArrayOfstring2):
  ArrayOfstring2; stdcall;
  function  echoInteger(const inputInteger: Integer): Integer; stdcall;
  function  echoIntegerArray(const inputIntegerArray: ArrayOfint):
  ArrayOfint; stdcall;
  function  echoFloat(const inputFloat: Single): Single; stdcall;
  function  echoFloatArray(const inputFloatArray: ArrayOffloat):
  ArrayOffloat; stdcall;
  function  echoStruct(const inputStruct: SOAPStruct): SOAPStruct; stdcall;
  function  echoStructArray(const inputStructArray:
  ArrayOfSOAPStruct): ArrayOfSOAPStruct; stdcall;
  procedure echoVoid; stdcall;
  function  echoBase64(const inputBase64: TByteDynArray):
  TByteDynArray; stdcall;
  function  echoDate(const inputDate: TXSDateTime): TXSDateTime; stdcall;
  function  echoHexBinary(const inputHexBinary: TXSHexBinary):
  TXSHexBinary; stdcall;
  function  echoDecimal(const inputDecimal: TXSDecimal): TXSDecimal;
  stdcall;
  function  echoBoolean(const inputBoolean: Boolean): Boolean; stdcall;
end;
```

These fourteen methods are used for returning the fourteen fundamental data types defined by the SOAPBuilders Interoperability Lab workgroup for testing. Some of them are the same as the native data types of Object Pascal.

Another subset of types is described in the SOAP standard; in order to map such types to Delphi data, you need to use special adapter objects. Their names all begin with the prefix TXS: you will surely end up using some of them, such as TXSDateTime, TXSDecimal, TXSHexBinary, etc. The role of an adapter is to convert data in SOAP form to Delphi data, and vice versa. Every such object has two basic methods — XSToNative and NativeToXS, along with a number of useful properties like, for instance, AsDate, AsByteArray, etc.

Finally, the third subset of data types includes the types exclusive to the particular service. The BASE service defines five such types, which you may have noticed earlier in the WSDL importer wizard. Data types, however, will be covered later.

At this point, we need to stress the relationship between the WSDL import wizard and COM. However similar they may look, the above interface *does not* correspond to any real COM object. Neither calling CreateOLEObject with the InteropTestPortType parameter, nor calling CreateCOMObject with the {426150D1-7C2C-A74F-954B-DB3ADC067CD8} GUID will have any kind of productive result. Consequently, you needn't worry about preserving the original content of the registry: none of these interfaces are registered in it. You can import dozens of various service definitions if you like; the only thing you'll have to delete later will be the .pas files that were generated.

Nevertheless, COM does come into play here: the declaration of the interface is always followed by a Get<service name> function; in our case this is

```
function GetInteropTestPortType(UseWSDL: Boolean=System.False; Addr:
string=''): InteropTestPortType;
```

Take a look at its implementation. You will see manipulations with a certain THTTPRIO object. As far as the technical aspect of the operation of this object is of particular interest to us in the context of the present discussion, we will explore the "inside" of this object, which serves as a bridge between the web service and COM, later. But for now, we can tell you that the Get function is meant to cater to those users who don't want to, so to speak, "turn the object inside out" in order to know how to use it. This function provides a ready-to-use InteropTestPortType object, sparing you the details about where it actually came from. As a result, the simplest communication session with the BASE web service looks as follows:

```
procedure TForm1.Button1Click(Sender: TObject);
var Port : InteropTestPortType;
```

```
begin
 try
  Port := GetInteropTestPortType;
  ShowMessage( Port.echoString('Hello, world!') );
 finally
  Port := nil;
 end;
end;
```

The `Port` variable gets the "real" COM instance, and therefore, after it has been used, it must always be reset to the `nil` value.

Now, add the **Button1** button to an empty form of your project and bind its `On-Click` event with this method. As a result, you will get your very first welcome to the world of web services.

In our example, we called the `GetInteropTestPortType` function without any parameters, though in fact it has two of them, even if they are optional. They are necessary when creating an object from a file different from the WSDL file or the URL used by the WSDL import wizard. Suppose you have a copy of the WSDL document used for debugging (for information on how this is possible, see below). The `UseWSDL` parameter must then be set to `True`, while the `Addr` parameter should point to the debugging file:

```
Port := GetInteropTestPortType( True,
'c:\MyFolder\InteropTestPortType.wsdl');
```

Now you can consider your first step into the world of web services completed. You now have enough knowledge to find the description of the desired service, create a client for it, and call the methods. But, surely, you know better than to be satisfied with just the simpleest examples — so let's move on.

Oh, RIO, RIO

RIO — which has nothing to do with Rio de Janeiro — is essential for understanding the SOAP client interface in Delphi. RIO stands for Remote Interfaced Object. This object "pretends" to be a web service. How is this possible? By now, we are all used to static declarations of COM interfaces and Object Pascal classes. The compiler reads the declaration — which is published, as a rule, in IDL — and generates calls for the Virtual Method Table (VMT) of the interface. If the declaration is valid, these calls will be successful irrespective of the languages used to implement the COM object or to call its application.

But we cannot always know the description of the web service interface in advance! As a consequence, we cannot rely on the compiler to do this job.

And here a daring idea suggests itself: why not create this Virtual Method Table dynamically instead of having it be static? The compiler knows the VMT structure because it has processed the PAS file generated by the above wizard that defines the service interfaces. And where these methods come from and how they will be implemented are of no concern to it.

Borland has managed to implement this idea by introducing TRIO. Initially, this Delphi object supports just one interface — IUnknown. But once you request some other interface from it via the QueryInterface method or, alternatively, use the syntax more commonly used by Object Pascal programmers

```
Obj := RIO as InteropTestPortType;
```

RIO will attempt to do the following:

1. Read the description of the required interface from the InvokeRegistry repository. This repository stores the descriptions of all web service interfaces; it will be expounded on later.

2. Generate the VMT and the adapter methods (or stubs) — which are intended for establishing consistency between the calling conventions and the types of the parameters of the given method — based on the obtained description.

3. Return a reference to the newly created VMT, and increment *its own* call counter by one — which implies that from this point on, RIO will operate as an object instance that supports the requested interface

The TRIO class itself is nothing more than a general implemention of the idea of a remote call. The Delphi Component palette has the THTTPRIO component, which is responsible for adapting RIO for transmitting method calls in the SOAP format on top of the HTTP transport protocol. Don't forget that there are other variations of coding and passing SOAP messages; in each of these cases, different TRIO descendants will come into play. For right now, however, we have just one representative of this family.

You can create an instance of this uncommon object in two ways:

1. As a traditional component, by placing a THTTPRIO instance from the Component Palette into a form and setting its properties in the design mode. In this case, the component owner will be the form, frame, or other component. This owner also will be responsible for freeing the THTTPRIO instance.

2. Dynamically, by calling the `Create` constructor with the `Owner=nil` parameter. It is this mechanism that is used by default in `GetInteropTestPortType` and other analogous functions generated by the WSDL import wizard. In this case, the full burden of responsibility for the object's life-cycle is placed on its creator.

Remember that freeing object instances is the cornerstone of COM. Every time the instance is requested, the `_addRef` method is invoked, incrementing the reference counter by one. By resetting the reference (to `zero`), you are thereby refusing the instance and instructing the Delphi runtime library (RTL) to call the `_Release` method and decrement the number of references. Once the value is `zero`, the object instance must be destroyed.

But the code of the `TRIO` component and its descendants are written in such a way that it will perform all the above actions *only* if it has no owner — a `TComponent` descendant. To put it differently, if you have created `RIO` as a traditional component, go on treating it as such and do not worry about the instances. If you are more at home with the COM paradigm, use `RIO` as a regular COM object.

Specifically for those who got lost in the maze of these rules, the normally hidden `RefCount` property is included into the **public** section, where it is listed as a read-only property:

```
property RefCount: Integer;
```

If you are not quite sure about your code, keep an eye on the `RefCount` value: before calling `TRIO.Free`, the reference number should be `zero`.

How to Connect to the Necessary Web Service

Now it's time to discuss the properties that point to the service that you intend your `THTTPRIO` object to connect to. Here again, two approaches are possible.

The first one is exactly the same as the logic of working with the importer wizard.

Three properties, when used in the this order,

```
property WSDLLocation: string;
property Service: string;
property Port: string;
```

will lead you to the required interface. First, you need to specify the WSDL location; the drop-down list will show you the addresses of already familiar services.

Do not forget that you are able to use not only the URL, but also the path to the local file on the disk to indicate the address.

Once the file is specified and its parsing is successfully completed, the collections of services and their ports available at this address will be added to the Service and Port properties.

The second approach can be used, as a rule, if both the client and the server have been created with either Delphi or Kylix. If you know the service inside out, then why perform this intermediate step and read the WSDL? Well, because you can address the port specified in the URL property directly. Remember that the address in question must be indicated in the `<port>` element of the WSDL file:

```
<service name="InteropTestPortTypeservice">
  <port name="InteropTestPortTypePort" binding=
  "tns:InteropTestPortTypebinding">
    <soap:address location="http://soap-server.borland.com/
    WebServices/Interop/cgi-bin/InteropService.exe/soap/
    InteropTestPortType" />
  </port>
</service>
```

For services built with Borland tools, this address resembles the address of the WSDL file, except that the /wsdl action has been replaced with the /soap action (as it is in the example given)

Naturally, the URL and WSDLLocation/Service/Port properties are mutually exclusive — setting one of them clears the value of the other.

Let's illustrate these properties with another simple example. Move the THTTPRIO component from the Component Palette into the form of our first **BASE** service client (you haven't closed it yet, have you?) and set its WSDLLocation/Service/Port properties to http://soap-server.borland.com/ WebServices/Interop/cgi-bin/InteropService.exe/wsdl/InteropTestPortType/, InteropTestPortTypeservice, and InteropTestPortTypePort, respectively. Add one more button and the following code to its OnClick:

```
procedure TForm1.Button2Click(Sender: TObject);
begin
    ShowMessage( (HTTPRIO1 as InteropTestPortType).echoString('Hello, world!') );
end;
```

This saves you the trouble of checking the call counter, since the release code of the Delphi RTL, which executes upon completion of the `Button2Click` method, will see to it that this counter is taken care of.

Tackling Communication Problems

The speed and reliability of various services is determined, first and foremost, by the transport used to deliver messages. In this case it is HTTP. For Delphi 6, HTTP is implemented by calling the WinInet.dll library that comes with Windows and Internet Explorer and contains the entire engine for working with the higher-level protocols built into IE — specifically, HTTP, HTTPS, FTP, and Gopher. Due to the fact that, at least in the course of the last six or so years, it is impossible to imagine Windows without the Internet, such an approach appears to be warranted. Moreover, WinInet is a relatively reliable and tested implementation of the above protocols.

On the other hand, independence from the type of platform, and especially independence from Microsoft, is only too welcome a gain. For Kylix, the HTTP implementation provided with the Indy libraries (which we discussed in previous chapters) was chosen. If you happen to take a look at the code of the SoapHTTPTrans.pas module (the Source\Soap folder), you will see many conditional compilation directives: `{$IFDEF USE_INDY}`. Having mastered certain skills, you can recompile the module into Indy- and Delphi-based HTTP implementations. Moreover, in various newsgroups on Delphi, and in particular at borland.public.delphi.webservices.soap, you also can find bindings to other HTTP implementations.

This became possible thanks to the module construct of `RIO`. Actually, the above brief overview is about all that needs to (or can) be said about the inherent properties of the `THTTPRIO` component. This component, however, has two child components: in the Object Inspector, these are listed as `Converter` and `HTTPWebNode`.

If you are looking for an explanation of all six components on the **WebServices** page of the Delphi Component palette, here are two more of them — `TOPToSoapDomConvert` and `THTTPReqResp`. These, as you may have already guessed, are the same as `Converter` and `HTTPWebNode`.

The first of them — `Converter` — is responsible for converting calls between the SOAP protocol and the application. All important information published about this component is included in its `Options` property. It is its options that for the most part affect its compatibility with other clients and servers of web services.

The second component — `THTTPReqResp` — is responsible for transmitting data. Its name in fact is derived from two HTTP terms: Request and Response.

You might be wondering: this is all very well and good, but what do I personally need it for? The answer is: to parameterize the connection options. Tasks that can be solved with these options include:

1. Setting the options for the proxy server. The property

```
property Proxy: string
```

indicates the address of such a server that is to be used for establishing the connection. Warning: the fact that this property is empty *does not mean* that the connection will be implemented without a proxy. It simply implies that the WinInet standard settings are to be applied; in other words, you will use the same settings as your Internet Explorer does.

If you have ever watched the process of configuring a proxy for Internet Explorer, you could not but have noticed the option with the same name as the property

```
property ProxyByPass: string;
```

If certain servers are to be connected to, bypassing the proxy, such servers can be listed in this property and delimited by semicolons.

Finally, the property

```
property Agent: string;
```

sets the value of the HTTP header of the same name. Some firewalls filter HTTP traffic depending on the value of this field, so make sure that you have permissions the Borland SOAP 1.1 agent (and DataSnap if you use `TWebConnection`).

2. Authorizing the service's users. If the service server or the proxy server requires authorization, the properties

```
property UserName: string;
property Password: string;
```

can be used to specify the required username and password. Many client applications simply cannot use a system dialog for entering a password; having set the above properties, you can avoid this.

> **NOTE**
>
> The THTTPRIO component's behavior depends on whether it has been placed in the form in the design mode or generated dynamically. In the first case, failure to provide a Username and Password will result in the server returning Error 401 and generating the corresponding exception. A dynamically created THTTPRIO apparently does not initialize the values of these properties: you will see a system authorization dialog, its appearance being determined by the web server type and the authorization mechanism in use.

The subject of certificates has already been covered extensively enough earlier for us to avoid dwelling here on the problems surrounding secure connections. If you intend to connect to a web server using SSL, it will suffice to simply change the protocol prefix from HTTP:// to HTTPS:// — it is up to the WinInet library to correctly recognize the setting.

> **NOTE**
>
> If writing the server part of the service is also your responsibility, you have to synchronously change the name of the protocol in the WSDL file. Failure to do this is a typical mistake.

The InvokeOptions property has the soIgnoreInvalidCerts checkbox. This checkbox is a very useful feature when you have to deal with a server with an expired certificate or a certificate that is invalid for some other reason. Checking this checkbox results in ignoring the certificate altogether, without displaying the dialog and informing the user.

However, the situation tends to become a bit more complicated if you also use client certificates for authorization. The THTTPReqResp class code does not include the means for choosing the required certificate from those currently available. Besides which, different WinInet implementations behave differently, as far as client certificates are concerned: some implementations simply do not support this functionality or contain errors, others automatically select the first available client certificate, and still others display a dialog prompting you to make a choice. All this should be borne in mind if you still want to protect the service using such an authorization method; obviously, you will have to partially rewrite the code of the SOAPHTTPTrans module. A WinInet function with the name InternetSetOption lets you select the context of the desired certificate.

> **NOTE**
>
> The same is true for another important parameter — the connection timeout value on the client side. This parameter also is impossible to regulate.

The THTTPReqResp component has a number of methods typical for HTTP: Connect, Send, Receive, etc. However, we don't need to examine them here because: a) these methods are not virtual and cannot be overridden, and b) the first time, they are called before the first call for service methods is made.

What is Invoke Registry? Registering Interfaces and Data Types

If you looked carefully at the description of our first interface, the observant reader certainly noticed the fact that InteropTestPortType is derived from IInvokable. What sort of interface is this and how it is distinct from the ancestor of all interfaces, IUnknown (or IInterface in Delphi)? Let's look at the source code of the **System** module:

```
{$M+}

  IInvokable = interface(IInterface)

  end;

{$M-}
```

It seems that it is the {$M+} directive (or {$TYPEINFO ON}) that makes all the difference. This compiler directive includes the generation of Runtime Type Information (RTTI).

RTTI is the mechanism that underlies the whole Delphi visual programming environment. Those class fields and methods which are declared as published, along with a number of other properties (the class name, instance sizes, etc.), are included in a special table, a pointer to which is supplied for every instance of a given class. Do you remember such TObject class methods as, for example, ClassName, ClassInfo, MethodAddress, and MethodName? Essentially, they are the means of navigation through RTTI.

When you are saving a form included in your project, the form itself, together with all the components that you placed in it, must be written to a DFM file. When opened next, the form shows the same values for all its published properties. How can this happen? Because while saving, information is extracted from the RTTI and translated into binary or text format (depending on how you store your forms). Unpublished properties cannot, in theory, be saved.

How can it happen then that for many, this is probably the first time hearing about the {$M} directive? This can be explained by the peculiarity of its work: if a parent class was compiled in an {$M+} state, all its descendants will be provided with the RTTI — even if published methods and properties explicitly appear in a descendant class. The TPersistent class serves as the "point of reference" for all classes, and therefore, all VCL components descend from it.

Now a few words need to be said about interfaces. We hope that with classes the picture is fairly clear: here is the class declaration, here is a class instance, and here is the RTTI. But what does the {$M+} directive mean when it comes before an interface declaration? It means that this interface, along with all the Delphi classes that implement it, will include information on the interface methods into the RTTI, as if they were published methods of the class itself.

This novelty was first introduced into Delphi 6 — and primarily for the purpose of developing web services and their clients. Indeed, the similarity between the tasks is obvious: while reading a form file, the Delphi environment recreates the object on the basis of its text description; the very same thing must be done by the service client, but using a WSDL file instead of a DFM file.

However, it is not enough to have just the RTTI; we also need a special repository to store information about all interfaces, classes, and data types that take part in the work of web services. There are two such repositories. The first one — which is a global object available as InvRegistry — stores the declarations of interfaces (interfaces must be registered here both the client and server) and of the classes implementing these interfaces (only for the server part). If you are generating interface modules via the wizard, they will be registered automatically: take a look at the initialization clause of the sample InteropTestPortType1.pas module.

The second object — RemClassRegistry — stores the declarations of registered data types. It would be wrong to conclude that the Delphi standard data types need not be registered, though. The thing is, they are already registered in the InvokeRegistry module. These standard types include Boolean, Char, Byte, SmallInt, Word, Integer, Cardinal, Int64, Single, Double, Extended, String, WideString, Currency, and Variant. The corresponding dynamic arrays of these types are also registered (with the exception of Char, Currency, and Variant).

Non-standard types and structures must be registered in your application. Again, the WSDL import wizard will do this job for you. In our example with the BASE service, the SOAPStruct structure as well as an array of such structures must both be registered.

And here we run into a slight inconvenience. While arrays are registered in the normal manner, in order to register structures, you need to create classes to describe these structures. The same holds true for all types that the Delphi RTL does not know how to convert into XML strings.

So let's add one more button and a few lines of code to our example:

```
procedure TForm1.Button3Click(Sender: TObject);
var ssTest : SOAPStruct;
begin
 Randomize;
 ssTest := SOAPStruct.Create;
 try
  ssTest.varString := 'Hello, world!';
  ssTest.varInt := Length( ssTest.varString );
  ssTest.varFloat := Random;
  ssTest := (HTTPRIO1 as InteropTestPortType).echoStruct( sstest );
  ShowMessage( ssTest.varString );
 finally
  ssTest.Free;
 end;
end;
```

You need to remember that non-standard types are classes, and treat them accordingly. After the ssTest instance is created and utilized, it must be destroyed.

There are some frequently used data types that need classes to describe them in order to function properly in the services. These types include date, time, and binary data array. Delphi 6 provides us with such classes — they are contained in the XSBuiltIns module (XSBuiltIns.pas) and are called TXSTime, TXSDate, TXSDateTime, and TXSHexBinary. The abbreviation XS in the names stands for XML Schema.

All XS classes share the same virtual methods

```
procedure XSToNative(Value: WideString);
function   NativeToXS: WideString;
```

They are essentially the converters that translate data from the internal format into string format. But in fact, you will hardly ever need to call these methods. It's much more convenient to just call the following AsSomething type methods:

```
property AsDateTime: TDateTime;
```

for date/time, and

```
property  AsByteArray: TbyteDynArray;
```

for a binary array, etc.

XS classes often serve as parameters for service interfaces generated using WSDL. In such cases, the ways of handling them are very similar to those that we have been using to work with SOAPStruct:

☐ Create a class instance.

☐ Assign it the necessary value via AsSomething.

☐ Pass it as a parameter. It will take care of its conversion itself.

☐ If the service returns a value of this type, read the result using the same method.

If your particular task cannot be solved by means of the wizard and the above types, then you will have to write a class to represent your data type yourself. The very first piece of advice to be given here is: don't do it. The problems of compatibility between different SOAP implementations have repeatedly been raised in our discussion. It is not a fact that other development facilities will be able to correctly represent and process your custom data type. Consequently, if it is possible, try to limit yourself to the wide-used types.

If, nevertheless, you cannot do without it, derive a child class from TRemotable (for arrays and structures) or from TRemotableXS (for data that needs to be converted to strings). These types are registered by calling RemClassRegistry.RegisterXSClass (for a class) or RemClassRegistry.RegisterXSInfo (for other types).

Summary

In this chapter, we learned to create a simple client application that uses the SOAP protocol. The power of web services lies in the fact that they are self-documenting programs. Having armed yourself with a single THTTPRIO component, you can "devour" WSDL files and test any free services that may appeal to you. However, providing various useful services is also increasingly developing into a profitable business. For starters, we recommend that you begin your search at **http://www.xmethods.net**.

And now we are ready to proceed to the next stage of the design process — developing the web service server.

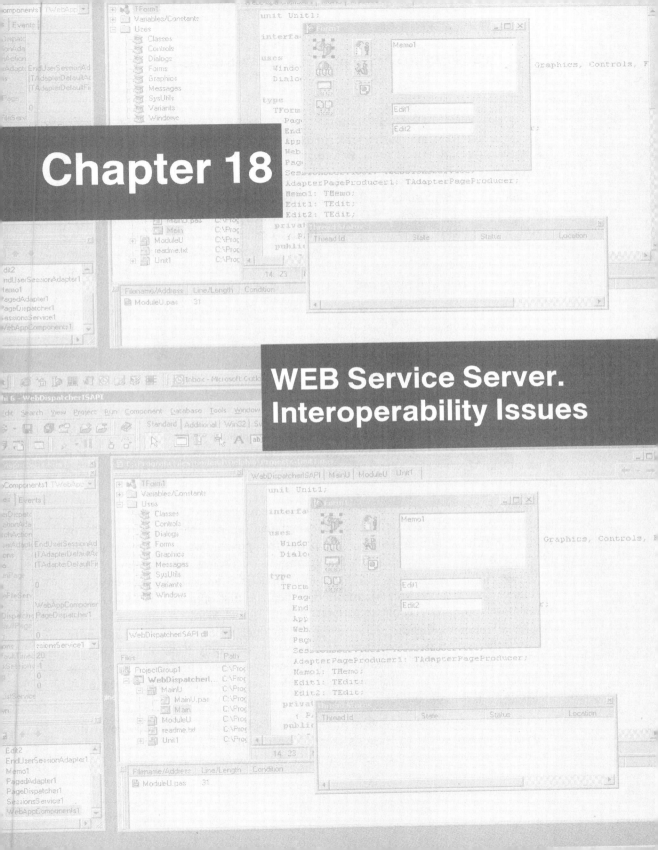

Chapter 18

WEB Service Server.
Interoperability Issues

I n this chapter, we will continue our discussion on creating web services. As a rule, developing the server part is a much more challenging and extensive task, since it is the server that is responsible for implementing all the functionality — the SOAP protocol just brings the results to the user.

Another critical issue to be dealt with in this chapter is interoperability. Here we will examine the Microsoft SOAP Toolkit, which is a tool used for publishing Automation objects as web services. Having created a second client and server pair with similar capabilities, we will be able to cross-connect them and see for ourselves that web services were not thought up by Borland, and that the solutions provided with Delphi 6 really can "talk" to other platforms.

Finally, this chapter covers a handy (and practically the only) tool for debugging web services — the SOAP Trace utility.

Creating a Test Example — the *SimpleEcho* Service

Among the server templates stored in the Object Repository, the first one — SOAP Server Application — is the most important. The other two templates — SOAP Server Data Module and SOAP Server Interface — are just constituent parts of the first one.

So, the very first decision to be made, once you have selected SOAP Server Application, is to choose the type of the server application. At first glance, the task of selecting the most appropriate one from the five possible varieties might appear difficult. In reality, however, it is fairly simple — let's just take it step by step. If you use Apache as the web server, then the Apache Shared Module is your obvious choice. If you work with Microsoft IIS, then the first option — ISAPI DLL — is the most appropriate application type. The CGI and WinCGI applications are executable modules that are launched in individual process, which significantly increases the system overhead; as a rule, they are used only if all other types are for some reason either unavailable or undesirable. And finally, if you want to debug the server part, Borland has included a special utility in Delphi 6 — the WebApp Debugger utility.

The wizard builds the main web module of the application (a data module of the TWebModule class) and then suggests creating an interface for the new web service. The answer to this question depends on what exactly you intend to publish. If you are just trying your hand at SOAP for the first time, answer "yes" without a moment's hesitation, especially since, if the answer is positive, Borland will offer you an interesting and instructive example. As for those readers who feel themselves experienced enough to embark upon developing a real, full-fledged application, by now you should know precisely which interfaces you are going to publish and how this will be done. For further information on the variations of publishing, see below; for now, we will proceed with designing our sample web service.

And so, Fig. 18.1 shows the dialog that allows you to create a new web service. The service name is the ID by which this service will be known to the clients. It stands to reason that the Delphi modules being built should also have the same ID. More specifically, Delphi will create to develop two modules: in our case, they will be called `SampleServiceInft.pas` and `SampleServiceImpl.pas`.

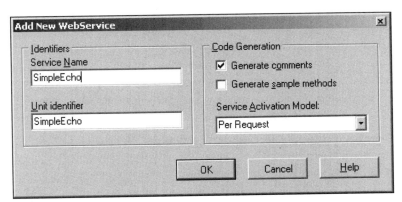

Fig. 18.1. The dialog window that lets you set the parameters
of the web service interface

Why two? The `Intf` (Interface) and `Impl` (Implementation) suffixes suggest the answer. The interface part of the service will be used by both the server and the client (if, of course, this client was written in Delphi — otherwise a WSDL file will suffice). It is because of these considerations that the interface in our example is separated from the code of the object implementing this interface.

NOTE

By all means, a WSDL file would also suffice for clients created in Delphi — how could such clients connect to services provided by other vendors otherwise? But the point is that the WSDL import wizard (see the description of the client part in the previous chapter) will build you an interface file almost identical to the one stored on the server (in our example, it is an analog of `SampleServiceInft.pas`). There is just one difference — a function that returns the RIO instance on the client side.

The **Generate sample methods** checkbox includes the following four methods into the code of the newly generated interface:

```
ISampleService = interface(IInvokable)
['{A5F9E9F3-4781-4465-900D-EC2BE6E17219}']
  { Methods of Invokable interface must not use }
  { the default calling convention; stdcall is recommended }
  function echoEnum(const Value: TEnumTest): TEnumTest; stdcall;
  function echoDoubleArray(const Value: TDoubleArray): TDoubleArray; stdcall;
  function echoMyEmployee(const Value: TMyEmployee): TMyEmployee; stdcall;
  function echoDouble(const Value: Double): Double; stdcall;
end;
```

The echo prefix rings a bell, no? As you probably remember, this is the name of the coresponding communication protocol; indeed, these methods are the same: all four methods send back the received input value as the result. Why four methods and not just one? Because there are four distinct types of parameters that illustrate the features characteristic to transmitting different complex data types. Experience in handling such data will come in handy in the later stages of our discussion.

In the SimpleEcho example service that we are creating, we will limit ourselves to using just two similar methods — `echoString` (which returns the sent string) and `echoStringArray` (which returns the sent array of strings). When it comes down to it, this chapter is not dedicated to the science of computing or, say, operations with a database. You already know how to make an application do those things, or at least you learned how from reading the previous chapters. Here we're going to learn to exchange ready-to-use results using SOAP. And so there's nothing strange in the fact that the codes for the service methods are extremely simple:

```
function TSimpleEcho.echoString(const Value: String): String;
begin
  Result := Value;
end;


function TSimpleEcho.echoStringArray(const Value: TStringDynArray):
TStringDynArray;
begin
  Result := Value;
end;
```

Once the interface is added, you will see your new web module with three components (Fig. 18.2).

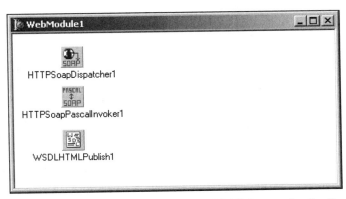

Fig. 18.2. The web module created by the SOAP Server Application wizard

Now, the server in its simplest form is ready for work. Compile your DLL (if you have chosen an ISAPI application) and place it into one of the web server folders. Just remember that the folder must have permission to launch scripts and executable files. If you store the application in the scripts folder automatically created by IIS specifically for these purposes, you should have no problems. If you choose to place the executable modules of the service into a separate folder, make sure that the access rights are properly set.

IMPORTANT NOTE

Recently, many viruses that attack the most vulnerable places in IIS have come to light. After penetrating into servers, they run their code on them and thus infect computers and distribute themselves throughout the net. Both the damages and the speed of their spreading can be enormous. For instance, while this chapter was being written, the debug server was attacked three times. This means that if your server is connected to the Internet and your system administrator has not taken adequate protection measures (or if you don't have a system administrator), be sure to visit the Microsoft security site — HotFix & Security Bulletin Service — at the address **http://www.microsoft.com/technet/treeview/ default.asp?url=/technet/security/current.asp**.

In particular, it is critically important that you install a hot fix, described at **http://www.microsoft.com/technet/treeview/default.asp?url=/technet/security/bulletin/ ms02-018.asp**. Working without one, you are running a grave risk.

Purposes and Options of the Server Part Components

Prior to moving to a discussion of more complex issues, you need to understand the role of these server components.

The TWebModule component, as you know, performs the role of a centralized dispatcher and handler for HTTP requests on the client side. The actions to which it responds are normally included into the Actions property. However, there are exceptions, or more precisely, additions to this rule: so-called auto-dispatching components. They are best understood if you view them as actions that are "external" in relation to the dispatcher. They have the same MethodType and PathInfo properties, which enable the dispatcher to forward an incoming request.

To register auto-dispatching components and the actions associated with them, simply make them child components of some dispatcher. The easiest way to do this is by placing them into TWebModule.

If you do this, the module passes the dispatching actions to two components — THTTPSoapDispatcher and TWSDLHTMLPublish.

In the previous chapter, we looked at two actions typical for services written in Delphi. The first action — /soap — provided direct access to the service interfaces. The second action — /wsdl — allowed you to get the file with the service's definition. Obviously, these actions are what the above components were intended for.

These components (as well as all other auto-dispatching components) all have the WebDispatch property, which specifies the dispatching rules. This property, in turn, is a class with these basic properties:

```
property PathInfo: string;
property MethodType: TMethodType;
property Enabled: Boolean;
```

These properties actually do not have very much practical use. The MethodType value is predefined in the SOAP standard: in order to request WSDL information, use the HTTP GET method, which addresses either a POST or M-POST port. Accordingly, you will see the mtAny value for TWSDLHTMLPublish and the mtPost value for THTTPSoapDispatcher in this property.

The PathInfo property will come in handy if, for some reason, you choose to rename an action. For instance, if you want to rename the part of the URL that is responsible for the path to the service from /soap to /shampoo, you can edit the value of PathInfo.

The *TWSDLHTMLPublish* Component

This long name is easier to understand if you divide it into separate parts: WSDL+HTML+Publish. That's right — it is used for publishing a service description in the easy-to-read HTML format. Providing self-documenting interfaces became a matter of "good manners" with SOAP application developers. If for some reason you don't want to publish the documentation for your service, you can safely remove the TWSDLHTMLPublish instance from the web module — it will not affect the performance of the other parts. However, this implies that you are going to use some custom technique to generate the WSDL file and pass it to your client.

The functionality of this component is fairly simple: it publishes *all* the content of the Invocation registry; this is guaranteed by the mere presence of TWSDLHTMLPublish. That's why you don't have to worry about customizing the component to work with each newly added interface; if these interfaces are correctly registered, they automatically appear in the published documentation.

Once again we remind you that the /wsdl action (in our case **http://localhost/ scripts/simpleecho.dll/wsdl**) outputs a page with interface descriptions (Fig. 18.3).

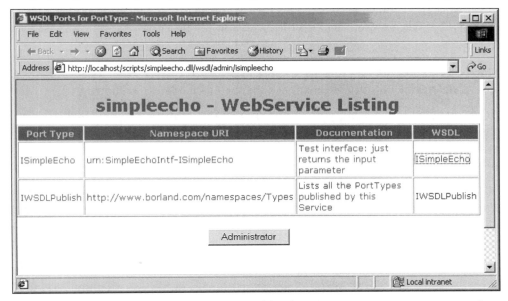

Fig. 18.3. An HTML document generated by the TWSDLHTMLPublish component, which describes the service ports

The code of a web module generated by the wizard also addresses a default action to `TWSDLHTMLPublish` (which is executed if no other characters follow the module name, which is either ISAPI or CGI). This means that in our case, we can access the service description page by simply typing in **http://localhost/scripts/simpleecho.dll**.

What are these columns in the above table? You will find that they resemble the parameters of the `RegisterInterface` method of the `InvokeRegistry` global object. Specifically, in the parameters of this method, you can specify a brief description of the interface (the Doc parameter), having amended the standard registration code (generated by the wizard) to:

```
InvRegistry.RegisterInterface(TypeInfo(ISimpleEcho),
'urn:SimpleEchoIntf-ISimpleEcho', '',
'Test interface: just returns the input parameter');
```

We can see this description in the table in Fig. 18.3.

The component under discussion lets you solve another important task — dynamically customizing the WSDL file. Suppose you were creating and editing your service under debugging conditions, and now you want to move it to a working server from the debugging one. To do this, you'd have to change the port addresses in WSDL — but how can this be done? Just use the property

```
Property AdminEnabled: Boolean;
```

which allows remote editing of WSDL via the browser. If it is set to `True`, the **Administrator** button appears under the list of interfaces, as shown in Fig. 18.3.

Having pressed this button, you end up in a simple port editor (Fig. 18.4). In fact, there is nothing else you can change at this stage: the port types and message format must be standardized in advance. In our case, only the port name and address are variables that can be added, removed, or modified.

In the example in the figure, we added one more port — TestPort — to the list of ports. If you go back and inspect the content of the WSDL document again, you will now see this port there.

How then are the newly entered ports remembered, since, as you may recall, the WSDL document is formed dynamically? Well, the administration parameters are written to a file called `<service name>_wsdladmin.ini`, which is stored in the same folder as the service itself. Every time the description is requested, the `TWSDLHTMLPublish` component views this file and adds the new ports to the document. Having configured them, you can recompile the application and disable the administration option by setting `AdminEnabled` to `False`. The INI file with the edited list of ports will not disappear: it will be shown reflecting the newly customized options.

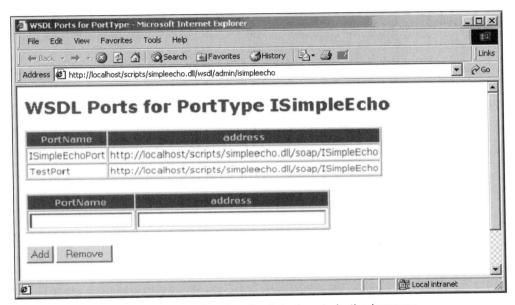

Fig. 18.4. Administering the list of ports in the browser

NOTE

Modules executed on the web server are, as a rule, executed in a system service mode (when there might not be an interactive user that has logged into the system) with the rights of and in the security context of the IUSR_<MACHINENAME> anonymous user. In such a case, there is no HKEY_CURRENT_USER registry subkey (since there is no current user), and access to the HKEY_LOCAL_MACHINE subkey is usually restricted, especially for this anonymous user who is a member of the guests group.

That's why the parameters are written in the INI file.

You should also pay particular attention to this: if your service has any customizable parameters, they will have to be written to the corresponding INI file, and not to the register.

The option with the long name — `poPublishLocationAsSecure` (the `PublishOptions` property) — allows you to insert just one character into the protocol name —

but it is a very important one. Since it is not possible to manually change the description file, the developer must find a way to inform the user of the service that the connection will be implemented in secure mode using SSL. Having set this option to `True`, the addresses of all the ports indicated in the service will have http:// replaced by https://.

The value of another property

```
property TargetNamespace: WideString;
```

is included into the `<definition>` root element of the service's WSDL file, and can serve as a part of the service's description.

The *THTTPSoapDispatcher* and *THTTPSoapPascalInvoker* Components

This pair of components is responsible for translating SOAP packages into calls for the methods of invokable interfaces.

The first component acts as a coordinator. Having received incoming HTTP requests, it caches them, recodes them, and extracts the SOAP envelope, which it subsequently sends to the linked `THTTPSoapPascalInvoker` component. Once a reply is received, the reverse conversion begins.

This component has neither important properties nor newly published events; it is simply the presence of `THTTPSoapDispatcher` in the web module which in itself is significant.

From the developer's viewpoint, `THTTPSoapPascalInvoker`, responsible for calling the methods, is by far more important.

First of all, you can control the process of invoking interface methods by declaring three event handlers:

```
property BeforeDispatchEvent: TBeforeDispatchEvent;
TBeforeDispatchEvent = procedure(const MethodName: string; const
Request: TStream) of object;
property AfterDispatchEvent: TAfterDispatchEvent;
TAfterDispatchEvent = procedure(const MethodName: string;
SOAPResponse: TStream) of object;
property OnExceptionEvent: TOnExceptionEvent;
TOnExceptionEvent = procedure(const MethodName: string; const Request:
TStream; const Response: TStream) of object;
```

And second, Invoker has a number of options (the `Options` property) that determine the compatibility parameters.

The SimpleEcho Service Client

To test our service, we now need a client part. We will use a minimally modified client from the BASE service that we looked at in the previous chapter, since functionally these clients are identical. (Fig. 18.5; the source code is provided on the companion CD.)

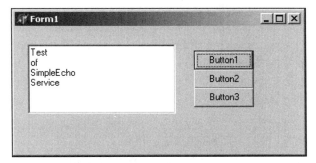

Fig. 18.5. The main window of the SimpleEcho service client

Let's now perform an operation that may not be so obvious. In order to describe the service on the client side, we need a file defining the service interface. We could take the ready-to-use `SimpleEchoIntf.pas` file generated by the SOAP Server Application Wizard and include it into the client project.

Alternatively, we can use a different approach: call the WSDL file import wizard again and create a description of the service interface. Note that the differences between these two approaches are minimal: the second approach provides us with the additional `GetISimpleEcho` function. Since we will need to use this function, we can exclude `SimpleEchoIntf.pas` from the server project, replacing it with the client file, which, for variety's sake, we will name `IntfSimpleEcho.pas`.

Processing Exceptions

If you now have a fairly good understanding of the logic of Invokable objects and interfaces, it will be easy for you to fully appreciate the principles of raising and processing exceptions in web services in Delphi. You just need to always remember that exceptions are just classes, and must be dealt with accordingly.

A class that is to be marshalled through the SOAP protocol must be compiled with RTTI. We have already decided that to do this, the interfaces should be derived from IInvokable, and the Delphi classes should descend from TRemotable. The parent exception class is called ERemotableException. All its descendant exception classes can be passed from the server to the client — if, of course, they have been correctly registered.

Now let's create our exception class. Here are the steps we must follow:

1. Define your custom exception (for our example, we will create EEchoException). The best place to define and register such an exception is the IntfSimpleEcho.pas declaration module; as you probably remember, it is shared by both the client and server projects.

   ```
   EEchoException = class(ERemotableException);
   ```

2. Register the exception by calling the RegisterXSClass method of the RemTypeRegistry global object:

   ```
   RemTypeRegistry.RegisterXSClass( EEchoException );
   ```

   The place for this code is the initialization section of the IntSimpleEcho.pas module.

3. Now both projects will "recognize" this class.

   At the appropriate moment, raise the exception in the server code. In our sample code, we need to modify the code of the echoString method (the SimpleEchoImpl.pas module) as follows:

   ```
   function TSimpleEcho.echoString(const Value: String): String;
   begin
     if AnsiCompareStr( Value, 'Error' ) = 0 then
      begin
       Result := 'Fault';
       raise EEchoException.Create( Value );
      end
     else
      Result := Value;
   end;
   ```

4. Having raised the exception, we pass it to the Delphi runtime library. And when we "catch" EechoException, it does the following:

   • Checks whether the exception is registered in the Remotable classes registry (if not, ERemotableException will be raised)

   • Packs the properties of the exception class into a so-called fault packet (which is sent by the service in response to the client's request if an exception occurs on the server side)

- Having interrupted execution of the current method of the service's interface, sends the packet to the client

5. On the client side, the runtime library checks the service's response. If a fault packet is received, an exception is generated: for registered exceptions, the appropriate (sent) exception class is raised, while for all unknown exceptions, `ERemotableException` is generated. This exception's properties are filled with the content of the fault packet.

6. So, the raised exception has been passed back to us. It is up to the client part developer to adequately process it. The modified code of the **Button2** button's click event handler in client application looks as follows:

```
procedure TForm1.Button2Click(Sender: TObject);
begin
  try
    ShowMessage(
      (HTTPRIO1 as ISimpleEcho).echoString( meMessage.Lines[0] ));
  except
    on E:EEchoException do
      begin
        ShowMessage( 'Must not contain string: ' + E.Message + #13#10
        + E.FaultActor + #13#10 + E.FaultCode + #13#10+ E.FaultDetail );
      end;
  end;
end;
```

Notice the three properties of the caught exception: `FaultActor`, `FaultCode`, and `FaultDetail`. They correspond to three elements of the fault packet, which are standardized in SOAP. Even if your service client was not written in Delphi, it will be able to read the information concerning what occurred. Consider a typical packet sent in such a situation:

```
<?xml version="1.0" ?>
<SOAP-ENV:Envelope xmlns:SOAP-
ENV="http://schemas.xmlsoap.org/soap/envelope/"
xmlns:xsd="http://www.w3.org/2001/XMLSchema"
xmlns:xsi="http://www.w3.org/2001/XMLSchema-instance" xmlns:SOAP-
ENC="http://schemas.xmlsoap.org/soap/encoding/">
  <SOAP-ENV:Body>
   <SOAP-ENV:Fault>
    <SOAP-ENV:faultcode>SOAP-ENV:Server</SOAP-ENV:faultcode>
```

```
<SOAP-ENV:faultstring>Error</SOAP-ENV:faultstring>
<NS1:detail xmlns:NS1="urn:intfsimpleecho"
xsi:type="NS1:EEchoException" />
</SOAP-ENV:Fault>
</SOAP-ENV:Body>
</SOAP-ENV:Envelope>
```

You can redefine the values of the properties when generating an exception; moreover, you are not limited to using just these three standard properties. The properties that you have added (to the exception class derived from `ERemotableException`) will also be packed and passed to the client.

Besides your custom exceptions, you should provide for the processing of `ESOAPDomConvertError`. This exception is raised within `TOPToSoapDomConvert` components (which are present in other components on both the server and the client side). Any serialization problem — i.e., SOAP packets being displayed at function calls and back — will cause it to occur. And so you can expect this exception any time there is a deviation from the SOAP standard — which, alas, is a common occurrence.

Some Comments on Using *TSOAPConnection*

There is only one component we have not yet covered in our discussion. It is the seventh component from the **WebServices** page of the Component palette — `TSOAPConnection`. This component belongs to the next hierarchy level. While all the components we mentioned before implement connections using SOAP, this one utilizes a ready-to-use SOAP implementation for transmitting DataSnap packets.

Borland engineers have confirmed the following critical deficiencies of the current `TSOAPConnection` implementation (http://groups.google.com/groups?q= TSOAPConnection+group:borland.public.delphi.webservices.soap&hl=ru&lr=&ie= UTF-8&inlang= ru&selm=3c6dabdb%241_1%40dnews&rnum=1):

1. In this case it is `IAppServer` that is an invokable interface. If you have derived a child from `IappServer` and added custom methods to this new interface, these methods cannot be invoked, because `TSOAPConnection` always calls `IappServer`, not its descendants.

2. If the server application contains more than one data module (and thus more than one class supporting `IAppServer`), there is no guarantee that `TSOAPConnection` will establish a connection with the correct data module; for the reason explained in the first item, this component cannot differentiate between these modules.

All of the above considerations lead to an obvious conclusion: as it is, the TSOAPConnection component cannot currently serve as a solution for actual applications. Besides which, we already have the TWebConnection component, which has the real advantage of being able to work on top of HTTP with high speed and reliability. However, all these faults will no doubt be addressed in the next update pack, and SOAP, in tandem with DataSnap, will yet be of help to developers that design distributed applications.

SOAP Development Tools: The Microsoft Approach

It would be quite strange to write a book devoted to the state-of-the-art solutions for providing cross-platform interoperability for applications and discuss just a single tool released by one company that can operate on just one platform. On the other hand, a comprehensive analysis of all the available software solutions, understandably, falls beyond the scope of a single book. Therefore, we will restrict ourselves to examining one more facility for dealing with services and, by studying the way these two alternative solutions interact with each other, we will be able to feel out and estimate the scope of feasible tasks and the various interoperability problems. This instrument is Microsoft SOAP Toolkit.

Microsoft was one of the first vendors to provide a development suite for SOAP. SOAP Toolkit version 1.0 was the first to appear, which used the currently out-of-date SDL language for defining requests. Originally, it was intended to test the new technology, preparing the ground for the .NET architecture. As it happened, it failed to become a full-fledged product. The next version — 2.0 — already used the standard WSDL language and has been significantly enhanced in terms of performance and user convenience. Lastly, the most recent version — beta version 3.0 — was released. It added a number of essential improvements and functional extensions.

Also, when discussing web services, we cannot but mention .NET, which is a principally new Microsoft architecture concept. For the most part, it is founded on the idea of web services. However, if we were to make it a goal for ourselves to conduct an in-depth discussion of .NET and the Visual Studio .NET development tool, this chapter and this book would become many times thicker. Borland prototype software containing new development tools for .NET have already been made public, and therefore we consider it unnecessary to provide a detailed description of .NET in this book devoted to Delphi 6.

So why did we choose MS SOAP Toolkit as an example of an alternative approach to working with SOAP and web services? To begin with, the SOAP Toolkit is freeware, which is nevertheless fully supported by Microsoft. Second, this toolkit can be used on almost every current Windows platform with only minor limitations, and does not have any specific requirements for installation. Third, it is closely associated with the COM paradigm, which can only be a plus for our readers. And finally, in its architecture, it is very similar to the approach implemented in Delphi 6.

In order to work with the toolkit's client part, we will need to consider a short script written in VBScript. We are sure that these scripts will not be particularly difficult to understand, even for those developers who are not familiar with the language. An instrument for interpreting such scripts — either the `cscript` or `wscript` utility — can be found on almost any Windows-based computer.

Brief Overview of Web Service Architecture with the SOAP Toolkit

Before starting the development process with the SOAP Toolkit, let's take a general look at the basic principles of its operation and the dataflow on the server and client side.

❑ The services proper, which provide the users with their interfaces, are COM objects. With Delphi 6, an object shown as a service must support interfaces descending from `IInvokable`. In the SOAP Toolkit, it is required that such an object support `IDispatch`, i.e., it must be an Automation object. Normally, this is an in-process server (a dynamic link library). Using **EXE** servers is also permissible.

The toolkit includes the WSDL Generator utility, which builds a file describing the service for an Automation object. You can choose any object from those registered on your computer and get the required description. Non-standard data types may become a problem here; for those interfaces whose methods are used for exchanging objects and/or structures, you need to take certain additional measures.

The specific feature of MS SOAP Toolkit is generating two files simultaneously — WSDL and WSML — rather than just a single WSDL file. The first file is a traditional description file organized in conformity with the WSDL 1.1 specification, but the purpose of the second file (its name is an abbreviation for Web

Services Meta Language) is very specific. It performs the same role as the Invo-cation registry for web services written with Delphi. This file maps a service port to a real COM object (indicated by its ProgID), while the port operations are mapped to calls for the object's methods:

```
servicemapping name='SimpleEcho'>
 <service name='SimpleEcho'>
 <using PROGID='SimpleEchoCOM.SimpleEcho'
 cachable='0' ID='SimpleEchoObject' />
 <port name='SimpleEchoSoapPort'>
   <operation name='echoStringArray'>
     <execute uses='SimpleEchoObject' method='echoStringArray' dispID='2'>
       <parameter callIndex='1' name='Value' elementName='Value' />
       <parameter callIndex='-1' name='retval' elementName='Result' />
     </execute>
   </operation>
     . . .
 </port>
 </service>
</servicemapping>
```

1. Special extension modules of the web server, called "listeners", are responsible for calling COM object. The toolkit contains two modules of this kind: the ISAPI extension and the ASP file. Having received a SOAP request from the web server, they interpret the WSDL and WSML files, and create an instance of a special `SOAPServer` object (or `SOAPServer30` in version 3.0). The function of this object is identical to that of `TSoapPascalInvoker`: it invokes the methods of the requested COM object.

The advantages of the first listener are the deficiencies of the second, and vice versa. The ISAPI listener is much faster; it caches all object instances being created. But at the same time, it does not support any customization on the server side.

An ASP listener is created in the form of a source file in a script language. Of course, the language being interpreted — irrespective of all optimization — cannot compete with the ISAPI dynamic library code in terms of performance. But on the other hand, you can see all the source code is right there in front of you, and you can, if you want, insert a fragment into it. This might be a section for extra checking and converting of procedures for parameters, initialization of variables and objects, a session management mechanism, etc.

Moreover, an ASP listener might not call any external objects. SOAP Toolkit users are provided with two APIs: one higher-level, and one lower-level. The second API lets the developer parse SOAP requests and generate responses; thus, all necessary service code can be written in a script language and be located directly in the ASP file.

A typical address of a port used in MS SOAP Toolkit might appear rather out of the ordinary:

```
<definitions>
...
<service name='SimpleEcho' >
 <port name='SimpleEchoSoapPort' binding='wsdlns:SimpleEchoSoapBinding' >
    <soap:address location='http://localhost/scripts/SimpleEcho.wsdl' />
 </port>
</service>
...
</definitions>
```

As we can see, the port address in WSDL points directly to the WSDL file, which as you may well have guessed, does not (and cannot) contain any executable code. You see, such files are stored in specially created IIS web folders. For these folders, the listener is registered as the tool to be invoked when the WSDL documents contained in this folder are requested. The ISAPI listener can be located elsewhere — outside the folder, or even outside the published IIS tree (usually C:\InetPub); this facilitates customization and helps in solving security problems.

Now let's once again stress the difference between two approaches above. With Delphi, each service is a separate extension module for the web server (either ISAPI or CGI). All the functional "stuffing" can be stored in this module. SOAP Toolkit uses one common extension module — a listener. This listener invokes methods of various COM objects, and they provide the service's functionality.

❒ The client side is very similar to the one we discussed in Delphi. The role of THTTPRIO here is performed by the SOAPClient (SOAPClient30) object. As soon as it is created, it should be initialized in order to make it emulate the service port:

```
Call soapclient.mssoapinit( _
    "http://localhost/scripts/SimpleEcho.dll/wsdl/ISimpleEcho", _
    "ISimpleEchoservice",_
  "ISimpleEchoPort")
```

Once the `mssoapinit` method is invoked and successfully completed, the `SOAPClient` object is ready to work: you can call port operations (which are actually methods of the source COM object on the server side) as custom `SOAPClient` methods.

The Client Part Script

For starters, let's create a simple client to connect to our sample SimpleEcho service. To do this, we will use the Microsoft SOAP Toolkit version 2. At the writing of this book, version 3 was still just a beta release, while version 2 had already had its second service pack released. Besides which, version 3 includes Microsoft XML parser version 4, which requires that certain modifications be introduced into the Delphi library modules in order for it to work (which we discussed in the previous chapter). You can download Microsoft SOAP Toolkit 2.0 SP2 at **http://msdn.microsoft.com/downloads/default.asp?URL=/code/sample.asp?url=/msdn-files/027/001/580/msdncompositedoc.xml**.

The system requirements are fairly simple: for server objects, it is either Windows NT 4.0 Service Pack 6, Windows 2000, or XP; and correspondingly, IIS 4, 5.0, or 5.1. For the client, you can use any Windows version higher than Windows 95, and Internet Explorer 5 or higher.

The only annoying limitation is that the WSDL Generator utility (wsdlgen.exe) requires that the Microsoft Visual Studio 6 development environment be available on your computer. However, this obstacle can be overcome if you use an analogous utility that works in command line mode instead — wsdlstb.exe.

The client code contains a little more that twenty lines. Create the SimpleEchoCli.vbs file and insert the code from Listing 18.1 into it (this file is, by the way, provided on the companion CD).

Listing 18.1. The SimpleEcho Service Client Code Generated with the SOAP Toolkit (in VBScript)

```
Sub CallEcho( ByVal Text )
Dim soapclient

set soapclient = CreateObject("MSSOAP.SoapClient")
```

```
On Error Resume Next

Call soapclient.mssoapinit( _
    "http://localhost/scripts/SimpleEcho.dll/wsdl/ISimpleEcho", _
    "ISimpleEchoservice",_
    "ISimpleEchoPort")
if err <> 0 then
  wscript.echo "Initialization failed " + err.description
  Exit Sub
end if


wscript.echo  soapclient.echoString( Text )
if err <> 0 then
  WScript.echo   err.description
  WScript.echo   "faultcode=" + soapclient.faultcode
  WScript.echo   "faultstring=" + soapclient.faultstring
  WScript.echo   "faultactor=" + soapclient.faultactor
  WScript.echo   "detail=" + soapclient.detail
end if
End Sub
rem -------------------------------------------------------
Dim Text
If WScript.Arguments.Count<1 Then
 Text = "Hello, World!"
Else
 Text = WScript.Arguments(0)
End If
Call CallEcho( Text )
```

The SOAPClient object is initialized inside the CallEcho procedure. This object is configured using the WSDL that was generated by our Delphi server of the SimpleEcho service (http://localhost/scripts/SimpleEcho.dll/wsdl/IsimpleEcho). In the following parameters — the service and port names — make sure that the proper case is used; unlike Delphi, this script is case-sensitive.

If the initialization has been successfully completed, the script calls the echoString method with the text passed to the procedure. This text is either a command line parameter of the script (if it was specified) or the traditional "Hello, World!".

If you get a fault (which, as you may remember, takes place if the input line contains the text 'Error'), the details on the occurrence — faultcode, faultstring, faultactor, and detail — will be shown to the user.

> **NOTE**
>
> Calling the `echoStringArray` method requires manual correction of the WSDL, since VBScript uses a highly specific mechanism for processing arrays. Make sure you are aware of this interoperability problem; for more information on it, refer to the documentation of the MS SOAP Toolkit.

You can launch the script using either the `wscript` (which outputs messages as standard Windows dialog boxes) or the `cscript` utility (which displays messages in the standard output file which, as a rule, is the window of the current session of the command interpreter).

Creating the *SimpleEchoCOM* COM Object and Publishing a Web Service Based on It

Now let's begin working on the server part of the service. The first thing we will need is the Automation object, whose interface will be called by a SOAP Toolkit listener.

As you may have read in the previous chapter, there is not an actual COM object behind the interfaces of Delphi web services. Thus we have to create the Automation object from scratch:

1. In the Delphi Object Repository (the **File\New\Others** menu), choose a new project of the **ActiveX Library** type and save it under the name of SimpleEchoCOM in the COMServer folder. This in-process server will hold the new object. (If you consider this step and the following ones to be unnecessary for your education, you can find a ready-to-use server in the set of examples on the CD included with the book.)

2. Again going into the Repository, select **New Automation Object**. Name it `SimpleEcho`, and then the `ISimpleEcho`, generated from `IDispatch`, will be added to the library. Save the file for the object implementation as SimpleEchoCOMImpl.pas (so as not to confuse it with SimpleEchoImpl.pas).

3. Add two methods of the `ISimpleEcho` interface to the type library, as shown in Fig. 18.6.

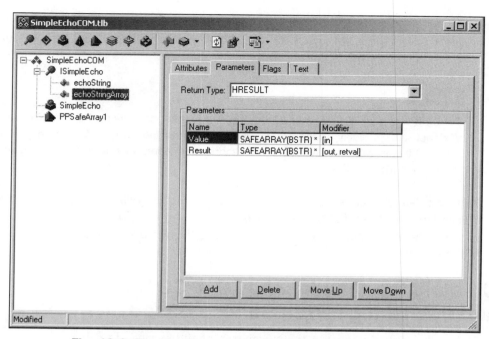

Fig. 18.6. The type library of the SimpleEchoCOM project

The string array that is sent to the echoStringArray method should have the SAFEARRAY(BSTR) * type. (We can't use the TStringDynArray class, since Delphi dynamic arrays are not supported in Automation; the closest analog is the SAFEARRAY type).

4. Add the code of the echoString and echoStringArray methods; they are very simple:

```
function TSimpleEcho.echoString(const Value: WideString): WideString;
begin
  Result := Value;
end;
function TSimpleEcho.echoStringArray(var Value: PSafeArray): PSafeArray;
begin
  SafeArrayCopy( Value, Result );
end;
```

5. Compile, save, and register (in the **Run\Register ActiveX Server** menu) the created object.

Now we can move on to creating and publishing the WSDL file for the new service, or rather, the old service with a new face.

If you don't have Microsoft Visual Studio installed, launch the wsdlstb.exe utility, and indicate in the command line the path to the COM object, the location of the ASP listener, and the folder where you want to put the WSDL and WSML files that you create. We'll put them in the scripts folder, where we already have the simpleecho.dll file. If you want to use the ISAPI listener (which makes more sense in this situation), in the generated file, you'll have to change the value of the `location` attribute of the service's port to http://localhost/scripts/ SimpleEcho.wsdl.

While the utility is running, you will be asked to enter the name of the interface (which we only have one of — `ISimpleEcho`) as well as the names of the methods that should be included in the description (include them both).

The generated file looks very much like the one written in Delphi that is given by the server. There is a difference, however, in the names of the service and the port (`SimpleEcho` is used in place of `ISimpleEchoservice`, and `SimpleEchoSoapPort` in place of `ISimpleechoPort`). Accordingly, you will have to make a few corrections in the WSDL and rename the old values. You can go another route, if you want, and change the connection parameters of both the Delphi client and the VBScript client.

Now we have two different servers and two clients at our disposal. This is more than enough to conduct at least a few experiments to check their interoperability. The example that we give you here, whose entire source code can be found on the appended CD, is fully interoperable, with one exception: the VBScript client does not support calling the `echoStringArray` method.

The main interoperability problems generally arise from the fact that the data types do not correspond. This is why it makes sense to go back to the BASE service (see *Chapter 17*), which, as you probably remember, is an "echo" of not two, but fourteen types of data. Issues of interoperability are sure to arise here. And when they do, there is another utility from the MS SOAP Toolkit, intended for debugging services, to which we can look for help.

Using the SOAP Trace Utility

Yet another reason for covering the MS SOAP Toolkit in this book is the fact that it contains the extremely useful SOAP Trace utility (MSSOAPT.EXE). It intercepts the HTTP traffic and writes it to a log. But as opposed to similar utilities, it not only has the ability to intercept HTTP requests and responses, but can also decode SOAP packets. By doing this, you can easily see what exactly you sent to the server and how the response looks in the original.

It's hard to overestimate the usefulness of SOAP Trace. While technology and web service standards are still being actively developed, a little roughness is inevitable. Looking at the SOAP messages will help to localize the problem.

Technically, the interception of traffic is a very simple process. The utility plays the role of a fake server. The WSDL files are modified to indicate the address of the host and port on which the utility "listens to" the exiting traffic. After receiving and logging the package, SOAP Trace forwards it to the "real" server.

The window for setting the interception parameters is shown in Fig. 18.7.

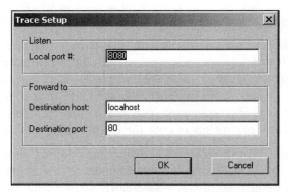

Fig. 18.7. Setting the parameters of the SOAP Trace utility

You can use SOAP Trace on both the client and the server side.

To use it on the server side, you just need to change the number of the port from 80 (the default HTTP port) to 8080 in the WSDL file, for example http://soap.myservices.com/scripts/.. to http://soap.myservices.com:8080/scripts/.

NOTE

Of course, you'll first have to check to see whether port 8080 is open, and if it's not, choose one of the available unused ports.

In this case, if you launch the utility with the parameters shown in Fig. 18.7, you don't have to change anything at all. The packets will be re-addressed from localhost:8080 to localhost:80, and this is exactly what we want to happen.

Launching SOAP Trace on the client side involves just a little bit more work. First, you need to modify WSDL so that it points to localhost:8080. In our example, this means changing http://soap.myservices.com/scripts/ to http://localhost:8080/scripts/.

Second, when entering the utility's parameters in the **Destination host** field, you need to give the true address of the server — soap.myservices.com. In this case, utility will readdress packets from localhost 8080 to soap.myservices.com.80. Note that you should only change the addresses of the host and the port; the rest of the URL stays the same.

The utility has two modes — one giving a formatted output (in XML, in compliance with SOAP rules) and one giving an unformatted output. The first mode is shown in Fig. 18.8. We hope you'll be able to easily recognize the client package calling the `echoString` method with the "test" parameter, as well as the corresponding sever response, in the figure below.

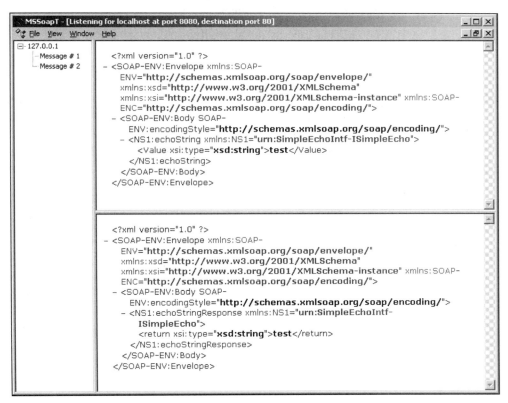

Fig. 18.8. The SOAP Trace utility using formatted output

The second mode is a dump of the HTTP request and the server response. It might be necessary if the client or server does not properly format the output and it can not be presented in the form of a proper XML document.

Summary

We have now finished looking at the functioning principles of web services and the tools for creating and debugging them. You should now be familiar with:

❑ The standards on which the world of web services is based

❑ Invokable interfaces and registering them

❑ The THTTPRio component and the principles used for configuring the client to the necessary service

❑ Creating server applications for web services

❑ The MS SOAP Toolkit package as an alternative means of creating and using services

❑ Tools for debugging used with the SOAP protocol — the SOAP Trace utility

Obviously, web services are not the only technology from Borland that provides a connection for and the stability of distributed applications. We covered other options in previous chapters, and will continue to cover them in the coming ones. However, web services alone promise to become a universal means for connecting discordant platforms into a united entity. This is why we recommend that you give them your steadfast attention.

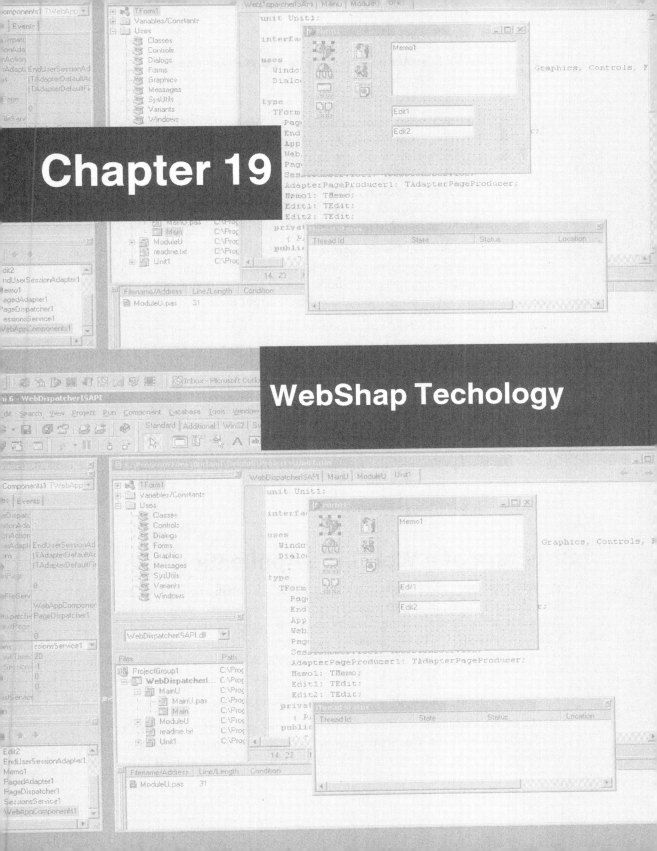

Chapter 19

WebShap Techology

M ost distributed applications include parts that are accessed via the Internet. Understandably, such applications exploit the capabilities of various web technologies in order to represent data and interact with users. Delphi provides distributed applications with this kind of functionality by integrating *WebSnap* technology. This technology is, in fact, an advanced and significantly extended version of another Delphi technology for handling web applications — WebBroker — which was used in earlier Delphi versions.

WebSnap applications use web pages on the basis of HTML or XML templates, thereby enabling the developer to considerably modify the functionality of the application without recompiling the source code. This feature may be vital for systems that are meant to serve thousands of concurrent users.

This chapter covers the following problems:

❑ The composition of a WebSnap application and the techniques for using standard WebSnap wizards

❑ The intended purposes of data modules and page modules

❑ The role of the TAdapter component

❑ Dispatching client requests

❑ Approaches to designing the interface and business logic for a WebSnap application

❑ The principles of using templates

Structure of a WebSnap Application

A WebSnap application needs to provide for the processing of requests sent by clients. Strictly speaking, all requests are received by the web server, which in turn passes them to the application for processing. By utilizing the functionality of specific components (to be discussed in more depth later), the application forwards the requests to its business logic repositories, which are implemented in the form of data modules and HTML or XML page modules.

Thus, a WebSnap application consists of two essential parts.

The first part manages the flows of requests and responses. This functionality is implemented by those WebSnap components that can process requests and return responses to the web server and, in addition, support of HTML pages, i.e., execute HTML tags and VBScript or JScript scripts, as well as dynamic page generation based on HTML and XML templates.

The second part of a WebSnap application is composed of web modules responsible for building the user interface, implementing access to data sources, and storing the business logic of the application.

Let us now take a closer look at each of these constituent parts.

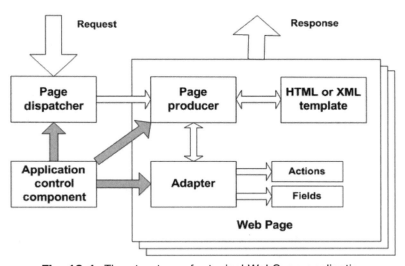

Fig. 19.1. The structure of a typical WebSnap application

To begin with, a request is received by the TPageDispatcher *dispatcher component*, which is "aware" of the functional purpose of each *page* of the application and, as a result of this knowledge, can forward the request to the appropriate pages for processing and response generation. The page module, in turn, ensures that the page adequately responds to the request.

In the design stage, each application page is supplied with its individual *template*. This is the template that will be available for editing in the development environment. This template is created either in HTML or in XML. If need be, the developer can implement more complicated functions by including VBScript or Jscript scripts.

While running, the request is passed to the *producer component* that is associated with this page. This component enables the generation of a page on the basis of the existing template.

> **NOTE**
>
> Various producer components can be found on the **Internet** page of the Delphi Component Palette.

If a template contains a script, its execution is provided by *adapter components*. Depending on the task to be solved, the developer can utilize several types of producer components that are stored in the **WebSnap** page of the Component palette. The TAdapterDispatcher component is used for coordinating the request flow so that each request can be forwarded to the appropriate adapter.

> **NOTE**
>
> Script compilation is done automatically by the special Script Engine processor.

And finally, the TWebAppComponents component coordinates the collective performance of all the above components. In addition, it is responsible for implementing the top-level business logic. TWebAppComponents links all parts of a WebSnap application into a single "technological chain," and the developer is able to change the links in this chain (that is to say, the above components) as he or she chooses, in order to meet the needs of the application's business logic. This is done by manipulating those properties of the component that reference the corresponding adapter and dispatcher components.

Processing Requests

Now, let's trace the path traveled by a request within the WebSnap application framework.

First, the request is passed to the page dispatcher that decides which web page will process it. For example, if the user has pressed a button on the main page, the request will be forwarded to the main-page module.

Here the request is processed by the appropriate producer component, which changes the page. If the user triggers any kind of complicated operation associated with a script by pressing a button, the request will be relayed to the adapter dispatcher component for processing. This component will then forward the request to the relevant adapter component. For instance, this can be the dataset adapter (the TDataSetAdapter component), which will implement access to the database in order to retrieve the dataset records.

Web Modules

As viewed by the developer, a WebSnap application is essentially a combination of specialized modules that can be used as containers for the necessary components. All these web modules are subdivided into two categories: page modules and data modules.

HTML page modules implement the user interface for the application. They perform two functions:

❐ Contain the producer component that dynamically generates the page on the basis of the HTML or XML template

❐ Contain the page template

Data modules are simply platforms for placing various non-visual components, and, in this sense, are similar to the data modules used in database applications (see *Chapter 5, "The Architecture of Database Applications"*).

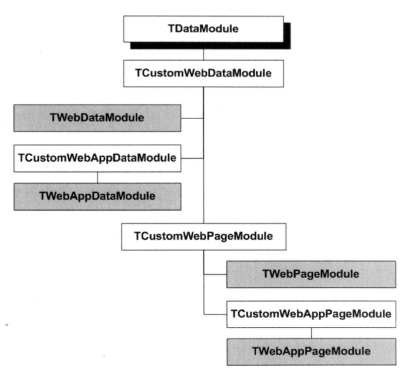

Fig. 19.2. The hierarchy of web module classes

In addition, web modules can also be *application modules*. In a WebSnap application, such modules perform the role of repositories for the components, and implement the most essential functions for the entire application. An application can only have one web module of this kind. Both a page module and a data module can act as an application module.

All web modules descend from the `TDataModule` class.

Data Modules

In a WebSnap application, a data module (like a traditional data module) serves as a platform for placing all types of non-visual components. This module can contain both WebSnap application controls and, for example, data access components.

The functionality of a data module is encapsulated by the `TWebDataModule` class, which not only implements a container for storing various non-visual components, but also manages requests. To process requests, this class is provided with two properties.

The property

```
property Request: TWebRequest;
```

represents the request sent to the WebSnap application. Using this property, the developer can access numerous request properties.

The property

```
property Response: TWebResponse;
```

represents a reference to the instance of the `TWebResponse` class. The properties and methods of this class let the developer customize and send a response to the web client.

Also, the data module can be utilized for managing the client access session. To this end, you need to use the property

```
property Session: TAbstractWebSession;
```

while the `TAbstractWebSession` class allows for the implementation of methods for setting the session timeout

```
property TimeoutMinutes: Integer;
```

and the termination time

```
procedure Terminate;
```

for its descendants.

Page Modules

A page module performs the task of building a single web page for the WebSnap application. In addition to the traditional files typically contained in any Delphi form, a page module also includes either an HTML template file (an HTML file) or an XML template file (XML file) that stores a description of the page in the corresponding format. Such templates can contain both standard language commands and fragments of VBScript or JScript scripts.

The Delphi Code Editor enables the display of these included files (Fig. 19.3). Note that a set of extra tabs in the bottom left part of the window not only allows you to view and edit the HTML template associated with this page (the **HTML Result** tab), but also, without compiling the entire application, lets you get an idea of what this page will look like at run time (the **Preview** tab). This function lets you quickly and easily create and optimize the user interface for the page.

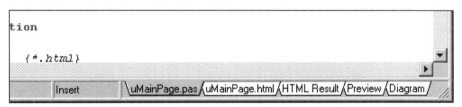

Fig. 19.3. A page module in the Delphi Code Editor window

The `TWebPageModule` class encapsulates the functionality of the Web page.

Every page module must contain the `TPageProducer` component. This component is absolutely essential, since it generates the page from the template at run time. `TPageProducer` is associated with the page module by the module property

```
property PageProducer: IProduceContent;
```

which must point to the producer component. Typically, any application page can perform various complex operations that can be implemented by different producer components. For instance, it can be the traditional `TPageProducer` component together with the `TDataSetPageProducer` component that implements access to the dataset of some database. In any event, the developer is able to redefine the `PageProducer` property of the page module dynamically, at run time.

The property

```
property DefaultAction: TAdapterActionName;
```

enables you to associate the page module with one of the adapter components, which can be manually imported to the module from the Component palette. The `TAdapterActionName` class allows you to specify a default adapter component together with its functions.

In addition to its unique properties, the page-module class also has regular properties typical of every web module: it also manages client requests. This is why the Web request and response properties are also available in this module:

```
property Request: TWebRequest;
property Response: TWebResponse;
```

In addition, the page module lets you manage client sessions by employing the property

```
property Session: TAbstractWebSession;
```

For a more detailed discussion of these properties, see the previous "*Data Modules*" section.

Application Modules

The basic functionality of a WebSnap application is implemented by its application module. This module must contain the components that encapsulate the functionalities of general application management and those that allow for processing requests.

A WebSnap application can only have just one application module, though the role of this module can be taken on by both a data module and a page module. The functionality of the application module is implemented by two classes.

The `TWebAppPageModule` class is an application page module. It is used if the application requires a main page in order to provide more efficient general management.

The `TWebAppDataModule` class is an application data module. It is not used in the user interface, and therefore is not available at run time.

Every application module inherits the properties and methods of the corresponding class of traditional page or data module (see Fig. 19.2). Consequently, it has all their capabilities that relate to processing requests and performing various operations.

In addition, the application module possesses the property

```
property AppServices: TComponent;
```

which must point to the TWebAppComponents component. This component is added automatically when the application module is being built in order to coordinate the performance of the other components.

Beside the TWebAppComponents component, every newly created application module is, by default, supplied with page dispatcher and adapter components.

> **NOTE**
>
> When it is being built, the application module, which is represented by a web page module, is automatically supplied with the TPageProducer component, just like any traditional page module.

Application Level Components

Beside specific WebSnap components, a WebSnap application can also use a number of extra components that implement various application level functions rather than operations related to processing individual requests and pages. It is these components that link all page and data modules together with their auxiliary components into a single consistent system.

In WebSnap technology, the functions performed by application-level components are as follows:

❐ Managing the process of the interaction of WebSnap components with each other and with client requests

❐ Storing all general information about the entire application

❐ Providing for the smooth performance of the application in multi-user mode and maintaining user lists

❐ Tracing interactions between the application and data files

Managing Application Components

The TWebAppComponents component is used to join all functional parts of a WebSnap application together into a single structure. It has a number of properties that point to certain other components necessary to the application. The developer can modify the application's functionality by simply replacing certain components at run time.

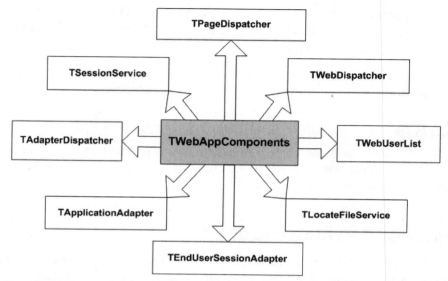

Fig. 19.4. The TWebAppComponents component coordinates interactions among various components of a WebSnap application

The TWebAppComponents component resides in the application module.

NOTE

When you import the first instances of the WebSnap components listed below, the properties of these first instances are automatically linked to the corresponding properties of the TWebAppComponents component.

The property

```
property AdapterDispatcher: IAdapterDispatcher;
```

specifies the TAdapterDispatcher component used in the application.

The property

```
property ApplicationAdapter: IWebApplicationInfo;
```

points to the TApplicationAdapter component that contains the parameters common to the entire application.

The property

```
property PageDispatcher: IPageDispatcher;
```

indicates the `TPageDispatcher` component that will manage requests and forward them to web pages for processing.

The property

```
property LocateFileService: ILocateFileService;
```

references the `TLocateFileService` component that provides the developer with event handler methods used for handling application files. These can include data, script, or page template files. When the application calls a file, the appropriate handler methods are invoked.

The property

```
property Sessions: ISessionsService;
```

specifies the reference to the `TSessionsService` component. This component handles application sessions in multi-user mode.

All application users, along with their passwords, can be listed in the `TWebUserList` component. And the property

```
property UserListService: IWebUserList;
```

lets the developer activate this list for the application to use it.

The parameters of the current application user are stored in the `TWebEndUser` component, and the component itself is linked to the application through the property

```
property EndUserAdapter: IWebEndUser;
```

Finally, the property

```
property DispatchActions: IWebDispatchActions;
```

associates the application with the `TWebDispatcher` component. As you probably remember, this component implements the processing of web requests passed to the application by a traditional data module. To this end, this component must encapsulate a list of specific actions.

Should any application level exception occur, the `TWebAppComponents` component handles this event, while the developer can use the handler method

```
type
    TWebExceptionEvent = procedure (Sender: TObject; E: Exception;
    var Handled: Boolean) of object;
property OnException: TwebExceptionEvent;
```

The Application Adapter and the Application Global Variable

A WebSnap application can use its own set of actions that are not associated with any of the adapter components of the page or data modules. This task is performed by the `TApplicationAdapter` component located in the application module.

Similar to any other adapter component, `TApplicationAdapter` has the property

```
property Actions: TAdapterDefaultActions;
```

for storing a collection of actions, and the property

```
property Data: TAdapterDefaultFields;
```

for representing a set of fields.

The difference, however, lies in the fact that the fields and actions of this component are available from every script of the application thanks to the functionality of the `Application` global variable. For example, when you are developing a new page module for the application, the line

```
<h1><%= Application.Title %></h1>
```

is automatically added to its HTML file, which, at run time, will display the general title of the application on every page.

In this example, we use the `Title` field. This field is generated for the component by default and shows the value of the published property

```
property ApplicationTitle: string;
```

of the component. At a later stage, you will be able to create fields of your own in order to use them on all pages of your application.

User Information

A WebSnap application can save and use information about its clients. This task is implemented by a number of specific components.

A full list of potential users is built by the `TWebUserList` component. This component has the property

```
property UserItems: TWebUserItems;
```

which stores an indexed list of `TWebUserItem` objects. Each element in this list corresponds to a single user.

The `TWebUserItem` class allows the developer to set three properties for the user. Two properties indicate the user name and password:

```
property UserName: string;
property Password: string;
```

The third property

```
property AccessRights: string;
```

contains a list of the access rights granted to the user. The names of the rights must be delimited by commas, semicolons, or spaces.

If the `TWebUserList` component is linked to the `TWebAppComponents` component (as discussed above), its event handler methods are automatically called when a new user logs on. All these event handler methods use the `UserID` parameter for user identification. This parameter is set automatically for every user.

> ### WARNING
>
> The `TWebUserList` component event handler methods do not let you influence the outcome of the process of user authorization; they are used only to program certain extra operations. The process of authorization will be examined later in this chapter.

Prior to and following user authorization, the following handler methods are invoked:

```
type
   TValidateUserHandledEvent = procedure(Strings: TStrings;
   var UserID: Variant; var Handled: Boolean) of object;
property OnBeforeValidateUser: TValidateUserHandledEvent;
```

and

```
type
   TValidateUserEvent = procedure(Strings: TStrings;  var UserID:
Variant) of object;
property OnAfterValidateUser: TValidateUserEvent;
```

When the user's access rights are being checked, the following pair of methods is called:

```
type
   TCheckAccessRightsHandledEvent = procedure(UserID: Variant;
   Rights:  string; var HasRight: Boolean; var Handled: Boolean) of object;
property OnBeforeCheckAccessRights: TCheckAccessRightsHandledEvent;
```

and

```
type
 TCheckAccessRightsEvent = procedure(UserID: Variant; Rights: string;
 var HasRight: Boolean) of object;

property OnAfterCheckAccessRights: TCheckAccessRightsEvent;
```

If the user name is not found in the list, the following handler method is called:

```
property OnUserIDNotFound: TCheckAccessRightsHandledEvent;
```

And if either an invalid user name or password has been entered, this handler method is called:

```
type
 TValidateUserErrorEvent = procedure(Error: TValidateUserError;
 Strings: TStrings; var UserID: Variant; var Handled: Boolean)
 of object;
property OnValidateUserError: TValidateUserErrorEvent;
```

Note that here you are able to specify the reaction of your application to the error using the TValidateUserError parameter:

```
TValidateUserError = (vuBlankPassword, vuBlankUserName,
vuUnknownUserName, vuUnknownPassword);
```

For example, in the simplest case, it can be done as follows:

```
procedure TSomePage.WebUserList1ValidateUserError(Error:
TValidateUserError; Strings: TStrings; var UserID: Variant;
var Handled: Boolean);
begin
 case Error of
  vuBlankPassword:    ShowMessage('Blank Password');
  vuBlankUserName:    ShowMessage('Blank User Name');
  vuUnknownPassword: ShowMessage('Wrong Password');
  vuUnknownUserName: ShowMessage('Wrong UserName');
 end;
end;
```

At run time, information about the current user is contained in the TEndUserAdapter component. For the scripts included in the application pages, this component provides the EndUser global variable.

Like any other adapter, the TEndUserAdapter component contains indexed lists of actions and fields in its standard properties:

```
property Actions: TAdapterDefaultActions;
```

and

```
property Data: TAdapterDefaultFields;
```

As a consequence, the developer is able to specify all necessary actions and variables for the current user. In addition, the component contains two predefined actions and two fields. By including them in the scripts of the pages, you can control the user's access to application resources.

The `LoginForm` action lets the developer handle the login page. This page is displayed by calling the method:

```
EndUser.LoginForm.Enabled
```

while the following property is used for indicating the name of the login page:

```
property LoginPage: string;
```

The `LogOut` action disconnects the current user.

The Boolean `LoggedIn` field informs the developer whether or not the user has successfully logged in. And the `DisplayName` field stores the user name.

Sessions

Any WebSnap application can serve multiple clients at the same time. This means that, besides the standard task of authorizing users, the application must be able to process requests sent by several clients when they arrive in random order. This problem is solved by introducing the `TSessionsService` component.

For every newly connected client, this component creates its own context in which all specific settings pertaining to this client are saved. This context is called a *session* and has a unique inner ID. At run time, a session list is stored in the component.

Thus, every single user request is identified with one, and only one, session; while the current request is being handled, the relevant session is also made current. Two handler methods are available to the developer when the current session changes:

```
type
  TStartSessionEvent = procedure(ASender: TObject;
  ASession: TAbstractWebSession) of object;
property OnStartSession: TStartSessionEvent;
```

and

```
type
  TEndSessionEvent = procedure(ASender: TObject;
  ASession:  TAbstractWebSession; AReason: TEndSessionReason) of object;
property OnEndSession: TEndSessionEvent;
```

As you can see from the above declaration, the current session can be terminated by the application or discontinued as soon as the specified timeout has expired:

```
type
  TEndSessionReason = (esTimeout, esTerminate);
```

The `TSessionsService` component can also be used to set a timeout for each session (that is to say, a fixed period of inactivity after which the session is terminated). The following property is used for this:

```
property DefaultTimeout: Integer;
```

In addition, the developer can specify the maximum permissible number of clients by setting a session quota through the property

```
property MaxSessions: Integer;
```

Based on the information on the current session, the `TEndUserSessionAdapter` component provides the current client's profile. This component is much like the `TEndUserAdapter` component, except that its collection of handler methods is more limited. Also, `TEndUserSessionAdapter` lets you obtain the client ID:

```
property UserID: Variant;
```

Managing Application Files

A WebSnap application actively uses auxiliary files. These files can be implemented in the form of web page templates or scripts. All these files are managed using the `TLocateFileService` component.

If the application is trying to locate an HTML file, the component calls the handler method

```
type
  TLocateFileServiceFindFileEvent = procedure(ASender: TObject;
  AComponent: TComponent; const AFileName: string; var AFoundFile:
  string; var AHandled: Boolean) of object;
property OnFindTemplateFile: TLocateFileServiceFindFileEvent;
```

And if you need a script file, the following handler method is called:

```
property OnFindIncludeFile: TLocateFileServiceFindFileEvent;
```

Both handlers get the full name of the file as their respective `AFileName` parameters and, if the search is successful, return the name of the located file in the `AFoundFile` parameter.

Dispatcher Components

Dispatcher components perform a key role in WebSnap applications. They manage client requests in the application. The WebSnap technology has two components that fit this category.

The `TPageDispatcher` component forwards requests to the appropriate application pages, without needing any additional customization. While the application module is being built, this component is placed in it and, at run time, automatically performs its functions.

In addition, the developer can use the event handler methods for the events that occur in the course of processing requests.

Once a request is received and the decision as to what application page is to process it is made, these handler methods are called:

```
type
  TDispatchPageHandledEvent = procedure(Sender: TObject;
  const  PageName: string; var Handled: Boolean) of object;
property OnBeforeDispatchPage: TdispatchPageHandledEvent;
```

and

```
type
  TDispatchPageEvent = procedure(Sender: TObject;
  const PageName:  string) of object;
property OnAfterDispatchPage: TdispatchPageEvent;
```

The pages are identified by their names passed in the `PageName` parameter.

While handling requests, the developer can control users' access to the page. To this end, he or she needs to use the handler methods:

```
type
  TLoginRequiredEvent = procedure(Sender: TObject; const PageName:
  string; var Required: Boolean) of object;
property OnIsLoginRequired: TLoginRequiredEvent;
```

If client authorization is required, the `Required` parameter must be set to `True`:

```
procedure TPageProducerPage2.PageDispatcherIsLoginRequired(Sender:
TObject; const PageName: String; var Required: Boolean);
begin
  Required := PageName = 'SecuredPage1';
end;
```

If a client's logon attempt failed, the following handler method is invoked:

```
type
  TPageAccessDeniedEvent = procedure(Sender: TObject; const PageName:
  string; Reason: TPageAccessDenied; var Handled: Boolean) of object;
  property OnPageAccessDenied: TPageAccessDeniedEvent;
```

If the dispatcher component cannot locate the page addressed by the request, the following handler method is called:

```
property OnPageNotFound: TDispatchPageHandledEvent;
```

The `TAdapterDispatcher` component links the events of the application page user interface to a specific adapter component, which is responsible for performing various complex operations based on VBScript or JScript scripts. This component also functions without any extra settings. Its handler methods enable the developer to trace calls of fields or actions of adapter components.

Producer Components

Producer components are mandatory elements in every WebSnap application. Their purpose is to generate HTML pages from either HTML or XML templates at run time. The family of producer components is available from the **Internet** page on the Component palette.

A producer component must be included in every page module used by a WebSnap application. By default, the `TPageProducer` component is used for building new page modules in WebSnap applications. This component is meant for working with HTML templates.

An HTML template is specified by the property

```
property HTMLDoc: TStrings;
```

which sets the template proper, or by the property

```
property HTMLFile: TFileName;
```

which indicates the name of the file containing the template.

If the template uses scripts, the property

```
property ScriptEngine: string;
```

lets you define the script language.

At run time, the developer can generate pages whenever necessary. To do this, he or she needs to use the method

```
function Content: string;
```

but here, you must always specify the page template via either the HTMLDoc or HTMLFile property. Alternatively, you can utilize two methods to generate the page content "on the fly."

The method

```
function ContentFromString(const S: string): string;
```

works with the template specified by the S parameter.

The method

```
function ContentFromStream(Stream: TStream): string;
```

first loads the template from the Stream stream.

Beside the TPageProducer component, four more special-purpose producer components are available from the **Internet** page. They are responsible for loading data for the page under generation from a connected dataset. For more details about these components, see *Chapter 16, "Web Server Applications. WebBroker Technology."*

Adapter Components

Adapter components provide WebSnap applications with a highly efficient and convenient mechanism for implementing their business logic. Adapters can store sets of customized *actions* and *fields*.

Actions are the procedures implemented for a given adapter. These procedures can be called by the application in response to certain events. For example, when you press a button, the code of the relevant script is executed and, after that, the TAdapterProducer component takes care of the execution of the adapter component's actions.

The fields of an adapter component are utilized for storing the variables necessary for the application pages to function and for executing actions.

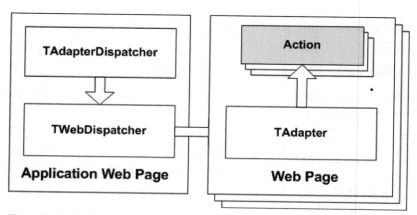

Fig. 19.5. The mechanism for invoking actions of adapter components

Among all adapter components used by the WebSnap technology, the `TAdapter` component is the most universal one.

An indexed list of adapter actions is encapsulated by the property

```
property Actions: TAdapterActions;
```

Once you have pressed the property button in the Object Inspector window, the Actions Editor window will be displayed (Fig. 19.6). Here you are able to create, remove, and customize action objects. Each action is introduced by the `TAdapterAction` class.

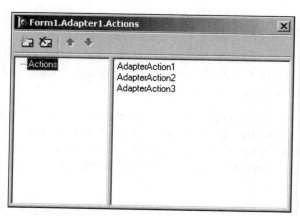

Fig. 19.6. The window for editing the actions of an adapter component

When implementing actions, the main role is performed by the handler method

```
type
 TActionExecuteEvent = procedure(Sender: TObject; Params: TStrings)
 of object;
 property OnExecute: TActionExecuteEvent;
```

which is activated when an action from the script included in the application page is executed. The developer here can guarantee the execution of all necessary operations. The `Params` parameter lets you use the required action variables.

If some parameters need to be passed for an action to execute, they can be accessed through the event handler method for getting parameters with the action

```
type
   TActionGetParamsEvent = procedure(Sender: TObject; Params: TStrings)
 of object;
 property OnGetParams: TActionGetParamsEvent;
```

The fields of adapter components allow for storing the values of the necessary variables. An indexed list of field objects is available from the property

```
property Data: TAdapterFields;
```

By pressing the property button in the Object Inspector, you activate an editor identical to the Actions Editor (see Fig. 19.6). While creating a new field object, the developer is able to choose the data type for this field from the list. Possible varieties of field types are described in Table 19.1.

Each separate field is described by the base `TAdapterField` class. Other, special-purpose types of fields listed in Table 19.1 have classes of their own, which inherit their basic functionalities from `TAdapterField`. The core difference between these types lies in their implementation of the event handler methods they use for setting and returning values, depending on the data types supported.

Table 19.1. The Field Types for the TAdapter Component

Class	Description
TAdapterField	A universal field for representing simple data types and strings.
TAdapterBooleanField	A special field for storing Boolean variables.
TAdapterFileField	A field for storing the names of the files used by the WebSnap application in its work.

continues

Table 19.1 Continued

Class	Description
TAdapterImageField	A field for representing binary arrays.
TAdapterMemoField	A field for representing Memo data.
TAdapterMultiValueField	A field used for storing a number of values or for storing one-dimensional arrays. Individual values can be accessed via the Index parameter.

Taking into account the important role of the TAdapterField class, let us discuss it in more depth.

Once the value of a field is changed, the following handler method is called:

```
type
  TAdapterFieldValueEvent = procedure (Sender: TObject;   Value:
Variant) of object;

property OnUpdateValue: TAdapterFieldValueEvent;
```

To make the field value available from the script, you need to specify it in the handler method:

```
type
  TAdapterFieldGetValueEvent = procedure (Sender: TObject;   var Value:
Variant) of object;

property OnGetValue: TAdapterFieldGetValueEvent;
```

Note that the principles of using these methods are similar to those employed for handling properties of Delphi classes. Here is a simple illustration:

```
procedure TPageProducerPage2.AdapterField1GetValue(Sender: TObject;
var Value: Variant);

begin
 Value := FSomeInternalValue;
end;
```

In addition, you can define a whole list of possible values for each field and use this list to build various controls (for instance, lists or radio groups). To do this, use the special-purpose adapter component, TStringsValuesList. It has the property

```
property Strings: TStrings;
```

in which, applying the `Name=Value` format, you can set the required values.

The `TAdapter` component points to the component that stores the list of values through its property

```
property ValuesList: TComponent;
```

Problems related to using adapter components in WebSnap applications will be further discussed in this chapter.

Designing a WebSnap Application

Delphi includes a number of special wizards for designing new WebSnap applications and their constituent parts, such as page modules and data modules. These wizards are available from the WebSnap page of the Delphi Repository.

The wizard for creating new applications is called by clicking the **WebSnap Application** icon. Its window is shown in Fig. 19.7.

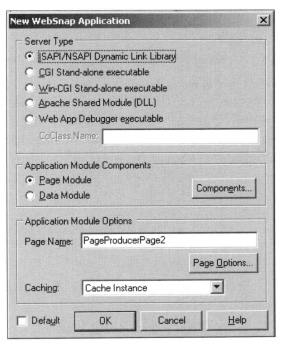

Fig. 19.7. The wizard for creating a WebSnap application

The **Server Type** radio group is for selecting the type for the application under design:

❏ **ISAPI/NSAPI Dynamic Link Library** — the dynamic library that operates within the Internet Information Server address space in multi-user mode

❏ **CGI standalone executable** — the executable Common Gateway Interface (CGI) file, which receives control commands through environment variables

❏ **Win-CGI standalone executable** — a variety of the CGI adapted for Windows

❏ **Apache Shared Module (DLL)** — the dynamic library that operates within the Apache server address space under the UNIX operating system in single-user mode

❏ **Web App Debugger executable** — the executable file that lets you debug your application using only Delphi functionalities (without using real web servers)

In the process of its work, the wizard will create the main page for the new application. Depending on which radio button has been selected from the **Application Module components** radio group, either an HTML page or data module will be used as the application module.

In the same section, you will see the **Components** button, and by pressing it, you will activate the **Web App Components** window (Fig. 19.8). This window enables you to select those WebSnap components that will be placed in the application module. The TApplicationAdapter, TPageDispatcher, and TAdapterDispatcher components are selected for you by default. Their purposes have already been explained earlier in this chapter.

NOTE

Beside the above components, the wizard always includes the mandatory TWebAppComponents component in every new application.

After that, enter the name for the new page into the **Page Name** text box instead of the default page name.

The **Caching** list lets you customize the behavior of the new module after processing a client's request, while the application is running. If this module is not that important or won't be used frequently, you can set the **Destroy Instance** value. In this case, once a request is processed, the module is instantly removed from memory. By setting the **Cache Instance** value you, on the contrary, cache the module after processing a request.

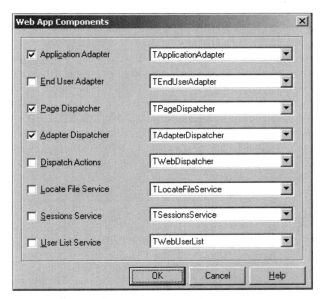

Fig. 19.8. The **Web App Components** window for selecting the components to be placed in the web module

We recommend that you always specify **Cache Instance** for the application module.

By pressing the **Page Options** button, you open the **Application Module Page Options** window, where you can set a number of extra options for the web module (Fig. 19.9).

Here, using the **Type** list of the **Producer** group, you can select the producer component that will generate the page at run time. If you mean to include scripts on this page, select a supported script language from the **Script Engine** list.

The group immediately below **Producer** changes its name depending on the type of producer component that you have just selected. Thus, if you specify TXSLPageProducer, the following group's name is **XSL**; otherwise, it is **HTML**. Here you need to set the parameters for the corresponding template.

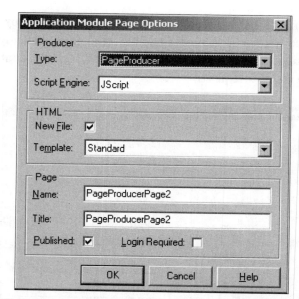

Fig. 19.9. The **Application Module Page Options** window lets you set several additional options for the web module under development

By checking the **New File** checkbox, you create an individual file for storing the template. Its name is identical to the name of the module of the Object Pascal source code and its extension is determined by the producer component selected (either HTML or XSL).

Then, define the template type via the **Template** list. The default template type is **Standard** and, by leaving it as it is, you ensure that the template file will be formed in compliance with the rules of the chosen script language. The **Blank** value forbids generation of the source template. The **Data Packet** value is used only for XSL templates, and therefore generates the appropriate template.

Enter the name and title for the new page in the **Name** and **Title** textboxes, respectively.

A checked **Published** checkbox enables the page to automatically respond to a request, on the condition that this request is addressed directly to this page.

By checking the **Login Required** checkbox, you activate the procedure of user authorization for users who try to log on to the page.

As soon as you have set all the options for your new application and pressed the **OK** button in the wizard window, the source files of the new Delphi project and the application module will be created.

The files of the application module (PAS, HTML, XML, or XSL), as well as those of all other web modules, can be accessed through the tabs in the bottom right part of the Delphi Editor.

If you choose to add new pages or data modules to the application, you can also use the wizard available from the Delphi Repository.

The controls contained in the window of the wizard responsible for building new applications have already been covered. The only extra, the **Creation** list, enables you to specify the method of creating the page. The **On Demand** value means that the page will be created only on demand, as soon as it is called for the first time. Alternatively, the **Always** value indicates that the page must be created in any event.

When designing a data module, it is only necessary to define the method of creating and caching this module.

Designing the Interface and Handling Data

Now that you have a fairly good idea about the structure of a WebSnap application, let's move ahead to a small practical exercise and discuss some of the details of using WebSnap components.

Using the appropriate wizard, let's create a new WebSnap application. Select Web App Debugger executable as the server type (see Fig. 19.7). Here, the executable application file will provide for the display of your application's web pages using Delphi exclusively. Set the name of the page as `MainPage`. Leave all the remaining parameters unchanged.

Now select the `TApplicationAdapter` component in the application page module and set its `ApplicationTitle` property to 'Simple WebSnap Application'. Note that from this point on, all newly added pages will display a common application title, since the following tag will be automatically inserted into their templates:

```
<h1><%= Application.Title %></h1>
```

where `Application` is the global application variable provided by the `TApplicationAdapter` component.

Once the project is saved and compiled, the application is ready to run and can be debugged. To this end, start the WebApp Debugger utility (Fig. 19.10) by selecting the item of the same name from the Delphi **Tools** menu.

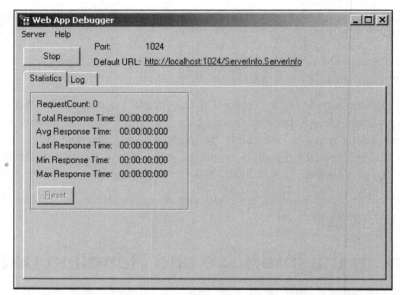

Fig. 19.10. The Web App Debugger utility for debugging WebSnap applications

If the server has not yet been started, start it via the **Start** button. Select the **Default URL** hyperlink and after that select the **ViewDetails** link in the Internet Explorer window. Here you need to choose a test application from the list, and the MainPage of the application will appear on the screen.

The same pattern will be utilized for testing in all subsequent development stages.

Issues related to developing a user interface on the basis of web pages are beyond the scope of our discussion. Those readers who wish to learn more about these problems can refer to the ample collection of literature on the subject. We just need to mention here that the Delphi Editor window lets you work with the template text directly. Should you need to utilize certain professional toolkits, you can simply replace the HTML or XML files of the application pages in the project folder with the files that you yourself created using specific editors, but make sure to keep the file names unchanged.

Navigating Application Pages

In this section, we are going to add a new page to the project using a wizard from the Delphi Repository. The process itself is easy enough. However, if a WebSnap application has more than one page, then the code fragment of the main page template that provides for navigation through the application pages begins to be executed.

Listing 19.1. The Code Fragment of the Template of the HTML Application's Main Page That Provides for Navigation through the Pages of the Application

```
<table cellspacing="0" cellpadding="0">
<td>
<%  e = new Enumerator(Pages)
    s = ''
    c = 0
    for (; !e.atEnd(); e.moveNext())
    {
      if (e.item().Published)
      {
        if (c>0) s += ' | '
        if (Page.Name != e.item().Name)
          s += '<a href="' + e.item().HREF + '">' + e.item().Title + '</a>'
        else
          s += e.item().Title
        c++
      }
    }
    if (c>1) Response.Write(s)
%>
</td>
</table>
```

This code fragment is embedded in the template of the main page of the application during its creation.

In this code, the new 'e' enumerator is created, which contains the application pages available for viewing. The page names are then added in the 's' line of the cycle and, if the 'c' page enumerator contains more than one page, a navigation bar is displayed on the main page of the application. This can be done with the `Response.Write(s)` method, where `Response` is the pointer to the response object.

Using the Fields and Actions of Adapter Components

WebSnap adapter components provide the developer with two very important tools for designing interactive user interfaces. These include an indexed list of the fields that are used for storing different types of variables at run time, and a list of actions that implement various functions of the application interface.

In order to illustrate these functionalities with an example, let's create a simple HTML page that would implement the viewing of text files. We start by adding a page, `TextFileViewer`, to the newly created application.

This page template is developed using Microsoft Front Page and contains a single-line editor for entering the file name, and a multi-line editor for viewing the file content. The template was saved as uTextFileViewer.html and imported to the project folder. In the process, the description of the page's caption was modified: it was copied from the source HTML file generated by Delphi while the uTextFileViewer.html file was being created.

The next step is to build into Delphi a new field for the adapter component of the page under design. Press the button of the `Data` property in the Object Inspector, and as soon as the Field Editor is displayed, use it to create a new field. You need to specify `TAdapterFileField` as the type of new field. This field will store the current name of the file. Then build another new field, but in this case, it should be a field of the `TAdapterMemoField` type. This field will be used for presenting a selected file.

Now we have to supply these new fields with `OnGetValue` event handler methods, as shown in Listing 19.2.

The `FileName` field returns the full name of the current file, and the `FileContent` field returns the content of this file in Memo format. Its `FileContentGetValue` handler method creates a file stream object using the value of the `FFileName` variable and fills the `FFileContent` variable.

Now we need to create an action that will implement the procedures of selecting a file and displaying it on the page as soon as the **Open** button is pressed. Open the Actions Editor for the adapter component by pressing the `Actions` button in the Object Inspector (see Fig. 19.6). Using this editor, generate a new `TAdapterAction` object and name it `SelectFileName`. Then create the `OnExecute` handler method and use it as a container for the code that calls the standard dialog for opening files (Listing 19.2).

Listing 19.2. The Source Code for the TextFileViewer Page Module

```
implementation

{$R *.dfm}   {*.html}

uses WebReq, WebCntxt, WebFact, Variants;

function TextFileViewer: TTextFileViewer;
begin
  Result := TTextFileViewer(WebContext.FindModuleClass(TTextFileViewer));
end;

procedure TTextFileViewer.FileNameGetValue(Sender: TObject;
var Value: Variant);
begin
 Value := FFileName;
end;

procedure TTextFileViewer.FileContentGetValue(Sender: TObject;
var Value: String);
begin
 if FFileName = ''
  then FFileContent := ''
  else
  try
   with TFileStream.Create(FFileName, fmOpenRead) do
```

```
  try
   SetString(FFileContent, nil, Size);
   Read(Pointer(FFileContent)^, Size);
  finally
   Free;
  end;
 except
  on E: Exception do FFileContent := E.Message;
 end;
 Value := FFileContent;
end;

procedure TTextFileViewer.SelectFileNameExecute(Sender: TObject;
Params: TStrings);
begin
 if dlgOpen.Execute
  then FFileName := dlgOpen.FileName;
end;

initialization
  if WebRequestHandler <> nil then
WebRequestHandler.AddWebModuleFactory(TWebPageModuleFactory.Create
TTextFileViewer, TWebPageInfo.Create([wpPublished {,
wpLoginRequired}], '.html'), crOnDemand, caCache));
 end.
```

Now you need to link all the newly created fields and actions to the controls of the uTextFileViewer.html page. The `FileName` field should be displayed in the `edFileName` single-line editor. This is done by declaring the control in the page template in the following way:

```
<input type="text" name="edFileName" size="38"
value=<%=FileViewerAdapter.FileName.Value%>>
```

The `FileContent` field should be displayed in the `meFileContent` multi-line editor. Its declaration must look like this:

```
<textarea rows="19" name="meFileContent" cols="82">
  <%=FileViewerAdapter.FileContent.Value%>
</textarea>
```

Pressing the `buOpen` button should invoke the `OnExecute` handler method for the `SelectFileName` action. To this end, include the following declarations in the page template:

```
<input type=hidden name="__action"
value="<%=FileViewerAdapter.SelectFileName.AsFieldValue%>">

<input type="submit" value="Open" name="buOpen"
onclick="F.__action.value=
'<%=FileViewerAdapter.SelectFileName.AsFieldValue%>'">
```

Here, the action of pressing the button is linked to the execution of the `SelectFileName` action. In other words, it is linked to the execution of its `OnExecute` handler method.

All actions inherit the properties of their common `IAdapterActionWrapper` interface. And the property

```
property AsFieldValue: WideString
```

returns the action's result in string format.

As a result, once the application is compiled and started, the `TextFileViewer` page lets you select files in a standard dialog and view them in the multi-line editor by just pressing the **Open** button. The name of the selected file will be displayed in a single-line editor.

Interaction with Databases

In this section, we will address issues of the interaction of WebSnap applications with databases. By way of illustration, let us consider an example where an HTML page is used for displaying data from the Country table of the Delphi demo database.

To achieve this result, we will start by adding a new page to our `Simple WebSnap Application` application discussed in the previous sections, and name it `DataViewer`. However, here we will utilize other adapter and producer components. Since in the most elementary case it is far more convenient to display data in tabular format rather than use the standard `TPageProducer` component, we will take advantage of the `TAdapterPageProducer` component. And, instead of the `TAdapter` component that has already done a good job in the above examples, we will employ the `TDataSetAdapter` component. Let's see how we can benefit from using these new components.

Specialized Controls

The TAdapterPageProducer component lets you take advantage of additional capabilities as far as creating web pages and linking the controls from these pages to the fields and actions of adapter components goes. Start by pressing the button of the component's property

```
property WebPageItems: TWebComponentList;
```

in the Object Inspector window. You will see a property editor window similar to the one presented in Fig. 19.11.

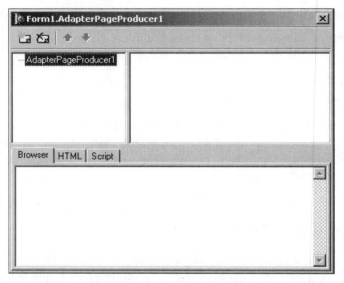

Fig. 19.11. The TAdapterPageProducer component editor window

At the top of the window, you will see a hierarchical list just as with editors for the fields and actions of adapter components (see Fig. 19.6). This list is used for creating, editing, and deleting web page controls. The bottom part of the window is taken up by a multipage notepad that displays the template text and appearance of the page.

The editor enables you to build the user interface with multiple nesting levels for the page. Only two types of objects at the root of the tree (whose name is identical to the name of the component) are available to the developer.

The TAdapterForm class encapsulates the functionalities of an HTML form. It can be used as a container for controls.

The `TLayoutGroup` class aligns the controls in several columns. Instances of this class can contain only HTML forms. If the `TLayoutGroup` class property

```
property DisplayColumns: Integer;
```

is set to `1` (which is its default value), all child forms (`TAdapterForm` class instances) are arranged on the page without alignment — one under another. Otherwise, the value of the property indicates the number of columns in which the forms will be placed from left to right.

The following controls of an HTML form can be handled through the `TAdapterPageProducer` component:

The `TAdapterFieldGroup` class provides for the presentation of the fields of a linked dataset in the form of a text list of field names and values. Only one record's field values can be displayed at a time. The necessary dataset is connected through the property

```
property Adapter: TComponent;
```

which points to the `TDataSetAdapter` component, and through it to the dataset component.

This class is always used in tandem with the `TAdapterCommandGroup` class, which is represented by a set of buttons enabling navigation around the dataset. Its property

```
property DisplayComponent: Tcomponent;
```

must point to the `TAdapterFieldGroup` class instance contained in the same form.

The `TAdapterGrid` class encapsulates a grid. To populate the grid with data, just indicate the required `TDataSetAdapter` component via the property

```
property Adapter: TComponent;
```

In addition, the properties

```
property TableAttributes: TGridAttributes;
```

and

```
property RowAttributes: TGridRowAttributes;
```

allow you to customize the appearance of the grid and of its rows.

The `TAdapterErrorList` class is not a visual control, which is why it is not available from the editor's hierarchical tree and can be displayed only in the right pane of the editor. It is used for handling potential exceptions that may occur in the process of working with datasets.

Viewing Data

In this example, we will limit our task simply to displaying data in tabular form. To do this, add an HTML form (an `TAdapterForm` class instance) in the `TAdapterPageProducer` editor window, and then place a table (a `TAdapterGrid` class instance) in this form. You can instantly see the result of these fairly simple operations in the same window: just select the **Browser** tab in the bottom pane of the editor; the text of the template can be accessed through the **Script** tab. However, at this stage, you can see neither data nor the table. Instead, an error message is displayed (Fig. 19.12).

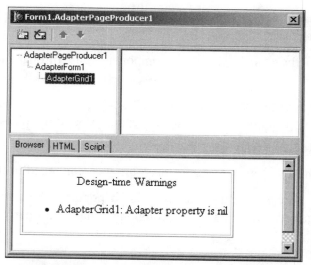

Fig. 19.12. The error message in the **Browser** tab of the `TAdapterPageProducer` component editor

Do not despair, however; everything is going according to plan. The problem is we still have not linked the table component to the dataset.

NOTE

Every newly created control in the `TAdapterPageProducer` component can be linked to a separate dataset (if it is intended for this task). This feature allows data from multiple sources to be displayed on a single page. Obviously, this approach is far more flexible than linking a dataset to the entire `TAdapterPageProducer` component.

This is not done directly, but through an intermediary adapter component. All controls of the `TAdapterPageProducer` component have the `Adapter` property, which allows you to link them to the adapter component. In our scenario, it should be the `TDataSetAdapter` component, since it knows how to interact with dataset components. It can be implemented through its property

```
property DataSet: TDataSet;
```

And due to the fact that this property has the `TdataSet` type, the adapter can handle components provided by various data access technologies (see *Part II, "Data Access Technologies"*). In our example, we will opt for ADO components. To do this, place the `TADOConnection` and `TADOTable` components into the module of the page under design and customize them for accessing the Country table of the Microsoft Access DBDEMOS.MDB database, which is a part of the Delphi demo database and is stored in the ..\\Program Files\Common Files\Borland Shared\ Data folder by default. (For more information about customizing these components, see *Chapter 7, "Using ADO with Delphi."*)

Now that we have performed all the above operations and linked the `TAdapterGrid` control to the `TDataSetAdapter` adapter — and through it to the `TADOTable` component — our page should begin to work properly, and the necessary data from the Country database table should appear in the **Browser** tab of the `TAdapterPageProducer` component editor.

You can also use other controls in this way.

Editing Data

To edit data contained in the Country table, add one more form to the hierarchical list of the `TAdapterPageProducer` component controls and create the `TAdapterFieldGroup` control in this new form. This control will allow all fields of the current record of the dataset to be displayed in separate single-line editors. Using the `Adapter` property, the field group object will connect to the adapter component, and via this component, it will link up with the dataset component.

In order to provide navigation through the dataset, add the `TAdapterCommandGroup` control, which is implemented as a set of buttons enabling you to move around the records, edit data, and save updates. It also should be linked to `TAdapterFieldGroup`. The link is established if the `DisplayComponent` property of the `TAdapterCommandGroup` class points to `TAdapterFieldGroup`.

As a result, once the application is compiled, you can use the **DataViewer** page for viewing and editing data from the Country table.

Handling Errors

WebSnap applications support several levels of handling errors.

On the application level, the `TWebAppComponents` component offers the handler method:

```
type
  TWebExceptionEvent = procedure (Sender: TObject; E: Exception;
  var Handled: Boolean) of object;

property OnException: TWebExceptionEvent
```

The `Handled` parameter manages the process of handling an error. If it is set to `True`, it means that the exception will be processed by this handler method.

Page-level exceptions can be processed using the adapter component property

```
property Errors: TBaseAdapterErrorsList;
```

It lets the developer obtain a list of the exceptions that have occurred in the process of the component's performance:

```
var ErrorsList: TStringList;
...
if Adapter1.Errors.ErrorCount > 0 then
  for i := 0 to Adapter1.Errors.ErrorCount - 1 do
    ErrorsList.Add(Adapter1.Errors.Errors[i].ErrorText);
```

The `TBaseAdapterErrorsList` class gives us the following properties and methods.

Its main property

```
property Errors[I: Integer]: IAdapterError;
```

is an indexed list of errors. The parameters of each error are available from the `IAdapterError` interface.

The total number of errors in the list is returned by the property

```
property ErrorCount: Integer;
```

The list can be cleared using the method

```
procedure ClearErrors;
```

For instance:

```
if Adapter1.Errors.ErrorCount > 0
then Adapter1.Errors.ClearErrors;
```

While developing the part of application business logic meant to trace invalid operations that your would-be clients are likely to cause with application pages, you will most likely find those methods that add a new error to the error list very useful:

```
procedure AddError(AException: Exception; AObject: TObject);
procedure AddError(AException: Exception; const AObjectName: string = '');
procedure AddError(const AMessage: string; AObject: TObject; AID: Integer = 0);
procedure AddError(const AMessage: string; const AObjectName: string =
''; AID: Integer = 0);
```

For example:

```
try
...
except
  on E: Exception do Adapter1.Errors.AddError(E);
end;
```

Authentificating Users

It is often necessary to provide web applications with the functionality of authentificating clients who try to connect or query certain pages. The WebSnap technology addresses this challenge by providing a collection of special components, a general description of which was covered earlier in this chapter.

By way of example, let us add the functionality of authentificating clients to our sample application. To do this, we need to:

❒ Integrate a list of user names and passwords into the application, or, alternatively, add a function that would enable us to obtain such a list from external sources (for instance, from a certain database or encrypted file)

❒ Create a page containing the controls that will be used for entering user names and passwords

❒ Provide interaction between the components and application pages

❒ Specify those application pages that can be accessed only by properly authorized users, and set necessary options for these pages

Let us now take a closer look at each of these stages.

User Lists and Sessions

The process of user authentification implies that the application will be able to match the user name and password entered by the user against those stored in the system. Such a list is encapsulated by the TWebUserList component. In the SimpleWebSnap Application application, you need to place this component in the application module. By pressing the button of the UserItems property in the Object Inspector, you activate a dialog where you can edit the list of users. You can specify a name, password, and access rights for each individual client.

The next step is to add the TSessionsService component to the application module in order to implement session management. This component does not require any specific settings for it to work.

Once the login procedure is over, information about the user and the current session can be accessed through the TEndUserSessionAdapter component. Therefore, it also needs to be placed in the application module.

Note that as soon as you place all three components into the page module, they are automatically linked to the TWebAppComponents component via the corresponding properties (as described above). In such a way, you implement general control over all the components that are responsible for user authentification.

Developing the Login Page

A login page is an ordinary web page that provides for entering user names and passwords. So, we'll begin by creating one more HTML page for our SimpleWebSnap Application application and select the TAdapterPageProducer producer component for it, as we did with the page used for accessing the database. Let us name our new page UserLogin.

However, this case is a bit different: the UserLogin page should not be available at design time. This can be done by checking the **Published** checkbox in the window of the wizard that lets you create new pages (Fig. 19.3).

After that, using the TAdapterPageProducer component editor, create an HTML form and place the TAdapterFieldGroup and TAdapterCommandGroup controls in it. Then link these components to each other through the DisplayComponent property. Now you are able to view the new page in the **Browser** tab (Fig. 19.13).

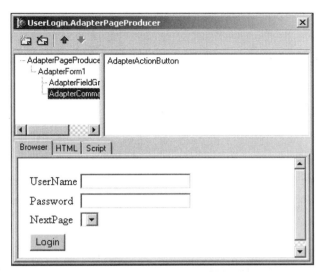

Fig. 19.13. A standard login page of a WebSnap application

Now we just need to place the `TLoginFormAdapter` component in the page module in order to provide for the proper performance of all newly created controls. It is this component that should be indicated in the `Adapter` property of the `TAdapterFieldGroup` class instance.

The next move is to link the predefined `Login` action of the `TLoginFormAdapter` component to the event of pressing the **Login** button. To this end, we will create a new `TAdapterActionButton` object for the `TAdapterCommandGroup` instance using the editor. Then, in the Object Inspector window, we need to select the `Login` action from the list contained in its `ActionName` property.

Finally, it is possible to modify the page template slightly. You see, when the page is being created, two fragments are automatically embedded in its template. One fragment provides for the appearance of the Login link on the page if the user has not yet entered his or her password. The second fragment builds a navigation bar to be used by clients for moving around available pages. Certainly there is no harm in keeping these fragments in the templates, but it seems to us that they are quite unnecessary. Thus, the template of the authentification page of the test application will look as follows.

Listing 19.3. The File of the HTML Login Page

```
<HTML>
<HEAD>
```

```
<TITLE>
<%= Page.Title %>
</TITLE>
</HEAD>
<BODY>
<H1><%= Application.Title %></H1>
<H2><%= Page.Title %></H2>
<#STYLES><#WARNINGS><#SERVERSCRIPT>
</BODY>
</HTML>
```

Once it is saved, the page is ready to function.

Customizing the Application

In conclusion, we need to link the newly created page to the application login procedure and specify the password protected pages.

In the following property of the TEndUserSessionAdapter component:

```
property LoginPage: string;
```

define the name for the login page — UserLogin in our case. Now, every user's attempt to log on to a protected page or click the Login link will automatically activate the new authentification page.

To protect any application page, just modify the parameters used for creating an instance of the page by the class factory. Let's do this for the **DataView** page. In the following fragment of the page's source code:

```
initialization
  if WebRequestHandler <> nil then
    WebRequestHandler.AddWebModuleFactory
( TWebPageModuleFactory.Create(TDataView,
TWebPageInfo.Create([wpPublished{, wpLoginRequired}], '.html'),
crOnDemand, caCache));
```

we need to remove the commentary from the wpLoginRequired parameter.

As a result, when an attempt is made to open this page at run time, a page prompting the user for his or her user name and password will be called automatically.

It should be mentioned, however, that the process of testing the authentification mechanism has a certain peculiarity to it. The login procedure involves using information about the application session. And this information is saved only if the application runs uninterrupted between page calls.

Since the test application has the Web App Debugger type, you need to start the application executable file manually from the Web App Debugger utility prior to calling `MainPage`.

Using XML and XSL

Along with HTML templates, a WebSnap application can also use XML templates. The `TXSLPageProducer` component is used for this: it dynamically generates pages based on templates in XML using XSL-style templates.

Discussion of the capabilities of XML and XSL falls far outside the scope of this book. Thus, in the examples that follow, we will restrict ourselves to considering just the simplest sample templates, focusing mostly on WebSnap's capabilities as far as using XML and XSL is concerned. More in-depth information on both can be found in *Chapter 14, "Using XML ."*

In order to illustrate how the WebSnap technology supports XML and how your applications can benefit from using this language, we will create a new `Simple XML WebSnap Application` application, similar to the one discussed in previous sections of this chapter. The application's main page will still be implemented in the form of an HTML standard main page that contains all the default components; they will do their job irrespective of the format used for the templates of other pages.

The next step is to add two new pages to the application. Since you want the application to use XML templates, you need to specify the `TXSLPageProducer` component in the wizard window (see Fig. 19.3) while developing the page.

From the following sections, you will learn how to generate pages on the basis of XML and XSL files, and by using data retrieved from the database.

Using XML Files and XSL Templates

First, let's see how XML files can be used for building WebSnap application pages.

Let's name the first page **ListViewer**. Except for the `TXSLPageProducer` component, it is very similar to a traditional page based on an HTML template. Also, notice that a new tab, **XSL**, has appeared at the bottom of the Delphi Editor window.

The process of customizing a page that you mean to use as an XML template involves two stages.

To begin with, you need to establish a link between the page and the XML file.

Then, place the TXMLDocument component into the page module and specify in its property

```
property FileName: DOMString;
```

the name of the file — SimpleXMLDataList.xml. This particular file contains a list of the capitals and their population from the Country table of the Delphi demo database. In order to provide portability for an application that uses this property:

❏ Place the XML files in the application folder without specifying their full address

❏ Or, use the URL as the full path to the file

NOTE

The SimpleXMLDataList.xml file is created using the Microsoft XML Integration in ADO 2.5 standard, which is utilized for exporting and importing data to and from ADO data sources.

❏ Once the TXMLDocument component is customized in such a way, it needs to be attached to the page. To do this, we will use the TXSLPageProducer component and its property

```
property XMLData: TComponent;
```

❏ In the second stage, we need to apply the style sheet contained in the XSL file to the page.

❏ In order to do this, import the required XSL file to the application folder and rename it according to the names of the files of the page under design. In our example, it is the ListViewer.XSL file. Alternatively, it is also possible to copy the XSL content in the source file and then move it directly to the Delphi Editor window and save the XSL page file.

❐ Now, if both the XML template and the XSL style sheet have no syntactical errors, the HTML code for the page under design — which was generated by the `TXSLPageProducer` component — is available in the **HTML Result** Editor window. And the **Preview** window shows the appearance of the page at run time.

❐ In our example, the XSL file allows us to use the easiest method of processing data — using two text columns (Listing 19.4).

Listing 19.4. An XSL File for the ListViewer Page of the Simple XML WebSnap Application

```
<xsl:stylesheet xmlns:xsl="http://www.w3.org/TR/WD-xsl">
 <xsl:template match = "*">
 <xsl:apply-templates />
 </xsl:template>
 <xsl:template match="/">
 <H2>Simple XML WebSnap Application</H2>
 <xsl:apply-templates select="//rs:data"/>
 </xsl:template>
 <xsl:template match="//rs:data">
     <TABLE BORDER="1">
         <TR>
            <TD BGCOLOR="gray" STYLE="font-weight:bold">Country</TD>
            <TD BGCOLOR="gray" STYLE="font-weight:bold">Capital</TD>
         </TR>
         <xsl:for-each select="z:row">
         <TR>
            <TD><xsl:value-of select="@Name"/></TD>
            <TD><xsl:value-of select="@Capital"/></TD>
         </TR>
         </xsl:for-each>
     </TABLE>
 </xsl:template>
</xsl:stylesheet>
```

Note that the elements

```
<xsl:apply-templates select="//rs:data"/>
```

and

```
<xsl:for-each select="z:row">
```

provide access to the nodes of the XML document that contain data, while the elements

```
<xsl:value-of select="@Name"/>
```

and

```
<xsl:value-of select="@Capital"/>
```

are for receiving the values of fields.

Using the Dataset and the XSL Template

Pages developed on the basis of XML and XSL can also integrate the functionality of handling data stored in various databases.

To illustrate this capability of the WebSnap technology, let us create one more page for our Simple XML WebSnap Application and call it **DataViewer**. As in the previous example, we will choose TXSLPageProducer as the provider component.

In this case, however, the role of the data source will be performed by an ADO dataset. To access data, we need to create an additional web data module and place the TADOConnection and TADOTable components in this module. The next step is to customize these components for accessing the Microsoft Access DBDEMOS.MDB database included in the Delphi demo database. (For more details on the ADO technology and ADO components, see *Chapter 7, "Using ADO with Delphi*.") In addition, we will have to use the TDataSetProvider component, which will provide for data transmission. (The role of the TDataSetProvider component is covered in more depth in *Chapter 8, "DataSnap Technology. Remote Access Mechanisms*.") The TADOTable component and TDataSetProvider component are linked via the DataSet property of the latter.

After that, the TXMLBroker component from the **Internet Express** page is imported into the data module of the new **DataViewer** page. Specify the name of the TDataSetProvider component contained in the data module for the ProviderName property of TXMLBroker. The TXMLBroker component, in turn, must be linked to the provider component of the page. This can be done by specifying a link to the TXMLBroker component in the XMLData property of the TXSLPageProducer component.

Now we have the entire chain of components that will be used to implement data transmission from the database to the XML page, fully customized. We now only need to create the XSL style sheet that is to be applied. This is done exactly as in the previous example. The XSL file used for this page describes a table that is to be filled with data.

Listing 19.5. An XSL File for the DataViewer Page of the Simple XML WebSnap Application

```
<xsl:stylesheet xmlns:xsl="http://www.w3.org/TR/WD-xsl">
<xsl:template match = "*">
<xsl:apply-templates />
</xsl:template>
<xsl:template match="/">
<H2>Simple XML WebSnap Application</H2>
<xsl:apply-templates select="//ROWDATA"/>
</xsl:template>
<xsl:template match="//ROWDATA">
        <TABLE BORDER="1">
            <TR>
            <TD BGCOLOR="gray" STYLE="font-weight:bold">Country</TD>
            <TD BGCOLOR="gray" STYLE="font-weight:bold">Capital</TD>
            </TR>
        <xsl:for-each select="ROW">
            <TR>
              <TD><xsl:value-of select="@Name"/></TD>
              <TD><xsl:value-of select="@Capital"/></TD>
            </TR>
        </xsl:for-each>
        </TABLE>
</xsl:template>
</xsl:stylesheet>
```

Note that, in this case, the `TXMLBroker` component passes the `TXSLPageProducer` producer component the XML data that describes the dataset in the form of a Delphi data packet. This is why the style template contains somewhat different elements for nodes that encapsulate data:

```
<xsl:apply-templates select="//ROWDATA"/>
<xsl:for-each select="ROW">
```

The Additional *TAdapterXMLBuilder* Component

Besides the standard WebSnap components, which have been extensively covered in this chapter, the developer can also use an extra component included in WebSnap sample codes for designing XML pages. The source files of the TAdapterXMLBuilder class are stored in the ..\Demos\WebSnap\XMLBuilder folder. The component is registered using the XMLBuilder.reg file. Once it is installed in the Component Palette, this component is available for selecting providers in the window of the wizard responsible for creating web pages (see Fig. 19.3).

Like the TAdapterPageProducer component, the TAdapterXMLBuilder component allows the developer to build the interface for a web page. The component editor window (which is activated by double-clicking the component) consists of two panes: the left pane contains a hierarchical tree of controls, and the right pane displays the constituent parts of the control selected in the hierarchical tree.

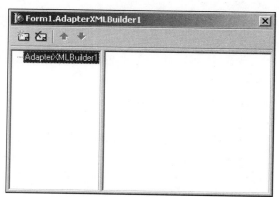

Fig. 19.14. The TAdapterXMLBuilder component editor window

Controls can be placed only in a form encapsulated by the TXMLForm class. Here you can use the same controls as those supported by the TAdapterPageProducer component, except for the class analogous to TLayoutGroup.

Due to the fact that, in this case, an XML template needs to be used for generating pages, the component requires the relevant XSL file for its work.

The property

```
property XSLTemplate: TXSLTemplate;
```

lets you link the component to the necessary XSL file. As you can see, however, it is done via another intermediary — TXSLTemplate component — rather than directly. This component is placed in the Component Palette together with the TAdapterXMLBuilder component. To indicate the required XSL file, the component has the property

```
property FileName: DOMString;
```

As a result, the component generates a new web page on the created tree of controls described in XML and using the necessary XSL template. The code, which is automatically built by the component, can be viewed via the **XML Tree** tab in the Delphi Editor.

Summary

WebSnap technology allows you to develop a wide range of various web applications. These include:

- ❏ ISAPI/NSAPI DLL
- ❏ CGI
- ❏ Win-CGI
- ❏ Apache Shared Module (DLL)
- ❏ Web App Debugger

The task of processing requests passed to a WebSnap application by a web server is performed by three components:

- ❏ Dispatcher components that coordinate requests, forwarding them to the appropriate pages
- ❏ Producer components that generate pages based on existing templates
- ❏ Adapter components that enable the developer to link the user interface of pages to certain programmed actions

Should a developer need to implement more complex functions for his or her application, he or she can write scripts using VBScript or JScript.

Application pages can be designed either by utilizing HTML or XML templates, or by using specialized components that let the developer build a page interface "on the fly."

On the CD

Following are the descriptions of the examples discussed throughout this book. Each example is stored in an individual folder, and should be regarded as a complete project that can be loaded into the development environment and compiled.

The folder names are combinations of the number of the chapter in which the example is found, and the number of the example going by the text of the chapter.

A number of applications use data from the Delphi demo database as their data source, which, during standard installation, is placed into the ..\Program Files\ Common Files\Borland Shared\Data folder. Prior to working with such applications, you will have to configure the relevant properties of the data access components yourself. These properties were intentionally set to nil, since the Delphi database can be stored elsewhere on your computer.

Description of the Demo Applications

Folder	Application
01_1	A group of projects. The server application project implements a COM server as part of the native server (the dynamic library), which provides two interfaces that have arithmetic functions. The client application project demonstrates using these interfaces.
02_1	A group of projects. The server application project implements a simple Automation server. The client application calls methods of the Automation server interface.
03_1	An example of creating a custom ActiveX control.
04_1	A group of projects. The project of an MTS server built from an MTS data module implements an elementary interface. The TADOConnection component should be configured to the demo database. The client application uses this interface. The name of the server computer must be specified for the TDCOMConnection component.
04_2	A group of projects. Two MTS server projects provide for the retrieval of information from the demo database. The TADOConnection components must be configured for the demo database. The additional project implements an MTS project for a distributed transaction. The TDCOMConnection component must be configured for working with the MTS object computer and, if necessary, define the object itself. The client application gets data from the MTS servers using a distributed transaction.
06_1	This application shows various approaches to using dbExpress components. The Interbase server is selected as the data source; it is accessed via its standard alias — BDE IBLocal. If this alias is not found, the path to the DBDEMOS.GDB demo database file for Interbase should be set manually in the TSQLConnection component.

continues

Description of the Demo Applications, *Contunued*

Folder	Application
07_1	A sample code illustrating how to use ADO components. The path to the data source should be defined by the user at run time.
09_1	A group of projects. An example of a distributed application designed on the basis of the DataSnap technology. The server application uses ADO components for accessing data; it is divided into two data modules, main and secondary. The path to the database is stored in an INI file. This application is described in *Chapter 9*. The client application uses `TClientDataSet` components. Described in *Chapter 10*.
11_1	A pair of applications using sockets for transmitting data.
12_1	An example of using CryptoAPI — a manager for the certificates installed in the system.
13_1	An application using a thread for calculation of π.
14_1	An example of loading an XML file to the `TtreeView` component as a tree-like structure.
14_2	Loading/unloading and viewing an ADO Recordset in XML.
14_3	An extended version of 14_1 that allows for editing.
15_1	An example of converting XML data into a Delphi data packet and using them as an XML document and a dataset.
16_1	An example of a simple web server application that uses the Delphi demo database. Before beginning your work, customize the `TADOTable` component. The Web App Debugger utility acts as a server.
16_2	An example of a simple web server application that uses the Delphi demo database. Before beginning your work with the application, you need to configure the `TADOTable` component. The MS IIS web server is used. The dynamic library is placed into the Scripts folder of the server (by default), and is called from the web browser as follows: **http://localhost/scripts/simplewebapp.dll**.
17_1	A simple example of the BASE client web service, which illustrates two ways of using the `THTTPRIO` component and using non-standard data types.
18_1	The SimpleEcho web service: an example containing two service servers and two service clients created using Delphi and the Microsoft SOAP Toolkit.
19_1	A web application based on the WebSnap technology and HTML templates. Allows you to view files and access databases for browsing and editing. Uses a user authentication mechanism. The Web App Debugger utility is used as the server.
19_2	A web application based on the WebSnap technology and XML templates. Lets you view files and provides access to databases for browsing and editing. The Web App Debugger utility is used as the server.

Index

Protected Internet, intranet, & Virtual Private Networks

A guide to methods of protection in network security

A systematic guide to the technologies, standards, protocols, and means used for the transparent security of information interaction in computer networks, this resource enables an independent understanding of the various methods of providing computer and information security when using modern network technology. The basic features of both web technologies and the distributed information processing technologies connected with them that are based on mobile programs are described, as are the network technologies that influence security. Also covered are the methods of attacking computer networks and practical guidelines for protecting a virtual network.

AUTHORS Alex Moldovyan, Nik Moldovyan, Doug Summerville, Vlad Zima   ISBN 1-931769-14-1
PRICE $44.95   PUB DATE October 2002   PAGES 400 pp   SOFTCOVER 7.375 x 9.25

Protect Your Information with Intrusion Detection

A reference and guide to the implementation of intrusion data systems and vulnerability analysis

This comprehensive reference provides a detailed overview of intrusion detection systems (IDS) offering the latest technology in information protection. Introducing network administrators to the problem of intrusion detection, it includes the principles of system technology and an in-depth classification in IDS. Topics covered include information gathering and exploitation, searching for vulnerabilities, distributed attack tools, remote and local penetrations, and password crackers, sniffers, and firewalls. Examples of actual information system break-ins provide practical reference.

AUTHOR Alex Lukatsky   ISBN 1-931769-11-7   PRICE $44.95   PUB DATE November 2002
PAGES 700 pp   SOFTCOVER 7.375 x 9.25

Windows .NET Domains & Active Directory

Intended for system administrators with a general knowledge of Windows 2000 or Windows XP/.NET, this reference covers all main system tools and program methods used for routine Active Directory administration and troubleshooting. Information important for understanding the Active Directory service architecture—LDAP protocol, DNS interoperation, and Active Directory concepts—is discussed in detail along with methods of performing common administrative tasks such as creating directory objects, audit, and backing up. This guide addresses troubleshooting problems that occur after deploying Windows .NET domains and system tools used for solving such problems. Also covered are Active Directory Service Interfaces with annotated listings of ready-to-use scripts that illustrate programming principles needed to help non-programmers learn the main ADSI concepts to begin their own scripts.

AUTHOR Alex Tchekmarev   ISBN 1-931769-00-1   PRICE $39.95   PUB DATE December 2002
PAGES 560 pp   SOFTCOVER 7.375 x 9.25

Modern Cryptography: Protect Your Data with Fast Block Ciphers

Methods of data conversion for the creation of ciphers
Covering the specific issues related to developing fast block ciphers using software and hardware implementation, this book provides a general picture of modern cryptography. Covered is the meaning of cryptography in informational society, including two-key cryptography, cryptographic protocols, digital electronic signatures, and several well-known single-key ciphers. Also detailed are the issues concerning and the methods of dealing with designing fast block ciphers and special types of attacks using random hardware faults.

AUTHORS Nik Goots, Boris Izotov, Alex Moldovyan, Nik Moldovyan   ISBN 1-931769-12-5
PRICE $49.95   PUB DATE January 2003   PAGES 400 pp   SOFTCOVER 7.375 x 9.25

A-LIST Publishing
295 East Swedesford Rd, PMB #285, Wayne, PA 19087
e-mail: mail@alistpublishing.com
www.alistpublishing.com
Fax: 702-977-5377